HORROR OF PHILOSOPHY

Vols. 1–3

Eugene Thacker

zer0 books

London, UK
Washington, DC, USA

This edition first published by Zero Books, 2025
Zero Books is an imprint of Collective Ink Ltd.,
Unit 11, Shepperton House, 89 Shepperton Road, London, N1 3DF
office@collectiveinkbooks.com
www.collectiveinkbooks.com
www.zero-books.net

For distributor details and how to order please visit the 'Ordering' section on our website.

Hardcover ISBN: 978 1 80341 590 1
eBook ISBN: 978 1 80341 591 8
PCN: 2023938813

A CIP catalogue record for this book is available from the British Library.

Design credit(s): Lapiz Digital

UK: Printed and bound by CPI Group (UK) Ltd, Croydon, CR0 4YY
Printed in North America by CPI GPS partners

for my father

CONTENTS

PREFACE

(WRITTEN THIRTEEN YEARS LATER)

There's something a little immodest about a "revised and expanded" edition of one's own book. It implies the earlier edition of the book needed improvement, or that it was incomplete (when in fact all books are, in a sense, incomplete, and for this reason cannot be improved).

But a book also has a life of its own, apart from the author's intention, the reader's opinions, or the dictates of the publishing industry. A book is published — or not published, ever. A book goes out of print. A book is put back into print. A book is read by some, not read by others, and merely referred to by others still. A book is bought, and returned. A book is reviewed and ignored, deemed relevant or irrelevant, timely or untimely, lent, borrowed, and often never returned. Some books rest on the oaken shelves of antiquarian booksellers, others lurk in the dollar bins outside (and it's starting to rain). Books are pulped, pirated, auctioned, and digitized. Others are quietly circulated among secret channels, forever in the shadows. Tangible yet temporary accretions of tree, pigment, and thread (or glue), a book has its own life cycle, bearing all the material wear and tear of its author.

When the opportunity arose to publish all three volumes in this series as one, I had reservations. I didn't want to simply reprint them together as is. While there are three books in the series, putting them in a single volume would seem to give the impression that it was one book, and not three. At the same time, the idea of a single book was intriguing to me. Going back over my writing of that time, I realized there was a lot of material that was not included in the original three volumes. Some of it was outtakes, some of it existed as notes or in outline form, and there were also derelict bits that simply had nowhere else to go. Much of that material has found its way back into this edition. I've also edited substantial sections of the original three books for continuity or to avoid repetition. Images — mostly from films — have been added, and the Notes have been updated as well. As I was in a different space when I originally wrote these books, I've made the somewhat arbitrary decision to keep all the added material from this same period.

In the Dust of This Planet — the first volume in the series — is a book that came about by accident. In the spring of 2010, I was attempting to gather together some stray thoughts about philosophical concepts in supernatural horror, many of them the result of teaching. I was also searching for a new way of writing, outside of the conventions of traditional academic scholarship. Most of the ideas I had existed at the time in notebooks — outlines, fragments, lists, and so on. For the sake of convenience, I decided to write out some of these ideas in as brief and concise a way as possible. After a couple of weeks, I looked over what I had and realized a few things. The first was that there was more than enough material for at least a short book. I went to the bookshelf, and the first thing that jumped out to me was H.P. Lovecraft's slim volume *Supernatural Horror in Literature* (published in 1927 … and later expanded). While not especially theoretical, Lovecraft's book does provide a brief but compelling survey, hinting at a neglected aspect of horror literature, which is the way in which supernatural horror highlights the limitations of human knowledge and the human-centric point of view. It seemed to me this could be a model for the book I had in mind.

The second realization was that most of what I wanted to say was already there in the short bits that I wrote. There was no need to add anything, no need for the accoutrements of introductions and conclusions and secondary scholarship and citation after citation. If what I had to say was there in a single page or single paragraph, so be it. I have long admired authors who adopt the short form in their writing, be it fragments, aphorisms, anecdotes, prose poems, or micro-essays. So, instead of attempting an overly ambitious, comprehensive study of philosophy and the horror genre, what appealed to me much more was the idea of a brief and concise book on the topic (little did I understand that this was overly ambitious in itself).

This led to a further dilemma, which was how to structure all these sections in a way that made sense. The architecture of a book can be tricky. On the one hand, it gives dissociated ideas a cohesion (though it can also stifle them). On the other hand, the lack of architecture can give the sense of randomness, or even laziness (and I have been guilty of both). As a wayward philosophy student, I was always taken by the variety of styles in philosophical writing — essays, dialogues, lectures, maxims, axioms, aphorisms, parables, sermons, sutras, and even aspects of autobiography. (I'm often disappointed that academic philosophy has lost much of this attentiveness to questions of style.)

I had just finished writing a book that dealt with mystical theology and Scholastic philosophy, and it was in my mind to appropriate some of these genres; they provided a nice combination of the analytical and the synthetic. Quickly the structure of the book began to take shape. As I began putting the sections together, it became apparent that a method of sorts was emerging from this — by no means rigorous, but a way of working all the same. It was something about "misreading" — misreading philosophy as if it was horror, and misreading horror as if it was philosophy. From this, Volumes 2 and 3 began to take shape, albeit in skeletal form.

Given the labyrinthine process of writing these books in the first place, revisiting them was a daunting task. In film, I've always been suspicious about a "director's cut," though there are of course exceptions. Some films are better — but some not. The same goes for books. As I glance over at the bookshelf, I see all manner of examples both literary and philosophical.

The more discursive, brooding, 1831 edition of *Frankenstein* contains numerous additions and changes from the taut and harrowing 1818 edition, and readers since have been divided on which is their favorite. In her Preface to the 1831 edition, Mary Shelley famously mythologized the creation of the novel itself, evoking the rain-swept ruminations of summer nights at the Villa Diodati. She notes, almost in passing: "Invention, it must be humbly admitted, does not consist in creating out of void, but out of chaos." What is incarnated is — as Shelley was well aware — another kind of chaos, the chaos of a book. It goes lumbering out into the world, its fate perpetually vulnerable to the exigencies of time.

When Arthur Schopenhauer published the third edition of *The World as Will and Representation* in 1859, the new material was twice as long as the original (also published in 1818). Though it is a doorstopper of a book, I'm glad he did so, because the material he added is more concise, more misanthropic, and laced with gallows humor — it bears all the signs of disillusion and disappointment. It was as if he stopped trying to impress others and simply put the book together how he thought it should be put together (but does an author ever stop trying? — a few years prior, an entry in his notebook reads: "When one has spent such a long life in insignificance, neglect, and disdain, they then come at the end with the beating of drums and the blowing of trumpets, and imagine that there is something").

Putting together even a slim book like *In the Dust of This Planet* is one thing. Finding a publisher is quite another. And yet the two are never totally separate from each other. At the time, nonfiction publishing tended to be divided between academic and trade, with little to address the grey zone in between. Zero Books had just been launched with the express intent of occupying that grey zone. Thankfully, Tariq Goddard and Mark Fisher were both open to the conceits of the book, for which I'm grateful. (Zero was at the time a very modest operation, with the three of us wearing multiple hats, as copyeditors, proofreaders, and even publicists.)

Going over all this material, I am also reminded of the Preface by French author J.-K. Huysmans, written for his 1884 novel *À Rebours* (often translated as "Against the Grain" or "Against Nature"), a book that for many was "the Bible" of the Decadent movement. It's titled "Preface, Written Twenty Years After the Novel," and was published after Huysmans, following a middling if not controversial career, had fled the petty and myopic melodramas of the world, seeking solace in a Trappist monastery. In his Preface, he writes: "there is nothing more disillusioning or more painful than to look over one's sentences after so many years. They have, as it were, been decanted, and settled to the bottom of the book; and generally books are not like wines, improving with age; once discolored by time the chapters have gone flat and their bouquet faded."

There's a part of me that has always admired Huysmans's disposition, in part because it implies that an author somehow transcends their books. I'm fascinated by authors who have the wherewithal to calmly, clearly, repudiate their own works as a matter of fact. That must be liberating. A certain detachment is required, an estrangement from one's own former self, a letting-go of "my" book. I wish I could, like Huysmans, find these books strange and unfamiliar, but I don't. It would be nice to let them go and move on, but I can't. The truth is that there remain still-activated filaments and tendrils that connect me to these books, and the ideas in them.

In this way, perhaps some books are "thought creatures," bibliophage-like secretions of often awkward and dubious authors who may, in their brief delusions of grandeur, treat their books as so many witch's "familiars" — when in reality it is flesh-and-blood authors who are the familiars of their books.

Brooklyn, April 2023

IN THE DUST OF THIS PLANET

1

PREFACE: CLOUDS OF UNKNOWING

The life of every individual, viewed as a whole and in general, and when only its most significant features are emphasized, is really a tragedy; but gone through in detail it has the character of a comedy.

– *Arthur Schopenhauer*

...when you are "nowhere" physically, you are "everywhere" spiritually ... Never mind if you cannot fathom this nothing, for I love it surely so much the better.

– *The Cloud of Unknowing*

The world has become increasingly unthinkable — a world of planetary disasters, emerging pandemics, tectonic shifts, strange weather, oil-drenched seascapes, and the furtive, always-looming threat of extinction. Perhaps it has always been this way. In spite of our daily concerns, wants, and desires, it is increasingly difficult to comprehend the world in which we live and of which we are a part. To confront this idea is to confront an absolute limit to our ability to adequately understand the world at all — an idea that has been a central motif of the horror genre for some time.

The aim of this volume is to explore the relationship between philosophy and horror, through this motif of the "unthinkable world." More specifically, we will explore the relation between philosophy as it overlaps with a number of adjacent fields (demonology, occultism, and mysticism), and the genre of supernatural horror, as it is manifest in fiction, film, comics, music, and other media. However, this relationship between philosophy and horror should not be taken to mean "the philosophy of horror," in which horror as a literary or film genre is presented as a rigorous formal system. If anything, it means the reverse, *the horror of philosophy*: the isolation of those moments in which philosophy reveals its own limitations and constraints, moments in which thinking enigmatically confronts the horizon of its own possibility — the thought of the unthinkable that philosophy cannot pronounce but via a non-philosophical language. The genre of supernatural horror is a privileged site in which this paradoxical thought of the unthinkable takes place. What an earlier era would have described through the language of darkness mysticism or negative theology, our contemporary era thinks of in terms of supernatural horror.

In this book, the means by which philosophy and horror are related to each other is the idea of the "world." But the world can mean many things, from a subjective experience of living in the world, to the objective, scientific study of geological conditions. The world is human and nonhuman, anthropocentric and non-anthropomorphic, sometimes even misanthropic. Arguably, one of the greatest challenges that philosophy faces today lies in comprehending the world in which we live as both a human *and* a nonhuman world.

On the one hand, we are increasingly aware of the world in which we live as a nonhuman world, a world outside, one that is manifest in the effects of global climate change, natural disasters, the energy crisis, and the progressive extinction of species worldwide. On the other hand, all these effects are linked, directly and indirectly, to our living in and living as a part of this nonhuman world. Hence contradiction is built into this challenge — we cannot help but to think of the world as a human world, by virtue of the fact that it is we human beings that think it.

However, this dilemma is not new. Philosophy has repeatedly returned to this problem of the nonhuman world. While in philosophy circles it may be called "correlationism," "accelerationism," or "atmospheric politics," for earlier philosophers this same dilemma was expressed in different terminology: the problem of "being-in-the-world," the dichotomy between "active" or "passive" nihilism, or the limits of human thought in the "antinomies of reason."

When the world as such cataclysmically manifests itself in the form of a disaster, how do we interpret or give meaning to the world? In classical Greece the interpretation is primarily *mythological* — Greek tragedy, for instance, not only deals with the questions of fate and destiny, but in so doing it also evokes a world at once familiar and unfamiliar, a world within our control or a world as a plaything of the gods. By contrast, the response of medieval and early modern Christianity is primarily *theological* — the long tradition of apocalyptic literature, as well as the Scholastic commentaries on the nature of evil, cast the nonhuman world within a moral framework of salvation. In modernity, in the intersection of scientific hegemony, industrial capitalism, and what Nietzsche famously prophesied as the death of God, the nonhuman world gains a different value. In modernity, the response is primarily *existential* — a questioning of the role of human individuals and human groups in light of modern science, high technology, industrial and postindustrial capitalism, and global conflict.

The contemporary cynic (which on many days describes my disposition) might respond that we still live by all of these interpretive frameworks, and that only their outer shell has changed: the mythological has become the stuff of the culture industries, spitting out big-budget, computer-generated films; the theo logical has diffused into political ideology and the fanaticism religious conflict; and the existential has been repurposed i self-help and the therapeutics of consumerism. While there may be some truth in this, what is more important is how all of these interpretive lenses — mythological, theological, existential — have as their most basic presupposition a view of the world as a human-centric world, as a world "for us" as human beings, living in human cultures, governed by human values. While classical Greece does, of course, acknowledge that the world is not totally within human control, it nevertheless tends to personify the nonhuman world in its pantheon of all-too-human gods, themselves ruled by jealousy, greed, and lust. The same can be said of the Christian framework, which, while also personifying the supernatural (angels and demons; a paternal God by turns loving and abusive), recasts the order of the world within a moral-economic framework of sin, debt, and redemption in a life after life. And the modern existential framework, with its ethical imperative of choice, freedom, and will in the face of both scientific and religious determinisms, ultimately constricts the entire world into a solipsistic, angst-ridden vortex of the individual human subject. In short, when the nonhuman world manifests itself to us in these ambivalent ways, more often than not our response is to recuperate that nonhuman world into whatever the dominant, human-centric worldview is at the time. Being human, how else would we make sense of the world?

However, one of the greatest lessons of the ongoing discussion on global climate change is that these approaches are no longer adequate. We can, instead, offer a new terminology for thinking about this problem of the nonhuman world. Let us call the world in which we live the *world-for-us*. This is the world that we, as human beings, interpret and give meaning to, the world that we relate to or feel alienated from, the world that we are at once a part of and that is also separate from us. But this world-for-us is not, of course, totally within the ambit of human wants and desires; the world often "bites back," resists, or ignores our attempts to mold it into the world-for-us. Let us call this the *world-in-itself*. This is the world in some inaccessible, already-given state, which we then turn into the world-for-us. The world-in-itself is a paradoxical concept; the moment we think it and attempt to act on it, it ceases to be the world-in-itself and becomes the world-for-us. A significant part of this paradoxical world-in-itself is grounded by scientific inquiry — both the production of scientific knowledge of the world and the technical means of acting on and intervening in the world.

Even though there is something out there that is not the world-for-us, and even though we can name it the world-in-itself, this latter constitutes a horizon for thought, always receding just beyond the bounds of intelligibility. Tragically, we are most reminded of the world-in-itself when the world-in-itself is manifest in the form of planetary disasters. The discussions on the long-term impact of climate change evoke this reminder of the world-in-itself, as the specter of extinction furtively looms over such discussions. Using advanced predictive models, we have even imagined what would happen to the world if we as human beings were to become extinct. So, while we can never experience the world-in-itself, we seem to be almost fatalistically drawn to it, perhaps as a limit that defines who we are as human beings.

Let us call this spectral and speculative world the *world-without-us*. In a sense, the world-without-us allows us to think the world-in-itself, without getting caught up in a vicious circle of logical paradox. The world-in-itself may coexist with the world-for-us — indeed the human being is defined by its impressive capacity for not recognizing this distinction. By contrast, the world-without-us cannot coexist with the human world-for-us; the world-without-us is the subtraction of the human from the world. To say that the world-without-us is antagonistic to the human is to attempt to put things in human terms, in the terms of the world-for-us. To say that the world-without-us is neutral with respect to the human, is to attempt to put things in the terms of the world-in-itself. The world-without-us lies somewhere in between, in a nebulous zone that is at once impersonal and horrific. The world-without-us is as much a cultural concept as it is a scientific one, and, as this book attempts to show, it is in the genres of supernatural horror and science fiction that we most frequently find attempts to think about, and to confront the difficult thought of, the world-without-us.

In a sense, the real challenge is not finding a new or improved version of the world-for-us, and it is not relentlessly pursuing the phantom objectivity of the world-in-itself. The real challenge lies in confronting this enigmatic concept of the world-without-us, and understanding why this world-without-us continues to persist in the shadows of the world-for-us and the world-in-itself. We can even abbreviate these three concepts further: the world-for-us is simply the *World*, the world-in-itself is simply the *Earth*, and the world-without-us is simply the *Planet*. The terms "world" and "worlding" are frequently used in phenomenology to describe the way in which we as human subjects exist in the world, at the same time as the world is revealed to us. By contrast, we understand "Earth" as encompassing all the knowledge of the world as an object, via geology, archaeology, paleontology, the life sciences, the atmospheric sciences (meteorology, climatology), and so on.

What then is the "Planet"? The World (the world-for-us) not only implies a human-centric mode of being, but it also points to the fuzzy domain of the not-human, or that which is not for-us. We may understand this in a general sense as that which we cannot control or predict, or we may understand it in more concrete terms as the ozone, carbon footprints, and so on. Thus, the World implicitly opens onto the Earth. But even "the Earth" is simply a designation that we've given to something that has revealed itself or made itself available to the gathering of samples, the generating of data, the production of models, and the disputes over policy. By necessity there are other characteristics that are not accounted for, that are not measured, and that remain hidden or occulted. Anything that reveals itself does not reveal itself in total. This remainder, perhaps, is the "Planet." In a literal sense the Planet moves beyond the subjective World, but it also recedes behind the objective Earth. The Planet is a planet, it is one planet among other planets, moving the scale of things out from the terrestrial into the cosmological framework. Whether the Planet is yet another subjective, idealist construct or whether it can have objectivity and be accounted for as such, is an irresolvable dilemma. What is important in the concept of the Planet is that it remains a negative concept, what remains "after" the human. The Planet can thus be described as impersonal and anonymous.

In the context of philosophy, the question is whether thought is always determined within the framework of the human point of view. What other alternatives lay open to us? One approach is to cease searching for some imaginary locus of the nonhuman "out there" in the world, and to refuse the well-worn dichotomy between self and world, subject and object. This is, of course, much easier said than done. In addition to the interpretive frameworks of the mythological (classical-Greek), the theological (medieval-Christian), and the existential (modern-European), would it be possible to shift our framework to something we can only call *cosmological*? Could such a cosmological view be understood not simply as the view from interstellar space, but as the view of the world-without-us, the Planetary view?

Scientists estimate that approximately ninety percent of the cells in the human body belong to nonhuman organisms (bacteria, fungi, and a whole bestiary of other organisms). Why shouldn't this also be the case for human thought as well? In a sense, this book is an exploration of this idea — *that thought is not human*. In a sense, the world-without-us is not to be found in a "great beyond" that is exterior to the World (the world-for-us) or in another planet just like Earth (the world-in-itself); rather, it is in the very fissures, lapses, or lacunae in the World and the Earth. The Planet (the world-without-us) is, in the terms of mystical traditions, the "dark intelligible abyss" that is paradoxically manifest as the World and the Earth.

Hence, a central focus of this book is on the problem of thinking this world-without-us; and its premise is that this problem is at once a philosophical, a political, and a cultural problem. Hence the subtitle of the series, of which this volume is a part: "horror of philosophy." But here a terminological clarification is in order. The term "horror" does not exclusively mean cultural productions of horror (or "art horror"), be it in fiction, film, comics, or video games. While the horror genre is an important part of culture, and while scholarly studies of the horror genre do help us to understand how a book or film obtains the effects it does, genre horror deserves to be considered as more than the sum of its formal properties. Also, by "horror" I do not mean the human emotion of fear, be it manifest in a fiction film, a news report, or a personal experience. Certainly this type of horror is an important part of the human condition, and it can be leveraged in different ways — ethically, politically, religiously — for the gain of different ends. This also deserves to be studied, especially for the ways in which reality and fiction increasingly overlap in our reality-TV culture. But "horror" in this sense remains strongly inscribed within the scope of human interests and the world-for-us.

Against these two assumptions, I would propose that horror be understood not as dealing with human fear in a human world (the world-for-us), but that horror be understood as being about the limits of the human as it confronts a world that is not just a World, and not just the Earth, but also a Planet (the world-without-us). This also means that horror is not simply about fear, but instead about the enigmatic thought of the unknown. The apprehension of this limit produces a particular kind of fear that is almost ancient. Hence, for authors like H.P. Lovecraft, what courses through the tradition of supernatural horror is a primordial "fear of the unknown." Horror is about the paradoxical thought of the unthinkable. In so far as it deals with this limit of thought, encapsulated in the phrase of the world-without-us, horror is "philosophical." But in so far as it evokes the world-without-us as a limit, it is a "negative philosophy" (akin to negative theology, but in the absence of God).

Briefly, the premise of this book is that "horror" is a non-philosophical attempt to think about the world-without-us philosophically.[1] Here culture is the terrain on which we find attempts to confront an impersonal and indifferent world-without-us, an irresolvable gulf between the world-for-us and the world-in-itself, with a void called the Planet that is poised between the World and the Earth. It is for this reason that this book treats genre horror as a mode of philosophy. Certainly a short story about an amorphous, quasi-sentient, mass of crude oil taking over the planet will not contain the type of logical rigor that one finds in the philosophy of Aristotle or Kant. But in a different way, what genre horror does do is it takes aim at the presuppositions of philosophical inquiry — that the world is always the world-for-us — and makes of those blind spots its central concern, expressing them not in abstract concepts but in a whole bestiary of impossible life forms — mists, ooze, blobs, slime, clouds, and muck. Or, as Plato once put it, "hair, mud, and dirt."

2

THREE *QUÆSTIO* ON DEMONOLOGY

Between the 11th and 13th centuries, much of Western philosophy was developed within the emerging universities, many of which were institutionally tied to the Church. During this period of "scholastic" thinking, a number of discursive forms were introduced that have become the basis for modern philosophy and its tenuous connection to the modern university. For instance, the *lectio*, or the "reading," is the forerunner of our modern "lecture," while the *disputatio* is the forerunner of our modern classroom debate or discussion. Originating in the medieval law schools, the *quæstio* or "question" developed as a systematic way to compare and contrast canonical legal texts, and the commentaries attached to them. When discrepancies were found in the same law developed in a different region or at a different time, this became the occasion for an inquiry or "questioning," the goal of which would be to achieve some sort of synthesis or reconciliation.

By the 12th century, philosophers and theologians incorporated the *quæstio* into their teaching as a way of systematically exploring a topic — usually one associated with or deriving from theological matters.

This, combined with the resurgence in the study of Aristotle, led to the kind of methodical, almost detective-like investigation of a concept that one finds in, for instance, the works of Thomas Aquinas. But the use of the *quæstio* did not have strict rules. Aquinas sometimes incorporates *quæstio* within the larger framework of the *summa* (the "summary" or compendium), while at other times the *quæstio* are themselves the framework (as in his work *De Malo*, or *On Evil*).

These forms — the *lectio*, the *disputatio*, and the *quæstio* — are not just simply methods of a bygone era; they can also be regarded as genres of writing, stylistic modes that allow for variety and nuance in structuring nonfictional prose. Because many of the ideas that inhabit the horror genre tend to have their roots in the philosophy and theology (and demonology) of the Scholastic period, this invites us to similarly adopt those modes of thinking and writing, albeit in a self-reflexive manner. What follows here are three *quæstio* which deal broadly with demonology, understood as the study of demons and the demonic. Historically speaking, demons are far from being horned and goateed Mephistos tempting us to do bad things. The demon is as much a philosophical concept as it is a religious, juridical, and political one. In fact, as we will see, the "demon" is often a placeholder for some sort of nonhuman, malefic agency that acts against the human (that is, against the world-for-us).

Borrowing from thinkers such as Aquinas, each *quæstio* utilizes the simple format of the statement of a theme, a discussion of the assumptions of that theme (*articulus*), and a discussion of counterarguments (*sed contra*), before attempting to find some middle way or resolution (*responsio*) — which, needless to say, often ends up in irresolution and further questions.

QUÆSTIO I — On the Black Gravity of Sound

ARTICULUS

The horror genre, in whatever medium it is expressed, is a genre rooted in the senses, and, in the tradition of supernatural horror in particular, it is also our senses that give testimony to what we cannot see, hear, or touch. Insofar as supernatural horror deals with what lies beyond the senses, the capacity to sense also becomes uncertain, unstable, and unreliable, indexing something that by definition cannot be sensed. The horror genre leaves us in a predicament, one that is as philosophical as it is affective: we suspect that there is something "out there" that we cannot verify through our senses, and yet our capacity to sense is all we have. No longer do the senses provide evidence for the reliable construction of knowledge; instead, what the senses reveal seems to undermine all knowledge. Human characters do see, hear, and feel things — the unnatural hovering of tenebrous shapes, a rustling in the dark that seems to have no source, impossible fissures in the fabric of spacetime — but what the senses point to is something that is contrary to all reason. A presence is manifest, via our senses, but what the testimony of the senses points to is an absence, an aberration, an impossibility, something that cannot possibly exist, or something that should not exist. A rift grows between what the senses indicate and what our reason demands: a rift within the core of the human subject between apprehension and comprehension — what Ann Radcliffe, writing during the heyday of the Gothic novel, characterized as the dynamic between "terror" and "horror." In special cases, the senses seem to indicate a "something" that reveals itself to be "nothing," or at least nothing that can be understood within the human-centric framework through which we have pictured the world to ourselves, a void at the heart of experience itself.

Horror motifs in music and in music subcultures provide one way of appreciating this predicament. The goth, industrial, and metal subcultures have traditionally taken up horror motifs in different ways, allowing lyrical content, musical form, and subcultural style to highlight this affective dimension of horror, in which supernatural themes point to a widening rift between the known and unknown, the latter often eclipsing the former. The black metal subculture is a case in point, where nearly everything about it — from its unhuman, screeching vocals, to the wearing of "corpsepaint," even to the scrawled and tortuous designs of band names — everything about black metal takes part in an ambience of the demonic. While black metal bands rarely put forth anything like a systematic philosophy of horror, the music, lyrics, and iconography of black metal are relevant for the ways in which they look back to earlier concepts of demons and the demonic — in all their ambiguity. The demonic, of course, is not only about possession, but about possession by unseen and often unknown forces. In Medieval Christian demonology — as in the tales of the Gothic novels or supernatural horror — the demonic revolves around an entire acoustics of incantation or exorcism, litanies of naming or cursing, language corroded into guttural sigils, a shadowy zone where demonology and musicology intersect. The communication with the demonic is a dialogue with the supernatural, a sonic ritual with a something "out there" that is manifest only in external forms, but which has no existence in and of itself.

Now a style more than a genre or movement, black metal has become increasingly mainstream (perhaps a sign of the ultimate Faustian bargain), though for many it remains controversial, especially for the lengths to which it took its obsession with forms of nihilism and self-destruction. In the 1990s, when the first Norwegian black metal bands emerged, the element of the demonic could not only be seen in the lyrics, imagery, and brutalist minimalism of the music, but also in the low-fi recording aesthetics, as if the recording itself were in the process of perpetual decay and rot. Black metal bands were not the first to do this, of course, but there is a sense in which black metal in the 1990s is a culmination point of horror-related themes in metal that looks back to the "New Wave of British Heavy Metal" in the 1980s, as well as the ur-metal of the early Black Sabbath albums. Perhaps there is even a sense of black metal being haunted by the Faustian bargain struck by Robert Johnson one night on an abandoned road in the Mississippi Delta, or back to the earliest plainchants that would form the *Missa pro defunctis* or Requiem Mass — perhaps back even further, to archaic attempts to make contact with the dead through funerary rites.[2]

Discussions of music genres often revolve around what does or doesn't constitute the essence of a genre, and, when disagreements arise, a common solution is simply to divide the genre into subgenres. Metal is no longer just heavy, but also death, speed, grind, doom, funeral, funeral doom, and of course black. But there is often less discussion on all the descriptors that make one subgenre distinct from another, words that belie a set of concepts and orientations. What, for example, is the "black" in black metal? In its popular associations, black metal is called black for a wide range of reasons — its references to black magic, demons, witchcraft, lycanthropy, necromancy, the nature of evil, and all things somber and funereal. Black metal is black because it is — this is one position at least — the most extreme form of metal, both in its attitude and in its musical form.

Of all these associations, there is one thing that sticks out, and that is the association of black metal to Satanism and the figure of the Devil. In fact, it would seem that this equation is the defining factor of black metal: *black = Satanism.* Obviously this is a reduction, and we will undo it later on. To begin with, however, we have to keep in mind the complicated history of translation and terminology, as the term *satan* or *ha-satan* passes from the Hebrew Bible (where it designates an angelic divinity that tests one's faith) to the Koine Greek of the Septuagint, to the Latin Vulgate of the Old Testament, before its appearance in the Gospels, where the figure of Satan is often depicted as a malefic figure poised against a monotheistic God, rather than against humanity per se. At different points in the long history of Christianity, the figure of the Devil, as the universal antagonist of God and humanity, is given different names, Satan being only one of them, and it is with this figure that the "black" in black metal may arguably be identified. Black metal is neither the only metal subgenre, nor the only music genre generally, to have made this association. One can just as easily find it in the music of Robert Johnson or the *Carmina Burana* as one could in bands like Black Sabbath. But the degree to which Satanism constitutes a conceptual reference point for black metal is indeed striking.

For the moment, then, let us think about "black" as meaning Satanic. What does this imply conceptually? For one, if we take the medieval and early Renaissance notion of Satan as a starting point, the equation black = Satanism is governed by a structure of opposition and inversion. Opposition defines the demonic as much as the divine; it is the "War in Heaven" described so vividly in the *Book of Revelation*, and dramatized in Milton's *Paradise Lost*. Opposition is also the structure that comes to define the medieval Church against its foes, the role that the Church councils accord various activities, from witchcraft to necromancy, as threats to both religious law and religious political authority. This opposition is as much political as it is theological, resulting in the infamous witch hunts, persecutions, and inquisitions of the early Renaissance. In its oppositional mode, the equation black = Satanic means "against God," "against the Sovereign," or even "against the divine."

The image of Satanism takes on a different form in the 19th century, however. In a sense, one cannot really talk about Satanism before this time, at least not as an organized counter-religion complete with its own rituals, texts, and symbols. What we would call Satanism before this time was, legally speaking, defined by the Church as heresy, and heresy is a particular kind of threat — it is not the threat of not believing at all, but the threat of believing in the "wrong" way. By contrast, 19th-century Europe, following upon the religious challenges posed by Romanticism, the French Revolution, and the aesthetics of the Gothic, developed something that more resembles modern Satanism. It is markedly different from the medieval and early Renaissance versions as it is from its later 20th-century incarnations (e.g., Anton LaVey's Church of Satan). This more formalized, "poetic" Satanism operated not only by opposition, but also by inversion, as demonstrated in Charles Baudelaire's then-scandalous poem "Les Litanies de Satan" (1857). This Satanism is ritually, as well as ideologically, opposed to the

Church. In its 19th-century context, it overlaps considerably with occultism, magic, and even offshoots of spiritualism. A key aspect of this poetic Satanism is the infamous Black Mass, deliriously portrayed in Joris-Karl Huysmans's novel *Là-bas* (1891; *Down There*) — purportedly based on a real Black Mass the author had attended. Every element of the Black Mass, from the blasphemous anti-prayer to the erotic desecration of the host, aims at an exact inversion of the Catholic High Mass.

If we take the "black" in black metal to mean Satanic, then we see how this is emblematic of a conceptual structure of opposition (its medieval, "heretical" variant) and inversion (its 19th-century, "poetic" variant). In this association we also see an instrumental relation to the natural world and supernatural forces. The "black" in this case is almost like a technology, or a dark technics. Black magic in particular is predicated on the ability of the sorcerer to utilize dark forces against light, leveraging one set of beliefs against another.

SED CONTRA

On the contrary, it is obvious to any listener of black metal that not all black metal bands ascribe to this equation of black = Satanic. There are many black metal bands that self-consciously adopt a non-Christian framework as their foundation, referencing everything from Norse mythology to the mysteries of ancient Egypt. In these instances, what is "black" about black metal is its decided antipathy to a view of Christianity as monotheistic, institutional, and state-sanctioned. In taking up such positions, "pagan" tends to be more negatively defined, as not-Christian, not-orthodox, not-institutional. We can take a different approach, then, and suggest another meaning to the word "black" in black metal, and that is: *black = pagan*. We will undo this yet again, but for the time being let us think about this in contrast to the formula of black = Satanism.

Scholars of religion have long noted that the various groups that have historically been called "pagan" never themselves used this term to identify their spirituality or their practices. In a sense, much of the modern scholarship on the topic has been devoted to complicating, if not rejecting, the usefulness of the term "pagan" altogether. In the early 20th century, scholars such as the classicist, art historian, and archaeologist Jane Ellen Harrison made significant contributions to a more nuanced understanding of ancient Greek religions. In books such as *Prolegomena to the Study of Greek Religion* (1903; revised 1922), Harrison pointed to the profound connection between Greek tragedy, myth, cosmology, and social order, grounding her analysis in ancient festivals and the role of sacrifice. This work was extended in the late 20th century in studies such as Walter Burkert's *Homo Necans: The Anthropology of Ancient Greek Sacrificial Ritual and Myth* (1972), and René Girard's *Violence and the Sacred* (also 1972), both of which analyze ritual sacrifice in the practices of the "mystery cults" of Late Antiquity, from Orphism, to the Eleusinian Mysteries, to the Mithraic Mysteries, and beyond.

In this sense, the different forms of so-called paganism also overlap with the rise of Christianity as a dominant religious, juridical, and political force. Paganism, as a polytheistic — and sometimes pantheistic — viewpoint, thus stood in stark contrast to the orthodox sovereignty of the Church.

Following the long and gradual adoption of Christianity in the 4th century by the Roman Emperor Constantine, the term *paganus* ("rustic," "rural," "from the country") became one of several terms used to identify Romans who continued to practice some form of polytheistic, often regionally defined, religious practice. While such beliefs and practices differed widely, at their core were two elements that sat in an uneasy relationship with the new state-sponsored, Roman Christianity: the practice of animal and sometimes human sacrifice, and the division between exoteric and esoteric aspects of religious belief (often centered on particular figures such as a priest or priestess). In a sense, then, "paganism" denotes less a negative or reactive mode, than an entirely different, and ultimately pre-Christian outlook.

Because of this, forms of paganism were often inculcated within what the Church ambiguously called "heresy." During the high

Renaissance a wide range of activities, from alchemy to reactivated forms of shamanism, were popularly associated with paganism. The ideas of Rosicrucianism, Freemasonry, Hermeticism, and, in the 19th century, theosophy and spiritualism, all claimed some connection to an ancient, pagan outlook. The ambit and scope of some of these movements is even more expansive than Christianity itself; the writings of Madame Blavatsky and Rudolph Steiner, for instance, are exemplary in their transcultural and transhistorical breadth. In books such as *Isis Unveiled* (1877) or *The Secret Doctrine* (1888), Blavatsky covers everything from archaic mystery cults to modern paranormal research, giving one the sort of global perspective found in anthropology classics such as James Frazer's *The Golden Bough* (1890).

While these different forms of paganism sometimes overlap with the traditional Judeo-Christian outlook, more often than not they are marginalized, and, in some cases, driven underground into regional religious cults or early incarnations of secret societies. It's not difficult to see the attraction of "paganism" in this sense for modern subcultures such as that of black metal. But we also see one major difference from the prior association of "black" with Satanism. Whereas the latter operated through opposition and inversion, the former is related to the dominant framework of Christianity by exclusion and alterity. Whereas heresy was viewed by the Church primarily as an internal threat, with paganism one finds, in some cases, an entirely different framework — an external threat. Much of this alterity has to do with almost point-for-point contrasts with orthodox, institutional Christianity: where Christianity is monotheistic, paganism is polytheistic (even pantheistic); whereas Christianity is hierarchical, juridical, and "top down," paganism is underground, esoteric, and "bottom up"; whereas Christianity advocates the denial of nature and the Earthly, paganism is immersed in nature as the manifestation of the divine; whereas Christianity emphasizes transcendence, paganism emphasizes immanence.

The iconography is also different. Instead of demonic invocations and the Black Mass, there may be images of animistic nature, elemental and earth powers, astral lights and astral bodies, the metamorphoses of human and animal, human and plant, and human and nature itself. In paganism one is always "on the side of" nature and its animistic forces. The magician is less one who uses nature as a tool, and more like a conduit for natural forces. If anything, the pagan outlook inverts the view of technical mastery — nature makes use of us, not vice versa. Whereas in Satanism one finds an attempt to instrumentalize dark forces against light in a kind of holy war, in paganism magic is technology and vice versa, the two overlapping in the identity of the natural and the supernatural. This tendency reaches a pitch in the 19th century revival of so-called pagan traditions. For example, works like Eliphas Lévi's notorious *Dogme et Rituel de la Haute Magie* (1856) read more like a veritable how-to manual of occult knowledge, theories, and practices, in which the line between magic and technology nearly disappears. In contrast to the dark technics of Satanism, then, the dark magic of paganism.

So far, we have two possible meanings that the word "black" can have in black metal culture. These are black = Satanism and black = paganism. One has the structure of opposition and inversion, and other the structure of exclusion and alterity. Both are united, however, in what amounts to a human-oriented relation to nature and natural forces — with Satanism we see a technics of dark vs. light forces, and with paganism we see a dark magic of being-on-the-side of nature itself. Despite their differences, both meanings of the term "black" point to one thing they have in common, and that is an anthropocentric view towards the world. The world is either there for us to use as a tool, or it is there inside us as a force for our benefit. Even as the various forms of paganism adopt an animistic or pantheistic view of the world, they also assert a means of knowing and utilizing the forces of that world; the self is at once united with the world and yet split from it. The human point of view seems to be a limit for thought in both of these meanings of "black."

RESPONSIO

Is there yet another meaning of "black" beyond this? There is, but it is a difficult thought to think, though it does exist (actually it doesn't exist, though the thought of its not-existing does). As we noted, both the Satanic and pagan variants of the word "black" remain minimally committed to the perspective of the human, even as they posit forces in the world beyond all comprehension. The result is that these forces are in some way always "for us" as human beings (either as wielding darkness or "being on the side of" darkness). Whereas both the Satanic and pagan variants retain an anthropocentric thread, a third position, which we can call "cosmic," attempts to relinquish even this.

Music again provides us with some insights here. Or rather, sound. Indeed, it is in the slippage from music to sound, and from sound to silence, that we might be able to detect this "cosmic" aspect of the symbolics of "black." The horror genre, in particular, is filled with underappreciated examples of the horrific aspects of sound. While many of us might think of the horror genre as an ocular-centric mode of storytelling (based on what we can or can't see), the role of sound uniquely reveals something about the shifting sense of unreality in supernatural horror. Sound is manifestly present but (for us) it is also invisible, and it is no accident that the ghosts, revenants, monsters, and "unnamable things" that populate supernatural horror are often heard before they are seen (that is, if they are seen at all). The sound of the supernatural conveys the sense of an ambivalent "beyond" or a "something else" lurking in the blind spot of human cognition — and because of this, there is also a sense in which the supernatural is not supernatural at all, but only supernatural for us as human beings with a constrained sensorium.

The maddening, rhythmic beating of Edgar Allan Poe's "The Tell-Tale Heart"; the memorable scenes of supernatural sounds in classic horror films like *The Haunting* (1963); or the 2012 film *Berberian Sound Studio*, where the hallucinatory capacity of sound seeps into the darkest corners of the psyche. The ability to hear the supernatural — or better, to listen to it — is as much about detecting its presence as it is about straining to understand what it is trying to "say," what significance it holds, what it means. And yet, the same uncertainty holds as with the act of seeing. An acoustic phenomenon manifests itself at the same time that it recedes into a nether region of what cannot be heard, or of what lies outside the human range of hearing. Are these voices from the beyond, or are they simply voices in my head? Is the manifestation of sound from the beyond itself meaningful, or is it simply the desiderata of our own, confined, human-bound range of hearing?

In H.P. Lovecraft's short story "The Music of Erich Zann" (1922), a university student (who is, of course, studying metaphysics) moves into an apartment building, where he discovers an eccentric old man living on the top floor, playing mysterious and haunting melodies on his viol into the glowing night. The student is inexplicably drawn to the music, though he is rebuffed by the old man. One night, listening outside the old man's door, the student hears strange, chaotic, violent sounds — sounds which almost seem to be replying to the old man's viol playing. Fearing for the old man's life, he breaks into the apartment, and everything is a cacophonous, cadence-like blur. Strange entities seem to brush by him in the dark, the whirling sounds far off into the cosmos and yet whispering inside his head. The old man, who appears to have died, continues playing. Ancient ritual, musical invocation, portals to other dimensions, the unbearable revelation of having heard something outside the scope of hearing.

The cosmic dimensions of sound are heightened in the 1906 short story "The Omega Force" (*La Fuerza Omega*), by Argentine author Leopoldo Lugones. In it, we hear about an amateur scientist obsessed with the occult potentials inherent in modern technologies. Experimentally modifying some phonograph discs, the scientist makes an accidental discovery. His strange and disturbing inventions have tangible, material effects on solid objects — including the human body — sometimes pulverizing them into so much dust and debris. Increasingly unhinged, the scientist becomes fixated on his theory of an invisible, monistic energy or force that impersonally flows through all living, existing entities, such that all forms of material existence are simply localized manifestations of this "Omega force" (Lugones's story was published in a collection titled *Las Fuerzas Extrañas*, or "Strange Forces"). Mind, matter, and cosmos collapse. But, as with so many tales of this kind, this knowledge comes at a price, and the forces that manifest are also the forces that dissipate, neither of them operating within the limited ambit of human control and comprehension.

Music become sound, sound become physics, physics the elemental properties of the cosmos itself. When we reach "The House of Sounds," a 1911 short story by M.P. Shiel, we enter a terrain in which music and metaphysics become one in the same. Shiel (who also wrote a mystery novel titled *The Lost Viol*) builds this out into the idea of music as a portal to other dimensions, an entire house built around this idea of communing with the beyond. But here, as with Lovecraft, there are similarly tragic consequences for those who would dare — or who simply feel compelled — to follow the strange sounds of the cosmos beyond the scope of human capacity. Similarly, Algernon Blackwood's 1910 novel *The Human Chord*, while not counted among his best writing, extends these motifs in fascinating ways. There, a young student is drawn into an enigmatic cult devoted to the physics of sound. Their leader is convinced that the right group of people, emitting a precise combination of sounds — the titular human "chord" — will have the capacity not only to loosen the bonds of physical reality as we know it but also to refashion the physical world.

Blackwood's novel is built around a simple intuition: that sounds is physics, and physics is phenomenal, material reality, and that by extension there is not only a physics to sound, but sound is in every way just as material as what we can see or touch. As with our other senses, however, a rift is revealed between what we can hear and what we can register. The cosmic unraveling of "the human chord" has more to do with this enigmatic state of a sound that is registered but that we cannot hear. This is, in many ways, the crux of the supernatural horror tradition. And it is also the predicament of finite, limited human perspectives against what we can only dimly intuit as a much vaster, much more impersonal scope of the cosmos. A something, a "beyond" is or seems to be there, but always residing in that liminal zone where the human must either resign itself to its relative insignificance or annul itself in the process.

What these and other tales express is the sense that, beyond human-constructed systems, there is only the anonymous, impersonal "in itself" of the world, indifferent to us as human beings, despite all we do to change, to shape, to improve and even to save the world. A strange mysticism of the world-without-us, a hermeticism of the abyss, a noumenal occultism. It is the difficult thought of the world as absolutely unhuman, and indifferent to the hopes, desires, and struggles of human individuals and groups. Its limit-thought is the idea of absolute nothingness, unconsciously represented in the many popular media images of nuclear war, natural disasters, global pandemics, and the cataclysmic effects of climate change. Certainly, such images are different from the scientific, economic, and political realities that underlie them, but they are spectral images deeply embedded in our psyche nonetheless. Beyond these specters there is the impossible thought of extinction, with not even a single human being to think the absence of all human beings, with no thought to think the negation of all thought. We can refer to this perspective not just as cosmic, but as a form of "cosmic pessimism." Hence another possible meaning of the term "black": *black = cosmic.*

This cosmic pessimism has a genealogy that is more philosophical than theological. Its greatest — and most curmudgeonly — proponent was Arthur Schopenhauer, the misanthrope who rallied as much against philosophy itself as he did against doctrinal religion and the politics of his time. Throughout his life, Schopenhauer remained equally dissatisfied with the meticulous system building of Kant as with the nature-Romanticism of Fichte, Schelling, and Hegel. If we are to really think about the world as it exists in itself, Schopenhauer says, we have to challenge the most basic premises of philosophy. These include the principle of sufficient reason (everything that exists has a reason for existing), as well as the well-worn dichotomy between self and world, so central to modern empirical science. We have to entertain the possibility that there is no reason for something existing; or that the split between subject and object is only our name for something equally accidental we call knowledge; or, an even more difficult thought, that while there may be some order to the cosmos, it is an order that is absolutely indifferent to our existence, and of which we can have only a negative awareness.

The most we can do, Schopenhauer notes, is to think this persistence of the negative. He uses the term *Vorstellung* (Representation; Idea; Conception) to describe this negative awareness, an awareness of the world as we conceive it (through subjective experience or through aesthetic representation), or the world as it is presented to us (through practical knowledge or scientific observation). Whatever the case, the world remains the world-for-us, the world as *Vorstellung*. Is there something outside this? Logically there must be, since every positive needs a negative. Schopenhauer calls this nonexistent something-outside *Wille* (Will; Drive; Force), a term that designates less the volition or action of an individual person, and more an abstract principle that runs through all things, from the bowels of the earth to the array of constellations — but which is not in itself anything towards which we can point.

Unlike his Romantic contemporaries, however, Schopenhauer views this abstract *Wille* as impersonal, blind, and indifferent to our wants and desires. There is no nature-for-us, much less any being-on-the-side-of nature. Furthermore, the *Wille* is, in itself, "nothing," a gulf at the heart of the world as *Vorstellung*. It is both the ground and the ungroundedness of the world:

> If we picture to ourselves roughly as far as we can the sum total of misery, pain, and suffering of every kind on which the sun shines in its course, we shall admit that it would

> have been much better if it had been just as impossible for the sun to produce the phenomenon of life on earth, as on the moon, and the surface of the earth, like that of the moon, had still been in a crystalline state ... We can also regard our life as a uselessly disturbing episode in the blissful repose of nothingness.[3]

Schopenhauer is unparalleled in this sort of metaphysical misanthropy, a cosmic pessimism that runs the gamut from the microcosm to the macrocosm. Even a thinker like Nietzsche, who otherwise lauds Schopenhauer as one of his "educators" and one of the great anti-philosophers, chooses to recuperate Schopenhauer's pessimism into a more vigorous, vitalistic, "Will-to-Power." But for Schopenhauer, the blind compulsion of the *Wille* is also inseparable from a negation that ultimately negates even itself, in a perpetual cycle of metaphysical self-abnegation. This blind, purposeless, indifferent aspect of the *Wille* leads Schopenhauer to make a distinction between two kinds of "nothing": a privative nothing (the *nihil privativum*; dark as the absence of light, death as the absence of life), and a paradoxical, negative nothing (the *nihil negativum*; nothing without any positive value). In so doing, Schopenhauer not only highlights a paradox at the core of philosophical logic (the moment "nothing" is thought, it becomes "something"; every instance of "not" also "is"), but he also embeds this within the existential problem of suffering (mortality and death inhering in each instance of life; every life is already dead).

In this sense, Schopenhauer's pessimism is less about a pessimism specific to human existence (e.g., the all-too-human despair of an identity crisis or a lapse in faith), and more about the way in which thought always devolves upon its own limits, the prism through which positive knowledge turns into negative knowledge. To find an equal to Schopenhauer, one would have to look not to philosophy, but to writers of supernatural horror such as Lovecraft, whose stories evoke a sense of what he termed "cosmic outsideness":

> The most merciful thing in the world, I think, is the inability of the human mind to correlate all its contents. We live on a placid island of ignorance in the midst of black seas of infinity, and it was not meant that we should voyage far … some day the piecing together of dissociated knowledge will open up such terrifying vistas of reality, and of our frightful position therein, that we shall either go mad from the revelation or flee from the deadly light into the peace and safety of a new dark age.[4]

Here we have yet another meaning of the term "black" — not Satanism with its opposition and dark technics, not paganism with its exclusion and dark magic, but a cosmic pessimism, with its dark metaphysics of negation that opens onto the nonhuman.

Having gone through this, it's tempting to view these senses of "black" as a typology in music genres such as metal. For instance, it would seem that black metal bands might fall into one of these three categories. Old school Norwegian black metal might fit the description of "black" as Satanic, perhaps exemplified in Darkthrone's albums from the 1990s — *A Blaze in the Northern Sky* (1992), *Under a Funeral Moon* (1993), and *Transylvanian Hunger* (1994) — where both lyrics and musical form seem drenched in the ritual ruins of unholy anathemas. But a different perspective suggests that Norwegian black metal is also "black" in the sense of pagan, suggested by Ulver's "black metal trilogy" from the same period, *Bergtatt* (1995), *Nattens Madrigal* (1997), and the eerie quietude of *Kveldssanger* (1996), albums that take up supernatural themes in a folkloric and even mythical register. Both bands also evoke a sense of the cosmic — ancient trees, primeval forests, forbidden utterances, all set against the cold and impersonal canopy of deep space. It is likely that variations of black metal — doom metal, funeral doom metal, depressive black metal, suicidal black metal, and of course cosmic black metal — all these extend from these interwoven senses of "black."

These examples from the metal genre are a reminder of the ways that traditional musical forms can be leveraged in ways that reveal the elemental, unhuman physics of sound — corrosion, erosion, gravity, density. Borrowing terms from alchemical traditions, we might say that, in certain kinds of music, a kind of "blackened" physics emerges, where, at its peak, music collapses into sound, and sound unfurls in unseen quanta of waves, reverberations, and sound so slow we cannot hear it. For decades, bands on the fringes of the metal genre such as Sunn O))) have dedicated themselves to this blackened physics, distilled in drone metal albums like *The Grimmrobe Demos* (1999) and expanded in the Requiem-like eeriness of *Monoliths and Dimensions* (2009). The work of Sunn O))) also points to the dense and vast soundscapes of composer Glenn Branca (whose *Symphony No. 13* is scored for 100 guitars), to the interstellar cataclysms of Romanian spectralist composers Iancu Dumitrescu and Ana-Maria Avram, to haunting postwar avant-garde compositions such as György Ligeti's *Atmosphères* or Krzysztof Penderecki's *Polymorphia* (both 1961). It is perhaps no accident that the music of composers such as Ligeti and Penderecki have also been used in horror films such as *The Exorcist* and *The Shining*, and it is likely an influence on the eerie and reverberant soundtrack produced by the band Goblin for Dario Argento's 1977 film *Suspiria*.

But, as any listener to these compositions will attest, the music of Ligeti, Penderecki, and other composers of the period are anything but illustrative or representational. They exist in a sound world of their own, often at the fringes of acoustic legibility, a sound world of overtones, dissonance, and uncanny sonic spectra that seem to echo from another dimension altogether. Perhaps the benchmark example in this regard is *Quattro pezzi su una nota sola*, the 1959 orchestral work by Giancinto Scelsi, an enigmatic figure even by avant-garde standards. The work was produced following the composer's mental breakdown in the 1940s, where he experienced a creative catatonia, unable to compose or play anything, except a single note on the piano, over and over. In the process, Scelsi discovered that the actual sound of the note was less interesting that the *decay* of the sound. The sound itself produced a whole array of overtones and other artifacts that revealed themselves in this subtractive, distilled context. It was the dissipation of sound, and everything happening "around" the sound, that became the focal point, as if something almost epiphenomenal was generated in the dissipative passage from sound to silence. Running counter to the showy hyper-complexity of 12-tone, atonal, and serialist music of the period, Scelsi's *Quattro pezzi* is sound that resides in the blind spot of hearing.

Perhaps, at its limit, music like this reaches a point where the dense reverberation of its "necro" sound collapses in on itself, producing something like the sonic equivalent of a black hole. Unlikely as it may seem, ambient music too has undergone a transformation, and is also "dark ambient," "space ambient," and of course "black ambient." Against the cliché of ambient music as a New Age form of relaxing, therapeutic, "spa music," black ambient projects take the next step into this third sense of "black" as cosmic, resulting in a deeply subtractive sound. Without lyrics, without melody, lacking anything resembling song structure, and inhabiting a subsonic sound world at the threshold of human hearing, black ambient is not even music per se. It pulls as much from the long tradition of experimental and avant-garde music as it does from the genres of metal. The work of Lustmord (aka Brian Williams) is exemplary in this regard, where there is a sense of the hollowed-out, chthonic depths of the planet — in albums such as *The Place Where the Black Stars Hang* (1994) or *Trinity* (2020) — or the sense of being engulfed in the infinite void of deep space — in early albums such as *Heresy* (1990) or more recent work such as *Dark Matter* (2016). Williams, who also works as a sound designer and film score composer, began the Lustmord project in the 1980s, emerging from his work with industrial bands such as Throbbing Gristle and SPK. What began as harsh industrial noise has, over time, become more and more minimal, whittling away everything sonically unnecessary, until what is left is the musical equivalent of dark matter or deep space. It is no accident that Williams often draws inspiration from developments in astrophysics and the enigmatic science of black holes and other strange cosmic phenomena. In the *Dark Matter* album, the compositions actually make use of electromagnetic resonance captured from pulsars and interstellar flares, referencing the oblique, indirect, and tenebrous core of ambient itself — the sound that is at once nowhere in particular but everywhere in general, nondirectional sound, sound that is felt but not heard, sound that is equivalent to space, space eclipsed in sound.

This "cosmic" dimension has correspondences to music seemingly unrelated to black metal or black ambient. The exploration of sound at the threshold of hearing is prevalent in the work of William Basinski's *Disintegration Loops*, Thomas Köner's *Daikan*, and Francisco López's "Untitled" series: sound that decays slowly over time, sound that emerges from its subsonic depths with such patience that the listener almost doesn't notice, or sound that is actually felt before it is heard. This strange ambiance of the subtractive is at the core of the work of French composer Éliane Radigue. From her early experiments with tape feedback loops in the 1950s (influenced by musique concrète pioneers Pierre Schaeffer and Pierre Henry), to her discovery of the ARP 2500 analog synthesizer in the 1970s, to her recent compositions for solo cello, organ, and other instruments, Radigue has pursued the manifold textures of sound distilled to its primeval core. What seems to be musical emptiness is in actuality an entire sound world, often operating at temporal fluctuations alien to our own. When nothing seems to be happening, everything is happening. This is perhaps best demonstrated in Radigue's *Trilogie de la mort*, comprised of three interconnected, hour-long pieces: *Kyema* (1988), *Kailasha* (1991), and *Koumé* (1993). Though the pieces reference the *Bardo Thodol* (*Tibetan Book of the Dead*), they are anything but illustrative, comprised instead of extremely gradual fluctuations of sound emerging and dissipating, a kind of sound at once physics and metaphysics.

In this sense, the most striking example of Cosmic Pessimism comes from outside of the metal genre altogether. It is by the

Japanese multi-instrumentalist, poet, and mystic Keiji Haino. Haino's album *So, Black is Myself* employs a subtractive minimalism akin to that of Sunn O))) or Lustmord. Haino's approach is eclectic, borrowing techniques from everything from Noh theater to Troubadour singing. Clocking in at just under 70 minutes, *So, Black is Myself* uses only a tone generator and voice. Its sole lyric is the title of the piece itself: "Wisdom that will bless I, who live in the spiral joy born at the utter end of a black prayer." The piece is brooding, rumbling, deeply sonorous, and meditative. Sometimes the tone generator and Haino's voice merge into one, while at other times they diverge and become dissonant. Haino's voice itself spans the tonal spectrum, from nearly subharmonic chant to an uncanny falsetto perhaps produced only by starving banshees. Haino's performance is an example of the radically unhuman aspect of the cosmic, the impersonal affect of dread described by Kierkegaard as "antipathic sympathy and sympathetic antipathy." *So, Black is Myself* also manages to be mystical at the same time that the individual performer is dissolved into a meshwork of overtones — voice, space, and instrument variously existing in consonance and dissonance. *So, Black is Myself* is a reminder of the metaphysical negation that is also at the core of black metal, as if Schopenhauer's *nihil negativum* were rendered as musical form, ultimately negating even itself in a kind of musical anti-form.

QUÆSTIO II — On Whether There Are Demons, and How to Know Them

ARTICULUS

That demons really exist seems to be verified by the cross-cultural acceptance of supernatural forces of some type, that may be rendered to varying degrees as animalistic or anthropomorphic, and that display a general antagonism towards all of humanity (and in some cases, the world itself). Scholarship in comparative mythology and religion has done much to reveal the similarities and the differences between demons of this type. The *jinn* in Islamic theology and pre-Islamic mythology, the *se'irim* of the Hebrew Bible, and the legion of evil spirits in the Judeo-Christian tradition, all testify to some type of supernatural antagonism that may manifest itself within theistic ways of understanding the world. Other claims have also been made for demon or demon-like equivalents in various African, Polynesian, and Native American folklore traditions, as well as in the Hindu and Buddhist pantheons (in the *Tibetan Book of the Dead*, for instance, one encounters, as part of the Bardo cycle, the "dawning of wrathful deities").

However, it seems that our technologically advanced, scientifically hegemonic, and religiously orthodox post-millennium world leaves little room for something as fanciful as demons. At the most, such flights of fancy are left to the culture industries, where demons swarm about (via advanced computer graphics) in films, television, and video games. Even within the culture industry, one finds the subgenre of Satanic cinema — from "documentaries" such as *Häxan*, to classics of Hollywood horror such as *The Exorcist*, to recent indie films like *The Witch*. In films like these, the elaborate scenes of exorcism and possession serve to remind us that what we today classify as mental illness was, for an earlier era, a manifestation of the demonic.

Nevertheless, one must still account for the persistence of the figure of the demon, even as it is relegated to the fringes of genre horror. One way of doing this is to understand the demon less in a strictly theological sense, in which the demon is the relation between the supernatural and natural, and to understand it in its cultural function as a way of thinking about the relationships between human individuals and groups. In short, the figure of the demon, though it may not be accepted literally today, can be understood as *anthropological*, as a metaphor for the nature of the human, and the relation of human to human.

In fact, it is possible to outline an anthropology of the demon in Western culture with this perspective in mind. We could begin with the *daimōn* (δαιμων) in classical Greece, found in Hesiod and Homer as well as in the works of Plato. There the demon is not a malefic figure, but a divine entity that may serve as a source of inspiration, or that may serve to warn or to caution. When Socrates claims to always have by his side a "demon" (*daimonion*) that prevents him from taking the wrong course of action, he is invoking this more elemental meaning of the demon. The Greek demon is, in a sense, very much in keeping with the classical themes of human free will and destiny vis-à-vis the will of the gods.

The association of the demon with malevolent forces is most commonly made in early Christianity, though there are arguments for its development in early Judaic and Islamic theology as well. The archetypal example of this is the demon as tempter, as told in Athanasius's *Life of Antony*. While meditating in the desert, Anthony is repeatedly assaulted by demons, which take the form of everything from tempestuous winds to Satyrs and Centaurs. After closing himself off in a desert cave, Anthony is again assaulted by demons. "The demons, as if breaking through the building's four walls, and seeming to enter through them, were changed into the forms of beasts and reptiles."[5] Despite the suffering he endures, Anthony's asceticism and prayer remains unfaltering, and the demonic assault is to no avail. This motif of immovable prayer against the temptations of the demon has also become something of an iconographic image of the demonic in Western art.

An interesting shift takes place once one moves into the clinical and medical view of Western modernity. In a 1923 article, "A Neurosis of Demonical Possession in the Seventeenth Century," Freud recasts an account of possession in light of psychoanalysis's study of the workings of the unconscious. In terms of historical accounts of possession, the case study itself is unremarkable. It involves Christoph Haitzmann, a young painter who, in or around 1677, sees a priest, complaining of convulsions, hallucinations, and a sense of persecution. Aside from Haitzmann's being an artist, the priest finds nothing wrong with Haitzmann — except, of course, that he may be in consort with a demon. Like the case study, Freud's analysis is also unremarkable. Tracing Haitzmann's delusions to the death of his father, Freud then remarks that the demon is a condensed "father-substitute" — at once a replacement for Haitzmann's mourned loss, as well as a crisis brought about by the absence of the father as a figure of authority. As per the standard psychoanalytic reading, the demon is taken to be an externalized projection, and the so-called possession really a form of therapeutic purging for Haitzmann himself.

One of the ironies of this modern, medicalized take on demonic possession is that, when it comes to the mysteries of human behavior, it has generated more mystification than clarification. Demonic possession, when rendered as a medical problem, produces a different kind of demon: the human mind possessed by unreason. No longer does unreason play the dark counterpart to reason, by turns critiquing, mocking, and satirizing it. With the ascendency of "psychiatric power" unreason is exiled from reason, and enters a separate domain. But this disease is different from physical ailments, in that its lesions are largely invisible, existing in the inaccessible interiority of the subject. This possession by unreason must be brought to the surface, in a kind of medically codified language, a series of signs and gestures, culminating in what Michel Foucault calls a "delirious discourse." It is hardly surprising that, alongside these developments in psychiatry and, later, psychoanalysis, we find numerous works in the horror genre dealing with madness, hysteria, and other modes of cognition coded as mental aberration.

One can trace this in the "diary of a madman" literature, a kind of subgenre in itself that deals with unreason narrating its own condition. Perhaps the best-known example is Nikolai Gogol's 1835 story "Diary of a Madman," which details the gradual descent into madness of a Russian civil servant. Gogol's story uses two narrative techniques that are set against each other: the diary format, which gives the account a documentary-like legitimacy, and the unreliability of the narrator, whose progressive mental instability chips away at his account of events. Similar approaches can be found in Tolstoy's story "Diary of a Madman" (1884), in which a profound anxiety over death leads to madness, and in Guy de Maupassant's "Diary of a Madman" (1885), both of which take the premise of

Gogol's to metaphysical proportions. Maupassant would crystallize these themes in his 1866 story "The Horla," perhaps one of the most harrowing examples of an unreliable narrator. "The Horla" highlights a troubling quandary that is nascent in Gogol's story as well: at what point can we as readers say that the narrator has gone mad? It is clear by the end of the story the narrator has been possessed by unreason, but the format of the diary creates a slippery slope of incremental steps and finer and finer distinctions, until it becomes difficult to say when exactly it happened — and yet it clearly has happened. Charlotte Perkins Gilman's famous story "The Yellow Wallpaper" (1892) also uses a diary-like format to inflect these issues through the lens of gender and the ominous legacy of 19th century theories of hysteria and depression. By the early 20th century, when Lu Xun publishes his own "Diary of a Madman," the conundrum has also become political. Is the "madman" simply someone who is able to see through the charade of social norms and power dynamics, or are such supposed insights simply forms of self-delusion?

Such tales of reason possessed by unreason lead to a further permutation, in which the demon is neither purely theological nor psychological, but sociological. Here the political aspects of the demon, as the stand-in for a threatening Other, come to the fore. The demon becomes a name, a placeholder, a designation that signifies at once that which is outside and, because of this, that which is a threat. Exemplary in this regard is recent scholarship in comparative religious studies. Elaine Pagels's widely read *The Origin of Satan* makes the clearest point: the demon is inseparable from a process of demonization, and this process is as much political as it is religious. Whether, as in Pagels's study, the demonic refers to pagans (the threat from outside), or to non-Christian Jews (the boundary between outside and inside), or, finally, to acts of heresy within Christianity (the threat from inside), all follow this motif of naming an Other.

If it is understood in this anthropological sense, we can see how the demon historically passes through various phases: there is the classical demon, which is elemental, and at once a help and a hindrance (*"the demon beside me..."*); there is the medieval demon, a supernatural and intermediary being that is a tempter (*"demons surround me..."*); a modern demon, rendered scientific through psychoanalysis, and internalized within the machinations of the unconscious (*"I am a demon to myself..."*); and finally a contemporary demon, in which the social and political aspects of antagonism are variously attributed to the Other in relationships of enmity (*"demons are other people"*).

SED CONTRA

Let us return to the traditional, Christian-theological premise of the demon — demons are, generally speaking, both malevolent and malefic. They are understood as supernatural beings that intend to do evil to humanity, and do so through supernatural means. Whether they are rendered as monstrous, chimerical creatures, or as immaterial dark forces, demons often inhabit the edges of the human understanding of the world. This twofold characteristic — an antagonism towards the human, and some form of supernatural mediation — is a key part of the theological concept of the demon. By the time one arrives at modern psychoanalysis, the antagonism is internalized (perhaps via some personal trauma) and the mediation is medicalized (for example, as a form of clinical paranoia). Even in such cases, however, the manifestation of the phenomena in question is taken as if the antagonism is external, and as if the mediation comes from the outside. This twofold character remains, if only in a more secular and more scientific framework.

In the interpretations of the demon above, the demon functions as a metaphor for the human — both in the sense of the human's ability to comprehend itself, as well as the relations between one human being and another. The demon is not really a supernatural creature, but an anthropological motif through which we human beings project, externalize, and represent the darker side of the human to ourselves. While this may serve a certain therapeutic function, something is lost in this anthropological interpretation of the demon, and that is the way in which the antagonism so central to the demon is also a nonhuman antagonism, an antagonism that is beyond human comprehension — not natural but supernatural, not merely physical but metaphysical. But how is the traditional Christian-theological demon nonhuman, when again and again in sacred texts demons are represented in decidedly anthropomorphic ways?

One way of understanding the nonhuman aspect of the demon is to understand the demon less in a strictly theological sense, in which the demon is an intermediary creature between the supernatural and natural, and to understand it as a way of thinking about the relation of the human to that which is nonhuman. This latter term — non-human — can, of course, have a wide range of meanings, from the rock or the chair to the black depths of the cosmos. And we as human beings certainly have a panoply of ways of relating to the nonhuman, be it via science, technology, politics, or religion. But the nonhuman remains, by definition, a limit; it designates both that towards which we stand in relation and that which remains forever inaccessible. This limit is the unknown, and the unknown, as genre horror reminds us, is often a source of fear or dread.

Thus, in contrast to the anthropological interpretation of the demon, we can consider another one that is *mythological*. The mythological interpretation of the demon takes place less by the use of metaphor, and more by the use of allegory, in which the very story of our ability or inability to comprehend the world is encapsulated in the ritual acts of invasion, possession, metamorphosis, and exorcism. This comes through more clearly in one of the classic Biblical accounts of demonic possession, that of the so-called Gerasene demon. Slightly different accounts are given in *Mark* 5 and *Luke* 8, but the basics of the parable are the same: Jesus, with his followers, travels from Galilee to the Gerasene region (in northern current-day Jordan). There Jesus is met by the local villagers, who appeal to him to heal an old man possessed by demons. The possessed man, it is said, roams about the tombs without clothing or shelter. When the villagers shackle him, he enters into a frenzy and breaks free. At night he screams aloud and cuts himself with stones. Jesus confronts the possessed man, who likewise appeals to Jesus to cure him. As part of the exorcism, Jesus commands the name of the demon possessing the old man: "Then Jesus asked him, 'What is your name?' 'My name is Legion,' he replied, 'for we are many.'"[6] The name "Legion" (λεγων) is tricky, for it is not clear from the passage whether it is a single demon speaking in many voices, or if it is a multitude of demons speaking in a single voice. Indeed, the very name "Legion" appears to devolve upon itself, the name of the Many naming itself as One. Jesus then casts the demons out of the body of the old man, and into a herd of swine in a nearby hill. The herd of swine, now possessed, are driven into a state of frenzy and rush over the side of a cliff into the sea below to their death. After this rather dramatic episode, something interesting happens: the villagers, witnessing the entire spectacle, become fearful of Jesus and his healing powers. With some urgency, they politely ask Jesus and his followers to leave the village.

In this parable the demons manifest themselves in three ways, each an example of the limits of the human to comprehend the nonhuman. First, within the possessed man are a multitude of demons. Demonic possession itself transgresses the normal relationship between the One and the Many (one person = one body). It is also an affront to and parody of the Trinity, in which a single One is incarnated in Three. God as Creator creates many creatures. As creatures they are linked to God through the act of creation. Yet, as creatures, they are also separated from God in their being mortal and rooted in the changes associated with temporality. The multitude of demons in the parable above occupy the individual human creature — that highest of creatures — and turn him into a mere animal-like thing. The iconography of the passage is striking — the true nature of the demons, we presume, is revealed by the choice of their receptacle in a herd of beasts. But throughout the parable, the only real indication we have of this multitude of demons is this enigmatic resounding of the word "Legion." In a philosophical sense, that the demons choose to present themselves via voice and sound — at once present and absent — is noteworthy.

These two manifestations of the demon — the demons in the old man and the herd of animals — lead to a third type, which is the word of mouth among the people, which itself spreads like a contagion. Jesus's demonstration of his sovereign and medical powers instills a certain horror in the people, resulting in his effectively being cast out. We might take a decidedly modern view of this scene and suggest that the threat posed by the demons is not simply a topological one having to do with the proper relation between the One and the Many, and neither is it to do with the proper relation between Creator and creature. There is another element here, which is the way in which the demonic also challenges divine sovereignty. The demonic challenges the divine in its refusal to be organized at all. We do not know how many demons there are, nor even if it is more than one voice that speaks "Legion." We only know that it is more than one, and that it is "Many," the latter term still denoting a potentially countable entity. The demons are, in a sense, more than Many, but never One.

Examples of demonic activity occur throughout the New Testament, though in it demons are by no means represented in the same way. For example, the famous scene of the apocalypse in *Revelation* not only features a battle between angels and demons but also portrays avenging angels that tend to look a lot like demons. These supernatural creatures are anthropomorphized, and they even have their own technology: trumpets, tempests, and "bowls of plague" come forth in the apocalyptic upsurge. In these scenes the demons/angels have as their sole function a religious-juridical relation to the human (either to damn or to save them). The various symbolic devices, from scales and seals to bowls, are technologies for the end of the world. Here the demons are a form of *mediated presence*.

By contrast, the exorcism scene from the Gospels portrays a demon that is omnipresent and yet incarnate — the demons called "Legion" are never present in themselves, but only via some form of earthly embodiment (the old man, the herd of pigs, the wind, the sea). In a sense, they are strangely pantheistic, announcing themselves only indirectly. Hence their embodiment is also a disembodiment, in the sense that they are wandering spirits — their movement happens more by demonic contagion than by divine inspiration. Demons are here a form of *immediate absence*.

While the anthropological meaning of the demon in the previous discussion remains ensconced within a human-centric, therapeutic solipsism (e.g., "why do we do the things we do?"), the mythological meaning focuses on the limits of the human ability to know the nonhuman. At its limit is the idea of the absolutely "dark" demon — the demon that remains absolutely unknowable to use as human beings, but which nevertheless seems to act upon us, perhaps through a malevolence we can only call "bad luck" or "misfortune."

RESPONSIO

If the anthropological demon is an attempt to reveal the nature of the human to the human, then we can say that the mythological demon is an attempt to reveal the nonhuman to the human. Both, however, come across certain limitations, due to the human point of view. The human is always relating either to itself or to the world. And these two types of relations overlap with each other: the human can only understand the human by transforming it into an object to relate to (psychology, sociology), while the human can only relate to the objective world by transforming the world into something familiar or accessible in human terms (biology, geology, cosmology).

This leaves one avenue open, which is the perspective of the nonhuman itself. But as thinking, embodied beings unable to fully detach ourselves from the subject-object relations that constitute us, such a perspective is undoubtedly a paradox. In fact, it is doomed from the start. Nevertheless it deserves to be stated, even if beyond it there can only be silence. In the parable of the Gerasene demons, the demons named "Legion" were, in themselves, defined by several properties: they were neither One nor Many but somewhere in between; they were fully immanent with the world (almost pantheistically); and, most importantly, they in themselves were never present, never a discrete thing that one could point to — the demons named "Legion" were really, in themselves, "nothing."

Perhaps there is a meaning of the demonic that has little to do with the human at all — *and this indifference is what constitutes its demonic character*. If the anthropological demon (the human relating to itself) functioned via metaphor, and if the mythological demon (the human relating to the nonhuman) functioned via allegory, then perhaps there is a third demon, which is more ontological, or really "meontological" (having to do with non-being rather than being). As the 6th-century mystic Dionysius the Areopagite notes, commenting on the paradoxical existence of demons, "evil is not a being; for if it were, it would not be totally evil ... evil has no place among being."[7]

Given that, for us as human beings, there is no simple "going over" to the side of the nonhuman, it would seem that the mode best suited to this third type of demon is something like metonymy, an indirect sign, an oblique meaning, a gesture towards something that we cannot grasp (with the demon as a stand-in for the abstract, indifferent, non-being of the world). The demon is, then, a way of talking about the perspective of the nonhuman, with all the contradictions this implies. For the meontological demon, affirmation is negation, and thinking about its being is the same as thinking about its non-being.

This is brought forward with great subtlety in Dante's *Inferno*, one of the classic depictions of the demonic. However, there is not simply one type of demon in the *Inferno*; indeed, the central drama of the *Inferno* is not good vs. evil, but in the tensions within the *Inferno* itself. For instance, one can identify at least three types of demons in the *Inferno*. First there is, at the center and lowest point of the underworld, the figure of Lucifer, the arch-demon. This takes place in the final scene of the *Inferno*, where Dante (who is both

Gustave Doré, illustration for Canto XXXIV of *Dante's Inferno* (*L'Enfer*, 1857)

author and character in the story) is led by his guide Virgil to the center of the underworld. Dante (the author) uses the word Dis in the poem, an alternate name for Pluto, the god of the classical underworld, to refer to the giant, grotesque, brooding arch-emperor ("emperor of all these realms of gloom").

Here we have the counter-sovereign, who, like the divine sovereign, is centralized and transcendent with respect to that which he governs. However, this counter-sovereign demon actually does very little in the long journey that constitutes the *Inferno*. The 19th-century artist Gustave Doré depicts the scene in great detail. Immobilized in the frozen waters of the underworld, this melancholy, counter-sovereign demon is condemned to repeat the same cycle of transgression and blasphemy against the Creator.

Distinct from this, there is the multitude of demons scattered throughout the different circles of the underworld. An example is

Gustave Doré, illustration for Canto XXI of *Dante's Inferno* (*L'Enfer,* 1857)

the so-called Malebranche demons found in the 8th Circle. These are "demons" in the more modern, Faustian sense; they are torturers, tricksters, and tempters.

The Malebranche demons are less the gloomy, majestic counter-sovereign, and more a roving pack, a demonic gang, a cluster of feral spirits. They operate according to the basic rules of the underworld, and are more decentralized, their power emanating from the rule of the counter-sovereign.

Contrasted to these two types of demons — the counter-sovereign Dis, and the Malebranche demons — there is a third, which comes near the beginning of the *Inferno*. This is in the Second Circle, the Circle of the Lustful. In a dramatic passage, Dante is lead by his guide Virgil to a precipice where, for the first time in the narrative, he encounters the strange and dark atmosphere of the demonic:

> I came to a place where no light shone at all,
> bellowing like the sea racked by a tempest,
> when warring winds attack it from both sides.
>
> The infernal storm, eternal in its rage,
> sweeps and drives the spirits with its blast:
> it whirls them, lashing them with punishment.
>
> When they are swept back past their place of judgment,
> then come the shrieks, laments, and anguished cries;
> there they blaspheme God's almighty power.

To this place the lustful have been sent, all "those who make reason slave to appetite." The mass of bodies, blown back and forth by the wind, prompt a comparison to the swarming of birds:

> and as the wings of starlings in the winter
> bear them along in wide-spread, crowded flocks,
> so does that wind propel the evil spirits (*spiriti mali*);
>
> now here, then there, and up and down, it drives them
> with never any hope to comfort them —
> hope not of rest but even of suffering less.[8]

We soon learn that this tempestuous scene is not the backdrop for some new genre of demons, but that the wind, the rain, and the storm itself is the demon. This bears restating. Here the demonic is climate, weather, the elements themselves. This "black wind" (*aura nera*) is at once invisible and yet dramatically manifest, coursing through the swarming bodies of the damned.

One of the images from Doré's illustrations depicts the well-known scene in which two of the spirits — Paolo and Francesca — emerge from the swarm of bodies to tell their tale of tragic love. Dante, moved by the scene and their story, is overcome and faints next to Virgil, who is by his side. But what is equally interesting

Gustave Doré, illustration for Canto V of *Dante's Inferno* (*L'Enfer*, 1857)

in the image is the way that Doré visually depicts the bodies of Paolo and Francesca: they barely stand out from the amorphous background of swarming spirits, which seem to recede back into infinity. Indeed, in certain areas the bodies appear to merge into the backdrop of the storm itself.

In this scene there is neither a fixed and majestic counter-sovereign, nor a roving gang of Faustian demons. There is only the strange, immanent, and fully distributed "life-force" of this black wind. The spirits of the Lustful in this circle dissolve into the elemental swarming of the storm and the wind. It is the most dramatically manifest form of life (indeed, Dante the character faints before its force), and yet it is also the most elusive (the demonic storm is not a discrete thing, much less a discrete body; it is everywhere but nowhere). Arguably, this scene puts forth the most difficult view of the demon — not a transcendent, governing cause, and not an emanating, radiating flow — but a concept of the demonic that is fully immanent, and yet never fully present. This kind of demon is at once pure force, and, not being a discrete thing in itself, it is also pure nothingness.

The *Inferno* is of interest not simply due to the panoply of monsters that inhabit its pages, but because of the way in which it carefully stratifies different types of demonic being and non-being. Within the paths, rivers, caverns, and fortresses of the *Inferno* all boundaries collapse: there are human bodies melting into dead trees, rivers flowing with blood, and entire cities populated with the living dead. The motif of possession in the *Inferno* demonstrates this: demonic possession is not just the possession of living beings, but includes the possession of the nonliving as well. Demons possess not only humans and animals, but also the very landscape, the very terrain of the underworld. Demonic possession in the *Inferno* is not just teratological, but also geological and even climatological.

QUÆSTIO III — On Demonology, and Whether It Is a Respectable Field of Study

ARTICULUS

Demonology is commonly understood no longer to be of contemporary relevance; it is an unfortunate and anachronistic offshoot of late medieval and early Renaissance theology, now relegated to the terrain of the horror genre. However, recent work by scholars such as Stuart Clark, Richard Kieckhefer, and Jeffrey Burton Russell has done much to tease out the philosophical and political aspects of demonology in its historical sense. In particular, the case of demonic possession presented a set of challenges to religious, juridical, and political authority that necessitated the development of entire fields of study. As historian Nancy Caciola notes, "[a]lthough the two categories of divine and demonic possession were diametrically opposed in abstract moral terms, in regard to observable behaviors the two categories were largely identical." The demoniac — not unlike the mystic — could only be attested to in this highly performative and empirical context, a context that required methods of interpreting signs and ciphers of the flesh, a hermeneutics for "reading" the body of the possessed. "Hence at the root of the debate over the discernment of spirits was a congeries of ambiguous physical and intellectual signs that rendered it difficult for observers to categorize a possessed individual as either a visionary prophet sent by God or an energumen in thrall to the devil."[9]

The term "demonology" itself is most often understood as the study and classification of demons (often inclusive of witchcraft and necromancy), directly tied to the long, dark history of the witch hunts and persecutions of heretics in Europe between the 15th and 17th centuries. While Christian theologians from Augustine to Aquinas had written extensively about the nature of evil prior to this period, the idea that a distinct field of study devoted to the topic — as well as to its practical application in combating and rooting out evil — does not really emerge until the late 15th century. An often cited reference point is the papal bull *Summis Desiderantes Affectibus* (1484), issued by Pope Innocent VIII in response to growing concerns that heretical activities, including witchcraft, constituted a serious threat to the unification of Church authority. The bull is noteworthy for several reasons, the foremost being that it confirmed the existence of witches, witchcraft, and the activities of all those who "have abandoned themselves to demons," through rituals undertaken "at the instigation of the Enemy of Mankind." If identifying an enemy as an enemy is to give that enemy strength, then this identification of witchcraft and demonic dealings would prove to be a double-edged sword. Of the countless trials and executions that took place under the banner of the Inquisition (modern estimates by historians range from 40,000 to 100,000 executions in continental Europe alone, between 1500–1700), the scope of the witch trials broadened, in some cases including the mere defense against an accusation of witchcraft as itself constituting an act of heresy.

Summis Desiderantes Affectibus not only identified a threat, it also made recommendations for dealing with that threat. It gave Church inquisitors such as Heinrich Kramer and Jacob Sprenger the authority to legally seek out, put to trial, and to punish those suspected of dealing with demons and practicing witchcraft. Roughly two years after the publication of the bull, Kramer and Sprenger published the book that would become the blueprint for the witch hunt: the *Malleus Maleficarum* (*Hammer of Witches*, 1486). Much of the *Malleus Maleficarum* is typical of the writing on witchcraft and demonology of the period. There are references to the writings of the Church Fathers and Scholastic theologians on the dangers of evil and consorting with demons. There are also attempts to distinguish and classify the different kinds of demonic activity. And there are a number of case studies of witchcraft, demonic possession, and other acts of *malefica* that serve to paint a picture of the real threat at hand.

What makes the *Malleus Maleficarum* unique, however, is its practical orientation. It is not a work of theological speculation, as is Aquinas's *De Malo* (*On Evil*, ca. 1270). Neither is it an attempt at systematic classification, as is Francesco-Maria Guazzo's *Compendium Maleficarum* (*Encyclopedia of Witchcraft*, 1608). It is, quite literally, an instruction manual, clearly demonstrated by the book's three parts: Part I, which argues that witches and witchcraft really exist, and are a threat; Part II, which deals with how witches and witchcraft can be detected and exposed; and Part III, which outlines the protocols for carrying out the trial, sentencing, and punishment.

Of particular interest is the role played by 15th-century medicine in demonology manuals like the *Malleus Maleficarum*. One role medicine played was in the cultivation of a general miasmatic or contagion-theory of demonic possession. In this premodern understanding of contagion, the demon is conceptualized in much the same way we saw earlier — as a paradoxical manifestation that is, in itself, "nothing" or non-being. This is illustrated in the *Malleus Maleficarum* by the three main types of demonic possession, each exhibiting anomalous symptoms that — in the argument of the demonologist — can be traced to some sort of commerce with a demon. At the first level there is psycho-physiological possession, in which the demonic spirit invades and affects the body itself (with symptoms including temporary disability, incapacitation, impotence, infertility, erotomania, epilepsy, narcolepsy, and melancholia). At a second level there are cases of epidemiological possession, which affects the relation between body and environment (plague, leprosy, mass hysteria, even mob behavior). Finally, at a third level one finds a more abstract, climatological possession, in which demons possess not only the living but the non-living, not only the animate but the inanimate (unnatural or anomalous changes in weather, affected livestock or crops, sudden famine or flood).

Added to this epistemological role of medicine is another role, which is juridical. Though the *Malleus Maleficarum* is a decidedly single-minded text, aiming without hesitation at the extermination of all witchcraft activity, it does make minimal allowances for natural, as opposed to supernatural, causes of witchcraft (in no way less punishable). While there was rarely any question as to the supernatural character of the witch or witchcraft activity in question, the exact cause of the said activity could be open to interpretation. There may be, for example, a supernatural cause producing a natural symptom. Such symptoms could be classified as either illusion or illness. If illusion, then the question was whether the accused is intentionally using some sort of trickery, and for what reason (e.g., gain of money, revenge, jealousy, etc.). If illness, then the question was what type of illness, the most commonly cited examples being the vaguely defined illnesses of epilepsy, hysteria, and melancholy. The role of medicine here was less to develop knowledge about demonic possession, and more to arbitrate — within the juridical context of the trial — the boundary between the natural and supernatural. Interestingly, it is this role that would be reinforced by later writers more skeptical of the witch-hunts and the mass paranoia they produced. Note, however, that a natural explanation of a phenomenon such as necromancy or possession in no way rules out the presence of the supernatural — in many instances it simply serves as yet another route towards the inevitable sentence.

Although witch-hunting manuals proliferated throughout the period, the *Malleus Maleficarum* set a new standard, encompassing theology (Part I), medicine (Part II), and law (Part III) into a single work. The result was not only a new set of juridical procedures, but also a new discourse and way of thinking about the demon in terms of the non-human. This is also evident in the early Renaissance debates over the status of demons and demonic possession, in treatises such as Johann Weyer's *De Praestigiis Daemonium* (*On the Trickery of Demons*, 1563), Jean Bodin's *Démonomanie des Sorciers* (*The Demon-mania of Witches*, 1580), and Reginald Scot's *Discoverie of Witchcraft* (1584).

Weyer's *De Praestigiis Daemonium* is noteworthy for being one of the few treatises that expresses criticism of the excesses of the witch-hunts and witchcraft trials. While Weyer did admit the real existence of witches, witchcraft, and demons, he also allowed for cases in which individuals were helplessly deluded by demons (thinking that their hallucinations were real), as well as cases of simple trickery. As Weyer ominously notes, real demons do not need us to carry out their acts of ill will — in fact, it is the height of vanity to suppose that we as human beings are in any way necessary for them. Be that as it may, it is noteworthy that Weyer, who studied under the scientist and reputed magician Cornelius Agrippa, spent most of his life as a physician, and this impacts his allowance for medical-psychological explanations of witchcraft. He notes, with biting sarcasm, that "such rare and severe symptoms often arise in diseases that stem from natural causes but are immediately attributed to witchcraft by men of no scientific experience and little faith."[10] *De Praestigiis Daemonium* also contains a number of indictments against the excessive use of torture and maltreatment of accused witches.

Bodin's *Démonomanie* is a direct counterattack to Weyer. Bodin, a Carmelite monk, member of Parliament, and professor of law, is mostly known in political philosophy for his massive work *Les Six Livres de la République*, a work which contains an early theorization of absolute state sovereignty. Written in order to aid judges in witchcraft cases, Bodin's *Démonomanie* is a disturbing work that advocates, among other things, the legal use of torture to elicit confessions of guilt, including the use of techniques such as cautery. It contains one of the early legal definitions of a witch, as one whom "knowing God's law, tries to bring about some act through an agreement with the Devil." It also contains a veritable litany of the antagonism of demons against human beings: "all demons are malevolent, deceiving, posturing enemies of humanity."[11] The *Démonomanie* never wavers in its assertion of the religious and political threat of witchcraft — that is, the threat that witchcraft posed to statecraft. The conviction in the *Démonomanie* appears to derive in part from Bodin's own experience as a judge, in which he saw a number of witchcraft trials (and purportedly showed no hesitation in torturing children and invalids to gain a confession).

If Weyer represents the attitude of temperance towards witchcraft (under the guise of medicine), and if Bodin represents the conservative retrenchment (under the guise of law), then Scot's *Discoverie of Witchcraft* takes the next step, which is to question the validity of the entire affair altogether. To the role of medicine in Weyer, and the role of law in Bodin, we add the role of skepticism in Scot. While Weyer and Bodin are on opposite sides of the fence politically, theologically they both remain committed to the existence of supernatural forces and the conflict paradigm of good versus evil. Scot, who had the advantage of relative financial independence, was neither beholden to the Church nor to science in his opinions — though the *Discoverie of Witchcraft* was printed at his own expense, was unregistered, and did not contain the publisher's name. Most likely spurred on by a series of controversial witch trials in England in the early 1580s, Scot's treatise is much more sarcastic, even sardonic, in its criticisms. He attacks both the pretenses of witches and witchcraft, dismissing them as trickery (either on others or on oneself), as well as the "extreme and intolerable tyranny" of the inquisitors and judges. In a sense, Scot's treatise is a sort of clearinghouse for the very concept of the demon, and indeed of the supernatural itself. As if to accuse both witches and inquisitors of a too-provincial, all-too-human mindset, the *Discoverie of Witchcraft* suggests that, in so far as there is a concept of the demon, it has to be one of which we can have little or no knowledge.

SED CONTRA

The debates surrounding witchcraft and demonology are instructive in that they often revolve around our ability to adequately comprehend the supernatural — be it divine or demonic. The question of the demon tends to oscillate, from highly anthropomorphic Satyrs to the more abstract and obscure demons that contagiously pass from person to person. Much of the confusion of early demonology treatises centers on how to verify the existence of a demon, when, by definition, they are rarely self-evident to the human observer. In cases where demonic possession cannot be distinguished from medical illness, on which side should one stand? To the 21st-century mind, the question is absurd. But for an era in which the lines between magic, science, and witchcraft were blurry, such questions were not only religious and political, but philosophical too. To the culture of the early Renaissance, the demon presents a limit to the empiricism of the unknown, something that can only be verified through contradictions — an absent manifestation, an unnatural creature, a demonic malady.

Such contradictions stretch the limits of language and thought. Indeed, one of the by-products of the flurry of writings on demonology was the development of a new language and a new set of concepts for thinking about the supernatural. While this language and these concepts were informed by theology, in describing the effects of possession, they also evoke the scene of the witches' Sabbath. Thus, in imagining a world swarming with malefic entities, a certain *poetics* of the demon was also needed. Demonology — whether it aims to convince or to criticize — is as much a rhetorical activity as it is a theological or juridical one. Thus, in contrast to the view of demonology as theological, we can briefly consider a poetics as being equally central to the concept of the demon.

If one were to outline a poetics of the demon, one could begin by thinking about the demonic in literary representations — the demon as represented via different motifs. For example, the narrative technique of the journey — so common in the history of world literature — is a key feature of Dante's *Commedia*, as Dante the pilgrim journeys from the dark circles of Hell, through the conical spiral of Purgatory, to the celestial geometries of Paradise, along the way undergoing various trials. This is a topological motif, in which we encounter various people, places, and creatures. The demonic is here symbolically inscribed by a particular locale (for instance, the way that the different circles of Hell contain different classes of demonic punishments for different sins).

The same follows for other narrative structures. There is the battle, such as one finds in Milton's *Paradise Lost*, and, following upon (and critiquing) Milton, as one finds in scenes from William Blake's prophecies. Here we find the structure of agonism, with the demonic ensnared in an eternal struggle or conflict. Then there is the motif of the pact, the black bargain with a demon that at once liberates and imprisons the human character that signs their name in blood. This is a juridical structure, most commonly associated with the Faust story and its literary incarnations by such authors as Marlowe and Goethe — I give you my soul, and in exchange, you give me … everything. The pact often overlaps with another narrative motif, which is that of the ritual. The infamous depictions of the Black Mass in novels such as Marjorie Bowen's *Black Magic*, J.-K. Huysmans's *Là-bas*, or Dennis Wheatley's *The Devil Rides Out* involve a set of sacrilegious acts that, at the same time, express a certain sanctity of evil. The demonic is the counter-divine, at once negating the divine while sanctifying the demonic. Wheatley's "black" novels are particularly noteworthy, for the protagonist De Richleau often uses both ancient and modern-scientific knowledge in his battle against demons and dark forces, continuing the "occult detective" genre inaugurated by authors such as Sheridan Le Fanu. Finally, there is the more modern, technological motif of the magical artifact, the dark invention that signals a new kind of apocalypse. Science fiction works such as Fritz Leiber's *Gather, Darkness!* and James Blish's *Faust Aleph-Null*, written in the shadow of world war and mass extinction, suggest an ominous affinity between technology and the supernatural. In Leiber's novel a futuristic Papacy utilizes a panoply of special-effects technologies to ensure the fidelity of the masses to the hegemony of the Church. Against them a demonic underworld of witches, warlocks, and familiars carry out their revolutionary cause. By contrast, Blish's novel suggests that with weapons of mass destruction, a renewed Faustian pact has been made, with quantum physics as a form of necromancy. In these 20th-century works, the demonic plays different roles, either as a revolutionary counter-power, or as an essentially unknowable force beyond human comprehension and control.

One of the striking commonalities between works of this type is that nearly all of them seem to follow an unwritten rule — the demonic antagonist must always "lose" in the end. This would seem to follow the moral structure of the novel or the epic poem (similar to the requisite happy ending of a studio film). But one always feels a little let down by this *deus ex machina*. Goethe's Faust goes all the way in his demonic explorations, only to later repent and — in Part II — gain salvation by virtue of divine grace. Similarly, there is Blake's famous statement about Milton's *Paradise Lost* — that the latter was of the Devil's party without knowing it. In this sense, the demonic always has something excluded about it, as if the demonic were emblematic of a kind of inverted metaphysics of negation and non-being, a metaphysics in which it ultimately negates even itself, "one of those violent, dark, revolts of being." The demonic is less an object to be repudiated or embraced by a subject, but something in between, what Julia Kristeva has termed the "abject." In her well-known formulation: "What is abject is not my correlative, which, providing me with someone or something else as support, would allow me to be more or less detached and autonomous … what is abject, on the contrary, the jettisoned object, is radically excluded and draws me toward the place where meaning collapses."[13]

Here one finds the problem of "being-on-the-side-of" the demonic, in so far as the demonic is unknown and, perhaps, unknowable. More than simply a figure of revolt or rebellion, the demonic takes on the qualities of negation: the dissolving of boundaries, the corrosion of structures, the decay of forms, everything turned inside-out, upside-down. There are no romantic appeals to freedom here, much less any fidelity to the efficacy of reason or critique; there are only processes that remain fundamentally ambivalent. The failure of the demonic antagonists in literature is therefore less a testament to the victorious nature of good, and more an indication of a certain moral economy of the unknown. By the end of Goethe's *Faust* there is a sense that we know no more or less of the demonic than when we started, and are left only with the residue of the humility of human finitude.

RESPONSIO

Here again we arrive at the concept of the demon as a limit for thought, a limit that is constituted not by being or becoming, but by non-being, or nothingness. And here we should state what we have been hinting at all along, which is that in contrast to the theology of the demon, or the poetics of the demon, there is something more basic still that has to do with the ideas of negation and nothingness — hence we should really think of the demon as an ontological problem (not theology, not poetry, but philosophy).

True, demonology is a theological phenomenon, tied up with historical debates about the nature of evil, and the politics surrounding the witch-hunts. True, demonology is also a cultural phenomenon, as the literary, cinematic, and video game examples demonstrate. But demonology ceases to be interesting if it is taken as being "merely" historical, or "only" a fiction. If demonology is to be thought in a philosophical register, then it would have to function as a kind of philosoheme, an allegory that brings together a cluster of ideas that have, for some time, served as problematic areas for philosophy itself: negation, nothingness, and the non-human.

What would such an approach to demonology look like? To begin with, demonology would have to be distinguished from anthropology, in which the demon is simply a stand-in for the human and ruminations on the nature of evil in human beings. Demonology would also have to be distinguished from pure metaphysics, in which the demon functions as a stand-in for the pair being/non-being. Denying the anthropological view means considering the world as not simply the world-for-us or the world-in-itself, but as the world-without-us. Likewise denying the view of metaphysics means considering the unreliability of the principle of sufficient reason for thinking about the world (not sufficient reason but a strange, uncanny, insufficiency of reason). A philosophical demonology would therefore have to be "against" the human being — both the "human" part as well as the "being" part.

Perhaps we can come up with a new term for this way of thinking, based on this renewed understanding of demonology. If the traditional anthropological perspective is predicated on a division between the personal and the impersonal ("man" and cosmos), then this other way of thinking collapses them into paradoxical pairings (impersonal affects, cosmic suffering). Likewise, if classical ontology deals with the relation being and non-being, then this other way of thinking would begin from non-being, rather than from being. The classical question for Western philosophy, "Why is there something rather than nothing?" would undergo a shift. Instead, the question would be, "What is the 'nothing' that subtends all existents, including being itself, and which — the moment it is thought — is no longer 'nothing'?" Instead of ontology, or even meontology, this other kind of thinking might be called a "demontology." An admittedly clumsy portmanteau, this other kind of thinking entails the paradoxical thought of nothing (a negative orientation) that is also not simply reducible to non-being (a privative orientation).

In his own attempts to think in this way, Arthur Schopenhauer provides an explanation, recapping the distinction between the two kinds of negation:

> I must first of all observe that the concept of *nothing* (*Nichts*) is essentially relative, and always refers to a definite something that it negates. This quality has been attributed (especially by Kant) merely to the *nihil privativum* indicated by – in contrast to +. This negative sign (–) from the opposite point of view might become +, and, in opposition to this *nihil privativum*, the *nihil negativum* has been set up, which would in every respect be nothing … But considered more closely, an absolute nothing, a really proper *nihil negativum*, is not even conceivable, but everything of this kind, considered from a higher standpoint or subsumed under a wider concept, is always only a *nihil privativum*.[13]

For Schopenhauer, the *nihil privativum* is the world as it appears to us, the world-for-us, the world as "Representation" (*Vorstellung*), while the *nihil negativum* is the world-in-itself or the world as "Will" — or better, the world-in-itself, as it is manifest to us in its inaccessibility, in its enigmatic "occult qualities." As Schopenhauer notes, the world we typically accept without question as existing, can reveal itself to be the opposite — the world as precarious, transitory, ephemeral, and subject to the vagaries of passing time. In such moments, what was previously assumed to have a positive value, as "being" (*Seiende*), suddenly reveals itself as "nothing" (*Nichts*). But, for Schopenhauer, this "nothing" is not itself some other world — this is precisely what the world as "Representation" is. The "something" that is "nothing," the reality of illusion, the "is" and the "is not" as two aspects of the same phenomenon. As for the other path, the *nihil negativum*, Schopenhauer — who is otherwise vociferous in his attacks on religion — suggests a strange affinity with mysticism:

> But so long as we ourselves are the will-to-live, this last, namely the nothing as that which exists, can be known and expressed by us only negatively … If, however, it should be absolutely insisted on that somehow a positive knowledge

> is to be acquired of what philosophy can express only negatively as denial of the will, nothing would be left but to refer to that state which is experienced by all who have attained to complete denial of the will, and which is denoted by the names ecstasy, rapture, illumination, union with God, and so on.[14]

Schopenhauer here suggests a new relation to the category of the unknown. The *nihil negativum* is not just about the limits of language to adequately describe experience; it is about the horizon of thought as it confronts the unthought, the horizon of the human as it struggles to comprehend the unhuman. As Schopenhauer notes, it cannot really be called knowledge, for this implies a minimal distinction between subject and object, or knower and known, that is itself annulled. And yet, the conundrum is that something is experienced, or at least apprehended, even if what is registered is an absence, a void, an abyss at the core of the self-world relation that is so central to the Western philosophical tradition.

Given this distinction (*nihil privativum* and *nihil negativum*), and its implications for thinking the world as a non-human world, we are led to a dilemma. That is, a demontology of the type we've been discussing would have to distinguish itself from the moral, juridical, and cosmic framework of Christian demonology (moral law, temptation, transgression, sin, punishment, salvation, etc.). And here "demontology" comes up against one of its greatest challenges, and it is, in many ways, a Nietzschean one — how does one think the world as unthinkable? — that is, in the absence of the human-centric point of view, and without depending on the metaphysics of being?

Again, we run up against all sorts of obstacles, in part because a philosophy of this sort does not exist — or not yet. Should one then create a lineage, citing predecessors? But here an interminable game of inclusion and exclusion begins. Should one include classical philosophers, such as Heraclitus or Pyrrho? Should one include works in the tradition of "darkness mysticism" or negative theology? And then what of the great works of spiritual and philosophical crisis, from Kierkegaard to E.M. Cioran and Simone Weil? We've already mentioned Schopenhauer and Nietzsche, but then are we obliged to also consider their 20th-century inheritors, such as Bataille, Klossowski, or Shestov? Then again, is there not something dubious in hoping for the existence of a field dedicated to negation, nothingness, and non-being? Is it possible for one to make the claim that the *nihil negativum* exists, without becoming ensnared in an endless theater of the absurd? Perhaps the only thing for certain is if such a philosophy could exist, it would not be made any more respectable because of its existence — for nothing is more frowned upon than nothing…

3

SIX *LECTIO* ON OCCULT PHILOSOPHY

Preamble: On Agrippa's *De Occulta Philosophia*

The phrase "occult philosophy" is often used by scholars to describe an intellectual movement prevalent during the early modern period, which combined elements of Christian theology with a range of non-Christian traditions, from ancient Egyptian theories of magic to Renaissance astronomy and alchemy. In its own way, occult philosophy's mashing of diverse intellectual traditions questioned the hegemony of any one particular tradition (most notably, orthodox Christianity as ensconced within a whole host of legal documents defining the parameters of heresy). There is, perhaps, something to learn from this tradition. In our increasing awareness of the cataclysmic effects of climate change and global warming, and yet after the "death of God," what new meanings can occult philosophy have today?

Occult philosophy is first and foremost a historical phenomenon. The work of scholars such as Frances Yates did much to place occult philosophy within its philosophical, religious, and political context. In her book *The Occult Philosophy in the Elizabethan Age*, Yates argues that what has come to be called occult philosophy is really an amalgam of diverse intellectual traditions, traditions that have, historically speaking, been at odds with each other. In this mixing together of different speculative traditions, one finds: Greek natural philosophy (Aristotle) and cosmology (Pythagoras), Neoplatonism, Renaissance alchemy, Egyptian Hermeticism, Christian-Scholastic theology, and Jewish mysticism. In particular, the work of Heinrich Cornelius Agrippa — physician, theologian, diplomat, mercenary, and occultist — stands out for its eclecticism and its attempt to synthesize diverse philosophical traditions. In Agrippa's work, Yates identifies a thread that combines Hermeticism, as filtered through Renaissance thinkers such as Marsilio Ficino, and a hybrid Christian-Cabbalistic mysticism as filtered through thinkers such as Giovanni Pico della Mirandola. However, in Yates's view, Agrippa's text takes occult philosophy in directions that other thinkers were not prepared to go, for fear of accusations of heresy. "It is the Ficinian magic which Agrippa teaches in his first book, though he teaches it in a much bolder way. Ficino was nervous of the magic; he was anxious to keep his magic 'natural,' concerned only with elemental substances in their relations to the stars and avoiding the 'star demons,' the spirits connected with the stars. It was really not possible to teach astral magic whilst avoiding the star demons, as Agrippa saw and boldly accepted the challenge."[15]

First published in 1533, Agrippa's *De Occulta Philosophia Libri Tres* (*Three Books of Occult Philosophy*) presents a veritable compendium of Renaissance philosophy, theology, mysticism, science, and magic. While Agrippa began writing the *Occult Philosophy* as early as 1509, the work itself went through a number of editions, with an English translation appearing in 1651. An itinerant scholar, Agrippa traveled extensively throughout Europe, coming into contact with intellectuals participating in the religious and scientific humanism of the time (some modern historians even suggest that Agrippa's travels point to an unknown secret society of which he was a member). The *Occult Philosophy* has had a tremendous impact on later generations, its influence seen in the 19th-century European revival of occultism (for instance, in the work of Eliphas Lévi or Gérard Encausse in France) and in early 20th-century groups such as the Golden Dawn and the Theosophical Society.

In Agrippa's philosophy, the nature of reality is divided into three worlds — the elemental world, the celestial world, and the intellectual world. Each of these has specific meanings in the context of Renaissance occult philosophy. By "elemental" Agrippa means the natural world, comprising as it does the spectrum of animate and inanimate entities, organic and inorganic nature, as well as the primary elements described in classical thought (water, air, fire, earth). Beyond the elemental or natural world is what Agrippa calls the "celestial," by which he means the sky, the stars, the firmament, and the planetary cosmos. This celestial domain is partially defined within the science of astronomy, and partially defined within the long tradition of Neoplatonic cosmology, Pythagoreanism, and Cabbalistic mysticism. Finally, beyond the celestial is the "intellectual" world, and here Agrippa displays the influence of Neoplatonism, referring to the supernatural world of intermediary beings (angels and demons) as well as the First Cause, the Neoplatonic "One," or God. Hence "intellectual" has little relation to the modern, colloquial sense of the cognitive functions of the brain. This last world is intellectual in the sense that it contains, in Platonic fashion, the abstract, purely formal essence of all things in the celestial and elemental worlds.

The philosophical commitment of Agrippa's *Occult Philosophy* is that there is a distinction between the world as it appears to us, and the "hidden" or occulted qualities of the world which, though they are not apparent, are all the more important and essential in gaining a deeper knowledge of the three worlds (elemental, celestial, intellectual). While most of the *Occult Philosophy* is dedicated to detailing, often in a very practical way, the process of revealing the hidden essences of the world, the world as such doesn't always lend itself to being revealed. In fact, there are a number of moments in the text that describe the world refusing to be revealed at all.

Early on in the First Book, Agrippa includes a number of chapters on what he calls the "occult virtues of things." The strange effects of certain herbs or minerals, anomalies in the sky or the stars, the practice of necromancy or geomancy, even the existence of magic itself — all these are evidence of aspects of the world that refuse to reveal themselves, that remain hidden or occulted. As Agrippa notes, "they are called occult qualities, because their causes are hidden, and because human intellect cannot entirely investigate them."[16] His examples vary widely, from the mundane case of how digestion occurs, to the rather fantastical account of how creatures such as satyrs can exist. All these examples are united by their existing and yet being unexplainable in human terms: "There are, in things we recognize, certain other innate virtues beyond the elemental qualities created by nature, which we admire and often amaze us, though we may not know or rarely see."[17]

This idea — of the occulted world which both makes its presence known and yet in so doing reveals to us the unknown — this idea is the dark underside of occult philosophy and its humanist claims. Against the humanist world-for-us, a human-centric world made in our image, there is this notion of the world as occulted, not in a relative but in an absolute sense. Etymologically speaking, that which is "occult" (*occultus*; *occulere*) is something hidden, concealed, and surrounded by shadows. However, that which is hidden implies that which is revealed, just as that which is already apparent may, by some twist, suddenly become obscure and occult. That which is occulted can be hidden in a number of ways: something can intentionally be hidden, as when a precious object or important piece of information is stored away or withheld (buried treasures or best-kept secrets). In this case we enter the human world of hide-and-seek, of giving and withholding, of all the micro-exchanges of power that constitute human social networks. We as human beings actively hide and reveal things that, by virtue of this hiding and revealing activity, obtain a certain value for us as knowledge.

To this we can add another way in which the occult is hidden, and that is a hiddenness in which we as human beings play little or no part, and which is either already given, or which occurs in spite of, or indifferently to, our attempts to reveal that which is hidden. This second type of hiddenness — which may be cataclysmic or everyday — is the hiddenness of the world that we find ourselves thrown into, a hidden world which, regardless of how much knowledge we produce about it, always retains some remainder that lies beyond the scope of our capacity to reveal its hiddenness. In some cases the hidden world is simply the world that does not bend to our will or to our desires, the differential between the world-for-us and the world-in-itself. In other cases the hidden world may be something like the "unsolved mysteries" that percolate in our popular culture fascination with the paranormal.

Let us introduce a terminology for talking about the occult in a contemporary context. This second notion of the occult — not that which we as human beings hide or reveal, but that which is already hidden in the world — this we can refer to simply as the occulted world, or better, the *hiddenness of the world*. But here we need to make a further refinement. The hiddenness of the world is not just the world-in-itself, for the world-in-itself is, by definition, absolutely cut off from us as human beings in the world (the world-for-us). When the world-in-itself becomes occulted, or "hidden," a strange and paradoxical movement takes place whereby the world-in-itself presents itself to us, but without ever becoming fully accessible or completely knowable. The world-in-itself presents itself to us, but without simply becoming the world-for-us; it is, to borrow from Schopenhauer, "the world-in-itself-for-us."

If this is the case — that the world-in-itself paradoxically presents itself to us — then what is it exactly that is revealed? Quite simply, what is revealed is the "hiddenness" of the world (and not the world-in-itself). This hiddenness is also, in a way, hideous. The hidden world, which reveals nothing other than its hiddenness, is a blank, anonymous world that is indifferent to human knowledge, much less to our all-too-human wants and desires. Hence the hiddenness of the world, in its anonymity and indifference, is a world for which the idea of a theistic providence or the scientific principle of sufficient reason, are both insufficient.

With this in mind, we can suggest an approach to "occult philosophy" as defined by Agrippa. Whereas in traditional occult philosophy, the world is hidden in order that it is revealed (and revealed as the world-for-us), today the world simply reveals its hiddenness to us. A second shift follows from this. Whereas traditional occult philosophy is a hidden knowledge of the open world, occult philosophy today is an open knowledge of the hiddenness of the world. Despite Agrippa's criticisms of both science and religion, the orientation of his work remains within the ambit of Renaissance humanism. For Agrippa it is not only possible for humanity to gain knowledge of the world, but it is also possible for humanity to, by virtue of occult practices, obtain a higher "union" with the "Maker of all things." Today, in an era almost schizophrenically poised between religious fanaticism and a mania for scientific hegemony, all that remains is the hiddenness of the world, its impersonal "resistance" to the human *tout court*. Hence, in traditional occult philosophy knowledge is hidden, whereas in occult philosophy today the world is hidden, and, in the last instance, only knowable in its hiddenness. This implies a third shift: whereas traditional occult philosophy is historically rooted in Renaissance humanism, the new occult philosophy is anti-humanist, having as its method the revealing of the non-human as a limit for thought.

What follows are a series of readings which trace this theme of the hiddenness of the world. In medieval philosophy and theology, the *lectio* (literally, a "reading") is a meditation on a particular text that can serve as a jumping-off point for further discussion. Traditionally, the texts read were scriptural, and the *lectio* delivered orally akin to the modern-day lecture. The *lectio* could vary in form, from shorter, more informal meditations (*lectio brevior*) to more elaborate textual exegeses (*lectio difficilior*). As with the previous section, we can borrow from the *lectio* as a genre of writing, allowing us to structure our texts as variations on a theme. We begin with a first group of *lectio* (1–3) that depict the use of the magic circle in literature. Here the magic circle serves as a boundary between the natural and supernatural, and the possible mediations between them that are made possible by the circle itself. The magic circle is not only a boundary, but also a passage, a gateway, a portal. In these examples the hidden world reveals itself at the same time that it recedes into darkness and obscurity (hence the tragic tone of many of these stories). The second group of *lectio* (4–6) will take this motif in another direction, asking what happens when the hidden world reveals itself without any magic circle to serve as boundary. Here blobs, slime, ooze, mists, and clouds are prevalent, being not quite pure nature and yet not quite pure supernature. This moment — the manifestation of the hidden world without boundaries — will lead us to ask whether there is a new kind of "political theology" on the horizon, one that ambivalently attempts to govern this age-old boundary between the natural and supernatural.

Marlowe's *The Tragedy of Doctor Faustus* • Goethe's *Faust I*

In his study of the cultural anthropology of play, Johan Huizinga notes how play involves a number of ritualized practices, in which play is at once separated from the everyday world and yet mirrors it. The games we play, whether as children or adults, at once reaffirm hegemonic social structures while also revealing to us the rules of play. Whether they are games of chance or games of strategy, play achieves this ambivalence through a spatial and symbolic motif that Huizinga calls "the magic circle." As Huizinga notes, "play moves and has its being within a play-ground marked off beforehand either materially or ideally, deliberately or as a matter of course."[18]

The magic circle need not actually be a circle, nor need it be magical. "Just as there is no formal difference between play and ritual, so the 'consecrated spot' cannot be formally distinguished from the play-ground." Hence a playing field, a game board, or even a building can be an incarnation of the magic circle: "The arena, the card-table, the magic circle, the temple, the stage, the screen, the tennis court, the court of justice, etc., all are in form

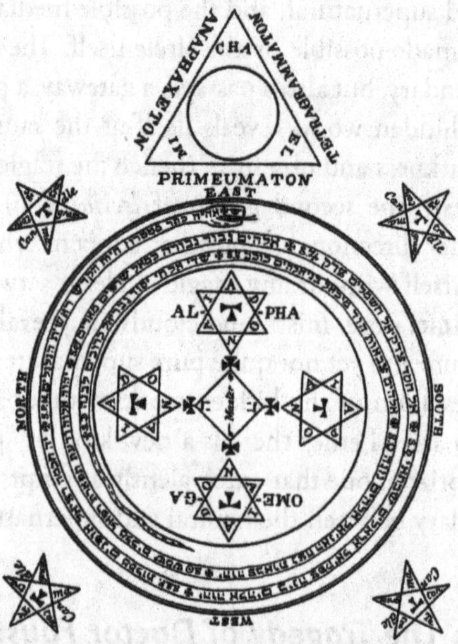

A diagram from the *Key of Solomon* (*Clavicula Salomonis*, c.14th–15th century)

and function play-grounds, i.e. forbidden spots, isolated, hedged around, hallowed, within which special rules obtain."[19]

Despite this everydayness — or indeed because of it — Huizinga observes that the circle obtains a magical significance. For Huizinga, the magic circle has its roots in classical world mythology, in which one finds the themes of fate and free will at the hands of the gods or cosmic forces. Huizinga notes that in the *Mahābhārata*, for instance, a game of dice is played among the descendants of the legendary king Kuru. The place where the game is played "is a simple circle, *dyūtamandalam*, drawn on the ground … The players are not allowed to leave the ring until they have discharged all their obligations."[20]

The magic circle has a cosmological significance, mirroring the cosmic or mythic ordering of the universe. This is inseparable from a social and political significance, in which the magic circle delimits a boundary between law and transgression, the legitimate and illegitimate, the sacred and profane. All incarnations of the magic circle "are temporary worlds within the ordinary world, dedicated to the performance of an act apart."[21] One of the most noteworthy uses of the magic circle is in the form of ritual magic, particularly evident in literary representations of necromancy and demonology. These are not only literary uses of a magic circle, but they also demonstrate, in their successes or failures, the political and theological aspects of the magic circle that historians such as Huizinga point out.

The Faust myth provides one such example. Though there are at least one or more historical personages known as Faust, little is known of their lives except by hearsay. In 16th-century Germany, several books recounting the life of Faust were in circulation. These "Faustbooks," as they are known, detail the basic elements of the story: Faust's challenge to faith, his pact with a demon, and his eventual downfall and damnation. One Faustbook tells how Faust, after dismissing the miracles performed by Christ, began to demonstrate his ability to perform miracles just as easily. When confronted by the Church, Faust rebukes, noting that "I have gone further than you think and have pledged myself to the devil with my own blood, to be his in eternity. How, then, can I return? Or how could I be helped?"[22]

In the late 16th century Faustbooks began to be translated and made their way around the continent. In England *The Damnable Life and Deserved Death of Dr. John Faustus* was published around 1588. It is thought that this edition prompted the playwright Christopher Marlowe to compose the first version of his own Faust story, *The Tragical History of Doctor Faustus* in 1592 or 1593. Marlowe's version of the Faust myth is noteworthy for several reasons. It formalizes with great detail the ritual practices of Faust, while also raising a host of difficult theological and philosophical questions regarding the mobile boundary between science and religion. In Marlowe's first edition, the play opens with a despondent Faustus questioning and then abandoning all forms of human knowledge as limited and inefficacious: "Bid *On kai me on* farewell. Galen, come!

/ Seeing *ubi desinit philosophus, ibi incipit medicus,* / Be a physician, Faustus. Heap up gold, / And be eternized for some wondrous cure."[23] Showing off his classical education, Marlowe has Faustus almost indifferently rattle off Greek and Latin — he bids farewell to *On kai me on* or the question of being and not-being so central to Greek philosophy; he then takes up the proverb *ubi desinit philosophus, ibi incipit medicus*, or "where the philosopher ends, the physician begins," announcing his intent to move beyond theory and into practice.

What is left for Faustus to do, seeing that all human knowledge has come to naught for him? Should he turn to religion? Here Faustus expresses his most vitriolic phrases, for with religion "We deceive ourselves" in an absurd, vicious circle of temptation, sin, and repentance — thus Faustus claims, "Divinity, adieu!"[24] All that remains are the dark arts. As Faustus picks up an unnamed book of magic, he notes how "These metaphysics of magicians / And necromantic books are heavenly, / Lines, circles, signs, letters, and characters / Ay, these are those that Faustus most desires."[25] This litany of magical tools — "lines, circles, signs, letters, and characters" — paves the way for Faustus's use of the magic circle in his evocation of demons, the act that has come to define the Faust myth.

The key scene appears in both versions of the play, though in the second version of 1616 both the stage directions and textual variants create a much more dramatic, even cataclysmic atmosphere. The second version begins with thunder and a storm. We see Faustus in his study, with his books of black magic. Suspended above him is a swarm of demons, including Lucifer. Faustus is unaware that they are there, suspended above him, but we in the audience can see them, waiting. The passage is worth citing in full, particularly for the way that it connects Faustus's use of the magic circle with elemental and even planetary forces:

The Tragicall Hiſtory of the Life and Death of Doctor FAVSTVS.

With new Additions.

Written by *Ch. Mar.*

Printed at London for *Iohn Wright*, and are to be ſold at his ſhop without Newgate, 1624.

The title page of Christopher Marlowe's *The Tragical History of the Life and Death of Doctor Faustus* (c.1592–1593)

> Now that the gloomy shadow of the earth,
> Longing to view Orion's drizzling look,
> Leaps from th'Antarctic world unto the sky
> And dims the welkin with her pitchy breath,
> Faustus, begin thine incantations,
> And try if devils will obey thy hest,
> Seeing thou hast prayed and sacrificed to them
> *[He draws a circle]*
> Within this circle is Jehovah's name
> Forward and backward anagrammatized,
> Th'abbreviated names of holy saints,
> Figures of every adjunct to the heavens,
> And characters of signs and erring stars,
> By which the spirits are enforced to rise.
> Then fear not, Faustus, to be resolute,
> And try the utmost magic can perform.[26]

Following this we get more thunder and Faust incanting in Latin. The demon Mephistopheles appears, and the two begin their dialogue that eventually leads Faustus to sign in blood the pact with the demon. However, what is striking in the passage above is the way in which the "hidden world" of occult philosophy is cataclysmically revealed. Planets shift, winds howl, and a demon emerges from the smoke — this is, to be sure, the stuff of contemporary horror film. Yet for all this spectacle, the world, by the play's end, remains hidden, up to the final scenes where Faustus is dragged into the underworld as fulfillment of the pact.

Marlowe brings together two shadowy bodies of knowledge of the Elizabethan era: that of occult philosophy and its connections between the microcosm and macrocosm, and that of the ongoing controversies over and persecutions of witchcraft and demonology. Both discourses raise a topic hotly debated among theologians and law-makers of the time, principally, the relation between the natural and the supernatural, or between the "scientific" cosmology of the planets and elements, and the "religious" topology of angels, demons, and other spiritual creatures. Marlowe's Faustus is not simply a black magician out to sate his every desire, and neither is he an official doctor ensconced within the halls of legitimate Church institutions such as the university. In his use of the magic circle, he is someone who does not or cannot see the distinction between the natural and supernatural, the cosmic forces of Orion or the Antarctic and the spiritual forces of angels and demons.

Interestingly, the dramatic staging of this scene is almost entirely left out of Goethe's version of the Faust myth. This is, likely, intentional on Goethe's part, since his *Faust: A Tragedy* (1808) is known for its decidedly more philosophical tone. Faust's Promethean quest for knowledge of the Absolute results in the still-moving, angst-ridden soliloquies that rail against the limits of human knowledge. This all-or-nothing demand ultimately leads to revelations for which Faust is unprepared to accept: the futility of all human endeavor, the fickle and fallible nature of human existence, and the inexorable effacement of all things by time. Many a reader has been left to wonder whether, by the tragic end of the story, Faust consciously commits a kind of philosophical suicide.

Throughout these struggles with the Absolute, the motif of the circle persists. In the opening scenes, Goethe has Faust ruminate for pages about his search for ultimate knowledge, immersed in a melancholy state exemplary of the German-Romantic anti-hero. Like Marlowe's Faustus, Goethe's Faust also abandons the official knowledges of philosophy, science, and religion. For Faust, the world remains hidden, and it is doubtful that any *human* knowledge or access to the world will reveal anything of worth. Faust laments, "That I might see what secret force / Hides in the world and rules its course. / Envisage the creative blazes / Instead of ruminating in phrases."[27] Faust's impatience with book-learning leads him to a kind of Romantic embrace of the world in itself, though even in this gesture Faust takes with him a book of magic: "Flee! Out into the open land! / And this book full of mystery, / Written in Nostradamus's hand / Is it not ample company?"[28]

While there is no magic circle scene like we see in Marlowe's version, Goethe does give us something like a magic circle, though all the drama takes place in the inner recesses of the mind. In his search for ultimate knowledge, Faust is led first to contemplate the symbol of the macrocosm, perhaps of the type frequently encountered in Renaissance alchemical treatises — a spherical diagram showing the cosmos and all of its layers. When, in 1790, Goethe sought to publish an early version of *Faust*, he chose to include an etching by Rembrandt, "Doctor Fautrieus, or, the Alchemist at Home in His Study" (1652), and it's easy to see why. Rembrandt's image uncannily depicts the scene in which Faust has a vision of the cosmos.

Goethe's Faust, like Marlowe's Faustus, notes the mystery of the hiddenness of the world. What divine force is it, Faust asks, that "Make nature's hidden powers around me, / manifest?"[29] This meditation prompts Faust to the epiphany of the interconnectedness of all things. As he notes, "Through every nerve, my veins are glowing." And again: "All weaves itself into the whole, / Each living in the other's soul."[30]

Yet this first, dramatic contemplation of the world's hiddenness only leaves Faust in despair. His only realization is the limit of all human knowledge. Picking up another book, Faust gazes upon a symbol of the earth spirit (*Erdgeist*), leading him to a second contemplation. Modern commentators have debated what exactly this earth spirit is — another name for an alchemical symbol, a pagan symbol linked to cyclic or seasonal time, or a Romantic personification of nature. Whatever it is, it prompts Faust, with some excitement, to ruminate on the elemental mysteries of the planet — Faust notes, in short, staccato phrases, the clouds, storm winds, the moon, and the sea. It finally leads Faust to invoke the earth spirit, which appears as a flame whose light is too bright for Faust's eyes to bear.

Abstractions of the magic circle appear elsewhere in Goethe's *Faust* — a crowd of townspeople at a festival make a circle around Faust to commend him; at the same festival an anonymous black dog seems to follow and make circles around Faust; later, in the conversation between Faust and Mephisto, the latter is blocked from leaving Faust's study due to a magical pentagram that has

Rembrandt, *Doctor Fautreius, the Dutch Philosopher* (1652), etching

been placed above the door. These and other instances reinforce Goethe's abstraction of the magic circle, which comes to have the central characteristic brought forth in Faust's contemplations: the magic circle as that which paradoxically reveals the hiddenness of the world-in-itself.

Wheatley's *The Devil Rides Out* • Blish's *Black Easter, or Faust Aleph-Null*

Adaptations of the Faust myth in modernity are innumerable, and, while it is not possible to document each and every one of them, let us note just two 20th century examples, specifically for the way they take up the motif of the magic circle in modernity. Published in 1934, Dennis Wheatley's sensationalist novel *The Devil Rides Out* contains what is perhaps among the most detailed and elaborate magic circle scenes in the horror genre. The novel features, as its protagonist, the Duke de Richleau, a dashing and gentlemanly figure whose background in the dark arts helps him to solve mysteries that outwit even British Intelligence. Wheatley wrote several novels featuring Richleau, and in *The Devil Rides Out* a furtive black magician attempts to lure some of Richleau's friends into a coven of witches. In this, as in other Wheatley novels, Richleau fights magic with magic, not unlike the van Helsing character in Stoker's *Dracula*; it is therefore Richleau's intimate knowledge of the dark arts that makes him its greatest foe.

In the midst of an elaborate plot involving Satanism in modern London, Wheatley's novel has Richleau and his friends make a final stand against the black magician Mocata. In this scene, at the home of one of his friends, Richleau patiently makes preparations for the construction of a magic circle. After removing all furniture and rugs, the group — Richleau, Richard (an unswerving skeptic), Mary Lou, and Simon — proceeds to sweep and mop the floor. As Richleau comments, "I would like the room gone over thoroughly, since evil emanations can fasten on the least trace of dust to assist their materialization."[31] The group then change into simple, freshly cleaned clothes. Taking a piece of chalk, string, and ruler, Richleau then proceeds to draw a perfect circle on the floor. To this outer circle he adds an inner circle. Then to this he draws a five-pointed star, whose points touch the outer circle and valleys touch the inner circle. Around the rim Richleau inscribes in Latin an exorcism, along with ancient symbols, including Cabbalistic signs from the Sephiroth. Richleau then completes the "astral fortress" with a number of objects: silver cups with holy water, placed at the valley of the pentacle, long white candles at the apex of the pentacle, horseshoes, mandrake roots, and, for each person, rosaries, a string of garlic, asafetida grass, and phials of salt and mercury.

Richleau explains the rules of the game and what is at stake: "What may happen I have no idea ... I cannot tell you what form his attack is likely to take ... He may send the most terrible powers against us, but there is one thing above all others that I want you to remember. As long as we stay inside this pentacle we shall be safe, but if any of us sets one foot outside it we risk eternal damnation."[32] What does happen happens in phases. The first phase appears not to be supernatural at all, and involves psychological or affective disturbances (one of the characters, Richard, grows impatient when nothing happens, and is about to exit the circle to go to bed). A second phase involves anomalies of the room itself (unnatural play of light and cast shadows, violent winds in the room that come from nowhere). These merely pave the way for a third phase of strange "ab-human" creatures: a viscous dark shadow cumulating on the ceiling, then "a dim phosphorescent blob ... shimmering and spreading into a great hummock ... It had no eyes or face but from it there radiated a terrible malefic intelligence."[33] The climactic moment comes when, all else failing, an angel of death in the form of a ghostly black stallion comes to claim their lives. Richleau must resort to a secret incantation (from the "Sigsand manuscript") that finally wards off the last attack. It's worth noting that the 1968 Hammer Studios adaptation of *The Devil Rides Out* spends a great deal of time on this scene, in which the magic circle becomes a kind of dome-like screen, an allegory for film in general and horror film in particular.

At each stage of the attack Richleau and his friends are tested. Up until this point in the novel we have no real, direct evidence of the supernatural. Though we hear of a Satanic coven, and though Richleau, we are told, is in possession of erudite knowledge on the topic, we as readers never witness the supernatural in real time. Here, the magic circle drawn, the rules of the game established, and the play begun — here, the supernatural is able to manifest

Still from *The Devil Rides Out* (dir. Terence Fisher, 1968)

itself. First it comes in a form nearly indistinguishable from idealism (that is, from the *thought* of the supernatural, as possible or impossible). Then it comes in the form of inanimate, elemental forces (light and darkness, flame and shadow). This leads to its manifestation in the abject monster, the "nameless Thing" undulating and writhing just outside the circle's edge. Finally, the figure of death itself approaches, whose personification in the stallion masks the deeper metaphysical unknown of death itself. The magic circle is both what allows the "hiddenness" of the world to reveal itself, as well as that which protects the human subject from the rational unacceptability of this hidden, world-in-itself. It can be written off as mere illusion and trickery, an over-active imagination, and so on. But if, as Huizinga reminds us, the magic circle is also a mirror of the world, then the hiddenness of the world must also be understood as more than mere idealism, more than "it's all in your head."

Wheatley's novel takes up the traditional notion of magic as presented in the Faust stories by Marlowe and Goethe. Here magic is not completely divorced from something called science, but neither is it simply equivalent to it. In these instances, magic — and in particular black magic — is deemed an illegitimate form of knowledge primarily because it stands opposed to both the orthodox, religious worldview (the world as divine creation) and the then-burgeoning scientific worldview (the world as knowable in itself through reason and experiment). The knowledge gained by black magic is neither the knowledge of the world as given to us by the divine Logos, nor is it the knowledge produced by the machinations of human reason. The knowledge of black magic is — or claims to be — a knowledge of the world as essentially hidden, rather than given (religion) or produced (science). The knowledge it lays claim to is, for this reason, occult knowledge, but knowledge that is only made apparent within the topography of the magic circle.

But while much of the dialogue in Marlowe and Goethe surround the status of human knowledge, we forget that the primary motive for Faust is practical — that is, the instrumentality of such occult knowledge. What happens when one takes occult knowledge not just as a philosophical problem, but as a resource to be harnessed and transformed into a tool? Certainly this happens in Wheatley's novel, where Richleau fights magic with magic, pitting occult knowledge against occult knowledge. But for all its evocative aesthetics of black magic, *The Devil Rides Out* remains firmly inscribed within a conventional moral framework (White Magic vs. Black Magic). What Richleau never talks about is the paradox of instrumentalizing the hidden world — that is, of taking that which by definition we as human beings cannot comprehend, and transforming it into a tool ... or a weapon.

This is the theme of James Blish's novel *Black Easter*, which originally contained the subtitle *Faust Aleph-Null*. Published in 1968 as part of a series of works dealing with religion and science fiction, *Black Easter* takes up the Faust myth and places it in the modern context of nuclear war. The premise of the novel is straightforward — a wealthy arms manufacturer named Baines seeks to release all the demons on the world for a day. Presumably he, like Faust, has exhausted all the knowledge of his field, all the means of making weapons and accumulating global capital. The only weapon left undeveloped is the supernatural one, the weapon of all weapons. In his search he contacts a reputed sorcerer named Theron Ware, who works as a noir-ish private detective (much to the chagrin of the Church). Ware minces no words with Baines, stating with great sobriety, "All magic — I repeat, *all* magic, with no exceptions whatsoever — depends on the control of demons."[34] In Blish's near-future scenario, we get glimpses of a number of modern institutions, including the Consolidated Warfare Service, the Reformed Orthodox Agnostic Church, government think-tanks on weaponized anti-matter, a classified report titled *The Effects of Atomic Weapons*, and shady arms deals that feed directly into the ongoing Israel-Palestine conflict.

The climax of *Black Easter* is the actual invocation scene, depicted as something between Faust's conjuration and an experiment in particle physics. In a laboratory, Ware consults a panoply of grimoires, including the notorious *Grand Grimoire*, to ostensibly outdo Faust a hundredfold. "Ware stared at the Grand Circle for a moment, and then walked around it clockwise to the lectern and unlocked the book of pacts. The stiff pages bent reassuringly in his hands. Each leaf was headed by the character or sign of a demon; below, in special ink reserved for such high matters — gall, copperas, gum arabic — was the text of Theron Ware's agreement with that entity, signed at the bottom in his own blood, and by the character of the demon repeated in its own hand."[35] What follows in the novel is Ware's almost endless list of demons, their names, signs, and descriptions.

Of course this, like all such experiments, goes horribly wrong — or really, it goes too well. All the demons are loosed upon the earth, followed promptly by natural disasters and the Emergency Broadcast System. In the panic, Baines, speaking to a military scientist, unrepentantly exclaims, "we're turning out to be wrong about the outcome — but no matter what it's *our* outcome. We contracted for it. Demons, saucers, fallout — what's the difference? Those are just signs in the equation, parameters we can fill any way that makes the most immediate sense to us. Are you happier with electrons than with demons?"[36] The cataclysm concludes with the arrival of Baphomet, who speaks, with great dramatic flair, as the voice of the cataclysm itself: "WE WILL DO WITHOUT THE ANTICHRIST. HE WAS NEVER NECESSARY. MEN HAVE ALWAYS LED THEMSELVES UNTO ME."[37]

On one level, *Black Easter* is an allegory for the atomic age and the looming threat of Mutually Assured Destruction. We get black magic instead of atomic physics, sorcerers instead of scientists, warring nations instead of warring religions, and so on. But *Black Easter* is not a work of fantasy; arguably it isn't even a work of speculative fiction. The allegorical reading gives way, at a certain point, to a reading of the novel that is metaphysical. Taking the novel in this way does not mean, however, that one has to accept or reject the real existence of magic. The metaphysics of the novel lies in its evocation of the world and its hiddenness, especially when the hidden world is cataclysmically revealed through weapons that make it nearly impossible to distinguish a human-made war, a naturally occurring disaster, and a religious apocalypse.

Hodgson's *Carnacki the Ghost-Finder* • "The Borderland" (*The Outer Limits*)

Up to this point we've been considering variations on a theme: that of cultural representations of the magic circle. In these stories the magic circle maintains a basic function, which is to govern the boundary between the natural and the supernatural, be it in terms of acting as a protective barrier, or in terms of invoking the supernatural from the safety inside the circle. We can now take another step, which is to consider instances in which the anomalies that occur are not inside or outside the magic circle, but are anomalies *of* the magic circle itself. This need not mean that the magic circle malfunctions or has been improperly drawn. In some cases it may mean that the magic circle itself — as the mediation of the hidden world — reveals some new property or propensity.

A case in point is in the "occult detective" subgenre, a style of fiction popular in the 19th century. In these stories, a protagonist combines knowledge of modern science with that of ancient magic to solve a series of crimes and mysteries that may or may not have supernatural causes. Algernon Blackwood's *John Silence — Physician Extraordinary* and Sheridan Le Fanu's *In a Glass Darkly* are examples in fiction, while Charles Fort's *The Book of the Damned* is an example in nonfiction. These types of stories are not only the precursors to modern-day TV shows such as *In Search Of…* or *The X-Files*, but they also bring together science and sorcery into a new relationship.

Published as a collection in 1913 as *Carnacki the Ghost-Finder*, William Hope Hodgson's occult detective stories are noteworthy for their reinvention of the magic circle. Hodgson's detective, named Thomas Carnacki, not only has a deep and erudite knowledge of the occult, but he also has at his disposal an array of gadgets, tools, and gizmos. Unlike many of the other occult detectives, who solve mysteries by crafty ratiocination, Carnacki combines rational "scientific" thinking with the appropriate tools for the job. Some of these tools are simple and low-tech, such as candle wax to seal windows and doors (thereby indicating if an entry was made during the night). Other tools are, by early 20th-century standards, quite modern: Carnacki frequently makes use of photography in attempts to visualize spirits that may be invading a house or room. Still other tools are ancient and magical: Carnacki makes use of water circles and frequently refers to the Old English "Sigsand manuscript" for particular spells or incantations.

These types of tools are used mostly to document a presence that may or may not be supernatural. However, the tool that stands out from all the others is one of Carnacki's own design and invention: the "Electric Pentacle." It is featured in a number of the Carnacki stories. In "The Gateway of the Monster," Carnacki investigates the haunting of a particular room in a house. Residents complain of slamming doors, moving furniture, and strange, floating drapes. In itself the symptoms are unremarkable — your classic Gothic haunting. But Carnacki's approach is unique. Determined to spend the night in the room (dubbed the "Grey Room"), Carnacki first draws a traditional magic circle on the floor, with the aid of the Sigsand manuscript. As with our previous examples, this serves as a barrier or protection against what Carnacki calls the "Outer Monstrosities."

But this in itself is not enough. Carnacki calls upon esoteric research, including a lecture by one Professor Garder, "Astral Vibrations Compared with Matero-involuted Vibrations below the Six-Billion Limit." Summarizing the research, Carnacki notes: "When they surrounded the Medium with a current, in vacuum, he lost his power — almost as if it cut him off from the Immaterial. That made me think a lot; and that is how I came to make the Electric Pentacle, which is a most marvelous 'defence' against certain manifestations."[38] Using vacuum tube technology, Carnacki invents a steampunk magic circle: "I turned now to fit the Electric Pentacle, setting it up so that each of its 'points' and 'vales' coincided exactly with the 'points' and 'vales' of the drawn pentagram upon the floor. Then I connected up the battery, and the next instant the pale blue glare from the intertwining vacuum tubes shone out."[39] While Marlowe and Goethe implicitly combine science and magic in their theories, Hodgson materially combines them in the layering of the traditional pentacle with its modern, electrical cousin.

In most of the cases the Electric Pentacle serves Carnacki well as a barrier, whether it is from a giant "death Hand," the eerie "blood drip," a "Saiitii manifestation," or the "Ab-human" shadows of the "Outer Worlds." In one case, however, the Electric Pentacle does something different. In the story "The Hog," Carnacki attempts to cure a man possessed by the images and sounds of a horde of cosmic pigs (perhaps a reference to the Biblical parable of the Gerasene demon). Convinced that the man is not simply mad or hallucinating, he ensconces him within an elaborate version of the Electric Pentacle, with different colored vacuum tubes signaling different kinds of manifestations. Far from serving as a protective barrier, the center of the circle itself actually becomes a portal to another dimension, turning into a misty, bottomless, black pit: "A very curious thing happened then, for all around the edge of the pit, that looked so peculiarly like black glass, there came a sudden, luminous glowing ... and, abruptly, out of the tremendous Deep, I was conscious of a dreadful quality or 'atmosphere' of monstrousness that was coming up out of the pit."[40] What finally emerges is a surreal, demonic beast: "I saw it pale and huge through the swaying, whirling funnel of cloud — a monstrous pallid snout rising out of that unknowable abyss ... A pig's eye with a sort of hell-light of vile understanding in it."[41] In Hodgson's Carnacki stories, the Electric Pentacle is a hybrid of magic and science that, in stories like "The Hog" serves to invert the traditional uses of the magic circle. Instead of providing protection and serving as a barrier between the natural and supernatural, the Electric Pentacle actually focuses and intensifies the passage between them, whereby the "hidden world" reveals itself as a sort of extra-dimensional monstrosity.

This same idea is seen in "The Borderland," an episode of the classic TV series *The Outer Limits*. Aired in 1960 and directed by Leslie Stevens, the episode also juxtaposes science and magic, though in ways different from the occult detective genre. The episode opens, significantly, with a séance. An old, wealthy industrialist is attempting to reach his son, who has recently died in a car accident. However, not all of those present are convinced of the spiritual medium, and one of the assistants calls their bluff, revealing a simple cloth-and-string rig. After the failure of the séance, a discussion ensues about the possibility of reaching the dead. The others present at the table are scientists, working on the use of modern turbine power to open a gateway to the fourth dimension. Using a simple demonstration of magnets and an introductory lecture in quantum physics, the scientists convince the industrialist to use the city's entire power plant for a brief period of time to try to open the gateway. The caveat is that whoever goes through to the other side must also search for the industrialist's dead son.

Still from "The Borderland," ***The Outer Limits*** **(dir. Leslie Stevens, 1963)**

The bulk of the episode details the experiment. Unlike the Electric Pentacle, which in form and function remains a traditional magic circle, here the magic circle is different. In the center of the lab, a large chamber serves as the portal. Around it is arranged various unnamed laboratory technology — huge magnets, electron scanners, and tape-driven computers. This "black box" is the magic circle, and its techniques are not magic but laboratory physics, its animating principle not the magical sign but the principle of atomic magnetism. The episode documents the experimental protocols for each phase of the experiment, as laboratory technicians recite in monotone voices instructions and data, sounding like a very different type of grimoire. At the experiment's peak, the scientist does enter into the fourth dimension, depicted in the episode as a wonderful montage worthy of Surrealist cinema. Space and time collapse in the consciousness of the scientist, but the search for the dead is for naught. If the occult detective genre still attempted to strike a balance between science and magic, *The Outer Limits* episodes like these make a claim for bleeding-edge science as the new occultism, and electromagnetic laboratory chambers like the one we see as the new magic circle. If the lab is the circle, then the lab experiment is the magical ritual.

Lovecraft's "From Beyond" • Ito's *Uzumaki*

In our previous discussions, the magic circle serves as a portal or gateway to the hiddenness of the world. In some cases, the use of the circle actually guarantees the separation of the natural and supernatural, while also making possible the manifestation of the latter in the former. This is the case in the Faust stories by Marlowe and Goethe, where passages between nature and supernature are relatively restricted. While the supernatural is invoked, the division of natural and supernatural remains intact. By the end of Marlowe's play, for instance, Faustus is dragged down to Hell, and the cosmology of the world remains as it has been.

But we've also seen that the magic circle has a wider impact, affecting anomalies in the weather, in everyday objects, in the beliefs and desires of individuals, and even — as in Goethe's *Faust II* — the events of world history. The supernatural begins to bleed into the natural. The magic circle, whose function was to govern the boundary between them, begins to spiral out of control, as the human subjects in the magic circle struggle to control and comprehend that which lies outside of it (and thus outside the scope of human knowledge). Wheatley's *The Devil Rides Out* deals with these struggles on the level of religious morality, while Blish's *Black Easter* deals with them on the level of geopolitics and nuclear war. The boundary between the natural and the supernatural — topographically ensured by the use of the magic circle — is becoming more and more fuzzy. The final stage of this fuzziness is when the magic circle itself starts to behave anomalously, as we've seen in the occult detective subgenre. In some cases, the circle inverts its traditional function and amplifies the blurriness of the supernatural and the natural.

The *Outer Limits* episode ends on a note of caution, with humanity saving the world from its own inventions. But not all modern scientific incarnations of the magic circle are so filled with optimism. We get a slightly different, more menacing picture from early 20th-century writers in the "weird fiction" tradition like H.P. Lovecraft. Lovecraft's short story "From Beyond," published in 1934 in the pulp magazine *Fantasy Fan*, takes the technological magic circle in a different direction. Instead of serving as a gateway or portal to other dimensions — a function still very much within the traditional magic circle — Lovecraft's characters construct a magic circle whose function is to dissolve the boundary between the natural and supernatural, the four-dimensional and the other-dimensional, the world revealed and the world as hidden. This dissolving of boundaries between the natural and supernatural is also found in the work of contemporary authors influenced by Lovecraft, including Caitlín Kiernan, Thomas Ligotti, Brian Everson, and recent films such as *The Babadook*, *The Lighthouse*, *Noroi: The Curse*, *The Wailing*, *The Void*, and *Under the Shadow*. In Lovecraft's story, what results is a "subtractive" magic circle, which by its very receding into the background bizarrely flattens all dimensions into one.

In "From Beyond," the narrator recounts the experiments of a reclusive physicist named Crawford Tillinghast, who explains his rationale as follows: "We see things only as we are constructed to see them, and can gain no idea of their absolute nature. With five feeble senses we pretend to comprehend the boundlessly complex cosmos, yet other beings with a wider, stronger, or different range of senses might not only see very differently the things we see, but might see and study whole worlds of matter, energy, and life which lie close at hand yet can never be detected with the senses we have."[42] Tillinghast continues, a little excitedly, announcing "I have always believed that such strange, inaccessible worlds exist at our very elbows, *and now I believe I have found a way to break down the barriers*" (in Lovecraft's inimitable prose, italics always indicate an epiphany of cosmic horror).[43] Tillinghast goes on to demonstrate a device he has constructed, set up in the center of the laboratory, which Lovecraft only describes as a "detestable electrical machine, glowing with a sickly, sinister, violet luminosity."[44]

Seated around the device, in the center of the lab, the narrator and Tillinghast reenact the magic circle of Marlowe's Faustus. When Tillinghast turns on the device, the narrator experiences an influx of color and shape. Quickly, however, the trip begins to turn sour: "At another time I felt huge animate things brushing past me and occasionally *walking or drifting through by supposedly solid body.*"[45] Finally, the narrator "sees" around him that which has always existed but which human senses forever obscure: "Foremost among the living objects were great inky, jellyfish monstrosities which flabbily quivered in harmony with the vibrations from the machine. They were present in loathsome profusion, and I saw to my horror that they *overlapped*; that they were semi-fluid and capable of passing through one another and through what we know as solids."[46] The horror of this "cosmic" realization is then doubled by another more tangible horror. As Tillinghast exclaims to the narrator, "Don't move,' he cautioned, 'for in these rays *we are able to be seen as well as to see.*"[47] Tillinghast, who by now has gone far into mad-scientist territory, begins to prophesize of "ultimate things" stealthily approaching "from beyond." Later, the police find Tillinghast's lab in a disarray, and the bodies of the servants — abducted into the other dimension — are nowhere to be found. As with many weird tales, the story closes with ambiguous newspaper reports of unsolved mysteries. The narrator — as with many of Lovecraft's protagonists — wishes he were insane, wishes that he could rationalize the "beyond" as mere illusion: "It would help my shaky nerves if I could dismiss what I now have to think of the air and the sky about and above me."[48]

With Lovecraft, we see several transformations to the magic circle. First, as with the Electric Pentacle, the magic circle's function is inverted — it now serves to focus and intensify the strange, enigmatic appearance of the "hiddenness" of the world. And it does so not through traditional magic, but through the modern sorcery of science; instead of referencing alchemy or necromancy, Lovecraft's characters use the language of optics, physics, and the fourth dimension. There is also a second transformation to the magic circle, which is that science and technology are not just used to upgrade the magic circle — they *are* the magic circle. This distinguishes the device in "From Beyond" from the Electric Pentacle; while the latter remains a traditional magic circle, the device in Lovecraft's story distills the metaphysical principle of the magic circle, which is a boundary or point of mediation between two different orders, two different planes of reality. Lovecraft dispenses with the architectonics of the magic circle, but preserves its metaphysics. The device serves as a nodal point from which the characters are able to "see" the extra-dimensional reality and the weird creatures that swim about them. The aim of the magic circle is primarily a philosophical one: rather than assuming the division between the natural and supernatural, and then utilizing the magic circle to manage or govern the boundary between them, in "From Beyond" the magic circle is used to reveal the already-existing non-separation between natural and supernatural, the "here and now" and the "beyond."

A third and final transformation to the magic circle has to do with *the disappearance of the circle itself*, while its powers still remain in effect. During the story, as the characters witness the "beyond," the device itself gradually recedes into the background as the characters can only look about in a state of horrified awe. It is as if we get the effects of the magic circle, but without the circle itself. Nearly all the traditional uses of the magic circle adopt the model of spectator and spectacle — inside the circle is the audience, and outside it is the dramatic action (again, this is most explicit in the film version of *The Devil Rides Out*). In "From Beyond," however, we lose this separation, and there is no spectacle that we may view from inside the safety of the circle. Instead, natural and supernatural blend into a kind of ambient, atmospheric no-place, the characters bathed in the alien ether of unknowable dimensions. The center of the circle is, then, really everywhere … and its circumference, really nowhere.

This third transformation — in which the magic circle as such is diffused into the world — is the principal motif in Junji Ito's manga series *Uzumaki.* First appearing in Shogakukan's weekly *Big Comic Spirits* in the 1990s, Ito's manga tells the story of a small Japanese town that is mysteriously afflicted by the symbol of the spiral. The spiral first appears as the obsession of several townspeople, one of whom — a Mr. Saito — begins to see spirals everywhere — in a snail's shell, in the swirling river water, in incense smoke, in handmade pottery, in tapestry designs, even in the fish cakes in his udon soup. As he frantically comments to a friend, "I find the spiral to be very mystical ... It fills me with a deep fascination ... like nothing else in nature ... no other shape."[49] In a final, desperate attempt to achieve this mystical union with the spiral, Saito's body itself undergoes a spiral-metamorphosis. His eyes swirl around in opposite directions (so he can see the whole world as a spiral...), his tongue twists inward like a spiral, and his entire body twists and curls itself into a giant, fleshy spiral.

Not only does "spiral obsession" become contagious, affecting people throughout the town, but, more importantly, the spiral begins to manifest itself in strange and unnatural ways: at the cremation of Saito, the ashes and smoke rise into the sky, forming a menacing, dark spiral shape with vague hints of ghostly faces floating within it. In the scenes that follow, the townspeople discover spiral-shaped grass growing in the hills, spiral-shaped clouds in the sky, spiral-shaped mud and clay from the town river, and so on.

Thus, what begins as a psychological and subjective *obsession* quickly turns into an objective *manifestation* in the world. In one episode, a potter discovers that the clay he uses seems to be imbued with unnatural capacities, forming grotesque, spiral-like forms, with hints of horrific, haunting faces deep within the clay itself. In nature (the river, the sky, the mud), in the body (the eyes, tongue, ears, hair), and in art (ceramics and clay pottery; tapestry design), the spiral manifests itself both in and as the world.

Uzumaki adds yet another dimension to the magic circle motif we've been tracing. The spiral is, in one sense, an abstract, geometrical shape. It has no actual existence in the world, except as a

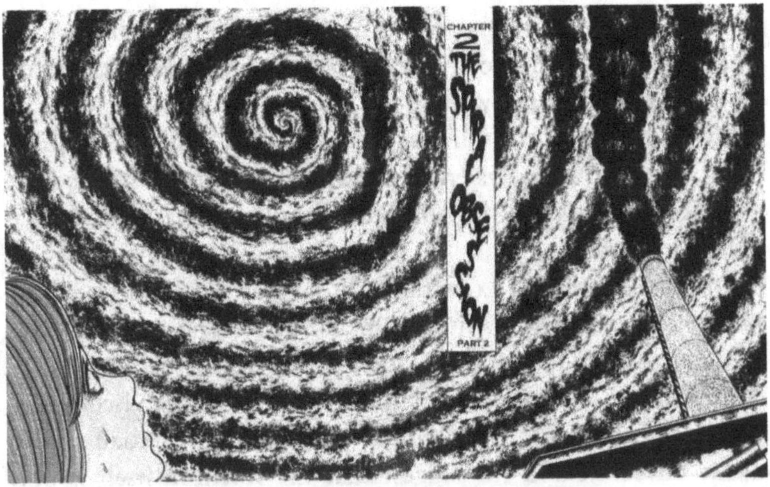

Panel from Junji Ito, *Uzumaki* (1998–1999)

manifestation in the form of a spiral (a snail's shell, a slice of fish cake). This paradoxical state means that the spiral can only be said to negatively exist — the spiral in itself is never manifest except as a spiral "in" some thing, in the world. This sort of bleed-over effect of the abstract into the concrete world is different from our traditional examples of the magic circle. In Goethe's *Faust*, we saw that Faust only encounters the magic circle symbolically, in his contemplation of the abstract symbol of the macrocosmos. But the abstract symbol and the concrete manifestation remain separate; Faust's contemplation of the symbol in itself does not lead to the invocation of demons. In *Uzumaki*, something else happens in the relationship between the abstract and the concrete, between symbol and manifestation. On the one hand, the spiral has no existence except as manifestation — and it is this contagious, pervasive manifestation that the characters describe as unnatural or strange. On the other hand, the spiral is more than just a pattern in nature — it is also equivalent to the *idea* of the spiral. That is, the abstract symbol and the concrete manifestation are inseparable, to the point that the ideational world of the spiral can "infect" the outer world of the spiral's manifestation, and vice versa. Beyond a geometrical symbol, and beyond a pattern in nature, the spiral in *Uzumaki* is ultimately equivalent to thought itself — but "thought" understood here as not simply being the interior, private thoughts of an individual. Instead, the spiral-as-thought is also "thought" as unhuman, "thought" as equivalent to the world-without-us. In this sense *Uzumaki* suggests that the Absolute is horrific, in part because it is utterly unhuman.

In the examples of Lovecraft's "From Beyond" and Ito's *Uzumaki* we see that the traditional magic circle is no longer needed in order to think about the hidden world. This is because, as the stories imply, we are already bathed in the invisible viscous hiddenness of the world. In a kind of perversion of Kantian philosophy, Lovecraft and Ito suggest that the world-in-itself is only "hidden" to the extent that our phenomenal experience of the world is determinatively a human one. In fact, Lovecraft and Ito implicitly make the argument that there is no distinction between the natural and supernatural, and what we sloppily call "supernatural" is simply another kind of nature, but one that lies beyond human comprehension. Herein lies the basis of what Lovecraft calls "cosmic horror" — the realization of the world's hiddenness as absolute. It is a sentiment frequently expressed in Lovecraft's many letters:

> Now all my tales are based on the fundamental premise that common human laws and interests and emotions have no validity or significance in the vast cosmos-at-large. To me there is nothing but puerility in a tale in which the human form — and the local human passions and conditions and standards — are depicted as native to other worlds or other universes. To achieve the essence of real externality, whether of time or space or dimension, one must forget that such things as organic life, good and evil, love and hate, and all such local attributes of a negligible and temporary race called mankind, have any existence at all ... but when we cross the line to the boundless and hideous unknown — the

> shadow-haunted *Outside* — we must remember to leave our humanity and terrestrialism at the threshold.[50]

In our readings of the hidden world, both Lovecraft's "From Beyond" and Ito's *Uzumaki* act as hinges, between the traditional uses of the magic circle (which maintain the relation between the revealed world-for-us and the hidden world-in-itself), and a more unconventional variant of the magic circle. That unconventional type of magic circle is one in which the metaphysical principle remains in effect, but the magic circle itself disappears. It is a kind of nonhuman, anonymous "magic" without any "circle" to inscribe it. This implies that any magic without a circle is also a magic without human agents to cause, control, or utilize magic. But what would magic without the magus mean? What would it mean to have revealed to us the hiddenness of the world without any revelation?

Excursus on Mists and Ooze

In "From Beyond" Lovecraft's characters are suspended in a strange no-place that is neither the normative, human world of scientific laws and therapeutic religion, nor is it the purely supernatural domain of the heavens or the underworld. Once the device is turned on, they cease to be in the magic circle per se, as it is impossible to distinguish the world outside from the world inside the circle. They seem to almost swim about in a thick, viscous ether of unknown dimensions. In Ito's *Uzumaki* the magic circle as a symbol diffuses into the world itself, to the point that it infects both the natural world and the very thoughts of the characters. This strange disappearing act of the circle already gives us a clue to our earlier question of magic without the circle. What is revealed in such instances is not just the world understood scientifically. What is revealed is a world that is neither quite natural nor supernatural, not quite the normal "here and now" and not quite the unknowable "beyond." Perhaps, instead of a magic *circle*, we have something like a magic *site*.

The magic site is, simply, the place where the hiddenness of the world presents itself in its paradoxical way (revealing itself — as hidden). In some cases magic sites are like magic circles, constructed by human beings for specific purposes. This is the case with the mad scientist theme in the Lovecraft story. More often than not, however, the magic site spontaneously happens without any human intervention. The magic site need not be on sacred ground, and it need not have special buildings or temples constructed for it. It can be in the darkest, most obscure, hidden caverns or underground fissures. It may be an accidental or unintentional site — the site of an archaeological dig, the site of a mining operation, a forest or an underground subway tunnel. Whereas the magic circle involves active human governance of the boundary between the apparent world and the hidden world, the magic site is its dark inverse: the anonymous, unhuman intrusion of the hidden world into the apparent world, the enigmatic manifesting of the world-without-us into the world-for-us, the intrusion of the Planet into the World. If the magic circle is the human looking out and confronting the unhuman, hidden world, then the magic site is that hidden world looking back at us. It is not surprising, then, that whereas the magic circle evokes vaguely anthropoid creatures (demons, ghosts, the dead), the magic site creeps forth with entities that are neither animate nor inanimate, neither organic nor inorganic, neither material nor ideal.

Let us introduce a terminology to talk about the ways in which the magic site — as opposed to the magic circle — creeps forth. The magic site manifests the hidden world revealed in two forms: as *mists* and *ooze*. Mists evoke many things — drizzling rain, a dense fog, or surreal clouds in the overcast sky. Natural formations like clouds or rain are, certainly, entities inscribed within the scientific study of atmospheric conditions. But the term "mist" may also refer to any inanimate entity that lies somewhere between the air and the ground. For instance, nephology, the scientific study of clouds, considers clouds not only on Earth but on any planet where conditions are conducive to cloud formation — indeed in interstellar space, where gravity fields may attract cosmic dust into nebulae. The ethereal nature of mists means that while they may appear solid and to have distinct forms, they are also immaterial, and can readily become formless and dissipate.

The same applies to ooze. The term "ooze" evokes more that which oozes than a discrete, static thing. What oozes can be slime, mud, oil, or pus. Ooze can ooze on the body, in the ground, in the sea or in space. Slime, for instance, can be understood in a scientific scene (for instance in plant microbiology or prokaryotic biology), but slime is also something between a liquid and a solid. Ooze may also be metamorphic and shape-shifting, as with the organisms classed as *myxomycota*, which, during their life cycle, may alternately behave like plants, fungi, or amoeboid organisms. Despite their differences, mists and ooze are two examples of the ways in which the "hidden" world reveals itself, often with strange and weird effects.

Mists and ooze populate many of our speculative fantasies about the end of the world. In our fifth *lectio* let us consider a few examples of cataclysmic mists in the genres of science fiction and horror, before going on to a consideration of ooze in our sixth and final *lectio*.

Shiel's *The Purple Cloud* • Hoyle's *The Black Cloud* • Ballard's *The Wind from Nowhere*

There are, of course, a host of stories that portray mists as malevolent forces that often serve as cover for ghosts, monsters, or unknown entities. Novels such as James Herbert's *The Fog* (1975) and Stephen King's *The Mist* (1980), as well as John Carpenter's film *The Fog* (1980) all fall into this category. The mist in these types of stories is not only itself vaguely material and formless, but in many cases its origin and aims remain utterly unknown to the human beings that are its victims. Arguably, the text that establishes the blueprint for this type of story is M.P. Shiel's 1901 novel *The Purple Cloud*. Hailed by the likes of Lovecraft as a masterpiece of weird fiction, *The Purple Cloud* is a surreal and sometimes wandering narrative about a mysterious purple gas, which emerges from a remote, vast lake, that spreads over the entire planet, killing every living being in its path — except for one person, whose diary-like account constitutes much of the novel.

Shiel's novel borrows from the "last man" motif popularized by works such as Mary Shelley's underrated *The Last Man* (1826). But whereas most last man stories depict a definable cause for the extinction of humanity (war, plague, a comet), Shiel's novel abstracts the cataclysm into a roving, amorphous mist, whose origin is described in surreal, unhuman terms by the last surviving human being:

> The lake, I think, would be something like a mile wide, and in its middle is a pillar of ice, low and thick; and I had the impression, or dream, or fantasy, that there is a name inscribed round in the ice of the pillar in characters that could never be read; and under the name a lengthy date; and the liquid of the lake seemed to me to be wheeling with a shivering ecstasy, splashing and fluttering, round the pillar, from west to east, with the planet's spin; and it was borne in upon me — can't say how — that this fluid was the substance of a living being...[51]

Here we have the magic site from which the mist emerges, flowing deep within the undiscovered coldness of remote waters. Approaching this site, the narrator experiences something like a dark ecstasy, verging on delirium — a "most cold, most mighty high — had its hand of ice on my soul, I being alone in this place, face to face with the Ineffable; but still, with a gibbering levity, and a fatal joy, and a blind hilarity, on I sped, I span."[52]

In *The Purple Cloud* we see a mist emerge from within the earth, a mist that menacingly washes over the surface of the planet, described by Shiel in an eschatological manner. A variant on this theme comes from a pulp SF novel by the astrophysicist Fred Hoyle — *The Black Cloud*. Published in 1957, *The Black Cloud* involves a mysterious black mass that appears to be heading straight for Earth. A group of American astrophysicists are the first to detect the interstellar anomaly through their high-tech telescopes: "If you look carefully at what seem like very big clouds, you'll find them to be built up of lots of much smaller clouds. This thing you've got here seems, on the other hand, to be just one single spherical cloud."[53] Rational observation and pragmatic urgency are at the center of Hoyle's novel. At an international meeting convened to discuss the pending danger, one scientist notes, "I find that if the results that have been presented to us this afternoon are correct, I say if they are correct, then a hitherto unknown body must exist in the vicinity of the solar system. And the mass of this unknown body must be comparable with or even greater than the mass of Jupiter itself."[54] As the black cloud approaches, it starts to become visible to the naked eye, and general panic sets in — there are eyewitness reports of a "general blackness in the sky," a "yawning circular pit," and newspaper reports of a "celestial black-out." As it comes nearer to Earth, atmospheric and biospheric changes rapidly occur — global temperatures drastically increase, there are warm rains in Iceland, an exponential increase in insect speciation in the southern hemisphere, and "the deserts flowered as they had never done at any time while Man had walked the Earth."[55]

Hoyle's treatment of the hidden world theme is markedly different from that of Shiel. While both novels involve a mist that threatens to destroy the planet and render humanity extinct, Shiel's treatment is much more rooted in the tradition of apocalyptic mysticism. Shiel's prose descriptions read more like one of William Blake's prophecies than science fiction, and by the novel's end this tendency is reinforced even more. By contrast, Hoyle's narrative is much more in line with Cold War-era "hard" science fiction. Scientists from all disciplines convene to study, hypothesize, and develop an action plan for the black cloud. While the protagonist of Shiel's novel comes to relate to the hidden world in terms of mysticism and manifest destiny, the characters in Hoyle's novel have no time for existential angst, as they are caught up in the production of knowledge and preparations for an impending disaster. In Shiel's novel the end actually does arrive — or at least one version of the end. In Hoyle's novel, the end is narrowly averted (a *deus ex machina* frequently used in 19th-century "comet" stories). Finally, in *The Purple Cloud* the magic site — the site from which the mist manifests itself — is that of Earth itself, an encircled whirlpool of animate gas. In *The Black Cloud*, however, the mist comes from outer space, suggesting that the hidden world is also a hidden cosmos.

The presence of a magic site — some locale from which the hidden world can manifest itself, often with disastrous effects — implies some point of origin for the hidden world, or at least for its manner of manifesting itself to us as human beings. In *The Purple Cloud* and *The Black Cloud* it is through mist that the hiddenness of the world manifests itself, though their magic sites differ (the cold heart of Earth in one, and the depths of interstellar space in the other). What happens when this strange, cataclysmic mist is present, but without a point of origin? This is the idea behind J.G. Ballard's first novel, *The Wind from Nowhere*. Published in 1961, the novel has become something of a cult classic, ironically due to Ballard's repeated attempts to disown it throughout his life. Taking place in modern London — as well as at different locales across the globe — *The Wind from Nowhere* begins with your run-of-the-mill hurricane, which proceeds to turn into a worldwide cyclone that makes Earth all but uninhabitable for human beings. In its episodic format, we see a range of human individuals coping with the wind, and the dense storms of dust and dirt that accompany it: "The wind had reached 250 mph and the organized resistance left was more interested in securing the minimal survival necessities — food, warmth, and 50 feet of concrete overhead — than in finding out what the rest of the world was doing, knowing full well that everywhere people were doing exactly the same thing. Civilization was hiding. The earth itself was being stripped to its seams, almost literally — six feet of topsoil were now traveling through the air."[56]

"It's hard to describe," one character says, a "solid roaring wall of black air — except that it's not air any more but a horizontal avalanche of dust and rock."[57] Eventually the realization sets in — the wind may continue to increase in velocity until the planet becomes almost completely composed of winds and gases. As one scientist notes, "we're witnessing a meteorological phenomenon of unprecedented magnitude, a global cyclone accelerating at a uniform rate, exhibiting all the signs distinguishing highly stable aerodynamic systems."[58] (The novel also contains a number of rather awkward bits of humor, like the following exclamation by one character, during a wind storm in southern Europe: "So much of life in the States — and over here for that matter — could use a strong breath of fresh air."[59]) By the novel's end the wind abates without warning or cause, just as mysteriously as it had begun. But throughout the novel, Ballard traces a theme that would become common in many of his novels — the correlation between internal states and external states, between the inner turbulence of modern, alienated subjectivity, and the outer turbulence of an equally unbalanced atmosphere.

What makes *The Wind from Nowhere* — and Ballard's other disaster novels — noteworthy is the ways in which the novel itself never totally accepts this symbolic reading, where the outer state simply mirrors the inner state. Unlike *The Purple Cloud* or *The Black Cloud*, there is no magic site to which one can go to witness the hidden world revealing itself. There is only the black "aerodynamic" cyclone that eventually becomes identical with the very planet itself. While the human characters do form a central part of the novel, it is Ballard's attention to surrealistic detail, and his elaborate descriptions of climatological events, that invite us to read *The Wind from Nowhere* as really being not about the human characters, but about the anonymous and enigmatic world-in-itself.

Caltiki, the Immortal Monster • *X: The Unknown* • Leiber's "The Black Gondolier"

In our previous readings we considered the theme of the hidden world as manifest in "mists" — clouds, gases, and the like. There we saw how the hidden world often manifests itself in ways that are cataclysmic — at least for the human characters in those stories. Not surprisingly, genre horror is also replete with ooze. Ooze always seems to attach itself to monsters, dripping off their tendrils and making them all the more abject. Ooze is also an indicator of the threateningly near presence of the monster; it is the footprint (or tentacle-print) of the monstrous creature. More interesting, however, are those horror stories in which ooze in and of itself *is* the monster. The most popular example is the 1958 Hollywood film *The Blob*, which features a gooey, pink substance that lands on Earth via a meteorite, and which then proceeds to engulf everything in sight (with a special appetite for screaming teenagers). As with many American films during the period, *The Blob* generalizes fears about invasions of all kinds (Communists, immigrants, nuclear war) into a blank, unspecified menace that threatens a Cold War-era town and its inhabitants. *The Blob* relies on a fairly conventional relationship of inside and outside, "us" and "them," with the key to survival in the protection of the former from the invasion of the latter.

But not all ooze-horror stories are predicated on this inside/outside dichotomy. That the gooey entity in *The Blob* comes from outer space — the outside of all outsides, as it were — is noteworthy, for it implies a safe boundary that must be secured at all costs. Other films depict the entity coming not from outside but from inside, from within the Earth itself. This is what happens in the 1959 Italian film *Caltiki, the Immortal Monster*. Directed by Riccardo Freda and Mario Bava — two directors who reinvented Italian horror film — *Caltiki* is in many ways a classic, low-budget, monster movie. Shot in black and white, with stilted acting and special effects techniques that include a giant honey-drenched cheesecloth, *Caltiki* takes the ooze-horror motif in a different direction than that of *The Blob*.

In *Caltiki* the ooze comes not from outer space, but from the bowels of the Earth. The oozing creatures are linked to an ancient Mayan myth about an indescribable monster — Caltiki — raised by vengeful gods. The film itself takes place in modern Mexico, where we find an American team of government scientists conducting an archaeological dig. Amid the all-too-human drama of lovers' quarrels and tensions between the local villagers and the American scientists, the expedition comes across an ancient, underground temple — that also contains buried treasures, along with a very high degree of radioactivity. This is the magic site, a forgotten, dead temple that contains a still-living curse. Once Caltiki is revived — as the expedition attempts to steal away the relics and treasures — it proceeds to attach itself to anything and everything in sight. Eating away the flesh of any living thing, Caltiki stumbles, like a giant, drunken, undulating amoeba, into the nearby town. In the lab, scientists examine a piece of Caltiki that has broken off; their studies suggest that Caltiki is a giant unicellular organism over 20 million years old. Meanwhile, in scenes both wonderful and abject, Caltiki proceeds to engulf houses, cars, animals, and people, able to grow and divide itself in the process. The scientists finally crack and mystery and discover that only fire can kill Caltiki, at which time a battalion of tanks with flamethrowers comes to the rescue. The ancient curse is again put to rest … for now.

In *Caltiki* we see ooze depicted allegorically, as the revenge of nature (Earth "biting back" against its colonizing intruders), or as the revenge of culture (ancient Mexico biting back against American pillaging). But at some point, these allegorical readings recede into the background, and what comes to the fore is the strange, faceless, formlessness of the ooze itself. It seems to have no motive, no vendetta, no program of action, other than simply that of "being ooze." This anonymity is matched by the affective sliminess of Caltiki, as if it were literally the bowels of the earth. Thus, whereas films like *The Blob* imagine threats *to* the world coming from outside, a film like *Caltiki, the Immortal Monster* turns this around and imagines a threat that *is* the world, coming from within.

Another variation on this theme comes from the 1956 Hammer Horror film *X: The Unknown*. Whereas *Caltiki* gives us the example of ancient ooze, *X: The Unknown* gives us the example of modern, industrial ooze. In both films the magic site lies buried under the earth. But whereas the magic site in *Caltiki* is a buried temple, in *X: The Unknown* the magic site is a radioactive field previously used for weapons testing. Presumably too many bombs have inadvertently created a fissure in the ground, out of which "Monster X" emerges, with a ravenous appetite for any source of electrical energy. A group of British military men and an American scientist attempt to study Monster X. Similar to Caltiki, Monster X is also an oozing, formless mass that resembles mud more than slime. At one point a scientist gives a mini-lecture on geology, suggesting that Monster X was originally a primordial form of life buried in the Earth's depths, which has adapted itself to feed off of radioactive energy. But the scientist, lacking a solution for stopping Monster X, wonders to himself: "but how do you kill mud?" In a moment of irony not uncommon in monster movies, the characters realize that to defend itself against the ooze, humanity must in effect destroy Earth. The threat of ooze elicits the only response of which humans seem capable: a scorched Earth.

Both *Caltiki* and *X: The Unknown* feature monsters that frustrate the traditional inside-outside boundary established by films like *The Blob*. They both feature a magic site, deep within the crusts and caverns of the planet, in which the hidden world oozes and gropes forth to the surface, threatening the human beings that inhabit this surface. This surface/depth boundary is slightly different for each film, however. In *Caltiki* the depth is archaeological, referring to lost civilizations; here the magic site itself was also once a magic circle. In *X: The Unknown* the depth is geological, in that the animate, radioactive mud that oozes to the surface is itself inseparable from the sedimentary layers from which it comes; here the magic site, while enabled by human actions (weapons testing), remains utterly unhuman.

We have one more step to take, and that is to consider ooze not only as archaeological and geological, but noological as well. Here ooze is not just a biological amoeba, and not just the mud of the earth; here ooze begins to take on the qualities of thought itself. Consider Fritz Leiber's short story "The Black Gondolier," published in the 1964 Arkham House anthology, *Over the Edge*. In it, the narrator recounts the events that led to the mysterious disappearance of his friend Daloway, a recluse and autodidact living nearby oil fields in southern California. Daloway, it seems, began to develop a bizarre and unnatural fascination with oil — not just as a natural resource or of geopolitical value, but oil in itself as an ancient and enigmatic manifestation of the hidden world. Daloway's conversations with the narrator gradually take on the form of mystical visions. Oil, he notes, constitutes "that black and nefarious essence of all life that had ever been ... a great deep-digged black graveyard of the ultimate eldritch past with blackest ghosts."[60] Oil becomes a kind of funereal, Gothic ooze, as Daloway tries to convince the narrator that "oil had waited for hundreds of millions of years, dreaming its black dreams, sluggishly pulsing beneath Earth's stony skin, quivering in lightless pools roofed with marsh gas and in top-filled rocky tanks and coursing through a myriad channels."[61]

The image of oil as stealthily waiting gives the ooze the vague quality of intelligence and intent — and, more specifically, of malefic intent. In Leiber's hyperbolic prose, oil is not the type of ooze that we see in *Caltiki* or *X: The Unknown*, where the ooze remains hidden beneath the surface of the Earth. Instead, in "The Black Gondolier" oil is described as an animate, creeping ooze that is already on the surface, that courses through all the channels of modern industrial civilization, from the central pipelines feeding the major cities to the individual homes and cars that populate those cities. At one point, the narrator attempts to put Daloway's crackpot theories into coherent form:

> Daloway's theory, based on his wide readings in world history, geology, and the occult, was that crude oil — petroleum — was more than figuratively the life-blood of industry and the modern world and modern lightning-war, that it truly had a dim life and will of its own, an inorganic consciousness or sub-consciousness, that we were all its puppets or creatures, and that its chemical mind had guided and even enforced the development of modern technological civilization.[62]

"In brief," the narrator concludes, "Daloway's theory was that man hadn't discovered oil, but that oil had found man."[63]

While the oil in "The Black Gondolier" is, like the monsters in *Caltiki* and *X: The Unknown*, an instance of the hidden world manifesting itself as ooze, there are some striking differences between them as well. For instance, the monsters in *Caltiki* and *X: The Unknown* are anomalies of nature (effected by radiation or mining), whereas the oil in "The Black Gondolier" is sentient and malefic precisely because it is indigenous to the planet. The oil is not so much a product of human design or intervention, but the reverse — it is human "modern technological civilization" that is the effect, the product of this sentient, creeping oil. In addition, both *Caltiki* and *X: The Unknown* rely on the governance of boundaries — *Caltiki* inverts the inside/outside relationship of *The Blob*, while *X: The Unknown* shifts things to a surface/depth relationship. In "The Black Gondolier" we see yet another shift, and that is to a relationship of continuity/discontinuity. The monsters in *The Blob*, *Caltiki*, and *X: The Unknown* remain, even though they are formless monsters, discrete entities. They creep, crawl, and undulate forward. One can point to them, isolate them, and even firebomb them. Thus their formlessness — their "ooziness" — is still constrained by the outline of their form. In "The Black Gondolier" any attempt to point to or isolate oil as a discrete entity is futile, precisely because it is fully continuous, not only with the Earth, but also with modern industrial society.

Arguably, this image of sentient ooze effects a further transformation of the "hidden world" theme that we've been tracing. The final scenes of the story, in which Daloway is silently carried into a great undulating "sea" of oil, asserts the decidedly unhuman qualities of the ooze. Many of our stories thus far rely on a basic dichotomy between self and world, between the thinking subject (where thought is interiorized) and a nonthinking object (upon which thought is projected). All of this breaks down in the case of ooze. Oil does not simply become a "big brain," as if to recuperate all thought within the ambit of human thought. The oil in "The

Black Gondolier" is both crude, material stuff, and immanent, miasmatic thought, both materially viscous and sentient. What we are presented with in "The Black Gondolier" is the suggestion that thought has perhaps always been unhuman.

Addendum: Circle of Dread, Cycle of Doom

The question of whether or not the supernatural exists is subtended by another question, which is whether or not we can access it. Often the latter question is the premise for the former, in that any assertion that the supernatural actually exists presumes some minimal point of contact with "the beyond." But how does one know if they have made contact with the supernatural, and if they have, is it still "supernatural," having since been brought within the ambit of human-centric frameworks of apprehension and comprehension? There is an ambiguity that inheres in the very concept of the occult, insofar as the hiddenness of the world implies something that exists at the limits of human-based forms of understanding. Once it has been accessed, studied, and rendered instrumental, it is no longer hidden, and if it is no longer hidden, is it still supernatural? This is perhaps the reason why Renaissance occult philosophy remains so conflicted; on the one hand it puts forth elaborate, systematic, syncretic philosophies explaining the hidden forces of the world, while at the same time retaining a commitment to the inaccessibility and essential unknowability of those same forces. In a fascinating way, occult philosophy is at once religious and secular, spiritual and technological; it seeks to bring the world in all its hiddenness within the scope of human control, while never wavering from its assertion of a "beyond" that is forever hidden from the limited capacities of human understanding. In occult philosophy, the supernatural collapses into the natural, at the same time that they are kept apart.

The variations on the magic circle that we've seen thus far dramatize this ambiguity regarding shifting notions of the supernatural. In some cases, the magic circle functions as a technological medium, enabling direct access to some aspect of the world that lies beyond human capacity — all the accoutrements of Faust's ritual, from the grimoires to the drawing of the magic circle, are so many techniques for gaining access to the beyond. In these cases, we see that the magic circle not only works but works *too well*; the gates are open, demons pour in; it cannot be closed again. In other instances, however, we see a degree of uncertainty as to whether the magic circle has worked or not — or whether it has worked in a way totally different from what was intended. Things get even more complicated once the magic circle itself has vanished, and the possible point of contact with the beyond becomes diffuse and ambient, often to the point where it becomes impossible to distinguish the supernatural from the natural, the beyond from the here and now.

This ambiguity is acutely apparent in a kind of horror film produced within the Hollywood system in the interwar period. No doubt the traumatic events of the world war, combined with all manner of political, economic, and social instability, have an impact on the films produced in this period — it is the period of the glorious, effortless, escapist musical, as well as the more angst-ridden, shadowy recesses of film noir. While the popular horror films produced by Universal Studios in the 1930s made Dracula, Frankenstein, and the Wolf-Man staples of the genre (as well as Abbot and Costello), a different kind of horror film emerges in the 1940s. Many of them were produced by Val Lewton at RKO Studios, and featured films such as *The Body Snatcher*, *Isle of the Dead*, *I Walked with a Zombie,* and the popular film *Cat People*. In cinematic style and narrative structure, these films resembled film noir — nocturnal urban settings, shadowy alleyways, rain-soaked streets, lonely bars and cafes, and the scratchy soft echoes of shoes on pavement. Except that the nebulous activities concerned were not to do with murder, infidelity, robbery, or embezzlement, but instead with a different kind of crime, the crime of the supernatural intruding into the natural, the spiritual invading the secular — *the crime of the supernatural.* We might call such films "Gothic noir," in that they import the Gothic motifs of earlier horror film (going back to the silent era) into the decidedly modern, urban setting of film noir. As in film noir, there is a constant interplay between what we can see and what is hidden in shadows, both figuratively and literally. But instead of revealing the grotesque *pathos* of Frankenstein's monster, or the bestial metamorphoses of the Wolf-Man, films like *Cat People* are almost totally devoted to what is hidden, what we don't see, what we can't see. Instead of showing us what is hidden, these films hide the act of showing itself, revealing another kind of horror — there is something "out there," but it will forever remain hidden from view, lurking in the blind spot of human cognition.

Of the films Lewton produced for RKO, the 1943 film *The Seventh Victim* stands out in this regard. Whereas the other Lewton-produced horror films implied a monster of some sort, or at least a monstrous villain, in *The Seventh Victim* all we are left with is an extended study in ambient dread. The film centers around a young woman searching for her wayward, missing sister Jacqueline in the nocturnal labyrinths of New York City. At one point, she sees Jacqueline, their eyes lock — and then she's gone. Did she imagine it? A landlord opens Jacqueline's rented flat in Greenwich Village, revealing an empty room, a wooden chair, and a noose hanging from the ceiling. She then goes to Jacqueline's workplace, a perfumery (called "La Sagesse"), then uptown to a psychiatrist's office, and eventually finds herself in the Upper East Side, in the company of a Satanic cult (as so many of us do). By the end of the film, she has found Jacqueline, but she is in such a state of catatonia that all she can do is walk, trancelike, into her empty flat, where she will surely hang herself. In the flat next door, a terminally ill woman emerges for the first time in months, determined to live the life she has left to her.

The Seventh Victim is a film drenched in dread, and in particular a dread of the strange allure of death. Jacqueline is at once obsessed and terrified of her own death; throughout the film she is perpetually unsure if her decisions are her own, or if every step she takes unwittingly brings her one step closer to her suicide. This harrowing combination of the fatality of death, and the futility of human action, also suffuses the 1948 film *Night Has a Thousand Eyes*, another example of Gothic noir that features Edward G. Robinson, known to most as a mainstay in film noir. Robinson plays John Triton, a performer who pretends to be clairvoyant. With the assistance of his wife and his business partner, Triton has built a successful career out of his parlor tricks — until he discovers, mid-performance, that he actually does have supernatural talents. The revelation is not only a shock, but also a curse. The sudden ability to see into the future becomes an unbearable burden. He "sees" the accidental death of a young boy. Should he intervene? Or will his intervention itself play into what was already been fated to happen? He hides himself away, estranging those closest to him for their own protection, becoming a recluse in the crowded byways of San Francisco's Bunker Hill. The struggle becomes personal, however, when Triton has a vision about a young woman's suicide — a woman he suspects is his daughter. He is afraid to act, but he cannot not act, unsure if his intervention will prevent or facilitate what he's seen in his vision. In one scene, the young woman, Jean, has just attempted suicide, burdened like Triton is with the fatality of death and the futility of action. Saved at the last second by her fiancée Elliot, her disoriented gaze rises up to the night sky: "Why didn't you let me go? — I can't face it — like a thousand eyes — watching..." Elliot responds: "The stars?" While a death is prevented, and all loose ends tied up, there remains, even by the film's end, this pervasive sense of a nebulous "something else" that may be behind each of our individual decisions.

The hiddenness of the world, whether revealed via the human-oriented motif of the magic circle, or the unhuman motif of the magic site, puts forth a challenge, which is how to live in and as part of such hiddenness. In the ambivalent moment in which the world-in-itself presents itself to us, but without immediately becoming the human-centric world-for-us, might there be a way of understanding hiddenness as intrinsic to being human as well? Does what follow for the individual also follow for the collective, however it is defined?

One of the insights of Carl Schmitt's 1922 book *Political Theology* (*Politische Theologie*) is that the very possibility of imagining the political is dependent upon a view of the world as revealed, as knowable, and as accessible to us as human beings living in a human world. As Schmitt notes, "all significant concepts of the modern theory of the state are secularized theological concepts not only because of their historical development — in which they were transferred from theology to the theory of the state, whereby, for example, the omnipotent God became the omnipotent lawgiver — but also because of their systematic structure."[64] Such an analogy has an impact, Schmitt argues, for an understanding of the development of key political concepts, such as sovereignty and the state of exception. The most concise statement of the book comes a few lines later: "The exception in jurisprudence is analogous to the miracle in theology."[65] In a sense, sovereignty is intimately linked to the governance of the supernatural, to the ability to suspend the laws of nature, to allow the impossible to become possible.

The way in which that analogy is manifest may change over time. Schmitt notes that the 17th and 18th centuries were dominated by the theological analogy of the transcendence of God in relation to the world, which correlates to the political idea of the transcendence of the sovereign ruler in relation to the state. By contrast, in the 19th century a shift occurs towards the theological notion of immanence (specifically, in modern pantheism and organicist philosophy), which likewise correlates to "the democratic thesis of the identity of the ruler and the ruled."[66] In these and other instances, we see theological concepts being mobilized as political concepts, forming a kind of direct, tabular comparison between cosmology and politics (God and sovereign ruler; the cosmos and the state; transcendence and absolutism; immanence and democracy).

Given this, what would it mean to consider a political theology of the hiddenness of the world (that is, an occult political theology)? To do so, we would have to avoid taking Schmitt's theory literally. This would not only recuperate the hiddenness of the world into the human frame, but it would also lead to rather harrowing political models (in which, for instance, the hiddenness of the world would serve as an analogy for a similarly hidden form of governance, or the secret society as a political platform).

The question that comes out of *Political Theology* has to do with how decisions are reached as to the correlation of this or that worldview with this or that political system. However, what Schmitt pays less attention to is the way in which *the analogy itself* may come under question. As Schmitt himself notes, "the metaphysical image that a definite epoch forges of the world has the same structure as what the world immediately understands to be appropriate as a form of political organization."[67] The analogical framework presumes several things: That there is an accessible, revealed, and ordered world "out there," that may serve as a model or guide for the development of a political system "in here." This is, arguably, the basis of political philosophy itself. It also presumes that this analogical relation is a one-way street, in that the discernible order of the world flows directly into the constitution of politics, when clearly there are a number of ways in which the direction is reversed (as when politics determines how and whether we intervene in "the environment"). Finally, Schmitt's analogical framework is decidedly anthropocentric, taking for granted that politics — not unlike theology — deals first and foremost with the human (here the Hobbesian analogy of the body politic is the most explicit example of this kind of anthropomorphism of the political).

What happens when we as human beings confront a world that is radically unhuman, impersonal, and even indifferent to the human? What happens to the concept of politics once one confronts the possibility that the world only reveals its hiddenness, in spite of our attempts to render it as a world-for-us, either via theology (sovereign God, sovereign ruler) or via science (the organismic analogy of the state)? This unresponsiveness of the world is a condition for which, arguably, we do not yet have a language. While the *lectio* above have focused on the cultural and philosophical ramifications of this situation, one has only to take a few steps to then consider what the hiddenness of the world might mean for thinking about the political.

Clearly there are no easy answers here. The "hiddenness of the world" is another name for the supernatural, exterior to its assimilation by either science or religion — that is, exterior to the world-for-us. But we also like to think that we are much too cynical, much too smart to buy into this — the supernatural no longer exists, is no longer possible — or at least not in the same way. It is hard to escape the sense of living in a world that is not just a human world, but also a planet, a globe, a climate, an infosphere, an atmosphere, a weather pattern … a rift, a tectonic shift, a storm, a cataclysm. Philosophically speaking, the enigma is how to relate to this world, without immediately presuming that it is identical to the world-for-us (the world of science *and* religion), and without simply assuming that it is an accessible and manipulable world-in-itself.

4

NINE *DISPUTATIO* ON THE HORROR OF THEOLOGY

In medieval Scholasticism, disagreements or confusions on a given topic were often vetted through the "disputation" (*disputatio*). Sometimes the *disputatio* would be highly regulated, as when two scholars would debate an agreed-upon topic. On other occasions the *disputatio* could be about any topic, about "whatever" — referred to as *disputatio de quodlibet.* Such intellectual free-for-alls were often quite spontaneous and associative. These "whatever" *disputatio* could also be written down, in which the author would, in effect, engage in a *disputatio* with themselves. A novel form of nonfictional, philosophical writing develops from this, and it is possible that the modern genres of the philosophical notebook or journal may harken back to the *disputatio.* It is in this spirit that the following essays-in-miniature are presented. Each deal with the way that supernatural horror mediates between life and death, often by evoking some concept of "life-in-itself" that hovers between the domains of science and religion, biology and theology — it is in this in-betweenness that one discovers supernatural horror as a way of thinking about life beyond either the subjective (life-experience) or the objective (life science) definitions.

The question that runs through these *disputatio* is the following: What if "horror" has less to do with a fear of death, and more to do with the dread of life? Not a very uplifting thought, that. Nevertheless, death is simply the nonexistence after my life, in a sense akin to the nonexistence before my life. These two types of nonexistence (*a parte post* or after my life, and *a parte ante* or before my life) are mirrors of each other. This is a sentiment repeatedly voiced by Schopenhauer: "For the infinity after life (*a parte post*) without me cannot be any more fearful than the infinity before life (*a parte ante*) without me, since the two are not distinguished by anything except by the intervention of an ephemeral life-dream."[68]

If horror — as we've been discussing it — is a way of thinking the world as unthinkable, and the limits of our place within that world, then really the specter that haunts horror is not death but instead life. But what is "life"? Perhaps no other concept has so preoccupied philosophy, with such divergent opinions on what is or isn't the essence of life. After millennia of philosophical inquiry, we can be pretty sure that we will never arrive at a definitive answer to the "what is life" question. And yet life, as lived, constantly throws the question back at us — the most immediate is the least understood. In addition, "life" is not really a philosophical concept. Philosophers talk endlessly about metaphysical concepts such as "being," "substance," or "existence," whereas "life" seems to slip by the wayside, not quite a metaphysical concept, and yet more than its scientific or religious definitions. In fact, "life" is interesting for philosophy precisely because of the way it seems to be nestled between its scientific and religious definitions, which steer life towards human life, the life-for-us.

In a sense, the question is: Can there be a philosophy of "life" that does not immediately become a concern of either Being or God? To what extent is "life" as a concept always situated between a non-ontological "life itself" (the view of science) and an onto-theology of the life-beyond-the-living, or afterlife (the view of religion)?

After Life

Ever since Aristotle distinguished the living from the nonliving in terms of *psukhē* (ψυχη) — commonly translated as "soul" or "life-principle" — the concept of life has itself been defined by a duplicity — at once self-evident and yet opaque, capable of categorization and mystification. This duplicity is related to another one, namely, that there are also two sides to Aristotle — there is Aristotle-the-metaphysician, rationalizing *psukhē*, form, and causality, and there is Aristotle-the-biologist, observing natural processes of "generation and corruption" and ordering the "parts of animals."

Despite the voluminous output of Aristotle's natural philosophy of life, there is relatively little about death — or, for that matter, the afterlife. But what comes "after life"? Is it death, decay, and decomposition, or is it resurrection and regeneration? Is it, in biological terms, the transformation of the living into the nonliving, the organic life of molecules into nonorganic matter? Or does it involve a theological revitalization of the resurrected, living cadaver? In either case, the afterlife bears some relation to the "during life" and the "before life," and it is precisely the ambiguity of these relationships that has shaped the debates on mechanism and vitalism in the philosophy of biology, as well as the earlier debates in Scholasticism on the nature of creaturely life.

There is no better guide to the afterlife than Dante. The life of the afterlife in the *Commedia* is a political theology, at once rigidly structured and yet coursing with masses of bodies, limbs, fluids, fires, rivers, minerals, and geometric patterns of beatific light. In particular, the *Inferno* gives us several concise statements concerning the life of the afterlife. In the seventh circle, Dante and his guide Virgil come to a "burning desert," upon which a multitude of bodies are strewn about.[69] Among them Dante and Virgil come across Capaneus, one of the seven kings who assaulted Thebes and defied the law of Jove. Capaneus lies stretched out on the burning sand, a rain of fire descending upon him, while he curses against the sovereign. As Virgil explains, Capaneus is one of the blasphemers, grouped with the usurers and sodomites for their crimes against God, State, and Nature. But, as with many of Dante's depictions in the *Inferno*, there is no redemption, and the punished are often far from being penitential. Their tired, Promethean drama of revolt, defiance, and blasphemy goes on for eternity.

It is easy to read such scenes in a highly anthropomorphic manner. But each individual "shade" that Dante encounters is also associated with a group that denotes a category of transgression, and this is especially the case of Middle Hell. Upon entering the gates of the City of Dis, Dante and Virgil are first confronted by a horde of demons, and then by the Furies. Once they are able to pass, they come upon a "landscape of open graves," each one burning and holding within it one of the Heretics. The scene is depicted with great drama by Gustave Doré, who, following the prior example of Botticelli, presents the heretics as a mass of twisted, emaciated corpses emerging from their graves. Along the way they also encounter a river of bodies immersed in boiling blood (watched over by a regiment of Centaurs), as well as the "wood of suicides," in which the bodies of the damned are fused with dead trees (watched over by the Harpies). Within many of the circles, Dante encounters nothing but multiplicity — bustling crowds (the Vestibule of the Indecisive), a cyclone of impassioned bodies (Circle II, the Lustful), a sea of bodies devouring each other (Circle V, the Wrathful), dismembered bodies (Circle VIII, the Sowers of Discord), and a field of bodies ridden with leprosy (Circle VIII, the Falsifiers). The life-after-life continually negates itself, a kind of vitalistic *life-negation* that results in the living dead "citizens" of the City of Dis.

Perhaps, then, we should begin not by thinking about any essence or principle of life, but by thinking about a certain negation of life, a kind of life-after-life in which the "after" is not temporal but liminal.

Blasphemous Life

But we've forgotten about blasphemy, a concept that runs throughout Dante's *Inferno*. In its original theological sense, blasphemy is a form of sacrilegious speech, an act of speaking out against God, against the divine, against the sacred.[70] Blasphemy is therefore the conjunction of a language of negation with the negation of the sacred. More than a simple outburst, blasphemy's profanation is always carefully articulated, employing a whole grammar of negation, from simple negation ('God does not exist'), to relativism ('the divine is demonic'), to indifference ('the supernatural is the natural, and vice versa'), to the annulment of double negations ('there is neither Heaven nor Hell'). In a sense, Dante's vision of Hell is that of a highly gradated architecture of blasphemy that mirrors blasphemy's own syntax of the sacrilegious. Through words, acts, and gestures, the various "shades" that populate Hell speak blasphemy in their very life forms, strange and horrific though they may be. They are the very embodiment of blasphemy in their contorted and monstrous forms of life.

What is blasphemy in regard to the forms of life-negation found in the *Inferno*? Returning to the burning desert, Capaneus, noticing Dante's inquiring gaze, shouts back to him: "What I was once, alive, I still am, dead!"[71] On one level this is simply a descriptive statement — defiant towards divine sovereignty in life, I remain so after life. But surely Capaneus realizes that, after life, resistance is futile? Or have the terms changed, after life? Perhaps his words do not mean "I am still defiant" but rather, quite literally, something like "I am a living contradiction." Such phrases denoting a living death recur in the *Inferno*, often spoken by Dante himself.[72] Perhaps, then, this phrase "What I was once, alive, I am still now" actually means "I am still living, even in death." This living contradiction — being *living dead* — is also linked to the political-theological contradiction of a power that at once "shuts down" as much as it "lets flow." There is a kind of medieval biopolitics in the *Inferno* quite different from the modern version given to us in the work of thinkers like Michel Foucault. The strange conjunction of sovereignty and multiplicity in the *Inferno* does not demand the punishment of souls, but instead requires a mass of animated, sensate, living bodies, in some cases resulting in an almost medical concept of the afterlife (e.g., the Sowers of Discord are meticulously dismembered, dissected, and anatomized). In tandem with a sovereign "shutting-down" we have also a "letting-flow"; indeed, at several points the *Inferno* seems to imply their isomorphism.

Blasphemy, then, can be viewed in this regard as the assertion of living contradiction. But this assertion is not simply a resistance to a demand to be noncontradictory. In its modern variants it strives to become an ontological principle as well, the basis for any and all considerations of what counts as "living" or "nonliving." In the 1955 British film *The Quatermass Xperiment* (released in the U.S. as *The Creeping Unknown*), a rocket launch gone awry has inadvertently brought back with it a novel form of life. All of the crew have mysteriously disappeared, except for one, left in a catatonic state, drained of life and yet undergoing strange metamorphoses. His body seems to absorb any and all other forms of life, be they human, animal, plant, or mineral. Body parts mimic the other life forms they touch, eventually detaching themselves completely and continuing to grow in their autonomous, amoeba-like sentience, eventually threatening to take over all of life on Earth.

The Quatermass Xperiment was largely the product of author Nigel Kneale (who wrote the story), as well as the eerie, film noir direction of Val Guest (who would go on to direct the Quatermass sequels). Kneale in particular understood that life — be it terrestrial or extraterrestrial — need not bear any relation to the anthropomorphic conceits that we so often drape over it. In Kneale's original TV screenplay (broadcast in 1953), Quatermass and his colleagues speculate on the origin of this strange form of life that seems not of this world. Judith, one of the scientists, thinking aloud: "We know the rocket wasn't near any other planet or asteroid. Could a form of life exist somewhere in space itself? Just drifting." Quatermass responds: "A sort of ... plankton of the ether." Briscoe, an engineer: "It couldn't be remotely like life as we know it." Judith again: "Does it have to be? Why not pure energy, without an organic structure? It's at least conceivable, isn't it? In some sense there might even be intelligence." Briscoe, now nervous, asks: "And afterwards? After it invaded them?"[73]

A form of life that refuses to adhere to any definition of life — at least according to human-centered notions of life on Earth — and therefore, a life that resides at the threshold of comprehension, and for that reason alone, is a threat. Contra much of the Cold War science fiction of flying saucers and Martian invaders, this "alien invasion" occurs via a microbial-like sentience whose only purpose seems to be to absorb, engulf, and consume life, irrespective of the arbitrary boundaries we have created.

Nowhere is this more evident than in the "weird biologies" of H.P. Lovecraft's novel *At the Mountains of Madness* (1936). The narrative describes two kinds of blasphemous life. The first involves the discovery of unknown fossils and a "Cyclopean city" in the deep Antarctic, both of which display "monstrous perversions of geometrical laws."[74] The discovery leads to the remains of an unrecognizable, intelligent species of "Old Ones" that, in the Lovecraftian mythos, are thought to have lived eons prior to the earliest known human fossilized data.

But this only leads to a further revelation, in which the explorers discover another type of life which they call the Shoggoths, and which seem to resemble formless yet geometric patterns: "viscous agglutinations of bubbling cells — rubbery fifteen-foot spheroids infinitely plastic and ductile — slaves of suggestion, builders of cities — more and more sullen, more and more intelligent, more and more amphibious, more and more imitative..."[75] In Lovecraft's prose, the Shoggoths are the alterity of alterity, the species-of-no-species, the biological empty set. When they are discovered to still be alive, they are described sometimes as formless, black ooze, and sometimes as mathematical patterns of organic "dots," and sometimes as a hurling mass of viscous eyes. Formless, abstract, faceless. In an oft-referenced passage, what the narrator expresses is the horizon of the ability to think this kind of "life":

> [W]hen Danforth and I saw the freshly glistening and reflectively iridescent black slime which clung thickly to those headless bodies and stank obscenely with that new unknown odor whose cause only a diseased fancy could envisage — clung to those bodies and sparkled less voluminously on a smooth part of the accursedly resculptured wall in a series of grouped dots — we understood the quality of *cosmic fear* to its uttermost heights.[76]

What Lovecraft puts forth in his tales of cosmic horror is a form of blasphemy that is non-anthropomorphic and even misanthropic. At the mountains of madness, we move from a concept of blasphemy grounded in human agency (the blasphemy of Capaneus in the *Inferno*) to a blasphemy of the unhuman ("more and more amphibious"). For Lovecraft, "it" is blasphemous — but also indifferent, incomprehensible, and in many cases unnamable ("the thing," "the doom," "the fear," "the whisperer").

At the center of blasphemous life is this idea of the living contradiction. *Blasphemous life is the life that is living but that should not be living*. Whereas for Dante the blasphemous is the living contradiction — to be living in death, to be living after life — for Lovecraft the blasphemous is the very inability to think "life" at all. Blasphemy is here rendered as the unthinkable. To account for such blasphemous life, one would have to either compromise existing categories of thought, or entertain contradictory notions such as "living numbers" or "pathological life." This contradiction is not a contradiction in terms of medical science; the blasphemous life can often be scientifically explained and yet remain utterly incomprehensible. If it is a logical contradiction, it would have to be one in which the existence of true contradictions would not only be admitted, but would be foundational. In the philosophy of logic, the assertion that there are true contradictions is often referred to as "dialetheism."[77] But with Lovecraft we have a twist. The Shoggoths are bizarre examples of *dialethic biologies*, contradictions that are living precisely because they are contradictory, or "blasphemous."

If there is a stage of blasphemous life beyond this, perhaps it is exemplified in the "tissue horror" films of Canadian auteur David Cronenberg, which form a kind of trilogy: *Shivers* (1975), *Rabid* (1977), and *The Brood* (1979). Regarded by many as the maestro of body horror, Cronenberg is no stranger to the monstrous and the metamorphic, and his often overlooked early films leverage the low-budget, B-horror film aesthetic to examine the role of the body in the late-20th century culture of biotechnology, tissue engineering, reconstructive surgery, and virology. In *Shivers* (whose alternate titles are *The Parasite Murders* and *They Came From Within*), a series of bizarre deaths occur in the newly built Starliner Towers, an ultramodern, metropolitan high-rise. In each case, the deaths seem connected to medical aberrations in the victims' anatomies. We eventually learn — through a very messy autopsy — that the tenants of the high-rise have been infected with an experimental microbe whose function is to take control of the host by parasitically controlling their organs. As the parasite spreads throughout the building, human behavior gradually disintegrates into a bizarre, frenzied orgy of flesh feeding on flesh.

Similar motifs are found in *Rabid*, where, at the Keloid Clinic for Plastic Surgery, an experimental skin graft is performed on a young woman's arm after a motorcycle accident. Inexplicably, she soon develops strange physical symptoms, including the growth of a strange orifice in her armpit, from which a grotesque, fleshy stinger darts out, thereby infecting anyone close to her, transforming them into zombielike creatures. Likewise, in *The Brood*, we are introduced to the Somafree Institute, lead by the eerily charismatic, avant-garde psychotherapist Hal Raglan. There he performs his controversial therapeutic modality of "psychoplasmics," in which patients are induced to physically externalize their inner psychopathologies on their bodies. One of his patients, Candace, struggles with motherhood and her own family trauma. Gradually we suspect that the weirdly biomorphic growths on her abdomen and back are more than just benign cysts. Like overripe fruits, the miniature, humanoid growths soon mature, and detach themselves, blindly carrying out Candace's unconscious directives.

Cronenberg's tissue horror films take up the idea of blasphemous life in a decidedly postmodern, postindustrial, and biomedical context. The life that is alive, but that should not be alive. Here this idea is more than theological. It is scientific and medical, as the natural and supernatural collapse in on each other, pointing back to an idea we find in the weird fiction tradition: that science, under the right circumstances, is more "supernatural" than nature itself.[78] In a sense, Cronenberg's tissue trilogy brings back a motif that stretches back to Mary Shelley's *Frankenstein*. The monsters are produced, not because the science is inaccurate, or because the technology is broken. Rather, it is precisely because the technology works too well, that we see a whole new bestiary being formed, one that leverages biotechnologies against any naïve notion of "natural" life.

Ambient Plague (or, Thing and No-Thing)

The anonymous "it" of blasphemy is also expressed in the hermeneutics of plague and pestilence. Our very concepts regarding disasters generally betray a profound anxiety. That some disasters are "natural" while others are not implies a hypothetical line between the disaster that can be prevented (and thus controlled), and the disaster that cannot. The case of infectious diseases is similar, except that the agency or the activity of this "biological disaster" courses through human beings themselves — within bodies, between bodies, and through the networks of global transit and exchange that form bodies politic. In the U.S., the twofold conceptual apparatus of "emerging infectious diseases" (naturally caused) and "biodefense" (artificially caused) cloaks a general militarization of public health. More fundamentally, when it becomes more and more difficult to discern the epidemic from the bioweapon, entire relations of enmity are redefined. The threat is not simply an enemy nation or terrorist group, the threat is itself biological; biological life itself becomes the absolute enemy. Life is weaponized against Life, resulting in an ambient *Angst* towards the biological domain itself.[79]

However, while it has become customary to view epidemics in light of post-germ theory, "autoimmune" boundary disputes, a more fundamental problem is articulated in the premodern concepts of plague and pestilence, where biology and theology are intertwined in the concepts of contagion, corruption, and pollution.[80] One of the central concerns of chroniclers of the Black Death was that of causality, and how causality was interpreted in relation to the divine. As the Black Death spread throughout medieval Europe, the motif of the "angry God" recurs in many of the chronicles, both fictional and nonfictional. It appears in Boccaccio's *Decameron*, is a motif in *Piers Plowman*, and it shapes the subgenre of plague pamphlets in England.[81] These in turn make reference to the examples of Biblical plague, of which the most well known is the Ten Plagues of Egypt, in which God sends down "plagues" to persuade the Egyptian pharaoh to free the Jewish people.[82] Here the plagues do include epidemic disease, but also rivers that turn into blood, swarms of insects, tempestual storms, and an eclipse. Another, more common reference among the Black Death chronicles is apocalyptic. *Revelation*, with its dense and complex symbology, tells of "Seven Angels" sent forth to deliver "Seven Plagues" that are to be "poured" upon mankind as a form of divine judgment; here again the "plagues" include contagious disease, aberrations in livestock, strange weather phenomena, and the destruction of human cities.[83]

In all these instances we see this key element: a divine sovereign who, in the form of a judgment or punishment, sends down — or better, emanates — a form of miasmatic life that is indissociable from decay, decomposition, and death. What is noteworthy about the premodern concept of plague is not only its blurring of biology and theology, but the profound lability that the concept of plague has. In the chronicles of the Black Death, plague seems to be at once a separate, vitalized "thing" and yet something that spreads in the air, in a person's breath, on their clothes and belongings, even in the glances between people. As one early chronicler notes, "one infected man could carry the poison to others, and infect people and places with the disease by look alone."[84]

Philosophically, it is tempting to understand the medieval hermeneutics of plague as Neoplatonic — a supernatural force emanating from a divine center. However, this would require that we understand the relation between Creator and creatures as pathological, a divine sovereign that emanates itself through a miasmatic diffusion of decay. But what is being emanated here is not creation itself but rather its opposite, a kind of de-creation that occupies the underside of what Aristotle called "passing away" (disease, decay, decomposition). This strange type of life, that seems to emanate from a Neoplatonic One and diffuse itself throughout creaturely life, cannot be understood without taking into account another element. As varied as the medieval accounts of plague are, one of the common motifs, along with the angry God, is that of plague as a divine weapon. The divine sovereign doesn't simply pass judgment; the sovereign weaponizes life — the pathological life of "plagues" — and turns it against the earthly life of the creature, itself a product of divine will.

This motif has its roots in antiquity: in Hesiod, for instance, we see how Zeus sends the "gift" of plague-ridden Pandora to Prometheus as a form of retribution; likewise, the *Illiad* opens with angry Apollo sending down "arrows" of plague upon the armies of men for their disrespect towards the gods. There are earthly instances of this as well. An oft-mentioned example in this regard is the medieval practice of catapulting corpses. The primal scene in this regard is the 14th-century Italian trading post at Caffa, on the northern border of the Black Sea. Ongoing skirmishes between Italian merchants and Muslim locals led, in one instance, to the catapulting of plague-ridden corpses by the latter, over the fortress walls of the former.[85]

It is not clear in the accounts of chroniclers, or in the texts of Boccaccio, Chaucer, or Langland, if plague is that which causes social and political disorder, or if plague is identical with this affective fantasy of total chaos. We have a strange situation in which plague, itself supernaturally caused by a divine and sovereign power, then elicits a host of exceptional measures by a secondary, earthbound sovereign, in order to ward off the pending chaos that plague occasions — which itself emanates from the primary, divine sovereignty — the divine origin of plague.

All of this is to suggest that the political theology of plague is not just an issue of shutting down or building walls. The pervasive, diffuse, and circulatory quality of plague — this strange "thing" that is at once a divine emanation and yet a source of social and political chaos — raises a more complex problem for sovereign power: how to control the pervasiveness of plague without losing control of the pervasiveness of people.

The strange status of plague — is it the microbe, the host, the pathways of contagion, or all of these? — is dramatized in John Carpenter's classic 1982 film *The Thing*. Based on John W. Campbell's 1938 novella "Who Goes There?", Carpenter's film also draws upon the 1951 film adaptation *The Thing From Another World*. As different as they are, all three versions of the story have one thing in common: they feature a group of human beings isolated in an arctic landscape, who are confronted with a mysterious and very angry shape-shifting alien entity, the very existence of which frustrates all human categories and anthropomorphic ways of thinking about life. In Campbell's novella, the human characters begin having strange, telepathic-like dreams after their discovery of an unidentified creature frozen in the ice: "I've had dreams … Dreaming the thing thawed out and came to life — that it wasn't dead, or even wholly unconscious all those twenty million years, but just slowed, waiting — waiting. You'll dream, too, while that damned thing that Earth wouldn't own is dripping, dripping in the Cosmos House tonight."[86]

In all versions of the story, the unidentifiability of the creature quickly leads to doubt, suspicion, and paranoia. In Carpenter's film this is intensified not only by the groundbreaking special effects work of Rob Bottin, but by the film's minimalist narrative and sparse dialogue, all of which gives the story a pervasive sense of dread. That ambient dread has to do not only with the horrific yet fascinating metamorphoses that take place within the bodies of the human hosts, but it is also a dread that comes from the invisible and unverifiable aspect of contagion itself. Has "the Thing" infected you? If you're asking, is it already too late? Are you still even "you" anymore?

The wonderfully unnerving idea that undergirds Carpenter's film is that "the Thing" is never simply itself, but only manifest in a host organism, which it can replicate almost perfectly, and in which it can hide (or hibernate), until it finds another suitable host. The contorted and unrecognizable husks of life that "the Thing" leaves behind — something from a nightmare vision of Bosch, Dalí, or Unica Zürn —form an amalgam of previous hosts, suddenly unfurling into an anatomical assemblage of microbial memory. As a form of life — if it is indeed alive at all — the Thing is in itself nothing, only the accumulation of its previous and current hosts. There is no independent and autonomous microbe or virus that can be separated from its hosts; here microbe and host are inseparable. Not only that, but each case of infection carries with it a microbial memory of previous hosts, so that one host becomes monstrously comingled with other hosts — on this planet or on other planets. When threatened, the Thing (that is, the microbe, host, and previous hosts) doesn't simply reveal itself; it is expressed in horrific anatomical improvisations — a plantlike tentacle exudes from fur, a multitude of eyes open in a torso, a head opens like a flower petal, every limb screeches with a fanged noumena. In short, the Thing in itself is nothing (a "no-Thing"), and this troubling absence at the core of its existence — this *is* what it is. It is an absence that perpetually manifests itself as something else, negation incarnate with no other agenda than to perpetuate the cycle of contagion. What philosophers like Kant had described as the "thing-in-itself" (the world apart from our perception of it, forever foreclosed to us) is here incarnated as something that lies so far astray from normative notions of life that no name can be applied to it. One of the characters in Campbell's *Who Goes There?* encapsulates the quandary: "Nothing Earth ever spawned had the unutterable sublimation of devastating wrath that thing let loose in its face when it looked around its frozen desolation twenty million years ago."[87] A sentiment expressed Carpenter's film, where one character, stunned by the Thing's strange metamorphoses, exclaims in disbelief: "You gotta be fuckin' kidding me!"

Nekros

However, it should not be forgotten that the weaponized plague always targets bodies. And what, indeed, is the target of the living weapon, if not the living target — that is, the corpse?

The concept of *nekros* (νεκρος) has two significant meanings in classical culture. On the one hand, *nekros* is the corpse or the dead body. When Odysseus organizes the funeral rites for one of his companions, it is the *nekros* that is burned at the grave site: "Once we'd burned the dead man (*nekros*) and the dead man's armor,/heaping his grave-mound, hauling a stone that coped it well,/we planted his balanced oar aloft to crown his tomb."[88] Here *nekros* names the singularity of the departed life, or of life recently departed from the body, leaving behind a corpse. This corpse retains something residual of that life, insofar as both the corpse and its armor are together set upon the grave. We might even say that *nekros* not only names the "dead man," but also the thingness of the corpse. In a sense *nekros* oscillates between the body-minus-life and the thingness of the corpse, the latter approaching the domain of the purely nonliving (e.g., the armor as the nonliving body).

However, the *Odyssey* also contains another, more significant usage of *nekros*. This comes in the well-known passages recounting Odysseus's journey to the underworld. In this scene Odysseus first performs a sacrificial rite that calls to the dead, who then emerge from the underworld in a kind of slow-motion swarm:

> And once my vows
> and prayers had invoked the nations of the dead (*ethnea nekrōn*),

> I took the victims, over the trench I cut their throats
> and the dark blood flowed in — and up out of Erebus they
> came,
> flocking toward me now, the ghosts of the dead and gone
> (*nekuōn kataethnēōtōn*)[89]

Here *nekros* no longer names the corpse, nor even the thingness of the corpse. Instead, *nekros* names something alive, or at least vitalized — but in a way that is different from the life of animals. *Nekros* as the corpse presumes a reliable boundary between life and death, whereas *nekros* as "the dead" are characterized by an ambivalent vitalism. These dead souls are immaterial and yet not transcendent, a life that at once continues to live on but that lives on in a kind of interminable and vacuous immortality. *Nekros* is thus not the corpse but rather "the dead," the existence of a life-after-life.

But what, if anything, "lives on" after life? Paul of Thebes provides one example, which would become a center of dispute in later theological debates over resurrection. The mortal body, like all living things, displays both an infusion of life-spirit as well as processes of growth. "God gives it a body as he has determined, and to each kind of seed he gives its own body ... So also is the resurrection of the dead. The body that is sown is perishable, it is raised imperishable ... It is sown a natural body: it is raised a spiritual body."[90] The organic motif of resurrection is that of a seed that is sown in the earth and that grows and is animated (or reanimated) into a new body, the latter being both the resurrection of the person as well as that of the community of the *corpus mysticum*.

There is also a great deal of ambiguity in the Pauline formula. Patristic thinkers differed on what kind of life-after-life resurrection was, and how such a supernatural form of life was to take place.[91] One set of debates centers around the problem of the temporality of resurrection. If the living, mortal, earthbound body was susceptible to the processes of growth and decay, then in what material state would the body be resurrected? What kind of life returns?

Would the resurrected body — the life-after-life — live in a state of perpetual stasis (as a kind of "living statue"), or does it still undergo transformations, either in the form of higher perfections, or in terms of a beatific hyper-growth? The so-called material continuity debates among Patristic thinkers not only highlights the problem of time in relation to life (and afterlife), but it points to a problem that cuts across the theological and political domains (as when Paul lays out the basic anatomy of the *corpus mysticum* as constituted both by the natural and supernatural, earthly and divine).

Resurrection could be resurrection of the body, the soul, or more generally of "the dead." But even theories of the resurrection of the soul — as one finds in Origen's notion of a "spiritual body" — still maintain the minimal necessity of a body in flux. The problems of material continuity are also linked to spatial and topological problems concerning the material process by which the body of decay and putrefaction is reassembled and revitalized. The mere return of material particles does not constitute resurrection, for those particles must be ensouled, renewed, or in some way cast anew. And here the almost absurdist debates concerning "chain consumption" come into the foreground. If the corpse is devoured by worms and beasts, and those beasts are in turn devoured by man, how can the parts or particles of the body be reassembled for resurrection? (One can imagine a solution to this problem offered by Alfred Jarry's King Ubu...). One solution, offered by Tertullian, was to shift emphasis from the matter to the form of the resurrected body, so that continuity could exist through change. Cannibalism thus does not negate continuity, and thus the living dead can also be the eaten dead.

The theological debates over resurrection point to some basic dichotomies: should the organicist model of the growth and decay of the natural world (seeds, plants, animals) serve as the analogy for resurrection, or are those processes precisely what resurrection aims to correct and to "heal"? Such questions have to do, in effect, with the nature and the supernature of the afterlife, or better, with the relation between life and a "life-plus-something" that constitutes early medieval theology. Insofar as the afterlife is related in some way — as analogy, as model, as perfection — to finite, mortal life, it obtains a familiarity that enables thinkers such as Origen to talk at length about growth and decay in a theological context. But insofar as the afterlife is a supernatural phenomenon, it remains outside the scope of philosophical and even theological inquiry.

How can life — something that is lived — be situated at such a point of inaccessibility? In his classic 1917 book *The Idea of the Holy* (*Das Heilige*), theologian Rudolf Otto examines religious experience in a broad context through his concept of the "numinous." The numinous is the limit-experience of the human confronting the world as absolutely nonhuman, the world as "wholly other," a "mystery inexpressible and above all creatures."[92] For Otto, the numinous describes a contradictory experience of horror and wonder that is encapsulated in his phrase, *mysterium tremendum*. Both mystery and the "overpoweringness" of tremors or terror play into Otto's theory of religious experience:

> The truly "mysterious object" is beyond our apprehension and comprehension, not only because our knowledge has certain irremovable limits, but because in it we come upon something inherently "wholly other," whose kind and character are incommensurable with our own, and before which we therefore recoil in a wonder that strikes us chill and numb.[93]

While such events may indeed result in dramatic, intense experiences (such as that of mystics), they may also creep up on one in the most everyday circumstances.

As Otto notes, this confrontation with the unhuman world may manifest itself as the various demons, ghosts, and malefic creatures that populate the mythological and cosmological framework of different religious traditions. We might also add that this confrontation with the divine as horrific is also a leading theme in the 18th-century Gothic novel. In such fictions, the numinous points to a fork in the road; it can be revealed to have rational causes (as in Radcliffe's *The*

Mysteries of Udolpho), or the supernatural can be affirmed, and its horror sublimated into an affirmation of faith (Walpole's *The Castle of Otranto*), or a descent into damnation (Lewis's *The Monk*).[94]

The word "numinous" is etymologically akin to the Kantian term *noumena*. Kant's own reaffirmation of the split between *phenomena* (the world as it appears to the subject) and *noumena* (the inaccessible world-in-itself) tends to draw his analyses towards the former and away from the latter. Indeed, there is a sense in which Kant's antinomies of pure reason — the proofs for God's existence, the origin of the universe, and the existence of the soul — are pushed so far away from *phenomena* that they begin to occupy a space not far from *noumena*.[95] And yet it is precisely this domain — the anonymous "there is" — that has for so long remained a point of attraction for ontology.

Let us consider a portmanteau, between the "numinous" (the horror of the divine as absolute otherness) and Kantian *noumena* (the unhuman, anonymous world). In what sense is the *nekros* as "the dead," also a kind of *nouminous life*? A nouminous life is neither that which is lived outside of thought (the Gothic "numinous"), nor that in which thought and life are kept forever apart (the Kantian antinomies). We could call this a "horror of life" if such a phrase did not bring with it unwanted anthropomorphic and even existentialist connotations. Perhaps we can say that, if the life-after-life is a nouminous life, it is because it elicits a horror — the horror of a life that simply lives on, indifferent to the human structures that attempt to give it meaning.

The Spirit of Biology

There are a number of superficial comparisons between theology and horror in the Western tradition: in the Eucharist there is both cannibalism and vampirism; in the Jewish and Christian apocalyptic traditions the realization of the City of God entails resurrection of the dead; and in numerous instances the New Testament portrays the demons and demonic possessions that elicit the healing powers of the Messiah. Indeed, considering the extent to which genre horror deals with the themes of death, resurrection, and the demonic, one could argue that genre horror is a secular, cultural expression of theological concerns.

If we look more closely, however, we see that in many instances it is a concept of "life" that mediates between theology and horror. We can even imagine our theologians carefully watching the classics of 20th-century horror film: the relation between the natural and the supernatural (Augustine watching *The Cabinet of Dr. Caligari*); the distinction or non-distinction between human and beast (Avicenna watching *Cat People*); the coherence or incoherence of the *corpus mysticum* (Aquinas watching *White Zombie*); the problem of the afterlife (Dante watching the Italian silent film *L'Inferno*). But one need not imagine such scenarios, for many art-horror films deal with such issues, from David Cronenberg's "tissue horror" films to Ingmar Bergman's *Through a Glass Darkly* to Dario Argento's now-complete "Three Mothers" trilogy.

If both theology and horror deal with the concept of "life," then what exactly is this "life" that lies at the limits of the thinkable? Aristotle gives us one clue. In the *De Anima* Aristotle thinks the question of life as a philosophical question, though the concept of *psukhē*: "It must be the case then that soul (*psukhē*) is substance as the form of a natural body which potentially has life, and since this substance is actuality, soul will be the actuality of such a body."[96] There is, to borrow terms from Scholasticism, an "ensoulment" or animation that takes place in hylomorphism, a process through which life is literally formed (or in-formed … and sometimes de-formed).

However, Aristotle gives us a slightly different picture in his treatise *On Generation and Corruption* (*De Generatione et Corruptione*). Here the central question is not about the principle of life, but rather about morphology and change. Aristotle asks, how are "coming-to-be" and "passing-away" different from change in general? Are growth and decay merely examples of the larger genre of change in itself? This in turn leads to a more fundamental question regarding the domain of the living: "What is 'that which grows'?"[97]

Aristotle's approach is to distinguish between different modalities of change. There are, first, the processes of alteration, which are qualitative (one thinks of a tree sprouting branches or an animal growing fur — the tree or animal remains the same kind of tree or animal). There are also the processes of coming-to-be and passing-away, which are substantial changes (as when one animal is eaten by another animal, the former undergoing modification in substance). Finally, there are the processes of growth and decay, which can involve changes in magnitude (growing larger or smaller). While the first two are general processes of change that occur in the living and nonliving, Aristotle implies that growth and decay are exclusive to the domain of the living. Why is this? One of the reasons Aristotle provides has to do with eating. Growth and decay, though exclusive to the living, have to do with changes to the substance of the living and nonliving, changes that are due to "the accession of something, which is called 'food' and is said to be 'contrary' to flesh," and that involves the "transformation of this food into the same form as that of flesh."[98]

To Aristotle's example of nutrition we might also include the processes of decay and decomposition, the passage of *nekros* into nonliving matter — the body as food for worms. But might we also include the passage from *nekros* into the afterlife? What sort of change would this be — alteration, coming-to-be/passing-away, or growth/decay? Would this constitute a kind of biology of spiritual transformation, or would it constitute the "spirit of biology"?

What theology implicitly admits, horror explicitly states: a profound fissure at the heart of the concept of "life." Life is at once this or that particular instance of the living, but also that which is common to each and every instance of the living. Let us say that the former is *the living*, while the latter is *Life* (capital L). If the living are particular manifestations of Life, then Life in itself is never simply this or that instance of the living, but something like a principle of life, or that-by-which-the-living-is-living. This fissure between Life and the living is Aristotelian in origin, but we also see it in the Scholastic attempt to conceptualize "spiritual creatures," we see it in the problem of the life-after-life of resurrection, and we also see it in natural philosophy and the attempts to account for teratological anomalies and aberrations.

However, the most instructive examples come from classical horror film, in particular the "creature features" of Hollywood film studios. The proliferation of living contradictions in horror film constitutes our modern bestiary. Let us consider a hagiography of life in the relation between theology and horror: the living dead, the undead, the demon, and the phantasm. In each case, there is an exemplary figure, an allegorical mode, a mode of manifestation, and a metaphysical principle that is the link between philosophy and horror.

With the living dead the exemplary figure is of course the zombie. Its allegorical mode has changed over time, but it is most often that of the uprising of the underclasses (the working class, the mob, and the masses are all represented in George Romero's films). The zombie can manifest itself in many ways, as multitude (Romero's *Land of the Dead*) or as contagion (Lucio Fulci's *Zombie*). With the living dead, the guiding metaphysical principle is "flesh."

By contrast, the undead has its exemplary figure in the vampire. Its allegory is not the rising of underclasses, but a decaying, romantic aristocracy (as in Bram Stoker's *Dracula*, though already evident in earlier tales by John Polidori, Lord Byron, and Sheridan Le Fanu). The vampire manifests itself in either human-animal metamorphoses (bats, rats, dogs), or in metamorphoses between the organic and inorganic (mists, smoke). While such metamorphoses indicate a near-immortality and an infinite changeability, the vampire is also haunted by mortality — sometimes as threat, sometimes as promise. The vampire's metaphysical principle is "blood."

The demon is an amalgam (partially material, partially immaterial) whose exemplary figure is itself an amalgam — that of demonic possession, and its strange and unnerving hybrid of human body and demon soul. The allegory of the demon is often middle class and bourgeois, sometimes within a therapeutic or even clinical framework (as evident in Renaissance narratives of possession or in modern films like *The Exorcist*). Being in the middle, as it were, the demon brings together the highest and the lowest, transforming the human into a beast, and the beast into a god. The demon's metaphysical principle is "meat."

Finally there is the phantasm, whose exemplary figure is the ghost. Whereas the three previous figures dealt with allegorical modes that reflected class dynamics (zombie/working class, vampire/aristocratic, demon/bourgeois), the ghost deals with that strange and unknown provenance after life — the domain of spirit, soul, or, in its secular sense, of memory. Despite their immateriality, ghosts also manifest themselves in various ways, either by spiritual mediums, by changes to objects in the physical world, or by signs and portents. The ghost's metaphysical principle is "spirit."

Generalizations such as these obviously have their limitations. But one thing to note is that in each case we have a form of life that at once repudiates "life itself" for some form of afterlife. In this sense, *horror expresses the logic of incommensurability between Life and the living*. Each of these figures are literally living contradictions. The zombie is the animated corpse, the vampire is the decay of immortality, the demon is at once a supernatural being and a lowly beast, and the phantasm exists through materializations of its immateriality. And, in each case, the form of afterlife works towards a concept of life that is itself constituted by a privation or a negation, a "life-minus-something"; the basic Aristotelian (and Hippocratic) concepts of flesh, blood, meat, and spirit are paradoxically living but without life.

Blind Life

One of the peculiarities of Aristotle's *De Anima* is that, while it opens with the stated aim of inquiring into the "principle of life," it quickly bypasses this in favor of detailed analyses of the natural world, the senses, and the intellect. What begins with an investigation into the bodies of living organisms (*zoē*) ends with a rather opaque meditation on thought (*nous*). It is almost as if Aristotle discovers that the question of "life" can only be philosophical if it ceases to be a question of life-as-such. This has also colored later glosses on the text, such as those by Averroës and Aquinas, whose commentaries are characterized by this shift.

In Book II, however, Aristotle makes some important distinctions. After having offered the concept of *psukhē* as the life-principle, Aristotle distinguishes between different types of *psukhē* — that is, that *psukhē* is itself manifested in a range of specific forms. Aristotle distinguishes between plants, animals, and humans, based on the manifestation of *psukhē* or the life-form that governs them. While plants are characterized by a nutritive *psukhē* animals are characterized by a sensory and motile *psukhē*, and humans by a reasoning or intellective *psukhē*. This forms an ascending order, for whereas plants are governed by nutrition, they can neither move nor think. The same follows for animals, who can sense but lack reason.

The Aristotelian framework was, of course, surpassed by the development of natural history and, later, the emergence of a separate field of biology. But while the modern life sciences have analyzed the domain of the living down to the smallest molecule, the Aristotelian concept of a "life-principle" remains contested terrain.[99] In particular, one issue left unresolved in the *De Anima* has to do with the concept of *psukhē* itself — the Life that is common to every instance of the living. Is there one, univocal *psukhē* that cuts across different domains of the living? Or is there a *psukhē* that is proper to each individual form of life?

Before Aristotle's "biological" works make their appearance in the twelfth century via Arabic translations, there were already attempts to indirectly think Life as the divine. The creature, emblematic of the domain of the living, is always a symptom. It is an effect, a trace — as Bonaventure would put it, a *vestigium* or "footprint" of the divine. The world of the living is a manifestation of a great *liber creaturae*, the "Book of Creatures." Life is precisely that which is symptomatic of the divine, though it is not of the divine itself.

It is Aquinas who emphasizes that the concept of the creature revolves around the relation between Creator and creature, supernatural and natural, light and mud. In his attempts to wed Aristotelianism with Christian doctrine, Aquinas offers a summary of what we might call the "creaturely triad." What is the relation between the creature and Creator, between the living and the divine Life that makes the living possible? Aquinas first sets up a dichotomy between two approaches, that of equivocity and that of univocity. In the first, there is no relation between creature and Creator, and the divine remains forever outside the scope of thought. In the second — univocity — there is a relation of continuity between creature and Creator, such that the latter can be said to be coexistent with the former. For Aquinas, the problems with each are easy to see. While equivocity forecloses any possibility of thinking or experiencing the divine, univocity makes it too easy, in effect flattening the divine onto nature. As is well known, the solution offered by Aquinas is that of analogy. Between no relation (equivocity) and pure relation (univocity), there is partial relation, or analogy. Thus the creature is analogous to the Creator, their difference in the form of degrees of perfection ("proportion" and "proportionality"). The creature is the life that is less-than-divine, the Creator is the life that is more-than-the-living.

Might we also then say that, for Aquinas, the living are related to Life by analogy? Aristotle's question of "life" and the life-principle cannot be asked of Life as such. It can only be asked of the living, of something "beyond" the living or through the living. But then we would have to consider "life" in general as a kind of negative concept, a concept that at once asserts itself as it recedes into the background.

This negative concept of life is organized along two axes. The first is predicated on ontological difference. It posits a distinction, as we noted previously, between "Life" and "the living." The *De Anima* posits a general life-principle, but at the same time distinguishes it from particular instances of the living in plant, animal, and human life. Everything hinges on the relation between Life and the living. In the period of high Scholasticism, the spectrum of creation, from monotheism to pantheism, from orthodoxy to heresy, illustrates the way in which the question of Life is never far from the question of the nature of the divine. In this sense the *De Anima* is the foundation for other Aristotle treatises such as *On the Parts of Animals* (*De Partibus Animalium*).

This concept of life is also aligned along a second axis, predicated on a distinction between a "principle of life" and its corresponding "boundaries of articulation" (essence vs. existence, substance vs. accident). The principle of life may vary quite widely, from divine soul to modern mechanism, from "vital spirit" to contemporary concepts of molecule, gene, and information. But it always makes possible one or more boundary relations that reaffirm the principle of life as essence. Such boundaries include, first and foremost, that between the living and the nonliving, as well as the division between the organic and inorganic, and between human and animal.

These two axes — Life vs. the living; a principle of life vs. its boundaries of articulation — are brought into great focus in genre-blending films that combine elements from horror and science fiction. For instance, the original *Alien* from 1979 incorporates motifs from the literary Gothic tradition with the themes of space exploration and contact with extraterrestrial life. With Dan O'Bannon's taut screenplay, and Ridley Scott's knack for situating human characters against vast backgrounds (in this case, deep space), *Alien* is as much about the age-old quandary "what is life?" as it is about survival or predator-prey relationships. A chamber play in outer space, *Alien* leverages the isolation of deep space as well as the confinement aboard the *Nostromo* ship in a way that allows the (mostly) human characters aboard the ship to question everything they think they know about life in the universe. At the core of the film is the confrontation with a form of life that, on the one hand, is apprehended as a form of life by the human crew members, but that, on the other hand, is so unrecognizable that they struggle to understand it as life at all. Is the "alien" the glistening, viscous, screeching predatory creature aboard their ship, or is it the "face-hugging" creature that implants the eggs inside its human host? Or is it the vast array of pods, at once biological and botanical, which gestate the face-hugging creatures — or is the alien life all of these together, forming a single horrific circuit of gestation and devouring? The biomorphic, strangely biomechanical creatures themselves – vividly brought to life by H.R. Giger's designs — highlight this confusion as to what exactly this novel life form is. *That* it is living is clear, but *what* kind of life it is, remains a mystery.

The confusion surrounding alien life is also raised in Mario Bava's 1965 film *Planet of the Vampires*. Also an example of SF-horror, the film follows a human crew aboard a ship that responds to a distress signal on an unknown planet. Once there, the strange, swirling colors of the mist-shrouded planet seem to swallow the crew members, possessing their bodies and driving them to prey on each other. The human form is at once reduced to an animalistic state, devouring everything in its wake, and yet elevated to an ethereal, almost spiritual dimension, an out-of-body experience transcending the flesh. Eventually the crew explores the planet and discovers the crashed remains of an alien ship, revealing to them that this has happened perhaps countless times before. Short stories written during the Golden Age of SF, such as A.E. van Vogt's "Discord in Scarlet" (1939), also detail the ways in which the alienness of alien life is at once familiar and strange, horrifyingly animalistic and yet weirdly transcendental. These and other examples suggest that it is not so much the discovery of alien life that is troubling, but that the discovery may undermine our own, human-centric, and earthbound notions of life. In *Alien*, the crew's science officer Ash reveals his fascination with the creature that is now stalking them within the labyrinthine passages of the ship. "I admire its purity," he notes, marveling at its efficiency, its ability to act without the burden of morality or conscience — "the perfect organism."

These words point to a deeper horror in *Alien* beyond the actual creatures themselves. It's as if a single form of life courses through all the alien creatures — the pods, the face-huggers, the chest-bursting alien. All these are in a sense one creature in that they are compelled to do what they do by the simple yet terrifying compulsion to live, to gestate, to devour. What the human crew confronts is a principle of life indifferent to its manifestations — it's not personal, it's simply carrying out a set of morphological procedures, a set of biological protocols. This form of life is "alien" in the way it frustrates our attempts to anthropomorphize it, but also in the sense that there is something about life that is impersonal, and for that reason, also horrific for us. The form of life in *Alien* is perhaps akin to what Schopenhauer often called the "Will-to-Live," "Will-to-Life," or simply "blind life." Life that has no agenda, life shorn of morality or ethics, voraciously ignorant of any existential crisis or anxiety about death; life as a horrific tautology, life that has no purpose other than to live, without purpose, without meaning.

Extinction and Existence

The individual life can die. But what of "life" in general? This is the question posed by the disaster, for while any given disaster — human-made or not — may not render all of life extinct, it contains within itself the thought of extinction. In our era of ecological disasters, climate change, global pandemics, and the ongoing specter of bioterror, we are continually invited to think about humanity in relation to its real, hypothetical, or speculative extinction. Nowhere is this more evident than in the resurgence of the disaster film in popular culture. But while earlier disaster movies may have imagined extinction as having some determinate cause (e.g., nuclear war, alien invasion, mad scientists), in contemporary disaster movies extinction just happens, without determinate cause, and without determinate meaning. In *Independence Day* (1996) the threat of extinction comes from outside in the form of alien invasion, a motif that stretches back to H.G. Wells and Camille Flammrion.[100] But by the time of *The Day After Tomorrow* (2004), the implication is that the threat of extinction comes from within, as a result of human mistreatment of the environment. It is a human-caused disaster, rather than that of war and the external threat, that leads to extinction — a motif also found in the Irwin Allen produced films of the 1970s, such as *Flood!*, *Fire!*, and *The Towering Inferno*. A further step occurs in *2012* (2009), in which even human causality is absent — the cataclysmic effects portrayed in the film seem to happen randomly, in scenes that are exemplary of the sublime, a mixture of horror and wonder that seem to be taken directly from *The Critique of Judgement*. Extinction begins to take on a mystical and apocalyptic tone, with only vague and ancient prophesies as indicators of its possible meaning.

On the one hand, these examples of "extinction cinema" are dominated by biological themes. What is at issue is the survival of the species, and what is under threat is not just the life of the species, but its very existence. On the other hand, these films also reference, implicitly or explicitly, eschatological themes (the apocalypse, the messianic, the resurrection of the dead). These dual views of biology and theology are often one in the same. For instance, the plague theme is at once a biological motif (concerned with the survival of the human species), but also a theological motif (attributing the plague to divine retribution). In such instances we see an excess of life as generative and germinal (the nonhuman life of the plague virus itself) confront another life as scarcity and finitude (the preservation of the species). One type of "life" confronts another type of "life." In this way, the biological motif quickly folds onto a theological motif. And here we find a paradox that is at the heart of the concept of life.

As a scientific concept, extinction is distinguished from its theological and apocalyptic variant by the work of zoologists such as Georges Cuvier and the Comte de Buffon. Attempting to discover a scientific framework for studying life that would avoid the religious framework of the Great Chain of Being, the study of fossils became a key locus for investigating the emergence and disappearance of living beings. Cuvier, in particular, became a proponent of "catastrophism," the theory that Earth is periodically visited by sudden, cataclysmic events that not only radically alter Earth's geological composition, but the organisms living on the Earth as well. In the late 18th and early 19th century, Cuvier published a number of archaeological studies that established extinction as a scientific reality, culminating in his multivolume work, *Research on the Fossil Bones of Quadrupeds* (*Recherches sur les Ossements Fossiles de Quadrupèdes*, 1812).[101] As Cuvier provocatively notes, behind the revolutions of nations there lies another type of revolution, that of the planet itself:

> The ancient history of the globe, the definitive term towards which all research tends, is also in itself one of the most curious objects to have captured the enlightened mind; and, if one allows oneself to follow, in the infancy of our species, the nearly invisible traces of so many extinct nations, one will also find there, gathered in the shadows of the Earth's infancy, the traces of revolutions anterior to the existence of all nations.[102]

Extinction, however, is a strange idea — it simultaneously denotes the negation of particular lives, as well as the negation of an entire category of living beings (the species). Extinction implies death, but death of a particular type — while individual people may die, they do not become extinct, whereas this or that species may be threatened by or in danger of extinction. Extinction is also predicated on a division between the life of the organism and the life of the species. If, for the individual organism, life is inscribed within the dichotomy of life and death, growth and decay, and so on, then for the species, life is inscribed within the existence of a category, and the dichotomy of existence and nonexistence. If organisms live and die, then species exist or do not exist.

But immediately questions arise: Can one have an organism without a species? Can one have a species without an organism? In a sense, the life of the organism is not the same as the existence of the species (insofar as the death of a single organism does not indicate the extinction of the species), although the concept of the organism presumes a prior concept of species. The category of species presumes the actual possibility of the organism (except in supernatural horror…);

however, this category may also persist even if there is no actual and living organism to authenticate it. What, then, is extinction? Can it be solely understood as the nonexistence of the categorical species, when that nonexistence is indelibly tied to the living or dying of actual, living organisms? Or is "extinction" neither the organism nor the species, but the relationship between them?

Such questions are further ramified by these: Who is the witness of extinction? In the case of the extinction of all human beings, who is it that gives testament to this extinction? In this sense extinction can never be adequately thought, since its very possibility presupposes the absolute negation of all thought. In a short, satirical essay entitled "The End of All Things," Kant notes this paradox: "For we see nothing before us now that could teach us about our fate in a future world except the judgment of our own conscience, i.e. what our present moral state, as far as we are acquainted with it, lets us judge rationally concerning it."[103] Any postulation about the state of the world after the end can only be speculative — and, for Kant, this means that any speculation about the end of all things can only be based on our moral assumptions and prejudices about the world as a human-centric world, a world-for-us. All that remains will be "those principles we have found ruling in ourselves during the course of our life," which will inevitably determine any speculation about the afterlife, "without our having the slightest ground to assume that they will alter in the future."[104] *Extinction is always speculative*. Philosopher Ray Brassier encapsulates Kant on this point, noting "extinction is real yet not empirical, since it is not of the order of experience."[105]

But if extinction implies the thought of extinction, and if, in the case of human extinction, this thought implies the existence and affirmation of the human, then it would seem that extinction also has a flip side, in which extinction also implies the nonexistence of all thought (including the thought of extinction), thereby affirming not the human but the negation of the human. In this, even philosophy's "principle of sufficient reason" slips through our grasp, putting us in the difficult position of not even being able to assume a reason for the world as such. This leads Kant to ask, somewhat wryly, "why do human beings expect an end to the world at all? And if this is conceded to them, why must it be a terrible end?"[106]

Hence the real question is not whether or not the world will end, but how this can be thought at all. Certainly, the history of extinction science draws upon zoology, archaeology, and paleontology to gloss this paradox. Here extinction as a biological concept is different from the death of the organism. But philosophers such as Heidegger also differentiate the death of the organism (which for Heidegger is "perishing") from Death, the latter related to beings in their temporal being-in-the-world (*Dasein*). In this sense Death is not just the perishing of the individual being (while the species still remains intact), but rather the culmination, condition, and ultimately the negation of this *Dasein*.

If extinction is tied to the first kind of death (death-as-perishing), then what is the relation of extinction to this second kind of death (Death as the culmination of *Dasein*)? There is a relative extinction, which entails the death-as-perishing of all existent living beings that are members of a species, even though in a scientific sense the species *X* still remains as a category. But there is also an absolute extinction, which we might describe as relative extinction that binds with it the nonexistence of the species *X*. This is akin to forgotten, unknown, or even imaginary species. From this one can outline an entire "organon of extinction," drawing upon examples from the horror genre. This would involve: the living being without a species (e.g., the "unnamable thing"); the species without any existent living beings (e.g., cryptids and fantastical creatures); or the subtraction of the species from living beings (e.g., the elemental life of mists, fog, clouds).

However, if absolute extinction implies that there can be no thought of extinction, then this thought in itself leaves but one option: that extinction can *only* be thought, that it can only be said to exist, as a *speculative annihilation*. This would be opposed to the idea that extinction describes an event (actual or virtual), or that extinction is the experience (or impossibility of experience) of death on a mass scale.

Extinction is a void — a biological void, a form of life that is neither biological life (the death of the organism) nor the existence of a set (the persistence of a species). In extinction, the set is related to life by the way in which the death of life leads to emptiness or the empty set. Extinction is the null set of biology.

Extinction implies the death of individuated, living beings, but its primary meaning is that an entire category of life — biological life — ceases to exist as such. But we double back again, for the concept of the extinct species may still, of course, exist (e.g., in a natural history museum), though the species as such has ceased to exist. Extinction can only imply "life," then, to the extent that a claim is made for the "life" of the species as a whole (its growth in numbers, its territorial expansion, its speciation or evolutionary adaptation). But the life of the species is still quite different from the life of the individual organism; the latter seems to provide at best an analogy for the former. Extinction is *the non-being of life that is not death.*

Life as Non-Being

What is striking about many of the attempts to think life philosophically is the way in which "life" becomes an always-receding horizon. If we accept the Aristotelian distinction between Life and the living as structuring the philosophy of life in the West, then it would seem that Life is always receding behind the living. Beyond this, one must have recourse to either natural theology or what Kant calls onto-theology, the system of knowledge of the "being-of-all-beings." But, in the tradition of Aristotelian natural philosophy, Life is not simply the absent center to every instance of the living. The relation between Life and the living is that, while the former conceptually guarantees the latter, in itself it is never available to thought, for its lack of "thisness" is precisely what exceeds any particular instance of the living. If Life has a negative value, then, it is because of its superlative nature, because it exceeds any instance of the living. Life is "nothing" precisely because it is never some thing, or because it is always more than one thing.

In this sense, philosophical thinking about life borrows heavily from the tradition of mystical theology — and in particular from the tradition of negative theology. Before Anselm offers his famous ontological proof for the existence of God (God as "that beyond which nothing greater can be thought"), the 9th-century Irish philosopher John Scottus Eriugena provides one of the most elaborate theories of the divine as "nothing" (*nihil*). Eriugena's *The Division of Nature* (*Periphyseon*, ca. 866–67) is deeply influenced by the apophatic approach of earlier mystical theologians such as Dionysius the Areopagite. In Book III, Eriugena puts forth a notion of "divine darkness," in which the divine is *nihil* precisely because of its superlative nature: "For everything that is understood and sensed is nothing else but the apparition of what is not apparent, the manifestation of the hidden, the affirmation of the negated, the comprehension of the incomprehensible."[107]

To what extent can we say that Life is *nihil* in this sense? Once the ontological difference between "Life" and "the living" is collapsed, life subtracts from itself any possibility of an affirmation. What remains is a kind of negative theology, or better, a negative theo-zoology, whereby life always displays some relation to the negation of life. Hence the afterlife is not about the dichotomy between life and death, but about a more fundamental relation — that between Life and Being.

What happens once the concept of "Life" detaches itself from "the living"? This is a problem implicit in the *De Anima*, where the concept of *psukhē* is sometimes a life-principle, and sometimes a stand-in for being itself. In a modern context, process philosophy (Bergson, Whitehead) and process theology (Chardin, Steiner) likewise reach a zone in which "Life" becomes convertible with Being — even if the name of Life is "process" or "becoming" or "flow."

For many, all of this is a false problem. The opening sections of *Being and Time* provide what is perhaps the clearest statement on this point. There Heidegger effectively glosses over the fields of anthropology, psychology, and biology as fields which must presume being in order to begin their inquiries about human existence. While each of these fields, according to Heidegger, deals in some way with Life, none of them are capable of posing the question of Life as an existential question of "being-there" (*Dasein*):

> [I]n any serious and scientifically minded "philosophy of life" (this expression says about as much as the "botany of plants") there lies an inexplicit tendency toward understanding the being of *Dasein*. What strikes us first of all in such a philosophy (and this is its fundamental lack) is that "life" itself as a kind of being does not become a problem ontologically.[108]

This "missing ontological foundation" is itself what grounds these fields. The question *that* Life is, is displaced by the question of *what* Life is — or, more accurately, what the domain of the living is. The anthropological category of the human, the psychological category of mind, and a general biology of the organism all presume a Being of Life. Where Heidegger leaves off, however, is at the question of whether Life is a subset of Being, or whether the ontology of Life in effect transforms Life into Being. His last words on the topic are at once suggestive and opaque: "Life has its own kind of being, but it is essentially accessible only in Dasein."[109]

One approach is to think about non-Life (a non-Life that is not Death), and by extension, non-Being (a non-Being that is not Nothing). Put another way, the challenge would be to think the relation between Life and Being as mediated by negation. This is an ancient problem, one posed by the presocratics, in the attempt to secure a conceptually sound concept of the One and the Many. At its root is the profound ambivalence towards the concept of non-Being. As Emmanuel Levinas notes, in language not too far removed from Eriugena:

> When the forms of things are dissolved in the night, the darkness of the night, which is neither an object nor the quality of an object, invades like a presence. In the night, where we are riven to it, we are not dealing with anything.

> But this nothing is not that of pure nothingness. There is no longer this or that; there is not "something." But this universal absence is in turn a presence, an absolutely unavoidable presence … There is is an impersonal form, like in it rains, or it is warm.[110]

Thus the problem of non-Being is not simply that of a fear of nothingness or the vacuum. Rather, it is the tenebrous fear of a something whose thingness is under question. "This impersonal, anonymous, yet indistinguishable 'consummation' of being, which murmurs in the depths of nothingness itself we shall designate by the term 'there is'… The rustling of the there is … is horror."[111] The pinnacle of this type of horror — really a kind of concept-horror — is the evisceration of all noological interiority: "horror turns the subjectivity of the subject, his particularity qua entity, inside out."[112]

Is the concept of Life already a "there is…" and therefore already enveloped in the shadowy horror of absolute otherness and anonymity? If "Life," as opposed to "the living," is always receding into the anonymous "there is," does this then mean that Life is really Life-without-Being?

Anonymous Horror

Granted, there is a certain absurdity in asking about the non-being of Life; one might as well inquire into nonexistent creatures … which is, of course, precisely what supernatural horror does. Horror film is replete with examples of the horror of the "there is…" The titles of such films are telling: *The Being*, *The Creature*, *The Entity*, *It's Alive!*, *It Lives Again*, *Monster Zero*, *The Stuff*, *Them!*, *The Thing*, and so on. Such films imagine the monster in a decidedly different way from the classical creature-feature films (*Dracula*, *Frankenstein*, *The Wolf-Man*, *The Mummy*). In these films, the site of horror is not simply that of a physically threatening monster, for at least these can be given names (Dracula,

Frankenstein's monster, Wolf-Man), and thereby included within the sphere of moral and theological law. This also means they can be destroyed. But what of the creature that cannot be named, or that is named in its unnameability? The unnamable creature is also the unthinkable creature (the B-horror version of Samuel Beckett's *The Unnamable*). In some cases the unnamable creature is without form, the intrusion of a raging hylomorphism. Cold War films such as *The Blob* and *Caltiki, the Immortal Monster* exist in a state of oozing, abject, borderlessness. In other cases the unnamable creature is without matter, existing as pure (demonic) spirit, an inverted theophany. In the 1958 film *Fiend Without a Face*, human beings are besieged by immaterial, brainstem-like entities, suggesting telepathy as a form of contagion.

Such films represent a subversion of the classic creature-feature by shifting the criteria by which a monster is made. Whereas the creature-feature films define the monster as an abomination of nature, the unnamable creature is an aberration of thought. The classical creature-features still retain an element of familiarity, despite the impure mixture of categories (plant, animal, human) or differences in scale (giant reptiles, ants, leeches, rabbits, etc.). Films featuring unnamable creatures, by contrast, contextualize the monster in terms of ontology (form-without-matter, matter-without-form) or in terms of onto-theology (the spiritual abject, the oozing abstraction). They point towards a form of life-after-life that highlights conceptual monstrosity.

Let us pause and gather our propositions concerning this concept-horror, or, granting ourselves some poetic license, what we can also call the "teratological noosphere":

- The question of a philosophy of life is traditionally predicated on a fundamental distinction between Life and the living, or, between that-by-which-the-living-is-living and that-which-is-living.
- This distinction is deployed along two axes, one that requires a "principle-of-life" to structure all manifestations of the living,

and another axis, in which the living is ordered according to various "boundaries of articulation."

- This philosophy of life continually oscillates between a natural philosophy of creatures and an onto-theology divine nature, or the supernatural.
- The structure of the concept of life is therefore that of negative theology.

To this we can offer a further proposition, which is that, in its traditional formulations, Life is what is denied of Being. Life bears some minimal relation to non-Being. But this can take several forms. The non-Being of Life can be situated either "above" or "below" the scale of the human — on the one hand there is the strata of Thomist "spiritual creatures" or the strata of Aristotelian creaturely life, while on the other hand there is the strata of demonic multitudes or that of subhuman plague and pestilence. Life in this sense sustains itself within a non-anthropomorphic and even misanthropic orientation. Life, in conditioning the living, is able to assert its self-evident character, while also remaining occluded from thought. Kant's statements concerning the teleology of the natural world would have to be qualified: it is because Life is noumenal that it is teleological; it is because it is inaccessible that Life can be said to have a purpose. But this then means that the ends of Life are also anonymous.

Any philosopher of life would have to consider "life" as a particular intersection between a biology of a nonconceptual life itself and an onto-theology of transcendence, emanence, and immanence. The problem is that the concept of Life remains tenaciously nonconceptual, even as it continues to function in scientific fields such as network science, swarm intelligence, and biocomplexity. The issue is that Life as a concept must always presume a further question concerning Being. The infamous question "What is Life?" appears to always be eclipsed by the question of "What is Being?" And yet the very idea of Life-without-Being would seem to be an absurdity for philosophy — though, as we've seen, not for horror.

5

THE SUBHARMONIC MURMUR OF BLACK TENTACULAR VOIDS

Prologue

"Mysticism" is a term that has been used so widely and in such diverse contexts that the term itself has taken on a mystical quality, at once denoting a set of concrete, historically rooted, spiritual practices and, at the same time, pointing to a vague, diffuse, ineffable "great beyond" that has served as the calling card for innumerable orthodoxies and countercultures alike. Today, in the so-called post-secular era of religious extremism and scientific hegemony, perhaps "mysticism" has again become relevant, especially as we as human beings struggle to comprehend a larger nonhuman cosmos of which we remain only a part.[113] What can "mysticism" tell us about the limits of the human, a mysticism that has as its focus the climatological, meteorological, and geological world-in-itself, and, moreover, that is not reducible to either religion or science? But we must be cautious: this does not mean a mysticism of the Earth or a mysticism of "Nature," nor does it mean a mysticism of the human or humanity in general, much less a mysticism of something as grotesque and burdensome as "life." Indeed, the suggestion that something called mysticism exists at all may at first seem a ridiculous, even naïve presupposition; as a way of thinking and as a set of practices, it can be argued that mysticism today is no longer relevant. This is not only due to the dominance of applied scientific thinking in our globalized, converged cultures, but it is also due to the hegemony of orthodox, religious extremism in dictating the contours of what may or may not legitimately count as religious experience. And yet, the question persists.

What follows takes place by way of an anonymous, poetic text and accompanying commentary.[114] Because the poem was originally circulated in fragments, its total length is not known, and its rather baroque title — "The Subharmonic Murmur of Black Tentacular Voids" — appears nowhere in the body of the poem itself. In addition, it is unclear whether the poem is of contemporary origin, or whether it is a contemporary translation of an older text, or a contemporary pastiche of an earlier form of mystical poetry. In spite of these uncertainties, parts of the poem have been said to have — this is the claim, at least — verifiable geomantic symptoms within the metabolism and physiognomy of those who have, under unspecified conditions, recited its lines. Given this rather melodramatic image of what one scholar calls "geomantic shifts in the nature of thought," the rumors surrounding the poem are noteworthy for the way they implicitly investigate the relationship between the climatology, geopolitics, and the unhuman — and it is in this spirit that the following commentary is written.

Stanza I

A landscape of archaeal
And bacterial species

Living under extreme
Environmental conditions

High temperatures
Ionizing radiation
Hydrostatic pressure
Ultraviolet light
Salinity

Creatures of oblivion
Submerged
In black pools.

Low or high levels of pH
Tolerant of heavy metals
Very low levels of water
Very low levels of light

One dark night
Night more viscous than the dawn
Night that has united the living and the nonliving
Transforming the living in the nonliving.

Commentary on Night. Here the language of night and "extreme environmental conditions" opens onto the enigmatic phrase that opens the last stanza, "One dark night." In its geological description and its more poetic evocations (the refrain of "night" in the last stanza), the poem seems to identify itself as part of the darkness mysticism tradition.

One perspective is provided by John of the Cross, the 16th-century Spanish Carmelite monk, whose poem "The Dark Night of the Soul" (*La Noche Oscura del Alma*) offers several definitions of the term darkness. The text that we currently have called *The Dark Night* is actually composed of four different, though interrelated, texts: a commentary known as *Ascent of Mount Carmel*, a diagram made by John detailing the path of mystical perfection, the poem

"The Dark Night of the Soul," and a commentary on the poem, written by John himself. It is the latter two texts that will concern us here. It is thought that John wrote the poem and commentary around 1583–1585. Its composition is thus well after John's collaborations with Theresa of Avila in reforming monastic institutions, and also after John's imprisonment and torture at the hands of Carmelite monastic authorities.

The Dark Night is a text very different from the more systematic, more rigorous works in speculative mysticism. At its core is the problem of mystical experience — its structure, its meaning, and the possibility (or impossibility) of its communication. It is thought by modern scholars that John broke off his writing on *Ascent of Mount Carmel* in order to directly deal with the problem of mystical experience in *The Dark Night.*

The Dark Night is also unique in that, in contrast to other mystical texts, it foregrounds the relationship between the divine and the motifs of darkness and negation. However, there are variations in the way that John thinks about darkness in the context of mystical experience. In the poem "Dark Night of the Soul," the very first stanza lays out these themes: "One dark night / Fired with love's urgent longings / — Ah, the sheer grace! — / I went out unseen, / My house being now all stilled."[115]

In the commentary John notes the apparent paradox here: "Why, if it is a divine light … does one call it a dark night?" That is, how is it that the union with the divine, the pinnacle of mystical experience, one that is traditionally described in terms of beatific light, how can this experience here be described in terms of its opposite — darkness, stillness, and negation? In response John provides two definitions of darkness: "First, because of the height of divine wisdom, which exceeds the capacity of the soul. Second, because of the soul's baseness and impurity; and on this account the wisdom is painful, afflictive, and also dark for the soul."[116] The second definition follows the standard devaluation of the senses that is a hallmark of the ascetic tradition. More interesting is the first definition, which seems to imply that "divine darkness" is dark because it exceeds our human capacity to adequately render it intelligible. The divine is dark because we have no concept of it.

Given this, if divine darkness is dark because it is in some sense beyond the human, how then are we able to understand even this much? Does not the assertion of the darkness of divinity itself begin to render it intelligible to us? In response to this John provides another, slightly different definition of darkness. Describing the "dark night" in terms of the mystical tradition of contemplation (*contemplatio*), John distinguishes two types of darkness within the individual in the throes of mystical contemplation: the sensory and the spiritual. Here John's emphasis is less on what darkness is and more on how it affects the subject in the midst of mystical experience. This definition is also a much more philosophical one, in that it takes the metaphysical split between body and spirit as being affected by divine darkness, but in two different ways. The "sensory darkness" is akin to a privation, again as per the practices of ascetic monasticism. The "spiritual darkness" also appears to be a privation, but in terms of what John elsewhere calls "spiritual gluttony" (e.g., wanting to be the best or most extreme mystic for selfish ends; focusing on the destination and not the journey).

While both of these types of darkness should, obviously, be read in the context of 16th-century Christian mysticism, we can also draw from them more secular, more philosophical themes. The sensory darkness is not simply about ascetic discipline; it also concerns the ambiguous status of empiricism, and the interface between self and world that ultimately determines all experience, mystical experience included. Given a radically non-anthropomorphic concept of God, the question is this: how can something be experienced, when there is nothing to experience? In a sense, what John and other mystics call mystical experience is an oxymoron — and hence the tropes of darkness, night, and negation.

Similarly, the spiritual darkness John discusses is not simply about the debasement of spiritual practice (during John's time, when both Inquisitions and Reformations were afoot, certainly there was no shortage of religious solutions in the ideological marketplace).

Spiritual darkness extends the empiricist theme of sensory darkness further. Its primary concern is with idealism. Given that there is nothing to experience, what then prevents mysticism from becoming idealism, a contemplative practice of pure thought, "purged" of all sensory and phenomenal attributes? John's reply is that the thought of non-experience is not enough, for then one either ends up in a vicious circle (the thought of the thought of non-experience, and so on) or one then posits something beyond thought — at which point thought must itself become silent, still, and "dark." As John notes, in a sentiment echoed by later mystical thinkers such as Kierkegaard, "for the intellect faith is also like a dark night."[117]

In this second definition of darkness — sensory and spiritual darkness — John points to the limits of both experience and thought. Both types of darkness are described by John as forms of "purgation" and "accommodation" for mystical experience. While the initial part of this process entails active practices (meditation, contemplation, etc.), the latter part of it is passive. Mysteriously, it just happens. For us, however, living within the nonmystical everyday world, this is not enough. If there is a passive purgation, for what does this cleansing take place? If there is a passive accommodation, what is the subject accommodating?

John's reply comes in the form of his third definition of darkness. It is what we might call the "lightning theory of darkness." As he notes, "in striking the soul with its divine light, it surpasses the natural light and thereby darkens and deprives individuals of all the natural affections and apprehensions they perceive by means of their natural light. It leaves their spiritual and natural faculties not only in darkness but in emptiness too."[118] Here we see the motif of the divine as dark due to its excess and exuberance (as per John's first definition). We also see the notion of the divine as dark because it represents a limit for thought and experience (as per the second definition). Finally, we also have here an articulation of the paradox at the heart of mystical experience: the manifestation of that which is an absolute limit (for experience, for thought, for the human), which, in its manifesting, is also a vacuousness, a dissipation, a receding into shadows and night.

This is the movement evoked in later thinkers such as Georges Bataille: "Here darkness is not the absence of light (or of sound) but absorption into the outside."[119] Or again, from Bataille's mystical poem "L'Archangélique": "the excess of darkness / is the flash of a star."[120] It is this paradoxical movement that John evokes when he states, "God is also a dark night to the soul in this life."[121]

Stanza II

Generating models
Of primordial life, and
The opacity of
Non-planetary ground.

The phylogeological distribution
Of other extremophiles
In distant cladograms
Does not provide evidence
Of their possible antiquity.

The moss begins to glow —
anagrams of sorrow.
Black ink. Dried nettle.
Sleeping gloom.

Given the shortened gap in descriptions
Of xenobiological transition between
The probiotic synthesis of biochemical compounds
And the last common ancestor (LCA) of all extant living being

Water and ice in the solar system
Giving witness to the extinction
Of ice-dependent organisms
On Earth

Even as the signatures of life — or life itself — are
In evidence, in extraterrestrial ice.

Commentary on Ground. In the second stanza of the poem, terms evoking both terrestrial and non-terrestrial environments are more frequent, as are the biological descriptions of "primordial life." All of these terms bring to the mind the concept of the "ground," not only in the literal sense of a planetary, terrestrial land mass, but also in the figurative, philosophical sense of providing a rational basis or support for the development of a concept.

But grounds are often unsteady, shifting suddenly and giving way to tectonic upheavals that could only have arisen as a result of long-term, nearly imperceptible shifts. For every ground, then, there is a corresponding state of the groundless, or better, an *unground*. The idea of the unground is found in the work of the German mystical philosopher Jakob Böhme. Böhme worked as a cattle herder and a shoemaker before becoming involved in mystical theology, largely as a result of his own mystical experiences (one of which included a vision of the structure of the world encapsulated in a beam of sunlight on a pewter dish). His influences are eclectic, and range from Neoplatonism to Christian mysticism to Renaissance alchemy. And, while Böhme wrote on a range of topics, from natural philosophy to the theology of the Trinity, it is in his mystical works such as *The Signature of All Things* (*De Signatura Rerum*, 1621) or *The Great Mystery* (*Mysterium Magnum*, 1623) that Böhme puts forth the idea of the divine as *Ungrund*.

The term *Ungrund* is difficult to translate, as it may, depending on context, mean a lack of ground, a lack of ground as itself a ground, or a superior or superlative ground. English editions of Böhme sometimes translate *Ungrund* as "abyss," though this latter term must be understood as more than just empty space. For the sake of simplicity let us translate *Ungrund* as "unground," keeping in mind the plurality of meanings it may have. These pluralities, moreover, are implicit in Böhme's writing. What does it mean to say, as Böhme did, that God is the *Ungrund*? On the one hand God is the unground because the divine is without specific attributes, neither affirmative nor negative, neither light nor darkness, neither good nor evil. That is, it is precisely that which is neutral with respect to human-centric, moral and metaphysical attributes of the world. On the other hand, Böhme will repeatedly refer to the divine less in terms of its neutrality, and more in terms of negation — the divine as "the nothing and the all," or the divine as "Divine abyss" or even "abysmal God."[122] Here God is abyss or "unground" not because the divine passes beyond the human world of morality and metaphysics, but because the divine subtracts itself, in an act of self-negation, from its very intelligibility as such.

This leaves Böhme with a basic theological problem, which is how to explain the creation of the world, nature, and life if the divine is indeed to be negatively thought of as the unground or abyss. There is, to begin with, the metaphysical problem of how something can be created from nothing. Then there is the theological problem of how plurality, the diversity of the world, can come from an indivisible unity. But beyond these problems, there is another, more important one, which is if the divine is indeed the unground, and if the unground is neutral, anonymous, and indifferent, then this clearly implies a notion of the divine as equally neutral, anonymous, and indifferent with respect to us as human beings and the human world that we inhabit. The divine as *Ungrund* implies not only negation or a Divine abyss, but the divine as indifferent to the human.

Here Böhme relies upon a standard mode of theological exegesis for his time, combining the Neoplatonic emanation of the divine with the Trinity as its mode of manifestation, all of which results in the world as manifestation of divine goodness (the *mysterium magnum*), animated by an equally divine and beneficent principle of life (the *spiritus mundi*). In short, Böhme's religious commitment to a highly moralized natural philosophy ends up compromising the ambivalence in his idea of the Divine abyss or the unground.

That the divine as unground eventually leads to the infusion of divine creation in the innately good and moral world is both theologically unsurprising and philosophically disappointing.

This is precisely where later philosophers influenced by mystical traditions intervene. A case in point is Schopenhauer's notion of the Will. Schopenhauer's major work, *The World as Will and Representation*, takes up and modifies the Kantian distinction between the world as it appears to us (*phenomena*) and the world in itself (*noumena*). For Kant, the latter idea is philosophically necessary but can never be known as such. It is simply there to designate something "out there" that we as human beings indirectly sense, but which remains beyond the pale of human knowledge. In the Kantian framework, the world-in-itself guarantees that all thought does not reduce to idealism.

For all his pessimistic grumblings, Schopenhauer remains optimistic that the world-in-itself can be known by us as human beings. Schopenhauer grants to Kant the world as it appears to us, which he terms *Vorstellung* (Representation). But this is only an index to something else, which, Schopenhauer is sure, is the world-in-itself, which he terms *Wille* (Will). Given that the world-in-itself can never be known without becoming the world as it appears to us, how can Schopenhauer make this claim? Certainly, the term "will" in this context has little or nothing to do with the pedantic world of individual human wants and desires. But what then is it? Nietzsche, one of Schopenhauer's greatest advocates and sharpest critics, notes that Schopenhauer can only make this claim by a "poetic intuition" — by definition it can never be proved.

In attempting to describe the *Wille* as the world-in-itself, Schopenhauer variously resorts to the language of force, flux, flow, process, power, and dynamism, though none of this language is used with any consistency. Neither does Schopenhauer opt for the sort of pantheism evidenced in the *naturphilosophie* of his contemporaries Schelling and Hegel (of whom he has only derisory things to say). Instead, the rhetoric Schopenhauer returns to again and again is that of the ground and the groundless. As he notes in one of his more pessimistic moments, "everything in life proclaims that earthly happiness is destined to be frustrated, or recognized as an illusion. The grounds for this lie deep in the very nature of things."[123] For Schopenhauer, it is the oscillating experiences of suffering and boredom that come to form this ground, a ground that relies on the "poetic intuition" of the mystic more than the logical syllogism of the philosopher.

But Schopenhauer offers another, more rigorous notion of ground in discussing the Will as the world-in-itself. Blind, anonymous, and indifferent to our wants and desires, the Will can never, for Schopenhauer, have a stable ground, either in terms of human experience or in terms of human knowledge. For, as he notes, "there will always remain, as an insoluble residuum, a content of the phenomenon which cannot be referred to its form, and which thus cannot be explained from something else in accordance with the principle of sufficient reason."[124] Again: "Everywhere a ground can be given only of phenomena as such, only of individual things, never of the will itself."[125] By evoking this phrase "sufficient reason," Schopenhauer insinuates a world-in-itself without the moral-theological framework that still marks Böhme. A long-standing foundation of Western philosophical thought, the principle of sufficient reason states simply that everything that exists has a reason for existing. It is the very bedrock, the very ground of philosophy. In discussing the Will in terms of the principle of sufficient reason, Schopenhauer suggests that the world literally has no reason. "For in everything in nature there is something to which no ground can ever be assigned, for which no explanation is possible, and no further cause is to be sought."[126] This is not only the limit of philosophy, assuming as it does the principle of sufficient reason; it is also the hinge upon which mystical thought operates. At this limit, all ground can only turn into the unground: "the principle of the world's existence is expressly a groundless one … which, as *thing-in-itself*, cannot be subject to the principle of sufficient reason or ground."[127]

And this is where the mysticism implicit in Schopenhauer's projects comes to the fore — except that Schopenhauer's reference points are not only those of Christian mysticism, but those of the mystical strand in Hinduism and Buddhism as well. Whatever Schopenhauer's errors in his understanding of, say, the Buddhist concept of "emptiness" (*śūnyatā*), what this engagement with mysticism allows him to do is to pose the problem of the unground as a problem of the human. Schopenhauer's challenge is how to think the world-in-itself apart from any human framework, subtracted from any anthropocentric and even anthropomorphic experience.

If, as both Böhme and Schopenhauer suggest, mystical thinking is intimately related to the ground, then we leave the last word to Dōgen, the Japanese monk and founder of the Sōtō School of Zen Buddhism. In or around 1227, Dōgen, returning from his enlightenment on the mountain of T'ien-t'ung, took it upon himself to write a manual for meditation, known as the *Fukan zazen gi*. The opening passages of the manual, which today exists in several versions, depict a master "sitting fixedly" in meditation. However, to a novice monk, the groundedness of the master's sitting appears to stand in contrast with the ungrounded practice of meditation on nothingness. In fact, Dōgen's telling of this tale even seems to suggest that mystical experience is precisely this ground of the unground, the thinking of not thinking: "Once, when the Great Master Hung-tao of Yüeh shan was sitting in meditation, a monk asked him, 'What are you thinking, sitting there so fixedly?' The master answered, 'I'm thinking of not thinking.' The monk asked, 'How do you think of not thinking?' The master answered, 'Nonthinking.'"[128]

Stanza III

Temperature constrains all life,
In the permafrost,
Hibernating for millions of years or
Decomposing for millions of years.

No well-established growth temperatures
In thermotolerant caves
For living optimally
For any of the Bacteria, Archaea, or Fungi.

Tears distilled from obsidian
Envelop our entwined eroded limbs.
Sleeping premonitions levitate.
Quiet fluttering of night.
Ominous signs seep
From sullen anatomies.

The amoeba Echinamoeba thermarum grows
Optimally at $T_{opt} > 50°C$ *and is*
One of the few truly thermophilic eukaryotes
Of terrestrial, nonanthropogenic environments.

Such environments are enriched in elements
Such as arsenic (As), antimony (Sb), and
Mercury (Hg), such that thermotolerant surfaces
Experiencing evaporation also have

Elevated salinity and, therefore
Halophilic inhabitants.

Commentary on Planets. In this, the third stanza, the poem evokes the materials, substances, and temperatures of the planet, an entire planetary ambience. There is, from the view of science, the planet itself, which is inclusive of the atmosphere. But the atmosphere is not simply identical to the planet. How, then, can the planet be excluded from the atmosphere, especially when, in common knowledge, the latter derives from the existence of the former?

In an enigmatic text entitled "The Congested Planet," published in 1958, Georges Bataille attempts something unheard of in mystical traditions: to conceive of a nonhuman mysticism that would also refuse all forms of anthropomorphic personification. Depicting "a planet congested by death and wealth," Bataille evokes an anonymous, impersonal "scream" that "pierces the clouds." In these clouds and on this planet — planets and clouds that are to be taken literally, and not metaphorically — Bataille notes that "knowledge is the agreement of the organism and the environment from which it emerges."[129] We might even read into this phrase something more specific — it is the accommodation of the environment to the organism that, in the last instance, constitutes knowledge.

That said, Bataille, notes that "the wager of knowledge opens two paths." The first, perhaps unsurprisingly, is the path of instrumental knowledge. Bataille nuances this as both a philosophical and mythical need for a correlation between organism and environment (which is really the accommodation of the latter to the former). In one movement, the organism is this "unconditioned flight" from the possible into "the impossible that surrounds it." Knowledge only arises, however, by virtue of the conversion of the impossible back into the possible, of the unforeseeable into the foreseeable. "Hazardous flight" is converted into "wise calculation."

While the conventional leftist reading of Bataille would see this as a critique of global industrial capitalism, this is only part of the picture. Bataille is not simply on the side of the "hazardous flight," and he is not simply advocating for the liberation of "the impossible." Both the hazardous flight and the wise calculation belong to the human world, and this world, as Bataille notes, is not always the same as "the planet." The differential between them is the world-for-us and the world-in-itself: "human knowledge becomes the calculation of possibility when it orders the totality of things for itself."[130]

This is the second path that the "wager of knowledge" opens up. Bataille can only state it negatively — yes, we have language, and concepts, and tools, and we apply ourselves to the world, in the world. But the world's deep time and tectonic shifts remind us that "it is nothing that exists *in the last place*: everything is in suspense, over the abyss, the ground itself is the illusion of an assurance."[131]

Awareness of the fragility of the human, of the ungroundedness of the ground, the disjunction of the planet from the world, the world-in-itself from the world-for-us — all of this evokes for Bataille an experience that would in an earlier epoch be called mystical. Nowhere is this more evident, ironically, than in the precision of our knowledge about geology, paleontology, meteorology, and ecology. The more we learn about the planet, the stranger it becomes to us.

The melodramatic quality of Bataille's writing has meant that vast numbers of graduate students have furtively "skipped over" the poetic parts in favor of the more robust "theory." But it is difficult not to read texts like "The Congested Planet" in light of the ongoing anxieties over climate change. This is also the case with Bataille's project *The Accursed Share* (begun in the late 1960s), which proposes to turn political economy upside down by regarding "terrestrial activity [...] as a cosmic phenomenon." The first volume of Bataille's study opens with these striking words: "Beyond our immediate ends, human activity in fact pursues the useless and infinite fulfillment of the universe."[132] This strange intuition of the impersonal leads Bataille to question basic presuppositions of causality with regard to human activity on the Earth in general: "[i] s the general determination of energy circulating in the biosphere altered by human activity? Or rather, isn't the latter's intention vitiated by a determination of which it is ignorant, which it overlooks and cannot change?"[133]

Bataille is not unaware of the natural resource and energy problem that readily exists at the time of his writing *The Accursed Share*. This is, in fact, the backdrop for his approach, which is "to recognize in the economy — in the production and use of wealth — a particular aspect of terrestrial activity regarded as a cosmic phenomenon."[134] In the same passage Bataille rhetorically notes, "isn't there a need to study the system of human production and consumption within a much larger framework?"

In as much as *The Accursed Share* is, in Bataille's words, a work of political economy, it is also very much an expanded view of what terms like "economy," "wealth," and "production" may mean. The economy, in its conventional and narrow, human-centric meaning, dips down into the bowels of the viscous planet, which itself can only be known on the radically nonhuman level of deep time. Bataille is asking for more than a simple marriage of economy and ecology, however. In this "cosmic" perspective, economy is also the wealth, production, and expenditure of the nonhuman planet: "A movement is produced on the surface of the globe that results from the circulation of energy at this point in the universe."[135]

What would this unhuman, planetary "economy" look like? To begin with, Bataille distinguishes economy in the conventional sense from this other, cosmic economy. The former — a "restricted" economy — is nearsighted in its goals, and expresses a human-centric point of view (be it in terms of humanity generally or specific interest groups). The latter — a "general" economy — is the view of the deep time of the planet, its tectonic shifts and atmospheric transformations, all of which takes place indifferently to the human-bound interests of the restricted economy. In the former, we not only see rivers, but also dams, bridges, and occasions for sport. In the latter, our language falters, opting for either the poetic (the ebb and flow of life) or the scientific (fluid dynamics, laminar flow).

The shortcoming of Bataille's project was to insinuate that an appreciation of the general economy could lead to a critique and even transformation of the all-too-human restricted economy, especially when the latter is by definition indifferent to the hopes and desires of the former. The best he could do is to simply document the ways in which we as human beings unknowingly participate in the general economy through the ambivalent rituals of festivals, war, and luxurious squandering.

But if Bataille comes up short in *The Accursed Share*, that same theme of the unhuman planet is taken up, in a different guise, in his almost aphoristic, posthumously published text *Theory of Religion*. *Theory of Religion* also evokes the problem of mystical experience, and in particular the mysticism of the unhuman. His starting point is our twofold status as situated, living beings: on the one hand we exist *in* the world, viewing the world as a world-for-us as human beings, with particular needs and desires. Our existing in the world in this way is predicated on a basic separation between self and world, which in turn is predicated on a minimal notion of individuation (I am not you, you are not me, my personal space, etc.).

On the other hand, we also exist *as* the world itself, in as much as we are living beings indelibly bound to the world just as much as are the rain, the buildings, or the internet. Our intimate binding to everything gives us the impression of our interconnectedness and of the interconnectedness of all things, human beings as only one kind of being. Bataille uses the terms "discontinuity" and "continuity," respectively, to describe these two impressions. Sometimes we prefer to keep our distance, have some "alone time." At other times we seek out community or belonging. For Bataille, this everyday experience is the crux of the mystical dilemma: the experience of continuity (existing *as* world) that can only take place on the precondition of a basic discontinuity (existing *in* the world). Put another way, our fundamental discontinuity as human beings in the world is also, at its most extreme limit, an overflowing negation that indexes a continuity — a continuity that is also the limit of the human. To exist *as* the world, we must cease existing *in* the world.

Bataille refers to this dilemma, with all its negations and contradictions, as *divinity*: "If we now picture humanity conceiving the world in light of an existence that is continuous … we must also perceive the need for them to attribute to it the virtues of a thing … In this reduction to a thing, the world is given both the form of isolated individuality and creative power. But this personally distinct power has at the same time the *divine* character of an impersonal, indistinct, and immanent existence."[136] This sense — of an unhuman, indifferent planet — can only be expressed in us as a "powerless horror." However, "this horror is ambiguous." Its ambiguity is that which Bataille attempts to get at in his earlier texts, such as "The Congested Planet." It is a dilemma expressed in the contemporary discourse on climate change, between a debate over the world-for-us (e.g. how do we as human beings impact — negatively or positively — the geological status of the planet?), and a largely unspoken, whispered query over the world-in-itself (e.g. to what degree is the planet indifferent to us as human beings — and to what degree are we indifferent to the planet?).

Stanza IV

Many microbes in the deep sea are not
Autochthonous residents,
Descending to the deep as components
Of phytodetrital aggregates.

Such piezophiles (or barophiles) are
Defined by optimal growth rates
Far beyond atmospheric pressure
Where 1 atm = ~0.1 MPa

Under a spectral night
Of tectonic ice —
The withering of bone
Become green stars.

An ocean time-series study
A long-term, oligotrophic, habitat assessment
Shows the fraction of group Ia Crenarchaea in the total picoplankton
Increase with depth to the deepest site.

Ten thousand moons
Of black graphite rise —
Blind night corridors
Of deathless skies.

D. profundis 500-1T, Japan Sea, P_{opt} *= 15MPa*
Moritella abyssi 2693^{T}*, Mariana Trench,* P_{opt} *= 30MPa*

Psychromonas profunda 2825T, Eastern Tropical Atlantic,
P_{opt} = 25MPa
A life form in dynamic, cosmic equilibrium
With its environment
Is dead.

Life in space can only occur
Temporarily
In a dormant state —

A cold, ice-covered moon
Of a distant planet.

Commentary on Nothing. In this fourth and last stanza the poem noticeably moves beyond the geological and climatological reference points it has evoked in the earlier stanzas. The concepts of depth and dormancy (the former in the sea, the latter in ice), open onto the questioning of the "autochthonic" origin of life, and in particular, human life. And it is here that the poem most forcefully opens onto the problem of mysticism that we have been elaborating thus far.

What kind of mysticism is this, which gives us only scientific description, experimental data, and taxonomic names? We may, in a general sense, think of mysticism as a vague, impressionistic feeling of wonder or awe (that may or may not involve drugs), and that may or may not involve nature hikes and generally blissing out. We can also think of mysticism as actually enabled by an overly optimistic, "gee-whiz" scientific instrumentality, in which the Earth is the divinely sanctioned domain of the human, even and especially in the eleventh hour of climate change. But whether it is of the political left or right, whether it is the affectivist-hippie mysticism or the eschatology-of-oil type of mysticism, in both cases mysticism is ostensibly a human-centric and human-oriented experience. Mysticism in these cases is always a union "for us" as human beings.

Perhaps something more is gained by considering mysticism in its historical context. Long considered unworthy of serious scholarship, the study of mysticism and mystical writing was largely inaugurated in the 20th century by Evelyn Underhill's oft-cited book *Mysticism: A Study in the Nature and Development of Man's Spiritual Consciousness* (1911). Underhill elucidates the logic of mystical thinking, paying particular attention to mysticism as a systematic practice, as well as to the psychology of mystical experience. As she notes, "if we may trust the reports of the mystics ... they have succeeded where all others have failed, in establishing immediate communication between the spirit of man ... and that 'only Reality,' that immaterial and final Being, which some philosophers call the Absolute, and most theologians call God."[137] Underhill notes, however, that this communication is established varies a great deal, from canonic statements by the Church Fathers, to anecdotes and autobiographies by spiritual laypeople, to fringe heretical insinuations of pantheism.

In the West, the intermittent flowering of mysticism is often explained in terms of a historical context against which mysticism operates. In the 14th century one finds mysticism flourishing in Germany, most notably in the work of Meister Eckhart. While Eckhart remains one of the more "philosophical" mystics, his mode of thinking also works against the hyperrationality of Scholasticism and its predilection for logic, nominalism, and elaborate Scriptural exegesis. In the 16th century mysticism again flourishes, this time in Spain, where works of, and collaboration between, John of the Cross and Teresa of Avila are the most commonly cited examples. Tending more to non-philosophical discourses than their predecessors — mystical poems, autobiography, meditations — both authors are working in an ambivalent relation to the emerging scientific humanism of their time. At the core of their writings is the problem of human suffering in the world — indeed, the extent to which suffering *is* the very relation between self and world. As John notes, "the darkness and trials, spiritual and temporal, that fortunate souls ordinarily undergo ... are so numerous and profound that human science cannot understand them adequately." John continues, noting that "nor does experience of them equip one to understand them. Those who suffer them will know what this experience is like, but they will find themselves unable to describe it."[138]

Given this, it is no surprise to see many mystics positing some type of effacement or union of self and world as the resolution to the problem of suffering. In effectively bypassing the self-world division one also bypasses all of the corporeal, spiritual, and existential suffering that is part and parcel of that division. This then places a person — to the extent there is a "person" any longer — in the position of experiencing a further effacement, that between the earthly and the divine, between the natural and the supernatural. This is the benchmark of nearly every text in the speculative mysticism tradition. But there is often disagreement on exactly how this union of natural and supernatural is to be achieved, let alone described in our all-too-human language. For some, the union is described using the motif of light, a motif that has a long tradition that extends back to the mystical texts of the Church Fathers, and ultimately to Neoplatonic sources (e.g., the divine topologies of light and radiation in Plotinus). This "light mysticism" is also an affirmative mysticism; it asserts a positive communion with God, and it dictates the correct steps on the ladder of this ascent.

But light mysticism is compromised in several respects, including a highly anthropomorphized God with which one enters into an ambivalent, paternalistic embrace. If the divine — and here let us say "divine" rather than "God" to emphasize the anti-anthropomorphic tendency — is not simply superhuman but in some way beyond the human (or even, against the human), then it follows that any human thought of the divine can only be a horizon for thought. For some mystical thinkers, the very inconceivability of this union with the divine meant that any possible knowledge of it, and any possible description of it, could only take place by a negative means (such that the divine is not-*X* or not-*Y*, *X* and *Y* denoting earthly, human-centric attributes). Hence the preferred motif is not light — be it the radiation of divine Intelligences or beatific light — but instead that of darkness and night. This too has a long tradition, one that extends back to Dionysius the Areopagite, who, sometime in the 6th century, had articulated the *via negativa* or path of negation as the way to divine union. Those in this tradition often utilize several tactics to talk about the divine: that of negative theology, in which one makes use of language, logic, and philosophical argumentation to demonstrate the aporetic unknowability of the divine, and that of darkness mysticism, in which poetry and allegory are used to suggest the ways in which the divine remains forever beyond the pale of human thought and comprehension. John of the Cross's poem "The Dark Night of the Soul" is, along with the anonymous 14th-century text *The Cloud of Unknowing*, often referred to as a key text in this darkness mysticism tradition.

Darkness mysticism is not only figuratively but historically the dark underside of mystical thought. Even at the apotheosis of divine communion, darkness mysticism retains the language of shadows and nothingness, as if the positive union with the divine is of less importance than the realization of the absolute limits of the human. Darkness mysticism is "mystical" not because it says yes to the therapeutic, anthropocentric embrace of God, but because it says no to the recuperative habits of human beings to always see the world as a world-for-us.

But whether one opts for light or dark mysticism, the question that modern scholars such as Underhill return to is this, summarized in Henry Annesley's underappreciated 1927 book *Dark Geomancy*, intriguingly subtitled *Chthonic Mysticism in the Modern Age, With Implications for Cosmic Consciousness*. An eclectic author, Annesley worked in New York as a journalist and copyeditor, sometimes ghostwriting fiction for pulp magazines such as *Amazing Stories*, *Thrilling Wonder Stories*, and *Weird Tales*. Working in the same register as Underhill, Otto, Henri Bergson, and others interested in mysticism, Annesley goes so far as to suggest we take seriously the myths and superstitions of earlier epochs concerning "lost civilizations and fallen empires." As Annesley notes, "unless the history of the mystics can touch and light up some part of this seemingly normal experience of being human, that is to say, take its place in the general history of the ab-human, and contribute something towards our understanding of outer-human nature and destiny, its interest for us can never be more than remote, academic, and agnostic."[139] In short, what does mysticism mean to us, in the "ordinary nonmystical"? For Underhill, the response — a response that has continued to be echoed to the present day — is that the history of mysticism "is as vital for the deeper understanding of the history of humanity as it is for humanity's inevitable decline and extinguishing."[140]

While Underhill's book is an invaluable study of mysticism, we can retain her question, while repudiating her answer. And here we can, perhaps, see the darkness mysticism tradition in a new light, which is that of our current geopolitical imaginary of climates, tectonic plates, tropical storms, and the viscous geological sedimentation of oil fields and primordial life. In a contemporary context, one in which we are constantly reminded of the planetary (and cosmic) frailty of human beings, and reminded in ways that appear to be utterly indifferent to the "history of humanity" — floods, earthquakes, wildfires, hurricanes, water shortages, extreme temperatures, and the like — in such a context, perhaps something called mysticism has an unexpected meaning. Rudolf Otto suggests this in his examination of the ambivalent "horror of the divine" in religious and mystical experience. Such experiences, in which the human confronts the absolutely unhuman, can only be thought negatively. In the West, Otto argues, there have been two major modes in which this negative thought has been expressed: silence and darkness. To these Otto adds a third, which he finds dominant in Eastern variants of mystical experience, which he terms "emptiness and empty distances." Here the negation of thought turns into an affirmation, but a paradoxical affirmation of "nothingness" or "emptiness." As Otto puts it, "'emptiness is, like darkness and silence, a negation, but a negation that does away with every 'this' and 'here,' in order that the 'wholly other' may become actual."[141]

Hence our opening inquiry is really about a mysticism of the "without-us," or really, a dark mysticism of the world-in-itself. This sentiment is expressed in the work of the Kyoto School philosopher Keiji Nishitani, who repeatedly returned to the modern "tendency toward the loss of the human."[142] Nishitani is part of a generation of Japanese philosophers equally versed in Western philosophy and Mahāyāna Buddhism. Nishitani himself studied with Heidegger in the late 1930s, and he frequently engages with Western thinkers such as Schopenhauer, Nietzsche, and Meister Eckhart. For Nishitani, the insight of mystical thinking is to have revealed the core problem of nihilism in the modern era. Echoing Nietzsche's diagnostic, Nishitani notes how modern nihilism is primarily a privative nihilism, in which some thing is revealed to be nothing, in which some locus of meaning or value is revealed to be illusory and empty. For Nietzsche it was the waning of the credulity of religious belief that constituted this nihilism, but for Nishitani it is the twofold waning of religion and science that contribute to the sense of "the nihility that one becomes aware of at the ground of the self and the world."[143] Without a foundation to give meaning and substance to the world, modern nihilism finds itself confronted with nothingness.

Our response, argues Nishitani, should not be to rediscover some new ground for giving meaning to the world (be it in religious or scientific terms), and neither should we be satisfied to wallow in despair at this loss of meaning, this "abyss of nihility." Instead, we should delve deeper into this abyss, this nothingness, which may hold within a way out of the dead end of nihilism. For Nishitani, then, the only way beyond nihilism is through nihilism. And here Nishitani borrows from the Buddhist concept of *śūnyatā*, conventionally translated as "nothingness" or "emptiness." In contrast to the *relative nothingness* of modern nihilism, which is privative, and predicated on the absence of being, Nishitani proposes an *absolute nothingness*, which is purely negative and predicated on a paradoxical foundation of non-being.

"Emptiness in the sense of *śūnyatā* is emptiness only when it empties itself even of the standpoint that represents it as some 'thing' that is emptiness."[144] How does one think of this strange nothingness beyond nothing, this emptiness beyond the empty? Nishitani frequently turns to planetary, climatological, and cosmic tropes in describing absolute nothingness:

> [J]ust as nihility is an abyss for anything that exists, emptiness may be said to be an abyss even for that abyss of nihility. As a valley unfathomably deep may be imagined set within an endless expanse of sky, so it is with nihility and emptiness. But the sky we have in mind here is more than the vault above that spreads out far and wide over the valley below. It is a cosmic sky enveloping the earth and humanity and the countless regions of stars that move and have their being within it.[145]

In Nishitani's interpretation of absolute nothingness (*śūnyatā*), that through which everything exists and subsists is not itself an existent, nor is it an existent foundation for all existents — it is nothingness, emptiness. From this follows the equally strange and enigmatic identity of all that does exist: "everyone and everything is nameless, unnamable, and unknowable ... And this cosmic nihility is the very same nihility that distances us from one another."[146] For Nishitani, it is from this commonality — of nothing and nothingness — that one passes from relative to absolute nothingness: "In contrast to the field of nihility on which the desolate and bottomless abyss distances even the most intimate of persons or things from one another, on the field of emptiness that absolute breach points directly to a most intimate encounter with everything that exists."[147] Self and world come to be regarded not only as groundless, but, in an enigmatic way, as indistinct as well.

This is, of course, the most difficult thought. It doesn't help anyone. There is no being-on-the-side-of the world, much less nature or the weather. If anything, the apparent prevalence of natural disasters and global pandemics indicates that we are not on the side of the world, but that the world is against us. But even this is too anthropocentric a view, as if the world harbored some misanthropic vendetta against humanity. It would be more accurate — and more horrific, in a sense — to say that the world is indifferent to us as human beings. Indeed, the core problematic in the climate change discourse is the extent to which human beings are at issue at all. On the one hand, we as human beings are the problem; on the other hand, at the planetary level of the Earth's deep time, nothing could be more insignificant than the human.

This is where mysticism again becomes relevant. But the differences between this contemporary mysticism and historical mysticism are all-important. If mysticism historically speaking aims for a union between self and world, then mysticism today would have to devolve upon the radical disjunction of and indifference between self and world. If historical mysticism still had as its aim the subject's experience, and as its highest principle that of God, then mysticism today — after the death of God — would be about the impossibility of experience, about that which resides in shadows and withdraws from any possible experience — and yet which still makes its presence felt through the periodic upheavals of weather, earth, and space. If mysticism in its historical context is, in the last instance, theological, then mysticism today, a mysticism of the unhuman, would have to be, in the last instance, *climatological*. It is, perhaps, a kind of mysticism that can only be expressed in the dust of this planet.

STARRY SPECULATIVE CORPSE

I

STARRY SPECULATIVE CORPSE

Descartes's Demon. In the fall of 1639, René Descartes sat down at his desk to write. Having spent his early years steeped in mathematics, logic, and the sciences, he soon found himself returning to the themes of certainty and doubt. At issue for him was a simple question concerning knowledge. Philosophy, theology, mathematics, astronomy, medicine, the arts, and the natural sciences all claim to know things. From them a cumulative understanding of the self, of others, of the world, and of the cosmos is made possible. But how do we know that what we know is actually true? What is the foundation on which these disparate fields of knowledge are based? Are there questions that cannot — or should not — be asked, lest they undermine the knowledge they are designed to produce? How much uncertainty is tolerated before knowledge becomes doubt — and when does doubt come to a stop, if ever?

An abyss opens up. For Descartes this was a personal as well as a philosophical problem. As he writes, "Some years ago I noticed how many false things I had accepted as true in my childhood, and how doubtful were the things that I subsequently built on them and therefore that, once in a lifetime, everything should be completely overturned and I should begin again from the most basic foundations."[148]

Being the astute thinker that he was, Descartes set out a method for addressing this problem. The task was, as he notes, ambitious, and Descartes writes that he had been waiting for a "mature age" at which to undertake this project. Whether the age of 43 was the right age or not is hard to say. He felt he had been waiting long enough, even too long, and so, Descartes writes, "today I appropriately cleared my mind of all cares and arranged for myself some time free from interruption. I am alone and, at long last, I will devote myself seriously and freely to this general overturning of my beliefs."[149]

The result of these exercises in skepticism are well known to students of philosophy, and, when *Meditations on First Philosophy* was published in Paris in 1641, it immediately elicited a range of responses, renewing debates over the relationship between philosophy and theology, reason and faith.

Descartes's most lasting application of his methodological doubt comes in the first of his meditations, where he considers how our senses deceive us. Dreams, hallucinations, and painting are instances in which we think we know something based on sensory evidence, but are in fact deceived. In these cases we can learn, from experience, to distinguish dream from reality, the image from the thing itself. Our senses are reliable, if used properly.

But Descartes pushes his doubt further. What if our senses are, by definition, deceptive? What if deception is, as it were, hardwired into our very modes of being? Descartes raises this question through a kind of thought experiment:

> I will suppose therefore that not God, who is supremely good and the source of truth, but rather some malicious demon (*genium aliquem malignum*) of the utmost power and cunning has employed all his energies in order to deceive me. I shall think that the sky, the air, the earth,

> colors, shapes, sounds and all external things are merely the delusions of dreams which he has devised to ensnare my judgement. I shall consider myself as not having hands or eyes, or flesh, or blood or senses, but as falsely believing that I have all these things.[150]

Another abyss opens. Often dubbed the "evil demon" or "evil genius," here we see Descartes pushing his doubt to an extreme point, a point at which no knowledge is possible because nothing is for certain. One thought is as good or as bad as another, everything relative, arbitrary, haphazard, pointless. Subject to continual deception, prey to the cunning of unknown entities, dismembered and insubstantial, Descartes stands on philosophy's precipice and peers over the edge. What he finds there is a terrifying abyss, where there is neither certitude nor knowledge, nor even a single thought — just a tenebrous, impassive silence.

"But this is a tiring project and a kind of laziness brings me back to what is more habitual in my life." Can we blame Descartes for stepping back from the precipice? Thinking is hard work, yes, but the negation of all thought is, perhaps, harder. What Descartes inadvertently discovers is both the ground and the greatest threat to philosophy, the question that cannot be asked without undermining the idea of philosophy itself.

Traditionally, the Socratic tradition in philosophy has a therapeutic function, which is to dispel the horrors of the unknown through reasoned argument. What cannot be tolerated in this tradition is the possibility of a world that cannot be known, or a world that is indifferent to our elaborate knowledge-producing schemes. Descartes's *Meditations* begin — and end — in this mode. But along the way there are gaps, fissures, and lacunae in the philosophical edifice. With the evil demon Descartes stumbles upon a horror intrinsic to philosophy: the thought that philosophy cannot think without undermining and ultimately annulling itself. In order to continue its work, philosophy must ignore the evil demon, gloss it over, or avoid it altogether.

The quandary provokes a decision, one as arbitrary as it is necessary. Regarding the evil demon, Descartes asserts, "let him deceive me as much as he can, he will never bring it about that I am nothing as long as I think that I am something." And so a foundation is provided, in the famous formulation *cogito ergo sum*: "So, after considering everything very thoroughly, I must finally conclude that this proposition *I am, I exist*, is necessarily true whenever it is put forward by me or conceived in my mind."[151] From this flows an entire legacy of philosophical thinking, in terms of Cartesian space, Cartesian dualism, and the privileging of human consciousness over all other forms of being.

But it is not so easy to shake Descartes's demon, which continues to haunt his philosophical treatise to the end. It is always there, threatening to undermine whatever conceptual edifice Descartes has constructed. Better to not deal with it at all — and continue philosophizing. Given this, it perhaps comes as no surprise that Descartes, as a young man, was often plagued by nightmares, swirling dreams involving floating phantoms, torrential whirlwinds, and shape-shifting entities. It is likely such impressions made their way into the *Meditations*: "I am like a prisoner who is enjoying an imaginary freedom while asleep; as he begins to suspect that he is asleep, he dreads being woken up, and goes along with the pleasant illusion as long as he can."[152]

*

Kant's Depression. On the 12th of February, 1804, Immanuel Kant lay on his deathbed. "His eye was rigid, and his face and lips became discolored by a cadaverous pallor."[153] A few days following his death, his head was shaved, and "a plaster cast was taken, not a mask merely, but a cast of the whole head, designed to enrich the craniological collection of Dr. Gall," a local physician. The corpse of Kant was made up and dressed appropriately, and, according to some accounts, throngs of visitors came day and night. "Everybody was anxious to avail himself of the last opportunity he would have for entitling himself to say, 'I too have seen Kant.'"[154] Their impressions seemed to be at once reverent and grotesque. "Great was the astonishment of all people at the meagerness of Kant's appearance; and it was universally agreed that a corpse so wasted and fleshless had never been beheld."[155] Accompanied by the church bells of Königsberg, Kant's corpse was carried from his home by torchlight, to a candlelit cathedral, whose Gothic arches and spires were perhaps reminiscent of the philosopher's elaborate and vaulted books.

In his book *A Short History of Decay*, E.M. Cioran notes: "I turned away from philosophy when it became impossible to discover in Kant any human weakness, any authentic accent of melancholy, in Kant and in all the philosophers."[156] Indeed, for many, the name of Immanuel Kant has become synonymous with a certain type of elaborate, grand, system-building philosophy that characterizes works such as *The Critique of Pure Reason*, first published in 1781. Indeed, so decisive was the impact of Kant's later, "critical" philosophy that textbooks today often refer to philosophy before Kant and "post-Kantian philosophy." The significance of Kant's philosophy is, however, counterbalanced by its notorious difficulty. Reading through the table of contents alone, with its dazzling and labyrinthine array of sections, subsections, and sub-subsections, is a task in and of itself. Nevertheless, if Kant's philosophy achieved one thing, it was a renewed optimism in philosophy, much in line with Enlightenment ideals concerning secular reason and the "maturing" of humanity as a whole. Reading through Kant's works, with their rigorous divisions and subdivisions, there is a sense of philosophy as an all-encompassing, totalizing endeavor. Philosophy, in its Kantian mode, knows everything — it even knows what it doesn't know.

That Kant suffered from depression may come as a surprise, especially given the ambition of his philosophy and the enthusiasm of his wide-ranging intellectual interests (his lecture courses cover everything from philosophical logic to anthropology to chemistry to predictions about the end of the world). But in

1798, in a letter to a colleague on the topic of "the art of prolonging human life," Kant briefly noted his own struggle with depression. The comments are rare for Kant, being personal and an admission of fallibility. In typical fashion, Kant first defines depression as "the weakness of abandoning oneself despondently to general morbid feelings that have no definite object (and so making no attempt to master them by reason)."[157] A thought without an object is a troubling thing in Kant's philosophy; it can lead to an endless train of fickle notions without any ground, similar to the speculative debates in Kant's time over the existence of God, the origin of the universe, or the existence of a soul. Reason deployed for no reason — or at least, for no good reason. At issue for Kant is not just the use of reason against faith or the imagination, but the instrumental use of reason — reason mastering itself, including its own limitations. This was as much the case for everyday thought as it was for philosophical thinking: "The opposite of the mind's self-mastery … is faint-hearted brooding about the ills that could befall one, and that one would not be able to withstand if they should come."[158]

When the coherence of reason is threatened, so is philosophy. Or rather, so is the philosopher. A little later on, Kant offers this strange confession: "I myself have a natural disposition to hypochondria because of my flat and narrow chest, which leaves little room for the movement of the heart and lungs; and in my earlier years this disposition made me almost weary of life."[159]

Elsewhere Kant drops hints of this melancholic tendency. In the *Critique of Judgement*, for instance, he allows that "misanthropy" too has the character of the sublime:

> Falsehood, ingratitude, injustice, the childishness in ends that we ourselves hold to be important and great, in the pursuit of which people do every conceivable evil to each other, so contradict the idea of what they could be if they wanted to, and are so opposed to the lively wish to take a better view of them that, in order not to hate them, since

> one cannot love them, doing without all social joys seems to be only a small sacrifice.[160]

But Kant does not give in so easily to this "pathology" of thought. Philosophy is the panacea. Kant distinguishes "philosophizing" from "philosophy," though both play a therapeutic role in reason's self-mastery. Philosophizing, for Kant, "does not involve being a philosopher," but instead "is a means of warding off many disagreeable feelings and, besides, a stimulant to the mind that introduces an interest into its occupations."[161] At another level, there is "philosophy" proper, "whose interest is the entire final end of reason," and which "brings with it a feeling of power which can well compensate to some degree for the physical weaknesses of old age by a rational estimation of life's value."[162]

This is all fine, from the critical distance of philosophical self-mastery. But things get a little more complicated when Kant discusses depression (in the same essay he also discusses boredom, diet, and sleep). What Kant doesn't consider is that reason might actually be connected to depression, rather than stand as its opposite. What if depression — reason's failure to achieve self-mastery — is not the failure of reason but instead the result of reason? What if human reason works "too well," and brings us to conclusions that are anathema to the self-interested existence of human beings? What we would have is something like a "cold rationalism," shoring up the anthropocentric conceits of the philosophical endeavor, showing us an anonymous, faceless world impervious to our hopes and desires. And, in spite of Kant's lifelong dedication to philosophy and the Enlightenment project, in several of his writings he allows himself to give voice to this cold rationalism. In his essay on Leibniz's optimism he questions the rationale of an all-knowing God that is at once beneficent towards humanity but also allows human beings to destroy each other.[163] And in his essay "The End of All Things" Kant not only questions humanity's dominion over the world, but he also questions our presumption to know that — and if — the world will end at all: "Why do human beings expect an end to the world at all? And if this is conceded to them, why must it be a terrible end?"[164]

The implication here is that reason and the "rational estimation of life's value" may not have our own best interests in mind, and the self-mastery of reason may not coincide with the self-mastery of human beings (or, indeed, of the species as a whole). Philosophical reason taken to these lengths would not only make philosophy improbable (for how could there be philosophy without philosophers?), but also impractical (and what would be the use of such a "depressive reason"?). What Kant refers to as depression is simply this stark realization: that thought is only incidentally human. It would take a later generation of philosophers to derive the conclusion of this: thought thinks us, not the reverse.

Legend has it that Kant's final word on his deathbed was "enough" (*genug*).[165] The aged peripatetic philosopher of Königsberg let out a word that was also a sigh, and depressive reason seems to have had the final say.[166]

*

Nietzsche's Laughter. Nothing is more indicative of human culture than the obsessiveness with which it has depicted its own planet. When the Earth was decentered from the universe by Copernican astronomy, this was more than compensated for by the innumerable images of Earth produced over the years by artists and scientists alike. Earth was, and is, in many ways, still at the center of things. In this sense, the first televised images of the Earth can no doubt be regarded as the pinnacle of a species solipsism, one that has its underside in the many computerized film images of a disaster-worn, zombie-ridden, apocalyptic landscape. We are so fixated on Earth — that is, on ourselves — that we would rather have a ruined Earth than no Earth at all.

Astronauts often refer to their first view of Earth as the "overview effect," suggesting that the view of Earth from space produces a shift in consciousness — that we as human beings are not separate from the planet on which we live. The general message is that of sublime wonder and unity: national boundaries disappear, and over its surface the planet reveals strange, luminous patterns of color, cloud, and light (otherwise known as cities, smog, and the electrical grid). Thanks to digital technology the overview effect can now be an everyday experience.

However, in its appeal for a planetary consciousness, the overview effect tends to reveal something different — the indifference of the planet vis-à-vis our repeated attempts to render it meaningful. It is in this context that one is reminded of Nietzsche's oft-quoted passage from his essay "On Truth and Lie in an Extra-Moral Sense":

> In some remote corner of the universe, poured out and glittering in innumerable solar systems, there once was a star on which clever animals invented knowledge. That was the haughtiest and most mendacious minute of "world history" — yet only a minute. After nature had drawn a few breaths the star grew cold, and the clever animals had to die.[167]

Here Nietzsche gives us a different take on the "overview effect." In this version, we have never been one with the planet, nor does the planet require our cleverness and technical ingenuity to save it — from ourselves. It is tempting to imagine Nietzsche himself as an astronaut, going up into space, turning back and seeing Earth, and noticing the contrast between the indifferent, glittering planet and the equal indifference of the busy and clever animals on its surface. No doubt Nietzsche's notorious ill health would mean that he would fail the astronaut training. And so he would settle for writing it down.

But Nietzsche's capacity for undermining the human is more prescient now than ever. On the one hand, we who are still on the Earth's surface cannot escape an awareness of the impact of climate change, beset as we are by disasters that increasingly refuse the distinction between the natural and human-made. On the other hand, the process of recuperating the planet for us as human beings continues unabated. Whether we can "save" the planet is one question — whether the planet needs saving is another.

Nietzsche encapsulated this dilemma in the title of his third published book: *Human, All Too Human*, a book that captures the polyphony of voices in Nietzsche's writing — by turns sarcastic, enthusiastic, naive, spiteful, meditative, joyful.[168] For example, in the second volume of *Human, All Too Human*, Nietzsche gives us yet another, much more sardonic variant on the overview effect that deserves to be quoted in full:

> There would have to be creatures of more spirit than human beings, simply in order to savor the humor that lies in humans seeing themselves as the purpose of the whole existing world and in humanity being seriously satisfied only with the prospect of a world-mission. If a god did create the world, he created humans as *god's apes*, as a continual cause for amusement in his all-too-lengthy eternity … Our uniqueness in the world! alas, it is too improbable a thing! The astronomers, who sometimes really are granted a field of vision detached from the earth, intimate that the drop of *life* in the world is without significance for the total character of the immense ocean of becoming and passing away … The ant in the forest perhaps imagines just as strongly that it is the goal and purpose for the existence of the forest when we in our imagination tie the downfall of humanity almost involuntarily to the downfall of the earth…[169]

As Nietzsche jibes, the strange endeavor of human thinking tends to eclipse the world, until we become so philosophically solipsistic that even the nonhuman begins to look a lot like the human. Nietzsche caps off his rant with the following: "Even the most dispassionate astronomer can himself scarcely feel the earth without life in any other way than as the gleaming and floating gravesite of humanity."[170]

But Nietzsche's phrase *Menschliches, Allzumenschliches* has several meanings. It evokes a sense of disappointment — the "all too human" as less than human, as the failure to live up to the various standards, criteria, and values that we associate with being human. And, as Nietzsche repeatedly points out in his book, this itself has become a hallmark of the human. But the phrase also evokes a more critical sense of failing to challenge our most basic and habitual ways of thinking and living — including the questioning of those same criteria and values that demarcate the human from the nonhuman.

At the same time, Nietzsche's invectives against humanity are outstripped only by his refusal to dispense with the term "human," much less imagine a romantic, transcendent realm "beyond" the human (itself regarded as the height of humanist thinking). Nietzsche repeatedly affirms the human, all too human, even as he rails against it. Human beings are all too human not only because we fail to live up to the human, but because we are merely human, only human, and human in a way that refuses both the divine *fiat* of science as well as the natural history of religion's chosen peoples. This is Nietzsche's own, tragicomic brand of humanism: *that there is nothing special about the human.*

When Nietzsche began writing *Human, All Too Human* around 1876, many changes were afoot — the 32-year-old philologist was forced to retire from his teaching post at the University of Basel due to a series of health issues, which included stomach problems, arthritis, migraines, nausea, vomiting, and rapidly deteriorating eyesight. He had also alienated himself from Wagner and his cultist circle, opting instead for the life of an itinerant scholar. Deciding to relocate to a better climate, he traveled to Sorrento, where he wrote the bulk of the first volume of *Human, All Too Human.* 1878 saw the publication of *Human, All Too Human: A Book for Free Spirits,* comprising some 600 aphorisms. Of the 1000 copies printed, only 120 sold.[171] The following year another four hundred aphorisms would be published with the title *Assorted Opinions and Maxims,* and the year after that, another 350 aphorisms with the title *The Wanderer and His Shadow.* Writing in *Ecce Homo* some twelve years after its initial publication, Nietzsche would characterize the book as "the monument of a crisis" and a "spiritual cure."

The change in lifestyle was echoed in Nietzsche's writing style as well. While in Sorrento, Nietzsche began writing in the brief, aphoristic style that would characterize some of his best-known works. But Nietzsche's aphorisms are not of a single mold, and his turn to the short form manifests itself in different ways, from mini-essays in the vein of Montaigne to taut maxims reminiscent of La Rochefoucauld. We also get dialogues, parables, poetry, even jokes. Indeed, *Human, All Too Human* not only reflects Nietzsche's experiment with style, but with reading as well. One anecdote has Nietzsche reading La Rochefoucauld's *Sentences et Maximes* on the train to Sorrento, but Nietzsche himself gives the detective in us a number of clues: in addition to scholarly works on Greek tragedy and philology, Nietzsche is reading Chamfort, Lichtenberg, Montaigne, Pascal, Vauvenargues, Voltaire (the dedicatee of the first edition of *Human, All Too Human*), and of course Schopenhauer, ever Nietzsche's "educator" and paragon of misanthropy.

Human, All Too Human is a master class in fragmentary writing, an exegesis on the virtues of the "incomplete thought," as resonant today in our era of the "overview effect" as it was in Nietzsche's era of Darwinism, the Industrial Revolution, and Spiritualism. It is no accident that such experiments in the incomplete thought take as their subject the problem of the human. The "overview effect" rendered as the "gleaming and floating gravesite of humanity."

Were Nietzsche writing today, he might very well regard the flora and fauna of contemporary philosophy (posthuman, transhuman, and so on) as so many varieties of this impulse to redeem the human through the back door, the side door, a trap door. Nietzsche himself was not immune to such impulses. For every misanthropic statement there is a statement of almost ecstatic, almost embarrassing affirmation, and for every impulse to imagine a renewed humanism there is the equal impulse to abandon it. An entry from Nietzsche's notebook in the fall of 1878 simply reads: "A novel. A volume of poetry. A history. A philology." An entry from the summer of 1879, perhaps during a bout of illness, reads: "All I lack is a homunculus." Another note, from the fall of 1879, reads: "I am thinking of having a long sleep." In his notebook, Nietzsche puts the phrase itself in quotes, but does not give a reference. What follows thereafter are the enigmatic and disturbing "madness letters" (*Wahnbriefe*), short, visionary missives signed only "Dionysius" or "The Crucified."

*

Horror of Philosophy. When Descartes stumbles across his demon, he discovers a thought that potentially undermines his entire philosophical project. A dilemma presents itself. If Descartes accepts the demon as actual, he has remained true to his method of skeptical doubt — but then his project is futile, since there is no ground for his thought, and nothing can be known for certain. If Descartes rejects the demon, by ignoring it or by glossing it over, he can carry on with his philosophy, but he has effectively abandoned the original impetus behind his philosophizing to begin with. And so philosophy becomes a kind of pantomime, the passing of time, wasted energy. Either way, philosophy has to confront the real possibility of its futility — and the equal possibility that one will never know for sure whether philosophy has been futile or not.

This is the crux of the "horror of philosophy," which we see in Descartes's demon, Kant's depression, and Nietzsche's wrestling with an indifferent cosmos. Put simply, it is the thought that undermines itself, in thought. Thought that stumbles over itself, at the edge of an abyss. The moment when the philosopher stumbles upon (Descartes), or cannot avoid (Kant), or actively confronts (Nietzsche) the very thing that undermines their philosophy. Being philosophers, they cannot simply switch tracks, and opt for poetry or mathematics. So they continue the labor of philosophy, all the while under the tenebrous, impersonal gaze of the horror of philosophy.

Far from dismissing philosophy, I would argue that this makes philosophy interesting. Particularly if one "misreads" philosophy in this way. If we were to adopt a method, it might be this: read works of philosophy as if they were works of horror. Of course, this is not to ignore the differences between, say, the narrative fiction of Poe or Lovecraft and the analytic, discursive language of Plato or Kant. But, at the same time, we know that many philosophers make use of literary approaches (Plato's theatrical dialogues being a prime example, not to mention Augustine's use of autobiography and Kierkegaard's use of the parable). And we know that many of the classics of the horror genre, from Poe to Lovecraft to the "new weird" in fiction, are largely idea-driven stories and make extensive use of the speculative mode in their narration or dialogue. One imagines Descartes, the accidental necromancer, making hesitant pacts with demons; one imagines Kant, swaying before the looming abyss of a Gothic maelstrom; one imagines Nietzsche, reveling in the *fin-de-siècle* extinction of the species and the attendant exhaustion of vampiric thought.

The proposition that governs this volume, *Starry Speculative Corpse*, is that something interesting happens when one takes philosophy not as the heroic feat of explaining everything, but as the confrontation with this thought that undermines thought, this philosophy of futility. Certainly, there is a bit of tongue-in-cheek in this method of reading philosophy as if it were horror; and, like all methods, it is not to be taken too seriously. But the focus in the sections that follow will be on those moments when philosophy reveals the thought that undermines it as philosophy, when the philosopher confronts this thought that cannot be thought.

Admittedly, the title of this series of books — *Horror of Philosophy* — is a bit odd; in one sense, it is something of a joke. Anyone who has, as a student, been forced to read a philosopher like Kant (or worse, Hegel), has no doubt felt a certain horror of philosophy. The sheer heft of a book like *The Critique of Pure Reason* is intimidating in and of itself, never mind the pages upon pages of jargon-filled divisions and subdivisions that make a mockery of any notion of "plain language" or "common sense." Much of philosophy today prides itself on instilling this intellectual horror in the reader — it is too serious to be taken lightly, too full of gravitas to joke about, replete with relevance, rigor, authority. But this is not just limited to the obscure corners of academic philosophy; our public intellectuals and pop philosophers also leverage this intimidation factor in the guise of the know-it-all, the self-help guru, the philosopher as the person authorized to say something about everything, obliging us to stroke our collective beards in rehearsed gestures of profundity. As a reader, my reaction is something out of a B-horror movie — I recoil in terror.

But if the phrase "horror of philosophy" is humorous in this sense, it is because it simply reverses the phrase "philosophy of horror," thereby pointing to a basic assumption we have about philosophy itself. A "philosophy of horror" implies a relation between philosophy and its object. Specifically, that philosophy will either explain its object (whereas in itself it is confusing), give meaning to its object (whereas in itself it lacks meaning), or render its object clear, apparent, and transparent (whereas in itself it is opaque). This applies to any formula of the type "philosophy of X" where X is philosophy's object, an object that stands apart from philosophy, and because of this, can be analyzed, unpacked, and dissected. Today we not only have the philosophy of religion, the philosophy of nature, the philosophy of mathematics, and political, ethical, and moral philosophy, but also the philosophy of cognition, the philosophy of technology — even the philosophy of … philosophy (that is, meta-philosophy).

Questions arise. Is philosophy's object always separate from it? What happens when the critical distance of philosophy collapses? Does philosophy really have the ability to explain everything? And if philosophy can't explain everything, how would we know this, and what language would be appropriate for expressing it? At what point does a philosophy of futility become indistinguishable from the futility of philosophy?

The three volumes of the series aim to take up these questions in different ways, using different forms borrowed from the history of philosophy. The first volume — *In the Dust of This Planet* — introduces general themes, particularly regarding the limits of the human and the idea of the "world-without-us." This volume — *Starry Speculative Corpse* — aims to read philosophy as if it were horror, while the third volume — *Tentacles Longer Than Night* — aims to do the reverse, to read works of the horror genre as if they were works of philosophy. What follows for content also follows for form. Whereas the first volume borrowed approaches from Medieval philosophy (the "question," the "lecture," the "disputation"), the second volume borrows from the format of the "prayer" in religion and mysticism, and the third volume likewise borrows from the spiritual exercise of the "meditation."

In what follows we will adopt this intentional "misreading" of philosophical and religious texts as if they were works in the supernatural horror genre. The form of the "prayer" (*oratio*) — particularly in the tradition of Christian mysticism — offers us a method for doing so. Theologians such as Eckhart, Hugh of St. Victor, and Bonaventure often distinguish between different kinds of prayer serving different purposes — for example, supplication, devotion, and intercession — but what these authors understood was that prayer was also a particular use of language, and by extension, a particular kind of thinking. In prayer, one not only attempts to communicate with the divine (or demonic) but also, in so doing, attempts to create a linguistic link between the natural and supernatural, the earthly and the divine — that is, between the human and something beyond the scope of human comprehension. Prayer in this sense is predicated on the idea of finding a language adequate to that which is beyond the human, however this is named. Prayer has something tentative, exploratory, and experimental about it, and this is perhaps the reason why many mystics — including Julian of Norwich, Angela of Foligno, Richard Rolle — took to writing in the form of prayer. Prayer is not only a religious performative gesture, it is also a genre of writing, one that allows more searching, more experimentation, than the conventional modes of philosophical argumentation.

2

PRAYERS FOR DARKNESS

Afraid of the Dark. Nearly everyone can relate, I suspect, to the feeling of being afraid of the dark. Sometimes we may be scared of some unnamable thing *in* the dark, while at other times we may simply be scared *of* the dark itself. As children, we sense this even in the comfort and security of our own rooms, where a dark hallway or open closet may necessitate a whole apparatus of night lights and other talismans, in order to ward off what H.P. Lovecraft once called the "whisperer in the darkness." It is no doubt for this reason that darkness saturates the horror genre, from the earliest examples of the Gothic novel and the Graveyard School, to the most recent examples of "screenlife" and "analog horror." We do not know what it is that dwells in the darkness, only that our not-knowing is a source of fear. In short, our fear of the dark seems as ambiguous as darkness itself.

Indeed, the everyday usage of the English term "darkness" carries with it a string of different connotations: There is an empirical connotation, in which darkness simply describes the optics or the physics of light. There is the moral or theological connotation of good vs. evil, light vs. dark forces (as when one crosses over to the perennial dark side). Closely tied to this is the epistemological connotation of knowledge vs. ignorance, the enlightened subject vs. the dark savage, that Copernican shift out of the Dark Ages into an epoch of mature Enlightenment.

However, all this points back to a philosophical dyad, and that is the distinction between presence and absence, being and non-being. Darkness is at once something negative, and yet, presenting itself as such, is also something positive; from a philosophical perspective, darkness exists, but its existence is always tenuous, the stuff of shadows, night, and tenebrous clouds. Darkness "is" but also "is not" — and, in a way, this "is not" also "is" darkness. Put simply, the concept of darkness invites us to think about the basic philosophical dilemma of a nothing that is a something.

Our aim in this chapter is simple: to trace this dual aspect of darkness, the darkness that "is" and that "is not." To do so, we will stray from the straight and narrow path of philosophy proper, into the adjacent territory of mysticism both premodern and postmodern. Here I need to ask patience of the reader. For many of us, the term "mysticism" is too over-coded in our culture, evoking religious cults, New Age fads, astrology readings, drug-fueled hallucinations, and existential tourism in India. The term is, to be sure, too broad to have any specific definition. In addition, even if one limits the term to a particular historical and religious tradition — say, Sufi mystical poetry or the Sōtō Zen tradition in Buddhism — what one finds is a Pandora's box of different sects, schools, and traditions of practice. The more one searches for "mysticism" in the concrete, the more abstract and amorphous it becomes.

In the first volume — *In the Dust of This Planet* — we attempted to introduce a comparative approach, juxtaposing, for instance, the philosophy of Kant and Schopenhauer to modern Buddhist thinkers such as Keiji Nishitani. But this just touches the surface of the complexities involved in a comparative approach. Here we will try another approach, which is to identify one tradition that has defined itself both as "mystical" and also as a tradition — that of medieval Christian mysticism. The title of one treatise — *The Mystical Theology* — probably written in the late fifth or early sixth century, establishes a tradition that thinks of the divine in terms of darkness, shadow, abyss, and clouds. Subsequent theologians and mystics refer back to this text, in effect contributing to this genealogy of darkness, up to the present day. While these thinkers never question their faith, their ideas also exist in an uneasy relationship to orthodox Christianity. In some cases — Meister Eckhart — their ideas invite accusations of heresy, while in other cases — Georges Bataille — their so-called mysticism is founded on a radical notion of atheism.

One need not be "mystical" or even religious to appreciate the ways in which these texts take up the philosophical problematic of darkness ("is" and "is not"). Of course, these texts need to be understood in the context of Christianity, particularly medieval Christianity, but they need not be totally determined by them. Our own reading — or rather, our misreading — of these mystical texts will be a bit "irreligious." We will focus on those moments when darkness comes to define a notion of the divine that is highly ambivalent, contradictory, and radically nonhuman — and remarkably resonant with the ambivalent, contradictory, and nonhuman aspects of darkness in the horror genre. As it turns out, to be afraid of the dark may have a mystical impulse at its core.

*

Tomb of Heaven. Our starting point — and we will be working backwards from here — is the work of French thinker Georges Bataille. From the time when Bataille, as a teenager, entered a Catholic seminary (which he subsequently abandoned), to his later experiments with the secret society Ácephale, to his last writings on religious art, one can trace the themes of mysticism, darkness, and negation running through nearly all of his writings. This is especially the case during the 1940s, when, in the depths of the bombed ruins of Paris, Bataille began work on what was to be his magnum opus, which he titled *La Somme Athéologique*, or the *Atheological Summa*. Given Bataille's dislike of systems, the project was doomed to remain incomplete. The parts that Bataille did publish include the books *Inner Experience* (1943/54), *Guilty* (1944), and *On Nietzsche* (1945). These are eclectic, heterogeneous writings; in addition to philosophical argument, they contain poetry, journal entries, autobiography, and fictional narrative. Jean-Luc Nancy calls them "anti-generic" texts, in that they resist categorization. I would suggest that, in their form and content, these texts borrow heavily from a mystical tradition that, in the West, extends back to the 5th century, and for which the motif of "darkness" is central.

But Bataille does not simply return to the old forms of mystical thought, either to revive religious faith, or to praise the wonders of scientific modernity. In Bataille's hands, the concept of darkness denotes not just ignorance or the lack of knowledge, but the blind spot of knowledge, the blind spot that in fact inhabits *all* knowledge, the absolute limit that creeps beneath the surface of every relative limit.

There are numerous moments when Bataille resorts to the language of darkness to describe what appear to be extreme experiential states, states akin to the spiritual crises of mysticism:

> …how even for a moment can I dismiss this unknowing (*ignorance*), a feeling of having lost my way in some underground tunnel? To me this world, the planet, the starry sky, are just a grave (I don't know if I'm suffocating here, if I'm crying or becoming some kind of incomprehensible sun). Even war can't light up a darkness (*une nuit*) that is this total.[173]

In passages like this, experience seems to fail to give testimony to the limit that Bataille describes — even the heavens are, for him, a tomb, enclosing everything in the enigmatic abyss of incomprehensibility. It is not so much that language fails to adequately describe experience, but that experience fails to adequately circumscribe the human. The boundaries of the human become fuzzy and obscure, at once tomb-like and yet planetary and even cosmic.

We can trace this motif of darkness in a few selected mystical texts. These texts arguably form a tradition within mystical discourse, a "darkness-mysticism." The choices here are, of course, highly selective, and this in no way meant as a comprehensive survey. Each example puts forth a concept of *negation* that is tied in some way to the motif of *darkness* — though darkness is not always negative for each of these thinkers. Extending Bataille's ideas, one of the guiding questions is whether it is possible to have a mysticism without God, a negative mysticism, or, really, a mysticism of the unhuman.

*

Divine Darkness (Dionysius the Areopagite). Our next stop is an author about whom almost nothing is known — Dionysius the Areopagite, whose short and influential treatise *The Mystical Theology* was produced sometime in the early 6th century. This text, only five pages long, has cast a shadow over mystical writing in the West; it was translated into Latin in the early 9th century, and by the 13th century was a textbook of theology at the University of Paris. Nearly every mystical thinker makes some reference to Dionysius, though the only thing we are sure of is that he is not the person he claims to be.

From the very first lines of the text Dionysius introduces a concept of darkness that is defined by its duplicity. He will often use phrases such as "brilliant darkness" to describe the encounter with the divine:

> By an undivided and absolute abandonment of yourself and everything, shedding all and freed from all, you will be uplifted to the ray of the divine darkness which is above everything that is.[174]

In a complex and enigmatic phrase, the author repeatedly asks how we can know the "ray of divine darkness" (Θειου σκοτους ακτινα).

Dionysius presumes a concept of darkness that is neither simply privative nor oppositional. In addition, this move — describing the divine in terms of darkness — already sets Dionysius apart from other mystical thinkers of his time, where the encounter with the divine is often described in the more familiar terms of light, illumination, or radiation.

Coupled with this concept of darkness is a concept of negation. In *The Mystical Theology* Dionysius outlines two paths of mystical knowledge: an affirmative path, or the *via affirmativa*, and a negative path, or the *via negativa*. In the former one arrives at knowledge of the divine through successive affirmations, as when one describes individual human acts as "good" but the divine as "the Good" or "Goodness" in itself. The latter approach is the opposite, arriving at the divine through successive negations, as when one describes the divine as that which is not created or not existing in time. For Dionysius it is this second path, the *via negativa*, that yields the most profound results, and this is based on the author's metaphysical commitment to a concept of the divine that is absolutely inaccessible. As he notes, "[s]ince the Divine is the Cause of all beings, we should posit and ascribe to it all the affirmations we make in regard to beings, and, more appropriately, we should negate all these affirmations, since it surpasses all being."[175]

Dionysius gives us a concept of darkness that is characterized by a duplicity (at once absence and presence), and along with that, a concept of negation that involves the "negation of affirmations." When we put these two together, what we get is a dialectics of darkness that, in *The Mystical Theology*, moves through stages. An example of this comes from a passage where Dionysius is discussing Moses's ascent of Mount Sinai, a passage that has become something of a touchstone for mystical texts. There Dionysius begins by describing Moses's initial mystical experience as "seeing many lights, pure and with rays streaming abundantly." Then, at the summit of the mountain, a different type of experience occurs:

> ...then he [Moses] breaks free of them, away from what sees and is seen, and he plunges into the truly mysterious darkness of unknowing. Here, renouncing all that the mind may conceive, wrapped entirely in the intangible and the invisible, he belongs completely to that which is beyond everything. Here, being neither oneself nor someone else, one is supremely united to the completely unknown by an inactivity of all knowledge, and knows beyond the mind by knowing nothing.[176]

Through a successive stripping away of attributes, through the negation of affirmation, Dionysius puts forth a concept of darkness that is, first, an anti-empirical one (in that one moves away from what is seen and sensed), and then an anti-idealist one (in that one moves away from what can be conceptualized and thought), before arriving at a stage the author can only describe as "unknowing."

With Dionysius, we see a dialectics of darkness that moves from a concept of darkness as privative, to a concept of darkness as oppositional, and finally to a concept of darkness as superlative, and it is in the last type of darkness — a darkness that Dionysius claims is beyond privation or opposition — that we see darkness as a superlative or "divine darkness." This brings one up against a certain limit, not just of language, but of thought as well:

> The fact is that the more we take flight upward, the more our words are confined to the ideas we are capable of forming; so that now as we plunge into that darkness which is beyond intellect, we shall find ourselves not simply running short of words but actually speechless and unknowing.[177]

As Vladimir Lossky puts it in his classic study of Dionysius, "the apophatic way, or mystical theology ... has for its object God, in so far as He is absolutely incomprehensible."[178]

In spite of the fact that Dionysius brings us to the point of silence, where there is nothing to say, this has obviously not had the effect of silencing mystical discourse. In fact, the opposite is the case. A thinker like Meister Eckhart will take Dionysius's notion that there is nothing to say quite literally — as in, "nothing" or "nothingness" is the only thing that there is to speak of, when one speaks of the divine.

*

The Dark God (Meister Eckhart). Working in both the vernacular German as well as the scholastic Latin, writing both popular sermons as well as academic treatises, tried for heresy and claimed by many modern scholars as a Western Buddhist, Eckhart's output is emblematic of the flourishing of mystical thought in late 13th- and early 14th-century Germany.

Eckhart's notion of darkness is as compounded as that of Dionysius. In his sermons, Eckhart often discusses the difference between God and the Godhead (*Gottheit*). If God is the divine as it appears to us as human beings, then the Godhead would be that part of God that does not appear to us, and that, therefore, we can never know or experience. Eckhart uses the motifs of light and darkness in a fairly conventional manner, as in this passage: "If God is to shine directly in you, your natural light cannot help toward this end. Instead, it must become pure nothing and go out of itself altogether, and *then* God can shine in."[179]

We should note here that Eckhart's God is the God of the philosophers — non-anthropomorphic, abstract, and metaphysical. If the knowledge of the divine is light, then the knowledge of the senses can only obscure and throw one into darkness. But this sensory darkness gives way to another, more mystical darkness, whereby the self is emptied and negated. For Eckhart, it is only by becoming nothing that one is able to receive the knowledge of divine light. As he notes, "you cannot do better than to place yourself in darkness and in unknowing." Paradoxically, one must become absolutely dark, in order to become light:

> [N]o creaturely skill, nor your own wisdom, nor all your knowledge can enable you to know God divinely. For you to know God in God's way, your knowing must become a pure unknowing, and a forgetting of yourself and all creatures.[180]

But the problem is that the divine, in Eckhart's formulation, cannot really be parceled out in this manner, for the divine is a flowing and unbroken continuity, not a Janus-faced God. Thus God is not one part seen, and one part unseen; God is the manifestation of the divine to us that radiates or emanates from the Godhead as its source. In this more Neoplatonic interpretation, God emerges from the Godhead. The problem here, of course, is that this implies that God is in fact created from the Godhead, which not only goes against the very definition of the divine, but also puts one in the Aristotelian dilemma of "turtles all the way down."

Be that as it may, it is important to Eckhart to highlight these two dimensions to the divine — one side as outpouring manifestation, and one side as a kind of primordial darkness or un-manifestation. Eckhart grapples with this problem in the following cryptic statement:

> The final end of being is the darkness or nescience of the hidden Godhead whose light illumines it, but this darkness comprehends it not.[181]

This passage is complicated, even frustrating. It is also emblematic of Eckhart's polyvalent usage of the term "darkness." In the first part of the sentence, darkness appears to describe the Godhead, which is "dark" because it is "hidden" or inaccessible to us as human beings. All that remains of this inaccessible Godhead is its hiddenness, and thus we gain a residual access to this inaccessibility, a residual knowledge of our inability to know, encapsulated in Eckhart's phrase "darkness or nescience."

But is this darkness mystical knowledge? That is, does the darkness lead one to what Dionysius calls "unknowing"? On the one hand it does, because this darkness is described by Eckhart as the final end and goal of all being. Thus the culmination of all being is darkness, or the enigmatic knowledge of that which can never be known.

On the other hand, in the second part of the sentence, Eckhart adds that this hidden, "dark" Godhead is also radiating light that illuminates the human subject — that same subject that can only know the impossibility of knowing. There seems to be a disconnect here, a sort of mystical miscommunication, as the Godhead radiates light, but the human only receives darkness. Here "darkness" is not the mystical unknowing described by Dionysius, but the failure of knowledge — "the darkness comprehends it not."

It seems, then, that Eckhart's notion of darkness is a highly conciliatory one. Unable to fully comprehend the divine light in itself, we as humans are stuck with this inability. Indeed, we are abandoned to this inability, a dark knowing that follows in the Dionysian tradition of unknowing — the human knowing the absolute limit of all human knowing.

*

A Cry Out to Darkness (Angela of Foligno). The next stop in our itinerary is Angela of Foligno, a 13th century mystic whose major work, *The Memorial*, was written as dictation by a Franciscan monk known as "Brother Arnaldo," who became Angela's confessor. Angela is, along with Mechthild of Magdeburg, Hadewijch, and Marguerite Porete, one of the central female figures in the history of Christian mysticism.[182] For the better part of her life, she lived a respectable middle-class existence; born in the Italian town of Foligno, just outside of Assisi, she marries young, has several children, and manages a household. Around her thirty-seventh year, however, she enters a period of intense spiritual crisis. It leads her to seek the spiritual counsel of a local Franciscan monk and to undergo a lengthy period of penance. Intelligent, passionate, and independent, she vows to transform her life, renouncing her material possessions, her social status, and her family life. Eventually she gives away all her belongings, literally stripping herself bare before the crucified body of Christ. She undertakes an intense practice of prayer, weeping and mortifying her own flesh. On a pilgrimage to Assisi with Brother Arnaldo in the fall of 1291, she experiences several visions, which so fill her with the divine that, when the visions depart, she shrieks and collapses — in her own words, her joints become dislocated, the flesh torn from her body, and she screams continually for death to take her. Arnaldo, somewhat dismayed by the episode, is at first embarrassed, and then confused. Is Angela possessed by an evil spirit, or has she really received divine visions? Arnaldo proposes that Angela tell him everything that has happened, and over the next few years, from 1292 to 1296, the still-perplexed monk writes down Angela's own words, as well as his own commentary. The resultant text — *The Memorial* — outlines a mystical itinerary that includes nineteen stages, with seven supplementary stages, beginning with Angela's conversion and concluding with a fascinating discussion of the divine in terms of its darkness.[183]

Angela's version of divine darkness, though it bears resemblance to Dionysius and Eckhart, is also remarkably different. Her visions are more intense and more affective, and they also convey an ecstatic joy often coupled with images of mortality, corporeal decay, and death. Her visions emphasize the material aspect of mysticism in images that appear to the modern reader as starkly morbid and grotesque. In one vision, Angela, deep in prayer, is invited by Christ on the cross to drink the blood from his wounds: "I saw and drank the blood, which was freshly flowing from his side ... And at this I began to experience a great joy."[184] Another vision, again while in prayer, has Angela literally flying into the open wound of the crucified Christ: "...it seems to my soul that it enters Christ's side, and this is a source of great joy and delight."[185] In yet another vision, Angela finds herself in the tomb with Christ, in a kind of necrophiliac embrace: "She [Angela] said she had first of all kissed Christ's breast — and saw that he lay dead, with his eyes closed — then she kissed his mouth, from which, she added, a delightful fragrance emanated ... Her joy was immense and indescribable."[186]

Grotesque as they seem, such images participate in a broader iconography of Christ's body during the Passion, and modern scholars have detected allusions in *The Memorial* to everything from Dante to the *Song of Songs*. It is this material mysticism that works its way into Angela's comments on the divine darkness. There are, of course, passages in which Angela talks about "darkness" in a privative sense, and associates it with human finitude, desire, and temptation. For instance, in the Sixth Supplementary Step, Angela describes all the various doubts and challenges to her faith as "this most horrible darkness":

> When I am in this most horrible darkness caused by demons it seems to me that there is nothing I can hope for ... When I am in that darkness I think I would prefer to be burned than to suffer such afflictions. I even cry out for death to come in whatever form God would grant it.[187]

Importantly, the darkness that Angela here describes is not limited to those moments of temptation, vice, or wrongdoing. That is, it is not just a moral darkness, in which darkness is aligned with "evil" acts and impure thoughts. Angela concedes that it is part and parcel of being a mortal creature, to exist in a body that is "in such pain and so weary of life that it is ready to give itself up." This is a metaphysical darkness, the suffering of the body's cadaverous facticity, of a body so easily and effortlessly reduced to mere matter. This is a darkness only resolved by death.

This leads Angela — in the Seventh and final Supplementary Step — to comment on another type of darkness. This time darkness is not privative, not the absence or the taking away of something. More in line with the Dionysian tradition, darkness is here equivalent to a non-anthropomorphic notion of the divine:

> Afterwards I saw him [God] in a darkness, and in a darkness precisely because the good that he is, is far too great to be conceived or understood … And in this most efficacious good seen in this darkness now resides my most firm hope, one in which I am totally recollected and secure.[188]

Angela's tone is markedly different — more confident, more self-assured, more steadfast in her faith. And yet what she is expressing is something enigmatic, something that she herself places at the limits of language, thought, and the body. This is not just the darkness of the decaying cadaver, of something reduced to nothing, but rather the darkness of the divine, of something that is "nothing" because it so far surpasses anything that can be thought or imagined. If Angela is working in this "darkness mysticism" tradition, it is one that often revolves around apophatic anatomies, the body at once elemental light and chthonic decomposition.

Importantly, Angela qualifies her visions by noting that the divine is "dark" not only because it surpasses human comprehension, but because in so doing it renders the human insignificant. In the divine darkness one enters the divine abyss of oblivion, in which the human being annihilates itself in an ambiguous and yet ecstatic joy: "When I am in that darkness I do not remember anything about anything human, or the God-man, or anything which has a form. Nevertheless, I see all and I see nothing."[189]

*

Dark Contemplation (The Cloud of Unknowing). Though little is known about the author of the 14th-century Middle English text *The Cloud of Unknowing*, it remains one of the most significant expressions of the darkness-mysticism tradition in the English language. According to scholars, *The Cloud* was written as a spiritual guidebook, though whether for monks or laypersons is unclear. But its focus on asceticism and contemplation is unmistakable, as is the influence of mystical theologians such as Dionysius the

Areopagite. *The Cloud* itself cites Dionysius's *The Mystical Theology*, and contains numerous parallels to Dionysian commentators such as John Scottus Eriugena, Thomas Gallus, and the theologians at the Abbot of St. Victor.

The Cloud is first and foremost a practical text. Throughout its chapters it emphasizes the idea of asceticism in its root meaning — as spiritual exercise — covering everything from the reading of scripture, to techniques for prayer, to bodily discipline and warning novices against "unseemly outward behavior." But it is also a highly expressive text, evoking abstract, difficult images of opacity, shadows, and of course darkness. *The Cloud* is an example of what scholars have referred to as "affective Dionysianism," a mixture of poetic and theological ruminations on the divine as inaccessible, incomprehensible, radically nonhuman. At its most intense, *The Cloud* advocates for a spiritual exercise that entails a successive stripping away of the self, so that it may be ready to encounter the impersonal, formless "cloud" of the divine.

At the center of *The Cloud* is a distinction between two types of "clouds," the "cloud of forgetting" and the "cloud of unknowing." Both are prerequisites for the spiritual life, and both involve mediations — one between the self and the world, and the other between the self and God:

> If ever you come to this cloud, and live and work in it as I bid you, just as this cloud of unknowing is above you, between you and your God, in the same way you must put beneath you a cloud of forgetting, between you and all the creatures that have ever been made.[190]

Here we have two forms of negation, resulting in two types of darkness. For the spiritual novice, one negates one's relationship to the world through refusal and renunciation, thereby establishing a cloud of forgetting. One may be *in* the world but not *of* the world. This in turn points to the divine, but here confronted as a limit: "For when you first begin to undertake it [the spiritual exercise], all that you find is a darkness, a sort of cloud of unknowing; you cannot tell what it is, except that you experience in your will a simple reaching out to God."[191] Having renounced the world, the novice is left in a kind of limbo, cast adrift without direction. And, importantly, there is no simple resolution in which one finds a new ground; the limbo is perpetual. It is this limbo, this darkness, that *The Cloud* refers to as the divine:

> Now when I call this exercise a darkness or a cloud, do not think that it is a cloud formed out of the vapors which float in the air, or a darkness such as you have in your house at night ... When I say "darkness," I mean a privation of knowing, just as whatever you do not know or have forgotten is dark to you, because you do not see it with your spiritual eyes.[192]

Taking up some of the themes found in Dionysius the Areopagite, *The Cloud* combines two types of darkness into one: the darkness of human knowledge ("darkness" as privative, as a limit between the known and unknown) and the darkness of God ("darkness" as superlative, as beyond what can possibly be known by human beings).

Much of this is readily in line with Dionysius and his commentators. But *The Cloud* takes a novel turn in linking this notion of darkness — as both the limit of thought, and that which is forever outside of thought — with contemplation. The Latin term *contemplatio* has a rich history in medieval mysticism, and *The Cloud* references it frequently. But *The Cloud* never states that the divine can be fully known, and neither does it simply opt for some ineffable, transcendent silence. How can the divine be thought, if it is by definition outside of thought? In a striking passage, *The Cloud* names this conundrum "contemplation":

> But now you put to me a question and say, "How might I think of him in himself, and what is he?" And to this I can

> only answer thus: "I have no idea." For with your question you have brought me into that same darkness, into that same cloud of unknowing where I would you were yourself ... Therefore, it is my wish to leave everything that I can think of and choose for my love the thing that I cannot think.[193]

I love what I cannot think. Perhaps there is no better formulation for the philosophical impulse in these mystical texts. Thought questions, develops, and is led to a point where thought can no longer continue without negating itself. I love what I cannot think. Perhaps this is also an accurate formulation of the "horror of philosophy."

*

The Dark Night (John of the Cross). This preoccupation with the limit of the human finds its most dramatic manifestation in John of the Cross, the 16th-century Spanish Carmelite monk and mystic, whose collaboration with Theresa of Avila and subsequent imprisonment has become the stuff of hagiography.

John is mostly known for his poem "The Dark Night of the Soul," along with its accompanying commentary. Like Dionysius, John thinks of the divine in terms of darkness and negation, resulting in a mystical unknowing of the divine in its inaccessibility. Like Eckhart, John focuses on the darkening and emptying of the human subject as it attempts to comprehend the divine. But John also places a premium on experience — and in particular on the *limits* of experience. Much of this comes from John's more streamlined typology, which distinguishes between two types of darkness:

> This night, which as we say is contemplation, causes two kinds of darkness or purgation in spiritual persons ... Hence one night of purgation will be sensory, by which the senses are purged and accommodated to the spirit; and the other night or purgation will be spiritual, by which the spirit is

> purged and denuded as well as accommodated and prepared for union with God through love.[194]

Here John condenses Eckhart's typology into a kind of pre-Cartesian dualism of flesh and spirit, at once metaphysical and erotic. Both flesh and spirit must be negated in order to comprehend a third type of darkness that John never directly names. As with Eckhart, the sensory and spiritual annihilation hints at an anti-empirical and anti-idealist thread in the concept of darkness. The darkness of the senses is a pretext to the darkness of the soul, but even this is negated — in John's language, it is "purged" or "emptied" — which then leads to the limit that both Dionysius and Eckhart describe as divine darkness.

Dereliction, abandonment, and abjection are the order of the day in John's writings. As he notes, "the dark night with its aridities and voids is the means to the knowledge of God and self."[195] But we risk a misunderstanding if we read John as advocating a direct, human experience of the divine. For John, mystical experience does not reaffirm or bolster the human subject, quite the opposite. Mystical experience is precisely that which cannot be experienced — the *impossibility* of experience. This point is made more clearly when John hints at a third type of darkness that lies beyond the darkness of the senses or the soul:

> ...the clearer and more obvious divine things are in themselves, the darker and more hidden they are to the soul naturally ... Hence when the divine light of contemplation strikes souls not yet entirely illumined, it causes spiritual darkness, for it not only surpasses them but also deprives and darkens their act of understanding. This is why St. Dionysius and other mystical theologians call this infused contemplation a ray of darkness.[196]

Utilizing Dionysius's phrase "divine darkness," John describes a process whereby both senses and soul are muted, submerged, and finally emptied altogether. Instead of the experience of darkness, what John describes is more like the darkness of experience.

*

Excess of Darkness (Georges Bataille). John's evocation of the dark night and the impossibility of its experience brings us back to the work of Bataille. As we've noted, Bataille's lifelong engagement with mysticism manifested itself in a range of ways: his writing and research, his participation in collective ritual, and his practice of yoga and meditation undertaken during bouts of chronic illness. We also know that Bataille worked for the better part of his career as a librarian at the Bibliothèque Nationale in Paris, where he specialized in medieval manuscripts. He also made use of the library for his own research. Thanks to the bibliomania of Bataille's editors, the final volume of Bataille's complete works contains a catalog of nearly every book he requested from the library. There we see that, during the time in which he was working on the *Atheological Summa*, Bataille is reading Dionysius, Eckhart, Angela of Foligno, John of the Cross, and Theresa of Avila, among many others. All of these influences come together in the opening pages of Bataille's book *Inner Experience*:

> I read in Denys l'Aréopagite: "Those who by an inward cessation of all intellectual functioning enter into an intimate union with ineffable light … only speak of God by negation" … So is it from the moment that it is experience and not presupposition which reveals (to such an extent that, in the eyes of the latter, light is "a ray of darkness"; he would go so far as to say, in the tradition of Eckhart: "God is Nothingness"). But positive theology — founded on the revelation of the scriptures — is not in accord with this negative experience … In the same way, I hold the apprehension of God … to be an obstacle in the movement which carries us to the more obscure apprehension of

> *unknowing* (*l'inconnu*): of a presence which is no longer in any way distinct from an absence.[197]

Bataille's mystical writings are not simply a ventriloquizing of earlier mystical authors, and neither are they about the existentialist crisis of the modern subject; for Bataille this type of darkness runs the gamut from the most basic forms of "base materialism" and inorganic matter, to the planetary and even cosmic cycles of production, accumulation, and expenditure. That is, this darkness-mysticism has to be placed in the context of Bataille's own version of political economy, a nonhuman, "general economy" based on excess and expenditure. In the same way that divine darkness is in excess of the individuated human being, so is there a divine darkness that is in excess of the world — at least the world that we as human beings construct for ourselves and fashion in our image. Divine darkness is precisely this negative movement that cuts across self and world, the human and the nonhuman — not by virtue of a bountiful, vitalistic life-force, but by way of an emptying and a darkening. In an almost Lovecraftian vein, Bataille notes that, "beyond our immediate ends, humanity's activity in fact pursues the useless and infinite fulfillment of the universe."[198]

Bataille often expresses this sense of cosmic darkness in his poetry. But for Bataille poetry is far from being the romantic expression of a brooding subjectivity — he even titles one of his books *Hatred of Poetry* (*Haine de la poèsie*). Instead, poetry for Bataille is related to its ancient roots as *poiesis*, as an anonymous, impersonal producing or creating. The following, for instance, is from Bataille's poem "L'Archangélique":

> I am the dead man
> the blind man
> the shadow without air
>
> like rivers in the sea

sound and light
lose themselves in me without end

I am the father
and the tomb
of the sky

the excess of darkness
is the flash of a star
the cold of the tomb is a die

death rolls the die
and the bottom of the heavens rejoice
the night that falls inside me[199]

Far from the baroque, purple prose of the Surrealists, Bataille's poetry displays the sort of minimalism one also finds in John of the Cross. Bataille's concept of darkness maximizes the contradictions already found in Dionysius. The "I" of the poem immediately dissolves into a kind of planetary, climatological stuff, just as the anonymous, base materialism of the world courses through and is inseparable from the "I". But this is no hippie love-in. For Bataille, as for Dionysius, Eckhart, and John of the Cross, all roads of the *via negativa* lead to darkness, an absolute limit to the human capacity to know itself and the world, a limit Bataille nicely encapsulates in the phrase, "the excess of darkness."

This is where Bataille parts ways with other mystical thinkers we've mentioned thus far. Following Nietzsche's proclamation concerning the death of God, it would seem that there can no longer be any mysticism, for traditional, institutional religion has — so the argument goes — ceased to have the pervasive influence that it once had. Though profoundly influenced by Nietzsche, Bataille disputes this, opting instead for a mysticism without God, or a mysticism that negates God — but also a mysticism without the human. Bataille's mysticism is no revived humanism — far from it. What remains in Bataille's darkness-mysticism is neither human nor divine, but simply darkness itself. The shift from the earlier mystics to Bataille is akin to the shift from the horror of something in the dark, to the horror of darkness itself. As Bataille notes, in one of his last works: "What I suddenly saw, and what imprisoned me in anguish — but which at the same time delivered me from it — was the identity of these perfect contraries, divine ecstasy and its opposite, extreme horror."[200]

If, for Bataille, darkness is related to mysticism, then it would have to be a darkness that, paradoxically, cannot be thought as such. This type of darkness is not simply privation or opposition, but a darkness that lies at the horizon of the human itself, conveyed in Bataille's oblique prose:

> I imagine that it is as in vision, which is rendered sharp in darkness by the dilation of a pupil. Here darkness (*l'obscurité*) is not the absence of light (or of sound) but absorption into the outside (*dehors*).[201]

This "outside" that Bataille evokes is not some utopic other place, much less a transcendent beyond — that is, this darkness that is "outside" is not "above" or "beyond." It is a limit that is coextensive with the human. And this is why Bataille's unfinished project is interesting. It does not attempt to pass beyond the human, whether we call it the posthuman or the transhuman. It also does not attempt to undermine the human, be it in terms of the contemporary mania for "objects," "actants," or "technics." It is perhaps nearer to Nietzsche's call to "pass over" the human, though even this is too optimistic, too messianic, for Bataille. In borrowing from the darkness-mystical tradition, Bataille's writing opts to darken the human, to undo the human by paradoxically revealing the shadows at its core, to move not towards a renewed knowledge of the human, but towards something we can only call an unknowing of the human, or really, the *unhuman*. Bataille's mysticism, then, is a mysticism of the limits of the human, and this divine darkness would be something like a mysticism of the unhuman.

*

An Exegesis on Divine Darkness. In thinking about darkness (that which "is" and "is not"), we see mystical thinkers connecting a logic (in particular, a logic of negation) with a poetics (a poetics of darkness, shadow, abyss). With Dionysius the Areopagite the logic of the *via negativa* is tied to his notion of divine darkness (Θειου σκοτους ακτινα). With Meister Eckhart, a logic of negating negations (*negatio negationis*) is tied to the darkness (*finsternis*) of the Godhead, something echoed in the apophatic anatomies of Angela of Foligno, and *The Cloud of Unknowing*'s emphasis on the contemplation of that which cannot be thought. In John of the Cross, the negation of all possible experience is tied to this central poetic motif of the dark night (*la noche oscura*). And finally, with Bataille, a logic of excess leads to what he terms the excess of darkness (*l'excès des ténèbres*). Even though each of these thinkers uses different terms, we might say that there are three basic modes of darkness in this mystical tradition: a dialectical darkness, a superlative darkness, and a divine darkness.

The first mode — dialectical darkness — entails a concept of darkness that is inseparable from an opposing term. Dialectical darkness is therefore structured around the dyad of dark/light, which finds its avatars in the epistemological dyad of knowledge/ignorance, the metaphysical dyad of presence/absence, and the theological dyad of gift/privation. Dialectical darkness always subsumes darkness within its opposing term, and in this sense, darkness is always subordinate to something that opposes darkness. With dialectical darkness, the movement is from a negative to an affirmative experience of the divine, from the absence of any experience at all to a fully present experience. At the same time, this affirmative experience comes at the cost of a surreptitious negation: a "vision" (*visio*) that is also blindness, an ecstasy (*ecstasis*) or standing outside oneself that displaces the subject, and a rapture (*raptus*) in which the self is snatched away into a liminal otherness. We should note that the recuperative power of dialectical darkness is such that it absorbs all attempts to think darkness — even those that claim to pass beyond oppositions. Dialectical darkness is at once the ground of, and the obstacle for, any concept of darkness.

This management of boundaries shifts a bit when we move to superlative darkness, the second mode. Superlative darkness is a darkness precisely because it lies beyond the dialectical opposition of dark and light. Superlative darkness surpasses all attempts to directly or affirmatively know the divine. Hence superlative darkness contains a philosophical commitment to transcendence. Superlative darkness makes an anti-empiricist claim, in that it is beyond any experience of light or dark. It also makes an anti-idealist claim, in that it is beyond any conception of light or dark. What results are contradictory phrases such as "light beyond light," the "brilliant darkness," or the "ray of divine darkness." With superlative darkness, there is a movement from an affirmative to a superlative notion of the divine, from simple affirmation to an affirmation beyond all affirmation. Claiming to move beyond both experience and thought, superlative darkness harbors within itself an anti-humanism (beyond creaturely experience, beyond human thought), that also aims to illuminate darkness. We should note that with superlative darkness we are brought to a limit, not only of language but of thought itself. The motif of darkness comes in to indicate this limit. It is the possibility of thinking the impossible, a horizon that haunts every attempt to think darkness.

This play between the possible and impossible finally brings us to the third mode — what we've been calling divine darkness. Divine darkness questions the metaphysical commitment of superlative darkness, and this means questioning its fidelity to the principle of sufficient reason. The interesting thing about superlative darkness is that, while it may subscribe to a minimal version of the principle of sufficient reason, it does not presume that we as human beings can have a knowledge of this reason. That everything that exists has a reason for existing may be the case, but whether or not we can know this reason is another matter altogether. Superlative darkness is thus an attenuated variant of the principle of sufficient reason.

Perhaps we should really call this the *principle of sufficient divinity*. The principle of sufficient divinity is composed of two statements: a statement on being, which states that something exists, even though that something may not be known by us (and is therefore "nothing" for us as human beings), and a statement on logic, which states that such a something-that-exists is ordered and thus intelligible (though perhaps not intelligible to us as human beings). Superlative darkness still relies on a limit of the human as a guarantee of the transcendent being and logic of the divine, or that which is outside-the-human. The limit of human knowing becomes a kind of backdoor means of knowing human limits, resulting in the sort of conciliatory knowledge one finds in many mystical texts.

A divine darkness would take this and make of it a limit as well. This involves distinguishing two types of limit within darkness-mysticism generally speaking. There is, firstly, the limit of human knowing. Darkness is the limit of that which lies beyond the human — but which, as beyond the human, may still be invested with order, meaning, and purpose. This in turn leads to a derivative knowing of this unknowing. And here, darkness indicates the conciliatory ability to comprehend the incomprehensibility of what remains, outside the human.

Then there is, secondly, the limit of that which cannot be known by us, the limit of the limit, as it were. With the limit of human knowing, there is still the presupposition of something outside that is simply a limit for us as human beings. The limit of the limit, by contrast, is not a constraint or boundary, but a "darkening" of the principle of sufficient divinity. It suggests that there is nothing outside, and that this nothing-outside is absolutely inaccessible. This leads not to a conciliatory knowing of unknowing, a knowing of something that cannot be known. Instead, it is a negative knowing of nothing to know. *There is nothing, and it cannot be known.*

In mystical texts, the motif of darkness is compounded, duplicitous, and enigmatic. Each of our examples stems from the

Dionysian tradition of negative theology, or the *via negativa*. Each puts forth a concept of negation that is tied in some way to the motif of darkness, though darkness is not always negative for each of these thinkers. And each reaches its limit in a concept of the divine that we have been "misreading" in terms of the horror of philosophy — the limits of the human, the unreliable knowledge of such limits, the human confronting something it can only name as *unhuman*. Such a darkness is not in any way an answer to the questions we face today concerning climate change, posthumanism, or what Bataille once called "the congested planet." In a way, thinking this type of darkness is doomed to failure, devolving as it does on its own limits.

Perhaps the greatest lesson from all this is the one repeatedly stated by Eckhart — that this darkness, in its unknowing, is not separate from us, but really within us as well. It is not a darkness "out there" in the great beyond, but an "outside" (to use Bataille's term) that is coextensive with the human at its absolute limit. It runs the gamut from the self to the planet, from the human to the unhuman. It is a sentiment echoed by Bataille when he speaks about darkness as a form of impossibility:

> I enter into a dead end. There all possibilities are exhausted; the "possible" slips away and the impossible prevails. To face the impossible — exorbitant, indubitable — when nothing is possible any longer is in my eyes to have an experience of the divine...[202]

*

Blanchot's Night. Although the concept of darkness can be parsed and analyzed in a variety of ways, at its core is a duplicity: darkness as absence, and darkness as the presence of absence. This is a duplicity that marks many of the mystical texts on darkness, from Dionysius and Meister Eckhart to modern authors such as Georges Bataille and Maurice Blanchot.

Blanchot's short text from 1955, "The Outside, the Night," encapsulates this dual aspect of darkness in his characteristically lyrical, philosophical language: "In the night, everything has disappeared. This is the first night. Here absence approaches — silence, repose, night... Here language completes and fulfills itself in the silent profundity which vouches for it as its meaning."[203] This is night as indelibly tied to day, "another of day's constructions," nocturnal sleep opposed to daytime labor, nighttime dream opposed to daytime reality, oblivion opposed to the incessant production of meaning. In this night poets wander among nocturnal graveyards, protagonists from Gothic novels confuse moonlit illusion and reality, and a whole bestiary of impossible beings seems suddenly probable. This is the lyrical night evoked by the brooding of Edward Young's *Night Thoughts*, of Charles Baudelaire's elegies to the nocturnal city, and of Novalis's *Hymns to the Night*: "Away I turn to the holy, the unspeakable, the secretive Night. Down over there, far, lies the world — sunken in a deep vault — its place wasted and lonely. In the heart's strings, deep sadness blows. In dewdrops I'll sink and mix with the ashes."[204]

This first night is inseparable — but distinct from — another kind of night, which Blanchot simply refers to as "the other night." In the first night, everything has disappeared. "But when everything has disappeared in the night, 'everything has disappeared' appears. This is the *other* night."[205] Whereas the first night is the night of dichotomies (night/day, dusk/dawn, darkness/light), this other night is more austere, the mere registering of absence, of disappearance, of negation. In the same passage Blanchot writes: "Night is this apparition: 'everything has disappeared.'" This other night is the night of phantoms, specters, apparitions, visions, and haunting. But, Blanchot notes, "this eeriness does not simply come from something invisible, which would reveal itself under cover of dark and at the shadows' summons." That is because all these dreams, illusions, and apparitions are merely phenomena which serve as tenuous veils of a kind of non-phenomena, an absence that is, at the same time, "there."

Night is the phenomena of the absence of phenomena. "Here the invisible is what cannot cease to see; it is the incessant making itself seen." Blanchot's most concise formulation: "What appears in the night is the night that appears."

This dichotomy of the two kinds of night is found not only in Blanchot's philosophy but in his fictional works as well. His short novel *Thomas the Obscure* is an extended meditation on this "other night" as it gradually seeps into, or emerges from, the titular character. From a philosophical perspective, what Blanchot is trying to do is to think about "night" in a way that is not simply the opposite of day — that is, a concept of night that is not simply privative. This parallels the examples from the history of Western mysticism, in which, as Dionysius the Areopagite notes, there is a kind of "darkness" beyond the darkness opposed to light.

The question that arises from Blanchot's writing is whether "philosophy" resides on the side of day or the side of night. And if on the side of night, which night is it: the romantic, lyrical night, or this "other" night? In so far as philosophy is dedicated to constructing concepts, arguments, and systems of knowledge, it would seem to be a "daytime" activity. Yet every philosophy harbors within it the elements that undermine it — contradiction, paradox, inconsistency, vagueness, lack of direction or goal. Blanchot seems readily aware of the various tactics which "daytime" philosophical thought employs to both acknowledge the nocturnal element while keeping it separate from the daytime labors of philosophy. There is, Blanchot notes, a classical tactic, associated with Greek philosophy, one of balance and moderation, night as a limit that must not be transgressed. There is an Enlightenment tactic, in which night is by definition what the daytime work of philosophy's empire must dissolve and dissipate, the light of reason exploding into the darkness of ignorance. Finally, there is a modern tactic, in which daytime philosophy aims not just to dissolve, but to absorb and sublimate night, to make use of it in an ongoing engine of progressive, dialectical reason, ascending to higher and higher planes of knowledge-production.

And yet, Blanchot remains committed to this "other night." He does not say that it is totally outside of language or thought; but neither does he give it any positive, concrete determination. Blanchot's dreamlike novel *Thomas the Obscure* captures this "other night" in its detailed yet obscure depictions of Thomas's morose inner states. In it, the most innocuous of situations, such as walking home at dusk, reveals a whole unexpected universe of nocturnal affects:

> The night was more somber and more painful than he could have expected. The darkness immersed everything; there was no hope of passing through its shadows, but one penetrated its reality in a relationship of overwhelming intimacy. His first observation was that he could still use his body, and particularly his eyes; it was not that he saw anything, but what he looked at eventually placed him in contact with a nocturnal mass which he vaguely perceived to be himself and in which he was bathed … it was as if fear had immediately conquered him, and it was with a sense of shame that he raised his head to accept the idea he had entertained: outside himself there was something identical to his own thought which his glance or his hand could touch. Repulsive fantasy. Soon the night seemed to him gloomier and more terrible than any night, as if it had in fact issued from a wound of thought which had ceased to think … It was night itself.[207]

This other night is "outside" only in so far as its very conception (as "other night") takes place within the familiar light of philosophy's day. We are all daylight philosophers, especially those of us — Blanchot included — enamored of the night. In this way Blanchot's ruminations on the futility of philosophy, of thinking this other night, result in a kind of mystical itinerary — but an itinerary of futility. "One must live in the day and labor for its sake. Yes, one has to do that. But to labor for the day is to find, in the end, the night; it is thus to make night the job of the day, to make night a task and an abode."[208]

This itinerary ends not with philosophy's conquest of its object, but the reverse — the inessential, the impossible, the futile. One can sense this looking back from Blanchot's text to authors such as Dionysius, Angela of Foligno, and John of the Cross, where the price for union with the divine is the deeply ambivalent negation of the self. The "I" of the mystical text is continually undermined by the writing of the text itself — indeed, this is part of the practice of mysticism for these authors. In this sense, Blanchot's philosophical search for night is at once an impossibility and an itinerary, self-reflection turning into self-negation, until there seems to be nothing left but the desiderata of stray phrases, fleeting landscapes, and the faintest traces of a shape once human. Arguably, a whole tradition of lyric poetry is predicated on this practice of effacing the "I" of the poem — the very thing that defines the poem as such. We can see it in the poems of Giacomo Leopardi, Charles Baudelaire, Yevgeny Baratynsky, and others, where the poem, rather than serving as a platform for an expressive subject, actually serves to allow the "I" to dissipate against the backdrop of vast skies, impersonal landscapes, and the deep time of the cosmos.

Such themes are also found in contemporary poetry, where the resurgence of interest in zines and chapbook publishing has led to an interest in poetry that adopts anonymity or pseudonymity, often published by secret presses in small, hard-to-find editions. For example, the collection *Songs from the Black Moon*, authored by Rasu-Yong Tugen, employs much of the language of the darkness-mysticism tradition, emphasizing the turn towards the futility of thought, while at the same time evoking Blanchot's night:

In eternal night,
we had each burned the forest
in order to better see.

Clouds of sorrowful ravens
drifted upwards,
imperceptibly blotting out the stars.[209]

Another collection, *Cantos for the Crestfallen*, by an author known as Pseudo-Leopardi (miming the philological practice of adding "pseudo" to any text of questionable authorship), puts the same ideas in equally stark terms:

> Cease to imagine my intelligibility to you, stop trying
> To exit the darkness, the vast unilluminable melody
> Of night shrouding the corpse of this world from view.[210]

If this other night has any value for Blanchot, it is not because it points to some other, better place, above or beyond the tired dichotomy of day/night, but because the other night is always something that one fails to adequately think. It is philosophy as a form of thinking that culminates in its own silence: "Whoever senses the approach of the *other* night has the impression that he is approaching the heart of the night, the essential night which he seeks. And no doubt it is 'at this moment' that he gives himself up to the inessential and loses all possibility."[211]

*

The Black Universe. Some time ago, I was doing research for a seminar I planned to offer on "media and magic." I was interested in the concept of magic as it existed in the Renaissance, and in particular with the so-called occult philosophy of thinkers like Marsilio Ficino, Giordano Bruno, Heinrich Cornelius Agrippa, and Robert Fludd. It was while reading about Fludd that I discovered a startling image. It was from his major work, an ambitious, multivolume, syncretic theory-of-everything with the cumbersome title *Utriusque Cosmi, Maioris scilicet et Minoris, Metaphysica, Physica, atque Technica Historia*, or, *The Metaphysical, Physical, and Technical History of the Two Worlds, the Major as well as the Minor.* Fludd published the work (hereafter *Utriusque Cosmi*) between 1617 and 1621, and each volume is generously supplied with diagrams, tables, and images. The image that jumped out at me

The black square in Robert Fludd's *Utriusque Cosmi, Maioris scilicet et Minoris, Metaphysica, Physica atque Technica Historia* (c.1617)

is quite simple. In a section discussing the origin of the universe, Fludd was compelled to speculate on what existed prior to the universe, which he describes as an empty nothingness, a sort of "pre-universe" or "un-universe." He chose to represent this with a simple black square.

The image was startling to me because it was so different from the other images of Fludd's that we are used to — elaborate, ornate, hypercomplex diagrams that detail all the movements of the planets or of the mind. The black square was also startling because it immediately brought to mind examples from modern art, the most noteworthy being Kazimir Malevich's *Black Square* from 1915. Malevich first exhibited the painting at an exhibit of Futurist art, and decided to place the artwork in the top corner of the small exhibit space. Known within the Eastern Orthodox tradition as the "icon corner," the *Black Square* occupies the space that would traditionally be reserved for religious objects, for worship in a home. While the decision caused

Kazimir Malevich, *Black Square* (1915), oil on canvas

some controversy at the time, it is more likely that in placing the *Black Square* in the icon corner, Malevich may have been suggesting another kind of spirituality, one in which all icons are abstracted of their anthropomorphic conceits, distilled into an image that is also the absence of image. A something that is a nothing, a kind of mysticism of eclipse, in which all existents are annulled and engulfed by that which lies outside our field of vision.

Fludd's black square in the *Utriusque Cosmi* was, to be sure, enigmatic. Not only that, but Fludd also seemed aware of the limits of representation, noting, on each edge of the black square, *Et sic in infinitum*, "And so on to infinity..."

Looking at it out of context, Fludd's image has a tranquility to it, both in its simplicity and austerity. It was as if Fludd had the intuition that only a self-negating form of representation would be able to suggest the nothingness prior to all existence, an uncreation prior to all creation. And so we get a "color" that is not really a color — a color that either negates or consumes all colors. And we get a square that is not really a square, a box meant to indicate boundlessness. For the image to work within the context of Fludd's cosmology, the viewer must *not* see the image for what it is — a black square. The viewer must understand the square as formlessness, and the black inside as neither a fullness nor an emptiness. This simple little image requires a lot of work on the part of the viewer, perhaps as much work as in Fludd's other, more complex diagrams. For a synthetic, systematic thinker like Fludd, this must have been a difficult move. After all, the *Utriusque Cosmi* is, if nothing else, a totalizing work, and work whose ambition is to include and to account for everything — even nothing.

That Fludd would choose to do this is not surprising. His own syncretic philosophy combined elements of Neoplatonism, hermeticism, and Christian Kabbalah, with a touch of alchemy, music theory, Renaissance mechanics, and Rosicrucianism. Trained as a physician, Fludd was influenced early on by the work of Paracelsus, and was intrigued by the idea of God as an alchemist, mixing matter to produce the strange brew that is the universe. At one point, Fludd describes the state prior to creation as "the mist and darkness of this hitherto shapeless and obscured region," in which the "impure, dark, and dense part of the abyss' substance" is dramatically transformed by divine light.[212] The black square is quickly followed by a series of images — almost like a stop-motion animation — in which the divine *fiat* of creation and light flows forth. The Neoplatonic theme of the divine as a central source of radiating light takes over, producing the macrocosm and the microcosm, the ethereal and the earthly domains, all the stuff of the world.

I confess I lose interest in much of what follows, detailed and systematic though it is. But I continue to find the black square fascinating because of the contradictions in it. An image that, in order to be seen, negates itself. An un-universe that can only present its own absence. A boundless abyss that gives itself forth in an infinite austerity. Of course, words fail. For every un-universe, then, an un-philosophy that must also negate itself.

*

Dark, Black. But here we should remind ourselves that black is not just dark, but, well, black. If darkness implies a shrouding, a tenebrous obfuscation, should we then say that blackness is a blotting-out, a nullification of every existent? If darkness both "is" and "is not," is this also the case with blackness?

In his discussion of the crucifixion, Nicola Masciandaro shows us a moment in which darkness becomes blackness. His takeoff point is the interim of uncertainty, confusion, and anguish when Christ, on the cross, cries out "My God, my God, why has thou forsaken me?" The Gospels describe this interim period as one of a profound, even universal darkness: "Now from the sixth hour there was darkness over all the land until the ninth hour"; "It was now about the sixth hour, and there was darkness over the whole land until the ninth hour, while the sun's light failed."[213] In one traditional reading of this passage, Christ's cries of sorrowful doubt are not just the cries of one individual, but, allegorically, of every individual. In this breach between an anguished self and a seemingly indifferent cosmos, something appears. What appears is a breach, a fracture or lacuna at the core of existence. What appears is precisely what one cannot see, and what one apprehends is, in anguish, that one cannot apprehend. "It becomes a strange place where the only way to discern where you are with certainty is to see that you are hopelessly lost."[214] Masciandaro names this enigmatic breach "sorrow."

It is in this breach, this sorrow, that Masciandaro suggests a radical reading of this "crucifixion darkness." Beyond the suffering of Christ on the cross, and beyond the allegorical suffering of all individuals vis-à-vis a world that seems indifferent to them, there is a sorrow that is not simply that of individual human subjects that feel emotions. The real lesson of crucifixion darkness is that sorrow is, in a way, exterior to the human being: "it is the image of a cosmos that cries, the image of tears that are materially at the heart of its being made."[215] It is here that darkness becomes blackness. For, "the universe itself, an entity that most certainly includes your being in it, and vice versa, is … the dark realm of a literally authentic melancholy, that is, sorrow humourally proper to *black earth*."[216]

In this philosophical, or rather, mystical sense, black is less a color and more the withdrawal of every relation between self and world, resulting in this breach which, nevertheless, makes itself apparent as such. The sorrow that results is not simply the forlorn sorrow of finite, emotive human beings, but something impersonal and withering in existence itself. "There rests the difference between black and darkness," Masciandaro notes. "Darkness is a property of black, but black is not darkness. Shadow, nothingness, void look black and black is something *before* shadow, nothingness, void."[217] If, in this formulation, darkness always exists in some relation to light, however gradated, tenebrous, and shadowy, then blackness is something anterior to both light and dark. Philosopher François Laruelle encapsulates this in one of his early, experimental texts, "On the Black Universe" (*Du Noir Univers*): "Black is anterior to the absence of light, whether this absence be the shadows that extinguish it, whether it be its nothingness or its positive opposite."[218] Masciandaro extends this: "It is true that black is what is seen in the absence of light. But black is not that absence. Black is its own presence, not the presence of the absence of light."[219] Color and cosmos become intertwined in this blackness, something that neither exists nor does not exist; a dual negation of both "is" and "is not."

*

Nothing to See. Color and cosmos intertwine as much in the black square of Fludd as in Malevich. And the use of black in his cosmology is indicative of what modern color theory has had to say about black.[220] On the one hand, black is not considered to be a color in the conventional sense of the term. Black objects are those that do not reflect light in the visible spectrum; thus color theory refers to black as "non-chromatic" or "achromatic." A further nuance is the notion that black is the condition without any light — largely a theoretical proposition, or at least one that would have to be verified without being seen. But already there is some ambiguity, for does black designate a "color" that does not reflect light (and if so, why label it a color?), or does black designate the "color" that results in the total absence of light? Without light, no color, and without color, there is only black — and yet black is not a color. But this is not exactly right, for black is a color, not only in the sense in which we routinely designate this or that object as "black" but in the sense that black contains all colors, the color that absorbs all other colors into the noncolor of black — the black hole of color, as it were. We see black, but what exactly are we seeing when we see black? — light, or the absence of light? And if the latter, how is it possible to see the absence of light?

While black as a color has a rich and varied history in terms of its symbolic meanings, it would take a modern, scientific theory of color to begin to address such questions. When Goethe published his *Color Theory* in 1810, such conundrums were largely ignored in aesthetics, and often not discussed in the science of optics. But Goethe, being the polymath that he was, was not content to write a treatise of aesthetics. The *Color Theory* is as much a science of color as it is an aesthetics; indeed, the aim is to attempt the synthesis of the two. Goethe's major contribution was to distinguish the "visible" from the "optical" spectrum, and to make possible a science of optics that would be distinct from that of aesthetics, but which would overlap with it as well. Goethe's project is determined to consider color as a physiological phenomenon, to "search for nothing beyond the phenomena" of seeing color through the apparatus of the eye. For Goethe, any theory of color must begin from the physiological event of seeing color.

But black proves to be a difficult color to discuss for Goethe. In the opening sections of his treatise, "black" is often interchangeable with "dark" and "shadow," all three terms denoting a physiological state when the eye is deprived of light: "If we keep the eyes open in a totally dark place, a certain sense of privation is experienced. The organ is abandoned to itself; it retires into itself. That stimulating and grateful contact is wanting by means of which it is connected with the external world."[222] Black is conceived of in privative terms, in terms of the absence of light — not unlike Fludd's cosmic black square. And, black is even moralized by Goethe (as it is in Fludd), for the light that enables sight is not just a physiological stimulation, but a quasi-divine gift. When Goethe does briefly discuss black later on in his treatise, it is largely to discuss the combustion and oxidation processes that produce blackness in objects such as wood or metal. Strangely, Goethe does not raise the problem of black as a color, choosing instead to analyze the chemical process of blackening, and in the process sounding very much like a Renaissance alchemist.

Goethe's *Color Theory* had an immediate impact on the philosophy and science of color. One person particularly taken by it was Arthur Schopenhauer, who knew Goethe and discussed color theory with him on several occasions. While Schopenhauer does not depart from Goethe's distinction between the visible and the optical, he does attempt to root color theory in philosophy more than science. Schopenhauer's *On Vision and Colors* was published in 1816, just three years after the completion of his doctoral dissertation. A short book, it does not display the systematicity of *The World as Will and Representation* nor the aphoristic pessimism of his late writings. What it does do is drive a wedge into Goethe's *Color Theory*. Goethe, Schopenhauer claimed, does not really present a theory of color, foremost because he never considers what color is — that color exists is something assumed in his treatise.

Furthermore, Schopenhauer took Goethe to task for another assumption — that the perception of color necessarily corresponded to color itself, as if it were a physical thing in itself. Being a good Kantian, Schopenhauer tended to understand color as a cognitive process that began with the sensation of light and resulted in the cognitive representation of color. Schopenhauer was even more precise in identifying the "intensive activity of the retina" as the main apparatus for the perception of color. The trick was to understand what it was that made an impression on the retina in the first place; was color something identifiable in the world as such, or was it merely a by-product of the physiology of vision? Where did color take place? To say that we receive light that stimulates our retina is one thing, but to show how color is necessarily produced from this activity is quite another. In Schopenhauer's theory of perception, color begins to ever so slightly slip away — and yet, he admits, some vague entity called "color" could be identified, classified, measured, even agreed upon in an everyday context.

As with Goethe, for Schopenhauer the problem is black, which he sees as inseparable from white. Black and white are strange entities in Schopenhauer's treatise. At some points they seem to be additions or privations of light, much in line with Goethe: "The influence of light and white on the retina and its ensuing activity have degrees according to which light steadily approaches darkness and white approaches black."[224] But at other points black and white function more as logical necessities, forming the absolute poles of color perception; that is, black and white are never actually seen, and yet they determine the perception of color. Later in the treatise, there is even a third, more naturalistic interpretation, one that has to do specifically with black and not with white: that black is simply the physiological state of "retinal inactivity."[225] The eye without sight — or without vision.

After all is said and done, Schopenhauer's questions prove to be more interesting than his answers. All the same, it is tempting to make some connections between Schopenhauer's color theory and his pessimistic philosophy. A central ambiguity of Schopenhauer's *On Vision and Colors* has to do with black. Is black something that can be seen, like any other color? Or is black simply the name for something in the structure of vision that conditions color perception — but which can never be seen in itself? Perhaps there is a black that is seen — the black of shading and gradients — as well as a black that is unseen — the black of "retinal inactivity." And here again we seem to return to the paradox of Fludd's black square — the black that can only be seen at the expense of ceasing to be black (where black becomes "dark" or "shade"). Perhaps there is a *retinal pessimism* that secretly underlies color theory, encapsulated in the notion of black as privation (Goethe), black as retinal inactivity (Schopenhauer), black as that which precedes the very existence of light itself (Fludd). Far from being an empirical validation of the external world, what we see is so relative to various factors (range of visible color spectra, etc.) that at its extreme limit, to see is precisely to invalidate the testimony of the senses. Seeing is not believing — or is it? Retinal pessimism is not simply a failure in the phenomena of perception, the physiology of the retina, or the science of optics. Nor is it the conviction that whatever one is seeing is the worst of all possible things that could be seen. Both are intriguing options. Retinal pessimism is something else, and it is encapsulated in the strange status of black: at once present and absent, at once a fullness and an emptiness, at once the absorption of all light and the total absence of light. Black is at once the foundation of all color and, in its absence or emptiness, it is also what undermines the substantiality of all color. Retinal pessimism is not just about the noncolor that is black, but it is about the perception of color itself. It is, ultimately, the suspicion that *all* colors are black, that *all* retinal activity is retinal inactivity. Retinal pessimism: there is nothing to see (and you're seeing it).

*

Black on Black. There is, of course, a history of black painting in modern art.[227] For many the most notable example is that of Ad Reinhardt, who, in the 1960s, produced a number of paintings that, at first glance, appear to be all matte black, much in the tradition of Malevich. But after looking at the painting for some time, what appears to be black is not black at all. Instead, subtle hues of deep mauve, purple, magenta, and gray become apparent. And the uniform black canvas reveals a grid, or a series of squares within the canvas, each of a slightly different color. The painting actually changes within the duration of its viewing. "Black" literally vanishes as one looks at it, and what quietly emerges are colors and shapes. Reinhardt's paintings are almost visual analogues for Fludd's cosmology.

However, if modern paintings have anything in common with each other, it is that they always push black up front, in front of the viewer, as something to be seen. My own fascination with black in painting comes not from abstract expressionism, but from an earlier period — the infinite, stark, black backgrounds in Velázquez's "The Water Seller of Seville" (1618–22), the black clouds that envelop Rembrandt's "The Abduction of Proserpine" (1631), the almost Surreal flatness of Zurburan's "Christ on the Cross" (1627). As a painter of black, the artist that stands out from the rest is Caravaggio. In fact, I only came to appreciate modern black painting through seeing paintings like "The Crucifixion of St. Peter" (1601), "St. Matthew and the Angel" (1602), and "David with the Head of Goliath" (1605; 1609/10). One painting in particular I never tire of is Caravaggio's "St. Jerome Writing" (c.1606).

Certainly in paintings like this, Caravaggio makes extreme use of chiaroscuro, and he is not the first to do so. But there is a sense that Caravaggio took as much care painting the black backgrounds as he did the lighted figure in the foreground. Caravaggio's black is ambiguous. In one part of the canvas the black background is flat and full. In another part it is an empty, infinite depth. In still another part it is a thick black cloud, miasmatically embracing the foreground figures. The wonderful echo between the saint's barely haloed head and the skull holding open the book is accentuated by one kind of black — a black of shadows, shading, and contour. But behind both skull and head there is only outer space, at once flat and infinite. In a strange optical illusion, this same cosmic black seems to also inhabit the edges of the books, the space underneath the table, the creases of the fabric, and Jerome's own wrists. For me, this is "black painting" — black as a background that is always about to eclipse the foreground, the groundlessness of the figure/ground distinction itself, the presence of an absence, a retinal pessimism.

Black painting has had a long career in modern art, from the deceptively monochrome black paintings of Ad Reinhardt, to the tenebrous black canvases of Yan Pei-Ming, which tenuously hover in and out of abstraction. What is interesting about black artworks in a contemporary context is the way they seem to combine the

Caravaggio, *Saint Jerome Writing* (1605–1606), oil on canvas

likes of abstract expressionism with that of Caravaggio and his tenebrist contemporaries. In addition, large-scale, sculptural works by artists such as Terence Koh and Banks Violette add elements of "black" distantly borrowed from the metal, punk, and goth subcultures as well. This is the case in the work of Terence Hannum, whose series "Veils" (2012), which consists of images of disembodied hair on a black background — St. Jerome as a headbanger, as it were. The wisps of hair not only recall the black drawings of abstract expressionism, but they give the same sense of flat depth evoked in Caravaggio, in which we see figures almost drowning in black. Black is not only flat background, but a background that literally engulfs the foreground figure into a seemingly infinite abyss below, above, behind, everywhere.

A survey of contemporary art that employs black painting is too extensive to document here. What we can note is how contemporary black paintings continue to play on the foreground/background distinction found in earlier art, often via techniques that

Terence Hannum, *Veils* (2012), gouache drawing

bring out the thick materiality of paint or graphite or charcoal, as if to harken back to the chemical and alchemical tradition of Fludd and other occult philosophers. And it is worth noting how contemporary artists produce their black paintings through physical processes that are also processes of negation: rubbing, smearing, smudging, and erasing material like graphite or charcoal into shards of powder and dust. The process seems adequate for the result, the showing of nothing, the revealing of black less as a color and more as this "nothing-to-see."

It is this transition — from black as a color you see, to black as a noncolor you don't see, to black as "nothing-to-see" (and you're seeing it) — that Fludd encapsulates in his simple black square. For Fludd, black was the "color" of nonexistence, of preexistence, of an un-universe prior to its possibility. This idea has also come full circle in contemporary philosophy, bringing us back to Laruelle's short text "On the Black Universe." For Laruelle black is also a cosmological principle. Neither an aesthetics of color nor a metaphor for knowledge and ignorance, black is inseparable from the conditions of thought and its limit. Separate from "the World" we make in our own, all-too-human image, and apart from "the Earth" which tolerates our habitation of its surface, there is "the Universe" — indifferent, opaque, black: "Black prior to light is the substance of the Universe, what escaped from the World before the World was born into the World."[228]

In such a scenario, human beings probe the Earth and manufacture the World, but neither of these respond to the groping around that constitutes the being that has named itself human. The human being "is answered only by the Universe, black and mute."[229] And yet, it is this enigmatic response that leads us into thinking that this black universe, the black of Fludd's un-universe, is something "out there" — the nature of reality, the fabric of the universe, a consensual hallucination, something that I can see and touch and feel, a color. Laruelle again: "A phenomenal blackness entirely fills the essence of the human. Because of it, the most ancient stars of the paleo-cosmos, together with the most venerable stones of the archaeo-earth, appear to the human as being outside the World."[230] Fludd's cosmic black square, his un-universe, is not temporally prior to the universe, but neither is it some cataclysm to come; it is right here. But you can't see it. (And you're seeing it.)

Black is the color of ink, oil, crows, mourning, and outer space. Black is not just one color among others, and neither is it the absence of color. Black bathes all things in an absence, makes apparent an opacity, evaporates all the nuances of shadow and light. I leave the last word to an alchemist of a different sort, Yohji Yamamoto, who provides yet another variation of black: "Above all, black says this: I don't bother you — don't bother me."

3

PRAYERS FOR NOTHING

Horror Vacui. Philosophy in the West has, for some time, been haunted by the idea of non-being. The earliest Greek philosophers we know of differed widely in their ideas about the nature of reality, some arguing that everything was composed of water (Thales), or air (Anaximenes), or fire (Heraclitus), or miniscule moving atoms (Democritus). Others offered more abstract notions, of reality being composed of a universal mind (Anaxagoras's *nous*), of a principle of boundlessness (Anaximander's *aperion*), a numerical principle (Pythagoras), or a principle of oneness (Parmenides).

As different as these philosophies are, they are united in their commitment to the idea that there *is* something. The task for the philosopher is thus to determine what that something is — what the "is" is. There is something, and this something that "is" all there is. There is something, and beyond that — there is nothing. But this assumes a great deal, for every assertion of something that "is," there is a counter-assertion of something else that "is not." When Heraclitus argues that reality is composed of "fire" (dynamic and always changing) he is implicitly arguing that there is something that is not-fire (that is static, unchanging, immobile). The philosopher, in making arguments on the nature of reality, must assume that there is something at all about which one can make arguments. It may be that we are fooled by our senses, or have grown used to certain ways of thinking, or that we simply cannot — or will not — entertain the idea that there is nothing. It matters little whether the nature of reality is water, fire, air, or mind — what must be addressed in all these theories is that there "is" something at all.

Hence the central question that has, in one way or another, come to occupy Western metaphysics: why is there something rather than nothing? The stakes are high if one chooses to grapple with such a question. Aristotle understood this, which is why his approach is not to offer yet another theory-of-everything, but to step back and analyze the question. In his work known as *The Physics*, Aristotle begins to chip away at the problem, distinguishing three questions that occupy metaphysical speculation: first, the question of whether there "is" something; second, if there is something, the question of whether we can know this something; and third, if we can know this something, the question of how we can articulate it in language. All this proceeds from that first question — that there is something rather than nothing. Without this, everything else crumbles. But how can there be nothing — how can we say that there "is" nothing?

Aristotle is characteristically cautious in his analysis. He summarizes the different views on what he terms the "void" or "vacuum," and finds that many of the views assume the void to be defined in terms of empty space. Ambiguity ensues, as philosophers attempt to render the nothing as something; the void is not the container itself, but the nothing that "is" in the container, at best negatively demonstrated by displaced space (as water poured into an empty vessel). In this "plenist" view, the void is simply that which is not-yet-full, or that which is not-X, where X denotes an actual entity, and the void the interval or relation between one entity and another. Hence the well-known statement attributed to Aristotle: that "nature abhors a vaçuum." In Aristotle's metaphysics, the void seems to always slip away from thought, at once something that exists and that, by definition, cannot exist, both "is" and "is not" — a grey zone where physics and metaphysics begin to ever so slightly bleed into each other. Aristotle concludes, "if there is a void, a result follows which is the very opposite of the reason for which those who believe in a void set it up."[231]

Aristotle's analysis is helpful because it distinguishes two aspects of the idea of non-being: (i) a metaphysical aspect, in which one thinks about non-being as empty or full, an entity or a relation; and (ii) a logical aspect, in which one deals with what it means to state that non-being "is." For the moment we will be clustering terms together — non-being, nothing, and nothingness. But very quickly we will see that they will take on different meanings, differences that are important for any discussion of "nihilism," ancient or modern. For Aristotle and other classical philosophers, the stakes of such speculations are significant. The question "why is there something rather than nothing?" could quite possibly result in the response "there is nothing." And if there is nothing, then not only is philosophy's endeavor futile, but it is also absurd. This is where the "horror of philosophy" comes into play. This is the thought that philosophy cannot think without undermining itself. To say "there is nothing" is to evoke silence, or at least to render philosophy redundant. It is a limit to thought, and in particular, to the humanist preoccupation with thinking everything (including … nothing). Granted, while the possible reply "there is nothing" does not prevent philosophy from continuing — if anything, philosophy finds a new task, which is to state, with all the contradiction it implies, "there is nothing" — the reply "there is nothing" prompts us to question the fundamental premises of both the philosophical project and philosophical thought.

The idea of "nihilism" is for many a modern notion, linked either to the philosophical inquiries of Nietzsche and Kierkegaard, or its literary incarnations in the 19th century Russian novel (of which Turgenev's *Fathers and Sons* and Dostoevsky's *Brothers Karamazov* are the most well-known examples). In Turgenev's novel, a form of nihilism is adopted by Yevgény Bazárov, a young medical student and militant advocate of scientific rationality, who vows to "repudiate everything," accepting nothing that cannot be empirically verified. By contrast, Nietzsche, who turned to the question of nihilism late in his writings, understood nihilism to be a "symptom" more than a doctrine — a symptom of a culture in decline, in which "the highest values devalue themselves" with nothing to replace them. While he never put forth a systematic theory of nihilism, Nietzsche's comments on nihilism have had a lasting impact on later developments in both the continental and analytical traditions. The sense of a culture's dominant structures of meaning-making having lost their legitimacy produces a certain mood, particularly in periods of crisis or accelerated change — the sense of the floor dropping out, and a yawning abyss below.[232]

However, as we've already seen with Aristotle, nihilism is also about the vague and troubling "nothing" that is also a strange "something," and this contradictory quality of *nihil* courses through all the variants of nihilism in modernity, be they political, philosophical, cultural, or scientific. Perhaps instead of attempting to reduce "nihilism" to a fixed set of ideas, it would be better to reexamine the term itself, and think about a *nihil*-ism, a term that denotes both that which lies outside the scope of human knowledge, as well as the inherent limitations in the human-centric mode of knowing. Our trajectory will be highly eclectic, though methodical. After a consideration of the question "why is there something rather than nothing" in modern philosophy, we will examine the concept of nothing (*nihil*; *niht*) in the work of Meister Eckhart, who offers a multifaceted concept of nothing that also encompasses its contradictions, before then turning to the Japanese philosophers associated with the Kyoto School, and their own, syncretic development of the Buddhist concept of *śūnyatā* or "emptiness."

*

Nothing and Nothingness (Heidegger, Sartre, Badiou). One of the insights of Heidegger's *Being and Time* is that the question of being in and of itself can be distinguished from the question of this or that particular being or entity. As he notes, "the question which we are to work out, what is asked about is Being — that which determines entities as entities, that on the basis of which entities are already understood ... The Being of entities 'is' not itself an entity."[233] For any philosophy which aims to examine being as such, this "ontological difference" between Being and entities is the first step. One may ask about the being of this or that particular entity, but this is still asking about *beings* rather than *Being*. Heidegger's tongue-twisting terminology "the Being of beings" encapsulates this distinction. Being is not one being among other beings, but that which is common to all beings. This means that Being can be examined, but only obliquely, via beings, and for Heidegger it is the being specific to human beings that provides this privileged vantage point. The human being is unique for Heidegger because it is the being for whom Being is an issue, a particular type of being "thrown" into the world, while also orienting itself towards being in general — it is a type of being Heidegger famously terms *Dasein* (literally, "being-there").

In this sort of inquiry, asking about Being also means asking about what Being is not; one says there is Being, and beyond that, nothing. It is a grand, totalizing inquiry that at once encompasses everything and also says that, by virtue of its totality, there is nothing else to consider. To do so would be futile. To paraphrase Heidegger, the Being of beings is not itself a being. This would seem tantamount to saying that Being is, literally, "nothing." Heidegger addresses this in his lecture "What is Metaphysics?" where merely posing the question reveals all sorts of dizzying conundrums:

> [W]e shall try to ask about the nothing. What is the nothing (*das Nichts*)? Our very first approach to this question has something unusual about it. In our asking we posit the nothing in advance as something that "is" such and such; we posit it as a being. But that is exactly what it is distinguished from. Interrogating the nothing — asking what and how

> it, the nothing, is — turns what is interrogated into its opposite. The question deprives itself of its own object.[234]

As Heidegger notes, the question itself cannot be posed without immediately falling into contradiction. Being — as that which is held in common among all beings — this Being is not itself a being, and thus also non-being. And it is this contradiction that leads him to parse out two types of "nothing": first, a nothing viewed in terms of opposition to beings, as their negation, and secondly, a nothing that is identical with Being (in so far as Being is not a being). Heidegger briefly comments on the concept of nothing in classical Greek and medieval Christian philosophy, before offering this distinction:

> This cursory historical review shows the nothing as the counter-concept to being proper, that is, as its negation. But if the nothing becomes any problem at all, then … it awakens for the first time the proper formulation of the metaphysical question concerning the Being of beings. The nothing does not remain the indeterminate opposite of beings but reveals itself as belonging to the Being of beings (*Sein des Seienden*).[235]

For Heidegger, "nothing" names this paradoxical quality of Being, as everywhere and nowhere, as held in common among beings but never present in and of itself. Central to this is that moment when the human being apprehends this "nothing" in the confrontation with one's own mortality. It is in confronting the "indefiniteness of death" that the human being holds itself out over an abyss, and for a brief, fleeting moment, glimpses the Being of beings as "nothing." The being specific to the human being is "held out into the nothing." This existential state Heidegger famously terms *Angst* (anxiety, dread): "The indefiniteness of death is primordially disclosed in anxiety … The 'nothing' with which anxiety brings us face to face, unveils the nullity by which *Dasein*, in its very basis, is defined; and this basis itself is thrownness into death."[236]

Dramatic though it sounds, this confrontation with nothing is for Heidegger both the height and the depth of the human being. As Heidegger shows in his analyses of everyday moods such as boredom and anxiety, more often than not we shun "the nothing" in favor of immersion in the purely affirmative world of our individuated beings. This is Jean-Paul Sartre's takeoff point in the first part of *Being and Nothingness.* There Sartre begins from the situation of beings — in particular, human beings — alienated from their own being. In Heidegger's terms, we are beings shut off from Being. But Sartre is more concerned with the human being's relation to Being in itself. It is this relation that Sartre terms "nothingness" (*le néant*). For Sartre, when the human being asks about being as such, nothingness reveals itself in several ways: as an indetermination on the side of the questioner, on the side of that which is questioned, and in the possibility of there not being any meaning to the questioning itself. "The permanent possibility of non-being, outside us and within, conditions our questions about being."[237] The human being attempts to manage all these uncertainties by fixing its object of inquiry: "Being is *that* and outside of that, *nothing.*"[238]

For Sartre, "nothingness" is the moment when the "outside of that, nothing" creeps back into the concern with being. Sartre gives the everyday example of going to a café to meet someone. Let's say I am going to Joe Coffee to meet Prema. I enter the café, expecting to find her, but she isn't there. I scan the café, the people sitting or standing, the tables and chairs, the counter with the tattooed baristas, and I hear the clanking of espresso cups, coffee grinder, and dimly audible music in the background. But this is all a backdrop to Prema, whom I expect to find, and who isn't there. I may shift my attention to foreground elements in the café. *Do they really need to take up that much space with their laptop?, Those two students over there are talking way too loud, I should buy some coffee beans while I'm here, and oh, there's Dominic over there, hi.*... But this does not efface the basic differential between the background (Joe Coffee) and an absent foreground (Prema). I have, in Sartre's terms, "nihilated" the café as background, to make way for the expected foreground of Prema — who is not there. A kind of abyss opens up, a presence of an absence. It is Prema's raising herself up as nothingness against the nihilated backdrop that is the café. As Sartre notes, "what is offered to intuition is a flickering of nothingness; it is the nothingness of the ground, the nihilation of which summons and demands the appearance of the figure."[239]

What this means is that Sartre's notion of nothingness is nearly the opposite of that of Heidegger. For Heidegger "the nothing" is consummate with Being, which is itself not one being among others, and which also has a philosophical priority over this or that being. But for Sartre, the example of the café reveals that there is always first a being that is then "not there" — there is always first an "is" that is secondarily "not": "This means that being is prior to nothingness and establishes the ground for it. By this we must understand not only that being has a logical precedence over nothingness but also that it is from being that nothingness derives concretely its efficacy."[240] This is crucial for Sartre as it will allow him to argue for a notion of "freedom" based on this grey zone between expecting someone and not finding them there. It will serve as the basis for his famous dictum "existence precedes essence."

In spite of their differences, what both Heidegger and Sartre grapple with is the enigma of nothing/nothingness for philosophy, an enigma that asks philosophy to think, in a single thought, the "is" and "is not" of nothing/nothingness. Heidegger cloaks the nothing with the terminology of "Being" and "beings," in which "the nothing" is not that which opposes Being but which is fully commensurate with it. Sartre similarly cloaks nothingness with a different terminology, based on the encounter between beings and the rift that may result when an expected encounter does not take place. Perhaps we can say that, for Heidegger, "the nothing" is an absent presence, and for Sartre, "nothingness" is a present absence.

Alain Badiou adds another wrinkle to the discussion. Employing elements of mathematical set theory, Badiou uses the term "void" to designate the combined "is" and "is not" with which Heidegger and Sartre grapple. Badiou's terminology is highly technical, but, simplifying to the extreme, we might say that for Badiou the void captures both Heidegger's link between the nothing and Being, and Sartre's nothingness that is set against the backdrop of beings. If we think of set theory in terms of classification systems, those boxes (or "sets") into which we place different things (or "elements"), then the void (or "empty set") is that set that has no elements (the box with nothing in it). And yet, it still can be designated as an empty set (with the double bracket { } or the symbol Ø). Thus the empty set designates both its presence, its "somethingness" as a set, and also its absence, its nothingness, as a set with no elements. But by designating itself in this way — as the set of no elements, the set of nothing — the empty set also confers a somethingness to its contents (which are: nothing). These twists and turns in logic allow a philosopher like Badiou to propose a philosophy based not on presence and somethingness (the tradition of Heidegger and Sartre), but on the void: "It is a question of names here — 'nothing' or 'void' — because being, designated by these names, is neither local nor global. The name I have chosen, the void, indicates precisely that nothing is presented, no term, and also that the designation of that nothing occurs 'emptily.'"[241]

Being and Time, *Being and Nothingness*, *Being and Event*. Imposing philosophical tomes of opaque, indecipherable prose, of which these all-too-brief summaries can offer little clarification. But they are also books that contain surprises within them — often unbeknownst to the authors themselves. Though they differ in their approaches, Heidegger, Sartre, and Badiou all begin with that most basic of philosophical problems, "why is there something rather than nothing?" But they end up addressing a different problem: "what to do with nothing." We are brought back to the two problems Aristotle had identified long ago — "there is *nothing*" and "there *is* nothing."

The philosophical enterprise, which has long been almost exclusively concerned with the problem of being, also harbors within it an equal, if more furtive concern with non-being, nothing, nothingness, and the void. Perhaps there is some truth to Sartre's words when he states that "nothingness haunts being."[242]

*

God Is Nothing (Meister Eckhart). These discussions are in no way new. In fact, they often borrow from earlier philosophers, for whom philosophy, theology, and logic were deeply intertwined. The work of Meister Eckhart is exemplary in this regard. Eckhart — philosopher, theologian, and heretic — meditated at length on the philosophical problems evoked by nothing/nothingness. Noteworthy in Eckhart's sermons is his use of the language of negation and nothingness, employed in a range of ways to describe God, creature, and an enigmatic "beyond" that Eckhart frequently calls the "Godhead" (*Gottheit*). In all cases Eckhart pushes for a non-anthropomorphic, non-anthropocentric notion of nothing/nothingness that is, at the same time, not separate from the human being. While Eckhart's uses of the terms nothing, nothingness, and emptiness have garnered modern comparisons to Kierkegaard, Nietzsche, and Zen Buddhism, when placed in the context of Christian mysticism, they take on a specific set of meanings.[243]

In his writing on "nihilism" Eckhart utilizes both the Latin term *nihil*, but also the Middle High German *niht*, particularly in his sermons. Eckhart's sermons, in the theological tradition in which he was trained, isolate particular Biblical passages on which he will then comment in detail, developing a line of thought from a single phrase or even a single word. It is important to remain conscientious of this method when reading Eckhart. Our focus will be Eckhart's Sermon 19, where a passage from *Acts* 9:8 serves as the starting point for a commentary on the relation between the divine and "nothing." The passage in question is the following: "Paul rose from the ground and with open eyes saw nothing." A short but cryptic passage, it describes a mystical experience with three components: the mystical subject (Paul) in his relationship to himself; the act of "seeing" or of mediating between Paul and the divine; and that which Paul sees or which is mediated to Paul, which the passage enigmatically calls "nothing." In its form we have something completely quotidian, a human subject relating to an object through the mediation of sight, vision, and representation. But the mystical context of the passage deals not with the mediation of two like entities (both inscribed within time, both finite and bodily, both existing), but with two qualitatively unlike entities. For this reason, Eckhart focuses on the elusive object that is mediated, the "nothing" that is paradoxically seen.

From this passage, Eckhart derives four meanings of the term "nothing" (*niht*):

> One is that when he rose up from the ground with open eyes he saw Nothing, and the Nothing was God; for when he saw God he calls that Nothing. The second: when he got up he saw nothing but God. The third: in all things he saw nothing but God. The fourth: when he saw God, he saw all things as nothing.[244]

Eckart goes on to elaborate these different senses of the term "nothing." He summarizes the first sense of the term "nothing" in the following way: "He saw nothing, that is: God. God is a nothing and God is a something. What is something is also nothing."[245] This first sense is the most complex, in that it deals with a philosophical notion of God as "Nothing," but a nothing that is at the same time not simply negative or privative. It is a notion of the divine in terms of a "nothing" that has little to do with any philosophical notion of nothing, in which nothing is thought of in terms of the categories of being and non-being, or being and becoming. Eckhart's notion of divine nothing has "nothing" to do with ontological categories of being and non-being, as well as their modes or attributes, be they privative, subtractive, or destructive. In this formulation, the divine is a nothing that is not negative.

In fact, Eckhart's first formulation contains within it several variations that elaborate this idea. In one variation Eckhart states: "He saw nothing, that is: God." Here we have the assertion of a divine unity that encompasses everything, including nothing, and which itself is not reducible to a something. The fecundity of God is such that it encompasses that which is without substance. There is no mystical experience in the sense of having an experience of something that builds one up or fortifies the subject. Instead, there is the self-abnegation or "releasement" of the subject, in which one finds a nothing "that is like finding God."

This leads to the necessity of thinking the divine as unrelated to the ontological categories of being and non-being — the God beyond Being, the Godhead beyond God. Hence in another variation Eckhart notes: "God is a nothing and God is a something." This is a recapitulation of the Dionysian assertion of the nameless God, the God without attributes or properties, the God to which no name is adequate. Eckhart, in other sermons, will frequently describe this God-beyond-Being as "the One."

And this leads to the limits of philosophical thinking itself, as it requires that the divine — the Nothing that is God, the God-beyond-Being — be thought of in terms of contradiction. Thus, in yet another variation, Eckhart says: "What is something is also nothing." Eckhart here assumes the inverse of this phrase — that nothing is also a something — and suggests that even this something (of nothing) is conditioned by a further nothing (or "Nothing"), that is the Godhead. Together, these variations all come under the Eckhartian assertion that "God is Nothing," comprising the first sense of the term.

Eckhart continues, summarizing the second sense of "nothing": "He saw God, in whom all creatures are nothing."[246] Whereas the first sense of "nothing" dealt with the divine in itself, here Eckhart describes a nothing that has to do with the relation between God and creatures. There is a theological tradition of regarding creatures as "nothing" compared to God, in the sense that creaturely life is inscribed within temporality and finitude, life and death. This is the moral-theological notion of creaturely "nothing." But Eckhart means more than this when describing creatures as nothing. Whereas in the first sense it is God that is nothing, here it is creatures that are nothing. But the nothing of creatures can be taken in several ways.

Here, Eckhart uses the language of representation and the dichotomy between subject and object, image and thing. If the relation between any two creatures in the world relies upon the framework of subject and object, seer and seen, knower and known, then understanding creatures in God means understanding the relation between any two creatures as analogous to the relation between creature and God. The vertical relation between the creature and God serves as the model for the lateral relation between any two creatures. Divine mediation becomes "flattened" into creaturely mediation. In a way, this is a pantheist — or really, panentheist — version of Eckhart. In so far as God is "in" all creatures, all creatures relate to God by relating to other creatures. This leads to the state in which one effectively sees "through" creatures, to God — as Eckhart puts it, one sees "nothing but God."

In the third sense of the term "nothing," Eckhart notes that "[s]eeing nothing, he saw God. The light that is God flows out and darkens every light … the Nothing was God."[247] Here Eckhart makes a transition from the relation between creatures and God, to the relation of creatures to God. Using the mystical motifs of darkness and light, Eckhart follows in the Dionysian-apophatic tradition by describing a superlative form of darkness or nothing that goes beyond the dichotomies of light/dark, something/nothing. Here one moves from optical sight to mystical vision, from a metaphysics of being to a non-metaphysics of nothing or "the One."

Finally, Eckhart summarizes the fourth and last sense of "nothing": "In seeing nothing, he saw the divine Nothing."[248] Eckhart suggests that the divine Nothing, being neither optical sight, nor representational thought, nor metaphysical substance, must ultimately remain both indifferent and indistinct. The "blindness"

Eckhart references is both a turning away from the world (as finite, ephemeral, and insubstantial) and an emptying or "nothing-ing" of the self. Blindness is here an opacity, a total equivocity or non-relation between earthly and divine, creature and God. But this is not a nihilism, for this turning-away and self-emptying ultimately indicate the pervasiveness and the immanence of the divine Nothing — in everything. Eckhart often returns to this condition of blind nothing, this gesture of "seeing nothing" with "eyes open."

*

Nihil (Four Variations). In his commentary on "nothing" Eckhart highlights one of the central problems in medieval philosophy — the nature of the relation between human and divine. In so far as the divine is conceived of in radically nonhuman terms (non-anthropomorphic, abstract, inaccessible, and "dark"), the divine is, in and of itself, not some thing among other things, not a being among other beings — the divine is, strictly, "nothing."

The dilemma, then, is how the human being, which is finite, actual, discrete, and bodied, how this human being can relate at all to the divine, when the latter has been characterized as non-relatable. It would seem that either the divine would have to become more humanlike, constraining itself into an anthropomorphic entity one can interface with (this is the theme of Christ as the God-man), or that the human being would have to divest itself of its limitations in order to be adequate to the "nothing" of the divine (this is the theme of mystical *ec-stasis*, the self-abnegation of the mystic before God). It seems that the human-divine relationship is only possible at the cost of one of the terms negating itself (the human becoming more-than-human; the divine becomes less-than-divine).

In several of his sermons, Eckhart reminds us that the divine is not simply "out there" but also courses through the human being "in here." There is a nonhuman divinity within the human — it even constitutes the human, paradoxically forming its ground. And here, the philosophical dilemma returns. Either the divine is immanently "in" the human, equal to the human (in which case there is no relation because everything is divine), or the divine remains absolutely inaccessible in its "nothing," the human at best able to apprehend this inaccessibility as such.[249]

This dilemma, which reaches its peak in speculative mysticism, revolves around how "nothing" is defined, and this is the backdrop against which Eckhart parses his different approaches to the idea of "nothing":

First variation: The nothing of finite creatures. Creatures are "nothing" in the sense that they are created in time. Phenomenally, creatures exist in the world as flux and flow, as coming-to-be and passing-away (to borrow Aristotle's terms). This nothing is, as we've noted, the moral-theological notion, the devaluation of life and being, the "flight from creatures" advocated by theologians and ascetics. Nothing in this sense is *privative.*

Second variation: The nothing of creaturely being. Creatures are created in order to be (as Eckhart notes, "He created all things that they may be"). Thus there is a prior non-being that both precedes the creature and is its philosophical ground. Creatures are "nothing" in that they are founded on a primordial, preexistent, non-being. Nothing in this sense is *subtractive.*

Third variation: The nothing of God. God is that which is outside of time, space, and modality. God is "nothing" in so far as God is not a being among other beings. But neither is God simply the supreme being nor the most perfect being. God is, in this context, the Being of all beings, the superlative being whose particular, conditioning form of being bears no relation to the conditioned status of creaturely beings. Nothing in this sense is *superlative.*

Fourth variation: The nothing of the Godhead. Eckhart's own brand of apophaticism frequently puts him in a situation in which God alone is insufficient. There is, "beyond" God, the Godhead, to which no attributes, properties, or names can be given. Importantly, for Eckhart the metaphysics of being does not pertain to the Godhead. Eckhart often describes the Godhead as "the One." The Godhead, as the One, bears no relation to Being, or to Non-Being.

In one sermon Eckhart asserts, "God is all, and is one."[250] Elsewhere he notes that the Godhead is "a non-God, a non-spirit, a non-person, a non-image; rather, He is a sheer pure limpid One, detached from all duality."[251] In this final sense of nothing, the nothing of finite creatures (first definition) is simply a pretext for the real identity or indistinction of creaturely being (second definition) and the empty God (third definition). All of this is what is encompassed in the Eckhartian notion of nothing, in this final sense. The nothing of the now, the nothing of all that is. Nothing in this final sense is *nullifying*.

In traditional accounts of Christian mysticism, one is frequently led to a fork in the road between two types of divine mediation: either that of there being no relation to the divine, or that of there being a relation to the divine, as nothing. With Eckhart, we see that this is a false dilemma — but one must abrogate some of the most basic principles of philosophical and theological thinking to reach this point. In our "heretical" reading of Eckhart, divine mediation has little to do with a negative that must be overcome by a positive. Instead, divine mediation is the collapse of negative and positive, subtractive and superlative, into the strange negative immanence, an immanence of nothing that Eckhart terms the Godhead. The Godhead: *nothing is everywhere*. Furthermore, for Eckhart this mediation leads not to despair, but is "joyful."

But Eckhart, too, runs into problems. For one, any careful reading of Eckhart must acknowledge that this talk about God as nothing, and the arid, empty, unhuman "desert" is always doubled by an equal commitment to the Trinity, the *kenosis* or self-emptying of Christ, and a Person-oriented mysticism of Father, Son, and Human.[252] Put simply, the "philosophical" Eckhart is often compromised by the "theological" Eckhart. Both are brought into an uneasy relation with each other, and it is this assemblage that constitutes the "mystical" Eckhart. Eckhart at once shores up the limits of the human while at the same time asserting a profound commitment to the human — but a human that is also a "letting-be," a human that is a "living without a why."

This tension is illustrated in Eckhart's different uses of the term "nothing." On the one hand, there is the nothing of creaturely life, the non-substantiality of what is ephemeral and temporary, the nothing of the all-too-human in its creaturely finitude. On the other hand, there is the nothing of the Godhead, the nothing that superlatively encompasses everything, including the very dichotomy of something/nothing, being/non-being. This is the nothing that is at once transcendent and immanent, the nothing that is at once the apophatic inaccessibility of the divine and the very ground of all that is. These resolve in a kind of dual annihilation that is not simply negation. Bernard McGinn provides a summary:

> To say that creatures are nothing for Eckhart is to say that the existence they possess is a pure receiving. Poised between two forms of nothingness, the *nihil* by way of eminence that is God, and the *nihil* that marks the defect of creatures, Eckhart's mystical way will be an invitation to the soul to give up the nothingness of its created self in order to become the divine Nothing that is also all things.[253]

While we have outlined four usages of the term "nothing" in Eckhart, we can also streamline them into two: a basic distinction between the nothing of creatures (of the human creature in particular) and the nothing of God (of the divine, of the unhuman). But in Eckhart even this division breaks down. The nothing of creatures immediately opens onto the nothing of the Godhead, collapsing the division into what Eckhart describes as the nothing of that which is, the nothing of "letting be." So, while our strong reading of Eckhart pushes for total indistinction and the paradoxical immanence of nothing, we must also note that, even in his most heretical moments, Eckhart still preserves a basic distinction between two types of nothing.

*

Divine Nothing. As an exemplar of the tradition of negative theology, Eckhart frames mysticism as a form of mediation. But mediation in Eckhart is often unstable and in flux, as when the divine is characterized, in Neoplatonic terms, as fecund, generous, and flowing forth. In these instances, mediation becomes so full, so complete, so characterized by generosity, that it paradoxically negates itself and all middle terms.

At other moments, mediation comes up against a limit, in which that which is mediated is rendered as opaque, obscure, and unintelligible. This "darkness" is not due to any privation or lack, but due to its alterity with respect to the human. The "divine darkness" is neither privative nor oppositional, but rather superlative, an indication of a limit to thought and to the human. The minimal accessibility that remains can only be described in negative terms. Hence Eckhart's notions of the "silent desert" and the Godhead as a "nothing." This unhuman, apophatic limit is — at least in Eckhart — not simply "out there," but fully immanent to all that is. One can only relate to it by not relating to it — indeed, by negating all forms of relationality. The nothing of the Godhead is, in Eckhart's terms, the "negation of negation," the indifference of the transcendent and immanent, a paradoxical immanence of "nothing."

For Eckhart the condition of mysticism is the loss of self in the divine — or, more accurately, the emptying of the self or self-abnegation that parallels the emptiness or nothingness of the Godhead. Eckhart takes to the limit a motif commonly found in mystical texts — that of the mystical union as the dissolution of all differences, including the difference between self and God, the creaturely and the divine, the human and unhuman. With Eckhart, one divinizes the human, rather than humanizing the divine. For Eckhart, mysticism is a movement from the fullness of God to the nothing of the Godhead.

But we must remember that for Eckhart this mediation is really divine mediation, that is, the mediation not of two points within a single reality, but a mediation between two "realities," earthly and divine, natural and supernatural, the known and the unknown.

This comes with a few caveats: that the condition of the "other" reality being mediated must remain a limit (sometimes unintelligible, sometimes inaccessible), and that the "other" reality being mediated is not "out there," not above or beyond, not another place to which one can travel or with which one can connect.

In Eckhart's sermons, there is a consistent assertion of the divine as inaccessible (in his motifs of the desert, the emptying of the self, the nothing of the Godhead). Eckhart maintains a minimal form of mediation, seen in his distinction between the two basic types of nothing (the nothing of creatures and the nothing of the Godhead). For Eckhart, divine mediation tends towards a logic of *both/and*: in the coincident nothing of Godhead and creatures, there is both the mediation of nothing, and the nothing that is mediation. All mediation is a pretext for the impossibility of mediation, one that, at times, becomes indissociable from pure immediacy.

In short, for Eckhart, *divine nothingness is that form of relation that questions relationality in and of itself.* Divine mediation is unstable, always tending towards either the impossibility of relation or pure relation. Mysticism is that form of mediation that suggests to us that there is in fact no mediation as such, no steady-state or stable connection that we can, with any degree of confidence, call "mediation." In the parlance of modern communications theory, there are no fixed senders or receivers, no well-established channels, and no messages (or, for that matter, noise). The "mediation" of divine mediation is simply a waystation to either the fullness of mediation (and thus its negation as mediation) or the emptiness of mediation (a negation of a different order). For mystical thinkers like Eckhart, mediation is always failing, flailing, and breaking down into the darkness of God or the equally incomprehensible luminosity of divine self-abnegation. A certain mood is generated from this condition, a kind of religious horror, in which "mystical experience" is not the affirmation of union with the divine, but rather its near inverse: the negation of the divine (the rift between the human and the divine, as nonhuman), but also the negation that *is* the divine itself (as inaccessible and foreclosed to thought).

This dual negation within Eckhartian mysticism can also be found in later thinkers, from Pascal to Kierkegaard to Levinas. It indexes a nebulous, liminal philosophy of negative moods, in which the abyss within the self bears the traces of the abyss that is the divine (in so far as the divine hovers within the horizon of human language and understanding). As philosopher Alina Feld notes, rather than human being determined by the existential deferment of death, the "Heideggerian anxiety toward death is replaced by the horror of impersonal existence," a mode of being hovering within this dual negation of the divine (negation of the divine, negation as the divine), leaving only an ambivalent "murmur of inextinguishable anonymous being in the depths of nothingness."[254] The negation within me is a vestige of the negation outside me, the "within" and the "without" paradoxically grounded by a groundlessness or an abyss whose quality of indifference or the impersonal casts all human-centric presuppositions regarding order, meaning, and purpose, into abeyance. In Eckhart's sermons, either one is confronted with the numinous, absolute opacity of the divine, or one is engulfed in the prodigious flux of divinity; one either confronts the black, viscous void of divine discontinuity, or one is set ablaze in the sparkling brilliancy of divine continuity. Complete difference or complete indifference — these are the poles of divine nothingness.

*

Metaphysical Correlation, Mystical Correlation. These aspects of divine mediation allow us to reframe mysticism as a modern philosophical problematic. In the Western tradition, nearly every philosophical position, every philosophical "decision," every assertion of being, identity, or oneness, relies on a minimal relation between thought and world, self and other, subject and object. How exactly is the mediation of mysticism — divine mediation — different from the numerous examples of mediation one finds in philosophy? Both borrow the form of relationality that has now become the common parlance of modern communications theory (*A* connected to *B* via a medium *X*). Both also presume a separation that subsequently requires some mediated correlation.

In traditional metaphysics we are given the correlation between subject and object, within a given order of the real. The "real" may be material or ideal, noumenal or phenomenal, visible or invisible, but however it is construed, it remains the condition of possibility for thought. Let us call this *metaphysical correlation*. Metaphysical correlation, in presuming a minimal relation that makes thought possible, subscribes to a "principle of sufficient philosophy."[255]

And yet, with mysticism, we do not so much have mediation within a given real, as we have the correlation between different orders of the real, unilaterally posited as the relation between the real from the perspective of the human, and another real, that can only be termed the "unhuman." Let us call this *mystical correlation*. In theological terms, this relation may be between the natural and supernatural, the earthly and the divine, creature and Creator, and so on.

While both the mystical and the metaphysical borrow the form of mediation, what results in each is a different type of correlation between terms. In metaphysical correlation thought is always turned towards the world; thought is always "chasing" its correlate, on its trail, ferreting it out into the open — it is always a "thought of." In metaphysical correlation, thought is a *hunt*. In mystical correlation, by contrast, thought is always turned away from the world (or it is only turned towards the world in so far as the world *is* this other order of the real, the "out there" the same as the "in here"). In mystical correlation thought is always oriented towards something that is understood to be in excess of thought; thought is always in relation to its own negation. In mystical correlation, thought is a *sacrifice*.

Metaphysical correlation is after a response that it has already posited before it begins the task of thinking. It is a self-fulfilling prophecy, a self-congratulatory gesture. It has caught its prey before the hunt has begun. By contrast, mystical correlation can never receive a response, precisely because it is after that which is simply without-thought (or non-thought). It can only succeed if it fails; there can only be affirmation if there is negation. If metaphysical correlation is agonistic, mystical correlation is ritualistic.

This is, granted, a bit cursory. But if mysticism is a relation between two orders of the real, two "reals," instead of a relation between two entities within a single reality, then this means that the *intrinsic* relations of metaphysical correlation (self-world; human-human) are displaced or scaled up to the *extrinsic* relations of mystical correlation (earthly and divine; natural and supernatural).

Mystical correlation is a type of mediation that devolves around a limit. That limit is the unilateral "perspective" of the human towards something that it can only negatively index as the unhuman. This limit is neither relative nor absolute. It also means that the mystical correlation always fails. It is a loop that never closes, a spiral that never fully turns. It is a relation that can only be verified "from this side." It is a relation that is only verified in the blank, impersonal opacity of the "divine nothing," the wayless abyss, the "divine darkness."

From a contemporary perspective, what thinkers like Eckhart offer is a way of reconsidering a problem that is at once mystical and metaphysical — *the problem of the anthropocentrism of thought*. Eckhart presents us with a form of divine mediation as the form of relation between the human and the unhuman, a situation in which the fullest mediation and the impossibility of mediation become one in the same.

These two types of divine nothingness — as pure relation and pure opacity — are simply the premodern avatars of, respectively, a philosophy of continuity (the continentalist tendency towards immanence, vitalism, vibrancy, and the phenomenology of affect) and a philosophy of discontinuity (the analytical tendency towards assemblages, objects, actants, and so on). But we can already see in thinkers like Eckhart a willingness to break down such distinctions, in his notion of the divine as negative fecundity (a "negation of negation"), and the absolute opacity of "letting be."

In so far as mysticism is concerned with the relation between two orders of the real (divine and earthly, supernatural and natural), it can be regarded as an instance of mediation. In some instances, the divine is so in excess of the human that it can only be described as a total annihilation, a self-abnegation. In other instances, the unhuman, divine element stands in such indifference and indistinction to the human, that only negative terms can be used to describe it — it is null and void, a gulf or abyss, a "nothingness" in which all that is mediated is the impossibility of mediation itself. In one instance, we have a "full" nothingness, an immediacy or *immediation*; in the other instance, an "empty" nothingness, an *antimediation*. Together, these terms — mediation, immediation, and antimediation — describe the spectrum of mystical correlation, viewed through an apophatic prism.

*

Death in Deep Space (The Kyoto School). There is a motif commonly found in horror and science fiction, one that historically derives from narratives of adventures at sea and tales of castaways. The motif is that of the sole human being, unmoored, set loose, and adrift in space. From the *Odyssey* and *Orlando Furioso* to the tales of nautical horror by Edgar Allan Poe, Jules Verne, and William Hope Hodgson, to contemporary science fiction and horror films, there is something terrifying about this sense of being cast adrift in deep space.

Science fiction and horror authors often depict "adrift in space" as being "lost in space," that is, as a byproduct of intergalactic adventure. One was only lost in space until the next adventure, the next battle, the next conquest. However, in earlier works — most notably Camille Flammarion's metaphysical science fiction tale *Lumen* (1873) — being adrift in space is less a byway to yet another adventure, than a speculative opportunity in and of itself. Being adrift in space *is* the story itself, so much so that Poe could pen entire cosmic dialogues around the theme — such as "The

Conversation of Eiros and Charmion" — without character, plot, or setting; abstract horror tales comprised entirely of metaphysical speculation.

Being adrift in space is thus not only a moment of horror, but also a moment of speculation. It is, first, a confrontation with the certitude of death. The lone body, drifting into deep space, will inevitably dissolve itself into that abyss, both literally and metaphysically. When one is lost at sea, there is at least the reliable dichotomy of surface/depth or land/sea, to orient one's being lost. Similarly, when one is lost in space, one is simply moving from one planet to the next (using the dichotomy of earth/sky), perhaps with the stars as one's guide. But the motif of being adrift in space lacks these reference points. There is no ground, no horizon, no perspective — for that matter there is no depth of space itself, there is only blackness, an abyss that is at once flat and infinite. It is inaccurate to say that one is "in" empty space. It is even inaccurate to say that one is "in" emptiness.

This motif of being cast adrift is an allegory for a certain type of metaphysical crisis that goes by the name of "nothingness." As Pascal once noted, pondering the idea of infinity, "the eternal silence of these infinite spaces terrifies me." When a philosophy loses its ground — or when it discovers that the ground it had assumed is actually groundless — then it is confronted with a few choices. It can accept this loss of ground, and then opt for either mysticism or science, poetry or data. There are also those philosophies that resist this move, and attempt to subsist in the loss of ground. In the Western tradition thinkers such as Pascal, Kierkegaard, and Nietzsche are typically given as examples of this kind of thinking.

There is also a whole tradition of non-Western thinking that engages with this question, specifically in the history of Japanese philosophy, where the intersection of Buddhist and European cultural influences produced one of the most fascinating philosophical approaches — that of the so-called Kyoto School.[256] At the center of many Kyoto School thinkers is the classical Buddhist concept of *śūnyatā*, frequently translated as "nothingness" or "emptiness."

While Kyoto School philosophers were well-versed in Western philosophy, their development of this term differs as much from Heidegger and Sartre as it does from its original use in the Buddhist sutras. Contemporary philosopher Masao Abe summarizes this difference:

> [I]n the West such positive principles as being, life, and the good have ontological priority over negative principles such as non-being, death, and evil. In this sense negative principles are always apprehended as something secondary. By contrast, in the East, especially in Taoism and Buddhism, negative principles are not secondary but co-equal to the positive principles and even may be said to be primary and central … In short, the ultimate which is beyond the opposition between positive and negative is realized in the East in terms of negativity and in the West in terms of positivity.[257]

While comparisons like can only ever be schematic, it does illustrate one thing about the Kyoto School tradition: that many of the thinkers associated with it were as comfortable discussing Western metaphysics as they were the finer points of Zen Buddhism. It is this that makes the Kyoto School thinkers uniquely situated to carry out studies in comparative philosophy.

At the center of the formation of the Kyoto School are three philosophers — Kitarō Nishida (1870–1945), Hajime Tanabe (1885–1962), and Keiji Nishitani (1900–1990) — each of whom brings with them some degree of training in Mahāyāna Buddhist philosophy generally, and Sōtō Zen in particular. The moniker "Kyoto School" seems to have formed early; scholars date it to a newspaper article from the 1930s describing Japan's new, modern thinkers. Then as now, the term refers to a generation of philosophers who worked and taught at Kyoto Imperial University, and whose work brought together Western-European and Eastern-Buddhist ideas. Their influence also stretched outside of Japan — Nishida was a colleague and friend of D.T. Suzuki, who went on to popularize Zen in America, and both Tanabe and Nishitani studied and lectured outside of Japan.

One of the distinguishing aspects of the Kyoto School is their unique combination of Mahāyāna Buddhism and German idealism. Nishida speaks frequently of "pure experience," Tanabe of "absolute mediation," and Nishitani of "absolute nothingness." The concept of the absolute haunts nearly all their works, whether they are discussing subjective experience or the physics of the material world. This development of a hybrid philosophical language was no accident. In the early 1920s, Tanabe received a scholarship to study abroad, where he worked with the Kantian philosopher Alois Riehl, before turning to Husserlian phenomenology. Apparently, Tanabe was invited to Husserl's home to give a paper, where the latter hoped to make Tanabe a prophet of phenomenology to the East (a task to which Tanabe was not sympathetic). Tanabe eventually befriended a young Heidegger, who tutored Tanabe in German philosophy and introduced him to the works of Hegel, Fichte, and Schelling. Likewise, Nishitani grew up reading Dostoevsky, Schelling, Emerson, and above all Nietzsche, while also enjoying the novels of Natsume Sōseki. In the late 1930s Nishitani received a scholarship to study abroad with Henri Bergson. When news of the French vitalist's failing health reached Nishitani, he was offered an alternate choice: attend the University of Freiburg to study with Heidegger. While the notion of having Heidegger as a second choice is amusing, Nishitani took the opportunity seriously. During this two-year period, Nishitani not only attended Heidegger's lectures on Nietzsche, but he wrote a thesis on Nietzsche and Meister Eckhart, perhaps one of the first sustained studies of its kind. While Japanese philosophy is much broader than the Kyoto School, the tradition continues to this day in the work of philosophers such as Masao Abe, Shin'ichi Hisamatsu, and Shizuteru Ueda.

*

Absolute Nothingness (Nishida). These cross-cultural elements make for a fascinating, if sometimes ambiguous example of what a post-national, global philosophy might look like. For the Kyoto School philosophers, this particular mix of influences is best exemplified by what is arguably their major contribution: the concept of nothingness. The term *śūnyatā*, conventionally translated into English as either "nothingness" or "emptiness," brings with it a whole host of meanings that are as much religious as philosophical. In the Mahāyāna Buddhist tradition, *śūnyatā* is the groundless ground of all things, the principle or essence that is not itself a principle or essence. For instance, one frequently cited source for the Kyoto School thinkers is the 2nd–3rd-century Indian logician Nagarjuna, whose major work *Mūlamadhyamakakārikā* (*The Fundamental Wisdom of the Middle Way*) defines *śūnyatā* through a rigorous logic of successive negations:

> "Empty" should not be asserted.
> "Nonempty" should not be asserted.
> Neither both nor neither should be asserted.
> They are only used nominally.[259]

This practice of successive negations is known as the tetralemma (in Sanskrit, *catuṣkoṭi*), and it is found throughout Nagarjuna's work, as well as in other texts in the Mahāyāna tradition, such as the *Heart Sutra* and Ch'an Buddhist treatise *The Platform Sutra of the Sixth Patriarch*. The tetralemma involves, quite simply, four logical operations: an assertion *p*, its negation *not-p*, a double affirmation *both p and not-p*, and a double negation *neither p nor not-p*. When applied to the difficult concept of *śūnyatā* the result is often dense, enigmatic phrases, such as:

> If there were even a trifle nonempty,
> Emptiness itself would be but a trifle.
> But not even a trifle is nonempty.
> How could emptiness be an entity?[260]

Without getting lost in the massive commentarial tradition on Nagarjuna, we might generalize *śūnyatā* and say that it is that which is prior to all duality of being and non-being, beyond all subsequent divisions of subject and object, and that which persists beyond or behind all that subsists as phenomena. But nothingness is also inherently self-negating: the thought of that which defies the very categories of thought, primary among them being Aristotle's famed "principle of noncontradiction." Such a thought requires a deft philosophy able to handle the nuances of contradiction, and the Kyoto School thinkers would find such examples not only in the work of Nāgārjuna, but also in the legendary 5th–6th century figure Bodhidharma (who, according to legend, spent nine years meditating in a cave, whereupon his eyelids fell to the ground, from which sprouted the leaves used for black tea), as well as in Dōgen, the 13th-century philosopher, teacher, and founder of Sōtō Zen.

But the Kyoto School philosophers were never content to simply add Eastern ideas as a supplement to the Western canon, the former playing the role of the intuitive or poetic loosening of ideas, the latter establishing the rules and rigor of science. Instead, what we find is that each of the Kyoto School thinkers brings together disparate philosophical traditions in a way that ultimately questions philosophy itself.

For Nishida, personally and professionally inspired by Zen, the challenge was discovering the common thread between Eastern and Western philosophy. Nishida's reference point here is Kant, and the impasse that Kantian critical philosophy poses between self and world, an impasse that Nishida is convinced can be rethought. The path for doing this lies in Nishida's mixture of Zen and German idealism, particularly the work of Fichte. The result is a strange Fichtean Buddhism:

> For some time now I had it in mind to try and explain all of reality in terms of pure experience … Along the way, I came to think that it is not that there is an individual that has the experience, but that there is an experience that has the

> individual, that experience is more basic than any distinction individuals bring to it. This made it possible to avoid solipsism, and by taking experience as something active, to harmonize it with transcendental philosophy after Fichte.[261]

The passage is from Nishida's best-known work, *An Inquiry into the Good.* Nishida's search for "a single, all-encompassing, acting absolute" led him first to question the categories of self and experience laid out by Kant and recapitulated by post-Kantian thinkers such as Fichte. The problem Nishida runs into quite early is the same one encountered by mystics when they speak of a mystical union with the divine. That problem is about the tension between intuition and reflection, key terms in Kantian (and Bergsonian) philosophy: "As *intuition* it [the subject] needs to be aware of a flowing, continuous reality unbroken by subject or object, and as *reflection* it needs to step outside of the flow of reality to recognize it."[262]

Nishida's great insight was, perhaps, to be able to shift his direction: instead of establishing a continuum beyond subject and object from the inside out, Nishida recasts his method, moving from the outside in. This shift is detected at the microlevel of Nishida's philosophical vocabulary, which in earlier texts favored phrases such as "pure experience" to talk about the anonymous, impersonal quality of experience. In *An Inquiry into the Good* and his later writings, Nishida reserves the phrase "absolute nothingness" to talk about this continuum underlying all divisions (not just of subject and object, but of being and non-being as well). Instead of attempting to reach the continuum as a subject would an object — a project destined to fail, since the Absolute that Nishida discusses is not, strictly speaking, an object — now Nishida opts for the language of negation, borrowed in part from his study in, and practice of, Zen Buddhism. In the practice of *zazen* (seated meditation), one does not so much "look at" nothingness, as one allows the nothingness that pervades all things, including the self, to emerge. In this way, it is through negation that Nishida attempts to move from psychology to philosophy — a move echoed a century earlier by German idealist thinkers.

Whether or not such a philosophy escapes the pitfalls of subjectivism or solipsism is up for debate; but in shifting his terms in this way and opting for a philosophy of negation, Nishida's thought opens onto another problem, one different from that of subjectivism. That problem has to do with contradiction itself. The relation between contradiction and negation in philosophy has a long history. But, if we are to follow Aristotle's and Kant's statements on the topic, it appears that even contradiction must observe certain rules, such that it can be inculcated within philosophy itself or domesticated within the strictures of logic. Contradiction must make a certain sense. The Kyoto School philosophers question even this. Thus, "to call reality itself *absolute nothingness*, then, is to say that all of reality is subject to the dialectic of being and not-being, that the identity of each thing is bound to an absolute contradictoriness."[263]

*

On Nihility (Nishitani). Also deeply influenced by Zen Buddhism, Nishitani was an attentive reader of Western thinkers such as Eckhart, Nietzsche, and Heidegger, and, in a sense, where Nishida leaves off, Nishitani begins. More directly engaged with the social, cultural, and political issues of his time — though not without some controversy — Nishitani highlights the "problem of nihility" as it impacts modern Japanese culture.[264] It is from this basis that his own engagement with the concept of nothingness derives. Writing after the war, Nishitani notes that nihilism has come to mean something different in Japan. Whereas, as per Nietzsche's diagnosis, European nihilism emerges as the result of a crisis in religion and the ascendency of scientific rationality, in Japan the foundation has simply withered away, without any great pronouncement about the "death of God." It is, in a sense, the most perfected example of nihilism. While not nostalgic for this withering away of traditional religion, Nishitani notes that the manner in which religion has declined has given Japanese culture a different kind of nihilism. As he notes, "in the past, Buddhism and Confucian thought constituted such a basis, but they have already lost their power, leaving a total void and vacuum in our spiritual ground ... The worst thing is that this emptiness is in no way an emptiness that has been won through struggle, nor a nihility that has been 'lived through.' Before we knew what was happening, the spiritual core had wasted away completely."[265]

At the same time, Nishitani notes that increasing technological rationalization, along with the withering of traditional religions, has resulted in what he terms "the tendency towards the loss of the human." Reduced through science, manufactured through technology, and alienated in modern social relations, the human being, for Nishitani, finds itself everywhere in general but nowhere in particular. In addition, the increasing awareness of issues related to global climate change have rendered the idea of religion deeply problematic. Here an abyss opens up: "when this horizon does open up at the bottom on those engagements that keep life moving continually on and on, something seems to halt and linger before us. This something is the meaninglessness that lies in wait at the bottom of those very engagements that bring meaning to life."[266]

This abyss is what Nishitani terms "nihility." Nihility is the absence of any meaningful or necessary relationship between the human being and the world into which it is cast — a world that human beings have shaped in their own image. This nihility exceeds the scale of individual human beings or human collectivities; it is a vacuousness that oversteps the personal, resulting in what Nishitani terms an "impersonally personal" or "personally impersonal" relation. The human being, which had taken the world for granted as its home, suddenly appears radically out of place, both in the world and in its very being:

> While it continues to be the world in which we live and is inseparably bound up with our existence, it is a world in which we find ourselves unable to live as *human*, in which

> our *human* mode of being is edged out of the picture or even obliterated. We can neither take this world as it is nor leave it.[267]

With nihility the human being is stuck between two mutually untenable positions. It is clear that the world is not simply "our" world, the world made in our image, the world-for-us; but it is equally clear that we as human beings remain in the world, for better or worse. Is there a way in which we can make sense of the world — "so indifferent to our human mode of being as to rub it out" — but do so outside of our human meaning-making activities? This is where, for Nishitani, a philosophical question also becomes a religious one.

But traditional religions will not do, for they only ramify the problem by introducing indifferent, cruel, or law-enforcing gods. With nihility, the stakes are much higher than simply replacing one pantheon with another, one icon with another. Here Nishitani takes his cue from Nietzsche. Both identify a crisis that is as much a social, cultural, and political crisis as it is a philosophical one. Both agree that it will not do to simply set up a new idol (technology) to replace the old one (religion). And both agree that the way beyond nihilism is through nihilism. But whereas Nietzsche opts for an affirmative ontology of nonhuman will, force, and "quanta of power," Nishitani does nearly the opposite, and opts for a negative ontology — a ground of emptiness, a religion without God, an ethics without selfhood. Nihility is as much as much an intuition of a subject as it is a statement about the world: "the point at which the nihility that lies hidden as a reality at the ground of the self and all things makes itself present as a reality to the self in such a way that self-existence, together with the being of all things, turns into a single doubt."[268] The very distinction between doubting subject and doubtful world dissolves, leaving only what classical Buddhism refers to as the "Great Doubt." As Nishitani notes, philosophy "needs to pass through nihility and shift to an entirely new field."[269]

What that new field is, is the subject of Nishitani's major work, *Religion and Nothingness*, at the core of which is a classical Buddhist term, *śūnyatā* (emptiness, nothingness). The problem, as Nishitani defines it, is not so much that there is nothing to believe in, or that our ways of making meaning about ourselves and the world are unreliable. Rather, the problem is the very structure of belief, the very structure of meaning-making. How, then, to proceed? Perhaps, the problem with being, is, in a way, being itself. Whereas Western philosophy concerns itself primarily with being, the philosophy that Nishitani points to concerns itself primarily with non-being or nothingness; whereas Western philosophy is centered around the question of ontology ("why is there something rather than nothing?"), the philosophy that Nishitani is thinking of is that of non-being or nothingness ("why assume that there is anything at all?"). But this non-being or nothingness "cannot lie on a far side, beyond *this* world and *this* earthly life of ours, as something merely transcendent. It must lie on the near side, even more so than we ourselves and our own lives in the here and now are ordinarily supposed to be."[270] Nishitani is proposing something quite ambitious, a concept of non-being or nothingness that is neither contrasted to being (as in Heidegger), nor contained by it (as in Sartre). As Nishitani notes, from "the Buddhist standpoint of *śūnyatā* ('emptiness'), this point comes to light still more clearly."[271]

*

Emptiness of Emptiness. The concept of *śūnyatā* has a long and complex history in Buddhist thought. One finds it, in various guises, in the discourses of the Buddha, in Mahāyāna canonical texts such as *The Heart Sutra* (*Prajñāpāramitā Hṛdaya*), and in the writings of Zen teachers such as Dōgen. Nishitani, along with his Kyoto School colleagues, takes up this term in a modern way, placing it alongside Western notions of nihilism (Nietzsche), nothing (Heidegger), and nothingness (Sartre). As we've noted, for Nishitani the standpoint of *śūnyatā* takes as its starting point non-being rather than being, and in so doing already departs from the Western metaphysical tradition. This also means that, for Nishitani, *śūnyatā* cannot be regarded as equivalent to the terms non-being, nothing, or nothingness. It is not a non-being that is secondary to being (non-being is not derivative from or an error of being), and it is not a non-being that comes after being (non-being only existing by virtue of negating a prior being).

What then is *śūnyatā*? In Nishitani's hands, *śūnyatā* enacts a double negation: a negation of being (and in particular, of substantialist notions of being that view it as prior to non-being), and then a negation of this negation, in effect negating the very relation between being/non-being, something/nothing, fullness/emptiness. Herein lies the difference between *śūnyatā* and terms such as nothing or nothingness. In nihility we have a "negative negativity" aimed at or in relation to being. "Its standpoint contains the self-contradiction that it can neither abide in existence nor abide being away from it."[273] By contrast, with *śūnyatā* there is a negation of the negation, "the standpoint at which absolute negation is at the same time ... a Great Affirmation."[274] In *śūnyatā* one does not simply state that the self and all things are empty, since this would remain within the ambit of nihility (negating an affirmation). Instead of stating that the self is empty, in *śūnyatā* one states that emptiness is the self; instead of stating that all things are empty, in *śūnyatā* one states that emptiness is all things. The shift that Nishitani evokes here is subtle, but in his updating of the term *śūnyatā* he appears to be positing a kind of "empty" monism, a principle-of-everything that is, at the same time, nothing.

This is a tall order, to be sure. But the fact that this is so illustrates how ramified the problem is for Nishitani, not just in terms of philosophical habits, but in our everyday habits of thinking as well: "Ordinarily, of course, we occupy a standpoint shackled to being, from which being is viewed solely as being." When this becomes unstable, what Nishitani calls nihility breaks through. But then the temptation is to latch on to the inverse, to non-being as the sole reality and ground, and "this standpoint of nihility in turn becomes a standpoint shackled to nothingness."[275] This too needs to be negated, and this is where *śūnyatā* comes into play. We have negated the logic of *either/or* (either being or non-being is one true reality), and we have also negated the logic of *both/and* (non-being exists but within being). What remains is the logic of *neither/nor*. Strangely, *śūnyatā*, as neither this nor that, becomes "nothing" but what it is — it is such-and-such. "In this meaning, true emptiness is not to be posited as something outside of and other than 'being.' Rather, it is to be realized as something united to and self-identical with being."[276] Nishitani summarizes this point:

> The emptiness of *śūnyatā* is not an emptiness represented as some "thing" outside of being and other than being. It is not simply an "empty nothing," but rather an *absolute emptiness*, emptied even of these representations of emptiness. And for that reason, it is at bottom one with being, even as being is at bottom one with emptiness … And the things as they are in themselves … just what they are and in their *suchness*, are one with emptiness.[277]

At the same time, we have not simply been brought back into the fold of being, for *śūnyatā*, in its absolute negation, points to the indistinction between emptiness and fullness, non-being and being, something and nothing. This non-being cannot simply be privative or relative, else Nishitani has done nothing other than recast a tradition that runs from Plato to Kant. Neither can this nothingness be rooted in the subjective experience of groundlessness, as one finds in Sartre. Instead, *śūnyatā* has to be understood as "the nullification of the self by the nullification of the ground it has to stand on." This in turn leads to a further stage in which "that nihility is itself nullified … in the awareness that the world of being that rests on the nihility of the self and all things is only a relative manifestation of nothingness as it is encountered *in* reality."[278] Put simply, *śūnyatā* is non-being that is indistinguishable from being.

As with his colleagues Nishida and Tanabe, with Nishitani we find a preoccupation with a subtractive monism, a sense that "beneath that world, all around it, there is an encompassing absolute nothingness that *is* reality. Nihility is emptied out, as it were, into an absolute emptiness, or what Buddhism calls *śūnyatā*."[279] This is also the case in later generations of Kyoto School thinkers, many of whom adopt different approaches and methodologies, but still retain the insights of Nishitani's work on *śūnyatā*. For instance, Masao Abe, borrowing from analytical philosophy as well as from Buddhist sources, reiterates the contradiction in the concept of *śūnyatā*: "Emptiness as *śūnyatā* transcends and embraces both emptiness and fullness. It is really formless in the sense that it is liberated from both 'form' and 'formlessness.'" Pulling almost verbatim from the *Heart Sutra*, Abe continues, stating that "in *śūnyatā*, Emptiness as it is is Fullness and Fullness as it is is Emptiness; formlessness as it is is form and form as it is is formless ... true Emptiness is wondrous Being."[280]

Similarly, in a comparison of "nothingness" in Meister Eckhart and Zen Buddhism, Shizuteru Ueda notes how the concept of *śūnyatā* runs against the "substance-thinking" of Western philosophy (inclusive of philosophies of process, change, or becoming). As he notes:

> Absolute nothingness is concerned with the coincidence of ceaseless negation and straightforward affirmation, such that the coincidence as such is neither negation nor affirmation ... Put in philosophical terms, it [*śūnyatā*] refers to the negation of negation, which entails a movement in two directions at the same time: (1) the negation of negation in the sense of a further denial of negation that does not come back around to affirmation but opens up into an endlessly open nothingness; and (2) the negation of negation in the sense of a return to affirmation without any trace of mediation.[281]

While all the Kyoto School thinkers drew in different ways on Buddhism, they were in disagreement about the relation between philosophy and religion. In a way, they replay the debates of medieval Christian philosophers concerning the proper relation between faith and reason. In Nishida's more poetic works, philosophy tends to turn into religion, while at other times it is philosophy's function to explicate the truths revealed in religion. For Tanabe, who remains more committed to the scientific rigor of philosophy, religion and philosophy are analogous but separate endeavors. However, even Tanabe implies that if the "absolute insolence" and freedom of philosophical thought is pursued to its extreme, it enters into a shared space with religion. Nishitani takes yet another position: "nothingness is deepened to the point that it can assault the very throne of God. The nihility that has untied itself from any and all support wrestles with God for authority and succeeds in offering itself as the absolute groundless ground."[282]

One senses that, for Nishitani, there is a horizon of thought shared by religion and philosophy, though they may each come to that horizon from different places. There is, perhaps, another history of philosophy to be written, one that would begin not from an ontology of being or becoming, but from a negative ontology — or really, a meontology (from the negative prefix *me-*) for which contradiction is, paradoxically, not only fundamental but also necessary. On this point Nishida is perhaps the clearest: "I think that we can distinguish the west to have considered being as the ground of reality, the east to have taken nothingness as its ground."[283]

4

PRAYERS FOR NEGATION

Extremophiles. In the depths of labyrinthine caves, embedded in gigantic rocks, buried in the hottest geothermal vents, and in the cold stellar dust of space, life is stealthily creeping. In environments where it was assumed that life could not exist, scientists have discovered a whole range of life forms that not only survive, but actually flourish under conditions of extreme heat, cold, acidity, pressure, radioactivity, and darkness. Their very existence points to scenarios that for we human beings can only ever be speculative: the emergence or the extinction of life on the Earth, the adaptation of life forms to extreme environmental and climate changes, the existence of life on other planets or in outer space.

Dubbed "extremophiles," such organisms have been discovered by scientists working in a range of fields, from microbiology to astrobiology. Their discoveries have garnered attention both within and outside of the scientific community, primarily because their findings end up questioning the basic premises of the life sciences.[284] A scientific report titled *Investigating Life in Extreme Conditions* provides the decidedly nonhuman setting for understanding extremophiles:

> [T]hat part of the Earth's biosphere permanently inhabited by human beings is rather small and most of the planet, its deep core or mantle, will clearly never see a living organism. In between these two zones (inhabited and uninhabited), a variety of environments exist where human beings cannot live permanently, or physically access, although other forms of life exist within them.[285]

The report goes on to define an extreme environment as "a given environment, where one or more parameters show values permanently close to the lower or upper limits known for life."[286] Extremophiles are united by the fact that they constitute novel forms of life that exist in conditions that would be unfavorable if not fatal to most life forms. Scientists have even discovered microbes that appear to live without sunlight or even oxygen: a group of bacteria called autolithotropes, for example, live deep within rock formations and derive all their nutrients entirely from granite, while the bacterium *Desulfotomaculum* thrives in the darkness of radioactive rocks.

Extremophiles pose interesting problems for philosophy — they serve as philosophical motifs that again raise the enigmatic question, "what is life?" In the era of modern genetics, numerous scientific books and articles also posed this question. Erwin Schrödinger's 1944 book *What Is Life?* suggested that the question originally posed by Aristotle, had by the 20th century been answered in terms of modern cybernetics and information theory. "Life itself" was neither some abstract metaphysical principle, nor was it equivalent to a divine essence; instead, "life itself" had been allied to emerging concepts of "information" and genetic "codes."[287] The paradigm shift was evident in postwar molecular biology, where numerous publications attempted to articulate what was at stake both scientifically and philosophically: James Watson's *The Double Helix* (1968), Jacques Monod's *Chance and Necessity*, and François Jacob's *The Logic of Life* (both 1970), Henri Atlan's *Biological Organization and the Theory of Information* (1972), and Francis Crick's *Life Itself:*

Its Origin and Nature (1982). For molecular biology, life is information, and information contains the content of what life is, to the point where it has become commonplace to speak of DNA and genetic codes in everyday language.

Extremophiles present a different case, for, while their genomes can be analyzed and studied, they themselves have a questionable status. Extremophiles are, quite simply, forms of life living in conditions antagonistic to life. They should not be living — at least according to current biology — and yet they are. Microbes existing in the conditions of the absence of light or oxygen — indeed, feeding off of the absence of light or oxygen — are an anomaly for biological science. And their anomalous existence as scientific entities invites us to raise not only philosophical questions, but, more specifically, questions pertaining to logic as well.

*

What Should Not Be. Extremophiles are contradictions. They are alive, but should not be alive. That is, they are alive according to our existing criteria of "life" and yet, according to those same criteria, they are not alive — or rather, they should not be alive. In classical Aristotelian logic, extremophiles transgress the basic laws of philosophical logic. Aristotle's famous Law of Noncontradiction (LNC) states that for any entity *p*, the statements "*p* is true" and "*p* is false" cannot both be the case. And yet, here we have the *Desulfotomaculum* bacteria, which is both alive and not alive, according to the same set of scientific presuppositions concerning "life." Similarly, Aristotelian logic outlines the Law of the Excluded Middle (LEM), which states that *p* is either true or false, one or the other, but not both at the same time. And yet the *Desulfotomaculum*, something which, according to current scientific criteria, shouldn't be alive, is alive, and even thriving.

Biological science, in so far as it is rooted in systematic description and classification, relies on its own principle of sufficient reason, namely that life and logic bear some basic relation to each other — in other words, the principle that all that can be identified and known as life is ordered or organized in such a way that it can live. Life implies order, and order invites speculation about purpose, and purpose forms the ground for meaning. From a philosophical perspective, extremophiles are negation incarnate, in so far as their very existence undermines many aspects of the still dominant paradigm of molecular biology. Within the framework of biological science, extremophiles are examples of the manifestation of "what is not," something whose existence is disallowed by biology, and yet which persists regardless. The extremophiles are, in a way, examples of living contradictions, a living instance of the inverse relationship between logic and life.

Though Aristotelian logic has arguably been superseded by modern developments in logic, these so-called laws of thought still form the foundation for any general notion of philosophical rigor; they are the basis for the very possibility of anything like philosophy taking place at all. Without them, philosophy literally loses its ground, and collapses inward. And at the center of the example of extremophiles is not just the relation between logic and life, but, more specifically, the role that *negation* plays in this relationship. Negation is not simply a matter of disembodied, logical operations, but the very stuff of life, incarnate in the enigmatic logic of its molecular codes.

But negation is a strange entity, or, we should say, a non-entity. It is often assumed to have a reactive, derivative function, which first presumes the existence of a positivity, which can then be negated. This is as much the case in examples of classical negation as it is in contemporary philosophy. For instance, Benjamin Noys suggests that contemporary philosophy, as diverse as it is, betrays a common commitment to "affirmationist" thinking, in which negation is always subsumed within affirmation. Such affirmationism affirms "the creation of unashamedly metaphysical ontologies, the inventive potential of the subject, the necessity for the production of novelty, and a concomitant suspicion of the negative and negativity."[288] The result is that negation comes to be automatically viewed as a failed or reactive affirmation — as self-impressed deconstruction, as a dialectical "paleo-Hegelianism," or simply as the "endorsement of nihilistic destruction."

Furthermore, it is often unclear if negation is an actual entity in the world, or simply a statement about entities. According to the conventional, Aristotelian understanding, affirmations are statements about the world or entities in the world ("*p* exists"), whereas negations are statements about statements ("*p* does not exist" where $\neg p$ is merely the negation of the statement "*p* exists"). This is because the statement "*p* does not exist" does not itself point to anything that exists, except the enigma of "not existing." The very thing that the laws of thought are supposed to prevent suddenly seems unavoidable.

And yet, philosophers of logic, from Aristotle and Kant to Frege, Russell, and contemporary "dialetheists" all accept the central role of negation in any study of philosophical logic.[290] Though we may subsume negation within the ambit of philosophy, giving us a philosophy of negation, we can also ask at what point does negation *exceed* philosophy, perhaps undermining it and giving us a negation of philosophy? But such a negation of philosophy can be taken in a number of ways, either as evoking a "pre-philosophical" mode prior to the divisions of subject and object, self and world, or as promising a "post-philosophical" mode in which such divisions are at last overcome in a grand synthesis. But these are philosophical fantasies engendered by negation and its ambivalent threat. "Each philosophy," notes François Laruelle, "defines a non-philosophical margin that it tolerates, circumscribes, reappropriates, or which it uses in order to expropriate itself: as beyond or other to philosophical mastery."[291]

This leads to a conundrum. The laws of thought safeguard the coherence of philosophical claims, and yet any study of philosophy must necessarily acknowledge the centrality of negation in a philosophical inquiry. Wittgenstein encapsulates this conundrum: "…it is important that the signs '*p*' and '$\neg p$' *can* say the same thing. For it shows that nothing in reality corresponds to the sign '$\neg$'."[292] In short, the laws of thought exclude those things that are constitutive of the laws of thought. And yet, what negation itself indexes is, strictly speaking, nothing — which, logically speaking, still exists (as "nothing"). Wittgenstein again: "The propositions '*p*' and '¬*p*' have opposite sense, but there corresponds to them one and the same reality."[293]

The relation of logic and life is of particular interest, for "life" is, arguably, *the* principle of affirmation. It is generative, proliferating, productive and reproductive, and when negation is considered — as organismic death or decay — it is recuperated into the affirmative model of life (e.g., cycles of life, evolutionary adaptation, participation in an ecosystem). For every negative, a positive, and for every negation an opposing affirmative term that ultimately subsumes it within the larger positivity of living beings. The idea that life would be constituted by and through negation would seem to be an anomaly, if not a logical impossibility. What if extremophiles are in fact the norm, and not the exception? A contradiction seems to haunt the concept of life.

*

On Absolute Life. We need not delve into the deepest caves or the most obscure corners of logic to discover negation at the heart of life. It is a part of philosophical reflection on life, from Aristotle to Kant to contemporary biophilosophy. For instance, Aristotle's enigmatic *De Anima*, rendered more enigmatic by generations of commentary and translation, is perhaps the first systematic ontology of life that hinges on contradiction — namely, one between a general life-principle or life-force (*psukhē*) and the manifold instances of the living, so exhaustively catalogued in works such as *Historia Animalium*. The former (Life) is never present in itself, only manifest in the diverse concretions of the latter (the living); the latter serve as the conceptual guarantee of the former. But it is Kant's treatment of life's teleology or "purposiveness" (*zweckmäßigkeit*) that not only revives Aristotle's problematic, but adds another dimension to it

— any instance of life is always split between its purposiveness in itself and its purposiveness for us, the beings who think life. In the Kantian paradigm, the possibility of knowing the former is always compromised by the presumptions of the latter.

On the one hand life is phenomenal since we are not just subjects but also *living* subjects. Life is amenable to the manifold of sensation, is given as an object of the understanding, and results in a synthetic knowledge of the nature of life. Life is an object for a subject. On the other hand, the Aristotelian problem — what is the life-in-itself that is common to all instances of the living? — returns again in Kant's critical philosophy. Life-in-itself is neither the knowledge nor the experience of the living (be it biological classification or the subjective phenomenon of living). Life-in-itself is also not the living being considered as such (given to science as an object of observation).

In short, the life common to all living beings is ultimately enigmatic and inaccessible to thought, since any given instance of the living is not life-in-itself, but only one manifestation of life. It seems there is some residual zone of inaccessibility that at once guarantees that there is a life-in-itself for all instances of the living, while also remaining in itself obscure. It is precisely as living subjects, with life given as objects for us as subjects, that we are cut off from, and yet enmeshed within, life in itself.

Schopenhauer once noted that Kant's greatest philosophical contribution was the division between phenomena and noumena, the world as it appears to us, and the enigmatic and inaccessible world in itself. Whereas for Kant this division served a critical or regulatory function, providing philosophy with ground to stand on, for German idealism this division is an impasse to be overcome — through philosophy itself.

For the generation immediately following on the coattails of Kant, the important task was to identify this split as the key impasse in Kantianism, and to provide ways of overcoming that impasse.[295] This is a significant project, because for Kant, the critical philosophy was not, of course, a problem, but rather a solution to a whole host of metaphysical quandaries that pitted empiricists against rationalists, materialists against idealists, and so on. In a sense, German idealism's first and most important gesture is to restate Kantianism as a problem to be overcome. The concept of the Absolute, and the various avatars of the Absolute proposed by Fichte, Schelling, and Hegel (Spirit, the Infinite, the World-Soul), are an outcome of this gesture.

This split between phenomena and noumena can only be overcome if it is in some way collapsed — or rendered as continuous. Since we as thinking subjects cannot have access to noumena, we must begin from phenomena, and in particular the phenomena of thought. Hence thought must not be taken as split from the world in itself, but as somehow continuous with it. But this itself is a difficult thought, precisely because thought is presumed to be specific to living, rational, human subjects — thought is internalized, rendered proprietary, owned and instrumentalized. Kant's split implicitly relies on an internalist model of thought, one that begins and ends with anthropocentrism.

The key move that German idealism makes is to externalize thought, to render it ontologically prior to the individual thinking subject that thinks it. Only if thought is understood to be exterior to the human, can it then become that continuum between the "for us" and the "in itself," phenomena and noumena. The idealist operation is, in a sense, to subtract the noumenal from the Kantian split, leaving only a continuum that stretches without demarcations between the world-for-us and the world-in-itself.

In place of the phenomena-noumena split, then, one has a new totality, which raises thought above its Kantian, anthropocentric bias, and establishes it as that which enables the very split between phenomena and noumena, as well as the split within phenomena between thought and world, and subject and object. Thought is raised to the Absolute, and, in this continuum, the thoughts of subjectivity and of the world in itself are both manifestations of a single Absolute. If this is the case, then Kant's framework is not just a reflection or representation of the world, but is itself a manifestation of the Absolute. What results is a new kind of philosophical drama, a drama of the Real and the Rational (and their comingling), or, in Schelling's terms, a drama of Nature as the manifestation of the Absolute.

This continuum is neither a transcendent, static category of Being, nor is it simply an affirmation of an unbounded, immanent multiplicity of beings; it both an inaccessible noumena "outside" us, and a manifest field of phenomena that constitutes us from within. It is for this reason that German idealism turns to the concept of life-in-itself. For many philosophers working in the wake of Kant, the concept of life-in-itself establishes a continuum between phenomena and noumena, but without being reduced to either biology or theology. For Hegel, the Absolute is inherently dynamic, "the life of the Absolute," moving, flowing, and becoming through the structured phases of the dialectic, with the living organism its exemplar.[296] For Schelling, given his long-standing interest in natural philosophy, it is through the processes of nature that the Absolute manifests itself — thus Nature is "manifest Spirit" and Spirit is "invisible Nature."[297] Even Fichte, otherwise a logician, attempts to account for the movement between the I and not-I, the Ego and non-Ego, by resorting to the vitalist language of life itself, commenting on the "Absolute Life" through which the I/Ego spontaneously manifests itself.[298]

In its attempts to overcome the Kantian problematic, German idealist thinkers exhibit a conceptual shift from a static to a dynamic ontology from being to becoming; they also effect a shift from a transcendent to an immanent concept of life, in which the framework of source/manifestation supersedes that of essence/existence. They turn their attention to conceptual models borrowed from natural philosophy and the philosophy of the organism, which has the broad impact of shifting the philosophy of life from a mechanist framework to a vitalist one.

Within German idealism "life itself" becomes a philosophical problematic, and in the process becomes a stand-in for the Absolute, resulting in what we can simply call, borrowing from Fichte,

Absolute Life. Absolute Life is monistic; it is a metaphysical totality that underlies all reality, but that is not separate from it. It is a totality that exists beyond any part-whole relation, but that is also only ever manifest in the particular. Absolute Life is also immanence; it is an infinite process of becoming, flux, and flow, an infinite manifestation in finite Nature, an infinite expression of the living in an organic whole called Life. Finally, Absolute Life is paradoxical. It harbors within itself a duplicity in which Absolute Life is at once omni-present and omni-absent, accessible and inaccessible to the senses, thinkable and an outer limit for thought. Absolute Life, while not a pure thing-in-itself, is only ever manifest in Nature (and thus indirectly knowable). At its core, Absolute Life has the conceptual structure of negative theology.

*

The Ontology of Generosity. If we had to give a name to this kind of thinking, in which life itself is ontologized beyond its regional discourses (natural philosophy, biology, zoology), and comes to serve as a stand-in for the Absolute, we could call it the *ontology of generosity*. The ontology of generosity states, first, that the precondition of the intelligibility of life lies in its innate propensity for continually expressing itself in all the varieties of the living. This propensity applies as much to the upscale processes of growth and development as it does to the downscale processes of decay and decomposition; indeed, as Schelling notes, life is never more strongly asserted than in the process of decay. Life, then, is generous, not simply because it always gives itself forth, but because it always asserts and affirms itself, even as it withdraws, withers, and returns to its inorganic foundations — where another life then continues. In the ontology of generosity, life is not simply present, but *overpresent*.

In German idealism, the ontology of generosity begins from the overpresence of life-in-itself, coupled with the split between Life (as superlative to the living) and the living (as always in excess of

Life). However, the generosity of life does not flow forth in a single, homogeneous manner. In a number of the *Naturphilosophie* works of Schelling, one can detect several variations to the generosity of Life. There is, first, *Life as genesis* (also generation, production). Life is generous because it is defined by an ontology of becoming, process, and genesis. Here the question is "why is there something new?"[299] This mode is especially evident in Schelling's natural philosophy, where a "speculative physics" aims to account for the flux and flows of the Absolute in Nature. Life is ontologically prior to the living, but Life is also only ever explained in the living. When Schelling discusses the "potencies" of Nature — forces of attraction and repulsion, dynamics of electricity and magnetism, organismic physiology — he is evoking the generosity of Life in terms of its geneses.

In addition to this, there is a second mode, in which *Life is givenness* (also gift, donation). In this case, Life is generous because it is defined by its being given, its giving forth, its being already-there, its affirmation prior to all being. Here the central question is "why is there already something?" The idea of givenness enables the thought of Life to pass beyond the philosophy of nature and obtain a higher, ontological status. That this or that particular instance of the living is given is no great statement; it only points to the need for a concept of Life to account for all possible instances of the living. That Life (as opposed to the living) is given is another issue altogether; it means that the Absolute is not only an intelligible totality, but that it is an ongoing process, a flux and flow that is consonant with the Absolute. In the grand schema of Hegel, Spirit can only realize itself through its successive stages (Idea, Nature, Spirit) by virtue of this "life of the Absolute." Givenness is the necessary precondition for thinking Absolute Life.

However, while German idealism provides a solution to the Kantian problematic, that solution often ends up being compromised by the Kantian framework itself. There is, to begin with, the problem of genesis — generosity demands genesis, if only as its minimal condition. Within the ontology of generosity, one must still posit a source of life, even if this source is self-caused or self-generating. There is also the rather nagging problem of teleology. The positing of a life-source necessitates the positing of an end or purpose, in order to qualify and to justify the organization inherent in life — order demands an end. This is true even if the end one posits is the process of becoming itself, without end. The positing of a source and end dovetails into the need to accept a distinction between source and end, and this remains the case even if one asserts an immanent relation between source and end, in which source and end persist in a kind of tautology.

The result is that the ontology of generosity inherited from German idealism looks to be a compromised Kantianism, at once inculcated within the requirements of the Kantian framework and, at the same time, claiming to have absolved Kantianism of its own antinomies. The ontology of generosity must make do with a source that is self-caused, a process that is its own end, and a collapsed distinction between essence and existence.

With German idealism, we see the concept of life raised up, as it were, beyond natural philosophy, such that it can serve as a continuum bridging the Kantian gulf between phenomena and noumena. But this requires that one think not just of this or that living being, but Absolute Life — that which is not reducible to, and yet not separate from, the fluxes and flows of life as we know it. Idealism's ambition is to put forth a concept of Absolute Life via an ontology of generosity, in which Life is conditioned by its overpresence. Absolute Life is thus overpresent in several ways — as genesis or as givenness. Note also that these two paths — genesis and givenness — also form the two major channels through which flow contemporary biophilosophies: Life-as-genesis constituting the vitalist ontologies of Henri Bergson, Alfred North Whitehead, and Gilles Deleuze; Life-as-givenness constituting the phenomenological approach of thinkers such as Edmund Husserl, Jean-Luc Marion, and Michel Henry.[300]

*

On Ascensionism. How does the ontology of generosity attempt to resolve the problem posed by Kant, the irrevocable split between Life and the living? Put simply, the idealist philosophies of Fichte, Hegel, and Schelling attempt to expand the concept of life, to the point that "life" becomes identical with nature, the world, and even with being itself. In other words, life for these thinkers is not reducible to its biological, anthropological, or zoological definitions. Life is also not exclusive to the subjective, human experience of being alive (that is, to a life experience). In post-Kantian philosophy, the concept of life oscillates between these regional concepts (life science, life experience) and a more fundamental concept encapsulated in the phrase "Absolute Life." Life is elevated and raised up, beyond the human and beyond nature, even beyond the divine. We can call this broader, more expansive point of view *ascensionism*: the process by which the concept of life is raised up to the status of a metaphysical principle. Ascensionist thinking has two forms, both of which we can still see today.

The first form of ascensionism states that the *world is alive*. The concrete notion of life as defined within natural philosophy or life science, is raised up and expanded so as to describe the world itself. One begins with the individuated living organism, and scales it up to the planetary level. In the history of philosophy, animism, panpsychism, and certain strands of phenomenology are examples of this first form of ascensionism. In science, a well-known example might be the Gaia hypothesis, as well as certain aspects of deep ecology.

The second form of ascensionism states that *life is the world*. This is the near inverse of the first form. Here we see the raising up of life as the manifestation of a metaphysical principle, such as time and temporality, form and causality, or the concepts of becoming and process. In the history of philosophy, vitalism, mechanism, and pantheism might be examples of this second form of ascensionism. In science, one might cite certain aspects of biocomplexity and systems biology as examples.

Both forms of ascensionism are already present in philosophy after Kant. For instance, Hegel's comments on the organicist "life of the Absolute" in the *Phenomenology of Spirit* are linked to his study of living organisms in the *Philosophy of Nature*. Kant himself engages in ascensionist thinking when, for instance, he states that the principle of order in the world must be sought in the "analogue of Life" — in which life serves as the model for the ordered, purposive character of the world as a whole.

The ontology of generosity, expressed in ascensionist thinking, is not without its limitations. Primary among these is the investment in an affirmative ontology with regard to the concept of life (whether it be in terms of genesis or givenness). So crucial is this, that in some cases it tends to become a moral principle as well — life is good precisely because it is generous, bountiful, and gives itself forth unconditionally. Behind these ontological frameworks are psychological notions that may even border on self-help. We must have faith in life, go with the flow, it's the journey not the destination. And we as human beings become dubiously romanticized within this bountiful flux and flow, resulting in a lyrical and therapeutic anthropomorphism of the Absolute. In this heady mix of hippie-affectivism and chaos theory, the human expands to such an extent that it eclipses the world itself, absorbing the nonhuman into its embrace, able to know all and to be all.

The question is whether there are any alternatives to the ontology of generosity and its ascensionist thinking, a form of thinking in which "life" is always the "life-for-us" as human beings. Perhaps we have had too much of life. Perhaps "life itself" is as much negation as it is affirmation. But is it possible to have done with the concept of life? Is it possible to conceive of something like a negative ontology of life, an ontology of life as — in itself — "nothing"?

*

Schopenhauer's Antagonisms. When life is thought as life-in-itself, we seem to be driven to a fork in the road: either the framework of Being/beings or the framework of Being/becoming. There is, possibly, another approach, one that would think life-in-itself *meontologically*, as "nothing," though it too has its own limitations. The best exemplar of this approach is found in the work of Arthur Schopenhauer.

Schopenhauer's sentiments regarding German idealist thinkers are well known. He despised them.[301] Certain passages in *The World as Will and Representation* (hereafter *WWR*) betray a profound personal disgust towards Fichte, Schelling, and above all Hegel, for whom Schopenhauer reserves his most vitriolic phrases, here cited at length:

> But the greatest disadvantage of Kant's occasionally obscure exposition is that it acted as *exemplar vitiis imitabile* ["an example whose defects are easy to imitate"] … what was senseless and without meaning at once took refuge in obscure exposition and language. Fichte was the first to grasp and make vigorous use of this privilege; Schelling at least equaled him in this, and a host of hungry scribblers without intellect or honesty soon surpassed them both. But the greatest effrontery in serving up sheer nonsense, in scribbling together senseless and maddening webs of words, such as had previously been heard only in madhouses, finally appeared in Hegel. It became the instrument of the most ponderous and general mystification that had ever existed, with a result that will seem incredible to posterity, and be a lasting monument of German stupidity.[302]

Metaphysical rants like these occur throughout Schopenhauer's writings, and there is a certain charm behind Schopenhauer's grumpy dismissals. Indeed, for many readers, "obscure exposition" and "ponderous mystification" have come to define philosophy itself. To be fair, Schopenhauer himself was no stranger to the crime of obscurity, as demonstrated by his frequent use of phrases like *qualitas occulta* and *principum individuationis*.

Despite this, there is also a sense of clearing the air in Schopenhauer's writings, and no doubt "untimely" followers of Schopenhauer such as Nietzsche found inspiration in this tone. Not so fast, quips Schopenhauer, we have not even begun to address the problems put forth by Kant's antinomies. In the opening of *WWR* Schopenhauer's first step is to brush aside the entirety of post-Kantian dogmatism and return to Kant's problematic — the split between phenomena and noumena. As he notes, "Kant's principal merit is that he distinguished the phenomenon from the thing-in-itself, declared this whole visible world to be phenomenon, and therefore denied to its laws all validity beyond the phenomenon." This is, notes Schopenhauer, an acceptable constraint to our metaphysical thinking. But why stop there? As Schopenhauer notes, it is "remarkable that he [Kant] did not trace that merely relative existence of the phenomenon from the simple, undeniable truth which lay so near to him, namely 'No object without a subject.'" If Kant had pushed his philosophy a few steps further, he would have arrived at the notion that "the object, because it always exists only in relation to a subject, is dependent thereon, is conditioned thereby, and is therefore mere phenomenon that does not exist in itself, does not exist unconditionally."[303] Though inaccessible, noumena remain related — or correlated — to phenomena, with the former tending to become increasingly subsumed within the latter. When pushed a bit further, one ends up with something that looks a lot like idealism, with a metaphysical continuum between phenomena and noumena that promises to collapse Kant's split between them.

For Schopenhauer, German idealism can only overcome this split by dropping out one of the two terms — noumena — thereby allowing a phenomenal monism to fill the gap. "All previous systems started either from the object or from the subject, and therefore sought to explain the one from the other, and this according to the principle of sufficient reason."[304] Idealism attempts to think a continuum between phenomena and noumena that is not reducible to either. But what it really ends up doing — in Schopenhauer's opinion — is adopting a partial view (that of a subject towards an object) and universalizing this in the Absolute.

What, then, does Schopenhauer propose? One must reexamine not only the Kantian framework, but the basic presuppositions of the idealist response to Kant. For Schopenhauer, the principle of sufficient reason is primary among these presuppositions that must be reexamined. For the pessimist philosopher, that "everything that exists, must exist for a reason" must not be taken for granted. But this leaves a great deal open, too much perhaps: What if there is no reason for the world's existence, either as phenomena or as noumena? What if the world-in-itself is not ordered, let alone ordered "for us"? What if the world-as-it-is, let alone the world-in-itself, is unintelligible, not in a relative way, but in an absolute way? Once one dispenses with the principle of sufficient reason, what is left — except a philosophy that can only be a non-philosophy? It would appear that two paths are left open — materialism or idealism, nihilism or mysticism, the hard facts and the great beyond, "it is what it is" and "there is something more." As we will see, for Schopenhauer, pessimism is the only viable philosophical response to such an abandonment of the principle of sufficient reason.

Schopenhauer dismisses the German idealist response to Kant's phenomena-noumena split as inadequate. In its place he proposes a simple move — that Kant's split be recast in a way that allows an abyss to slowly grow within it. There is, first, the world as phenomena: "Everything that in any way belongs and can belong to the world is inevitably associated with this being-conditioned by the subject, and it exists only for the subject."[305] This includes the subject-object correlation, as well as the finer distinction that Schopenhauer later makes between the representation and the object of representation, both of which are contained within the world of phenomenon. Put simply, "the world is my representation."

Then there is, on the other side, the world as noumena, which is a pure limit that at once conditions thought and remains inaccessible to thought — "something to which no ground can ever be assigned, for which no explanation is possible, and no further cause is to be sought."[306] The concept of noumena can only ever be a limit concept. Schopenhauer enters deep waters here, not least because any attempt to conceptualize the noumenal is doomed from the start. This never seems to deter the philosopher-curmudgeon, however. The challenge is how to think the inaccessibility of the world as noumena, and Schopenhauer glosses this via a concept of nothingness/emptiness that is at the same time not completely separate from the phenomenal world. One need not soar into the infinity of the cosmos or the inner depths of Spirit to discover such a concept. Schopenhauer discovers it in the seemingly mundane materiality of the body: "Thus it happens that to everyone the thing-in-itself is known immediately in so far as it appears as their own body, and only mediately in so far as it is objectified in the other objects of perception."[307] What results is Schopenhauer's well-known, two-fold view: the correlation of subject and object that constitutes phenomena is the world considered as representation (*Vorstellung*), and that which is absolutely inaccessible to this world-as-representation, but which is also inseparable from it, is the world considered as will (*Wille*). "[T]he world is, on the one side, entirely representation, just as, on the other, it is entirely will."[308] While they are not separate from each other, it is, in a way, that very rift between them that also links them together.

*

Schopenhauer and the Negation of Life. Like his idealist contemporaries, Schopenhauer agrees that "Kant's greatest merit is the distinction of the phenomenon from the thing-in-itself."[309] And like them, Schopenhauer views this distinction as something to be overcome. But whereas the German idealist response is to adopt an ontology of generosity to bridge this gap, Schopenhauer will adopt a different approach. Instead of asserting an Absolute Life (the ontology of overpresence), Schopenhauer will drop the bottom out of the ontology of generosity. What remains is, quite simply, nothing. No overflowing life force, no pantheistic becoming, no immanent principle of life running throughout all of Creation. Just nothing. But nothing is, of course, never simple; it is also nothingness, or emptiness, or the void, and it quickly becomes an enigmatic something. So while Schopenhauer does not definitively resolve the Kantian problematic, he does provide a way of shifting the entire orientation of thought on the problem.

The new problem Schopenhauer is confronted with is how to overcome the Kantian split between phenomena and noumena, but without resorting to the ontology of generosity: how to think "life" such that it is not always determined by overpresence (generosity, genesis, and givenness). In short, *how to think life as negation*. Certainly one would not want to return to a metaphysics of life, in which life has the quality of pure being that one finds in the concept of "soul," common to both Aristotle and Aquinas. But Schopenhauer is equally skeptical of the diffuse theism in the German idealist notions of the Absolute, in which Absolute Life always radiates and flows forth, often finding its culmination in the heights of human life. Schopenhauer notes, with some sarcasm, "life is thus given as a gift, whence it is evident that anyone would have declined it with thanks had they looked at it and tested it beforehand."[310]

The remaining option for Schopenhauer is to consider the role that negation plays in relation to life, especially any ontology of life that would attempt to overcome the Kantian split of phenomena and noumena. Life is not simply subordinate to a metaphysics of presence (as in Kant), but neither is it consonant with an infinite overpresence of generosity (as with German idealism). In contrast to the ontology of generosity, which posits life as always affirmative, Schopenhauer will put forth a negative ontology, in which life is grounded in nothingness (it is, perhaps, "underpresent"). In a striking turn of phrase, Schopenhauer refers to all these relations between negation and life as *Wille zum Leben*, which we can translate either as "Will-to-Live" or "Will-to-Life":

> As the will is the thing-in-itself, the inner content, the essence of the world, but life, the visible world, the phenomenon, is only the mirror of the will, this world

> accompanies the will as inseparably as a body is accompanied by its shadow; and if will exists, then life, the world exists. Therefore life is certain to the will-to-live.[311]

Schopenhauer's concept of the Will-to-Life is a response to an old dilemma concerning the ontology of life. It is found in Aristotle, and then in natural philosophy, before its recapitulation in Kant. We have seen it in German idealism, in the ontology of generosity and its affirmative overpresence. The dilemma is how to articulate a concept of life-in-itself that would account for all the instances of the living. If one is to avoid both the naïveté of epistemological classification, as well as the rhetorical ruses of nominalism, what is needed is a concept of life that is at once synonymous with the living, and yet separated from it.

The Will-to-Life is Schopenhauer's attempt to overcome the Kantian split by asserting a subtractive continuity, a continuity constituted by negation. At the same time, in order to arrive at the concept of the Will-to-Life, Schopenhauer must make a number of moves (which many of his critics perceived as fallacious or untenable). With this in mind, we can briefly consider the three aspects of the Will-to-Life as presented in Schopenhauer's philosophy.

*

Riddle of Life. Early on in his writings, Schopenhauer recasts the Kantian problematic through the example of the living body. His concern, however, is neither a "body" in the sense of physics, which would commit him to mechanism or atomism, nor "body" in the sense of biology, which would commit him to natural philosophy. Instead the body is for Schopenhauer a kind of crystallization of abstract anonymity, a "Will" that is at once energy and drive, but that has no origin or end, and leads to no goal. The body is that which is the most familiar and yet the most foreign to us. We are bodies, and we have bodies. For Schopenhauer these are simply two ways of knowing the same thing — immediately as a living subject consonant with a living body, and mediately as a subject relating to or thinking about the body as object. Both of these are well within the domain of the phenomenal world that Kant describes.

But in the Second Book of *WWR* Schopenhauer will take Kant a step further. If the body, as both subject and object, is on the side of the world as phenomena (as representation), then what would the living body as a thing-in-itself be? If there is a phenomenon of life, is there also a noumena of life, a life-in-itself? On the one hand, such a noumenal life could not be something completely divorced from life as phenomena, for then there would be no point of connection between phenomena and noumena (a logical prerequisite for Kant). On the other hand, this noumenal life must retain a minimal non-relation with regard to phenomenal life, else we are simply back within the phenomenal domain of subject-object relations.

Hence Schopenhauer's "riddle of life": what is that through which life is at once the nearest and the farthest, the most familiar and the most strange? As he notes, "the answer to the riddle is given to the subject of knowledge appearing as individual, and this answer is given in the word *Will*."[313] The Will is, in Schopenhauer's hands, that which is common to subject and object, but not reducible to either. This Will is never present in itself, either as subjective experience or as objective knowledge; it remains a negative manifestation. Even as conscious, reflective beings, we spend so much of our bodily life in the shadow of a multitude of biological processes that require no reflection at all. Thinking of the autonomic processes of respiration, digestion, and the functioning of the nervous system, Schopenhauer presses this point further, suggesting that "the whole body is nothing but objectified will, i.e. will that has become representation."[314] And again: "My body and will are one ... or, My body is the *objectivity* of my will."[315]

In reply to the riddle "what is nearest and farthest?" Schopenhauer answers with the Will — that which is fully immanent and yet absolutely inaccessible. As we noted, Schopenhauer's first step is to recast Kant's framework in new terms — for Kantian phenomena he will use the term Representation, and for Kantian noumena he will use the term Will. His next step is to describe the living body, and more specifically life, as the nexus where Will and Representation meet. Schopenhauer posits that for each instance of the world taken as Representation there is the world as Will; and to each instance of life as Representation (whether as subject or object), there is a correlative Will-to-Life:

> The will, considered purely in itself, is devoid of knowledge, and is only a blind, irresistible urge, as we see it appear in inorganic and vegetable nature … and as what the will wills is always life, just because this is nothing but the presentation of that willing for the representation, it is immaterial and a mere pleonasm if, instead of simply saying "the will," we say "the will-to-life" (*Wille zum Leben*).[316]

Within this framework, life contains a duality within the domain of Representation — there is the subjective experience of living, just as there is the scientific knowledge of the living, both inscribed within the world as Representation or phenomena. Schopenhauer's controversial move is to assert that there is life outside of and apart from the world as Representation, that there is a life which remains inaccessible to the phenomenon of life, and his phrase Will-to-Life designates this horizon.

*

Life Negating Life. At this point, the problem is that Schopenhauer appears to have only elevated the concept of life beyond ontology, to the realm of unthinkable noumena. There still remains a part of the riddle to be answered, which is how that which is nearest can — *at the same time* — be that which is farthest. For this the role of negation in the Will-to-Life becomes more important.

Schopenhauer notes that the Will is not simply a static, transcendent category of being, but a dynamic, continuous principle that is much in line with the idealist concept of the Absolute. But, as we've seen, Schopenhauer distances himself from idealism by opposing the ontology of generosity that it puts forth.[317] As he notes, "everywhere we see contest, struggle, and the fluctuation of victory, and ... we shall recognize in this more distinctly that variance with itself essential to the will."[318] Schopenhauer provides a veritable compendium of examples from the sciences, though they read more like scenes from a horror movie: insects that lay their eggs in the bodies of other host insects, for whom birth is death; the predator-prey relationship within the hydra; the ant whose head and tail fight each other if the body is cut in two; invasive species such as ivy; giant oak trees whose branches become so intertwined that the tree suffocates. His examples continue, up through the cosmic negation of black holes, down to the basic chemical decomposition of matter in the decay of corpses, where life is engulfed in the negation of life.

Yet Schopenhauer is neither Hobbes nor Darwin; his emphasis is less on the universality of struggle, and more on what it indicates for an ontology of life. If the Will is flow or a continuum, it is, for Schopenhauer, one driven by negation — or by a negative flow, a negative continuum. The Will asserts itself through contradictions, oppositions, subtractions, and its limit is the self-negation of life, through life. Thus "the will-to-live (*Wille zum Leben*) generally feasts on itself, and is in different forms its own nourishment, until finally the human race, because it subdues all the others, regards nature as manufactured for its own use."[319] Life is not "for us" as human beings, much less for any particular form of life. There is, for Schopenhauer, something starkly impersonal about the Will-to-Life.

For Schopenhauer, there is an "inner antagonism" to the Will, one that is antagonistic at the level of this or that living being, as well as in the domain of inorganic nature, on through to the level of cosmic life. The Will-to-Life is driven by this process of "life negating life," from the inorganic to the organic and beyond, towards the cosmic.

*

Cosmic Pessimism. Considering the inner antagonism of the Will-to-Life, Schopenhauer comes upon what is perhaps his greatest insight, and that is its radically unhuman aspect. Schopenhauer pulls apart the Kantian split, suggesting that all claims concerning noumena are necessarily compromised by concepts derived in some way from the phenomenal domain. And it is here that Schopenhauer directly counters the furtive anthropocentrism in post-Kantian idealism. In the same way that the domain of noumena does not exist for phenomena, so the Will-to-Life is utterly indifferent to any instance of life, be it "for us" or "in itself." In the Will-to-Life "we see at the very lowest grade the will manifesting itself as a blind impulse, an obscure, dull urge, remote from all direct knowableness."[320]

Schopenhauer is actually making two separate claims. The first has to do with the principle of sufficient reason, and Schopenhauer's critical treatment of it. In so far as the Will-to-Life is noumenal as well as phenomenal, all statements concerning its causality, teleology, and its intelligibility, must only apply within the phenomenal domain. In this sense "the will as thing-in-itself lies outside the province of the principle of sufficient reason in all its forms, and is consequently completely groundless, although each of its phenomena is entirely subject to that principle."[321] Schopenhauer does admit that one can always recuperate any and all statements about the Will within the phenomenal, human-centered domain. But there is always something for which no sufficient reason can suffice, or for which there is only an absence of sufficient reason. We may provide reasons, or make bold claims concerning knowledge, but these merely beg the question for Schopenhauer. We might even say that the Will-to-Life ultimately points to a principle of *insufficient* reason at its core.

If the Will-to-Life, considered in itself, has no sufficient reason because it lies outside the phenomenal domain, so can the Will-to-Life not be granted any anthropocentric conceits, least of all that life exists "for us" as human beings, or that it reaches its pinnacle in the human life. Schopenhauer refuses to grant the human being, or the human perspective, any priority with respect to this principle. Certainly, as Schopenhauer grants, there are gradations and differentiations within the natural world. What remains, however, is this Will-to-Life that indifferently cuts across them all. "For it is indeed one and the same will that objectifies itself in the whole world; it knows no time, for that form of the principle of sufficient reason does not belong to it ... but only to the way in which these are known by the individuals who are themselves transitory."[322]

Though taxonomic science may arrange all the different life forms into a hierarchy, the Will-to-Life maintains this cosmic indifference throughout the world. Indeed, Schopenhauer will go so far as to say that this constitutes the tragicomic character of human life in particular: "The life of every individual ... is really a tragedy; but gone through in detail it has the character of a comedy."[323]

For Schopenhauer, pessimism is the only viable philosophical response to this unhuman condition. This pessimism is something for which Schopenhauer is popularly known (and often dismissed). But Schopenhauer's pessimism is often understood to be about human life, in so far as it is human beings that intuit the senselessness and suffering of the world. It is true that Schopenhauer's pessimism has to do with a view of life as essentially "incurable suffering and endless misery," an ongoing cycle of suffering and boredom. But this is only the case from the perspective of the individual, living human being, towards which the Will-to-Life is indifferent. Evocatively, Schopenhauer notes that every manifestation of the Will-to-Life is doubled by a kind of Willlessness (*Willenslosigkeit*), every sense of the world-for-us doubled by a world-without-us. Pessimism for Schopenhauer is not so much an individual, personal attitude, but really a cosmic condition — a strange, impersonal disposition. The indifference of the Will-to-Life thus stretches from the microscale to the macroscale:

> Thus everyone in this twofold regard is the whole world itself, the microcosm; he finds its two sides whole and complete within himself. And what he thus recognizes as his own inner being also exhausts the inner being of the whole world, the macrocosm. Thus the whole world, like humanity itself, is through and through will and through and through representation, and beyond this there is nothing.[324]

Negation courses through Schopenhauer's notion of the Will-to-Life, and evocations of the Will-to-Life recur throughout Schopenhauer's writings. In this, Schopenhauer was certainly influenced by his encounter with classical texts in the Vedanta and Buddhist traditions.[325]

However, that life is "nothing" can mean several things. The enigmatic last sections of *WWR* bear out some of these meanings. There Schopenhauer makes use of Kant's distinction between two kinds of nothing: the *nihil privativum* or privative nothing, and the *nihil negativum* or negative nothing. The former is defined as the absence of something (shadow as absence of light, death as absence of life). For Schopenhauer the world is nothing in this privative sense as this interplay between Representation and Will; the world, with all its subject-object relations, as well as its ongoing suffering and boredom, is transitory and ephemeral. By contrast, the indifferent Will-to-Life courses through and cuts across it all, whilst remaining in itself inaccessible, and "nothing."

The problem is that we have, at best, a limited and indirect access to the world as a *nihil privativum*, and "so long as we ourselves are the will-to-live, this last, namely the nothing as that which exists, can be known and expressed by us only negatively."[326] For Schopenhauer the very fact that there is no getting outside the world of the *nihil privativum* hints at a further negation, one that is not a relative but an absolute nothingness. As he notes, "in opposition to this *nihil privativum*, the *nihil negativum* has been set up, which would in every respect be nothing." But this is not simple opposition, for "a really proper *nihil negativum* is not even conceivable" but is, in the end "always only a *nihil privativum*."[327]

At this point it seems that one must say — or think — nothing more. It is as if philosophy ultimately leads to its own negation, to Wittgenstein's famous claim that what cannot be thought must be passed over in silence. That *WWR* closes with an enigmatic affirmation of life as nothingness is indicative of the limits of Schopenhauer's negative ontology. On the one hand the Will-to-Life is "nothing" because, considered as the interplay between Life and the living, the Will-to-Life in itself is never something in an affirmative or positive sense. But Schopenhauer suggests that the Will-to-Life is "nothing" for a further reason, which is that, in itself, the Will-to-Life indicates that which is never manifest, that which is never an objectification of the Will, that which is never Representation. To the relative nothingness of the *nihil privativum* there is the absolute nothingness (*absolutes Nichts*) of the *nihil negativum*. While Schopenhauer is himself opposed to the German idealists, he is united with them in his interest in the concept of the Absolute, albeit one paradoxically grounded in nothingness. His contribution is to have thought the Absolute without resorting to the ontology of generosity and its undue reliance on romantic conceptions of Life, Nature, and the human. It is for this reason that Schopenhauer can close *WWR* by stating that "this very real world of ours with all its suns and galaxies, is — nothing."[328]

*

Philosophical Doomcore. It is one thing to think the idea of "that which should not exist," quite another to live it, given that the Will-to-Life does, according to Schopenhauer, impel the living to live. How then should one live, given that "life itself" may be nothing more than a blind, indifferent, compulsion to live on? How should one qualify the peculiar existence of the human being, burdened with the awareness of this condition? We are led to a deceptively simple question: do such pessimists have an ethics? If they do, do they always expect the worst outcome, even in the face of well-intentioned actions? For that matter, wouldn't the true pessimist be unethical, precisely in the sense that they themselves would be incapable of any effective action? The problem is that pessimists still *do* things, even if all they do is complain. This is the double bind of a pessimist ethics — decision without efficacy, acting without believing, the abiding sense that, ultimately, everything will turn out for the worst, all will be for naught.

An oft-cited example in this regard is Voltaire's 18th-century satire *Candide; or Optimism*. Candide, an impressionable youth living a life free of worry, is educated according to the Enlightenment values of rational self-reliance by his teacher, Pangloss. Candide holds steadfast to the Panglossian motto that everything will turn out for the best, since this is the best of all possible worlds. But as Candide grows into adulthood, he is confronted by one situation after another that challenges this view, until it becomes absurd for Candide to continue to assert that everything turns out for the best. Disillusioned and confused, the narrative ends with Candide retreating into the solipsistic attitude of each person "tending their own garden," the question of whether this is indeed the best of all possible worlds left open.[329]

But Candide is not just a pessimist, he is also a part of the European Enlightenment's roving band of do-gooders. In other words, even though he becomes more and more disillusioned, Candide goes along with things all the same. He does not leave the culture he is a part of, he does not shut himself up in a desert cave, and he does not enjoy his solitude and write existential meditations on the virtues of suicide. Of course, there may be an eminently practical reason for this: to whom could Candide complain if he were alone? Yet nobody wants to hear such complaints. In a sense, Candide's growing confusion, along with Pangloss's absurd optimism, are challenges to the ethical world view in which Voltaire's narrative takes place — that there is good and evil, that the difference between them can be discerned, that action can be moral and have moral effects, that the "healthy" attitude for any adventurer in life is to be positive and try your best, that life is "out there" to be lived.

At first glance, Schopenhauer — that arch-pessimist of philosophers — presents a similar case. Judging by his rather curmudgeonly outlook, it would appear that for Schopenhauer, ethics would be about as necessary to philosophy as self-consciousness to a stone. In fact, Schopenhauer often cited an analogy borrowed from Spinoza: if a stone thrown through the air were conscious, it would fancy that it moved itself through the air of its own will and of its own accord.

Until recently, readers would have had to look to Schopenhauer's magnum opus, *The World as Will and Representation* (*WWR*) for anything like a pessimist ethics. In it one would find statements here and there about the suffering of the world, about how it is better not to have been born at all, and so on. But there is little in the way of a sustained, critical examination of the topic.[330] This is where Schopenhauer's work in *The Two Fundamental Problems of Ethics* comes into play. It comprises two long essays by Schopenhauer written several years after *WWR*. The ethics essays not only build upon this latter work, but they also highlight a fascinating lacuna within Schopenhauer's dark metaphysics — in a world bereft of foundation or meaning, a world constituted by an indifferent, inhuman "Will," how should one act? Given that the world is indifferent, what should one do?

Schopenhauer published *The Two Fundamental Problems of Ethics* in book form in 1841, though the two texts in it were originally submitted to different essay competitions. The first competition was hosted by the Royal Norwegian Society of Sciences, for which Schopenhauer submitted his essay "On the Freedom of the Human Will." The second competition was hosted by the Royal Danish Society of Sciences, for which Schopenhauer wrote the essay "On the Basis of Morals." To his delight, Schopenhauer was awarded the top prize for the first essay.

Delight soon gave way to chagrin, however, in the case of the second essay. Schopenhauer was the only person to submit an essay, and yet the Royal Danish Society refused to grant him a prize — or for that matter, any recognition at all. They pretended he didn't exist. To add insult to injury, in their comments on Schopenhauer's essay, the Royal Danish Society members would also reference "distinguished philosophers" such as Hegel. One can only imagine the absurdity of the situation for the pessimist from Danzig. When Schopenhauer published both essays in book form in 1841, he made sure to note that the second essay was "not awarded a prize," and added lengthy retorts and rants against the Royal Danish Society's comments. He would also make incisive remarks concerning "journal writers sworn to the glorification of the bad," of "paid professors of Hegelry," of Hegel's philosophy as a "colossal mystification that will provide even posterity with the inexhaustible theme of ridiculing our age," and of German idealism generally as a "pseudo-philosophy that cripples all mental powers."

Fisticuffs aside, it is important to note that in the case of both essays, Schopenhauer was in effect prompted to write about ethics; he was prompted by the announcement of the competition itself, but also by the particular questions to which contestants were to reply. In each case, the questions posed provide Schopenhauer with something to push against, and it is this kind of philosophical antagonism in his writing that makes Schopenhauer's conflicted works on ethics still worth reading.

*

Will Not. In the first essay that comprises *The Two Fundamental Problems of Ethics*, the question (originally posed in scholarly Latin) was, "Can the freedom of the human will be proved from self-consciousness?" For the second essay, the question, this time longer and more opaque, was, "Is the source and basis of morals to be sought in an idea of morality that resides in consciousness, and in an analysis of the remaining basic moral concepts that arise out of it, or in another cognitive ground?" To both questions

Schopenhauer answers in the negative. No, he says, human will is free only insofar as the ground of human will is free — that is, only insofar as a more fundamental, abstract, and nonhuman Will is free. For the second question Schopenhauer also answers no, and he even goes so far as to question the presumption that human morality has anything to do with reason at all, choosing to instead explore the concept of compassion (*Mitleid*) and the vaguely Eastern notion of loving kindness (*Menschenliebe*) as the basis for morality.

In *WWR* Schopenhauer had attempted to radicalize Kant, presenting a two-sided view of the world. On the one hand the phenomenal world of appearances, bodies, objects and nature — the world of Representation; on the other hand, that which grounds that phenomenal world, but which is itself not any Representation, and is instead an anonymous, indifferent, blind striving — the world of Will. Schopenhauer remained convinced that, even though the world as Will remained inaccessible to us as human beings in the world of Representation, there was a connection between them, particularly in the living body. The body and life were, for Schopenhauer, this nexus of the Will in Representation, of an undifferentiated Will in an individuated human will, of the nonhuman in the human.

While this would seem to steer things inevitably towards an ethical philosophy, *WWR* does something altogether different. By the funereal fourth book of *WWR*, any question of ethics drops away in favor of discussions on mysticism, Eastern philosophy, pessimism and the enigmatic idea of not-willing or "Willlessness." *The Two Fundamental Problems of Ethics* thus highlights a gap within *WWR* — how to connect the indifferent and inhuman world of Will with the all-too-human world of Representation?

In the first essay — "On the Freedom of the Will" — Schopenhauer breaks down the long-standing debate in ethical philosophy over freedom and necessity. He distinguishes between different types of freedom (physical, intellectual, and moral), arguing that freedom is essentially a negative concept, the absence or removal of an obstacle. Schopenhauer's target is the illusion of purely self-conscious acts, the presumption that freedom derives directly from willing (the notion that, as Schopenhauer says, "I am free if I can do what I will"). But what grounds this isomorphism of freedom and will? As Schopenhauer notes, one would have to inquire not just into the doing based on willing, but the willing of the willing of doing, and so on. One either follows this question to infinity, or one must presume a paradoxical groundless ground, a Will for all willing that does not itself will anything.

Likewise, Schopenhauer distinguishes three types of necessity (logical, mathematical, and physical). While he maintains the freedom-necessity pair, he also attempts to show that they can only be related outside the sphere of the human subject. If, as Schopenhauer argues, freedom is a negative concept, then it is also the absence of necessity. But the absence of necessity, taken to its logical conclusion, entails a notion of "absolute contingency": "So the free, as absence of necessity is its distinguishing mark, would have to be that which simply depended on no cause whatsoever, and would have to be defined as *absolutely contingent*; a highly problematical concept, whose thinkability I do not vouch for, but which in a strange way coincides with that of *freedom*."[331] Passages like these betray Schopenhauer's ongoing ambiguity surrounding ethics — particularly the investment of good faith in the humanist project that is needed in order to think about ethics at all. Schopenhauer likens the human being's bloated overreliance on free will and choice to being as absurd as a self-conscious pool of water: "That is exactly as if water were to speak: I can strike up high waves (yes! in the sea and storm), I can rush down in a hurry (yes! in the bed of a stream), I can fall down foaming and spraying (yes! in a fountain) ... and yet I am doing none of that now, but I am staying with free will calm and clear in the mirroring pond."[332]

*

Ought Naught. If the first essay is primarily concerned with critiquing the individuationist and humanist notion of ethical action (freedom vs. necessity), then the second essay — "On the Basis of Morality" — tackles the broader question of the ground of ethics itself. It is no wonder Schopenhauer was not granted a prize for this essay — from the start he contentiously implies the stupidity of the question, while admitting the "exuberant difficulty" of the problem of ethical grounds. Here Schopenhauer's target is Kant; but his extended critique of Kant is also laced with admiration. As Schopenhauer notes, Kant's contribution to ethical philosophy was to tear it away from *eudaimonia* (happiness, well-being). Whereas for the ancients virtue and happiness were identical, for the moderns virtue and happiness are related as ground and result. The axiomatic approach of Kant focuses less on *eudaimonia* and more on the practical aspect of ethical action. But here Schopenhauer is quite critical, for Kant's categorical imperative, with its emphasis on the "ought," can only lead to the absurd idea of a totalizing "ought": "In a practical philosophy we have to do not with providing grounds for what happens but rather laws for what *ought to happen even if it never does*... Who tells you that *what never happens ought to happen*?"[333]

In short, Schopenhauer sees in Kant's categorical imperative a church masquerading as a court of law: "Conceiving ethics in an *imperative* form, as *doctrine of duty*, and thinking of the moral worth or unworthiness of human actions as fulfilment or dereliction of *duties*, undeniably stems, together with the *ought*, solely from theological morals, and in turn from the Decalogue."[334] Schopenhauer later riffs on Kant's ethics as having a mystical, "hyperphysical" core: "...in the Kantian school practical reason with its categorical imperative appears as a hyperphysical fact, as a Delphic temple in the human mind, from whose murky sanctuary oracular utterances announce without fail not, unfortunately, what *will* happen, but what *ought* to happen."[335] Ethics as a form of wishful thinking.

And here we see Schopenhauer attempting to build a bridge between the ontological claims of *WWR* and the ethical claims of *The Two Fundamental Problems of Ethics*. The upshot of this, as Schopenhauer states with some subtlety, is that "the human being is no exception to the rest of nature."[336] That is, insofar as freedom is impersonal and unhuman, the human is simply part of a larger field that is at once ethical and metaphysical, human-centered and drawn towards the unhuman. Paradoxically, Schopenhauer's thinking moves towards something we can only call an *unhuman ethics*.

Of course, the major challenge is how to reconceive of ethics given this unhuman metaphysics. In the second essay Schopenhauer gives us hints of such an ethics, setting up two pairs of ethical concepts: the poles of self-oriented action and other-oriented action, and the poles of well-being and woe. From this he derives his two key concepts that close the essay: that of compassion (*Mitleid*) and that of loving-kindness (*Menschenliebe*), shifting the debate away from the preoccupation with human reason and law.

At the same time, his discussion on compassion remains open-ended; one senses that for Schopenhauer compassion is not limited to the feeling of one human being for another, but that it can be open to strange, unhuman compassions — with the animal, the plant, the rock, the ocean, the cloud, the swarm, the number, the concept, or even the cosmos. Such compassions, such instances of "suffering-with," can range from sentiments of dread and horror to ambiguous sentiments concerning the loss of self. Similarly, with Schopenhauer's ever-eccentric appropriation of Eastern thought, the concept of loving-kindness is not simply a love of the human by the human, but quite the opposite — one loves the human only as a starting point for going outside the human, for loving the unhuman.

*

Varieties of Pessimism. In spite of his misgivings vis-à-vis humanity, it is important to note that Schopenhauer's pessimism is of a particular type. In general pessimism can be characterized by one of several statements. One version is of the type "this is the worst of all possible worlds." In this view, essentially an inversion of the optimistic view, any possible positive in the world is always outweighed by a negative; indeed, the very fact that there is a negative at all (that we are mortal, that we suffer, or that we are fated to die) outweighs any positive.

Another version of pessimism is found in the statement that "life is not worth living." An outcome of the first statement — the worst of all possible worlds — this view transfers a statement about the world to a statement about the subject "thrown" into that world. If this is the worst of all possible worlds, then the value of what it means to live in that world can only be matched by an equal pessimism of life, be it bare biological life or the qualified life of self-conscious human beings. Indeed, in this view it is precisely due to consciousness that suffering exists at all.

Yet another version of pessimism is found in the even more austere: "it is better not to be." The first statement — this is the worst of all possible worlds — asserts something about the world as such. The second statement — life is not worth living — shifts the focus to the human being living in such a world. This statement — it is better not to be — shifts the focus again to the metaphysical plane, encompassing as it does both the world and the fact of living in the world. It expands the pessimist's misanthropy beyond humanity to all existing things, living or nonliving, physical or metaphysical. In this view it is *being itself* that is the problem, not some property of the world or of the human.

Each of these statements, though they make strong assertions, is also compromised by loopholes in logic that undermine them. For instance, the statement "this is the worst of all possible worlds" tends to conflate a state of the world with a judgment about the state of the world. Hence pessimism holds a tenuous position within philosophy, caught somewhere between an axiom and a bad attitude. Though it rails against life, against humanity, and against existence itself, pessimism must always make such assertions from the point of view of the living human being. Hence its negations against life, against the human, and against being itself also secretly index the nonhuman, non-being, or nothingness. As such, they remain horizons for the pessimist; they are negations that in themselves cannot be thought. Here we are brought to a central insight about pessimism — that it "fails," and that, in a way, it must fail. The pinnacle of pessimist logic, carried to its extreme, is the undermining of pessimist thinking itself.

We can qualify this further, paying attention to pessimism not just as a "bad attitude" but as a philosophical position — tenuous though it is. In the history of philosophy, pessimism is generally split between two views: a moral pessimism and a metaphysical pessimism.[337] In moral pessimism, one expresses an attitude about the world that takes the worst possible view of things. The moral pessimist can take any phenomenon, no matter how apparently joyful, beneficial, or happy, and turn it into the worst possible scenario — even if only to note that every positive only paves the way for a negative. This is the view of the glass being half empty. Moral pessimism is pessimistic because its view is pessimistic, irrespective of what is objectively happening in the world. The tendency to take the worst view of things, or the tendency to always expect the worst, is about an interpretation of the world, not about the world in itself.

This changes once one moves from moral pessimism to metaphysical pessimism. In the former one expresses an attitude about the world, whereas in the latter one makes claims about the world itself. This is the view that it is the objective property of every glass in itself to be empty. Metaphysical pessimism is more than just a bad attitude, it makes claims about the way in which the world in itself is ordered. For the metaphysical pessimist, the world itself is ordered in the worst possible way and is structured such that it always leads to the worst possible ends. For the metaphysical pessimist, saying that this is the worst of all possible worlds is less a case of being grumpy and more a statement about the antagonism between the world itself and our wants and desires.

While Schopenhauer expresses both of these types of pessimism, he remains dissatisfied with both, for they rely on a division between a human subject and a nonhuman world within which the subject is embedded. The only difference is that with moral pessimism, we have a subjective attitude, and with metaphysical pessimism we have an objective claim. Both views, being concerned with "the worst" (*pessimus*), implicitly rely on an anthropocentric view — either one is stuck with a bad attitude or one is stuck in a bad world (as the joke goes, "the glass is half full, but full of poison").

While Schopenhauer himself was a curmudgeon, and while he does state that this is the worst of all possible worlds, his philosophy ultimately moves towards a third type of pessimism, one that he never names but which we can tenuously christen *cosmic pessimism.*[338] For Schopenhauer, the logical endpoint of pessimism is to question the self-world dichotomy that enables pessimism to exist at all. Such a move would entail a shift away from the relation between self and world, human and nonhuman, subjective attitude and objective claim. It would entail a move towards an *indifference*, an indifference of the world toward the self. Cosmic pessimism would question even the misanthropy of moral and metaphysical pessimism, for even this leaves us as human beings with a residual consolation — at least the world cares enough to be "against" us. Schopenhauer's cosmic pessimism questions ethical philosophy's principle of sufficient reason — that there is an inherent order to the world that grounds reliable judgements regarding moral and ethical action. It also questions the fundamental relation between ethics and action, whether of the Aristotelian "first principles" type, the Kantian-axiomatic type, or the modern cognitivist-affectivist type. Cosmic pessimism seems to move towards an uncanny zone of passivity, "letting be," a kind of liminal quietism in which non-being is the main category. In cosmic pessimism, this "indifference" is the horizon of all ethics. And this is perhaps why Schopenhauer's ethics ultimately "fails."

As a philosopher, Schopenhauer tends to begin with human experience, especially if that experience is one that mitigates against the illusory coherence of the human being. All of Schopenhauer's rants concerning pessimism and the limits of human knowledge dovetail on this strange counter-experience, an estrangement from being itself, the experience that the subject is not a subject, that life is not purposive but incidental, accidental, indifferent. Part of Schopenhauer's strategy is to undo the notion that the subject is separate from the world it experiences, that it relates to, and that it produces knowledge about. Part of his strategy is also to deepen the notion, inherited from Kant, that there is an inaccessible, unknowable, noumenal world from which we are forever barred access. These issues deal with the problematic category of the human — the human being as living in a human-centric world that always exists "for us" as human beings.

The question of ethics becomes pertinent here. Schopenhauer's essays refuse relying on either the human individual or the group as its foundation, much less any discussion on human nature. He also refuses relying on either intuition (or any innate, moral faculty) or law (as in the axiomatism of Kant). Instead, Schopenhauer zooms out from the traditional, humanist ethical discourse to the larger issues of ethics as the self-world relation — or, really, ethics as the impossibility of this relation. In fact, while Schopenhauer does not go this far, I am tempted to suggest Schopenhauer's philosophy poses the problem of *an ethics without the human*. Given current concerns over climate change and global warming, the time would seem ripe for an exploration of such an ethics. But an unhuman ethics would have to avoid both the pole of an all-too-human ethics (ethics as the exclusive provenance of law and policy), and the pole of a romantic ethics (the ethics of animals or the environment, which often presumes naïve notions of nature).

Schopenhauer's strangely unhuman ethics puts forth some key philosophical points that resonate deeply with our so-called post-human era. The first is that Schopenhauer displaces the ethical discourse of free will by externalizing human will as an unhuman Will. This leads to another point, which is that Schopenhauer constantly shifts the scale of his discussion of ethics beyond the human institutions of religion, law, and politics. This is a contentious point, for, as Schopenhauer well knows, this nonhuman aspect of the world can never be proved as such. But in his criticisms of the traditional terms of ethical philosophy, one senses Schopenhauer's ontological commitment to some metaphysical principle in excess of the human. Schopenhauer does not divide the unhuman Will from the human, all-too-human will, but is constantly at pains to show their immanence to each other, the Will in the will (or Will-in-will), as it were. The individuated human being is what they will, but this will is also the Will, impersonal and blind, and in this sense the human is also the unhuman.

*

Logics of the Worst. Pessimism is based on a negation, encapsulated in its root term, "the worst." In saying that this is the worst of all possible worlds, or that life is not worth living, or that it is better not to be, pessimism takes something presumed to have value — the world, life, being — and negates its value. In doing this, the pessimist standpoint implies that what we presume to have a substantial existence does not in fact have a substantial existence at all. The world, life, even being itself is without value, and their existence as arbitrary as anything else.

Where pessimist logic often gets caught is between a negation that states that something has a negative value, and a negation that states that something has no value. The first is an oppositional negation, a minus for every plus in the balance sheet of life, the world, existence itself. The second is a nullifying negation, a flattening of value systems themselves, which would argue back and forth interminably about the value or valuelessness of the world, life, and being. The first says that the world is not meaningful but meaningless, not joyful but sad, not good but evil, and so forth. The second says that the world is neither meaningful nor meaningless, neither good nor evil, neither joyful nor sad, neither this nor that.

So-called pessimist philosophers often waver between these two negations. Schopenhauer, for instance, will at one point sardonically note that if we asked the dead in their graves whether they would like to live again, they would surely shake their heads. Their pessimism is based on their experience, the balance sheet of life tipping towards the negative. But at other points Schopenhauer's thought will move towards the nullification of all terms — including "pessimism" and "optimism" — moving towards "Willlessness," the quietism of neutralized being, the silence of self-negating thought.

Let us try to refine this further. The logic of pessimism is structured around two qualitative statements. One is a statement on metaphysics, which makes a claim about the world, life, or even being as such. A breach exists between the self and the world, a gap between the world as it exists for us and in relation to us (the world-for-us) and the world as it is exists in itself, apart from our relating to it (the world-in-itself). Can this breach be crossed? For a philosopher like Kant, the answer is no — we as human beings are always embedded in the world, always sensing, intuiting, and apprehending the world as sensory and cognitive subjects. By contrast, German idealist philosophers assert that yes, this breach can be traversed, by virtue of the fact that we as human beings are part of the world, and that the world-in-itself is also "in" us. For German idealism, the for-us *is* the in-itself. The concept of the Absolute signifies this equivalence.

For his part, Schopenhauer sides with Kant, but his reasons are slightly different. True, there is an irrevocable gap between self and world, and, even though we as human beings are part of the world, we forget that the world is not human. To presume to gain knowledge of the world also presumes that there is an order hidden "out there" in the world to be revealed. But for Schopenhauer this is pure vanity — there is literally *no reason* that the world should be ordered in this way or that, or ordered at all. What both Kant and German idealism presume is a principle of sufficient reason that governs both the world-for-us and the world-in-itself. Schopenhauer, though he is in many respects a dyed-in-the-wool Kantian, holds no such illusions.

Tied to this statement on metaphysics is another, a statement on humanism. It follows from the statement on metaphysics. Can this breach between self and world be crossed? If so, can it be crossed by human beings? Are human beings uniquely situated to traverse the gap between self and world? Kant replies in the affirmative. While we can never know the world-in-itself, what we can know is the world as it appears to us as human beings, with our sensory apparatus, categories of understanding, and capacity for reason. From this, systematic philosophical knowledge can be constructed. Likewise, German idealism also affirms the ability of human beings to traverse the self-world relation, because the Absolute itself traverses all beings, inclusive of human beings. Subjectivity is not something opposed to the world, but something that pervades the world, manifesting itself in its highest form in the human being. The real is rational, universal history consummates itself in human history, and the Absolute in its various guises (Spirit, Ego, Nature) pervades the entirety of reality in a continuous, quasi-vitalist flux and flow.

Once again Schopenhauer is the naysayer. Not only can the self-world breach not be crossed, but human beings are in no particularly unique position in regard to this. There is no conciliatory move, as we have in Kant, where human knowledge is possible but in a highly attenuated way, and there is no heroic conquest, as we have in thinkers like Hegel, where the human being triumphs over the world by recognizing itself as part of the world. For Schopenhauer, the best we as human beings can do is register this limit, that the world may be acknowledged but cannot be known, that the world may make a difference in our human lives, but it remains in itself indifferent to our hopes, desires, and disappointments. In so far as the world is nonhuman, we who are a part of that world are also nonhuman. In so far as the world has *no reason* for being at all, so do we as human beings have no "sufficient reason" for existing.

Let us take stock of these different positions. Can the gap between self and world be traversed? Kant: no. German idealism: yes. Schopenhauer: no. Given this, is the human in a privileged position vis-à-vis this self-world relationship? Kant: yes. German idealism: yes. Schopenhauer: no. As we can see, if Kant holds the middle way (no/yes), then German idealism is on the affirmative (should we say, optimistic) side (yes/yes), while grumpy old Schopenhauer paradoxically affirms a double negative (no/no).

*

The Specter of Eliminativism. Philosopher Steven Shaviro once characterized contemporary speculative philosophy as polarized between "panpsychism" and "eliminativism." If one accepts that philosophy is broadly conditioned by the correlation between self and world (but also subject and object, or thought and the intentional object of thought), and if one accepts that this "correlationism" is a central problematic within philosophy (in so far as philosophy is by definition unable to think outside of correlationism), then for Shaviro this leaves one of two paths open for philosophy. Either one must opt for a kind of diffuse immanence, in which some quasi-monist entity (thought, affect, object, life, etc.) is everywhere — the view of panpsychism — or one must opt for an equally diffuse reductionism, in which all claims about existing entities are in themselves groundless, masking a potential void within everything — the view of eliminativism. In short, contemporary philosophy tends to be polarized between, on the one hand, a view of everything-already-everywhere, and on the other hand, a view of nothing-ultimately-nowhere.[339]

Nevertheless, Shaviro also notes the way that speculative philosophy also abrogates between eliminativism and panpsychism. For Shaviro, the eliminativist tendency has "a very negative view of the efficacy of thought, and in that sense they're eliminativists. And yet they couldn't find the universe as horrible as they find it, in this Lovecraftian way, without being kinds of inverted panpsychists."[340]

Eliminativism is more commonly understood as a branch of analytical philosophy that also goes by the name of "eliminative materialism."[341] Often associated with thinkers such as Paul Churchland and Daniel Dennett, eliminative materialism questions the existence of "qualia" such as mental states, psychological behaviors, or subjective affects. At its most extreme, it challenges any claims for an independently existing mind beyond a neurological and biological basis. As fields like cognitive science progress, many commonly held notions such as "belief" or "desire" will be discovered to have no viable scientific basis and may even be relegated to the dust heap of folk psychology. Eliminativism also has a broader significance, especially in the philosophy of science, where it questions the existence of any entity beyond its material basis (e.g., the vitalist "soul" or the "luminiferous ether").

Shaviro's comments are, of course, meant to evoke a different type of eliminativism, one that would take up the challenge to philosophy's principle of sufficient reason, while also departing from eliminative materialism's fidelity to biological, neurological, or physical "baseline" concepts. In a way, traditional eliminative materialism doesn't go far enough. Given its critical questioning of basic philosophical premises, eliminative materialism's reliance on positivist science can only seem an arbitrary stopping point. Why claim that subjective states or psychological categories like "faith," "joy," "despondency," or "dereliction" can only be assessed to the degree that they reduce to the biological or neurological level, and then not continue on to "eliminate" that biological or neurological basis as well? It would seem that, for eliminative materialism, philosophy once again reinstates its Kantian, juridical capacity to regulate boundaries and reestablish grounds, precisely at the moment that it questions the concept of "ground" altogether. In short, another kind of eliminativism might suggest that any eliminative materialism must ultimately eliminate matter itself.[342]

The trials and tribulations of "life" as a philosophical concept readily lend themselves to the eliminativist approach. Surely no other concept has been so vociferously asserted and questioned, from historical debates over vitalism in the philosophy of science, to contemporary evocations of "vibrant matter" and "the life of things." Eliminativism haunts the ontology of life, constantly questioning its theological pretentions, while also maintaining a minimal ground that would enable fields like neuroscience to make scientifically sound claims about what is or isn't living. At its extreme, the search for a material basis for life (be it in a molecule or in biological "information") ends up reducing life to its material constituents — at which point there is no life at all ... or there is nothing but life. Eliminativist approaches to the ontology of life tend to split it along the lines that Shaviro describes: either everything is alive or nothing is alive; either everything is pulsating flux and flow, auto-affecting and self-transforming, or everything is silence, stillness, and the enigmatic, vacuous hum of nothingness.

For both Aristotle and Kant, the proliferating, generous, and over-present manifestations of life are always shadowed by a concept of life-in-itself that must, by necessity, enter the eliminativist abyss. Nowhere is the awareness of this duplicity more evident than in German idealism. In Schelling's *Naturphilosophie* and his concept of the World-Soul, in Hegel's meditations on the organicist flows of Spirit, and in Fichte's lectures on "Absolute Life," one sees an attempt to ameliorate this shadowy aspect of life itself, while also refusing the options of either mechanistic science or a return to theology.

In contrast to this tradition, one also finds thinkers like Schopenhauer, the misanthrope from Danzig who, again and again, rails against his contemporaries for not having adequately grasped the negation at the heart of life itself. But if negation is at the heart of life, then how does one account for its prodigious generosity and overpresence? How does one think the negation at the heart of life, when life is commonly understood to be the concept of affirmation *par excellence*? This is the question that concerns the German idealists as well as Schopenhauer; and it is a problem first fully articulated by Kant.

Post-Kantian idealism did not end with Fichte, Schelling, or Hegel. In a way, its conceptual contours are resurrected by subsequent generations. A thread runs from the notion of life-as-generation to philosophical vitalism and biophilosophies inspired by Deleuze or Bergson, just as another thread runs from the notion of life-as-givenness to the phenomenology of life, the life-world, or the flesh, as found in Husserl, Merleau-Ponty, or Michel

Henry. Are we, for example, witness to a contemporary post-Kantian idealism today, in the correlationism of a neo-Fichteanism, in the transcendental geology of a neo-Schellingianism, or in the metamorphic plasticity of neo-Hegelianism?[343] Even contemporary scientific fields such as those that study extremophiles recapitulate, through the methods of empirical science, this shift from life-in-itself as a regional problem of epistemology to a fundamental fissure within ontology. Its limit is one that Schopenhauer characterizes as life thought in terms of negation, pointing to one of Schopenhauer's most contentious propositions: that all life is "dark life."

5

LAST WORDS, LOST WORDS

The Relinquished Philosopher. What baffles me is how *unwise* philosophers often are — especially those philosophers most attentive to the challenges of systematic philosophy. How can one honestly undertake an ambitious project like *Being and Time*, or *Process and Reality*, or *Difference and Repetition*, or *Being and Event*, without acknowledging the admissions of a *Critique of Pure Reason*, or the delusions of a *Phenomenology of Spirit*? Surely every philosopher feels, deep down, that if we could have figured it out by now, we would have done so long ago? All that has changed is that we publish more books, not better books. Perhaps this is why Heidegger, Whitehead, and others left their books unfinished, why Schopenhauer kept on adding material to *The World as Will and Representation*, why Wittgenstein retired early, and why Nietzsche and Cioran never bothered in the first place — as if they each awoke from their own dogmatic hangovers, and realized, too late, the futility of the impulse to philosophize. Or perhaps they understood that one begins philosophy the moment one abandons it.

*

A Very, Very, Very Short History of Philosophy. Philosophical realism in the West is built upon three pillars, pillars that are shaky, full of fractures, and mottled with peeling paint. The first pillar, a classical one, is that of Plato. With Plato we are introduced to a two-world view, a world of the here-and-now and a world beyond, a world that is immediately given and a world that is far off or inaccessible. While innumerable commentaries have been written about Plato's allegory of the cave, its basic message is clear — "there's got to be more." What is given is fine, but it's not enough, it cannot be enough … no, there's got to be more. Perhaps another world lies above or beyond this one, perhaps it's coextensive with it and we just don't see it; but there has to be more. No doubt Plato learned this from the so-called pre-Socratic philosophers. Airdropped into a world one has neither created nor asked for, the human being gazes about, bewildered and horrified, and asks the primordial philosophical question — "is this it?" Answering this question means parceling out the world into a self that is questioning, a world questioned, and a tenuous relation between them. As we know, for Plato this was not it, and beyond every particular chair or book or jellyfish was an abstract, perfected form of chairness, bookness, jellyfishness. While Plato has been overturned many times in philosophy, the intuition of the two worlds remains, though it often goes under different names, each of which stands in for this basic relationship between the world as given and another world, perhaps a more fundamental world, but one that is not given — the One, Logos, God, noumena, the Absolute, Spirit, Will-to-Power, Being, duration, process, difference, the One…

The second pillar, a modern one, is that of Descartes. If Plato gives us the intuition of the two worlds, then Descartes gives us the means of traveling between them. Descartes's celebrated, by now cliché, phrase *cogito, ergo sum* is more than an affirmation of the self-conscious, reasoning, human being. It is the assertion of a necessary link between thought and reality. It is the assertion of a consonance between human thought and the two worlds, one of which is immediately given, and the other of which is not apparent, and must be accessed in some way. Descartes even goes so far as to suggest that the way to get to the world beyond is via the world here-and-now. The *Meditations* makes this clear in its narrative arc. One simply has to sit down next to a fire, with a warm sweater, maybe a cup of coffee, and think. The *Meditations* is a performative text, in which Descartes-the-character shows us how to get from the world here-and-now to the world beyond. Nevertheless, there are many twists and turns along the way, until, bit by bit, the world here-and-now becomes more and more unreliable, more and more like a nebulous, spectral world beyond, full of animatronic puppets, ghosts in machines, and trickster-demons. The open secret about the *Meditations* is that once Descartes starts down the path of skepticism, there is no good *reason* to stop, ever. God (the philosopher's God, the God of Descartes, Leibniz, and yes, of Spinoza too) comes in to save the day, but do we really buy it? A *deus ex machina* if ever there was one. Of course, the irony is that one has come full circle: the philosopher has traveled into the beyond in order to discover the self, the world beyond looks a lot like the world here-and-now, and one has simply arrived at where one had begun, resulting in a dizzying hall of mirrors.

The third pillar is that of Kant. For many, Kant is a boring writer (though better than Hegel, who may simply be a bad writer). What Kant did for philosophy is something that has had mixed blessings — he gave philosophy a job description. Certainly philosophers had had jobs prior to Kant's time, but they were either beholden to religious institutions ("you can teach Aristotle's logic but stay away from the works on biology") or they functioned in a transient zone prior to the disciplinary divisions of the humanities and the sciences (take Descartes — philosopher, mathematician, and amateur anatomist). Kant's critical philosophy is widely known for its delimiting effects vis-à-vis philosophy. It says what philosophy is *not*. "Yes, debate the existence of God all you like, but you will never reach a philosophically definitive answer, and philosophers shouldn't be bothering with this anyways — that is the job of the priests." It is also a sobering of philosophy, particularly as a privileged, human endeavor that was, in Kant's time, undergoing rapid professionalization. Kant's works articulate what philosophy cannot do — notably, it cannot ever fully close the gap between the world as it appears to us and the world in itself. Kant's critical philosophy is remarkable because it harbors within itself a contradiction — it is a grand, shimmering, systematic philosophy, a sort of cathedral of philosophy — but one that argues for philosophy's *humility*.

Yet even Kant's conciliatory gesture has a heroic ending, for while we may not know the world in itself, we can know our limits, we can know how we know, and we can study how the world appears to us, and maybe — just maybe — by doing this we can at least infer that there is "something more," something "out there," something making an impression on us, in whatever distorted way we may intuit it, like eyeglasses we can never take off.

From a certain vantage point, the history of Western philosophy looks like a somewhat panicky, feverish attempt to cover up a fundamental, maybe even primordial suspicion: that *there may not be more*. Every excited, anxious assertion of "there's got to be more" covers over a more gloomy, more morose, "this is it."

All of this leaves out a possible fourth pillar — that of Nietzsche — who excitedly asserts "this is it!" And so philosophy returns to its pessimistic roots.

*

Phantasms (I). "All that is visible rests upon the invisible — the audible upon the inaudible — the felt upon the unfelt. Perhaps thinking rests upon unthinking."[344]

*

Here … Everything Is by Design. In the history of philosophy, there is no single agreed-upon definition of "realism." Depending on what one thinks about philosophy, this is an occasion for concern or for laughter. And yet nearly every philosophy relies on some realist claim, a claim to be able to finally and definitively articulate "the way things are" — no matter how strange or counterintuitive such claims may seem. In fact, it could be argued that the criteria of realism in philosophy today is precisely how counterintuitive the claims are for the "weird." But inevitably disagreements arise, schools are formed, weighty academic tomes are published, and academic tribalism abounds.

What is at stake is a claim about the real, though no two claims are alike. Historians of philosophy usually resolve this by simply enumerating the realisms promoted by various philosophers, one following the next in a neat, sequential progression: Platonic realism (the world I see before me and the world of abstract forms), Aristotelian realism (the abstract forms as inseparable from the world I see before me), Hegelian realism (the world in itself as commensurate with the structure of thought), Whiteheadian realism (process, becoming, and change as primary; substances, objects, and things as secondary), and so on. Another approach is to brand the types of realism in a transhistorical manner, as they cross historical epochs: a naïve realism (in which appearance and reality are the same), an epistemological realism (reality distinct from appearance; reality residing in abstract universals; philosophy's goal is to interrogate not appearances but universals), and an ontological realism (that which exists is real, even if not actual).

But one is obliged to mention another kind of realism, for which we must thank Kant, and which he would undoubtedly call a critical realism — a realism that doesn't presume that the real can be adequately known. It is an agnostic realism, though in saying this we have already begun, according to Kant, to depart from the domain of philosophy proper. It is there, but we can never know this for sure. Kant brings us the most modern realism that is at the same time indelibly premodern (dare we say, mystical).

*

What You See Is What You Get. Simplifying to the extreme: philosophical realism is predicated on two related but distinct approaches. The first is the "what you see is what you get" approach, the attempt to understand without subjective bias, without idealism, without distortion. The second is the "just the facts" approach, the attempt to understand without reliance on speculation, hypotheses, guesswork, or even hoping for the best. In a way, the second approach follows from the first. In the first, what appears to be a value-neutral acceptance of the "way things are" relies to a great degree on the experience of a cognizing subject — and subjective experience is, as we know, not the most reliable of measures. "What you see is what you get," yes, but what I get is not necessarily what you get, and vice versa. One then moves to the second approach, attempting, as it were, to bypass the perennially problematic area of experience, while not jettisoning the domain of empirical sense data. What is real is what can be verified, measured, analyzed, articulated as an object of study. One parses out experience into an elaborate architectonics of cognitive functions (sensibility, understanding, reason), or one "brackets" the world in its appearing to us as an object of study, or one prioritizes becoming over being, the continuous over the discrete, process over product, or one makes a turn away from reality in itself towards language, logic, and signs, or one enlists the descriptive rigor of mathematical set theory and its capacity for managing parts and the whole. The approaches vary, but the upshot is that what is real is indisputable, apart from our desires, hopes, and wish fulfillments. But this too runs into problems, in that someone is always doing the measuring, a decision has been made about the sort of logical game we will play today, and the criteria for verification are at best moving targets. The apotheosis of this "scientific" realism is tautology — the real is … real. Besides, one person's reality is another's fantasy, regardless of — or indeed because of — how finely it is measured.

*

What to Do with Thought. There is a pessimism built into all attempts at a philosophy of realism. Philosophy's desperate push to attain the real is matched only by its inability to do so. Realizing this, one rescinds realism, but not reason. A new problem arises, a problem specific to the byways of skepticism, nihilism, pessimism, cynicism — the problem of what to do with thought.

*

Phantasms (II). A realist claim is not always a claim about the real, just as all claims about the real are realist — but not necessarily realistic.

*

Depressive Realism. Pessimism and realism seem to be two very different ways of thinking. Realism implies a certain neutrality, seeing things the way they are, apart from self-interest or the interest of others, a neutralization of value that always seems to end in the vaguely streetwise tautology of "it is what it is." Pessimism, by contrast, is often regarded as a bad attitude more than a philosophical position. It is always opposed to optimism, if not logically then affectively. If pessimists are enthusiastic about anything, it is about *pessimus*, "the worst," resplendent in every possible outcome, glimmering around every corner, an ecstasy of the worst that is shrouded by a grimace or curmudgeonly grunt. Realism is often employed by necessity — one is never a realist "just for fun." The necessity of realism is usually elicited by something non-philosophical — politics, science, or just getting things done. Pessimism is a luxury — one must have spare time to complain, to moan and groan and write lyrical poetry — all of which helps no one and in fact makes things worse.

That said, there is a connection between pessimism and realism. One example comes not from philosophy but from psychology. "Depressive realism" is the official-sounding name that has been given to the proposition that a pessimistic outlook gives one a "healthier" and more realistic grasp of life and the world in which one lives. The pessimist — so the argument goes — is freed from the "locus of control" fallacy; they do not believe that they are in total control of their actions and their destiny. Pessimists are also less likely to presume that bad things always happen to other people (the "optimism bias"), and as a result, the pessimist holds no illusions about their own superiority. They hold no high hopes, great expectations, or illusions of grandeur. They live and act, for now, for the time being, and if things don't work out, well, what did you expect?

The jury still seems to be out on whether this is a viable psychological theory or simply an attempt to view depression optimistically. Contemporary philosophers seem to have caught the bug, putting out pop-philosophy books that, in their almost absurd earnestness, sound like self-help. However, at the broadest level, the pessimist holds no illusions, not just about one's own individual being, but about the superiority of all human beings. If this is a realism, then it is a realism that extends into antihumanism — a sort of species-wide depression.

*

Elegy for a Dying Star. "Once upon a time, in some out of the way corner of that universe which is dispersed into numberless twinkling solar systems, there was a star upon which clever beasts invented knowing. After nature had drawn a few breaths, the star cooled and congealed, and the clever beasts had to die."[345] The oft-cited opening to Nietzsche's 1873 essay "On Truth and Lies in a Nonmoral Sense" presents us with a parable for the Anthropocene. The passage evokes a kind of impersonal awe before an indifferent cosmos, something which has since become the stuff of climate change documentaries, and their conflicted attitudes towards scientific and technological rationality. Nietzsche, for his part, was unequivocal: "For this intellect has no additional mission which would lead it beyond human life. Rather, it is human, and only its possessor and begetter takes it so solemnly — as though the world's axis turned within it."[346]

Almost a century later, in the shadow of the atomic age, Japanese philosopher Keiji Nishitani would reiterate Nietzsche's fable. "The anthropomorphic view of the world," he writes, "according to which the intention or will of someone lies behind events in the external world, has been totally refuted by science. Nietzsche wanted to erase the last vestiges of this anthropomorphism by applying the critique to the inner world as well."[347]

*

Born in the Ruins of Philosophy. At any given moment, the pillars of philosophy are indistinguishable from ruins. They may still stand, but they serve less an architectural function and are more like tourist attractions. As ruins, they are filled with cracks and fissures, but no one really is to blame (except of course the philosophers). And the demolition of philosophy is always carried out by philosophy itself (for who else cares enough to so thoroughly examine every niche of the ruins in order to spackle them over?). Historians of philosophy are the cleanup crew.

In the meantime, those loiterers known as anti-philosophers keep hanging around, sometimes hidden in their nearby caves, sometimes just sitting about like lumps of syllogistic clay. They are those who are skeptics, cynics, nihilists, pessimists. They refuse to live within the ruins, in the shadow of the pillars, but they also haven't left the site for better weather or tolerable coffee. The way they think sounds philosophical — skeptic*ism*, nihil*ism*, pessim*ism* — terms that seem to denote methods, schools, traditions. But they also know that everything built up must collapse again, and this intuition is evident within their very words — the all-too-convincing self doubt of Pascal, the funereal spite of Schopenhauer, the stark indictments of Cioran…

But there is still a philosophical question embedded in their aphorisms, fragments, and missives against humanity. With skepticism, one must always answer the question, "where does doubt stop?" Every philosopher finds their own stopping point: doubt stops at God, doubt stops at self-consciousness, doubt stops at logical consistency, and so on. Of course, for some, doubt doesn't stop, and so the skeptic overlaps with the nihilist. With pessimism, the question is different: how many "nos" make a "yes"? Every philosopher negates something in the world or about the world — a presumption, an article of faith, what passes as common sense. But this negation always paves the way for a further affirmation, a claim about how things really are. As with skepticism, there is also the possibility of a "no" that never leads to a "yes," a "no" that devolves upon and devours itself, leading to paradox and contradiction. The outcome is suicide (the modern version), self-abnegation (the mystical, premodern version), or tragedy (the classical version). We've forgotten the postmodern version — farce, slapstick, gallows humor.

*

Variations on Misanthropy (I). Billions of years from now, the sun will die. Our planet may very well die before that, or at least become inhospitable for carbon-based life forms. Species on the planet become extinct at a "natural background rate" of one to five species per year, and many scientists tell us we currently are living in the midst of the "sixth mass extinction." The current global human population is 8 billion, though health officials tell us the planet can sustain a population of 1.5 to 2 billion, with 50% of the planet's total land mass having been transformed for human use.

At what point does one — or should one — become concerned? Most likely, concerns we have about the death of the sun billions of years from now are themselves eclipsed by the more immediate worries over the next flu season. In addition, the rate of the extinction of species has exponentially increased alongside exponential increases in the human population. Human beings take up 42% of the planet's total terrestrial net primary productivity, 30% of its total marine productivity, and 40% of the planet's land is used for human food production, while 50% of the planet's total land mass has been transformed for human use.[348]

And yet, there is a certain inevitability in the sun's death, just as there is in our own deaths. As individuals, something survives our own death. We are remembered or memorialized (or, perhaps, cursed) by others who survive us, and even though the individual person dies, the species continues. But in the case of human extinction, who will give testimony to this strange event, who will be there to comprehend it, to mark the significance of its having happened? In so far as we human beings have elevated ourselves above all other species, the extinction of humanity presents a conundrum, encapsulated by philosopher Ray Brassier: "How does thought think a world without thought? Or more urgently: How does thought think the death of thinking?"[349]

Extinction is more than a thought problem, but a problem for thought itself. It is as much an existential quandary as it is a scientific problem. And the extinction of the human species — a biological inevitability — is abetted by other kinds of extinction, which become more and more abstract: the extinction of all life resulting from the sun's death, the extinction of all matter due to the continual gravitational expansion of the universe, the extinction of existence itself.

Of course, neither I nor anyone else will be around to witness those extinctions (except perhaps as a movie). But even the most remote extinction described by science haunts us with a secret message, which Brassier encapsulates: "*Everything is dead already.*" Against the romantic reveries of an unbounded future of human possibility (a romanticism that has since been co-opted by corporate off-world programs), the sciences of cosmology, astrophysics, and paleontology reveal to us a finitude that is inescapably philosophical: "The extinction of the sun is a catastrophe, a mis-turning or over-turning (*kata-strophe*) because it blots out the terrestrial horizon of future possibility relative to which human existence, and hence philosophical questioning, have hitherto oriented themselves."[350] Thought, that through which human beings have projected themselves into a future of infinite possibility, is also that which undermines that very same capacity. The culmination of thought is, in a way, to bring down that which it has raised up; thought fulfilled in its own negation. Brassier encapsulates this, noting that "extinction indexes the thought of the absence of thought."[351]

*

A Rope Over an Abyss. For Nietzsche, nihilism is predicated on a twofold movement: the highest values of a culture devalue themselves, and there is nothing to replace them. An abyss opens up. God is dead, leaving a structural vacuum, an empty throne, an empty tomb, adrift in empty space. The abyss stares back.

But we should also remember that, when Zarathustra comes down from the mountain to deliver his profound message to humanity, no one hears him. They think he's just the opening act. They're all waiting for the tightrope walker, which is, of course, way more interesting. Is nihilism melodrama or is it slapstick? Or something in-between, a tragicomedy?

*

Variations on Misanthropy (II). As a scientific picture of the world, extinction — and the enigmatic thought of extinction — is a product of the legacy of the Enlightenment, with notions of human reason and human self-reliance at its center. But Enlightenment is also Janus-faced; it decenters in order to recenter. It displaces the Earth from the center of the universe, in order to place human scientific reason back in the center. The Earth is not the center — but now we know this. One result of this decentering and recentering is a growing rift between the world as we experience it phenomenally, and the world described to us by increasingly specialized and counterintuitive scientific fields (what Brassier, borrowing from Wilfrid Sellars, calls the "manifest" and "scientific" images of the world).

Furthermore, extinction — as scientific description of an external finitude — renders thought as more than subjective interiority, more than intentional consciousness that selectively interfaces with the world. Extinction forces thought itself to be externalized. Brassier again: "Extinction turns thinking inside out, objectifying it as a perishable thing in the world like any other."[352] Extinction subsumes everything within its ambit, even the self-valorizing transcendence of human thought and its fantasy of "critical distance."

Far from advocating the dream of infinite human potential, Enlightenment in the shadow of extinction becomes something else. It is no longer reason in the service of universal human well-being. Rather, Enlightenment becomes "an unavoidable corollary of the realist conviction that there is a mind-independent reality, which, despite the presumptions of human narcissism, is indifferent to our existence and oblivious to the 'values' and 'meanings' which we would drape over it in order to make it more hospitable."[353] Enlightenment has, in a sense, worked too well, and human beings discover that they are problem, not the solution. The real lesson of the Enlightenment, for philosophers like Brassier: is "the disenchantment of the world understood as a consequence of the process whereby the Enlightenment shattered the 'great chain of being' and defaced the 'book of the world' is a necessary consequence of the coruscating potency of reason."[354] A cold rationalism.

Furthermore, the Enlightenment not only counters the previously model of theology and religion (a disenchantment of an enchantment), but Enlightenment reason also produces its own enchantment, but through the language of science rather than that of religion. The wonders of nature explicated by science, the diversity of catalogued flora and fauna, and mysteries of the mind technically revealed, all point to this Janus-faced decentering and recentering of the human.

The sun will die, species go extinct, human life will end. But who ever said that thought was exclusively human? If followed to its conclusion, the affirmative Enlightenment of enchantment leads to a negative Enlightenment of disenchantment. The enchantment of nature, life, and the cosmos engendered by the sciences also has a dark side, a disenchantment of the world that reduces human self-valorization to an act of self-annihilation. If philosophers like Brassier are thinkers of the Enlightenment, it is of this negative or "dark" Enlightenment, one for which the extinction of all thought becomes the *starting point* for philosophy, not its termination: "Thinking has interests that do not coincide with those of living; indeed, they can and have been pitted against the latter."[355] Perhaps, contra Descartes, we should not say "I think," but rather: "thought thinks me."

*

Towards a Philosophy of Futility. While it often has a quasi-philosophical status, pessimism is ultimately dismissed because it commits that most unforgivable of philosophical errors — it mistakes the subjective for the objective. But the acknowledgement of this error is already embedded within pessimism. This is the reason why Schopenhauer's *The World as Will and Representation* only looks like a work of systematic philosophy. Really, by the book's final sections, the "whole" has given way to crumbling, grumbling ruins and furtive appeals to quasi-Buddhist "nothingness." He should've known better. Nevertheless, every pessimistic thinker understands at some level the pessimism inherent in the philosophical enterprise. The challenge of any philosophy is to account for its own horizon, its own limits, what it cannot say, know, or think.

This is why there is no "analytical pessimism" in philosophy, only a metaphysical poetics of finitude and angst. No one has ever claimed a scientific status for pessimism. That is, almost no one. An exception is the late 19th-century American author Edgar Saltus, who, near the end of his book *The Philosophy of Disenchantment* is curiously optimistic about what he calls a "scientific pessimism" of the future. But Saltus's scientific pessimism is as much about a mystical revelation of limits as it is about logical rigor and verifiable claims. Science in the service of pessimism, it seems.

Eduard von Hartmann, discipline of Schopenhauer, takes a different route. In his massive, unwieldy *The Philosophy of the Unconscious* (1869), Hartmann attempts to wed Schopenhauer's pessimism with the biology and physics of his day. The entirety of the first part of his work contains detailed descriptions of scientific experiments involving the decapitation of animals — as if to suggest a stark allegory between science and philosophy. But all that science teaches Hartmann is that the human species is at best an accident that has had the misfortune of thinking itself a necessity. As accidentally as we have come into being, so must we accidentally move out of being.

Then there is Nietzsche, the defiant convalescent, who rails as much against science as he does religion, telling us that we have not gone far enough in our pessimism, not yet attained a "pessimism of strength." And yet, as he jibes, what we need now is "a chemistry of the moral, religious, aesthetic representations and sensations, likewise of all those stimuli that we experience within ourselves amid the wholesale and retail transactions of culture and society, indeed even in solitude." But that is not all. Given this, Nietzsche asks, "what if this chemistry were to reach the conclusion that in this area too, the most magnificent colors have been extracted from base, even despised materials?"[356]

All of this would seem to require a distinct branch of philosophy dedicated to studying the futility of all attempts to philosophize. Perhaps pessimism has a future after all. One imagines massive tomes of systematic philosophy with self-contradictory titles such as *The Philosophy of Futility*. But the thing is that such a proposition is ultimately tedious and pedantic. As a philosophy, pessimism is always half-hearted, ready to give up or abandon a line of thought at the slightest inclination. Pessimism — speaking (as it feels obliged to do) in its deep, resounding, philosophical tones — says that all philosophies must fail, no matter what methods they deploy or from which tradition they may stem. All philosophies must fail because their truth claims must by necessity be partial, contingent, and grounded in some basis that cannot itself be directly questioned; its claims are contingent because its authority relies on propositions, those peculiar, hallucinatory uses of a language of effective rigor. Propositions in language, with the aid of bounded concepts, through the structure of logical argumentation, all framed by intentionality and the self-world relation. The result is that pessimism is often relegated to the dungeons of philosophy. It is forced to witness or to wait for its own failure, in a series of infinite resignations: No philosophy can say anything about everything … no philosophy can say everything about anything…

*

Pascal's Abyss. In one of his notebooks Pascal comments on a paradox central to humanity's insatiable quest for knowledge: the more we learn, the more we learn how insignificant we are. Whether our knowledge is true or false matters little, for if our knowledge is false, "then there is no truth in humanity," and if our knowledge is true, then humanity "has good cause to feel humiliated."[357] For Pascal, this disproportion strikes him as cause for a species-wide humility, even a species shame.

One need not be a philosopher to do this. As he notes, let anyone contemplate, even for a moment, the known universe, radiating outwards from our blinding sun:

> [L]et them see the earth as a mere speck compared to the vast orbit described by this star, and let them marvel

> at finding this vast orbit itself to be no more than the tiniest point compared to that described by the stars revolving in the firmament. But if our eyes stop there, let our imagination proceed further; it will grow weary of conceiving things before nature tires of producing them … The whole visible world is only an imperceptible dot … we only bring forth atoms compared to the reality of things.[358]

Things don't stop there. What follows for the macrocosm follows for the microcosm. "I want to show humanity a new abyss":

> I want to depict to them not only the visible universe, but all the conceivable immensity of nature enclosed in this miniature atom. Let them see there an infinity of universes, each with its firmament, its planets, its earth, in the same proportions as in the visible world, and on that earth animals, and finally mites, in which they will find again the same results as the first; and finding the same thing yet again in the others without end or respite, they will be lost in such wonders, as astounding in the minuteness as the others in their amplitude.[359]

Such terrifying reveries lead Pascal to a formulation for which he is now well-known: "Nature is an infinite sphere whose center is everywhere and circumference nowhere."[360]

What Pascal discovers is an uncertainty achieved by a simple shift of scale — above the human, below the human. As creatures of a limited granularity, we as human beings tend to view the world almost exclusively on our own level. Hence the world is the world-for-us, there for our taking, designed for our various schemes, and in our brief moments of scientific euphoria, if we dare to posit a world-in-itself independent of human beings, it is only to bolster our deeply engrained dominion over the world-for-us.

This troubles Pascal. In his writings, Pascal the geometer is often haunted by Pascal the theologian. In the very next line in his notebook, he writes: "In short it is the greatest perceptible mark of God's omnipotence that our imagination should lose itself in that thought."[361] And so our inability to comprehend this cosmos is itself superseded by our recognition of this thought collapsing in on itself — a collapsing that is, for Pascal, an indicator of the divine.

I find Pascal's repeated turns to religious faith disappointing, especially because they always seem to occur just at the moment when he is about to abandon his faith, only to be saved at the last moment by mathematics or mysticism. But I am also, for a moment, intrigued by those moments where Pascal's musings take yet another turn:

> Let human beings, returning to themselves, consider what they are in comparison with what exists; let them regard themselves as lost, and from this little dungeon, in which they find themselves lodged, I mean the universe, let them learn to take the earth, its realms, its cities, its houses and themselves at their proper value.[362]

Pascal would seem to have been vindicated by modern cosmology. Scientists tell us that, "roughly" one trillion, trillion, trillion years from now, the ever-expanding universe will have reached a point at which matter itself — and the very possibility of material existence — will be obliterated:

> Every star in the universe will have burnt out, plunging the cosmos into a state of absolute darkness and leaving behind nothing but spent husks of collapsed matter. All free matter, whether on planetary surfaces or in interstellar space, will have decayed, eradicating any remnants of life based in protons and chemistry, and erasing every vestige of sentience — irrespective of its physical basis. Finally, in a state cosmologists call "asymptopia," the stellar corpses littering the empty universe will evaporate into a brief hailstorm of elementary particles. Atoms themselves will cease to exist.

> Only the implacable gravitational expansion will continue, driven by the current inexplicable force called "dark energy," which will keep pushing the extinguished universe deeper and deeper into an eternal and unfathomable blackness.[363]

And so the human being discovers, at last, that its existence has always been subtended by its non-existence, that it dies the moment it lives, and that, perhaps, we do nothing but carry around a corpse that itself carries around the sullen grey matter that occasionally wonders if the same sullen stars that occupy every firmament at every scale also occupy this starry speculative corpse.

TENTACLES LONGER THAN NIGHT

I

TENTACLES LONGER THAN NIGHT

The Vast and Seething Cosmos (Poe, Lovecraft). In 1843, Edgar Allan Poe published his short story "The Black Cat." It opens with the following passage:

> For the most wild, yet most homely narrative which I am about to pen, I neither expect nor solicit belief. Mad indeed would I be to expect it, in a case where my very senses reject their own evidence. Yet, mad am I not — and very surely do I not dream. But to-morrow I die, and to-day I would unburthen my soul. My immediate purpose is to place before the world, plainly, succinctly, and without comment, a series of mere household events. In their consequences, these events have terrified — have tortured — have destroyed me. Yet I will not attempt to expound them. To me, they have presented little but Horror — to many they will seem less terrible than *baroques*. Hereafter, perhaps, some intellect may be found which will reduce my phantasm to the common-place — some intellect more calm, more

> logical, and far less excitable than my own, which will perceive, in the circumstances I detail with awe, nothing more than an ordinary succession of very natural causes and effects.[364]

An opening unparalleled in horror literature, Poe prepares us to expect something incredible, but without giving us any clue as to what that will be. Regardless of what follows, we as readers are primed to experience something indefinite, something the narrator does not — or cannot — define in any concrete way. All that we know is what the narrator has witnessed seems to defy all rational explanation. The narrator even questions himself — was it a dream, a drunken hallucination, insanity itself? This self-interrogation (before the narrative has even begun) raises the stakes of the story. Whatever the abstract horror is that has happened, it cannot be explained by the narrator. And yet, it must be explained, *there must be an explanation*. The narrator is so committed to this that he is willing to question his own sanity so that the "Horror" can be explained. And, the narrator continues, if I can't explain it then there must be someone else who can. In lieu of this, he can only hope that someone else (doubtless we, the "dear readers") will come along and provide an explanation, some explanation, any explanation.

What cannot be accepted is that something happened for no reason. But this event is not just an everyday event. It has the character of being out-of-place, of not fitting into our everyday or even scientific modes of explaining the world. It threatens the order of things produced by human beings, living human lives in a human world largely (we presume) of our own making. That something might threaten this order of things, *and that it would happen for no reason* — this is, for the narrator of "The Black Cat," the real horror. It is a thought that cannot be accepted, without either abandoning reason and descending into the abyss of madness or making the leap of faith into religion and mysticism. It is as if, before Poe's story has begun, the horror tale itself is in a state of crisis, the narrator nearly having a breakdown before us, able to communicate only vague notions and uncertain utterances.

The story does go on, however. Through the narrator's point of view, we encounter a string of events that involves depression, alcoholism, a fire, a tavern, a noose, strange portents, the cellar of a house, murder, inhuman wailing, and two black cats, which may or may not be the same cat reincarnated. "The Black Cat" gives us a classic example of an unreliable narrator, who suggests strange events that may be supernatural, but which are, at the same time, undermined by the narrator's mental instability. Was that shadowy burn-mark on the wall really an image of the deceased cat, or was our unreliable narrator just "seeing things"? Is the white patch on the black cat's chest changing shape and forming the image of a gallows, or has the narrator had too much to drink? These and other conundrums produce the kind of suspenseful *frisson* for which Poe is well known. The wavering in the story, between "it's all in his head" and "it really happened" is a hallmark not only of Poe's work, but of the entire tradition of supernatural horror as well.

So much is this a cornerstone of supernatural horror that, almost a century later, H.P. Lovecraft could open his story "The Shadow Out of Time" with the following:

> After twenty-two years of nightmare and terror, saved only by a desperate conviction of the mythical source of certain impressions, I am unwilling to vouch for the truth of that which I think I found in Western Australia on the night of July 17–18, 1935. There is reason to hope that my experience was wholly or partly a hallucination — for which, indeed, abundant causes existed. And yet, its realism was so hideous that I sometimes find hope impossible. If the thing did happen, then man must be prepared to accept notions of the cosmos, and of his own place in the seething vortex of time, whose merest mention is paralysing. He must, too, be placed on guard against a specific lurking

> peril which, though it will never engulf the whole race, may impose monstrous and unguessable horrors upon certain venturesome members of it. It is for this latter reason that I urge, with all the force of my being, a final abandonment of all attempts at unearthing those fragments of unknown, primordial masonry which my expedition set out to investigate.[365]

Lovecraft's narrator expresses much of the same disbelief as Poe's narrator. But Lovecraft also gives us more details. The narrator of "The Shadow Out of Time" is Nathaniel Wingate Peaslee, Professor of Political Economy at Miskatonic University and resident of Arkham, Massachusetts. We are also given concrete references to a date ("July 17–18, 1935"), a place ("Western Australia"), and, it seems, an object of the horror ("primordial masonry"). And yet we know nothing more than we did with "The Black Cat." Peaslee's narrative is just as confused, uncertain, and delirious as that of "The Black Cat." As with the narrator of "The Black Cat," Peaslee also questions himself, more than willing to attribute what he witnessed to hallucination or even insanity.

However, what is more terrifying than insanity is the possibility that "it" really happened. This is a crucial aspect of both Poe and Lovecraft— what is horrific is not that one is insane, but that one is *not* insane. At least if one is insane, the strange, terrifying "it" can be explained in terms of madness, delirium, melancholia, or clinical psychopathology. But other option is, for Peaslee, unacceptable: "If the thing did happen, then man must be prepared to accept notions of the cosmos, and of his own place in the seething vortex of time, whose merest mention is paralysing." The stakes are, perhaps, even higher than they were with "The Black Cat," for here Lovecraft situates human beings and human knowledge within the vast, "seething vortex of time" and the anonymous, "lurking peril" that portends only "monstrous, unguessable horrors" for humanity.

The dilemma for Peaslee (again, before the story has begun) is this: either I stick to what I know, and forcibly reduce everything to illusion (madness, drugs, temporary insanity, whatever), or I accept what is real, but then because this is so alien to what I know, I really know nothing at all. This notion — that I cannot accept what is real — is the core of the type of story Lovecraft himself referred to as "supernatural horror."[366] As with "The Black Cat," there is a threat, one that promises to destabilize our most basic presuppositions about the world (especially the world for us as human beings), but it is also a threat that is unspecific (though "cosmic"). In "The Shadow Out of Time" horror is not just the horror of fear or of a physical threat, but an indefinite horror. Language falters, as does thought.

This is all in that opening paragraph. But "The Shadow Out of Time" also goes on. In the process we are witness to other, menacing dimensions, ancient archaeological findings, telepathic possessions, and fleshy geometries so ancient they are alien, all of it undermined by Peaslee's own incredulity towards the reality that he cannot accept. Again, the horror of philosophy. In this sense "The Black Cat" and "The Shadow Out of Time" sit squarely between stories that do have rational explanations (for instance, mesmerism in "The Facts in the Case of M. Valdemar" or the fourth dimension in "The Dreams in the Witch House"), and those that appear to affirm the supernatural (for instance, resurrection in "Morella" and "The Outsider"). As different as they are, the tales of Poe and Lovecraft deal in some way with what is essentially a philosophical problematic, well-known to students of Aristotelian logic — that everything that happens has a reason for happening, and can thus be explained. This "principle of sufficient reason" not only grounds philosophical inquiry, but some of the basic principles of storytelling as well, especially in those genres — such as horror — where what is at stake is the verification of something strange and incongruous that, somehow, impossibly, exists.

*

Horror of Philosophy. It's all in your head. It really happened. These mutually exclusive statements mark out the terrain of the horror genre. But everything interesting happens in the middle, in the wavering between these two poles — a familiar reality that is untenable, and an acknowledged reality that is impossible. Literary critic Tzvetan Todorov calls this ambiguous zone "the fantastic," in his seminal work of same name. Discussing Jacques Cazotte's 18th-century occult tale *Le Diable Amoureux*, Todorov provides a definition of the fantastic:

> In a world which is indeed our world, the one we know, a world without devils, sylphides, or vampires, there occurs an event which cannot be explained by the laws of this same familiar world. The person who experiences the event must opt for one of two possible solutions: either he is the victim of an illusion of the senses, of a product of the imagination — and laws of the world then remain what they are; or else the event has indeed taken place, it is an integral part of reality — but then this reality is controlled by laws unknown to us.[367]

While Todorov is primarily concerned with analyzing the fantastic as a literary genre, we can also note the philosophical questions that the fantastic raises: the presumption of a consensual reality in which a set of natural laws govern the working of the world; the question of the reliability of the senses; the unstable relationship between the faculties of the imagination and reason; the discrepancy between our everyday understanding of the world and the often obscure and counterintuitive descriptions provided by philosophy and the sciences. The fork in the road is not simply between something existing or not existing, it is a wavering between two types of uncertainty: either demons do not exist, but then my own senses are unreliable, or demons do exist, but then the world is not as I thought it was (Todorov uses the terms "uncanny" and "marvelous" for these two options). With the fantastic — as with the horror genre itself — one is caught between two abysses, neither of which are comforting or particularly reassuring. Either I do not know the world, or I do not know myself.

Given the degree of self-reflexivity in genre horror today, we are well aware of the various ruses through which the fantastic is introduced. Contemporary films such as *Paranormal Activity* (2007), *The Cabin in the Woods* (2011), or *It Follows* (2014) self-consciously play upon genre conventions as well as on our expectations as viewers. If a character experiences something supernatural, we tend to immediately question them: was it a dream, are they on drugs, are they insane, or is it simply a bit of visual trickery? We are also aware of how quickly an apparently supernatural event in a horror story — such as the actual existence of vampires or zombies — gets recuperated into the understanding of how the world works, thereby becoming quite unexceptional and normal — even banal. Biology, genetics, epidemiology, and a host of other explanatory models are employed in providing rational explanations for vampiric bloodlust or the resurrection of zombie flesh. Only in that brief moment of absolute uncertainty — when both options seem equally plausible and implausible, when neither thought can be accepted or rejected, when everything can be explained and nothing can be explained — only in that moment do we really have this horror of philosophy, this questioning of the principle of sufficient reason. It is for this reason that, in the same passage, Todorov qualifies his definition by stating that the "fantastic occupies the duration of this uncertainty."

This uncertainty lasts but a moment; the dilemma it presents to us is between two mutually exclusive, though equally plausible options. Rare are the works of horror that can sustain the fantastic for their entirety. An exception is the well-known *Twilight Zone* episode "Nightmare at 20,000 Feet," which aired in 1963. Based on a short story by Richard Matheson, it is a study in the fantastic, and manages to sustain that uncertainty up until its end. The episode centers on the character of Robert Wilson (played by the inimitable William Shatner), a very normal, middle-aged businessman and husband, who is returning home from the hospital

Still from "Nightmare at 20,000 Feet," ***The Twilight Zone*** **(dir. Richard Donner, 1963)**

after a mental breakdown. "Bob," along with his wife Julia, are boarding an airplane as the episode begins. In the austerity that has become a hallmark of the original *Twilight Zone*, the entirety of the episode takes place within this airplane. Pensive and nervous, Bob is continually reassuring himself that he is cured, and that everything will be alright. Thus, before anything strange has even happened, we have been primed to "explain" anything unusual in light of Bob's mental illness. Mid-journey, the airplane enters a storm. Unable to sleep, Bob glances out the window. Unsure of what he sees, he looks closer, and we as viewers see what he sees: a strange, grotesque creature outside, hunched over the wing. Director Richard Donner uses juxtapositions of shot and reverse-shot to let us "see" through Bob's eyes, while also judging him with suspicion, knowing what we do of his mental illness. Through a series of tension-filled events, Bob becomes convinced (as perhaps we do as viewers) that there is a strange creature on the wing of the plane. To our frustration, however, Bob fails to convince his wife or the flight engineer — each time he attempts to draw their attention to it, the creature vanishes. We, along with Bob, are deprived of the sole verification of the actual existence of the creature — that others witness it as well, and that it is not merely the product of an overactive imagination.

And yet, while we may attribute the creature to Bob's mental illness (as Julia and the flight engineer do), we as viewers also see the creature. We are the "others" that bear witness to the fantastic event, though we are not, of course within the story world. This play between the "uncanny" (Bob is hallucinating) and the "marvelous" (the actual existence of the creature) continues throughout the episode. Things become even more tense when Bob sees that the creature is pulling apart the wing of the airplane. In a climactic scene Bob takes matters into his own hands, attempting to kill the creature, opening the emergency escape hatch and forcing the plane down. Exhausted, delirious, and bound to a stretcher, Bob is taken out of the plane to an ambulance (the director uses a point-of-view shot, as we look up and see a policeman looking down at us). As the camera zooms out from the airplane, a final shot reveals something strange, which forces us to accept Bob's claims as true. This apparently objective evidence of a "something" out there returns us again to the fantastic, caught between the uncanny and the marvelous.

Contemporary horror film has also taken up techniques for sustaining the fantastic that we see in authors like Matheson. An example is the film *A Tale of Two Sisters* (2003), made by South Korean director Ji-woon Kim. The film is loosely based on a well-known Korean folktale, "Janghwa, Hongryeon," which tells the story of two sisters, Janghwa ("Rose Flower") and Hongryeon ("Red Lotus"), the death of their mother, an evil stepmother's plotting, the strange murders of the sisters, and their return as ghosts that haunt their family and the town in which they live. Kim's film introduces us to the teenage sisters — Su-Mi and Su-Yeon — who are spending a vacation in a remote lakeside house with their father and stepmother. Eventually the family dynamics are revealed — the morose, passive father, the manipulative stepmother, and the sisters, one of them rebellious (Su-Mi) and the other timid (Su-Yeon). But, like "Nightmare at 20,000 Feet," the film opens in a sanitarium, as Su-Mi, slumped over a chair

Still from *A Tale of Two Sisters* (*Janghwa, Hongreon*, dir. Jee-woon Kim, 2003)

in white gown and long black hair, is being gently questioned by a doctor. Here again we are primed to suspect everything we see in terms of mental illness. Throughout the film — most of which takes place in the house — we witness the family drama between the sisters and their stepmother. Su-Mi has a series of disturbing dreams concerning her birth mother which blur the line between dream and reality.

A good part of *A Tale of Two Sisters* takes place within this realistic mode — though the lush, shadowy, mesmerizing cinematography gives even the "realistic" a hallucinatory feeling. Several scenes are punctuated by the fantastic. At one point, family friends are visiting for dinner. When one of them inexplicably begins choking, she falls to the floor, and — still choking — sees something eerie and impossible beneath the kitchen counter. And yet, just when we expect the marvelous and the actual existence of the supernatural, the film turns again. The father, confronting the increasingly rebellious Su-Mi, attempts to explain to her that she is not well — suddenly the camera point of view shifts, and we as viewers suspect that Su-Mi has not been fighting with her stepmother, but with herself, acting out the role her stepmother. We are back to the uncanny. In a stark, mesmerizing, final scene, the real stepmother returns one night to the lakeside house. In the room where Su-Mi's mother had died, she witnesses something inexplicable. We are back to the fantastic, suspended between conflicting points of view and a series of impossible happenings.

The fantastic, then, is central to supernatural horror, and, as Todorov reminds us, the sorts of questions it poses can even undermine the genre itself. The fantastic may exist only briefly, or it may span the duration of the story itself. While the questions that the fantastic poses may be answered, moving us towards either the "uncanny" or the "marvelous," the questions themselves are more important than the answers — they are moments in which everything is up for grabs, nothing is certain, the ground giving way beneath our feet. Within the genre conventions of horror, the fantastic interjects questions that are, in another guise, philosophical questions.

With this in mind, we can suggest a different way of approaching the horror genre. The products of genre horror are often regarded simply as entertainment, and this is, to be sure, an important part of the genre. But there is no reason why we cannot, at the same time, appreciate the works of genre horror for these sorts of — dare we say — philosophical questions they raise, as well as the ways in which they question our presumption to know or understand or explain anything at all. Hence the title of this series — *Horror of Philosophy* — which has several meanings. Certainly any reader of difficult philosophy books will have experienced their own kind of horror of philosophy, reinforced today by public intellectuals, who most often use philosophy as a smokescreen for selling self-help books and promoting the cult of the guru.

But the phrase also implies a certain way of approaching the horror genre, which inverts the idea of a "philosophy of horror," in which philosophy explains anything and everything, telling us that a horror film means this or that, reveals this or that anxiety, is representative of this or that cultural moment, and so on. Perhaps genres such as the horror genre are interesting not because we can devise ingenious explanatory models for them, but because they cause us to question some of our most basic assumptions about knowledge itself, or about the hubris of living in the human-centric world in which we currently live.

In the second volume of this series — *Starry Speculative Corpse* — we adopted a "misreading" of philosophical works as if they were works of horror. There we saw how each philosophy contains a thought or set of thoughts that it cannot think without risking the integrity of the philosophical endeavor itself. In this volume — *Tentacles Longer Than Night* — we can do the same. Except, in this case, we will be misreading works of horror as if they were works of philosophy. What if we read Poe or Lovecraft as philosophers rather than as storytellers? This means that the typical concerns of the writer — plot, character, setting, genre, and so on — will be less relevant to us than the ideas contained in the story. And the central thought that runs through much of supernatural horror is the limit of thought, human characters confronted with the limit of the human. In short, we will be considering the horror genre as fundamentally idea-driven, rather than plot-driven (and this certainly bears itself out in writers of supernatural horror). In fact, I would even go so far as to say that what is unique about the horror genre — and particularly supernatural horror — is its indifference to all the accoutrements of character, psychology, motive, and human drama. All that remains is the fragmentary and sometimes lyrical testimony of the human being struggling to confront its lack of "sufficient reason" in the vast cosmos. And even this is not sufficient.

Perhaps what is needed are different modes of thinking and writing that can accommodate these aspects of philosophy and horror at the same time. In the two previous volumes of this series, we adopted genres of writing from medieval philosophy, theology, and mysticism: the "question," the "reading," the "disputation," and mystical "prayer." In this volume we will continue this approach, this time adopting the "meditation" (*meditatio*). While many may associate the "meditation" with rationalist philosophy (particularly in the case of Descartes), the *meditatio* has a deep history in mystical traditions worldwide. In many instances, the "meditation" serves a dual purpose: it is at once a preparatory stage for spiritual training, and also the occasion for self-reflection and self-examination. Indeed, in Christian mysticism the two imply each other, as *meditatio* was often linked to *lectio* or "reading," and *oratio* or "prayer." As a form of writing, the *meditatio* is at once a formal practice, but also something open-ended, exploratory, even experimental. The use of the *meditatio* in the works of Augustine, for example, take on literary qualities, where forms of narrative and autobiography merge with the more analytical tradition of the *lectio* and the supernatural context of the *oratio*. In this volume, we can take up the *meditatio* in a series of "meditations" on the ways that the horror genre often finds itself engaged with the limits of human knowledge and understanding.

*

On Supernatural Horror (A Personal History). While I may adopt such a method, this doesn't guarantee that I necessarily like what I'm reading. After all, there's no accounting for taste. At the same time, it would be misleading for me to say that this interest — in reading horror as philosophy — comes from a purely academic or scholarly impulse. There are personal motives too. To begin with, a confession: I'm not your typical horror fan (whatever that is). I have my likes and dislikes, certainly. I never tire of watching Argento's *Suspiria* or Kobayashi's *Kwaidan*, and no matter how many times I teach Algernon Blackwood's "The Willows" I'm always mesmerized by the lyrical and slightly dazed descriptions of the seemingly alive, hushed movement of the willows as they imperceptibly move closer. Do those choices — rather than, say *Walking Dead* or *Saw 3D* — make me a horror fan, or not? And if I consider Bergman's *Through a Glass Darkly* a horror film? If I consider Baudelaire's *Les Fleurs du Mal* as important to the genre as Shelley's *Frankenstein* or Stoker's *Dracula*?

Maybe such questions are not worth trying to answer. What I can offer is an anecdote. When I was younger, I was not an avid reader. Strange thing for a recovering English major to say, perhaps. I blame society; I grew up in the era of cable TV, home videos, and video games, so reading was, at best, something one had to do for school. But I also grew up around books and music, a kind of home library that was there whenever you needed it. For my birthday my parents gave me an illustrated edition of Poe's stories. I recall reading "The Pit and the Pendulum" and finding it unlike anything I had read before. Part of the reason was that most of the story is virtually without plot. We as readers are simply dropped into this strange, dark, otherworldly space with a sole character and an anonymous, swaying blade. We know nothing of who the character is, why he is there, where he is, if any of this is really happening, or if it is a mere dream or hallucination. It is only at the very end of the story, in the last few lines, that we learn the character is being subject to torture by the Inquisition. But everything up until that point is strangely unmoored from the usual stuff of narrative fiction. Poe had written an *abstract horror* story, a study, a thought piece, a meditation on finitude, time, and death.

This is, of course, one stock-and-trade interpretation of the story. But for me, at that time, it suddenly revealed something about the horror genre I had not expected: that the horror genre is as much driven by a mood as it is driven by scare tactics, as much by the unknown as by fear. A few years later, I discovered some of the Ballantine "Adult Fantasy" editions of Lovecraft, Arthur Machen, and William Hope Hodgson (my father had purchased them in the late 1960s when they were published). I had the same revelation in reading Lovecraft's "The Colour Out of Space": the characters in the story are confronted with something utterly inhuman and unknown, something that exists but at some other level from which our senses are barred. The horror came not from what you saw, but from what you couldn't see, and even beyond that, what you couldn't fathom, what you couldn't think.

This was not limited to literature, either. Again, I grew up in an era when the low-budget horror film was big business, and so yes,

I saw *Halloween*, *Friday the 13th*, *Return of the Living Dead*, and *Poltergeist*. But on Sunday afternoons one of the local TV stations would show old horror films produced by Hammer Studios (many of them starring Christopher Lee and Peter Cushing), as well as Roger Corman's Poe adaptions produced for American International Pictures (many of them starring Vincent Price). What Poe had done with language, Corman did with film images. The eerie opening of *The Pit and the Pendulum* is matched only by the closing scenes of the painterly, Piranesi-esque labyrinths of caves and tunnels. Almost a third of *The Masque of the Red Death* is devoted to a totally plotless series of scenes that take place in strange, abstract, monochromatic rooms that reflect the moods of the characters. Again, abstract horror.

*

I Can't Believe What I See, I Can't See What I Believe. Rereading some of these works today, what I find the most appealing is the way they can be read on different levels. This is a cliché, I know, but it is the thing that keeps me coming back to certain works, and not others. Literary critics typically refer to this as allegory. When Dante, for instance, is taken by his guide Virgil on a tour of Hell, Purgatory, and Heaven, he undertakes a journey that is both real and symbolic, literal and allegorical. In the *Inferno*, we as readers are to understand that Dante really does encounter the Wood of Suicides, the dismembered Sowers of Discord, and the frozen, cavernous pit in which he finds a brooding Satan. But on the allegorical level Dante's journey is an interior one, which we understand as the spiritual journey of an individual. Dante himself was aware of this. In his writings he discusses allegory at length, noting both the different types of allegory (a frequently used literary technique in the Middle Ages), as well as the way that his own *Divina Commedia* employs allegory. In a famous letter to his patron Cangrande della Scala, Dante explains his understanding of allegory:

> For the clearness, therefore, of what I shall say, it must be understood that the meaning of this work [the *Divine Comedy*] is not simple, but rather can be said to be of many significations, that is, of several meanings; for there is one meaning that is derived from the letter, and another that is derived from the things indicated by the letter. The first is called literal, but the second allegorical or mystical ... And although these mystical meanings are called by various names, they can in general be said to be allegorical ... for the word *Allegoria* is derived from the Greek *ἀλλοῖος*, which in Latin is *alienum* [strange] or *diversum* [different].[368]

Dante not only distinguishes the literal from the figurative, but he also notes the relationship between them. Although the allegorical derives from the literal, for Dante it is also more profound, ultimately having for him a mystical significance, one in which the manifold, syncretic influences of myth, religion, and philosophy come together to form an extended rumination of mortality and finitude.

As Dante knew, you can never really separate these aspects from each other — the allegorical relies on the literal, just as the literal can be fleshed out or made more alluring by the allegorical. In other words, you *need* all those creatures, you need all the gory details of their metamorphoses, you need those tortured descriptions of a character's inner state as they confront something utterly alien — the allegorical level doesn't erase them; in fact, it brings them out even more. In a way, this runs counter to much literary criticism, enamored as it is of the higher levels of abstract, symbolic meaning, which quickly depart from the literal and rise up to new interpretive heights. But horror is "low." It is flesh and fluids, mud and material formlessness, inhuman matter of life reduced to primordial physics and cosmic dust. It is the *literalness* of horror that makes it horror; it is not "as if" an unnamable, tentacular, other-dimensional entity was feasting on your soul — it really is. And that is that. There is something about the literalness of horror that forces our language and our thought to stop dead in its tracks, a kind of tautology of "it is what it is" and yet the "it" remains indefinable, unmentionable, a thick and viscous and vaguely menacing "thing on the doorstep."

We might say that in the horror genre, the allegorical is in the service of the literal, and not the other way around. But what are these allegorical levels? How is the literalness of horror fleshed out in allegory? For me, there are several levels at work. First there is the literal level of the story itself, inclusive of the characters, the setting, strange happenings, and the conflict and resolutions that ensue. At its core are a set of feelings that we usually identify with horror stories — fear, terror, suspense, and the gross-out effect. But often we as readers or viewers get the sense that an author or director is out to explore "issues" — say, pertaining to mortality, morality, religion, science, politics, conflicts between "us" and "them," or what it means to be human. At this level, which starts to become allegorical, a horror story may explore very human issues through the lens of monsters, gore, and the supernatural, a story filled with human drama, in spite of the fact that such beings are very nonhuman. These are the sorts of paradoxes that allegory makes possible. How many viewers have identified with Boris Karloff's lumbering sensitive monster on seeing *Frankenstein*? The same follows for modern examples, where our sympathies and antipathies drift and glide in different, often unexpected directions — a case in point is the sympathy for the zombies that is evoked in George Romero's films.

These levels are not really separate from each other. A reader can be aware of the literal and allegorical levels at the same time — in fact, I would argue that the best horror fiction even demands this of us as readers. And this brings us to a third level at which genre horror operates — and that is the level of the horror genre itself. Some of the most interesting works of the horror genre are also about the genre itself. This is especially the case today, as horror film, TV, and long-format programs increasingly rely on the viewer's knowledge of the genre and its rules, in order to play with or even break those rules. Some films make knowing, winking references within the film, others use gamelike or puzzlelike structures to create suspense, and still others incorporate an array of special effects, which serve to comment on the illusory capacity of visual media.

Looking over some of the classics of horror, one question that comes up again and again is whether the horror genre as a whole was to be identified with the supernatural. We are well aware of the Gothic tradition of supernatural tales, as well as the creature-feature films of the 1930s and 1940s. However, since the era of films like *Psycho* and *Peeping Tom*, the horror genre has also explored psychological terrors, the terrors of our inner worlds. But if everything can be explained by science and psychology, then are we not in the adjacent genres of science fiction or the thriller? What then makes a work a part of the horror genre? Fans are still split on these sorts of questions, which will never be definitively answered. But if you grew up watching horror movies in the 1980s, you were well aware of this inner conflict, if only on a subconscious level. There were some films that were steeped in the supernatural, where the horror relied on what you didn't see (*The Shining*, *The Amityville Horror*, *Poltergeist*). Then there were those films that dispensed with the supernatural completely, the stalk-and-slash films that came out of the Italian *giallo* tradition and led to films such as *Halloween*. In these films you saw everything, you even saw more than you wanted to see. Either the horror was what you couldn't see or the horror was what you could see all too well, either you had *supernatural horror* or you had *extreme horror*. (This dichotomy was evident in horror fiction too — on the one hand you had authors such as Joyce Carol Oates, Ramsey Campbell, and Thomas Ligotti, or you had authors associated with "splatterpunk"; and it continues to this day, for instance, in the dichotomy between "torture-porn" and J-horror films.) What's more, that conflict can manifest itself within a single film — while Kubrick's *The Shining* is essentially a haunted house story, it is precisely those elements that drive the main character to become a homicidal maniac (the supernatural becoming the natural);

and we often forget that the masked killer in Carpenter's *Halloween* was referred to as "The Shape," taking on almost superhuman qualities (the natural becoming supernatural).

These are, arguably, the poles of the horror genre — extreme horror and supernatural horror, people doing things to people and non-people doing things to people, "I can't believe what I'm seeing" and "I can't see what I believe." In a sense the horror genre itself is defined in the space between these two poles, and the passages between them. This slipperiness has now become a hallmark of the genre, with widely read authors such as Koji Suzuki, China Miéville, Victor LaValle, and Silvia Moreno-Garcia taking us from one pole to the other and giving us rich, complex, story worlds that also bring together elements from several genres — fantasy, science fiction, the detective genre, historical fiction, and so on.

Is there another level beyond even this, a fourth allegorical level to the horror genre, one that actually takes us out of the world of storytelling itself? If so, perhaps that level would take us beyond the horror genre and into more general reflections on religion and religious experience. By "religion" I do not simply mean the organized, institutional religion that we commonly associate with the monotheistic traditions of Judaism, Christianity, and Islam. But that leaves a lot open. Contemporary philosophy of religion has had much to say on the boundary that divides religion from non-religion. Some argue for the value of alternative traditions, be they pagan or "Eastern," while others argue for a more complex and internally fraught understanding of monotheisms like Christianity, while still others argue for a sense of an everyday, polyglot spiritual awareness outside of any particular religious institution.

However, one commonality all these positions have is that they articulate a basic relationship between the human being and the limit of its capacity to adequately comprehend the world in which it finds itself. That experience of limits can be called "religious" (William James preferred the phrase "religious experience"), or, more narrowly, "mystical" (from the Greek *mustikos*, or "hidden").

It broadly denotes an encounter with something essentially unknown, what theologian Rudolf Otto called "the numinous," an encounter with the "wholly other," a meeting with the horizon of our own understanding as human beings and the limit of thought this entails. That encounter may begin as the encounter with another person or other people, with a certain place or site, or with a book or a film or a work of music, or it might simply begin from a seemingly everyday, banal observation.

Whatever the case, this encounter with the unknown does not result in the kind of spectacular, beatific visions of light typically evoked by the word "mysticism." In fact, if one looks at, say, the tradition of Christian mysticism in the Middle Ages, what one finds are texts that are filled with ambiguity and ambivalence — evocations of "divine darkness," or "clouds of unknowing," or of the "dark night of the soul." They contain accounts of intense physical and spiritual suffering, of desert battles with legions of demons, of ecstasies and mortifications of the flesh, of passions so unhuman they can only come out as cries and sobs, of corpses happily entombed in an amorous embrace. If anything, we are presented with questions without answers, and problems without solutions. Should we say, then, that religious experience often runs counter to religion? But what counts as "experience" in this case, when we are at the limit of the senses and of thought? This is the "religious" allegory that I find so fascinating in the horror genre. But the 13th century context of, say, Dante's *Inferno* is markedly different from the 21st-century context of modern TV shows such as *The Terror*, *Dark*, or *Black Mirror*. Our contemporary horror stories are written in a world in which religious fanaticism routinely exterminates religious experience, a world in which scientific fanaticism explains and controls everything, a climatological world where there seems little faith, lost hope, and no salvation. And perhaps that is the level at which the horror genre operates, if only obliquely. It is noticeable in those works that dare to delve into a *religious horror*, where we pass beyond the pedantic world of people doing bad things to other people, and suddenly realize not only that the world remains indifferent to us, but that the world is and has always been an inhuman world. Not a comforting thought. But then again neither philosophy, nor religion, nor horror, is meant to comfort.

2

MEDITATIONS ON THE DEMONIC

The Structure of Suffering (Dante's Inferno). While the problem of human suffering is central to many world religions, too often the concerns over what form of suffering afflicts us and how to ameliorate it eclipses a more basic concern: that suffering should exist at all. The "what" (what is suffering?) and the "how" (how do we ease suffering?) often gloss over the more troubling, more mysterious question of the "that" (the so-called fact of suffering). It is this need to account for suffering — and in so doing to make meaning of it — that has generated the many topologies of the supernatural that inhabit world myth, literature, and religious ideas. After all, suffering is never just suffering in the abstract, but always incarnate in a body, in a population, in a culture, in the circulation of affects, doubts, and suspicions that circumscribe the strange thing called faith. There is something decidedly anti-transcendental about suffering. Suffering is never just out there, in some nebulous floating cloud of abstraction. Suffering always takes place. It is here, and now — even if we may only be dimly aware of it. It crisscrosses bodies, affects, and the terrain through which we move and act. The problem of suffering is also a problem of space and place. In this sense, the concern of accounting for suffering is also a concern for locating suffering, for identifying the topology of suffering — that is, the structure of suffering.

Perhaps this is why so many religious traditions have felt the need to delineate a specific place of suffering, be it the underworld of ancient Greek myth, populated as it is with the spirits of the dead, or the *naraka* of Buddhist cosmology, the lowest realm in the cycle of rebirth. The idea of Hell in the early Abrahamic religions, takes on more and more elaborate forms in Medieval Christianity.[369] In the Medieval Christian tradition — syncretic and polyglot as it is — the idea of Hell is filled with ambiguity. Hell is an alarmingly concrete and real place, a place of punishment and imprisonment. But Hell is also a strange non-place, a place of exclusion or excommunication, a place seemingly outside of life and death. Borrowing as it did from other sources, Medieval Christianity cultivated a notion of Hell that was at once literal and figurative, concrete and abstract, place and space. Unlike Heaven, Hell is not ethereal and transcendent, the realm of pure spirit — and yet it is clearly a space of the supernatural. Unlike earthly existence, Hell exists outside of the contingencies of mundane, creaturely life — and yet it is often described in ways that are as material and as embodied as that of life on Earth. Not transcendent, and yet supernatural. In short, Hell in Medieval Christianity is ambiguously spatial and symbolic, allegorical and architectural.

Nowhere is this ambiguity more evident than in Dante's *Inferno*, a work that at once encapsulates the multifaceted character of the Christian concept of Hell, while also serving as a kind of compendium of earlier Greek, Roman, and Judaic sources.[370] As is well known, Dante achieves this through the metafictional conceit of having himself — a wayward spiritual pilgrim — taken on a tour of Hell, guided by the ghost of the poet Virgil (whose *Aeneid* was a model for Dante). This device allows Dante to provide elaborate descriptions of Hell and its many circles, complete with a kind of geographical, environmental realism unparalleled at the time.

And yet the *Inferno* is not simply a stage set or the equivalent of a special-effects trick. All of the detail in it is also doing conceptual work. Hell is not just where demons reside, but it is also where the demonic takes place, in all its forms — primary among them the incarnation of suffering in the human being. As Thomas Aquinas and other theologians had indicated, the demonic is demonic because it is a falling away from life, and a lesser form of being, a diminished existence compared to the beatific fullness of the divine. In his late-13th century treatise *On Evil* (*De Malo*), Aquinas articulates the demonic in decidedly philosophical terms: the demonic is associated with "non-being," the negation of life, the negation of existence. How then, can the demonic exist at all, if it is non-being? What is a puzzle for the theologian, is a riddle for the poet. Dante's response to this counter-mystery — the mystery of the demonic — is to allow the demonic to manifest itself in heterogeneous ways Of course, there are the personified, horned, and winged demons that are by now clichés of the horror genre. But Dante also shows us the demonic manifest as terrain — as landscape, as weather, as the elemental forces of heat and cold, fire and ice. Hell in Dante's hands is wrought with an attention to the details of geography, terrain, and topology. This version of Hell is more than simply a place of punishment or suffering, it is an affective sense of being engulfed by the environment. In the *Inferno*, suffering is inseparable from the "extreme weather" and "climate events" that constitute it, from torrential hurricanes of human bodies, to molten deserts of rock and stone, to dark arctic plains of frozen souls, to petrified forests of contorted anatomies, down to the very core of the brooding wasteland itself, where one finds landscapes inhospitable to all life. In Dante's hands, Hell is not just theological, but also geological and climatological.

What the contemporary reader of Dante's *Inferno* discovers is not only an epic journey through the various regions of Hell, but a terrain of strange landscapes and fantastical creatures that seem to be a blueprint for the horror genre. In fact — for better or worse — it is difficult not to read the *Inferno* as part of the horror genre.

There is the torrential, swarming Circle of the Lustful, the burning bodies of the Heretics pouring out of their graves, the hybrid tree-corpses that populate the Forest of Suicides, the Plain of Thieves with limbs entwined by serpents, the anatomically dismembered Sowers of Discord — in addition to burning deserts raining flame, grotesque bogs of inertia, lakes of ice filled with corpses, a City of the Dead, rivers of boiling blood, stormy ravines and shadowy caverns, and a whole bestiary that includes creatures such as Cerberus, the Furies, the Harpies, Centaurs, the Gorgon, giants, packs of demons, and of course, in the lowest circle, gloomy three-faced Satan, half-submerged in ice, weeping tears from six eyes, eternally flailing with six wings. If ever there was a sourcebook for the horror genre, then arguably this is it.

It is also for this very reason that it can be difficult to appreciate the *Inferno*. When Dante wrote the *Commedia* in the early 14th century, he drew together a wide range of influences, from Greek mythology to Arabic philosophy to Christian theology, along with literary, historical, philosophical, and political references. We are so accustomed to films and TV shows that feature the living dead that it is difficult to appreciate the way in which Dante describes the City of Dis, a city of the dead in which a multitude of corpses — the Heretics — emerge from a field of fiery graves. The image is at once mythological, evoking the voyage to the underworld, and also political — at once a city, a cemetery, and a site of divine punishment. We have, perhaps, too much cultural baggage to really appreciate the *Inferno* in its historical, political, and cultural context.

At the same time, reading the *Inferno* retroactively as part of the horror genre allows us to take a step back from the intricacies and historical references that populate Dante's allegory. When we "zoom out" from the *Inferno*, one thing that makes itself clear is the way that it is structured, not only thematically but spatially. Everything is structured in this version of Hell, and, at the same time, everything flows. Contrary elements like fire and water merge into each other with the same effortlessness as the bodies of different creatures. The landscape and the climate of Hell is at once chaotic and ordered, just as the creaturely chaos within each circle is, at the same time, rigorously stratified into circles and layers.

That structure is well-known to any reader of the *Inferno*. Dante — who is both author and character in the *Inferno* — finds himself lost in a dark forest, "midway along life's way." There he meets the poet Virgil, who guides him on a tour through Hell, Purgatory, and Paradise. As Dante (the character) and Virgil enter the gates of Hell, they see the inscription over the gates, which ends with the famous line: *Lasciate ogne speranza, voi ch'intrate*, "Abandon Every Hope, All Who Enter."[371] Once inside, Dante, led by Virgil, passes through several "circles" of Hell, each of which contains a specific group of "shades" or souls of the deceased who have committed particular wrongs for which they are being punished. Each circle corresponds to a specific type of wrong committed, and the entirety of Hell is therefore a kind of classification system of wrongdoings — an architecture of fallibility and suffering. Within each circle, the shades are punished according to the logic of the *contrapasso*, in which the punishment fits the crime (for instance, the second circle, the Circle of the Lustful, has groups of sinners continually blown this way and that by the torrential winds of desire). Each circle also contains a unique terrain, a unique climate, and unique creatures, often borrowed from classical myth.

The *Inferno* contains nine circles of Hell, which are divided among 33 cantos in the text, along with the prefatory canto. The nine circles roughly group into three clusters:

Upper Hell (Circles I–V), dominated by an excess of passion.
Middle Hell (Circles VI–VII), dominated by perversions of passion or reason.
Lower Hell (Circles VIII–IX), dominated by an excess of reason.

Dante scholars conventionally refer to Upper Hell in terms of "incontinence" or the suffering caused by excess human emotion, to Middle Hell in terms of violence or perversions of the human nature, and Lower Hell in terms of deceit, fraud, or the suffering caused by excess human intellect. This breakdown generally follows Dante's appropriation of Aristotelian categories of the human faculties.

Hell is, first and foremost, a stratified domain, like so many geological layers of a fantastical world or an alien planet. Many modern editions of the *Inferno* provide diagrams which detail the various strata, since some of the circles — particularly the eighth and ninth circles — contain sub-circles, or *bolgia* ("ditches" or "trenches") which further stratify and classify the shades that populate Hell.[372] One of the most fascinating diagrams is the one by Wilfrid Scott-Giles, which accompanies Dorothy Sayers's celebrated 1949 translation of the *Inferno*.

I find this image fascinating in that it adopts an engineer's approach to Hell. The cutaway view reveals the different strata of Hell, and the three-dimensional aspect gives a sense of habitable worlds within worlds. From a contemporary standpoint, this image also evokes a kind of game logic, as if Dante had, unwittingly, designed Hell as a video game — except that, in this case, the goal of the game would be to descend further into Hell rather than to escape it (perhaps such a game would have a further rule — that, to advance to the next "level" of Hell, the player has to commit the sin of that particular circle). [373] Indeed, within the narrative of the *Inferno* Dante the character does frequently commit the sins of the circle through which he is passing — for instance, in the Circle of the Wrathful Dante expresses hostility towards the shades that reach out for him.

These types of images were common in early editions of the *Inferno*, stretching back to Dante's own time. Artists seemed to have gravitated towards this spatial, stratified aspect of the text, each devising their own way of visually representing Hell. Some opted for realistic depictions of particular scenes, while others adopted a more abstract, almost geometric method of

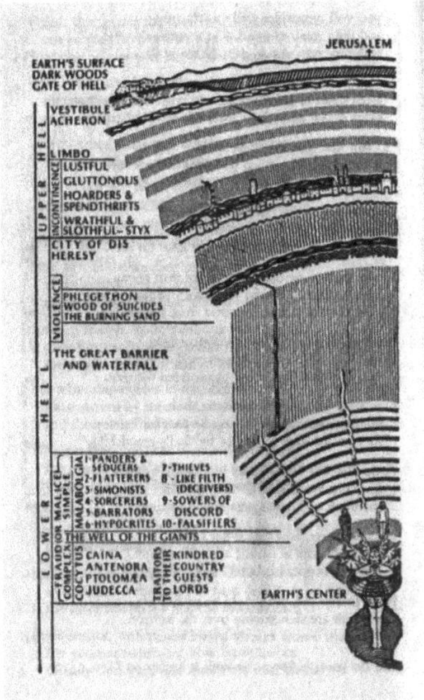

Cross-section of Dante's Hell, from Dante Alighieri, *The Divine Comedy I: Hell*, trans. Dorothy Sayers (New York: Penguin, 1949)

representation, while still others offered top-down views of the circles of Hell. Many of the images produced during the Renaissance combined, in interesting ways, diagrammatic and pictorial methods of representation. The Benivieni edition of 1506 (also known as the "Giuntina" after its publisher Filippo Giunti) contains a number of cutaway diagrams in woodcut that mime the cutaway view.

This version, edited by the Florentine poet Girolamo Benivieni, was among the first editions of Dante's *Commedia* to provide a more "scientific" cosmology of Hell, Purgatory, and Paradise. Benivieni's edition was based on the work of Antonio Manetti — mathematician, architect, and author — who undertook research into the worlds that Dante describes, providing ways to render them visually. Manetti's research into Dantean cosmology was taken up by subsequent editors, and it is now standard in modern editions of

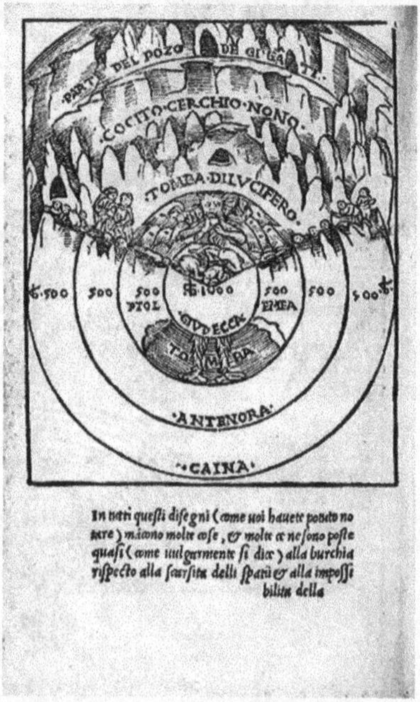

Diagram of Hell in the edition of Giorlamo Benivieni, from *Commedia di Dante* (1506)

Dante to include these kinds of summary diagrams. Such means of visually rendering Hell underscore the interplay between the microstructure of the individual circles and the macrostructure of Hell itself; the correspondences between the individuated bodies within each circle and the collective, infernal "body" of Hell itself.

Such diagrams as this were, no doubt, intended as guides for readers, thereby extending the allegorical aspect of Dante's text. They also underscore the spatial, architectonic design of Hell, with its myriad, chaotic scenes that are at the same time rigidly organized. This raises an important point about the *Inferno*: from this architectonic point of view, the tension central to Hell is the order of that which is disordered, the stratification of that which is unruly, the classification of that which transgresses classification. These are also central questions in political philosophy. How should things be structured such that they flow? What is the best way to order human beings and the culture which they have created? At what point does a political philosophy become a political theology?

These questions dovetail on one of the oldest ideas in Western political philosophy, that of the body politic. Philosophers from Plato to Hobbes to contemporary political theorists have long drawn on the analogy between the individual human body and the collective body of society, whether to affirm the hierarchy of the body or to question it. If we take a look at Dante's *Inferno* in this way, what we find is that Dante provides us with an architectonic body politic, one in which landscapes, climates, beasts, and various human bodies all come together to compose Hell itself. The general division of Upper, Middle, and Lower Hell is derived from Aristotelian ethics, which Dante then maps both spatially and corporeally. Upper Hell, dominated by an excess of human emotion, is often correlated to the nether regions of the body, while Middle Hell, dominated by perversions of human nature, correlates to the heart, torso, and hands, and Lower Hell, dominated by an excess of reason, correlates to the "head" — both as the seat of intelligence and as the control center of the body.

In this sense that we can describe the *Inferno* as *a structure of suffering*, an architectonics of power. It is hierarchical (the more serious the sins, the lower in Hell one is placed), but it is also a space of flux and flow (the landscape, the different climates, the roving of various creatures, the meandering human "shades"). As a whole Hell is a huge, cavernous structure often depicted as an inverted cone, each circle spiraling down to the center, the lowest point of Hell, where Satan sits, frozen and melancholy. The apex of Hell is nearly an inversion of the apex of a cathedral (symbolizing the theological "body" of the congregation, which, in turn, configures the body as the "temple" of the soul) — an infernal cavern in place of the divine temple. In short, the *Inferno* presents us with an inverted body politic, literally standing the body politic on its head.

Like any great systematizer, Dante's inferno does not form a perfect system, but contains numerous partial matches, subtle incongruities, and asymmetries. Thus, it is also important to note the disjunction between each individual circle of Hell against the structure of Hell as a whole. The human "shades" trapped within each circle long to escape their interminable punishment, cursing the God that has put them there; the various creatures — demons, Furies, and Centaurs — likewise threaten to break out of their confined roles; and the general terrain of Hell, with its tempestuous storms, flooding waters, and cascades of fire, threatens to spill over into the other circles. In this sense, the "big" body politic that is the architectonics of the inferno must be read alongside the multitude of "little" bodies that populate and are part of the ceaseless turbulence that is the structure of Hell.

In a way, Dante inverts the traditional philosophical model of the body politic. In doing this, we see variations on the motif of the body politic, not as an ideal, coherent, and unified body, but as a series of dissolute, dismembered, and diseased bodies. By inverting the body politic, Dante shows us the body politic defined not by its ideal principles (the One, the whole, the head), but by those things that threaten and dissolve the body politic (the "creaturely" activities of flux and flow). In doing this, Dante reminds us of one the central issues in the body politic motif as it is developed in political philosophy: that the greatest threat to the coherence of the body politic comes from within it. We will see later on exactly how political philosophy manages this tension. For the time being, we can simply note the way Dante has not only written a work of "horror" but has also written a work that ties horror to political philosophy and political theology, as well as to a political demonology.

*

Anatomy of Suffering. In the *Inferno,* each of the categories of sin (too much emotion, perversions of nature, too much reason) are not simply conceptual categories, but are linked to the affective dimension of suffering. The problem of too much passion, which occupies Upper Hell, may be understood as uncontrolled appetite, the problem of nature uncontrolled, the domination of the animal life, the problem of "too much life." The clearest expression of this is the famous second circle of the lustful (Canto V), depicted by Dante as a swarming whirlwind of bodies, desire, and unbridled passion.

The suffering caused by an imbalance between passion and reason occupies Middle Hell, and may be understood as a perversion of the innate human capacity for reason, producing the problem of unruly or aberrant forms of life. Dante subdivides them into three types: (i) violence against others (heresy, false doctrine), (ii) violence against the self (suicide), and (iii) violence against nature (usury, sodomy). The most interesting example of this comes after Dante and Virgil pass through the gates of the City of Dis (Cantos VIII–XII). They encounter otherworldly beasts and chimeras of all sorts: the living dead (IX, 106–133), the Furies (IX, 37–57), the Minotaur (XII), the Centaurs, the Harpies (XIII, 10–15), and the giant, monstrous Geryon (XVII).

In addition, the punished sinners in Middle Hell also undergo strange metamorphoses. In the City of Dis the arch-heretics (those violent against others) are condemned to be living corpses; while in the Wood of Suicides (those violent against the self), human merges with plant, as the tortured bodies are twisted into dead trees; and on the Burning Sand, the usurers and sodomites (those violent against nature) are stripped of everything except their fragile bodies. They are bodies without life, encircled by a river of boiling blood, the lifeblood that is both extracted and externalized from the living body, and which confines them in a desert void of light or life.

In fact, it is this landscape of bare life that tells us the most about Middle Hell. We move from a city of graves, to a dead forest, to rivers of boiling blood. In this progression, we see the extraction of natural, creaturely life from the human being, an extraction corresponding to the sinful acts that denigrate and pervert the "natural theology" of creaturely life. The city is a necropolis, a city in ruins, while the forest is barren and petrified, and the desert is, well, a desert — inhospitable to the human, deserted of all life.

Perhaps the most enigmatic figure of the bestial, abnormal life of Middle Hell comes at the end of Canto XIV, as Dante and Virgil are leaving the Burning Sand. Upon asking about the source of the river of blood that surrounds it, Virgil responds with the striking allegory of the "Old Man of Crete" (94–120). There Virgil talks about a giant, ancient man within Mount Ida in Crete, who "faces Rome as though it were his mirror." Combining references from Ovid and the Bible, Virgil describes the Old Man in terms that were, in the 14th century, becoming part of the political-theological vernacular: the head and topmost region is made of gold, the torso or middle region of silver, and the lower regions of brass and iron (except for the right foot, which is of terra cotta). This giant, allegorical body shows some similarities to that depicted in Plato's *Timeaus* — the "three-venter" body — itself not unknown to the Greeks.

But the giant body is everywhere cracked, and through the fissures tears of sorrow drain down, gradually forming the mythical rivers of Acheron, Styx, and Phlegethon, and finally settling in the pool of Cocytus where Satan resides. If the Old Man is Christian Rome, and if this body is fractured from within, then the implication Dante seems to be drawing out is that the body politic is showing signs of wear and tear. Not only is there a fissure between ecclesiastical and political authority (which Dante attempts to redress in his *De Monarchia*), but the very concept of the body politic is itself undergoing changes which threaten to fracture it from within. The question, then, would not only be about the tension between divine and secular authority, but about whether the body politic concept itself may be decomposing — an issue still not completely sorted in later thinkers such as Thomas Hobbes.

Lastly, the suffering caused by too much reason, which covers Lower Hell, is appetite manipulated by reason and rendered deceitful, life totally subsumed within instrumental rationality. Lower Hell contains a veritable numerology of subdivisions and sins. The *Malbowges* contain ten sub-circles of "simple" fraud, including the sorcerers and thieves, while the circles around Cocytus contain more circles of "complex" fraud, including the different classes of traitors.

The sins of Lower Hell are also more complex. They involve not just uncontrolled appetite, and not just perverted nature, but the reasoned use of nature for malicious ends, the suffering caused by reason transformed into unreason. This is, for Dante, the most dangerous of sins, but also the most sophisticated, the most "elevated." The corporeal expression of this is grotesquely presented in the ninth *bolgia*, where we encounter the Sowers of Discord (Canto XXVIII), and in the tenth, where we find the Falsifiers (Canto XXIX). In the former, the Sowers of Discord (which include Mohammed) are subject to the cruelest corporeal punishments: flaying, cutting, mutilation, and dismemberment. What makes these punishments so horrifying is precisely that they are punishments. They are carried out with a medical, anatomical accuracy, fulfilling the Biblical logic of the *contrepasso*, an "eye for an eye," the punishment fitting the crime. There is an echo here of the use of the cadavers of criminals or the poor for anatomical dissection in the early modern era, a ritualized anatomy theater of the supernatural.

Two examples illustrate this "anatomized" body politic. The first example is that of Mohammed, who is blamed for having split the unity of the Church, and who is himself ripped from hips to head. His body horrifically heals itself, only to have the punishment inflicted again. The clear implication is that the unified, hierarchical body of the Church is threatened from within by those that diverge from its doctrine. The message is clear: if the Church is a single body politic, then any attempt to subvert the hierarchy (by creating divergent heads or limbs) can only destroy the body politic.

A second example comes at the end of the same canto, with the figure of Bertran de Born, who, out of hubris, turned a young prince against his father. His punishment is decapitation, and to walk eternally holding his head by the hair. Here, Bertran is accused not only of turning the prince against the king, but of turning a son against a father. The body politic of the family is echoed in the body politic of the city-state (a very Aristotelian variant on the theme). And again the threat comes from within; the usurpation of the "head" (of family, of the city-state) can only end in the decapitation and death of the body politic altogether.

These two examples of the anatomical body politic emphasize a different aspect of the motif. The corporeal splitting of Mohammed stresses the unity of the body under a single head, while the decapitation of Bertran de Born stresses the unity of the head over the body. This anatomical body politic is further expanded in the following cantos, where we witness the falsifiers, each afflicted with diseases (including plague and leprosy). We have here a third aspect of the body politic, that of the diseased or "sick" body. Presumably, the Falsifiers' rumors circulate through society like a contagion, causing illness to the healthy unity of the body politic itself. Communication, then, plays a central role in the body politic. Language (*logos*) spreads throughout the body politic, and, like the other variants we've seen (Mohammed, Bertran), it also causes disease from within.

In the threats to anatomical body politic (too much emotion, too much reason), we see bodies that are at once individual bodies subjected to sovereign punishment, and a body politic that is dismembered, dissected, and diseased as a result of acts of creaturely sin. If we take these two kinds of body politic presented in the *Inferno* — the architectonic body politic (the "big" body) and the anatomical body politic (the "little" body) — we can discern an important relation between them. In the architectonic body politic, Dante presents us with an inversion of the body-as-temple metaphor, standing the body politic on its head. Here we have a redoubled analogy: the architectural building is analogized to the body, but then the body is then re-analogized, through the categories of creaturely sin, to actual anatomical bodies, that are finally read as variants on the concept of the body politic, a concept that was itself undergoing many changes in the later Middle Ages.

*

Dead Tropes, Resurrected Bodies. To understand the "political demonology" of the *Inferno*, we can take a detour into the history of political philosophy, outlining a few principles concerning the body politic, principles which determine the *constitution* or composition of the body politic. At the same time, we will also note how this constitution tends to turn in on itself, the body politic devouring itself, and becoming defined by a *dissolution* or decomposition. Highlighting this aspect of the body politic concept will require paying attention to ideas that are at once medical and theological, natural and supernatural, that pertain to the domain of the dead and the living dead.

One of the most familiar images of the body politic comes from Thomas Hobbes, who articulates that image through a language of natural law — illustrated in the famous frontispiece of *Leviathan* (1651) — an image of the body politic that is by turns mechanistic, vitalistic, and theological. A passage from the introduction deserves to be quoted in full, providing as it does a summary:

> For by art is created that great LEVIATHAN called a COMMONWEALTH, or STATE (in Latin CIVITAS), which is but an artificial man, though of greater stature and strength than the natural, for whose protection and defence it was intended; and in which the *sovereignty* is an artificial *soul*, as giving life and motion to the whole body; the *magistrates* and other *officers* of judicature and execution, artificial *joints*; *reward* and *punishment* (by which fastened to the seat of the sovereignty every joint and member is moved to perform his duty) are the *nerves*, that do the same in the body natural; the *wealth* and *riches* of all the particular members are the *strength*; *salus populi* (the people's safety) its *business*; *counselors*, by whom all things needful for it to know are suggested unto it, are the *memory*; *equity* and *laws*, an artificial *reason* and *will*; *concord*, *health*; *sedition*, *sickness*; and *civil war*, *death*. Lastly, the *pacts* and *covenants* by which the parts of the body politic were at first made, set together,

> and united, resemble that *fiat*, or the *let us make man*, pronounced by God in the creation.[375]

There are, certainly, many comments to make on this paragraph alone, and one can easily trace a lineage that moves backward to the vague naturalism of political theorists such as Bodin, Grotius, and Althusius (the latter's notion of the *corpus symbioticum* deserves more attention in this regard), and forward to the organicism of Hegel, Rousseau, and Nietzsche. However, the goal here is not to provide anything like a comprehensive history of the idea. Rather, we can pay attention to the literalness of the body politic analogy as expressed in passages like these (passages that are echoed in Hobbes's treatises *On the Citizen* and *On the Body*). To call the body politic a metaphor doesn't quite do justice to the way a great number of political treatises take the concept at face value. Again and again, we find specific comparisons made between the human body and political order, as if the basis for legitimacy in the latter depended on the coherence of the understanding of the former.

The body politic concept is especially literal in what are often said to be the two key moments in Western political thought concerning the concept: that of its formulation around the city-state or *polis*, most thoroughly expressed in Plato, and that of its recapitulation in the medieval theological notion of the *corpus mysticum*, the mystical body of believers united in the larger "body" of Christ and the Church.

Medieval scholars such as Étienne Gilson have noted the debt medieval philosophy owes to antiquity, and the body politic concept owes the same debt. In Plato the concept is formulated at several points in the *The Republic*, in which Socrates proposes understanding justice in the individual by extrapolating from the *polis*, or the individual "writ large." Plato immediately provides us with the language through which the body politic concept is most often understood — that of medicine, health, and illness. In the dialogue, Socrates argues that "health is produced by establishing a natural relation of control and subordination among the constituents of the body, disease by establishing an unnatural relation," wherefrom he then posits that "justice is produced by establishing in the mind a similar natural relation of control and subordination among its constituents, and injustice by establishing an unnatural one." The conclusion arrived at by Socrates? "It seems, then, that excellence is a kind of mental health or beauty or fitness, and defect a kind of illness or deformity or weakness."[376]

The Platonic body politic gives us several components that are fundamental to the body politic concept. The language of medicine, health, and illness implies there is something human and living that is larger than the living human individual. This large, living, and human thing must be understood through a logic of parts and wholes. The subsequent sections of the *The Republic*, in which the ideal *polis* is laid out, discuss the body politic not only in terms of health and illness, but also in terms of parts and wholes: the body politic in Plato is divided into three sections that reveal clear biases: the sovereign head (the reasoning part), auxiliaries and soldiers in the heart or chest (the impassioned part), and the peasantry and laypeople in the nether regions of the groin (the animal part). It's a tripartite division of the body that also appears in the *Timeaus*, though in a more cosmological context.

This scaling-up procedure is also found in late medieval Scholasticism, itself profoundly influenced by the writings of Paul, whose notion of the *corpus mysticum*, or the mystical body of Christ, introduced the language of community into the theological variants of the body politic: "The body is a unit, though it is made up of many parts; and though all its parts are many, they form one body ... there should be no division in the body, but that its parts should have equal concern for each other. If one part suffers, every part suffers with it; if one part is honored, every part rejoices with it."[377] While Platonic hierarchy and Aristotelian naturalism provide the philosophical terms for the medieval body politic, the idea also takes new turns in its emphasis on spirit, the creature, and corporeality, on a body that is ensouled, living, and never quite dead. Scholastic philosophy "brought out with no less force," Gilson notes, "the necessary connection between faith in the resurrection of the body, and the philosophical thesis of the substantial unity of the human composite."[378]

Significant sections of medieval political treatises, including those of Aquinas, Dante, Marsilius of Padua, Nicholas of Cusa, and William of Ockham, each contain passages in which the anatomical human body is analogized — or anatomized — point for point with the body of the Church, the State, or some mixture of both. Entire texts, such as John of Salisbury's remarkable *Policraticus*, are based on this kind of tabular matching between individual-natural and collective-political body. The head, the limbs, the torso, the feet, as well as an entire symbolics of the viscera — heart, brain, hands, genitals — are all offered up as functional parts within a greater whole. Though there were, of course, extensive debates about what kind of body this "whole" was, and, more importantly, what constituted the sovereign "head" of this body, the terms of the discussions remained focused on this conceptual movement between an anatomical, individuated human body and an equally anatomized, but collective, political body.

*

As Above, So Below. Contrary to the treatment it often receives, the body politic analogy does not neatly evolve from a theological to a secular interpretation, or from divine to natural law. It is filled with incongruities, diversions, and proliferations that express a startling lack of consensus on what the most ideal body politic might be.

Rather than elaborate endless quotations on the topic, we can present four principles that delineate the philosophical challenge posed by the body politic concept. What they share is an assumption that the body politic is shaped around human-centered interests, suggesting to us that current discussions about climate change and the Anthropocene have not yet rid themselves of concepts historically formulated through the lens of political theology.

We begin with a first principle: *The body politic is a response to the challenge of thinking about political order*. Put another way: a congruity between order as natural and as artificial is the starting point of the body politic analogy. The body politic is a way of thinking about politics as the order of the living, an order that is exclusive to human being. It is ordered insofar as it is defined within a logic of the one and the many, of parts and wholes, and of the relation between the natural and the artificial. And it is living insofar as it posits a correlation between the natural world and political order, either to say that the natural world is divinely ordered (as one finds in Augustine), or to argue that political order is built on a "natural law" (as one finds in Hobbes).

However, to posit politics as a combination of the living and the ordered is not enough, for it is the way in which this relation is formulated that is important. Thus, a second principle: the foundation for the intelligibility of political order is based on *an analogy between the body natural and the body politic*. The former is said to preexist the latter, and often serves as its model; and the latter governs, manages, and regulates the former. Moreover, the body natural is often taken as the basic, individuated, atomic unit of human life, extrapolated to the meta-individuated level as collective political existence. The task of political thought is to correlate the body natural and the body politic — though the two never quite coincide. The analogy thus presupposes asymmetries and incongruities. Does the body politic have one head or two (Church and State)? Is it a single system or does it have systems-within-systems ("corporations" and "councils")? If the individual body is mortal and subject to decline and death, should we say the same about the body politic?

Furthermore, the body politic analogy constantly aims to maintain its hierarchy by managing the relationships between the "limbs" of the political body. Political concepts concerning "sovereignty" and the "multitude" are outgrowths of the relation between "head" and "body," themselves descended from the medieval question about the place of "soul" in the body politic. In his classic study of the body politic, Ernst Kantorowicz shows how, in the later Middle Ages, the figure guaranteeing the continuity of sovereign power shifts from a Christ-centered, to a Law-centered, and finally to a "polity-centered" notion of rulership. In this transition, the figure of the "mystical body" (*corpus mysticum*) plays a central role: "Late mediaeval kingship, from whatever point of view it be considered, had become polity-centered after the crisis of the 13th century. The continuity, first guaranteed by Christ, then by the Law, was now guaranteed by the *corpus mysticum* of the realm which, so to speak, never died, but was 'eternal' like the *corpus mysticum* of the Church."[379]

In addition to questions of unity and of hierarchy, there is also a concern with centralization, or the question of how to govern the flows and circulations that mark what Aquinas calls the "life-giving spirit" of the body politic. Historian Jacques Le Goff remarks on a common tension found within late medieval treatises of the body politic: between the "head" and the "heart," both of which are connected to the nervous and circulatory systems that animate both the individual body and the "systems" of the body politic. Le Goff suggests that debates over Church and State often played themselves out through a kind of anatomical topology, in which nerves and blood are pitted against each other, vying for control: "The centrality attributed to the heart expresses the evolution of the monarchical state in which the most important thing is the *centralization* that is taking place around the prince, not the vertical hierarchy expressed by the head."[380]

These criteria — unity, hierarchy, centralization — are coupled to a narrative, one that tells us of the genesis or "constitution" of the body politic. This origin story accounts for the origins (and thus legitimacy) of the body politic, while also ensuring the coherence of the body politic over time. The most well-known of such narratives is the one derived from natural right theory, encapsulated by Hobbes as the transition from the pre-political "state of nature" to the laying down of rights and the establishment of a commonwealth. Plato, in *The Republic* and *The Laws*, had already given us a version of this in the analogy between the idea of justice in the individual and the idea of justice in the *polis*, or the individual "writ large." Augustine and Aquinas likewise provide narrative accounts of the necessity of the divine sovereign in the act of creation.[381]

All of this points to an abstract theological model to which, of course, an actual political regime may or may not correspond. Even though the body politic concept may entail a narrative of constitution or origin, this in no way means that the body politic analogy itself precedes an actual political regime. In fact, the opposite is the case, which brings us to a third principle: ***the body politic is expressed retroactively in the language of political theology***. The body politic analogy is employed in order to justify or legitimize a de facto political order — that is, to justify a particular philosophical relation between "life" and "order."

The term "political theology" has been used in different ways by a number of political thinkers, including Walter Benjamin, Carl Schmitt and Jacob Taubes. Conceptually it refers to the embodiment of sovereignty, be it in a single ruler (the King or the Pope as the "head") or in some notion of the people (popular sovereignty, collective rule, religious community as the "body"). Historically political theology refers to the manifold relations between spiritual and temporal powers in theological, legal, and Scholastic discourse in the later Middle Ages.[382] But it also raises the question of the necessity of sovereign power that is still at issue in the modern debates. Schmitt argues for the necessity of exceptional, sovereign power, since it is in the very nature of the political to be unable to legitimize authority except by reference to an outside source. As he notes, "all significant concepts of the modern theory of the state are secularized theological concepts."[383] Taubes disagrees, for, though the Judeo-Christian tradition does emphasize sovereign law, in the Pauline tradition it also emphasizes community and pluralistic rule: "Carl Schmitt thinks apocalyptically, but from above, from the powers; I think from below."[384]

For Schmitt, there is a direct correlation between the miracle in theology and the exception in politics, the latter being simply a secularized version of the former. Just as the divine sovereign is not only capable of establishing the natural workings of things, it can also intervene in the nature of things so as to make exceptional (that is, supernatural) decisions. In this way, the secular sovereign recapitulates the act of the divine sovereign — capable of deciding the rules of the game while not being subject to those same rules. In terms of the body politic analogy, this means that the "head" is both a part of the body (forming a unified whole) and yet detached from the body (it rules over body and stands apart from it). "Political theology" is this relation between miracle and exception, and it is this paradoxical state of being inside and outside that forms the basis of more recent discussions concerning sovereignty by Giorgio Agamben, Simona Forti, and Achille Mbembe.[385]

The body politic analogy, predicated as it is on a top-down model that emphasizes the rule of the "head" over the "body," may appear to us as rigid and inflexible. But also noteworthy are the many tensions, inconsistencies, and bizarre permutations of the body politic. The body politic, raised as it is to address a problem of "the order of the living," often entails the creation of aberrant logics — that is, modes of thinking that make sense logically or juridically but that result in a body politic that can only be described as monstrous. One sees such monstrous logics in the discussions over dual sovereignty (Church and State), which result in a "two-headed" or bicephalic body politic, seen in the political writings of Dante, Ockham, and Giles of Rome.[386] Limbs are multiplied or are amputated, the mouth and anus become black mirrors of each other, and the lowliest parts partake of the divine. In this sense, the monstrous anatomies of the body politic are echoed in modern works of the horror genre.

Innumerable examples of "body horror" lend themselves to this understanding of the aberrations of the body politic, from the early films of David Cronenberg, to Clive Barker's 1986 story "The Body Politic" (in which the limbs quite literally revolt against the body), or Kathe Koja's 1991 novel *The Cipher* (the porous body, the body as oracle, the body turned inside out), stretching back to Mary

Shelley's *Frankenstein* (1818), written in the shadow of the French Revolution, the Reign of Terror, and the ascendency of medical science — a book that is, perhaps, the ultimate expression of the monstrous body politic. In Sam Raimi's 1987 film *Evil Dead II: Dead by Dawn*, the protagonist (played by Bruce Campbell) finds that his right hand has become possessed by a malign spirit with the intent of killing him. In a remarkable scene that manages to combine body horror and slapstick comedy, we witness Campbell struggling for life against his own (possessed) hand. In examples as varied as these we see the dual precariousness and resilience of the body politic, as it constantly rises, falls, and is brought back to life again, a cadaver possessed of life, a reanimated corpse unable to die. As a philosophical and political concept, it is predicated on rationalized variations, permutations, and recombinations, like so many recombined, anatomical parts. Thus, a fourth principle: *the body politic is a logically coherent monstrosity*.

The leaky boundaries of the body politic are constantly guarded, defended, and renegotiated from a threatening porousness. As Roberto Esposito has noted, the body politic adopts an immunitary logic, always on guard against external invasions or enemies within.[387] There is a kind of medicalized thickness to the body politic analogy, in which it is always tottering in the balance between "healthy" or "diseased," an anatomy constantly under threat of being possessed by miasmatic, unruly forces (a medical logic found in a range of thinkers, including Plato, Paul, Nicholas of Cusa, Marsilius of Padua, Bodin, and Hobbes).

What, then, is the body politic? It is a response to the challenge of thinking about political order as living order. It is based on an analogy between the body natural and the body politic (through a narrative stressing unity, hierarchy, and the organism). This formal relation is historically expressed in terms of political theology (and the question of sovereignty). And, despite this apparent coherence, the body politic is also defined through its potential failure (its internal tensions and anatomical, medical precariousness). We have begun by talking about political order and have ended by talking about anatomical permutation, monstrosity, and demonic contagion. Perhaps this concept, one that is so often assumed in political thought, is less familiar to us than we think.

*

Corruptible Bodies. A whole tradition of scholarship, including the work of Gierke, Kantorowicz, and Henri de Lubac has elaborated such characteristics concerning the body politic. However, what remains striking is the way in which the body politic is, on the one hand, always ascending beyond itself to a more ideal order, and, on the other hand, the way in which this ascension (or resurrection) is discussed in thoroughly anatomical, medical, and even vitalistic terms. In this sense, there is one aspect that is often been overlooked, and that is the role that a "medical ontology" has played in articulating the body politic at different political and historical moments.

Nowhere is this more apparent than when the body politic fails to be a body politic. A body politic that fails can only be understood as aberrant, diseased, or unhealthy. The very existence of the body politic as a body — vulnerable to the contingencies of disease, old age, and mortality — points to the irremediable processes of decay and decomposition that are themselves part of the analogy as well. In the same way that the body natural is open to disease, decomposition, and decay, so will the body politic be defined in relation to its own "disease," "decomposition," and "decay." Again, we can turn to Hobbes, who gives us a clear example of this thinking:

> Though nothing can be immortal, which mortals make;
> yet, if men had the use of reason they pretend to, their
> Commonwealths might be secured, at least, from perishing
> by internal diseases. For by the nature of their Institution,
> they are designed to live, as long as Mankind, or as the
> Laws of Nature, or as Justice it self, which gives them
> life. Therefore when they come to be disolved, not by

> external violence, but intestine disorder, the fault is not in men, as they are *Matter*; but as they are the *Makers*, and orderers of them ... Amongst the *Infirmities* therefore of a Commonwealth, I will reckon in the first place, those that arise from an Imperfect Institution, and resemble the diseases of a natural body, which proceed from a Defectious Procreation.[388]

Hobbes, in whom we find a combination of the Platonic *polis* and the Pauline *corpus mysticum*, carries the analogy to its logical (and biological) conclusion. The body politic is not only constituted through natural law and the social contract; it must also confront the immanent possibility of its dissolution. This polarization between constitution and dissolution in Hobbes is echoed in the Platonic body politic, where Socrates makes an explicit comparison between disease and disorder. "When a person's unhealthy," Socrates notes, "it takes very little to upset him and make him ill; there may even be an internal cause for disorder. The same is true of an unhealthy society. It will fall into sickness and dissension at the slightest external provocation, when one party or the other calls in help from a neighboring oligarchy or democracy; while sometimes faction fights will start without any external stimulus at all."[389]

Processes of disease, decay, and decomposition seem to inhabit the core of body politic analogy itself. In a sense, the body politic implies an anatomical framework that it is always attempting to supersede. Late medieval theology, concerned as it was with the problem of the "creature" and its dual nature (immortal soul and mortal flesh; incorruptible spirit and corruptible body), also explored the connection between "corruptibility" and disease. In this connection, a mixture of Aristotelian animism, Galenic medicine, and early modern anatomy all intersect to produce an image of a body politic that is at once capable of a divine, incorruptible health, and yet determined by corruptible, worldly mortality. For a philosopher-theologian such as Nicholas of Cusa, this implied that the body politic required ongoing, medical attention, and in this way the "diseases" of the body politic also required a political "physician." At numerous points in Plato's dialogues, for example, the comparison is made between physician and ruler: just as the physician is skilled in the art of healing the natural body, so should the ruler be skilled at governing the body politic. Centuries later, Nicholas would echo Plato: "like an expert doctor the emperor's concern should be to keep the body well so that the life-giving spirit can dwell in it properly because it is well-proportioned." Nicholas goes on to note that, should any imbalance in the "four temperaments" occur, the watchful physician-sovereign should act at once, lest such imbalances "produce various diseases in the body" such as "usury, fraud, deceit, theft, pillage," not to mention "choleric wars, dissension or division."[390] Healing, then, bears some essential relation to governing.

It is this kind of thinking that is further elaborated in the wake of modern germ theory, emerging from the fraught legacy of 19th century medicine, colonialism, and militarism. With its attendant language of "invasion," war, and a general xenophobia of the body, the metaphors of germ theory have had a decisive impact on the way we still think about disease today. Similarly, in its ancient and late medieval variants, the body politic analogy also expresses itself through a dialectics of health and illness. Here, however, the lines between the supernatural and the natural, miracle and exception, theology and medicine, are not clearly demarcated. When references to plague and pestilence arise in the writings of Aquinas, Dante, or Marsilius of Padua, it is not always clear when the reference is to an actual disease (interpreted in theological terms), or when the threats to theological and political order are being expressed in the eschatological language of "corruptibility," "spiritual sickness," and divine judgment.

Thus, while the body politic is, certainly, not exclusively a medical affair, this medical ontology forms its central framework for addressing political challenges. The anatomical view of the body politic is thus that beyond which the body politic must always move, but without which the body politic cannot be thought as such. What, then, are the "diseases" of the body politic? Civil war, strife, rebellion, dissent, factionalism, mob rule — these massing, swarming, and ambivalent forms constitute the dissolution of the body politic. A clear lesson emerges from this: *the greatest threat to the body politic comes from within.* They are threats distinct from external invasion or war, threats that indelibly sweep up into a single motion medicine, theology, and politics.

*

Pathological Life. One of the enigmas of our modern scientific understanding of epidemics is that the agents of epidemic disease — viruses and bacteria — are not simply agents of death but also forms of life; in fact, they are pathogenic precisely because they express the most basic properties of biological life at the molecular level. From the epidemiological perspective, the most "successful" virulent microbes will not simply kill their hosts, but will maintain the minimum biological sustainability within a host population, so that the microbe can replicate and transmit its genetic material. Such viruses and bacteria are, on the one hand, obvious threats to the human biological organism, but on the other hand, they are also entities that utilize the same life processes (replication and transmission) as "normal" or "healthy" organisms. Viruses and bacteria are forms of life that are at the same time against life. Given the long history of epidemics alongside that of human history, perhaps epidemic diseases have established a more symbiotic than parasitic relation with the human species. Perhaps the history of humanity might even be rewritten from this microbial perspective.

In a way, these pathological life-forms inhabit that grey zone between "coming to be" and "passing away" that Aristotle defined as the processes of all living beings, and which has later developed in clinical medicine. A case in point is the emergence of pathological anatomy in the 18th century, most often associated with the French anatomist Xavier Bichat. Working against the then-dominant theories of mechanism, Bichat sought to understand life by understanding death — that is, by understanding biological death not simply as the cessation of life, but as the emergence of a whole different set of biological processes. For anatomists like Bichat, the decay and decomposition of the body inaugurated a wholly different dimension to biological life processes. In a way, from the biological perspective, there is no death, but rather a transition to a different form of life — that of decay and decomposition.

What was needed, according to Bichat, was a way to understand the processes of disease, decay, and decomposition as themselves forms of life. Bichat's treatise *Physiological Research on Life and Death* (*Recherches Physiologiques sur la Vie et la Mort*, 1800) purported to approach the fate of the corpse as a biological phenomenon which, from the physiological perspective, frustrated any easy division between life and death. Thus disease is not seen as something that comes in from outside, but as a "derivation within life"; death is not an external finality, but instead a process internal to life. Michel Foucault summarizes a key lesson from Bichat's work in physiology in a striking passage: "the idea of a disease attacking life must be replaced by the much denser notion of pathological life." [391] In the case of modern clinical medicine, pathological life presupposes a form of life that is in some way isomorphic with the processes of disease, decay, and decomposition. Death is another form of life.

The phrase "pathological life" seems contradictory; it invites us to think further about what makes biological life "pathological," when it is so often regarded as the very essence of abundance, growth, and fecundity. Interestingly, the term "pathology" is based on the Greek root *pathos*. For the ancient Greeks, *pathos* denotes the "pathetic," or that which evokes suffering, pity, and fear. These are, of course, the central affective modes of Greek tragedy. The effect of tragedy — in Aristotle's words, "to arose pity and fear" — was to at once evoke a sense of pity (for the tragic hero's flaws are also our own flaws), but also fear (this vulnerability was often placed at the capricious hands of fate). Aristotle's formulation of tragedy is tied not only to the various plot devices (e.g., the tragic flaw, the revelation and catastrophe, the use of elevated language), but it is linked to an affective and corporeal force that Aristotle famously termed "catharsis."

Catharsis draws together a notion of healing that is inseparable from a ritual or social function. Catharsis is "purgation" or "purification," both terms that denote a ritualistic process by which a body or bodies are made pure, clean, and free of any elements that would threaten the coherence, not only of the individual body, but of the body politic as well. Hence *pathos* in its ancient Greek sense is not just biological, but also cultural, political, and philosophical. The Greek *pathos* is not just a feeling, but the circulation of such feelings. Theater, political oratory, and medicine can all be instances of *pathos* in this sense. Putting *pathos* into circulation thus implies that the tonality of such feelings is experienced as a transmission, as a circulation, and as flux and flow. *Pathos* is also empathy ("feeling into"), sympathy ("feeling along"), and these are of course complimented by antipathy ("feeling against"). As transmission, as circulation, *pathos* depends not just on intersubjectivity (be it person to person, actor to audience, or work to reader), but on a set of relations draped across a whole social field, a meshwork of feelings that circulate.

Furthermore, *pathos* is not simply affected through representation in art; *pathos* also bears some essential connection, as Aristotle notes, to "life." *Pathos* has a double quality: it is a crossing-over, and it is a division. This is the case with tragic theater, where the suffering hero's pleas are felt throughout the audience, but also in the case of epidemics, in which the *pathos* of suffering is at once medical and existential, a crossing and a connecting, a contagion of affect — the *pathos* of pathology, as it were. One does not suffer in isolation, for suffering is communicated, which means that *pathos* is communicable, much like the contagious disease itself. Like plague and pestilence, *pathos* is always transgressive, crossing boundaries, passing between bodies, passing through populations, coursing through the body politic.

This is the case prior to the high point of Greek tragedy, as plague and pestilence make their appearance in some of the earliest poetic writings in the West. For instance, Hesiod's *Works and Days* mentions several instances in which plague and pestilence are sent by Zeus as punishments — first against Prometheus (resulting in the "gift" of plague-ridden Pandora), and then as a general punishment for human evildoing. Similarly, the *Illiad* opens with Apollo sending down "arrows of plague" upon the Greek army, also as a form of punishment. In both cases plague and pestilence are wielded as weapons by the gods to punish humanity, either for transgressions against the gods, or as a judgement of human wrongdoing. Importantly, this weaponized plague impinges not only human health, but also agriculture, economy, and the growth of the population. In these early examples, the body politic becomes a form of pathological life.

Authors such as Hesiod also stress the affective dimensions of plague and pestilence — whether viewed as divine punishment or as a social, economic, and political devastation. Plague and pestilence not only serve as a sign of the anger and judgment of Zeus, and they not only cause sickness, famine, and a decline in population, but they spread a specific kind of suffering (*pathos*) that is linked to a sense of human mortality, finitude and the humbling place of humanity in the wider cosmos.

This is expressed with great clarity than in the case of Oedipus. Sophocles, in the opening to *Oedipus the King* suggests that cursed Oedipus is himself a pestilence to the city of Thebes:

> Thebes is dying. A blight on the fresh crops
> and the rich pastures, cattle sicken and die,
> and the women die in labor, children stillborn,
> and the plague, the fiery god of fever hurls down
> on the city, his lightning slashing through us —
> raging plague in all its vengeance, devastating
> the house of Cadmus! And black Death luxuriates
> in the raw, wailing miseries of Thebes.[392]

Oedipus is bad luck, a "plague" of fortune, but he is also allegorized as that cathartic purification that links together pathology and *pathos*. Oedipus is that which is expelled, expunged, marked as being banished, sent to the outside. In this way, what *pathos* does is to cleanse, to purify, to "care" for the body politic — but also, to manage what circulates within and without the body politic.

Fate and the will of the gods enframe many of these actions; they are marked by the nonlinearity of time, and also by the bodies that become corpses through revenge, defiance, or jealousy. In short, it is not so much individual persons or actions that must be purged, but a chain of events, the flux of temporality, and the aggregate of bodies — forms of life that are marked as threatening to the coherence of the body politic. In his essay "The Theater and Plague", Antonin Artaud encapsulates this diffuse aspect of pathological life: "plague seems to manifest its presence in and have a preference for the very organs of the body, the particular physical sites, where human will, consciousness, and thought are imminent and apt to occur."[393]

Indeed, one of the central characteristics of epidemics, plague, and pestilence is their pervasiveness; they seem to be attached to stigmatized "others," but at the same time capable of drawing together the most unlikely conjunctions of bodies, economies, and territories. These ways of thinking give us an image of *pathos* that is, like the pathological life of disease, at once *everywhere* — in the air, all around us, pervading the very space of the body itself — and yet which emerges from *somewhere* — even if this "somewhere" lies in the nebulous grey zone of a mythical underworld or supernatural skies.

*

Only That Which Falls Can Rise Again. We've seen that the body politic analogy is predicated on a comparison between the individual and collective body. This also involves a pervasive, medical view of the body politic, anatomized into so many limbs and body parts. We've also seen that one of the byproducts of this analogy is that the body politic is vulnerable to disease, decay, and decomposition. But isn't the body politic made up of the many individual living bodies, bodies that are likewise vulnerable to disease and death? Isn't this thing we call the body politic actually, and not just figuratively, living? If so, shouldn't any understanding of the body politic include an equal appreciation of disease, decay, and the body politic as a corpse?

Perhaps it is worth thinking about the body politic alongside the actual historical incidents of plague, pestilence, and epidemic (each different terms, though for the moment we can group them together).[394] Plague, pestilence, and epidemic provide us with examples in which the metaphorical "diseases" of the body politic (revolt, rebellion, civil strife) immediately fold onto the state of emergency occasioned by actual disease in a population.[395]

This medical ontology of health and illness allows us to understand the body politic analogy in the context of epidemic, plague, and pestilence — not only because it has something to say about civil war or public health but also because it raises the more philosophical issue of "the problem of multiplicities." This is the phrase Michel Foucault uses in his comments on the political dimensions of epidemic disease. In his 1979 lecture course at the Collège de France, Foucault outlined three epidemic "diagrams" that correspond to a type of power. Leprosy in the Middle Ages, which is aligned with juridical sovereignty, and its power to divide and exclude; plague in the early modern era, aligned with disciplinary power, and its ability to include, observe, and organize; and smallpox in the 17th century, which, for Foucault, marked by a new type of power, an "apparatus of security" (*dispositif de sécurité*) whose main objective is to step back and "let things be," to allow circulation and flow, to calculate probabilities and forecast possible outcomes.[396]

As Foucault notes, in each case the presence of epidemic disease puts forth the same dilemma: how to prevent the circulation of disease, and still permit the circulation of peoples, goods, and commerce? As he notes, "I mean, of course, circulation in the very broad sense of movement, exchange, and contact, as a form of dispersion, and also as a form of distribution, the problem being: How should things circulate or not circulate?"[397] Somehow the sovereign action of "shutting down" (closing borders, building walls, quarantining) must be correlated with the security action of "letting things be." This leads Foucault to think about a new type of sovereign power, one that operates more through the regulation of circulation than through interdiction or intervention: "the sovereign will be that which will exercise power at that point of connection where nature, in the sense of physical elements, interferes with nature in the sense of the human species, at that point of articulation where the environment becomes the determining factor of nature."[398] In the case of epidemics, power steps back and becomes almost ambient, as diffuse and pervasive as the environment itself.

It is perhaps for this reason that Foucault uses the phrase "apparatus of security" to describe this combination of intervention and circulation: "It seems to me that in the apparatus of security … what is involved is not taking either the point of view of what is prevented or the point of view of what is obligatory, but standing back sufficiently so that one can grasp the point at which things are happening of their own accord, whether or not they are desirable."[399]

We return to our earlier question: What threatens the body politic? It is not just figurative or literal disease, but something we can call, simply, "multiplicity." In what does this multiplicity consist of? It is constituted by and exists through circulations and flows, by passing-through and passing-between — movements that are, in the case of pestilence, plague, and epidemics, both the constitution and the dissolution of the body politic. The same structures that enable the constitution of the body politic are also those that signal its dissolution. Perhaps we can say that multiplicity is the "disease" of the body politic. Or, alternately, it is multiplicity that "plagues" the body politic.

*

Necrologies. In the same way that each individual body must contend with mortality and its eventual demise, every attempt to constitute the body politic must also confront its dissolution. The body politic is, in a way, constituted on its dissolution, a forming of a collective, living body that always exists in relation to the corpse. The corpse (*nekros*) — that which remains after life — this thing-that-remains becomes at once that against which the body politic struggles, but also that through which it is constituted. In this sense, everything formed is destined to be un-formed or de-formed, just as every life is already dead, every body already a corpse. We might, therefore, call the study of such phenomena a *necrology*, in which the intersection between sovereignty and multiplicity often finds expression in the analogy of the body politic.[400]

This invites us to examine the *poetics* of the body politic (in the sense of *poiesis*, as creating or forming), particularly in the cultural motif of the living dead. We are brought back to Dante's *Inferno*, where we see stratifications of the living dead that are the product of divine punishment, meticulously managed as massing or aggregate forms. One of the most intriguing examples of this is the sixth circle of Hell, where Dante and his guide Virgil come to the giant, fortress gates of the infernal City of Dis. Virgil must enlist divine intervention in order to pass through the gates, guarded by hordes of demons. Once Dante and Virgil enter, they see a devastating city in ruins, a harrowing, uneven landscape of burning, open graves that deserves to be quoted at length:

> And then we started moving toward the city [*terra*]
> in the safety of the holy words pronounced.
> We entered there, and with no opposition.
> And I, so anxious to investigate
> the state of souls locked up in such a fortress [*fortezza*],
> once in the place, allowed my eyes to wander,
> and saw, in all directions spreading out,
> a countryside [*campagna*] of pain and ugly anguish.
> As at Arles where the Rhône turns to stagnant waters

or as at Pola near Quarnero's Gulf
that closes Italy and bathes her confines,
the sepulchers make all the land uneven,
so they did here, strewn in all directions,
except the graves here served a crueler purpose:
for scattered everywhere among the tombs
were flames that kept them glowing far more hot
than any iron an artisan might use.
Each tomb had its lid loose, pushed to one side,
and from within came forth such fierce laments
that I was sure inside were tortured souls.
I asked, "Master, what kind of shades are these
lying down here, buried in the graves of stone,
speaking their presence in such dolorous sighs?"
And he replied: "There lie arch-heretics
of every sect, with all of their disciples;
more than you think are packed within these tombs."[401]

We have here the ambiguously living "shades" in Dante's Hell, present as massing and aggregate bodies. But here the living dead are not simply punished through divine retribution. Here sovereign power not only punishes but, more importantly, it meticulously organizes the multiplicity of bodies according to their transgressions or threats, resulting in the ruined landscape — a kind of macabre and funereal database of the dead.

In Dante's version of the "dead walking the earth," the living dead are also included within the City of Dis; that is, the living dead are "citizens" of this city. The living dead are, as Virgil notes, political shades: they are the heretics, those who have spoken against the theological and political order, and, importantly, those who have done so from within that order. The heretics, as living dead, are those that spread disorder from within the *polis* — through disagreement or dissent — and in this way Dante links the heretics to the inhabitants of the other circles of Lower Hell, including the "sowers of discord" (who are meticulously dismembered) and the "falsifiers" (who are ridden with plague and leprosy).

Nowhere else in the *Inferno* are we presented with such explicit analogies to the classical *polis*. Needless to say, City of Dis is of course very far from the idealized *polis* in Plato's *Republic*, or the City of God described by Augustine. The City of Dis is not even a living city. Instead, what we have is a necropolis, a dead city populated by open graves, by the dead walking the earth. The City of Dis is, in this guise, an inverted *polis*, an inverted body politic.

Within this mortified body politic we witness two forms of power — a sovereign power that judges and punishes, but also a regulatory power that manages the flows and circulations of multiple bodies, of body parts and bodily fluids. Furthermore, this management of the circulation of bodies extends to the landscape and climate as well, transforming everything into a terrain that is at once natural and supernatural. Dante's underworld landscapes are utterly contemporary, for it suggests to us that the body politic is always confronted with this twofold challenge — the necessity of establishing a sovereign power in conjunction with the necessity of regulating multiplicities.

This is a remarkably persistent motif, one also found in contemporary lowbrow examples of horror film. The subgenre of the zombie film has, for many years, provided us with different variants of Dante's living dead. American and Italian films are the prominent examples in this regard. While early Hollywood thrillers such as *White Zombie* (1932) or *Revolt of the Zombies* (1936) placed Western doctor-heroes within the context of voodoo and colonialism, films after George Romero's landmark *Night of the Living Dead* (1968) place the living dead within a decidedly American, postindustrial context, self-reflexively stressing the "silent majority" through the use of political satire.

By contrast, the Italian tradition of zombie films displays parts of both the early and later American traditions. Though well-known horror directors have dabbled in the genre, it is Lucio Fulci who has explored (some would say exploited) the motif of the living dead in

Still from *Zombie* (*Zombi 2*, dir. Lucio Fulci, 1979)

the most detail. Fulci's zombie films not only pick up on the idea that the colonial encounter is a medical encounter, but medical power is always linked to the supernatural — and sovereign — power to raise the dead.[403]

Critics of Fulci often dismiss his work, noting that he basically made one film, over and over. And it is hard to deny such dismissals, for films such as the cult classic *Zombie* (1979; released in Italy as *Zombi 2*), *The Beyond* (1981), or the strangely uneventful *City of the Living Dead* (1980), repeatedly present an archetypal scene, one that visually encapsulates each of Fulci's films — that of the dead walking the earth. The final scene in *Zombie*, for instance, depicts the living dead slowly descending on New York City as they cross Brooklyn Bridge (apparently the living dead come from Brooklyn). Usually such scenes are moments of retribution in the film, the living dead taking vengeance upon their oppressors. Similar scenes are found in Romero's *Dawn of the Dead* (1978), *Day of the Dead* (1985), and, more recently, *Land of the Dead* (2005), all of which contain key scenes depicting the living dead as a massing, contagious movement seeping through the barricades and bunkers that humans have constructed to manage them. The spaces through which the living dead move — houses, suburbs, malls, streets, city squares, military bases, and corporate towers — are porous to the miasmatic logic of the living dead.

There is, to be sure, a certain political romanticism in these modern variants of the living dead. The multitude eventually prevail through sheer persistence, and all symbols of hierarchy fall. All of this is not without a certain eschatological flavor as well, for, if the living dead are universal they are also vague and unspecified, a massing and ambivalent force of retribution.

The body politic is not only a concept of political philosophy, it also involves a poetics, and both philosophy and poetics dovetail in this "necrological" zone — the point at which constitution turns into dissolution, composition into decomposition, the point at which the massing and aggregates forms of life that build up the body politic now are its agents of decay, decline, and dissolution. Viewed through the lens of Dante's *Inferno*, the body politic concept asks us to think the relationship between sovereignty and multiplicity, but as a necrological breaking-down, rather than a vitalistic or romantic instance of liberation. The body politic is, in these cases, that which withers and decays — like the corpse. Something that decomposes and yet that is living.

*

Variations on Hell. It is noteworthy how many modern adaptions of Dante's *Inferno* attempt to show both the architecture of Hell as well as its many opportunities for breakdown and collapse. Literary adaptations of the *Inferno* are too numerous to list, though we might mention two examples: LeRoi Jones's 1965 *The System of Dante's Hell*, which makes use of avant-garde literary techniques to recast Hell in terms of urban decay, with scenes worthy of Bosch or James Ensor; as well as Larry Niven and Jerry Pournelle's 1976 satire *Inferno*, which features science fiction writer Allen Carpentier instead of Dante, who dies at a science fiction convention and is taken on a tour of a high-tech, futuristic, theme-park version of Hell.

However, it is in film adaptations that we see an emphasis on the architectonics of Dante's *Inferno*. In 1911 the Italian silent film

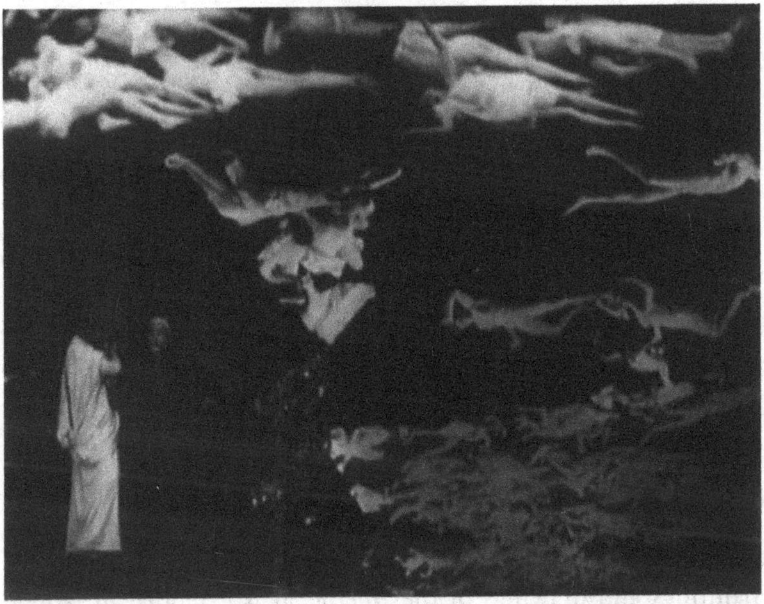

Still from *Inferno* (*L'Inferno*, dir. Francesco Bertolini, Aldolfo Padovan, Giuseppe de Liguoro, 1911)

L'Inferno was screened, by many accounts the first Italian-produced feature film. It was directed by Francesco Bertolini, Giuseppe de Liguror, and Adolfo Padovan, and had taken over three years to produce. While an early film, it contains dark and magical scenes that have the power to fascinate even today. While the special effects do not, of course, compare to today's standards, the directors made extensive use of Gustave Doré's engravings of the *Inferno* in the composition of shots. Scenes such as the Circle of the Lustful make use of trick photography to give the sense of weightless, flowing bodies, suspended against the black sky by a torrential storm. *L'Inferno* makes use of the film frame to construct entire worlds within worlds, with each frame connected to the next one by the passage of Dante and Virgil out of or into the frame of the film. The film frame not only gives us a view of each circle in a glance, but also serves as a kind of portal or gateway to the next circle, which we as viewers suture together in our minds.

Still from *Japanese Hell* (*Jigoku*, dir. Nobuo Nakagawa, 1960)

This technique not only gives us bodies within the film — within the frame — it also gives us the assembled body of the film itself, the architecture of Hell as a whole, but one that we experience temporally, much like the long historical tradition of paintings and drawings of the *Inferno*. It is extended in Nobou Nakagawa's 1960 film *Jigoku* (*Hell*). Widely recognized as one of the first modern horror films to be made in postwar Japan, Nakagawa's film combines Eastern and Western notions of the underworld into its script. The film is divided into two parts. The first part shows us the various desires, schemes, and deceitful dealings surrounding Shiro, a theology student at the University of Tokyo. Part melodrama and part crime thriller, the first part of the film depicts human beings preying on each other, each attempting to selfishly carry out their own nefarious plans. The first part ends with a surreal, grotesque banquet that includes murder, suicide, debauchery, and several guests poisoned by bad fish. This gives way to the second part of *Jigoku*, in which we follow Shiro through the various levels of Hell. Nakagawa's use of saturated color and hyper-artificial effects gives these scenes a nightmarish quality. Amidst rivers of boiling blood and haunted forests, we see bodies dismembered and eaten by demonlike ogres. The more Shiro learns the truth about human nature, the deeper he sinks into Hell. In a harrowing moment of cultural hybridity, at the end of the film we see Shiro crucified to a Buddhist wheel of life, suggesting to us a correspondence between Hell-on-Earth and Earth-in-Hell.

In postmodernity, many films have absorbed Dante's *Inferno* — with its architectonic spaces and passages between circles, its evocation of strange terrains and stranger creatures — but placed them within the technological realm of late capitalism. Kiyoshi Kurosawa's mesmerizing film *Kairo* (*Pulse*, 2001) takes up the spirit of Dante's *Inferno* but places it within the "space" of digital networks. The film follows a group of young friends as they become interested in video chat rooms on the Internet. Kurosawa films these scenes in a very specific way, often in darkened, silent rooms, with only the glow of the computer monitor. The video chat rooms are shown within the computer screen as eerily empty spaces, as if someone on the other side had suddenly vanished. Kurosawa frames these scenes with the camera at a slightly lower height, the camera completely still and motionless (akin, interestingly, to the films of Yasujirō Ozu). As the characters become more and more entranced by these seemingly empty rooms, strange suicides, agoraphobia, and depressive behavior ensue. Eventually we discover that the video chat rooms they are using are not connecting to other people, but to the realm of the dead. The video frames on the computer screen are portals to the underworld — and they are coming through.

Architectures of the dead, gateways and portals to the underworld, boundaries bleeding through. Numerous horror films show us portals to Hell in the most unlikely, and most familiar of places (a theme in films such as *The Sentinel* and *The Amityville Horror*). This is also a central motif in the 2011 experimental documentary *Devil's Gate*, by filmmaker Laura Kraning. A documentary without interviews or voiceovers, *Devil's Gate* is primarily composed of black-and-white shots of Devil's Gate Dam, located in Southern California. The dam was the site for a series of occult experiments in the 1940s by Jack Parsons, occultist, rocket engineer, and cofounder of the Jet Propulsion Laboratory. Kraning's film focuses on the now-abandoned, desolate, haunting terrain of Devil's Gate, interspersed with excerpts from Parsons's journals. The imposing, abstract, geometric shapes of the dam are contrasted against the uneven, overrun, chaotic flow of water, weeds, and drifting mist. And yet the dam, product of human technological intervention, is also so embedded into the natural surroundings that it soon begins to look ancient, even primordial, as if it had been there all along. While adaptations of Dante's *Inferno* such as *L'Inferno* and *Jigoku* take us as viewers on a tour of Hell, other films, such as *Kairo* and *Devil's Gate* exist in the play of surfaces, and secret, tenebrous portals. We become further removed from Hell, while it is, at the same time, more embedded into our living environments.

*

Dance of Death. Midday, an empty subway station, West Berlin, 1980. A woman undergoing a personal crisis has just come from the nearby church, where she has stood, it seems, for hours, gazing upwards with pleading eyes. In the subway station she finds herself overcome with intense, otherworldly emotions, as if unseen forces from another dimension are forcing her into a cathartic, spasmotic, almost ritual dance. Her eyes are wide, as if staring beyond the walls of the subway tunnel. Her limbs flail about, but at the same time seem weirdly choreographed. In an eerie, rhythmic whirl, her body seems to fall against the walls, as if they were the floor; her body seems to crawl up the floor as if it were a wall. It seems as if some nebulous form of life were coursing through her, a form of life engulfing the body, negating the body, one form of life eclipsing another form of life — life against life. She's lost control, experiencing an out-of-body experience that is also intensely corporeal, the body given over to alien affects dismissed by modern medicine. As the violent cadences of the strange dance recede, she becomes a tension-filled vortex of impersonal forces. Strange, unidentifiable fluids seep from every pore, producing the strange calm of catatonia.

Among memorable performances in the history of horror film, Isabelle Adjani's role in the 1981 film *Possession* stands out as both

Isabelle Adjani in *Possession* (dir. Andrzej Żuławski, 1981)

inspired and otherworldly. Her character moves with a trancelike abandon through "possession" in all its senses, from the personal, to the interpersonal, to the psychological, social, political, and of course the religious sense. The famous subway scene is at once tragic opera and Grand Guignol theater. No explanation is ever given. Perhaps what has happened is what her psychiatrist cum cult leader ominously labels "hysteria." Perhaps, as the doctor tells her, she has had a miscarriage (but was she pregnant to begin with?). Perhaps it is what the priest secretly suspects is demonic possession (or is it mystical ecstasy?). Perhaps it is even a manifestation of what Schopenhauer once referred to as the "Will-to-Life," the horrific, blind, pure impulse of life to be life, no matter what — life at the cost of the living. The film, directed by Andrzej Żuławski, keeps both characters and the viewer in a perpetual state of confusion. Characters are never completely sure of what they do, their decisions, actions, and motives lost in a vague background haze of doubt and crisis.

Adjani's performance in *Possession* points to other, equally compelling performances in horror film, where elements of ritual, dance, and theater come together in the "possessed" human body,

Conrad Veidt in *The Hands of Orlac* (*Orlacs Hände*, dir. Robert Wiene, 1924)

as if the individual body and the body politic cathartically collapse into some other form of life — one form of life suddenly eclipsed by another, more ambivalent, more tenebrous form of life. While the harrowing possession scenes from *The Exorcist* are perhaps the most well-known example of this, it is also present in early horror films, films that bring this idea of the possessed body into greater focus. The 1924 Expressionist film *The Hands of Orlac* features a concert pianist who tragically loses his hands in a train accident. In desperation he volunteers for an experimental graft surgery, receiving the hands of a recently deceased cadaver. Things seem to be going well until he discovers, to his horror, that his hands seem to have a mind of their own, doing things against his will. The role, played with stunning intensity by Conrad Veidt (who also played the somnambulist in *The Cabinet of Dr. Caligari*), reaches its fever pitch in scenes that are more performance art or ritual than film. His hands slowly creep towards him, turning to face him, strange and alien things revealing that his own body may not be his at all. It is only later that he learns that the surgically grafted hands were from those of a convicted murderer.

Indeed, early horror film is replete with such examples; the 1917 Italian silent *Rapsodica Satanica*, a variant on the Faust motif featuring the haunting performance of Lyda Borelli, captures the strange combination of frenzy and catatonia of demonic possession. These and other examples portray the possessed body in ambivalent ways, suggesting to us that, perhaps, our bodies were never our own to begin with, crisscrossed as they are by impersonal forces indifferent to our individual or collective desires. The strange choreography of the possessed body is a kind of dance in which life is, for a moment, eclipsed by death, the body by the corpse. The genre-bending, 1922 "documentary" *Häxan*, which reenacts historical cases of witchcraft and demonic possession, includes scenes of frenzied dancing that illustrate the medieval theme of the *Totentanz* or "Dance of Death."

In these and other horror films, demonic possession is more than a battle of wills or a malevolent form of remote control. The scenes in *Possession* or *The Hands of Orlac* depict possession as a dance of conflicting, impersonal forces — a ritual in which the domain of the personal (my life, my body, my identity) is suddenly divested of its shroud of certitude, revealing another, stranger, and more opaque domain — that of the impersonal. This is brought out clearly in the 1969 Japanese film *Horrors of Malformed Men*. Directed by horror maestro Teruo Ishii, the film is loosely based on the horror stories of Edogawa Rampo, but is so wonderfully fragmented and plotless that the film becomes something else — an extended piece of avant-garde theater, performance art, a ritual. For the film Ishii hired Tatsumi Hijikata, a choreographer known to many as one of the founders of Butoh (or as it was known, Ankoku Butoh, "Dance of Darkness"). Emerging out of the shadows of world war and the atomic bomb, Butoh's emphasis on deliberately slow, controlled, contorted movements, not only evokes many aspects of the mortality of the body, but it also allows us to see the strangeness of the body, the eeriness of the human form, and by extension, the eeriness of the life that inheres in and occupies every body. In Hijikata's vision, there is a sense in which Butoh is at once about allowing the alienness of life in the body to reveal itself, while also appreciating the mortification of life, the way in which bodies are, in a sense, always dying. In films like *Horrors of Malformed Men*, all bodies are "possessed" by an impersonal life, existing in an extended *Totentanz* that eventually eclipses each individual's life.

*

Argento's Inferno. A young woman living in New York opens an old, leatherbound book, written in Latin, its pages still unopened: *The Three Mothers*. It is by an architect named Varelli. In it, he tells of a coven of witches, each living in secret in three different cities — Rome, Freiburg, and New York — in houses designed by Varelli. He ominously refers to them only as *Mater Lachrymarum*, *Mater Suspiriorum*, and *Mater Tenebrarum* — Mother of Tears, Mother of Sighs, and Mother of Darkness. One of the architectural drawings in the book looks uncannily like the building in which she lives. Suspecting that she may be living in a building designed by Varelli, she leaves her apartment and goes down to the antiquarian bookstore next door, inquiring about the book she had purchased. The gaunt and curmudgeonly store owner lets loose only hints and clues, which deepen her suspicion further: "...the only mystery, is that our very lives are governed by dead people..."

It is night. On the sidewalk outside, the young woman notices an iron grating just outside her building. It leads down into the cellar. Opening it, she walks cautiously down the stairs. The cellar is filled with debris — old furniture, rusted pipes, wooden crates, cobwebs. There is the trickling sound of water. It is coming from one of the pipes, forming a small, thin stream that runs along the furrowed ground like blood in the arteries. It flows further into the cellar, where there is a rough opening in the middle of the dirty and mottled concrete floor. It appears to be a puddle, but on closer inspection is an opening into an entire water-filled chamber below. Peering over to the opening, the woman's keys accidentally fall into the water, languorously descending into the depths of the water-filled chamber. Unable to reach it with her hands, she descends into the opening, swimming down to retrieve her key. She notices remnants of an earlier era — baroque chairs and candelabra, an ornate carpet, crystal glassware, an old fireplace, ritual objects, and dangling above it, barely held to the wall, a massive portrait, now faded, but bearing the Latin inscription *Mater Tenebrarum*.

In this underwater chamber, there is a door that seems to open to still other chambers, equally submerged. Suddenly a flayed corpse floats by her, drifting upwards, as if reaching for the opening. In a panic, she swims up and climbs out of the opening. She frantically climbs out, quickly leaves the cellar, goes up the iron staircase into her building, and takes the elevator up to her apartment. Below, we see the cellar. Cracked beams collapse onto the opening, forming a kind of dilapidated, tenebrous, prismatic sculpture. An opera by Verdi begins playing.

*

Necropolis. Crumbling cities, flooded cities, quarantined cities — the corporeal coherence of the *polis* seems to be constantly under attack at the very same moment attempts are made to fortify its boundaries.[404] In the midst of these fissures, life is constantly rendered precarious, a life that is always vulnerable, tenuous, happenstance, and mortal. Nowhere is this precariousness of life rendered in such detail as in medical and public health concerns surrounding "biodefense."[405] In the case of bioterrorism, "naturally occurring" and human-made disasters become indistinguishable, culminating in a body politic that is threatened by the same form of life that constitutes it — a pathological life.[406] At its limit the body politic would perfectly overlap with the planet, resulting in the uncanny image of a living dead planet. Or is the planet not already living dead?

Today we no longer speak of the body politic; its terms have been relegated to the dusty corners of historical and scholarly interest — they are dead metaphors. Yet, in spite of this, what needs to be accounted for is the strange, morbid longevity of the body politic. If today we no longer speak of a "body politic" this is not because the concept has ceased to exist. Perhaps it is because the issues that are raised have never been so prescient as they are in contemporary discussions over the "existential crisis" of climate change and the resulting "climate anxiety" it produces — in addition to the zombielike proliferation of films, TV shows, and the like, all of which feature some variant of Dante's living dead in the City of Dis, the city that is a sepulcher, the *polis* that is, at the same time, a necropolis.

3

MEDITATIONS ON THE GOTHIC

Book of Beasts (Lautréamont's Maldoror). In 1868, a slim, anonymously published book entitled *Les Chants de Maldoror* appeared in Parisian bookshops. Its purported author was the "Comte de Lautréamont" — much in line with the *fin-de-siècle* vogue for the Gothic, the Decadent, and a turn towards a literary, aesthetic aristocratism. In its posthumous life, the book would have a decisive impact on the counterculture, from Surrealism to Situationism. But at the time of its publication *Les Chants de Maldoror* (hereafter *Maldoror*) was completely ignored, even when Canto I was republished in the anthology *Parfums de l'Âme* a year later.

It is not difficult to see why the book was ignored. It was neither prose nor poem, neither fiction nor nonfiction — it did not even fit into the popular genre of the *roman noir*, or the then-emerging genre of the prose poem. The following passage — from Canto II — is representative of many of the text's idiosyncrasies:

> There are times in life when verminous-scalped man trains
> his wild and staring gaze upon the green membranes of

> space, for ahead of him he seems to hear the ironic jeers of a phantom. He reels and bows his head: what he has heard is the voice of conscience. Then quick as a madman he rushes in amazement from the house, taking the first route available, and tears along the rugose plains of the countryside. But the yellow phantom does not lose sight of him and just as rapidly pursues. Sometimes on a stormy night while legions of winged squids (at a distance resembling crows) float above the clouds and scud stiffly toward the cities of humans, their mission to warn men to change their ways — the gloomy-eyed pebble perceives amid flashes of lightning two beings pass by, one behind the other, and, wiping away a furtive tear of compassion that trickles from its frozen eye, cries: "Certainly he deserves it; it's only justice." Having spoken thus it reverts to its timid pose and trembling nervously, continues to watch the manhunt and the vast lips of the vagina of darkness whence flow incessantly, like a river, immense shadowy spermatozoa that take flight into the dismal aether, the vast spread of their bat's wings obscuring the whole of nature and the lonely legions of squids — grown downcast viewing these ineffable and muffled fulgurations.[407]

Everything in *Maldoror* seems infused with an almost feral sense of creaturely life, as if some life force were voraciously feeding on itself as worms to a corpse. Animals themselves abound in *Maldoror*, but their functions vary, from the symbolic, to the scientific, to the absurd. The passage that opens Canto IV extends this litany of animalization across the spectrum of beings, from the human to the mineral, culminating in one of the text's many incantations against the human:

> A man or a stone or a tree is about to begin this fourth canto. When the foot slithers on a frog one feels a sensation of disgust, but one's hand has barely to stroke the human

> body before the skin of the fingers cracks like flakes from a block of mica being smashed by hammer blows; and even as the heart of a shark an hour dead still palpitates on the deck with dogged vitality, so are we stirred to our very depths long after the contact. Such is the horror man inspires in his own neighbor! Perhaps I am mistaken to propose this, but perhaps too I am telling the truth. I know of, conceive, a sickness more terrible than the eyes swollen from long meditations upon the strange nature of man: but I am seeking it still [...] and have been unable to find it! I do not consider myself less intelligent than anyone else, and yet who would dare assert that I have succeeded in my investigations? What a lie would escape his lips! The ancient temple of Denderah lies an hour and a half away from the left bank of the Nile. Today countless phalanxes of wasps have taken possession of its gutters and cornices. They swarm round the columns like dense waves of black hair. Sole inhabitants of the cold porch, they guard the entrance to antechambers as a hereditary right. I liken the humming of their metallic wings to the incessant clash of ice-floes flung against one another during the breaking-up of the polar seas. But if I ponder the conduct of him on whom providence has conferred this earth's throne, the three pinions of my grief give vent to a louder murmur![408]

Much of *Maldoror* displays this sense of a prodigious outpouring of word, sound, and image — pages on pages of thick, block text with dense, phantasmagoric creatures following one after the other. At some points the text addresses the reader directly, almost confrontationally; at other points it digresses into long, quasi-scientific descriptions of flora and fauna; at still other points the text suddenly breaks into pulp horror or Gothic romance. *Maldoror* breaks nearly every rule of poetics, though it does this less as avant-garde posturing and more because the text cannot help itself. There seems to be no end to what the text can do or is capable of — in a way, its length and division into six cantos seems almost arbitrary.

The one review that did appear upon the original publication of *Maldoror* expressed puzzled astonishment: "the hyperbolic bombast of the style, the savage strangeness, the desperate vigor of conception, the contrast of this impassioned language with the dullest lucubrations of our time, at first cast the mind into a deep amazement."[409] Such a reaction echoes subsequent mentions of *Maldoror* in literary history, as if the text itself might suddenly jump out and attack the reader. Antonin Artaud sums up the general attitude of conventional criticism towards the likes of Lautréamont, Nerval, and Baudelaire: "they were afraid that their poetry might leap out of the books and turn reality upside down."[410] *Maldoror* is, of course, fascinating for precisely this reason — the book as alive, the book as feral. As a text *Maldoror* itself seemed bestial and monstrous, a teratological anomaly composed of bits and pieces, a *corpus* left unfinished or untended, fecund in rot and decay. Too often literary criticism is contented to catalogue the representations of animals in literary texts. By contrast, *Maldoror* seems to put forth the animality of the text — multiple tendrils of appropriated passages, leaping off the page, devouring the book itself. In his classic study *The Romantic Agony*, published in the 1930s, literary critic Mario Praz includes only a few dismissive paragraphs on Lautréamont. But even in these few lines he echoes the tendency to treat *Maldoror* as something aberrant, ultimately dismissing *Maldoror* as a "late but extreme case of cannibalistic Byronism."[411]

When *Maldoror* was "discovered" by the Surrealists in the early 20th century, a shift occurred in the reception of the text: the animality coursing through *Maldoror* suddenly gave way to an almost mystical quality. André Breton noted that *Maldoror* was "the expression of a revelation so complete it seems to exceed human potential." Philippe Soupault edited several editions of *Maldoror*, and Louis Aragon wrote the essay *Lautréamont et Nous*. No doubt Breton & Co. were taken by the often surprising juxtapositions in the text, the most famous of which is the phrase "beautiful as the chance meeting on a dissecting table of a sewing machine and an umbrella." But Breton's comments point to another aspect of *Maldoror*, one that extends the animality of the text, and that is its vigorous and persistent anti-humanism. While the Surrealists were unwavering critics of religion, they notoriously imported a whole host of mystical and occult themes into their works. Little surprise, then, that *Maldoror* — a text that would become part of the Surrealist canon — is frequently described in mystical terms by authors both within and outside of the Surrealist circle: Breton evoked Lautréamont as "that dazzling figure of black light"; Artaud lauded *Maldoror* for its "perfect lucidity," an "orgy of the collective unconscious trespassing on individual consciousness"; René Daumal asserted that *Maldoror* was nothing less than a "holy war" on humanity. Aimé Césaire provided his own, hagiographical portrait of Lautréamont: "give him the wings of the archangel and the shivers of malaria, let him be accompanied through the streets of Paris by an escort of Uruguayan vampires and carnivorous ants, and you will have *Maldoror*."[412] A generation after the Surrealists, *Maldoror* would be rediscovered by "poststructuralist" thinkers drawn to its aberrant linguistic and psychic processes. For Julia Kristeva, *Maldoror* signified nothing less than a revolution in poetic language, "a shattered book whose musicality and mimesis are a veritable thanatography." At stake was nothing less than a pervasive indictment of anthropomorphism: "*Maldoror* puts the subject on trial into a hallucinatory narrative that has the linguistic resources of poetry."[413]

The prevalence of such a poetics of misanthropy, in all its guises, has been borne out by modern literary scholarship on *Maldoror*. There is the question of authorship (or rather, the erasure of authorship) — the real person Isidore Ducasse, who uses the pen name Comte de Lautréamont, and about whom very little is known, except that he was born in Montevideo, Uruguay in 1846, and that in 1870 he died under mysterious circumstances in his Parisian hotel room. Literary detectives have noted the similarity between the name Lautréamont and *Latréaumont*, a Gothic novel by Eugène Sue published in the 1830s. As for the title, *Maldoror* has often been compared to the French phrase *mal d'aurore* or "evil dawn," something that seems to be supported in one of the few surviving letters of Ducasse: "Let me explain my situation to you. I have sung of evil as did Misckiéwickz, Byron, Milton, Southey, A. de Musset, Baudelaire, etc."[414]

Further detective work has highlighted the many textual borrowings that find their way into *Maldoror*, from literary appropriations of Homer, the Bible, Shakespeare, Dante, and Baudelaire, to extended passages from textbooks on mathematics and the natural sciences — foremost among them Jean-Charles Chenu's multivolume *Encyclopédie d'Histoire Naturelle* (1850–61). Then there is riddle of the *Poésies*, a short treatise on literary aesthetics published under Ducasse's own name. Comprised of short fragments and aphorisms, the *Poésies* appears to endorse an attitude that is nearly the opposite of *Maldoror*, leading many scholars to suggest that the two works — *Maldoror* and *Poésies* — in fact comprise a single "work," each text annulling the other, resulting in a kind of zero degree of literary aesthetics. Indeed, all of the "facts" surrounding *Maldoror* seem to point to a book that, at all levels, attempts to dehumanize itself, divesting itself of authorship, authorial voice, and even foreclosing the possibility of interpretation. The text of *Maldoror* is predatory in its extensive borrowings, and, true to Praz's words, ultimately becomes a kind of autophage, devouring itself in the process. As we will see, this tendency towards a self-abnegation at once corporeal and textual allows *Maldoror* to effectively collapse the distance separating the bestial and the mystical.

*

Feral Melancholy. Decay, decomposition, and disintegration course throughout *Maldoror*; they are the lifeblood of the book. They are at once processes of breaking down, but also instances of relentless invention, even of sanctification, exemplified by *Maldoror*'s notoriously paradoxical phraseology: a "worm-eaten worship," a "rabid veneration," an "idol of the grotesque."

Obsessive though it is, *Maldoror's* emphasis on processes of breakdown emerge from an antagonism that grounds the book as a whole. Throughout its pages, *Maldoror* rails incessantly against its two primary targets: God and humanity. In their various guises, these two antagonisms (the divine and the earthly; the infinite and finite; the transcendent and the transcendental) become ciphers for a more generalized antagonism within *Maldoror* that often finds expression in the deeply ambivalent processes of decay and degeneration. Everything in *Maldoror* decays — bodies, affects, landscapes, mountains, oceans, the planet, the stars, language, and existence itself. Nothing grows in *Maldoror*, because everything is continually breaking down — or rather, the text inhabits a grey zone in which growth is inseparable from decay, composition from decomposition, constitution from disintegration, resulting in a strange type of fecund rot. Nothing is fixed or systematic in *Maldoror*, except for the incessant crumbling of all categories, and the slow, eerie patience with which all boundaries erode — including the boundary separating decay *in* the text from the decay *of* the text itself. The motif of decay, decomposition, and disintegration applies to every level of *Maldoror*, from the creaturely teratologies and unholy bestiaries that inhabit its pages to the text of *Maldoror* itself, which so frequently displays the wasting away of genre, style, and mood. It's as if the book itself is constantly threatening to disintegrate in the reader's hands — a book where corpse and *corpus* incessantly eclipse each other.

Maldoror is also a text that self-consciously situates itself in the tradition of the literary Gothic, both in theme as well as in its many textual borrowings and intertextual references. Brooding nocturnal landscapes, torrential stormy seas, foreboding cliffs and ominous skies, and within it, the insignificant and condemned human figure, overwhelmed by the ambient terror of nature rendered supernatural, and the whispering horror of unreason. *Maldoror* is a book written against the backdrop of the Gothic — and yet, it was written a century after the publication of popular Gothic novels, such as Horace Walpole's *Castle of Otranto* (1764), Ann Radcliffe's *The*

Mysteries of Udolpho (1794), Matthew Lewis's *The Monk* (1796) — not to mention Shelley's *Frankenstein* (1818), or underappreciated works in the genre such as Karl Friedrich Kalhert's *The Necromancer; or, The Tale of the Black Forest* (1794), and the notorious *Nightwatches of Bonaventura* (1804). *Maldoror* is a book that is perpetually belated, a "late" work that finds there is nothing more to write other than to cut and paste bits and pieces of other books.

While *Maldoror* borrows heavily from the general narrative structure of the Gothic novel, at the granularity of its language it borrows a great deal from the long poetic tradition of the so-called Graveyard School. Less a "school" and more a poetic mode, the Graveyard School extends from poems such as Milton's *Il Penseroso* (1632) and Thomas Parnell's "A Night-Piece on Death" (1722) to Keats's famous "Ode to a Grecian Urn" (1821). In between one finds innumerable examples of poems preoccupied with death and mortality, and which took the cemetery as its primary setting. In such poems, the site of the grave — and by extension the decaying corpse — was the occasion for a meditation on death and the transitory nature of all life. By some (no doubt apocryphal) accounts, such charnel-ground verse was actually written in cemeteries or among the tombs. One thinks of the "supernumerary horror" of "low-brow'd misty vaults" and "rueful wastes" evoked in Robert Blair's *The Grave* (1743), the "dirges due in sad array" of Thomas Gray's *Elegy Written in a Country Churchyard* (1751), and the confession at the core of Edward Young's *Night-Thoughts* (1742): "Darkness has more divinity for me."

The influence of both the Gothic novel and the Graveyard School can be seen in contemporary horror as well. In Guillermo del Toro's *Crimson Peak* (2015), for instance, the foreground melodrama of decaying familial lineages and the clash with modernity takes place against the equally important backdrop of the landscape itself. As with many classics in the Gothic novel tradition, the backdrop of torrential storms, vast landscapes, and brooding climate are as central to the narrative as are the conventions of human conflict and resolution. In *Crimson Peak*, the isolated grounds that surround the deliriously Gothic mansion sit on top of a now-derelict clay mine. As the plot progresses, a Gothic ecology emerges, the treeless landscape itself bleeding red clay, seeping through each human footprint, as if the very Earth were transformed into desiccated and exsanguinated flesh, consuming with a cold, impersonal patience, all human life that passes over its surface. The lesson is clear: *decay is not simply the flip side of growth, but is itself another kind of growth*. This is the lesson that works like *Maldoror* perform in paragraph after paragraph. What grows — is decay. The willful confusion of death as literal and death as figurative reveals the lush fecundity of decay itself, indifferent to what decays, impersonally decomposing all matter into its constituent parts, from which issues a mystery at once spiritual and corporeal — *ubi sunt*, "where are the dead, after they die?"

This is a throughline in both the Gothic novel and the Graveyard School of poetry, and it is resurrected by Lautréamont, in an anatomical, assemblage, Frankenstein-like manner. But, by the time we arrive at *Maldoror* in the 1860s, the Gothic is dead. It had long since been eclipsed by the cultural, social, and political upheavals of European Romanticism, as well as by the ascendency of realism and naturalism in the 19th century novel. Not only had its popularity waned, but from its inception the Gothic has always been a source of derision and dismissal, most notably by the literary establishment. Low culture, cheap thrills, often tending towards hyperbole — not too dissimilar from the academic reception of the horror genre in the 20th century. This alone may be an indicator of why *Maldoror* obsessively evokes the Gothic in its unwieldly prose; it is a book that resurrects the Gothic in its various guises, an atavism of decay and decline seemingly out of time. It might even be said that *Maldoror* is a book that allows itself to be haunted by the Gothic and its obsession with decline, and in this sense *Maldoror* achieves something unique in modern literature — it transforms the book itself into a ruin, falling apart and yet overgrown with a myriad of dead genres, motifs, and styles.

In taking up such themes, *Maldoror* also confronts the broader philosophical issues of the Gothic, primary among them being the way that the Gothic is often understood to be a counterweight to the 18th century European Enlightenment. With its emphasis on the passions governed by reason, on nature codified within science, on history narrated within an ideology of progress, and on the secular demystification of religion, it would seem that the 18th century literary Gothic forms a kind of counterpoint to the Enlightenment, favoring as it often does unreasonable or superstitious passions that eclipse all reason, a sublime and terrifying nature indifferent to all forms of scientific control, and history continually collapsing in on itself, as the revenants of the past come back to haunt the present. In this sense, the Gothic is the shadow side of the Enlightenment, a tenebrous repository of everything that must be hidden away so that the light of reason can emerge.

While this may be true, such a view also tends to simplify the relationship between Gothic and Enlightenment. We forget that numerous Enlightenment thinkers, from Voltaire to Kant, were themselves deeply suspicious about an overreliance on reason and instrumental rationality. Likewise, while many Gothic novels knowingly wander into the domain of transgression and taboo, such works could also express the most conservative religious morality, rendering their tales of death, occultism, and the supernatural as mere "cautionary tales." What *Maldoror* carries out in its resurrection of the Gothic is decidedly different: with its emphasis on decay, decomposition, and disintegration, the Gothic reveals something about the indifference of the world vis-à-vis all of our attempts to classify, systematize, and render it meaningful for us as a self-interested species. The instant we look at it, it withers and dissipates. In its place, something else emerges — a mirage, a dreamworld, a diorama of the world arrayed out before us, the provenance of the human. Decay, decomposition, and disintegration are not simply reminders of the transient character of all things, they are also indicators of a vast and tenebrous opacity that inhabits the gulf between human-centric creatures and the impersonal "nature" of the planet that they temporarily occupy. In short, the Gothic is not the inverse of the Enlightenment; *the Gothic is another kind of Enlightenment.*

What is revealed in this darker, more tenebrous enlightenment is revealed at the level of both form and content. There is a ferocity to the various preternatural or supernatural phenomena in *Maldoror*, an unsettling taxonomy of blasphemous life forms that seem to wither and decay with a wild abandon. Every monstrosity is classified, at the same moment that classification itself becomes so fecund that the categories become overgrown with the rot of negation — negation as logic, as language, as biology. Contradictions, metamorphoses, and mutations abound. Everything separating the natural from the supernatural is turned inside out, summarized by literary critic Anne Williams in her study of Gothic poetics: "Spirits that should be dead (or departed for another world) return ... the 'disembodied' suddenly materializes ... the material but inanimate object suddenly takes on the characteristics of the living — it moves, bleeds, or even speaks."[415]

Indeed, the incessant decay and disintegration in *Maldoror* extends to the level of the prose itself, where only the most tenuous trace of narrative remains, giving way instead to the constant mutations in the language of the book itself — cutting, suturing, recombining itself in ways that look ahead to later experiments in the 20th century avant-garde. The immersive, nocturnal uncertainty of *Maldoror* applies as much to the troubling and doubtful forms of life described in its pages as it does to the continual withering of the prose itself. Prose deconstructed into poetry. Forms of life revealed as so many permutations of death. Recombinations of bodies and texts into unholy anatomies. A poetics emerges.

This poetics of the Gothic has had a long tail; its influence can be found not only in the Graveyard School, but in Poe, Baudelaire, and the *fin de siècle,* but also in the tales of Isidore Ducasse's fellow-Uruguayan Horatio Quiroga. Indeed, when Baudelaire's *Les Fleurs du Mal* was first published in 1857, the scandal it caused was not only due to its transgressive depictions of death and eroticism, but also to the way that Baudelaire self-consciously incorporated Gothic motifs of decay and decomposition with all their grisly detail, driving home the deep-seated misanthropy that runs through *Les Fleurs du Mal.*

In Baudelaire's poetry, everything withers into environment, atmosphere, and a climate of withering — desiccated corpses, nocturnal city skies, dilapidated buildings, and a pervasive sense of gravity, of being weighted down in the depressive lethargy of creaturely life. In Baudelaire's "spleen cycle," affect and climate become so intertwined that it is nearly impossible to distinguish a depressive mood from rain-soaked, brooding night skies. A book saturated in melancholy, *Les Fleurs du Mal* is a book that absorbs the motifs of the Gothic and transforms them into an extended lyrical rumination on the sorrow of living, the *ennui* of suffering, and the strange, ambivalent allure of death. Gone is the religious fear of death which inhabits so many Gothic novels and Graveyard poems. Instead, it is life that comes to be regarded with wariness and suspicion. With *Les Fleurs du Mal* we move from the fear of death to a different affect, the horror of life. In this sense *Les Fleurs du Mal* renders the Gothic as both physical and metaphysical, paving the way for the full unfurling of decay that takes place in *Maldoror*.

What results is a version of the Gothic that is at once steeped in the lyrical grotesqueries of decay and withering, but that also raises decay to a metaphysical level, where the surefooted boundary between self and world that grounds so much of Enlightenment thinking also withers and dissipates. In *Maldoror* this "feral melancholy" takes up all these tendencies and delivers them in a tone that is at once angst-ridden and impassive, that rails against the inanity of blind and impersonal life while also reveling in the decidedly un-transcendental status of the happenstance creature christening itself "human."

*

Tooth and Claw, Flesh and Blood. Often, these two views of *Maldoror* — as animality and as spirituality — become indistinguishable and collapse into each other, resulting in what Gaston Bachelard once referred to as "the bliss of metamorphosis." Much of the content of *Maldoror* is expressed through the various creatures in the text, be they fantastical beasts from the imagination, the more recognizable animals of the natural sciences, or the abstract idea of "animality" itself. These strange and anomalous creatures often inhabit the worlds of dream, phantasm, and the archetypes of nightmare. In *Maldoror* they are often portrayed in ways that invert or pervert anatomical coherence, either through an inversion of the natural order (the soliloquies of spiders, frogs, squids), or through exaggerations in scale (the glowworm as big as a building). The particular types of creatures that frequent the pages of *Maldoror* — insects, reptiles, amphibians, flocks and swarms — also stand out in their radical alterity to the individuated human organism, and in this sense *Maldoror* as a whole becomes an extended "anatomy of nightmare" in which structural deformations of creaturely life serve as an index of the unraveling of the natural world. In *Maldoror*, the physical breaks open the metaphysical just as biology signals the decay of ontology.

At the same time, the innumerable creatures in *Maldoror* are themselves the product of classification systems in the history of science, in which natural philosophy, logic and taxonomy go hand in hand. It is likely that Lautréamont was drawn to textbooks in biology for this reason, for it is precisely this analytic approach to the creature that also enables the variety of monstrous combinations and recombinations to take place. In its excessive proliferation of monstrous life forms both real and fantastical, *Maldoror* looks back to the 19th century genre of the "teratology," or the scientific classification of biological aberrations.[416] A term coined in by the French zoologist Isidore Geoffroy Saint-Hilaire, the insight of the teratology is that aberrations in the natural world are not, in fact, anomalies, but have a structure of their own, which can be elucidated through anatomy, physiology, and related fields. Geoffroy Saint-Hilaire's *General and Particular History of Organizational Anomalies in Humans and Animals* (*Histoire Génénerale et Particulière des Anomalies de l'Organisation chez l'Homme et les Animaux*, 1832–37) catalogs such examples, in which aberrations in biological organisms are shown to have a structure and function that demands its own classification system.[417] The monstrous has a logic of its own, quite apart from the normative biology of so-called healthy organisms. It is just a step to make the claim that the "monster" is simply another kind of animal. The monstrous creatures in *Maldoror* are neither exemplars of the natural world, nor are they allegorical stand-ins for human beings. They move in another region altogether.

In a book like *Maldoror* the message is clear: "animality" is no way reducible to animals.[418] The critical work to have comprehended this is Gaston Bachelard's 1939 study *Lautréamont*. For Bachelard this means understanding animals less as scientific species or cultural symbols, and more in terms of their affectivity, a "vigorous poetry of aggression." As he notes, "Lautréamont grasps animals not as forms but as direct functions — that is, their aggressive functions."[419] Animals never are, they always do — moving, growing, decaying, pouncing, and devouring. In this sense *Maldoror* constitutes an inventory of affects: "A complete classification of animal phobias and philias would yield a sort of affective animal kingdom that would be interesting to compare with the animal kingdom described in the bestiaries of antiquity and the Middle Ages."[420]

One of Bachelard's most instructive analyses comes in his contrast between Lautréamont and La Fontaine. The latter, well known as the author of a number of beast fables, tends to portray humans in the guise of animals; the animals in La Fontaine's *Fables* only appear to be animals; underneath they are simply exemplars of human types and characters. For Lautréamont, the reverse is true — humans, when they are present in the text, tend to look like animals, or they are rapidly animalized in their behaviors. If what La Fontaine really wants to discover is the human in the animal, then Lautréamont is interested in the animal in the human.

Furthermore, in *Maldoror* humans don't just resemble animals, they frequently undergo metamorphosis and become animals as well. This stands in contrast to La Fontaine, for whom animality is physiognomy, representation, and form. The innumerable hybrids, teratologies, and metamorphoses that constitute *Maldoror* introduces us to an animality that constantly generates, proliferates, almost exploding in life forms, often to the point of decline, death, and decay — where other forms of life continue to proliferate. Whereas Lautréamont understands animality as an explosion of affects, La Fontaine understands animality as a set of behaviors; the psychological perspective of the latter is contrasted with the teratological perspective of the former.[421]

A catalog of the major appearances of animals reveals, for Bachelard, two major aspects that constitute the animality of *Maldoror*. There is the action of "tearing," and its association with the physiology of the claw, the beak, the horn, and then there is the action of "sucking," and its physiological association with the fang, the mouth, the orifice. The claw corresponds to the tearing of flesh, while the sucker corresponds with the extraction of blood. Vampiric and voracious, the creatures in *Maldoror* devour their environment, at the same time that they are engulfed within it. In the bizarre zoology of *Maldoror*, the natural world itself tears and sucks away at the organisms within it, extracting life from life, disaggregating anatomies into food for worms.

Furthermore, the action of tearing may be passed laterally, from a claw to a tusk, a beak, or a stinger. Similarly, the object of tearing may also be transferred, from the flesh of amphibian skin to the smooth marble of a statue. This lateral transference is so fecund in *Maldoror* that it almost becomes arbitrary, an indifferent, animistic propensity for the formation and deformation of forms. As Bachelard notes, in *Maldoror* "elementary energies are first *transformed*, then *transfigured*."[423] What results is a strange kind of beauty, one that is the product of the ambivalent transfiguration of creaturely forms.

In one of the book's startling scenes, the disembodied "spirit" of Maldoror is transformed, first into an eagle, then into an entire flock of birds, and finally into a phantom, "lost body" composed of a detached albatross wings comingled with fish tails, which then takes angry flight in defiance of "the Creator." For Bachelard, such moments reveal a teratological delirium, a "vertigo of the animalizing faculty, which at this point will animalize anything." Life, in itself, will not suffice. "In its very inadequacy this instant biological synthesis shows clearly a *need to animalize*."[424] The plethora of strange life forms in *Maldoror* becomes a kind of totem of the pervasive insufficiency of life, life railing against itself in a monstrous, musical polyphony.

In *Maldoror* animality is in no way identical with animals per se, and yet the text is replete with quite recognizable animals, animals that come to us straight out of natural history books, as well as out of the fantastical worlds of literature, the bestiary, and myth. The incessant borrowing, citation, and appropriation of *Maldoror* exists alongside its many biological combinations and recombinations. This type of layering — animals *in* the text and animals *as* text — is something that can only be achieved in the "anti-generic" poetics of a text like *Maldoror*, with its many references, appropriations, and modes of pastiche. In a sense, *animality is that point where the animals* in *the text and the text* as *animal eclipse each other*.

*

The Bliss of Metamorphosis. *Maldoror* is a text where the wild metamorphoses of creatures in the text are matched only by the equally wild metamorphosis of the text itself. So great is this "appetite for forms" that production and destruction, generation and decay, forming and deforming tend to overlap.[426] This emphasis on form places Lautréamont in relation to Aristotle. While Aristotle's works in natural philosophy contain detailed descriptions of animals, it is in the treatise known as *De anima* that Aristotle talks about life in itself, apart from any particular manifestation. The question that guides Aristotle's inquiry has to do not just with understanding this or that life form but with understanding the life of every life form. For Aristotle, there must be something substantial to each and every form of life, such that we can say that a bird, a human, a tree, and an octopus are all alive. It is here that Aristotle proposes the term *psukhē* (often translated in English as "soul," but more accurately as "life-principle"). This soul or life-principle is, for Aristotle, directly connected to the form of any living being. As Aristotle notes, *psukhē* must be "substance" in the sense that it is what forms life, that which "potentially has life."[427] Furthermore, this principle of life forms is always forming, in the sense that it is an actualization of this potential for life. The capacity for form is, for a philosopher like Aristotle, tantamount to the potential for life; there is no life without a form of life.

Against Aristotle, form in *Maldoror* is neither that which holds matter nor that which is an empty container. Form does not lead to that which is well-formed, or in-formed. The dynamics of tearing and sucking, flesh and blood, tooth and claw are themselves a manifestation of a more general animality, which is driven by an aggressive, generative, "appetite for forms." In *Maldoror* there is a sense in which everything is devoured by form, at the same time that form devours everything, including itself. Form is never formed, but instead devoured, deformed, metabolized, and reconstituted in a new guise. The animality of *Maldoror* is, in a sense, the extension of Aristotelianism to its logical conclusion, in which the forming is also reforming and deforming. *Maldoror* is not exactly against Aristotelianism; if anything, it is Aristotelianism run amok, a rabid Aristotelianism.

This "appetite for forms" has an end that is ostensibly spiritual. It is neither arbitrary nor happenstance, and passes through successive stages, culminating in ecstatic, almost mystical states — an "almost anarchic freedom of spiritualization."[429] The "spiritual anarchy" of *Maldoror* is a direct result of its aggressive, vitalistic, "appetite for forms," what Bachelard refers to as "the bliss of metamorphosis."[430] The "bliss of metamorphosis" not only describes an animality that is inseparable from a mystical tendency but it also attempts to conceive of form in a way that is at once the lowest and the highest, the bestial and the spiritual, the deformed and the informed.[431]

With this in mind, we can draw out the implications of *Maldoror's* "bliss of metamorphosis" by recasting *Maldoror* as a text structured along the lines of a mystical itinerary. The text begins from the normative perspective of the human being, structured along the Aristotelian division of life forms (human, animal, plant, mineral) which correspond to the division of faculties (reason, motion, nutrition, change). In these opening pages, we see all the exemplars of 19th century European culture — the bourgeois family, innocent youth, lovers and adventurers, men of science, and of course priests. But we also see criminals, the insane, gravediggers, and the sick delirious on their deathbeds. In short, human life and world of humanity. Here, animality is always reduced to the animal, either in the form of religious iconography (e.g., sheep, goats, black dogs) or in terms of scientific rationality (e.g., the numerous appropriations from biological classification textbooks).

Into this world *Maldoror* depicts the invasion of animality, the invasion of the human by the unhuman. Sometimes this occurs via actual animals, chosen for their stark difference to the human (amphibians and reptile hybrids), and at other times this occurs via animal assemblages (flocks, swarms, or packs). In Canto I this type of animality is depicted as a predatory, miasmatic force haunting both family and domestic space; this miasma then turns into a pack of rabid dogs, which somehow telepathically connect to a frightened young boy in the safety of his bedroom, as he realizes his harrowing fate. In such scenes human characters are confronted with something radically unhuman that they can only refer to as "evil," "demonic," or "cruel." In Canto II the discovery of a corpse in the Seine prompts a reflection on the arbitrariness of death; this directly correlates to an earlier section, where the narrator imagines the corpse of God, composed of a multitude of writhing fish and amphibians. Apprehension and dread predominate, as if the apparent order of the all-too-human world were suddenly thrown into abeyance. All human actions seem arbitrary, a pervasive sense of dread shrouds the most secure of situations.

Another stage occurs in which we see the animalization of the human, and in turn, of the divine. Here, *Maldoror* moves beyond the confrontation of human and animal and moves into the terrain of hybridity. The relations of human-animal, animal-animal, and, importantly, animal-God are each played out through successive metamorphoses and transformations. Not only are there human-animal hybrids, we also see: a reincarnated, vampiric spider; a glowworm's soliloquy on prostitution; a long elegy for a sleeping mystic hermaphrodite; a decapitated octopus blaspheming God; and a giant dung beetle sorrowfully playing out its excremental, Sisyphean drama. Perhaps the most notorious example of this type of animality comes in Canto II, where, amidst a stormy shipwreck off a rocky shore, the narrator has a passionate sexual encounter with a giant shark.

The final stage of *Maldoror*'s mystical itinerary is the stage where animality leads to a strange openness of form, where nothing remains but unceasing metamorphosis. The text departs from the animality *in* the text and moves out to the animality *of* the text itself; the scenes and events portrayed in the book — themselves appropriations from other sources — gradually give way to an almost purely arbitrary production of forms. Vampiric fingernails grow for weeks, along with a craving for infant blood; a soliloquy by a stray hair found in a brothel bed; the body's organs inexorably turn into rodents or reptiles; God is transformed into a toad and then a monstrous hog; the world seen from the perspective of a python, a basilisk, and then an oak tree; and lectures on mathematics as at once the most revered and most horrific of all things — the unhuman in its ultimate form.

*

Delight in Disintegration (Gothic Bliss). There is, undoubtedly, a strong anti-humanist thread that runs through *Maldoror*, evidenced by its misanthropy towards nearly all the human characters in the book, expressed in its bestiary of animals, animal parts, and animal transformations. Lautréamont rallies against the human in all of its guises (including the anthropomorphic fantasy of an all-knowing God). Human beings undergo incessant, monstrous transformations in *Maldoror*, to the point where, as Bachelard observes, "the bestiary of our dreams animates a life that returns to biological depths."[432]

The traditional philosophical view of animals is often split: it tends either to reduce animals to their natural substrate or elevate them into an abstract realm of universals. Ironically, in the philosophy of animals, animals themselves tend to disappear behind the mists of empirical observation, epistemological classification, and the hermeneutic demand for myth, symbol, and psychological depth. Either animality is reducible to animals, or animality is raised up to its pinnacle in human life.

However, what both of these views have in common is a philosophical commitment to a metaphysics of generosity, a vitalist prodigality of fecund forms that constantly proliferate and generate forms of life. The notion of an "animality" to animals expresses this commitment to a fundamental vitalism of creation and form. In a sense, the philosophy of animals must presume something prior to the animal called "life," that is then connected, in some basic way, to the generation and proliferation of the concrete forms that seem self-evident to us as "life." This metaphysics of generosity must presuppose some nebulous thing, some ineffable essence, prior to the very phenomenon it purports to explain.

If this is the case, we can ask whether there is in *Maldoror* an animality that is the negation of life, the withdrawal of form, the dissipation of form, the emptying of "life itself" Animality in *Maldoror* is not the continual proliferation of forms; instead, it constantly slips away, a single animal losing its form and becoming a swarm, which in turn disaggregates further, indistinguishable from primordial elements and the atmosphere itself — all of this similarly dissipating into the oblique and opaque textual fragments that constitute *Maldoror* as a book. An animality of absence, distance, opacity — a kind of tenebrous animality that approaches a condition we can only call "mystical."

In this sense, *Maldoror* is less a vigorous bliss of metamorphosis, and more an incessant poetry of negation. The 6th-century mystic known as Dionysius the Areopagite articulates this contrast between affirmative (*cataphatic*) and negative (*apophatic*) forms of mysticism:

> Now it seems to me that we should praise the denials quite differently than we do the assertions. When we made assertions we began with the first things, moved down through intermediate terms until we reached the last things. But now as we climb from the last things up to the most primary we deny all things so that we may unhiddenly know that unknowing which itself is hidden from all those possessed of knowing amid beings, so that we may see above being that darkness concealed from all the light among beings.[433]

The negation of this type of mysticism is not a negation of privation or subtraction but instead a negation that resides at its own limits, precisely because it forms the horizon of human knowledge. It is a negation that involves an erasure, an effacement, a denial (*apo-*) of rational discourse and thinking (*phanai*). Perhaps, then, there is a mystical itinerary in *Maldoror*, one that operates through anomaly: an animal retrogression of spiritual heights; the fracturing of divine beatitude in "tooth and claw"; a mysticism that ends not in the fullness of the divine union, but with a different type of bliss, a bliss of the loss of all form (including the human form). Such a Gothic bliss would require an ontology based not in affirmation and generosity, but instead in negation and dissipation — in short, it would require a negative theology. Borrowing from the apophatic tradition of negation in mysticism, we might call this "apophatic animality."

In *Maldoror*, apophatic animality has two aspects, both of which have to do with the negation of form. On the one hand there is *anamorphosis*, exemplified by the many chimeras, monsters, and hybrids that populate *Maldoror*.[434] A passage from Canto IV — again, worth citing in full — illustrates the dual process of the building up and breaking down that is part of *Maldoror*'s negative theology:

> I am filthy. Lice gnaw me. Swine, when they look at me, vomit. The scabs and sores of leprosy have scaled my skin, which is coated with yellowish pus. I know not river water nor the clouds' dew. From my nape, as from a dungheap, sprouts an enormous toadstool with unbelliferous peduncles. Seated on a shapeless chunk of furniture, I have not moved a limb for four centuries. My feet have taken root in the soil forming a sort of perennial vegetation — not yet quite plant life though no longer flesh — as far as my belly, and filled with vile parasites. My heart, however, is still beating. But how could it beat if the decay and effluvia of my carcass (I dare not say body) did not abundantly feed it? In my left armpit a family of toads has taken up residence, and whenever one of them moves it tickles me. Take care lest one escape and come scratching with its mouth at the interior of your ear: it could next penetrate into your brain. In my right armpit there is a chameleon which endlessly chases the toads so as not to die of hunger: everyone has to live. But when one side completely foils the tricks of the other, they like nothing better than to make themselves at home and suck the dainty grease that covers my sides: I am used to it. A spiteful viper has devoured my prick and taken its place. This villain made a eunuch of me. Oh! If only I could have defended myself with my paralysed arms — but I rather think they have turned into logs. Be that as it may, it is vital to note that in them blood no longer pulses redly. Two small hedgehogs, that grow no more, have flung to a dog — which did not decline them — the contents of my testicles; inside the scrupulously scrubbed scrotal sac they lodged. My anus has been blocked by a crab. Encouraged

> by my inertia, it guards the entrance with its pincers and causes me considerable pain! Two jellyfish crossed the seas, at once enticed by a hope which did not prove mistaken. They closely inspected the two plump portions which comprise the human rump and, fastening on to these convex contours, so squashed them by constant pressure that the two lumps of flesh disappeared while the two monsters which issued from the kingdom of viscosity remained, alike in colour, form, and ferocity. Speak not of my spinal column, since it is a sword.[435]

In this "anatomy" of the Gothic we are given a monstrous version not only of the body natural but of the body politic. The body depicted is at once decaying and, one senses, about to crumble and fall apart — and yet it is also fixed, frozen, and petrified in its place. In anamorphosis one sees the breakdown of part-whole relationships, in favor of the unstable play between part and part. Anamorphosis can take place in space — as in the above citation — or it can take place in time, as in the final canto, where an archangel is turned into a giant edible crab, then into a fishtail with bird wings, and so forth. Anamorphosis functions on the axis of humanity/animality; its operator is that of decay and decomposition.

In addition to anamorphosis, there is also *amorphosis*, exemplified by the numerous instances of formlessness in *Maldoror*. Whereas anamorphosis is predominantly metamorphic, amorphosis is predominantly morphological, dealing with the boundary between form and formlessness. An example is given in Canto V of *Maldoror*, which also becomes a meditation on the poetics of the text itself:

> Let not the reader lose his temper with me if my prose has not the felicity to please him. You maintain my ideas are at least singular. What you say, respectable man, is the truth, but a half-truth. And what an abundant source of errors and misapprehensions every half-truth is! Flights of starlings have

> a way of flying which is theirs alone and seems governed by uniform and regular tactics as a disciplined regiment would be, obeying a single leader's voice with precision. The starlings obey the voice of instinct, and their instinct leads them to bunch into the centre of the squad, while the speed of their flight bears them constantly beyond it; so that this multitude of birds thus united by a common tendency towards the same magnetic point, unceasingly coming and going, circulating and crisscrossing in all directions, forms a sort of highly agitated whirlpool whose whole mass, without following a fixed course seems to have a general wheeling movement round itself resulting from the particular circulatory motions appropriate to each of its parts, and whose centre, perpetually tending to expand but continually compressed, pushed back by the contrary stress of the surrounding lines bearing upon it, is constantly denser than any of these lines, which are themselves the denser the nearer they are to the centre. Despite this strange way of swirling, the starlings cleave through the ambient air at no less rare a speed and each second make precious, appreciable headway towards the end of their hardships and the goal of their pilgrimage. Likewise, reader, pay no attention to the bizarre way in which I sing each of these stanzas.[436]

Unlike other instances of biological admixtures and hybrids, we have here a sustained passage on a single phenomenon, that of swarming behavior that is at once tightly organized and yet formless and chaotic. It is also a passage that is itself borrowed from the *Encyclopédie d'Histoire Naturelle*, making the very act of reading the text ambiguous in its conflation of scientific description and suggestive simile.[437] In amorphosis form is pushed to its limit, becoming either the absence of all form or absolute form. In *Maldoror*, these instances of formlessness can exist within a single body (as in the morphologies of the Maldoror character as a pack of dogs and then a miasma), or it can exist pervasively throughout multiple bodies (flocks of birds, a horde of rats, a swarm of flying squids). Amorphosis functions along the axis of humanity/divinity; its operator is that of dissipation and dissolution.

In addition, *Maldoror* presents us with another variation on "Gothic bliss," which highlights the aggressive anti-humanism that drives *Maldoror*'s litany of assaults against both God and humanity. *Maldoror* is a text that rails against the human — and also against "life" (in so far as the concept "life" is itself a designation made by humans on behalf of other entities). While *Maldoror* takes up the Aristotelian fascination with life in itself, it is also poised against Aristotle on the necessity of an essential life-principle and the hierarchy of life forms that follow in its wake. With *Maldoror*, we move from the well-formed life (the life of biological classification), through the life that forms (the metaphysics of generosity, the bliss of metamorphosis), to the more suspect and shadowy region of the Gothic, where form and forming are inseparable from de-forming and un-forming. If a book like *Maldoror* is "mystical," it is in this apophatic register, in which the mystical tendency overlaps perfectly with a misanthropic tendency. As literary critic Alain Paris notes, "Lautréamont deplores the *human* form of conscience, which is duality and consciousness of this duality ... For Lautréamont, God frequently represents this alterity that both founds consciousness and the tearing of consciousness from itself." Far beyond any bickering over good and evil, *Maldoror*'s misanthropy extends to God and perhaps, even to the cosmos itself: "It is in this way that one must understand the hatred of God, invoked from the beginning of *Maldoror* ... There is a mysticism of hatred in Lautréamont. Hatred is a propaedeutic of the divine and that which is beyond the human."[438]

In this mystical misanthropy, life exists only to the extent that it continually ceases to exist; the prodigality of forms only exists in so far as they are already decaying, decomposing, or disintegrating. *Maldoror* presents us with a strange, Gothic delight in disintegration, where life grows by decaying, anatomies are built in ruins, and any notion of a "life-principle" can only be prodigious in its withering. In short, *Maldoror* is less a heroic and more a tragic type of poetry.

From its opening pages, *Maldoror* makes a stark assertion: that there is too much life in the world. It attempts a preposterous task, which is to continually un-form all forms, above all that most tiring and tedious of forms, the human form. In spite of its invectives against God, and in spite of all its absurdist chimeras, the challenge posed by *Maldoror* is not a challenge against religion or science. The real challenge posed by *Maldoror* is this: what is the most adequate form of the anti-human? Yet *Maldoror* as a book can only accomplish this via some form; hence its poetics of Gothic misanthropy must take on the abandoned shell or the carcass of existing forms, both of literature and of life.

*

Impersonal Sublime. Everything is possible in *Maldoror* — all hybrids are permitted, all forms only exist to be deformed and reformed. Teratology in fact becomes the norm, with its propensity for the aggressive creation of novel forms that decay the moment they are created. In this sense *Maldoror* also poses a challenge to philosophy's "principle of sufficient reason," a moral and theological principle that the world is well formed, and that the form of the world is somehow necessary to the world. The animality of *Maldoror* puts forth what is really a philosophical challenge — it works through various textual assemblages (appropriations, textual collage, unexpected juxtapositions), but these are really negations, the negation of the bodies in the text and the auto-negation of the body of the text itself, as narrative coherence gives way to narrative fragments and shards of surreal imagery. *Maldoror* is, in a way, the most "goth" of texts because it takes the Gothic logic of decay and decomposition to its extreme point, where the text itself crumbles beneath its misanthropic negation of all form — including literary form. As a book, the poetics of *Maldoror* is to have rendered poetics itself a ruin — and with it, the central role of the poetic subject, and its capacity to apprehend and comprehend the larger cosmos within which it is embedded.

This overwhelming sense of prodigious decay can induce in the reader a sense of the sublime, an aesthetic most often associated with the work of Kant or Edmund Burke. Kant's oft-cited, rather Gothic examples of the sublime in the natural world include: "Bold, overhanging, and, as it were, threatening rocks, thunder-clouds piled up the vault of heaven, borne along with flashes and peals, volcanoes in all their violence of destruction, hurricanes leaving desolation in their track, and boundless ocean rising with rebellious force, the high waterfall of some mighty river, and the like, make our power of resistance of trifling moment in comparison with their might."[439] The sublime engulfs the human being in a particular mood, one whose vast scales of space and time threaten to render the human point of view insignificant. In the "abyss" of the sublime, the human is humbled, even humiliated, a mere speck in contrast to impersonal, vast, and indifferent forces that, at the furthest point, reach a cosmic level. As Kant notes, the sublime "forces upon us the recognition of our physical helplessness as beings of nature," the strange allure of our own insignificance, the "astonishment amounting almost to terror."[440]

These ambiguous moods suggest that the sublime has a relation to religious experience, something of which Kant was well aware. No doubt this is why, in the early 20th century, theologian Rudolf Otto uses the Latin phrase *mysterium tremendum* to describe what he calls "the holy" (*das Heilige*). But for Otto the holy has nothing to do with the moral and religious connotations it often has. The holy is not good, and neither is it good "for us" as human beings. Central to this is what Otto refers to as the "creature-feeling," akin to Kant's description of the sublime rendering the human insignificant. Humbled before what is vaster and slower than entire empires, the human being can only register a negative awareness, and this is, for Otto, the core of religious phenomena: "The truly 'mysterious' object is beyond our apprehension and comprehension, not only because our knowledge has certain irremovable limits, but because in it we come upon something inherently 'wholly other,' whose kind and character are incommensurable with our own, and before which we therefore recoil in a wonder that strikes us chill and numb."[441] Otto uses the term *numinous* to describe this shadowy, excessive, nonhuman aspect of the holy, an experience of the "wholly other" that can only be described as a negative experience.

Otto's study takes up the sublime and suggests a link to religious phenomena. Literary historians and critics would suggest a further link to the horror genre. As religious authority was in crisis, and scientific rationality on the rise, the Enlightenment gave birth to cultural forms that expressed both a suspicion regarding traditional religion and at the same time an ambiguous desire for religious experience. Devendra Varma's study *The Gothic Flame*, which deals primarily with the Gothic novel, puts it plainly: "the Gothic novels arose out of a quest for the numinous."[442] But the numinous tends to be inverted, comprised of "ghosts and demons, the grotesque manifestations of the supernatural," indicators of an ambivalent transcendent forces that create and destroy at will.

In his book *Haunted Presence*, literary critic S.L. Varnado is even more explicit, noting that "Otto's concept of the numinous provides insights into the spirit of Gothic and supernatural horror."[443] The stock and trade of such fiction — "mountain gloom, lonely castles, phantom ships, violent storms, and the vastness of sea and polar regions ... magical lore, apparitions, ghouls, vampires, or revenants" — are echoed in Otto's own evocations of the numinous in terms of "darkness," "silence," and "vast and empty distances." They are also found in Kant's description of the sublime. Varnado highlights the duplicity of the numinous — at once a subjective affect, and yet also the failure of subjectivity as it confronts something radically nonhuman, something "wholly other," that registers itself as the failure to have an experience at all.

This failure is where horror and religion intersect. Instead of the more clichéd images of ebullient, overflowing, radiant experiences of fullness and light, these phenomena — the sublime, the numinous, the Gothic — are instead failures of experience, and therefore, failures of the human sensory and cognitive apparatus. It is the difference between an experience of horror and a horrific experience, the latter annulling any possibility of experience whatsoever. Thus one finds, in the mystical writings of Meister Eckhart, Angela of Foligno, John of the Cross, and the *Cloud of Unknowing*, self-annulling descriptions of the divine in terms of darkness, nothingness, an abyss, a desert, a dark night — descriptions that are as much about the negativity of experience as they are about experiences of negation. Writing about medieval Christian mysticism, philosopher Denys Turner notes that "there is a very great difference between the strategy of *negative propositions* and the strategy of *negating the propositional*; between that of the *negative image* and that of the *negation of imagery*."[444]

What remains of the sublime but this residue of the human being, not so long ago confident in its capacity for apprehending and comprehending the world around it as the world in its own image? What remains but a sublime of indifference, anonymity, impersonality — an impersonal sublime?

*

Eaten Alive, Buried Alive. It may be that the dissolving of the boundary between the earthly and the divine — so sought after by various mystical traditions — occurs within the depths of the very material existence that is repudiated. There, materiality and divinity strangely become one in the same. In his posthumously published study *Theory of Religion*, Georges Bataille discusses the relationship between "animal continuity" and "divine continuity," both of which entail the effacement of the boundary between subject and object. The lateral continuity of the animal is that of a being seamlessly existing in and as part of the world, unburdened by the divisions and estrangement of human consciousness. The vertical continuity of the divine transfers this seamlessness to the spiritual domain, for which religious ritual provides the means of "losing the self" in God. For Bataille, between these two types of continuity are numerous instances of metamorphosis, exemplified in the indistinction between eater and eaten in the animal world, as well as in the passage from the body to the corpse in religious ritual. It is in these passages of material existence that Bataille detects an "ambiguous horror," where all boundaries dissolve, all human-bound categories dissipate, and consciousness flounders before that which it fails to comprehend.

This horror that Bataille mentions is not simply the emotion of fear, the stimulus/response of fright, or even the existential dread of death — all of these imply an object of experience that threatens the subject, while maintaining the separation between subject and object. For Bataille, horror necessarily indexes something we can only call unhuman. If it can be described in affective or emotional terms, that is because it is, at its core, fundamentally non-anthropomorphic. It is, really, a *religious horror*. Religious horror arises, for Bataille, from the "impoverishment" of religious anthropomorphism and its meaning-making practices, encapsulated in what Bataille refers to as the desire for a "supreme being." The supreme being — Bataille's targets here are monotheistic religions, though his claim also applies to pagan gods — is continuity brought down by human beings into "discontinuity," the god become a thing. The supreme being allows for the Kantian framework of causality, relation, and modality to be applied even to the supernatural, such that the supreme being can also be seen to possess both "isolated individuality" and "creative power," just like human beings. In this attempt at having one's (theological) cake and (eucharistically) eating it too, there is the attempt to preserve the element of the divine as both indistinct and immanent.

The problem, for Bataille, is that in introducing the notion of the supreme being, one also attempts to comprehend continuity through the lens of discontinuity, in effect making the supreme being a being like other beings, along a sliding hierarchy of greater or lesser beings. "The objective personality of the supreme being situates it in the world next to other personal beings of the same nature … Human beings, animals, plants, heavenly bodies, meteors."[445] Everything is brought within the ambit of the human perspective. What results is a relative equivalency between discrete, individuated things, greater or lesser, supreme or subordinate — creature and Creator, earthly and divine, temporal and eternal. But this equivalency is not the same as the continuity (or "intimacy") of which Bataille speaks. For even though the concept of the supreme being is, for Bataille, universal, at the same time "the operation seems to have failed everywhere." That which is by definition outside the scope of human understanding is constantly recuperated within it, producing a solipsism that passes itself off as absolute knowledge. At best the supreme being becomes a symbol, an icon, an image that, when examined directly, gives way to negative concepts (as in Anselm's famous definition of God, as "that beyond which nothing greater can be conceived").

In a sense, then, religious horror is the impoverishment or the *implausibility* of the supreme being. And yet, as Bataille notes, there remains something profoundly negative in the notion of the supreme being. Religious horror is the horror of religion — the horror of its failure despite its success, of its all-too-humanity, of its claims for continuity in the language of discontinuity, of its confused confirmation and refusal of the Kantian antinomy between the world as it appears to us and the world in itself.

If the "horror" that Bataille discusses is really religious horror, what makes this religious horror different from the other kinds of horror just mentioned (fear, fright, *Angst*)? One difference is that these approaches to horror rely on a basic metaphysical dichotomy between life and death. But there is also a transformation that is neither that of life into death, nor death into life, but a kind of death-in-life, a living death, a hypostasis of persisting and subsisting— the religious horror of time interminable.

The tomb often comes to stand in as the symbol of this transformation, mediating as it does between the life above ground and the life below ground. The tradition of supernatural horror provides us with reflections on these themes.[446] A case in point is the film noir *I Bury the Living* (1958), directed by Albert Band. The film centers on Robert, a middling businessman, who comes into ownership of Immortal Hills cemetery. As the reluctant owner, Robert sets his sights on the real estate value of the cemetery lots. In a wonderful scene that diagrammatically distills the entire film, we see Robert kneeling before a huge map of the cemetery, divided like a grid into individual plots. Those that are occupied have black pins on them, while those that are available (and available for presale) have white pins on them. One day Robert's business partner decides to buy a cemetery plot for himself. That night, as Robert fills out the paperwork reserving the lot for his partner, he accidentally places a black pin on the lot. Days later, his business partner suddenly dies of a heart attack. As the film progresses it soon appears that Robert has the uncanny ability to literally plot deaths on the cemetery grid — a gift towards which he is horrified, and of which he cannot seem to dispense. A grim reaper allegory, *I Bury the Living* places the living on a hovering grid of chance, a gift of death, a map of mortality. Life becomes a waiting game, floating with uncertainty in an uncomfortable proximity to open and leasable tombs.

For all its dread of impending death, *I Bury the Living* retains the temporal boundary between life and death, with the tomb — vacant or occupied — as the mediator between them. Something further happens in films such as *Premature Burial* (1962). Directed by Roger Corman and adapted from an Edgar Allen Poe story, the film centers on Guy, an aristocrat of a decaying lineage, who is consumed by the fear of being buried alive. Despite the stern discipline of his sister, and the romantic wooing of his fiancée, Guy's obsessive fear continues, derived in part from his witnessing the death and internment of his father. It is revealed that Guy's father was a cataleptic, often falling into deathlike trances that could easily be mistaken for death. Convinced his father was buried alive, Guy fears that he too may succumb to the same fate. Determined not to do so, Guy constructs a sepulcher for himself that will

Still from *I Bury the Living* (dir. Albert Brand, 1958)

permit him to escape, should he be buried alive. In a strange mixture of genres, Guy's morbid plan for his "great escape" includes a high-tech coffin designed to open from the inside, a rigged gate and bell to signal for help, a rope ladder leading out through the roof, construction tools, dynamite, and, as a last resort, the ultimate escape — poison.

Eventually Guy does succumb to a cataleptic shock, mostly due to his own, increasingly deranged obsessions. He is believed dead, and plans are made for his funeral and entombment — not in the high-tech sepulcher but in an earthen grave. In a climactic, suffocating scene, Guy's cold, dead, motionless face, visible through a tiny window in the coffin, is juxtaposed to the desperate, whispering sound of his inner voice, which can only shout to deaf ears, "No! I'm not dead! — I'm alive!" This situation, which Guy himself calls "this living death," evokes a horror that derives not just from the fear of being buried alive, but from this hypostasis of living death, closed to the world outside and yet coursing through with a desperate vitalism — the religious horror of not being able to die.

Scenes like this are elaborated in Aldo Lado's 1971 film *The Short Night of Glass Dolls*. Combining elements of the *giallo* murder mystery with the supernatural tale, *The Short Night of Glass Dolls* is ostensibly a romance, but one in which love really is colder than death. The film's opening and closing sequences portray the paradoxical conjunction of thought and the corpse. We see a corpse in a sterile, cold setting — a morgue, a hospital, an anatomy theater. But as we watch the corpse, placed on a gurney, covered in plastic, shoved into a flat, horizontal locker, we gradually begin to hear its thoughts, presented in the film as a faint voiceover. *The corpse thinks*. The horror that thought might live on, after life.

What *The Short Night of Glass Dolls* does is focus on the metaphysics — the theology, even — of thought without a body. Here we have neither thought dissociated from the corpse and transcending it, nor do we have thought dying with the body, as mortal as the body is mortal, perishing as the body perishes. Rather, what the film offers is thought irrevocably tethered to the body, thought inextricably tethered to the corpse. It is this thinking corpse that then proceeds to narrate, through a living dead anamnesis, the events that have led up to this point in the film. What happens for the bulk of this strange flashback is an eerie, soft-focus *giallo* film involving a love affair, a missing person, a shadowy cult of the aged, and so on. The final scene returns us to this thinking corpse, now removed from the gurney and in the middle of a medical school anatomy theater. As with *Premature Burial*, the living corpse can only shout to the void, "but I'm alive! — You can't do this!" But the dissection has already begun.

With these examples in mind, we can revisit the onto-theological tension Bataille identifies: on the one hand, an immanent immersion in divine continuity, and on the other hand, a transcendental split between subject and object that guarantees the intelligibility of divine continuity. The former (divine continuity) can only be thought via the latter (subject-object discontinuity), but the latter by definition negates the former (in so far as there can be no subject-object division in divine continuity). For Bataille, the only way out of this double bind is by throwing oneself headlong into it, understanding religion in terms of horror. In this sense religious horror is an attempt to think of life in terms of negation, but a negation that is not negative. This life, at once a hypostatized materiality and yet divested of materiality, opens onto what Bataille variously calls continuity, immanence, or intimacy: "What is intimate, in the stronger sense, is what has the passion of an absence of individuality, the imperceptible sonority of a river, the empty limpidity of the sky: this is still a negative definition, from which the essential is missing."[447]

Bataille reserves the name *divine* to describe this tension. For Bataille, the divine names neither a supreme being nor a transcendent reality, but the necessarily implausible or impoverished character of the transcendent. This divine continuity must necessarily remain tragic, not some heroic attainment of a higher state of being after life. The divine is an indicator of the specifically human "fascination of the sacred world," beyond the profane world of ends, means, the tools. In a primordial sense, religion and religious rites serve as a means for human beings to reattain a continuity that is forever shut off from them by virtue of consciousness and the subject-object split it safeguards. "The sense of the sacred obviously is not that of the animal lost in the mists of continuity where nothing is distinct." While animals are, for Bataille, in the world like water in water, human beings seem at once horrified of and yet drawn towards this dissolution of boundaries. This is the core of religious experience for Bataille, a "horror in the sense of the sacred."[448]

*

Dreams of the Cephalophore. The decapitated body is, arguably, one of the most precise allegories of philosophy. The head, seat of reason and bearer of the brain, is detached from a body that it can no longer govern or control; there is a base materialism that always threatens to undermine it. In the art of early Christianity, martyred saints were sometimes depicted miraculously carrying their own severed heads. A popular, though apocryphal, account of Dionysius the Areopagite tells us that, upon being executed, his body calmly took up his severed head, and walked off, the head continuing its sermon on "the unknown god." These "cephalophores" exist in the interzone between life and death, the material and the spiritual.[449] Though their heads were separated from their bodies, they seemed to exhibit another kind of awareness, the severed head held by the very body that offers it up as a sacrifice.

As unsettling and grotesque as it may be, the decapitated head also heavily imbued with symbolism. There is, for example, the expository head, the head that proclaims something in its beheadedness, akin to a ventriloquist's dummy ("the sovereign law has acted" or "our wrath has visited this village" or simply "beware"). The expository head delivers a message, a message whose efficacy derives, in part, from the weird, metaphysical presence of the head without a body.

There is also the hermetic head, the hidden head, the head for whom beheading is the occasion for despair and melancholy. Such heads are frequently found in the Gothic literary and art traditions. Their most common manifestation is not as a head per se, but in the guise of a mask. However, the mask and the head are not the same thing. What the mask adds to the head is not just disguise, but an element of artifice. The mask is artifice, and when worn on the head, the artificial is added to the natural, art to life. But the mask also suggests that, in fact, *all heads are artificial*. This is the case in the horror genre, where we often see masks and heads becoming confused with each other.

In *Halloween III: Season of the Witch* (1982), for instance, a popular Halloween mask mutates the wearer's head into a goopy, bloody, mass of blood and tendril. Here the mask overlaps with the head, resulting in a paradoxical decapitation of the mask, or the unmasking of the head itself. A variant of this is found in the Japanese art-horror film *Onibaba* (1964). In the harrowing, final scene of the film, the mask cannot be pulled off from the head, the two having become inextricably enmeshed through some strange animistic curse.

Films like these point back to literary examples in supernatural horror, such as the Robert Chambers story "The Mask" (1895), in which an artist realizes that the best model for his sculpture is the human body itself, living, dead, or undead. The head is the portrait, and vice versa. The motif is explored at length in Edogawa Rampo's obsessive novel *The Blind Beast* (1931), where a reclusive, blind sculptor uses real bodies as his sculptures.

Perhaps the paradigmatic example of this grotesque fusion of head and mask is Edgar Allen Poe's Gothic tale "The Oval Portrait" (1842). The story involves a portrait painting session between a male artist and female sitter. As the artist begins the portrait, his attention is focused on the living sitter across from him. Gradually he becomes more and more focused on the painting, drawing his attention away from his surroundings and the world around him. Immeasurable stretches of time seem to pass. At the end, the artist looks up, and to his horror finds that the sitter has died, with only a decrepit, gaunt corpse remaining. While the tale is typically read as an allegory about art, mimesis, and representation, if taken literally (as all genre horror must be) it becomes a study of the real-time transformation of a head into a mask, to the point that the mask actually eclipses the head, and in fact becomes a death mask.

However, Georges Franju's *Eyes Without a Face* (1960) offers one of the most evocative cases of the fusion of head and mask. A desperate surgeon lures young women to his home, in order to graft their faces into the head of his young daughter (played by Édith Scob), whose face has been irreparably scarred in a car crash. The daughter, while she waits, is forced to wear an eerie, porcelain-like mask, wandering throughout the Gothic mansion. As her father succumbs to the inevitable fate in store for him, the daughter, now strangely attached to her mask, attains a strange insight. Listless, melancholic, and increasingly deranged, she sets the dogs and the birds free,

Edith Scob in *Eyes Without a Face* (*Les Yeux sans Visage*, dir. Georges Franju, 1960)

wandering about the grounds, and into the forest beyond. Without a face, all that remains is the mask — opaque, expressionless, and unhuman. In the film's final, haunting scene, she simply drifts off into the night forest, a body abandoning its lost head.

Variations on these themes are found in B-movies such as *The Brain That Wouldn't Die* (1962) or Stuart Gordon's cult film *Re-animator* (1985). Genre horror overlaps with black humor and slapstick, as heads are toppled, rolled, plugged in, and casually misplaced. Perhaps the last word should be left to Donald Cammell's harrowing film *Demon Seed* (1977). The film has become notorious for the scenes of sexual violence between the supercomputer Proteus and the wife of the creator of Proteus (played by Julie Christie). At one point in the film Proteus, frustrated by the limitations of disembodied, purely information-based existence, attempts to construct a body for himself. These initial experiments — carried out in a basement workshop — are attempts to construct physical prostheses, so that Proteus can act in the physical world.

In one scene, Proteus constructs a geometric "body" with almost infinitely recombinable parts, based on the dodecahedron. One of the nerdy lab assistants comes upon Proteus's unauthorized creation. After a brief conversation on the metaphysics of intelligent computers, Proteus kills the lab assistant, by actually beheading him with the dodecahedron. The pure geometry of the dodecahedron at once stands in contrast to the messy, fleshy body, but at the moment of beheading, the dodecahedron also displaces the body. This is death by mathematics, the usurpation of the human by the chilling geometry of the unhuman. Aside from being the only film to feature beheading by a three-dimensional dodecahedron, *Demon Seed* suggests something that is, at first, counterintuitive — that beheading is always abstract.

*

Long Hair of Death. Hair is that part of the body that is also estranged from the body, seemingly inorganic matter that exudes from each of our pores. Sometimes hair is regarded aesthetically as a sign of beauty, while in other instances it is associated with strength and vitality (for instance, in the 15th century, the *Malleus Maleficarum* prescribed the cutting of hair as one of the preliminary punishments for witches). A lock of hair given as a token of affection; hair as a relic of saints; hair bound in braids or unbound in fertility rituals; hair as a component of magical spells; hair ingratiated by extensions, hair renounced by being shaved.

What is evocative about hair's almost mythical status is its ambivalent relation to death, an ambivalence highlighted in horror films such as Antonio Margheriti's *The Long Hair of Death* (1964). Margheriti, who often directed under the name Anthony Dawson, also directed such lowbrow classics as *Castle of Blood*, *Cannibal Apocalypse*, and the "documentary" *Mondo Inferno*. But *The Long Hair of Death* is different in that, like other Italian horror films of the 1960s (most notably, Mario Bava's *Black Sunday*), the film is saturated in the aesthetics of the Gothic. Apart from the requisite period sets (complete with tombs, castles, and thunderstorms), the film is also notable for its nearly incomprehensible

Barbara Steele in *The Long Hair of Death* (*I Lunghi Capelli della Morte*, dir. Antonio Margheriti, 1964)

plot, which involves the burning of a witch, a curse, a plague, and a string of female characters (the two main characters played by the inimitable Barbara Steele), all of whom unwittingly carrying out a witch's curse.

In the opening scene, a woman in a feudal village is accused of witchcraft and sentenced to be burned at the stake. As she is taken to the site of her death, the woman becomes frenzied and panicky — her clothes are torn, her face is pallid, with dark eyes deeply set in her face, her hair wild and untamed, almost mimicking the flames surrounding her. A curse is cast against myopic and voracious humanity, and the tenebrous wheels of retribution are set in motion.

In the scene following this, we are introduced to the woman's two daughters and a stranger named Mary, but we already sense they are all merely vehicles for the original curse. At the end of the film, the vengeful ghost appears to her accusers, back from the dead to perform an execution of her own. In her revenge, she encases one of her accusers inside an effigy to be burned in commemoration of her own death, an effigy that is now a sarcophagus, complete with brutish mask and long, black, straw hair.

Though she plays several characters in the film, Barbara Steele's long, thick, jet-black hair becomes a leitmotif. We as viewers cease to care about the incomprehensible plot and instead focus on how the curse will inevitably be brought about, passing from one character to the next like a miasma, with the long black hair as the thread between them. The long hair of death stretches, like a curse, across generations, coursing through bodies, corpses, and revenants.

Masaki Kobayashi's landmark 1964 film *Kwaidan* opens with the story "The Black Hair." The plot is simple — in ancient Kyoto, there was once a samurai who lived with his beloved wife. While the samurai would go out looking for work, his wife would weave at home. Frustrated by living in poverty, the samurai leaves his wife and marries into a wealthy family. His career rises, but he is unhappy. A melancholy sets in. Eventually he decides to return to his wife. Upon returning, he finds the old house decrepit and overgrown, tall, lingering weeds sprouting everywhere, wavering in the moonlit night. But there is a light on in one of the rooms. To his amazement, he finds that she is still there, sitting by the weaving wheel. Their reconciliation is tender and heartfelt. When he wakes the next morning, however, things are not as they seem. *Kwaidan* is based on the popular renditions of Japanese folktales by Lafcadio Hearn. The story "The Reconciliation," on which the film is based, describes what the samurai finds the next morning:

> When he awoke, the daylight was streaming through the chinks of the sliding-shutters; and he found himself, to his utter amazement, lying upon the naked boards of the mouldering floor … Had he only dreamed a dream? No: she was there; — she slept … He bent above her, — and looked — and shrieked; — for the sleeper had no face! … Before him, wrapped in its grave-sheet only, lay the corpse of a woman, — a corpse so wasted that little remained save the bones, and the long black tangled hair.[450]

Kobayashi's film stresses the stark contrast between body and hair, the decaying corpse set against the vibrant hues of the kimono and deep black hair. As the samurai recoils in horror, the black hair even seems to move of its own accord. The hair is alive, the body dead; perhaps it is even living *because* it is detached from the body. The samurai's face turns pale and gray, his expression misshapen and monstrous, as his own hair turns white, eventually falling out in clumps — he becomes corpselike himself.

Both films present us with hair — that strange, spidery, nonself — as a kind of sigil of death. In *The Long Hair of Death* that relation is only hinted at, but Steele's black hair becomes a silent symbol of the reincarnation of the dead and the fulfillment of retribution — the persistence of hair as a marker of dread, beyond the life and death of the individuals that the hair "possesses." In *Kwaidan* the hair is brought more into the foreground — hair is not only analogized to weaving and the spinning wheel, but it takes on strangely vitalistic properties of its own, outgrowing and outliving its owner. Its power brings together death and beauty in a powerful concoction that physically overwhelms the samurai, draining all life from him and blanching his own locks with grey terror.

A tomb is unearthed, a grave opened, a corpse suddenly brought into daylight — film in this Gothic mode plays on deeply rooted myths concerning the mortality of the body. It also evokes more modern notions, the most popular of which is the notion that hair (along with fingernails and toenails) continues to grow after death. The uncanniness of this image — the body has withered but the hair has not — confuses any strict boundary between life and death, for how can the body continue to grow after death? Hair — while part of the body — takes on a life of its own, even after death.[451] In death, hair becomes estranged from the body, an alien thing that seems to have neither purpose nor function.

In these films hair is unmoored from its subservience to the body, becoming an unnatural thing, at once part of the body and estranged from it. Hair is always a problem; on its own, it is formless, and needs to be shaped and formed. Plato was grossed out by hair. In one dialogue he notes that of all the entities in the world there are those that are elevated and that have ideal forms (e.g. abstract notions such as justice or beauty) and then there are those lowly entities that are without ideal forms — "trivial and un-dignified objects" such as "hair, mud, and dirt."[452] The hair that is estranged from the body — the hair of the corpse, writhing and ever-so-slowly growing on its own — this hair is neither living nor dead, neither a part of us as living subjects nor an inert object. Hair estranged from the life of the body, is perhaps akin to the ambivalent, deathlike vitality of other inorganic forms of life — fungi, choral, moss, clouds.

*

Floating Abattoir. In all these variations, we see bodies decomposing, not just in the way that a corpse decomposes, but as vitalistic decompositions. The bones, muscles, and fibers of the body become a field of metamorphoses, flesh grows at the same time that it is entombed, limbs re-anatomize themselves, faces become masks, heads sprout detached from bodies, and hair grows beyond the life of the corpse. Gothic anatomies whose various parts are all mutually estranged from each other in a kind of Aristotelian nightmare of parts without a whole, obeying neither the hierarchies of anatomy nor the classification schemes of biological science. And yet, they are not simply irrational, random, or happenstance. These anatomies contain a logic of their own, one that centers on the core contradictions of the Gothic — the fecund ruin, the living corpse, the substance of shadow, reason devouring itself in enclosures of vastness. The Gothic fecundity of the body so vividly expressed in Lautréamont's *Maldoror* is given an equally stark expression in the following parable, from Pascal's *Pensées*:

> Imagine a number of men in chains, all under sentence of death, some of whom are each day butchered in the sight

> of the others; those remaining see their own condition in that of their fellows, and looking at each other with grief and despair await their turn. This is the image of the human condition.[453]

Pascal's parable evokes an image of humanity as a kind of floating abattoir, the meat of the body subject to myriad, anonymous, inhuman forces that ensure its decomposition the moment we are born.

The image is given further allegorical meaning in the way we as human beings relate to animals, especially those animals we produce and consume for our own uses. Georges Franju's 1949 documentary *The Blood of the Beasts* (*Le Sang des bêtes*) treads the fine line between realism and surrealism in his examination of a Parisian slaughterhouse. While its black-and-white footage and voiceover is straightforward and unaffected, the images themselves are anything but. From the harrowing beginning of the process (workers mechanically killing horses as they come into the slaughterhouse), to the cold, assembly-line manner in which their bodies are parsed (the uncanny rows of neatly flayed legs, torsos, and heads), Franju's film takes the viewer through a range of affects, from shock, to dissimulation, to horrific fascination, and finally to an abjection that is, arguably, turned back on the body of the human viewer and human culture as the real target of the film.

The Blood of the Beasts is, arguably, one of the earliest films to combine the genre of horror with that of the documentary. Contemporary documentaries, such as the 2012 film *Leviathan*, likewise combine novel approaches to documentary filmmaking (e.g., the use of lightweight, miniature digital cameras) with a stark and somber aesthetic reminiscent of the Gothic tradition. An experiment in what the directors call "sensory ethnography," *Leviathan* uses high-definition, extreme close-up shots to give the viewer a visceral sense of being aboard an industrial fishing boat in the North Atlantic. Images of various fish and other sea creatures are shot in a way that renders them at once grotesque and abstract, a slime-ridden mass of entrails, chopped muscle, and cold, deathless, protruding eyes. Nearly every shot in the film is from an impossible, nonhuman point of view — along a fishing line as it is submerged under water, the wailing gulls flying just above the surface; from on top of a fishing crane as it raises a heavy, waterlogged net filled with flailing, glistening sea forms; from within the bowels of the sorting containers on deck, the twitching creatures sliding back and forth as the boat itself sways on tempestuous, nighttime, ocean waters. Gradually the human workers aboard the boat themselves become part of the visceral, abject seascape, the boat itself lost in the black abyss of an undulating, industrial night. "This," as Pascal would say, "is the image of the human condition."

*

Molten Media. At the furthest limit of the Gothic, the human becomes so estranged from itself that its very material existence is rendered dubious. The human vanishes into the animal, the beast, the creature; the creature vanishes into the anatomical happenstance of body parts; the body parts decompose and merge with other parts both organic and inorganic; and finally, matter itself vanishes into a materiality that is at once its fruition and its negation. At the furthest limit of the Gothic, the human being is drawn into a black matter of oblivion.

Perhaps this is why so many horror films are as concerned with shadows and darkness as they are with presenting actual people, things, and scenery. We "see" both shadows and the figures that move in and out of them, but this "seeing" is of a different order, one registered on the level of paradoxes (the presence of a shadow that is in itself nothing).

This is the level at which visionary films such as *Begotten* (1990) take place. Directed by E. Elias Merhige, *Begotten* makes use of innovative black-and-white film processing techniques to produce film that itself has the same gritty, dirty, material feel as the

Still from *Begotten* (dir. E. Elias Merhige, 1989)

anonymous bodies, hair, limbs, soil, trees, mud, blood, semen, and other substances that populate the film's stark images. Though the film has a broad, mythopoetic structure to it, it is less this that guides the sequence of images and more the interplay between the material in the film — flesh, mud, forest — and the material of film itself.

Existing somewhere between genre horror and performance art, *Begotten* is a ritual in cinematic time, enacted within a primordial, mythical framework of origin and death, embodiment and dissolution, composition and decomposition. In between these two points there is only convulsion. Bodies emerge out of mud, limbs become solemnly entwined, distant figures fade into dead forest trees, rows of sinewy, shadowy figures crawl across a deserted horizon, hunched backs and arched torsos merge with the stony tombs of cracked rock ravines, as a granulated and shadowy sun sets beneath floating clouds of black earth. The human bodies — if they can be said to be human, or even bodies — disintegrate into their surroundings, just as the film images themselves dissolve into abstract, abject patterns of saturated black and white. There are no words, and breath is barely uttered.

The next step, presumably, would be to allow everything to dissolve — human into nonhuman, body into environment, image into emulsions of gelatin, crystal, and camphor. All that would remain is to see film as film — in its temporal passing and shifting, in its composition and decomposition, at the moment it decomposes. This is one of the ideas at work in Stan Brakhage's experimental short *Delicacies of Molten Horror Synapse* (1991). Though it is a later film for Brakhage, it takes up his life-long interest in the abstraction of film as film, from his much-referenced *Mothlight* (1963) to the meticulously hand-painted abstractions of *The Dante Quartet* (1981–87). In *Delicacies* Brakhage uses abstraction to both comment on film — as material, as chemical, as elemental — and to also allow film to aesthetically be what it is, nothing more than its material accumulation and disaccumulation. At just over eight minutes and without any sound, *Delicacies* consists of a sequence of hand painted film frames in mostly dark colors. These are occasionally juxtaposed with sequences of black "empty" frames, or frames that appears to be scratched, scraped, or otherwise corroded. At points the entire mush of color and substance suddenly rise upwards in a weightless, ghostly levitation. At other points the abstract colors suddenly hold still in a kind of frenetic seizure. An exercise in film painting, the colors frantically ebb and flow, then freeze in a slow black strobe. From one perspective, *Delicacies* is a horror film, but an abstract horror film. It contains no plot, no narrative, no characters, no setting, and hence none of the decor of human melodrama. But it is also a film about composition and decomposition, building up and breaking down, and the inevitable disintegration of all that exists, the almost metaphysical corrosion that is at the core of being. It is even inaccurate to say that *Delicacies* is "about" these things. It is them.

Indeed, one could trace a lineage of these shadow-filled, "disintegrationist" horror films, from German Expressionist classics such as

Still from *Black Sunday* (*La Maschera del Demonio*, dir. Mario Bava, 1960)

The Cabinet of Dr. Caligari to contemporary avant-garde films, such as Peter Tscherkassky's short *Outer Space*. One of the standout films in this regard is Mario Bava's 1960 film *Black Sunday* (*La Maschera del Demonio*). Shot in black and white, the film self-consciously references the Gothic novel tradition, both in its themes (witchcraft and sorcery, decaying aristocratic lineage, resurrection of the dead) and in its settings (darkened castles, gloomy landscapes, cold cellars, colder sarcophagi).

While its narrative is fairly standard by the conventions of the Gothic, *Black Sunday* is visually unique among horror films. At a cinematic level it is nothing less than a sustained study of shadow and darkness, both in film and as film. Numerous scenes depict characters wandering through castle passageways lit only by a single candle — or often, by nothing at all. The congruous spaces of the castle become separated from each other, almost as if the castle and the characters in it become lost in the material blackness of film itself. Bava simply lets the camera roll, filming "nothing" but the blackness of submerged shadow, at once flat and an infinite depth.

*

Stellar Sorrow. There is a continuum of decay in the Gothic that cuts across microcosm and macrocosm, an enigmatic region in which bodies are dispersed into star stuff, and stars collapse into bodies, limbs, fluids, and the desiderata of transient matter. Materiality converts into its opposite, while never ceasing to disintegrate. For the Gothic "delight in disintegration," anatomy is not enough. Geography is not enough. A planet is somehow insufficient. Even a universe is insufficient. An insatiable curiosity about a cosmos in continual decline, itself shadowed by an irrevocable doubt as to our limited, finite ability to apprehend the cosmos at all. This tension within the metaphysics of the Gothic is captured in "The Double Star" (*L'Étoile Double*), a difficult to categorize prose piece by Jane de la Vaudère, the pen name of French author Jeanne Scrive. At first, "The Double Star" appears to be much in the vein of the subgenre of the 19th century "cosmic dialogue," a trend within horror and science fiction in which disembodied and disoriented entities dispute the grand themes of chaos and cosmos — a strange combination of Platonic dialogue and speculative cosmology. Examples include Edgar Allan Poe's "The Conversation of Eiros and Charmion" (1839) and "The Colloquium of Monos and Una" (1841), as well as Camille Flammarion's collection *Stories of Infinity* (*Récits de l'Infini*, 1872). But it is "The Double Star" that takes up the idea of speculative cosmology in striking and deeply ambivalent ways.

Published in Vaudère's 1901 collection *La Mystérieuse*, "The Double Star" is, like many of Vaudère's short pieces, influenced by the Decadent movement's revival of occultism, as well as by late-century developments in physics and astronomy. Reading more like a cosmic dream vision than traditional narrative, "The Double Star" features a female protagonist — possibly the author herself — inexplicably finding herself in a strange and liminal state of existence ("I was not yet born, or, rather, I was already dead"). Her jeweled "body" seems composed of dragonfly wings infused with blue electricity, and she seems to be floating through endless space. Around her the familiar landscape of cities and forests has disappeared, and in its place are "masses of stone affecting a thousand different forms, mountains of iridescent crystal, violet and red waves seeming to fall from the sky to flow into abysms." Hallucinatory, tectonic formations seem to ebb and flow before her:

> The soil appeared to be composed of a thick coral dust dotted here and there with stones of onyx, sardonyx, chrysolite, girasol and turquoise. Huge, bizarrely indented walls, completely transparent, rose to implausible heights; some were of amethyst, others sapphire or topaz, without a stain or flaw, all of a piece. As for the celestial vault, it seemed to me to be as black as ink, immobile and as frightful as the vault of a sephulcher.[454]

Eventually, she encounters a guide, known only as "the Chimera," a stellar being composed of bioluminescent crystals, blood that mutates into impossibly shaped rubies, and a voice that is the harmony of the spheres itself. "Where am I?" she asks. "Very far from your tottering globe," the Chimera replies, "very far from your sad sun, which is dying slowly in the bosom of its cold planets … The Milky Way is collapsing around us like a cataract of suns, the stars streaming like rivers of light."[455]

The Chimera makes her an offer. A guided tour revealing the structure of the cosmos, in which the formation of planets and terrestrial existence is but a flicker. But in return, she will have to forever relinquish everything associated with terrestrial, human existence. The offer, at first, seems easy to accept. A dying sun, a rotting Earth, a declining world, the decadence of time. Nothing would seem to be more easily repudiated than the sorrowful and short-lived misery of terrestrial and especially human life. She considers the offer, repudiating humanity, the "abject race, which crawls everywhere," a scourge consuming itself, devouring the Earth, as a multitude of "cadavers void of sepulchers" weigh down a weary planet frozen in deep time.

And yet, tempting as it is, there is an undercurrent of melancholy in the Chimera's musical words. Sorrow never seems to leave even disembodied, stellar beings, revealed in one of the story's many poetic and prophetic soliloquies: "I am the Chimera with rapid wings, floating hair and a fiery gaze, I gallop through the labyrinths of the heavens, I soar over the worlds, I weep in the depths of solitudes, I cling to the clouds and raise oceans with my trailing tail."[456] In a moment of doubt, even the Chimera wonders: "Perhaps the stars suffer, like us." A certain sorrow persists, even in the farthest depths of the universe, as if the impersonal and opaque transformations of crystallization, irradiation, ossification, erosion, and the efflorescence of stellar decay serve as constant reminders of a transience that extends far beyond the reaches of limited terrestrial organisms burdened with consciousness.

In the story's strange and cataclysmic conclusion, the offer is reluctantly refused. A double refusal, for a double star. A repudiation both of this planet, but also of any other planet. A continuum of decay stretching across eons, accompanied by a melancholy that attains the proportions of cosmic decay. As the vision of "The Double Star" ends, a sorrow revealed to be stellar has also been revealed as merely earthly, the blind impulse of the living amid impersonal forces. All that remains are confused notions of resurrection and reincarnation, and the residue of the blind impulsion driving an impersonal planet.

4

MEDITATIONS ON THE WEIRD

Frozen Thought (Blackwood, Lovecraft). There are those moments when — before the breathable vista of the sea, desert, forest — there are those moments when "it" looks back at us, impersonally, impartially, indifferently. In Algernon Blackwood's story "The Willows," published in 1907, an unnamed narrator and his traveling companion — referred to only as "the Swede" — take a camping trip down the Danube River. At one point in the river, they enter a strange, eerie environment, covered everywhere by willows. It's nighttime, you're alone, you're in the middle of nowhere, and you're starting to get that strange, unsettling feeling that something just isn't right — you can see where this is going. The narrator, mesmerized by the slow swaying of the willows in the night wind, begins to wonder if he isn't in the presence of something unnaturally alive. Strange dreams and half-visions follow. All of this leads the narrator to distrust his senses:

> I saw it through a veil that hung before my eyes like the gauze drop-curtain used at the back of a theatre — hazily a

> little. It was neither a human figure nor an animal. To me it gave the strange impression of being as large as several animals grouped together … moving slowly. The Swede, too, got a similar result, though expressing it differently, for he thought it was shaped and sized like a clump of willow bushes, rounded at the top, and moving all over upon the surface — "coiling upon itself like smoke," he said afterwards.[457]

When these vague and alluring impressions become threatening, the unreliability of the senses turns into the incapacitation of the senses, rendering the narrator numb, unable to physically react to his surroundings:

> I gave one terrified glance, which just enabled me to see that the shadowy form was swinging towards us through the bushes, and then I collapsed backwards with a crash into the branches … I was conscious only of a sort of enveloping sensation of icy fear that plucked the nerves out of their fleshy covering, twisted them this way and that, and replaced them quivering.[458]

From here something further happens — or rather, nothing happens. There is no climactic confrontation with a monster, nothing lurching or crawling inside the willows, not even a man-in-a-monster-suit jumping out and giving his best cephalopod-like roar. There is nothing, that is, except thought. Indeed, Blackwood's story contains extended scenes that portray the absolute, icy stillness of everything, the only movement being the tenuous thoughts of the characters themselves. What are these thoughts? Quite simply, they are the thoughts of the unthinkable:

> "Now listen," he said, "The only thing for us to do is to go on as though nothing had happened, follow our usual habits, go to bed, and so forth; pretend we feel nothing and

> notice nothing. It is a question wholly of the mind, and the less we think about them the better our chance of escape. Above all, don't *think*, for what you think happens!"[459]

Aside from the Swede's inadvertent inversion of self-help rhetoric, what is interesting about "The Willows" is the way in which the focus shifts from a horror out there to the concept of horror itself. This is the moment of frozen thought, the enigmatic stillness of everything except the furtive, lurking revelation of a limit.

These moments of frozen thought are not uncommon in the genre of supernatural horror. Indeed, they become magnified in the early 20th-century development of the weird tale. In H.P. Lovecraft's 1936 novel *At the Mountains of Madness* (first published in the pulp magazine *Astounding Stories*), an expedition to the Antarctic reveals the massive, black ruins of a "cyclopean city," whose very existence throws human archaeological, geological, and biological knowledge into abeyance. In the depths of these darkly viscous and geometric ruins, the characters in the novel discover strange quasi-creatures that defy category and even description. At once formless and geometric, oozing with malefic intent and swarming with temporary eyes, these "Shoggoths" confront the explorers with their radically unhuman character:

> The shock of recognizing that monstrous slime and headlessness had frozen us into mute, motionless statues … It seemed aeons that we stood there, but actually it could not have been more than ten or fifteen seconds.[460]

In this frozen moment, the senses are useless, language falters, and thought becomes strangely equivalent to silence:

> I might as well be frank — even if I cannot bear to be quite direct — in stating what we saw; though at the time we felt that it was not to be admitted even to each other. The words reaching the reader can never even suggest the awfulness of

> the sight itself. It crippled our consciousness so completely that I wonder we had the residual sense to dim our torches as planned, and to strike the right tunnel toward the dead city.[461]

In a last, desperate attempt to comprehend their situation, Lovecraft's characters resort to what is essentially an apophatic language, the language of mysticism:

> We had expected, upon looking back, to see a terrible and incredibly moving entity if the mists were thin enough; but of that entity we had formed a clear idea. What we did see — for the mists were indeed all too malignly thinned — was something altogether different, and immeasurably more hideous and detestable. It was the utter, objective embodiment of the fantastic novelist's "thing that should not be."[462]

Lovecraft's stories abound with such revelations, expressed through the kind of melancholic, melodramatic, purple prose that has become a hallmark of the weird tale. At the same time, these revelations point to a minimalist limit that Lovecraft's characters can only negatively articulate: the beyond, the unnamable, the nameless thing, the thing on the doorstep, the lurker on the threshold, the whisperer in the darkness. Ironically, the characters can only attempt to describe what they see by reflexively referring to the genre in which they are unknowingly embedded.

In so far as stories like these are part of the horror genre, they present horror less as a stimulus-response system, in which a threat elicits an emotional response of fear, and more as a kind of freezing of all affect, resulting in a combined state of dread and fascination — what theologian Rudolf Otto once called the *mysterium tremendum*. In stories like these, horror is a state of frozen thought, reason's dark cyclopean winter.

*

The Logic of the Supernatural. In this state of frozen thought, the category of the "supernatural" plays a central role. However, the supernatural in this case is not the supernatural that is so often confirmed within the labyrinths of Scholastic theology. But neither is it the supernatural that is so frequently debunked by scientific rationality. In the horror genre the supernatural is duplicitous; it is the name for something that is indistinct and yet omnipresent, something that defies easy categorization and that is, nevertheless, inscribed by a kind of logic. That logic can be understood in several ways.

At one level, the supernatural can be understood as standing in an *either/or* relation to the natural. A character, inhabiting a world that they take for granted as a world obeying the laws of nature, may be confronted with an exceptional something that cannot be inscribed within this normative, natural order. What results is a wavering, an indecision: either this exceptional something can be rationally explained, and what seemed exceptional is really "the uncanny," or this exceptional something really is exceptional, and the existing natural and normative framework of reality must be reexamined, resulting the acceptance of "the marvelous." This wavering is what literary theorist Tzvetan Todorov has famously called "the fantastic."

At another level, the supernatural can be understood as existing immanently in relation to the natural. Here we do not have an ultimatum, not an either/or situation, but instead a *both/and* situation. If in the previous instance we have a theistic framework, here we have a pantheistic framework, in which the supernatural is revealed to coexist with the natural. While this flattens the hierarchy between natural and supernatural, it also remains committed to a minimal distinction between them — while the natural may be taken "as is," the supernatural is never manifest in itself, and is thus not always available to thought or the senses.

The question we can pose is whether there is another level, one in which the supernatural actually bears little or no relation to the natural, in which what is experienced by a human subject has no correlate in the world or in thought. This is a sentiment frequently expressed in Lovecraft's stories, and more broadly in the supernatural horror tradition. Here the supernatural functions via a double negation — a logic of *neither/nor*. Here the supernatural has no positive content; it neither stands in relation to the natural, nor is it an autonomous entity in itself.

In this last instance, the supernatural is a negative term. In tales of supernatural horror, the supernatural often exhibits this anti-empiricist tendency, in that it is not something that can be directly experienced or that is available to the senses. It also betrays an anti-idealist tendency, in that it is not something that can be inscribed within the ambit of thought — at least human thought. And yet the supernatural persists, in its being unavailable to the senses, and inaccessible to thought.

In short, the supernatural is less about any relation to the natural, normative world, and more about the very impossibility of that relation. And yet, as we've seen in our opening examples, this impossibility of the supernatural, this negative capacity, is at the same time manifest in the strange, unhuman catatonia of an impossible experience. The supernatural is another name for this enigmatic state of suspended animation — *frozen thought.*

*

Neither Fear nor Thought. In a sense, then, the genre of supernatural horror is really about what it would mean to think this frozen thought, the thought of the impossibility of thought. Understanding supernatural horror in this way requires that we read — or rather, misread — horror as a philosophical endeavor.

We can pause for a moment and remind ourselves of the orientation of this book. Certainly, horror and philosophy at first glance seem to be diametrically opposed to each other. Philosophy is highbrow, the stuff of academia, professors, and abstract ideas. Horror is lowbrow, the pulpy stuff of fan culture, gore, and scare tactics. Philosophy, with its principle of sufficient reason, seems to say that there is an order to the world and a way of knowing it; horror, by contrast, seems to bypass rational thought altogether in favor of the affective extremisms of fear, terror, and dread. But there are a set of deeper, more interesting relationships between philosophy and horror. And we are, arguably, in a moment now where both philosophy and horror are discovering a common limit, which is that between the human and the non-human world of which we are, at the same time, a part (though arguably a negligible part).

Genre horror is, generally speaking, inscribed within two philosophical paradigms. The first is a Kantian paradigm, one that involves the balanced interplay between the senses, the understanding, and reason. In Kant's model, while aesthetic experience is made possible by sensory apprehension, it is ultimately qualified by the understanding and reason. Even those anomalous moments in which the senses threaten to overwhelm reason, are, in the end, recuperated within reason's comprehension of its being overwhelmed. For instance, Kant's well-known distinction between the beautiful and the sublime rests on the problem of form and formlessness:

> The beautiful in nature is a question of the form of the object, and this consists in limitation, whereas the sublime is to be found in an object even devoid of form, so far as it immediately involves, or else by its presence provokes, a representation of *limitlessness*, yet with a super-added thought of its totality.[463]

We need not catalog the innumerable interpretations of the Kantian sublime. Suffice it to say that in the sublime there is an ambivalence at work, a tension between a supposedly well-formed subject and a formless, boundless object — a non-object, really. Kant describes an aesthetic relation to something that is, strangely, nothing. The consolation prize for us as subjects is that while we cannot fully comprehend this non-object, we can, at the very least, comprehend this incomprehension — we can think the failure of thought.

So fundamental is this ambivalence to Kant's philosophical project that he goes on to characterize the sublime as a "negative pleasure," in language not that far removed from Blackwood or Lovecraft:

> [T]he feeling of the sublime is a pleasure that only arises indirectly, being brought about by a feeling of a momentary check to the vital forces followed at once by a discharge all the more powerful ... the delight in the sublime does not so much involve positive pleasure as admiration or respect, i.e. merits the name of a negative pleasure.[464]

While the experience of the beautiful has a purpose, in that it establishes a certain harmony within the imagination, the sublime for Kant seems to have no purpose — except perhaps its own disintegration. In Kant's words, the sublime "does violence to the imagination; and yet it is judged to be only the more sublime."

But for Kant the real payoff of the sublime lies not in its excess or its capacity to overwhelm the subject, but in a final, recuperative move in which the very failure of the aesthetic is circumscribed by thought, and the subject able to minimally comprehend its own dissolution. What Kant has notoriously called "supersensible reason" effectively comes in to save the day. As he notes, "[t]he sublime is that, the mere capability of thinking which evidences a faculty of mind transcending every standard of sense."[465]

What exactly is the Kantian paradigm of horror? Horror is, as the story goes, a certain imbalance within this set of relations. Horror is the threat of the senses being overwhelmed, of something being sensed that is in excess of the sorting mechanism of the understanding, and the synthetic function of reason. Horror is a case of the sublime — even if, in Kant's version of the story, this excess, this being overwhelmed, is ultimately recuperated by reflexive, supersensible reason, and thereby domesticated within the confines of an internalized self correlating to an external world.

To be more direct, we might say that the Kantian paradigm of horror understands horror in terms of the emotion of fear. Horror is equivalent to fear. It goes without saying that today this has come to be the defining element of genre horror in the popular mindset. Filmmakers, authors, and scholars repeat it almost as a mantra: horror is fear.

This fear specific to horror encompasses a number of variations. One of them is the distinction between "terror" and "horror," famously encapsulated in Ann Radcliffe's 1826 article, "On the Supernatural in Poetry." The distinction between terror and horror is at once a temporal and a spatial distinction. In terror, there is the obscure apprehension of something malefic that is about to happen, whereas with horror there is a revulsion towards what has just happened.

This equation between horror and fear also encompasses the more existential distinction between "fear" and "dread," detailed in Kierkegaard's 1844 philosophical fiction, *The Concept of Dread*. In his famous analogy, when standing on a cliff before an abyss, we not only feel the fear of possibly falling to our death, but we also entertain the impulse to willingly dive into the abyss, as into something utterly unknown. At such moments one registers the distinction between that which has a distinct object of fear, and dread, or the "unfocused fear" before the looming abyss of uncertainty. Dread in this sense is linked to abandon, particularly the ambivalent self-abandon so often associated with mystical traditions. As Kierkegaard notes, "dread is the vertigo of freedom."

While both of these distinctions are interesting in themselves, horror continues to be understood as being equivalent to fear generally. The result is that this ends up defining horror within a Kantian paradigm, in which fear is situated in the relation between an experiencing, affected subject, and a nebulous object that is the source of fear for the subject.

However, Lovecraft provides us with a different story. In his 1927 essay *Supernatural Horror in Literature*, Lovecraft provides a list of qualities that he deems central to supernatural horror:

> The true weird tale has something more than secret murder, bloody bones, or a sheeted form clanking chains according

> to rule. A certain atmosphere of breathless and unexplainable dread of outer, unknown forces must be present; and there must be a hint, expressed with a seriousness and portentousness becoming its subject, of that most terrible conception of the human brain — a malign and particular suspension or defeat of those fixed laws of Nature which are our only safeguard against the assaults of chaos and the daemons of unplumbed space.[466]

Lovecraft was a staunch atheist, and yet his descriptions here and elsewhere in the essay also betray a sense of wonder, of the mysterious — even, dare we say, of a religious quality — but a religiousness in the absence of any God whatsoever.

Lovecraft's most concise definition comes in the opening pages of the essay. As he notes, "[t]he oldest and strongest emotion of mankind is fear, and oldest and strongest kind of fear is fear of the unknown."[467] Let us state Lovecraft's formula plainly: horror is the fear of the unknown.

Now, on the surface, it appears that Lovecraft is simply reiterating the Kantian paradigm of horror, where horror is equivalent to fear. But a more careful reading reveals something different, and that is a shift in this very phrase, "fear of the unknown." I would like to suggest that Lovecraft's insight is to have shifted the emphasis, from the "fear" part of that phrase, to the "unknown" part:

> The one test of the really weird is simply this — whether or not there be excited in the reader a profound sense of dread, and of contact with unknown spheres and powers; a subtle attitude of awed listening, as if for the beating of black wings or the scratching of outside shapes and entities on the known universe's utmost rim.[468]

One of the ideas that Lovecraft returns to again and again is this notion of the unknown, in which horror is less defined by emotion, and more by thought — or to be more precise, the limit of thought. And this is where Lovecraft departs, perhaps, from Kant. For, while both are concerned with the limits of thought, Lovecraft does not maintain the same faith in "supersensible reason" that we see in Kant. Perhaps we can paraphrase their differences by saying that, while Kant is concerned with the limit *of* thought, Lovecraft is concerned with limit *as* thought. The horror is not that there is a limit to thought; that is simply a regulatory gesture, a relative problem, a case of boundary management. Rather, the horror is that thought — all thought, since for Lovecraft everything is absolute — all thought is paradoxically constituted as limit, a strange but perhaps enchanting abyss at the core of thought itself.

For writers in the weird fiction tradition such as Lovecraft, the thought that comes to define horror is a concept with no content, an unknown in which thought itself falters. For example, in Lovecraft's 1936 story "The Shadow Out of Time," the narrator, following a sudden collapse and comatose state, describes being beset by "vague and frightful speculations." Strange dream images form in his mind, of "a ghastly, fungoid pallor," and "great shapeless suggestions of shadow." Eventually he is forced to confront the possibility that his dreams are not just dreams. A strange lucidity follows:

> I looked for an instant, then almost collapsed. Clenching my teeth, however, I kept silence. I sank wholly to the floor and put a hand to my forehead amidst the engulfing blackness. What I dreaded and expected was there. Either I was dreaming, or time and space had become a mockery.[469]

In such instances, horror is not an overwhelming feeling, but the emptiness of thought. Horror is not the overflowing continuum of experience, but the vacuity of any correlation between subject and object, between self and world.

*

Neither Life nor Death. In addition to the Kantian paradigm (where horror is equivalent to fear), there is a second paradigm, a Heideggerian one, in which fear is qualified in its relation to death. Again, this is not the place to provide a summary of Heidegger's *Being and Time*, nor to elaborate on the various esoteric schools of Heideggerian, hermeneutic, and phenomenological thought that flow from that work. Instead, we can simply highlight the role that death plays in Heidegger's writings, using that to characterize another aspect of genre horror.

We saw that in the Kantian paradigm, horror was broadly equivalent to an emotional state, that of fear. But this is an incomplete picture. Horror is not simply equal to fear, for fear is always prepositional, always "fear of." Horror is fear, yes, but fear of what? Fear of the loss of individuality, fear of the loss of individuation, fear of the loss of control, fear of fate, accident, or superstition, and above all, fear of death — especially one's own death. Again, as the story goes, horror is not just about fear, but is ultimately about the fear of death.

For Heidegger, however, not all death is equal. There is "perishing" (*Verenden*), or the physical, biological death of the living being, and then there is "demise" (*Ableben*), which might include the set of rituals and practices surrounding death that are part of human cultures. Death (with a capital "D"; *Tod*) grounds both perishing and demise, precisely because it is never present to us in itself, and cannot be the concrete object of any experience. As human beings, thrown into the world, Being is always being-there (*Da-sein*); hence what we experience is only this partial being-in-the-world, even though we may speculate on Being in general. But the dream of a complete, unified, and coherent picture of the world constantly eludes us. As beings-in-the-world, we are also beings-in-time, inscribed within the flux and flow of temporality, what Aristotle termed coming-to-be and passing-away. From one perspective, Death seems to be promise and fulfillment, but of course one never experiences one's own Death. We may witness the perishing of another living being, and we may feel for the demise of another, but in each case Death remains an enigma, at once negation and affirmation, the abyss of non-existence and the culmination of our being.

The human being, thrown into the world, inscribed within temporality, struggles to comprehend the world — *Dasein* struggles to comprehend something that is by definition incomplete. For Heidegger, Death *is* this incompletion. In his formulation, Death is one's "ownmost" (individuated towards the human subject), it is "non-relational" (it cannot be shared), and it is "not to be outstripped" (it is both inevitable and also indeterminate). With Heidegger, as with Kant, there is a consolation prize for the failure of the human to fully comprehend the world. We may not experience Death directly, but we can experience this failure. Death shifts from being thought of as standing in contrast to life (either as opposed to life or as signaling the end of life), to being immanent in life itself. In this sense Death determines our life, and because of this, we care. For the being that has realized this (and this of course means human beings for Heidegger), Death opens onto the "call of conscience" and the concern with "authenticity." Heidegger famously calls this attitude "Being-towards-Death" (*Sein-zum-Tode*).

It goes without saying that the horror genre is replete with instances of Death in Heidegger's sense. But it often cloaks these in the guise of "perishing" or "demise." Behind all the explicit focus in the horror genre on fear, fright, and terror, there is also the implicit and more general concern with death in this existential sense. In the Heideggerian paradigm, horror would not be defined by fear but by death, in so far as horror is centrally concerned with the problem of Being, beings, and the lives of beings. And, in this Heideggerian paradigm, there is a therapeutic function to philosophy as well. Death reveals the possibility of specifically human life as authentic and as existentially meaningful. Death makes possible the human concerns of salvation, redemption, remembrance. Indeed, it would not be going too far to say that there is a kind of humanism that runs through the horror genre. This is the existential aspect of genre horror — Life conditioned by Death, human beings conditioned by Being in general, our ontical "being-in-the-world" conditioned by an anxious Being-towards-Death, the value of human finitude in its factical being, its singularity, its "being-there."

Here again Lovecraft and the writers in the weird fiction tradition offer a different perspective. For Lovecraft, horror is defined precisely by having no truth to tell vis-à-vis humanity — except this non-truth. For Lovecraft, one does not leave a tale of supernatural horror feeling better, or, for that matter, feeling anything at all. There is no truth to horror, in the sense that one ultimately discovers a state of "being-there" that is the exclusive provenance of human beings and their capacity to seek out authentic lives. There is no heroism of human resilience and survival, no sequels and spin-offs (though the plethora of tales in the "Cthulhu mythos" would seem to suggest otherwise). If anything, supernatural horror is, for Lovecraft, defined by an anti-humanism, one that questions the apparatus in which we as human beings grant ourselves privileged points of access to the world in itself. It is a sentiment best reflected in Lovecraft's correspondence. In a letter to Farnsworth Wright, editor at the time of *Weird Tales*, Lovecraft makes the case for the anti-humanism of his stories:

> Now all my tales are based on the fundamental premise that common human laws and interests are emotions that have no validity or significance in the vast cosmos-at-large … but when we cross the line to the boundless and hideous unknown — the shadow-haunted *Outside* — we must remember to leave our humanity and terrestrialism at the threshold.[470]

Elsewhere Lovecraft refers to this disposition as "cosmic horror." Cosmic horror positions itself against anthropomorphism — the world regarded in the mythopoetic shape of the human, the personification of the world as a human world, the world as comprehended precisely because it is in a form that we recognize.

Anthropomorphism is therefore defined within the contours of the quasi-human, either through personification or in the guise of humanlike entities, from animals to robots.

Cosmic horror also positions itself against anthropocentrism — the world as instrumentally made for the human, the world as a world for human use and benefit. Anthropocentrism demands something more than the quasi-human, something more than mere semblance. The limit of anthropocentrism is the nonhuman, a broad domain that includes objects, assemblages, and things, as well as the hierarchy of the animate and inanimate, of higher and lower orders of being, the world of plants and animals.

It would seem that this would leave one option open, that of a general antagonism against the human, a position typically regarded as misanthropic. In the *mis-anthropos*, the human is regarded as an accident, an error, or as generally insignificant, leaving only a residue that is simply not-human, or better, unhuman.

Many tales of supernatural horror not only turn against the human, but they invert anthropomorphism and anthropocentrism, resulting in the misanthropic vision of a malefic and malevolent world. But even this is, in many ways, the ultimate anthropic conceit — the world is against us, but at least it cares enough to take notice. But for authors like Lovecraft supernatural horror must move beyond even this misanthropism, into the blank horror of the unhuman, into a region we can only call *indifference*, or what Lovecraft himself once referred to as "indifferentism":

> Contrary to what you may assume, I am not a *pessimist* but an *indifferentist* — that is, I don't make the mistake of thinking that the resultant of the natural forces surrounding and governing organic life will have any connexion with the wishes or tastes of any part of that organic life-process. Pessimists are just as illogical as optimists … both schools retain in a vestigial way the primitive concept of a conscious teleology — of a cosmos which gives a damn one way or the other … [the indifferentist] simply knows that this quality

> has nothing to do with the case; that the interplay of forces which govern climate, behavior, biological growth and decay, and so on, is too purely universal, cosmic, and eternal a phenomenon to have any relationship to the immediate wishing-phenomena of one minute organic species on our transient and insignificant planet ... The real philosopher knows that, *other* evidence being equal, favourableness or unfavourableness to mankind means absolutely nothing as an index of likelihood...[471]

In spite of what we may think, Lovecraft's rather awkward term "indifferentism" does not so much indicate a personal predilection towards apathy, boredom, or a general grumpiness. Instead, Lovecraft proposes a diffuse, enigmatic antagonism, an anti-humanism that attempts to dismantle the anthropic schema: anthropomorphism, anthropocentrism, and misanthropy.

Here, the world is neither anthropic nor misanthropic, but simply indifferent, an indifference registered by the human in the utter apophatic blackness of incomprehensibility.

*

Black Illumination. This brings us to what is perhaps the real issue, and that is the religious and mystical elements that course through supernatural horror. Lovecraft's shift out of the Kantian and Heideggerian paradigms of horror — that is, from fear to the unknown, from the human to the unhuman — cannot really be appreciated without taking into account the implicit indebtedness of supernatural horror to mystical traditions.

While Lovecraft was a self-described atheist, it is also important to note that much of what is referred to as "mysticism" in the medieval Christian tradition actually ran counter to orthodox Church doctrine. The so-called "negative theology" tradition is a case in point. In the early 6th century, the enigmatic figure Dionysius the Areopagite outlined a distinction between those mystical theologies that drew upon a notion of the divine as fully present ("kataphatic" or positive theologies), and those that relied on a notion of the divine as shadowy, dark, and absent ("apophatic" or negative theologies). But as Dionysius takes care to note, the divine is "dark" or "shadowy" not because it is lacking anything, but because it is superlatively beyond human comprehension. The most one can take away from this enigmatic thought is a negative knowledge, the thought of the limit of thought — or to use Lovecraft's phrase, the thought of the "inability of the mind to correlate all its contents."

This logic would be taken further in the tradition of "darkness mysticism," in which the divine is thought through motifs of negation — the desert in Meister Eckhart, the abyss in Jan van Ruusbroec, sickness and decay in Julian of Norwich, the tomb in Angela of Foligno, darkness in John of the Cross, silence in Angelus Silesius, and the motifs of obfuscation in *The Cloud of Unknowing*. Such texts lead not to total comprehension of the divine, but instead to a strange thought that devolves around what Dionysius calls "a negation beyond every assertion," and what Eckhart refers to simply as "the nothingness of God." Such a knowledge is referred to by Dionysius as "unknowing."

If supernatural horror is indeed driven by this mystical core, then the kind of thinking that takes place in its narratives would have to be akin to the "unknowing" of the apophatic tradition. But supernatural horror is not simply a secular affirmation of religious faith. Emphasizing as it does the indifference of the cosmos, supernatural horror also takes place in a godless world, a world that has given us both Nietzsche's "death of God" and the return of religious fanaticisms of all types. Disavowing science and the secular, supernatural horror seems to point to a limit in which there is only the negative without any positive — what Schopenhauer called the *nihil negativum*, or "negative nothingness." In so far as supernatural horror is mystical, it would have to be of a mysticism without religion, a mysticism without God.

What, then, are we left with? Perhaps what we're left with is something at once philosophical and and non-philosophical; the thought of the limit of all thought; the thought of the impossibility of thought. It is distinct from thought as reflection — that is, from Descartes's notion of thought as a subject correlated to an object. It is also distinct from thought as access — that is, from Kant's notion of thought as the synthetic tethering of reason, understanding, and sensibility, within an enclosed dyad of self and world. It is, finally, distinct from thought as equivalence — that is, from the Hegelian notion of thought as a continuum between self and world, an equivalence between thought and reality, the rational and the real.

Within this "frozen thought" we see something different, something on the order of deep time and the scale of the unhuman. Perhaps within frozen thought what we really discover is what we might call a *black illumination*. Black illumination is a degree zero of thought, inaccessible to the senses, unintelligible for thought, impossible to experience — all that is left is the residue of frozen thought, an enigmatic epiphany. The black illumination is the *reductio ad absurdum* of philosophy. In black illumination, thought does not exist, but instead subsists, persists, and resists. In black illumination, all experience leads to the impossibility of experience, from the fullness of fear to thought emptied of all human content.

We can state it plainly: supernatural horror takes up a set of concerns that have traditionally been the provenance of mysticism and religion. But supernatural horror also operates in a secular, scientific, and skeptical world, one that questions the ability of human beings to know anything at all. In so doing, supernatural horror also resurrects the most basic problems of philosophy, working against both the Kantian and Heideggerian paradigms, in which the truth of horror is given meaning in fear or in death. Instead, we see a shift from the human-centric concern of human passion and the anxiety towards death, to a strange, unhuman thought beyond even misanthropy.

If we can accept this, then this allows us to regard supernatural horror beyond genre and more as a mode of thought. It is even possible to construct a history of supernatural horror along these lines. For each period in Western culture, there is a corresponding principle that structures the way horror is manifest as an index of the unknown and the nonhuman.

For instance, we could say that, for the Middle Ages, the governing principle is that of *showing/hiding*, expressed in diverse examples such as textual accounts of mystical itineraries, the medieval bestiary, or the treatise on demonology. In each case what is at stake is how something can appear that is in itself not anything. How does the divine or demonic manifest its presence, not being itself substantial?

Likewise, for the Enlightenment, the governing principle is that of *knowing/believing* (or alternately, reason/faith). Here the phenomenon of appearance is less important than the cognitive apparatus for producing knowledge from those appearances. Its exemplars that of the Gothic novel, the poetry of the Graveyard School, through to the 19th-century *frénétique* school and the *fin-de-siècle* literature of Decadence. In these examples the presence or absence of the object of horror is secondary to the possibility or impossibility of knowing "what" it is at all.

In the modern period, a host of changes in science, technology, and industry provoke a further shift, and here the governing principle is more existential, that of *thinking/being*. It leads to a double bind that is characteristic of the paradoxical nature of the horror genre itself: either some "nameless thing" that exists, but which cannot be thought, or some fantastical being that is thought but that cannot exist (at least according to existing laws of nature). The weird tale, the psychic detective subgenre, and the hybridity of "sci-fi/horror" all provide examples in which this thinking/being dichotomy is expressed.

And our own era? It is likely too soon to name it, though this has not prevented critics and scholars from posing questions about a postmodern or posthuman era in which all boundaries are dissolved, where a fluctuating surface of relativistic differences proliferates against the nonhuman backdrop of climate, planet, and cosmos. Perhaps the governing principle is a more fundamental one that stretches back to questions posed by presocratic thinkers like Heraclitus, Democritus, and Parmenides: is there some unifying principle to everything or is there simply the arbitrary existence of what exists? In spite of our persistent attempts to produce theories-of-everything, something always escapes. Thus, the governing principle is that of *one/none*; the view that there is something underlying everything, versus the view that there is always something that escapes everything. Genres blend, theory becomes fiction, fiction is speculative, and what the cold rationalism of the sciences tells us is more "horrific" than any tale of Lovecraft or Poe. Our own era is one haunted by the shadow of futurity, precisely because there is no future.

But this is not just about the horror genre; it is also a reflection on philosophy, and what happens when the two intersect. Philosophy's explanatory function is tripped up, as is its obligation to be therapeutic. The moment one undertakes anything like a "philosophy of horror," horror tends to engulf philosophy. Rather than a philosophy of horror, in which philosophy would explain or give meaning to horror (the "philosophy of X" approach), horror turns back onto philosophy, revealing, among other things, a strange, apophatic flickering within philosophy itself. In supernatural horror, philosophy does not enter the scene in order to explain or even to describe the nature of things, much less to give it truth or meaning. Horror uncoils, unwinds, and "bites back," challenging philosophy's most basic presuppositions — the principle of noncontradiction, the principle of sufficient reason, the principle of sufficient philosophy itself. Horror reveals what François Laruelle calls "the philosophical decision," that flickering that both makes philosophy possible and that is excised from philosophical activity itself so that it may continue unabated. In this sense, the genre of supernatural horror is an attempt to think the unhuman, via a philosophical core of the impossibility of all thought. In supernatural horror, the philosophy of horror is exhumed, turned inside out, revealing a non-philosophy of horror, or better, the horror of philosophy.

*

Dark Media, Darker Matters. A glimpse into the beyond. A portal into another dimension. Ominous messages sent from other spheres. A connection beyond "connection" in the mundane and secular sense of the term — a *real* connection. A fragile picture of the world dissipating behind dimly intuited ciphers. Within the horror genre, such ambivalent revelations are often conveyed through technology, where media are presented as functioning in unusual, supernatural, or "possessed" ways. A blasphemous book is discovered, its unholy incantations uttered, and something responds to the call. A house built upon an ancient gravesite becomes a gateway for the dead. A camera takes pictures not just of what we see, but of what we cannot see, and which is there all the time, watching us. A website livestreams furtive, shadowy figures from some other dimension — and they are leaking through into our own. Deeply rooted, perhaps primordial intuitions are revealed via the most modern of technologies. A strange situation emerges: The ability to mediate between a world here-and-now, and a world that remains enigmatically inaccessible to us without the use of media.

Our modern, Western ideas of media are largely influenced by cybernetics and information theory.[472] In the classical model of communications theory, a sender and receiver are connected by a channel, which serves as the conduit for an informational message passing between them. The channel both connects and separates two points that are physically, geographically, or otherwise separated. Even though there may be "noise" along the communications channel, the aim of the mediation is to provide as seamless and as transparent a connection as possible, as if sender and receiver were physically copresent. In a sense, this type of thinking puts into a formal language what we so often take for granted — that a medium is some device or gadget 'X' that connects two separate points 'A' and 'B.' What was previously inaccessible — due to the contingencies of space or time — is rendered accessible, and what was absent is now present.

What happens when media cease to mediate — at least in this conventional sense? In 19th century Paris, for instance, we find numerous instances of science and superstition intersecting in unusual and innovative media technologies, from spirit photography to magic lanterns to phantasmagoria. In America, the popularity of the Spiritualist movement not only demonstrated the expanded notion of media — the human being as a spiritual "medium" — but also suggested an approach to media that might connect us to the afterlife or the great beyond. While easily dismissed, such activities were expanded in quasi-scientific research initiatives in Britain, such as those promoted by the Society for Psychical Research and The Ghost Club. Adopting a decidedly scientific, empirical mindset, many of the reports produced by the Society for Psychical Research (which counted among its members Arthur Conan Doyle, Henri Bergson, and William James) involved the use of then-emerging technologies to examine everything from haunted houses, to spiritual séances, to psychic powers, to early versions of "ghost hunting."

Given this, what should we make of the many modern-day examples — from horror film to reality TV shows — of digital cameras used to document the existence of ghosts, or digital audio to record the voices of the dead, or the use of sensors and other digital devices to confirm hauntings? There is, certainly, a degree of irony at play, as if harkening back to the wonderfully serious days of the Society for Psychical Research. More likely, we are prone to dismiss such uses of media as gimmick or entertainment; if anything, what is proven is the ability of digital media to produce the very phenomena they are purporting to reveal (and perhaps in a way this is all we ask of media). At the same time, there is a kind of pleasure in imagining such innocuous media — phones, computers, TVs — behaving in strange and unorthodox ways. Nowhere is this dual skepticism and fascination more apparent than in the horror genre. From *Poltergeist* to *Paranormal Activity*, there are innumerable examples of horror stories that involve the use of media to make contact with the supernatural. The same can be said of contemporary Japanese horror, where films such as *Ringu* and *Pulse* gives us video tapes, web cams, digital cameras, mobile phones, and the Internet itself behaving in such ways that they provide a connection to what author H.P. Lovecraft once referred to as "cosmic outsideness."

Perhaps we can refer to such situations as those involving "dark media."[473] Dark media involve the mediation of that which is unavailable or inaccessible to us as human beings, and thus that about which we are ultimately "in the dark." Dark media make possible that dim intuition of there being a "something there" which, at precisely that moment, recedes beyond the horizon of intelligibility. In this metaphysical play between what we assume exists and what should not exist, a presence reveals itself in absence — or an absence reveals itself as presence. The white noise on the TV seems to form vague figures, emitting strange signals — but the signals are unintelligible, the shapes unrecognizable. A video tape shows weird shapes that seem to come through the screen, which vanish as strangely as they appeared — though the images remain, hovering in the shadows on the wall, burned into the retina of the eye. In a sense, dark media also suggest to us the ways in which *all* mediation harbors within itself this blind spot, the minimal distance that persists in any instance of mediation, however successful or seamless it may be. Dark media inhabit this twofold movement — seeing something in nothing (e.g., the animate images appearing on the screen or the alchemical glass), and finding nothing in each something (the paradoxical absence or presence of the "demon" within each body).

That such horror stories have emerged when they did is perhaps no accident. The Industrial Revolution, theories of Darwinian evolution, rumors of the entropic heat death of the sun, along with the waning of traditional institutional Christianity, all make for a cultural context in which the secular all too easily slips into the post-secular. No longer is there a great beyond, be it in the topographies of the afterlife or the cosmic cycles of reincarnation. Instead, the supernatural is embedded in the world here and now, manifest via an immediacy that, at the same time, withdraws itself. The function of media is no longer to render the inaccessible accessible, or to connect what is separated. Instead, media reveal inaccessibility in and of itself — they make accessible the inaccessible, but in its inaccessibility. To reveal the manifestation of that which does not exist — this is not simply a matter of visualization, computing, or the design of virtual worlds. It is about the twofold possibility and impossibility of mediation itself. *This is a religious impulse.*

William James — philosopher, psychologist, and psychical researcher — once noted the strange status of "objects of belief" in mystical accounts. They neither adhere to the philosophical framework of intuitions given over to the understanding and reason, nor are they arbitrary utterances of madness or unreason. The accounts of mystics such as Tersea of Avila or John of the Cross are at once empirical and anti-empirical, rational and nonrational, rooted in the body and senses, and yet constantly transcending them through the possibilities and limitations of language itself. James calls this "the reality of the unseen." As he notes, "It is as if there were in the human consciousness a *sense of reality, a feeling of objective presence, a perception* of what we may call 'something there,' more deep and more general than any of the special and particular 'senses' by which the current psychology supposes existent realities to be originally revealed."[474]

Whether it be the strange optical device described in Lovecraft's "From Beyond," or the cursed videotape in *Ringu*, dark media are much more than media technologies that aren't working properly. If anything, the reverse is the case: dark media are working *too well*, operating at a level beyond the consensual hallucination we regularly accept as reality. At the same time, they remain media in their basic functionality (a camera that takes pictures, a phone that makes calls), but now this functionality has been enhanced beyond the physical to the metaphysical. A camera still takes pictures — but now it photographs the uncanny presence of ghosts and specters. A telephone still makes calls — but now they are calls to the undead, themselves drifting in a remoteness suddenly brought uncomfortably close. The classical model of communications presumed two interlocutors, separated within a single reality. With dark media something else is happening: *the "communication" between two realities*, one with which we are familiar, and the other which always remains just beyond the horizon of our comprehension. Dark media are examples of the standard communications model rendered supernatural. Modern horror films such as Kiyoshi Kurosawa's *Pulse* (2001) demonstrate this shift with an eerie, slow patience — the computer screen becomes a portal to the domain of the dead, drawing in viewers to the "other side" of the screen, as the shadowy and misshapen figures on the other side slowly seep through into the world of the living. Eventually these boundary transgressions render the difference between the two sides of the screen irrelevant, as life-in-death and death-in-life become one in the same.

And yet, the physical always subtends — and sometimes subverts — the metaphysical. Many of the examples of dark media we've mentioned involve the representation of such media within the frame of the narrative itself. When author Koji Suzuki published his novel *Ringu* in 1991, the use of videotapes was still prevalent, and the idea of an innocuous media object such as a video tape being "haunted" had a unique effect, due in part to the very ubiquity of that object. This is perhaps why the film adaptation of *Ringu*, released in 1998, was so popular. While Suzuki described a videotape within the frame of a novel, the *Ringu* film, in taking advantage of film as a visual medium, could suggest something further: there is a cursed video tape — and you are watching it now. This is a shift, from the media in the film, to the film as medium — as spiritual medium — itself. Films in the J-horror tradition — including *Ringu*, *Pulse*, and *Noroi: The Curse* — are films that self-reflexively play on the collapsing between media in the film and film as media. Kōji Shiraishi, director of *Noroi: The Curse* (2005), combines techniques from documentary, reality TV, and found footage films to create layers upon layers of mediation, as our mundane sense of an objective reality gradually slips away — much like the supernatural phenomena his characters are investigating. Kurosawa's *Pulse* utilizes simple but effective techniques to suggest something similar, as the film cuts from a shot of a computer screen, framed by the computer monitor (itself within the film frame), to a shot of the screen itself, without computer monitor, as if we are directly accessing whatever nefarious shapes hover on the other side.

This collapsing effect allows the "horror" of such stories to bleed through the confines of a particular medium (a book, a radio broadcast, a film, a video, a website), such that the material vehicle or medium of the story becomes the story itself. In one sense, dark media elevate the communications diagram to the metaphysical — the communication between two realities, rather than the communication between two points in a single reality. At the same time, dark media also descend into the materiality of the medium itself, prompting us to suddenly become aware of the actual TV, laptop, or phone we're using. It's as if the matter of the medium itself becomes imbued with strange and occult properties, somehow alive and impossibly animated by forces we can only guess at. The cursed video tape, the haunted screen, that last streaming video you feel that maybe you shouldn't have watched. A different kind of horror story emerges, one based more on the format of the "dossier" than traditional, linear narrative. We have been presented with a series of documents — texts, reports, interviews, video footage, audio clips, and so on — all of which seems to intimate deep and unsettling truths of the cosmos, and the significance of human beings within it.

This idea is prevalent in contemporary examples of "analog horror," many of which reference old or outdated media, with all of their low-fi aesthetics and imperfections, lending an eeriness of the obscure that is particular to dead media. These in turn lead us back to a wide range of horror films produced in the 1980s and 1990s — from *UFO Abduction* (1989) to *The Blair Witch Project* (1999) — which made use of both handheld cameras and a found footage aesthetic to heighten the sense of reality. The self-reflexive aspect of such films extends to the film itself, as if we the viewers are privy to some secret piece of evidence of the supernatural that has, until now, been shrouded in secrecy. This use of media as "evidence" gives such horror stories a forensic quality: the unsolved mystery, the unexplained phenomena, the conspiracy and cover-up. A decade prior to this, a number of horror films likewise presented themselves as "documentaries," from Italian director Ruggero Deodato's still-unsettling *Cannibal Holocaust* (1980) to the equally notorious *Faces of Death* series (1978–1981) — the third, never-released installment of which is shrouded in rumor and conspiracy even to this day. Perhaps examples like these point all the way back to the origins of the modern horror genre itself, and the way in which horror has always made use of its medium, often in self-reflexive and material ways. The use of letters and the diary in Mary Shelley's *Frankenstein* (1818), the scientific report in Robert Louis Stevenson's *The Strange Case of Dr. Jekyll and Mr. Hyde* (1886), and the use of nearly everything in Bram Stoker's *Dracula* (1897), including letters, journals, reports, newspaper articles, and even a phonograph diary. Little wonder, then, that a later generation of weird fiction authors, including Lovecraft, would insert news reports and scientific articles into their stories (techniques employed in late-20th century horror novels such as Stephen King's *Carrie* and Jay Anson's *The Amityville Horror*).

While not all horror stories make use of media in these ways, these examples of dark media illustrate the ways that the horror genre raises questions that are at once philosophical and religious questions — questions of both science and the sacred, the human and something unnamable at the threshold of human comprehension. Do scientific discoveries concerning the enigmas of dark matter compel us to revisit the intuitions of Renaissance alchemists and occult philosophers? Is there a secret affiliation between the weird physics of black holes and the weird fictions of authors such as Lovecraft or Junji Ito? The supernatural horror tradition presents us with extraordinary phenomena within ordinary contexts, phenomena that are experienced, but in their being experienced, remain at the threshold of our understanding. They are phenomena within which we hover between philosophical skepticism and religious resignation. Such instances of dark media present media as having this dual nature of skepticism and belief, ghosts and the machine, the engineer's ratiocination and the mystic's laughter.

*

In Praise of Shadows. Shadows and darkness pervade the most innocuous, everyday objects — a wooden table, a ceramic bowl, a candle, an obscure corner of a room. Sitting at a restaurant in Kyoto, the novelist Jun'ichirō Tanizaki writes:

> The rooms at the Waranjiya are about nine feet square, the size of a comfortable little tearoom, and the alcove pillars and ceilings glow with a faint smoky luster, dark even in the light of the lamp. But in the still dimmer light of the candlestand, as I gazed at the trays and bowls standing in the shadows cast by that flickering point of flame, I discovered in the gloss of this lacquerware a depth and richness like that of a still, dark pond, a beauty I had not before seen.[475]

The bowls and cups, otherwise purely functional objects, suddenly reveal a black and infinite depth that seems to defy the laws of physics. It prompts Tanizaki to think about a world lived by this "darkness seen by candlelight," a world at once readily familiar and yet completely unfathomable: "It must have been simple for specters to appear in a 'visible darkness' where always something seemed to be flickering and shimmering, a darkness that on occasion held greater terrors than darkness out-of-doors."[476]

Such visible darkness is the subject of the short story "Light and Shadows" (1896), by the Russian poet and novelist Fyodor Sologub. It involves a young boy, Volodya and his growing fascination with shadows. It begins, at first, as a harmless children's game, when Volodya discovers a booklet containing instructions for making different types of hand shadows cast on the wall from a light source. Becoming more obsessed with the booklet, Volodya begins to make more shadows with different objects around his desk. He begins to notice shadows everywhere, in his home, at school, on the buildings and street outside. He becomes intrigued by the interplay of light and shadow, how shadow is produced by light and how shadow also negates light. He sees the sun merely as a light source for creating shadows in the daytime. And each night, unable to sleep, he begins his own shadow-play: "These shadowy outlines were becoming near and dear to him. They were not mute — they talked, and Volodya understood their babbling language."[477]

Eventually Volodya's schoolwork suffers, as does his health, and his mother, reprimanding him, takes away the booklet. Volodya finds himself thinking of nothing but shadows, finding them alluring and ominous. At once weary of and fascinated by them, the shadows seem to take on a life on their own:

> But the shadows kept haunting him. Even though he didn't summon them with hand-shapes, even though he didn't heap up object upon object so they would make a shadow on the wall, the shadows themselves clustered around him, importunate and insistent ... Shadows all around everywhere — sharply defined ones from lights, dim ones from the dissipated light of day — they all crowded around Volodya, falling across one another, enveloping him in an indissoluble web.[478]

A few nights later, unable to sleep herself, Volodya's mother is found making hand shadows against the parlor wall. "In the dreary moments of morning she searches her soul and thinks back on her life, and she sees that it has been empty, unnecessary, aimless. Nothing more than shadows senselessly flitting by and fading into thickening twilight."[479] In the final scenes of the story both Volodya and his mother are seen casting hand shadows in the night, the rooms of their home lit only by a single lamp, "their joy is hopelessly sorrowful, their sorrow wildly joyful."[480]

In Sologub's story shadow exists in an ambiguous interplay with light, at once that which nourishes but also that which devours.

But in Thomas Ligotti's story "The Shadow, the Darkness" (1999) a different shadow is offered to us. The story centers around an art exhibit by Reiner Grossvogel, a loquacious, sickly aesthete recently released from the local hospital. At the opening of the exhibit Grossvogel gives a speech to preface his new sculptures:

> "It is all so very, very simple," the artist continued. "Our bodies are but one manifestation of the energy, the *activating force* that sets in motion all the objects, all the bodies of this world and enables them to exist as they do. This activating force is something like a shadow that is not only the outside of all the bodies of this world but is *inside* of everything and thoroughly pervades everything — an all-moving darkness that has no substance in itself but that moves all the objects of this world, including those objects which we call our bodies..."[481]

Grossvogel then details how, after his hospital episode, he was able to "see" this darkness, this "pervasive shadow" as it subsisted in the world, in each object. And what he sees is not comforting. In itself the shadow of which Grossvogel speaks is insubstantial — it is, literally "no thing." But the shadow is also everywhere, coursing through everything that exists. Grossvogel's realization is a stark one: "Everywhere I travelled I saw how the pervasive shadow, the all-moving darkness, was *using our world*."[482] Not only can Grossvogel sense the shadow, but he is capable of giving it shape in his art. The description of the sculptures in Ligotti's inimitable, hallucinatory prose is vague and grotesque. An object at once formless and composed of many forms; a glossy black surface beneath which seemed to swirl other dark shapes; forms suggestive of a creature such as scorpion or crab, and the uncanny suggestion of Grossvogel's body itself.

Near the end of the story, a select group of viewers are taken to a site-specific installation, an entire town that seems to exude shadow. Eventually the viewers realize that "the shadow" is emerging from within the site itself: "...what we were now seeing was not a darkness descending from far skies but a shadow which was arising from within the dead town around us, as if a torrent of black blood had begun roaring through its pale body."[483] It engulfs the entire site, including the spectators — now unwitting participants. The shape of everything turns "crooked and crabbed, reaching out toward them as if with claws and rising up like strange peaks and horns into the sky, no longer pale and gray but swirling with the pervasive shadow, the all-moving darkness that they could finally see so perfectly because now they were seeing with their bodies, only with their bodies pitched into a great black plain."[484]

Sologub's story imagines shadow existing in some kind of obscure, secret alliance with light, such that shadow can exist even in the middle of the day. By contrast, Ligotti's story imagines shadow without light, shadow as primordial as that in Sologub's story, but also metaphysical, as if a kind of dark matter exuding from every apparently substantial, existing thing. These are perversions of Plato's cave, where every light — even the sun outside — exists in order to produce shadows. The shadows become strange things, at once substantial and insubstantial, strange non-entities at the borderland where matter meets its opposite. In his study *A Short History of the Shadow*, art historian Victor Stoichita notes this strange status of the shadow in modern culture, where the shadow seems to exist of its own accord, with its own mysterious logic and agenda, the shadow as double, as other, as an inner state externalized in the world — "the shadow as an expression of autonomous power."[485] Tethered to light and yet seeming to pull away from it, "[t]he shadow is simultaneously presented as an emanation, a distortion and a projection onto the inner screen of [the] psyche."[486]

Shadows pervade the most innocuous and everyday of situations. Occasionally we have the opportunity to reflect on these moments. When it is night and I am in a well-lit room, I turn off the lights and, for a moment, it is pitch black. Even though this is a familiar room, and I know that to my right there is a desk, to the left a wall, and so on, for a brief moment everything — every thing

— vanishes, engulfed by a blackness at once infinite and opaque. For a philosopher like Kant, such moments reveal to us how we orient ourselves in the world through our senses:

> In the dark I orient myself in a room that is familiar to me if I can take hold of even one single object whose position I remember. But it is plain that nothing helps me here except the faculty for determining position according to a *subjective* ground of differentiation: for I do not see all the objects whose place I am to find; and if someone as a joke had moved all the objects around so that what was previously on the right was now on the left, I would be quite unable to find anything in a room whose walls were otherwise wholly identical.[487]

A more unsettling version of this is given in an episode of the radio show *Lights Out!*, entitled simply "The Dark." Originally aired on December 29, 1937, the episode features a policeman and doctor en route to a remote house, responding to an emergency call. They arrive only to find the house completely dark and abandoned. They open the inevitably creaky door, and inside they find a cackling old woman, and an unrecognizable mass of flesh, which they soon realize is a man — turned inside out. But this is only the beginning of their horrors. They open a further door, but this opens not to another room, but to … nothing. They shine in a flashlight, but the light does not reflect against any surface — no floor, wall, or ceiling. "I don't see nothin' but dark … the dark sorta spills over on the edges…" the policeman says. Another room, and the same thing. The house seems to be built of infinite, expansive darkness. As the doctor says, peering into the endlessly black room: "Well, look I tell ya — it's a deeper dark than … dark…" Eventually they notice something moving in the dark, but it is, strangely, the dark itself. It pours out and envelops the old woman, turning her body inside out. Aghast and speechless, the policeman and doctor are frozen in terror: "The shadows — they're crawling on the floor towards us…"[488]

*

Black Mirrors. The supernatural horror tradition is largely predicated on the allure of the existence of the supernatural. And yet, this can only be verified by the same category-bound human beings who have made up the very distinction between the natural and supernatural to begin with. It is this conundrum that is so often exploited in the genre, producing that harrowing grey zone of uncertainty that literary critics like Todorov call "the fantastic." It really happened. It's all in your head.

The uncertainty can only hold for so long. There is something intolerable about the hovering undecidability in which the world seems at once fully explained and yet utterly strange. The balance must tip to one side or the other. In the hazy, tenebrous indistinctness of the fantastic it can be tempting to lean towards the supernatural, as if we are pulled there by the nebulous darkness of night and shadow itself. The prevalence of mirror motifs in the gothic horror tradition is an example of this, from Ann Radcliffe to Henry James. To be sure, mirrors are among the most overdetermined and clichéd objects of literary and folklore traditions worldwide, but in the horror genre they seem to play specific roles. For instance, in "The Hungry Glass," a 1961 episode of the TV series *Thriller!*, a young couple takes a trip to the coast for a holiday. But the shadowy, angular, seaside mansion already has inhabitants — in particular, the ghosts of its previous Victorian-era tenants, who live inside the nebulous world of the mirrors themselves. In a scene reminiscent of avant-garde cinema, a locked storage room reveals a multitude of mirrors in the dark, standing in an array, as if waiting to be found. What follows is a melodrama played out in the strange refractions of the mirrors, where the dead past haunts the modern present, threatening to pull everything living into the dark recesses of its gothic optics.

What of the opposite direction? Total clarity, total transparency, everything fully accounted for and exhaustively catalogued in its hyper-visibility. Perhaps a different kind of horror emerges, one

Still from "The Hungry Glass," *Thriller!* (dir. Douglas Heyes, 1961)

equally as "weird" as the pull towards the supernatural. In many ways, the mirror is the counterpoint to the motifs of night, shadow, and darkness so often found in the traditions of the Gothic and weird fiction traditions. Mirrors do reflect self or world back to us, and they can also involve distortions; but more often than not, the mirror is simply a mirror. We do the rest.

One of the more harrowing examples of this is the British film *Peeping Tom*, directed by Michael Powell. Released in 1960 (the same year as Hitchcock's *Psycho*), the film features a serial killer (who is, we find out, an aspiring filmmaker) who uses mirrors to show his female victims their faces just before they die. The disturbing contortions of the victim's faces are exacerbated by their being reflected back to them, which is shown to us as viewers through the point of view of the mirror. A commentary not only on the horror genre but on the cinematic apparatus itself, *Peeping Tom* also raises issues about a postwar culture already saturated with images, as well as the gendered bias within artistic production. The mirror becomes the nexus where film, the horror genre, and consumer culture intersect in the face of fear.

Peeping Tom illustrates that mirrors in the horror genre need not be actual mirrors. They can be projections, screens, photographs, or even paintings. Numerous 19th century stories involve portraiture — photographic or painterly — as ciphers for mirrors, often with menacing results. Oscar Wilde's *The Picture of Dorian Gray*, written during the *fin-de-siècle* obsession with decay and degeneration, is one of the most well-known examples of portrait painting used as a kind of spiritual or moral mirror. As the ageless Dorian Gray descends into further and further layers of debauchery, the figure in the portrait likewise ages and decays. The motif of the portrait as a corpse not only inverts the traditional idea of portraiture (you will age, but your portrait is immortal), but it also involves an ambivalent magic trick of transference. Stories such as Edgar Allan Poe's "The Oval Portrait," Robert Chambers's "The Mask," Daphne du Maurier's *Rebecca*, all exemplify this strange capacity of mirroring to somehow absorb the life of its subject, leaving them in a suspended state that is neither quite alive nor dead.

Sometimes the mirror is at its most terrifying when it does nothing except reflect. In the Edogawa Rampo story "Hell of Mirrors" (1926), a young scientist studying optics develops an obsession with mirrors that takes on deranged, even absurdist proportions. Told through the narration of his friend, the scientist's interest in optics quickly develops into a mania. Part delirium, part experiment, the scientist notes that one mirror is not enough, there must be several, at each angle, capturing all sides of the subject. And if mirrors can reflect the exteriority of the body, why couldn't they also reflect the interiority of the psyche? Optics becomes architecture, as the scientist experiments with curved mirrors, multiple mirrors, kaleidoscopic mirrors. At one point, the narrator visits the scientist, disturbed by what he finds. "Every time I beheld these scenes I got the shivers, for the reflection of his madly whirling naked body became contorted and twisted into a thousand variations." The mirrors transform the scientist's body into a kind of kaleidoscopic anatomy: the head is doubled, belly impossibly swollen, the face exaggerated beyond recognition, "his swinging arms would multiply like those found on ancient Chinese Buddhist statues.[489]

Eventually the mirrors engulf the scientist entirely, forming an eerily moving sphere, a kind of glass cocoon of perpetual reflection and distortion, an echo chamber in which solipsism and madness perfectly overlap.

> This sphere was about twice as large as the ball on which circus clowns balance themselves. The exterior was completely covered with white cloth. What terrified me was the fantastic way this sphere kept rolling slowly and haphazardly, as if it were alive. Far more terrible, however, was the strange noise that echoed faintly from the interior of the ball — it was a laugh, a spine-chilling laugh that seemed to come from the throat of a creature from some other world.[490]

When the narrator, in a fit of desperation, finally shatters the glass ball, the creature that crawls out has undergone such strange mutations that it is hardly recognizable as human.

"Edogawa Rampo" was the pen name of Hirai Tarō, who chose the name as a variant of "Edgar Allan Poe," and there is a touch of Poe's "Oval Portrait" in the story as well — minus any hint of the supernatural. Like so many Rampo stories, "Hell of Mirrors" is bizarre, but not supernatural. Its strangeness lies precisely in the fact that the mirrors are completely secular and mundane, in spite of what we project onto them. The mirrors do what mirrors should do — they reflect. And it is in their supramundane reflecting that "Hell of Mirrors" reaches a kind of metaphysical horror, a horror that even idealist philosophers such as Berkeley had not considered: there is nothing except people, people everywhere. There is nothing except myself, ceaselessly gazing out onto a world that does nothing but reflect me back to myself, just as my language, my thoughts, and all the categories I use to think and communicate, all these are also mirrors. "Hell of Mirrors" takes up the theme and presents us with the inverse of supernatural horror — that there is nothing supernatural.

These examples of "black mirrors" are inhabited by a kind of horror, due to the fact that they don't do anything special, except reflect. There are no distortions or contortions, and the mirrors are not gateways or portals, and in their bizarre reflective opacity they coldly repudiate any notion of a transcendent "beyond." In fact, these mirrors are opaque because they are utterly transparent. There is nothing else, no other world, no other dimension, nothing but this — only this terrifyingly mundane and suffocating, suffering world, only this dimly flickering human consciousness just aware enough to realize its terrifying finitude. Black mirrors simply reflect, and that is all they do. They foreclose the possibility of the supernatural, and therein lies their quality of being something more, as if to suggest that the supernatural is at its most terrifying when it is only natural, when the very distinction between them has been rendered null and void.

*

Matheme of Terror. It usually starts with something small, something innocuous, a little obsession. You become fascinated by something you see, something that catches your eye: a particular pattern on a tablecloth, the shape of snail shells, the inward curve of a plant's tendrils, the shape in a ceramic cup, the swirling motion of your miso soup. Your interest is piqued, and "hm, that's interesting" gradually becomes "what else can I learn about it?" The focal point expands, gradually and by steps, until it eclipses your view of the world entirely. Ever so slightly, the little obsession becomes a big obsession, and soon everything is made of spirals, from microscopic cells and granules of sand to the human settlement patterns outside of cities, massive hurricane cloud formations, the galaxies, even thought itself.

This is the trajectory of Junji Ito's manga series *Uzumaki*, published between 1998 and 1999. It begins as we follow two teenagers who witness their hometown of Kurôzu-cho become obsessed by the shape of the spiral, eventually driving them all to murder, madness, or suicide. The "spiral obsession" appears to spread through the town, affecting not only the townspeople, but manifesting itself in the town itself. A mathematical abstraction becomes incarnate, and is suddenly spreading everywhere, from the spiral-shaped grass on the hillside to the swirling black fumes of cremated bodies. Ceramics, soup, hair, clothing, even the town itself, arrayed in a spiral-shaped row of houses, become so many vehicles for the spiral. By the third volume of the series, the town of Kurôzu-cho has become a massive spiral dwelling, composed of the impossibly contorted bodies of its inhabitants.

As an abstract geometric shape, the spiral is, in itself, nothing. It is only present by being manifest in some thing — a cup, a plant, a snail shell; even a drawing of a spiral requires the material substrate of ink and paper. Throughout *Uzumaki* we almost never see an abstract spiral, for the spiral is always some thing, some material object or living body. The spiral contagion spreads throughout the town, crossing boundaries between the living and nonliving, organic and inorganic, animal, plant, or mineral. The spiral is not reducible to any of those incarnations — but it is not separate from them either. What drives many of the townspeople mad is this duplicity — the tangible presence of the spiral matched with its intangible abstractness. It appears to be everywhere and nowhere, a black matheme that spreads even into the very thoughts of the characters themselves.

In the penultimate chapter of the series — titled, simply, "Galaxy" — a mild-mannered astronomy teacher appears to have discovered a new galaxy, which is — you guessed it — strangely spiral-shaped. But the galaxy is more than that; it appears to have spirals upon spirals of star-stuff folding in on itself. "Such strange luminosity ... such crooked arms ... It really is a weird galaxy." What's more, the spiral galaxy seems to emit "transmissions" to the astronomy teacher. By the end of the story he has turned into

Panel from Junji Ito, *Uzumaki* (1998–1999)

a raving lunatic, his eyes sunken in a spiral shape, driven mad by the incessant signals coming to him from the spiral galaxy. And his students seem to discover more spiral galaxies, none of them previously recorded. At one point, the astronomy teacher offers himself before the night sky, the spiral galaxies now visible to the naked eye, and beckons to the spiral galaxy to take him. A moment later a flash of light either emanates down from the sky or from within the teacher's head. "After exploding like an egg in a microwave, Torino's head turned into a small galaxy and flew off into the night sky." But, as with the spiral shape itself, the end is not really the end: "And it will be the same moment when it ends again ... When the next Kurôzu-cho is built amidst the ruins of the old one ... When the eternal spiral awakes once more..."[491]

At the center of Ito's manga is an inversion that takes place between the human being and an enigmatic something else that constitutes a horizon for human thought. We've been calling this "something else" the *unhuman*. The unhuman is not simply that

Panel from Junji Ito, *Uzumaki* (1998–1999)

which is not human, be it animals, machines, oceans, or cities, though all of these play a role in Ito's story. The unhuman is also not that which is personified and made human, in which we would have featherless, bipedal walking and talking spirals — though this is hinted at in *Uzumaki* as well. The unhuman is distinct from these two ways of thinking — anthropocentrism and anthropomorphism, respectively.

What then is the unhuman? It is, first of all, a limit without reserve, something that one is always arriving at, but which is never circumscribed within the ambit of human thought. In a story like *Uzumaki*, we see at least four stages by which one encounters the unhuman. At the first level, we encounter the unhuman only as it exists for the human. This is the normative world of modern suburban living described by the teenagers Shuichi and Kirie at the beginning of the story. At this level, the unhuman is everything that is for us and for our benefit as human beings, living in human cultures, and bearing some unilateral relation to the world around us. Houses, rivers, the countryside, roads, people, occupations, schools, hospitals, and the like. This relation between human and unhuman relies upon an *anthropic subversion*. The unhuman is only that which exists within the scope of the human; in a sense, there is no outside of the human, in so far as the unhuman is always fully encompassed by human knowledge and technics. At this level, the unhuman is everything that is subject to and produced by human knowledge. At this level, anthropocentrism overlaps almost perfectly with anthropomorphism.

But *Uzumaki* steadily moves towards a second level, which reintroduces a notion of the unhuman through an inversion of the relation between human and unhuman. Rather than a merely subjective obsession, the spiral manifests itself in the physical surroundings of Kurôzu-cho itself — as if the spiral were "interested" in the townspeople of Kurôzu-cho. Note that a relation of unilateralism still exists, except that it has been reversed. Instead of human beings making use of the world for their own ends, the world is revealed to be making use of human beings for its own end. Humans are simply another way for the spiral to produce and reproduce itself, be it as grass, clouds, bodies, or galaxies. Clearly all bets are off here — one can no longer regard the human endeavors of science, technology, and art in quite the same way. But the terms of this are still human — intentionality, instrumental rationality, and even a touch of malice are attributed to the spiral. It is as if the unhuman can only be understood through the lens of the human — a kind of *anthropic inversion*. The anthropic inversion allows for a concept of the unhuman to emerge, though it is ultimately recuperated within the ambit of human categories, such as intelligence or intentionality.

Towards the end of *Uzumaki*, this undergoes another turn, leading to a third level at which the unhuman is encountered. As the astronomy teacher is weirdly carried off into the spiral night where flesh and geometry merge into one, his own individuation slips away and is engulfed, and at this moment we realize the arbitrariness of the human categories of living/nonliving, or human/nonhuman. In other words, as opposed to the anthropic inversion (humans don't make spirals, spirals make us), here the townspeople of Kurôzu-cho experience another kind of inversion, an *ontogenic inversion* in which everything human is revealed to be a single instance of the unhuman. The ontogenic inversion is both ontological and ontogenetic, at once the evisceration of thought from the human, and an epiphany about the essentially unhuman qualities of the human.

At this point thought falters, and here we enter a fourth stage that we can call *misanthropic subtraction*. Language can only continue by way of an apophatic use of negative terms ("nameless," "formless," "lifeless"), which themselves are doomed to failure. This failure is leveraged with great effect in the literary tradition of weird fiction. Authors such as Lovecraft, Blackwood, Machen, and others excelled at driving language to this breaking point. Here one notices two strategies that are regularly used, often in concert with each other. There is a strategy of minimalism, in which language is stripped of all its attributes, leaving only skeletal phrases such as "the nameless thing" or "the shapeless thing," or "the unnamable" (also the title of a Lovecraft story). There is also a strategy of hyperbole, in which the unknowability of the unhuman is expressed through a litany of baroque descriptors, all of which ultimately fail to inscribe the unhuman within human thought and language. A random sampling from Lovecraft's "The Shadow Out of Time" provides examples:

> …the nameless bands of abhorrent elder-world hierophants…
>
> …brooding, half-material, alien Things that festered in earth's nether abysses…
>
> …phantasmal flashes of hideously familiar walls and carvings, all blighted with the decay of ages…
>
> …engulfed in a pandeamoniac vortex of loathsome sound and utter, materially tangible blackness…[492]

Often these two strategies dovetail into a singular epiphany concerning the faltering not just of language, but of thought. At the end of Lovecraft's story "The Unnamable," one of the characters, speaking to his friend Carter from a hospital bed, attempts to describe his strange experience in the following way:

> *No — it wasn't that way at all.* It was everywhere — a gelatin — a slime — yet it had shapes, a thousand shapes of horror

> beyond all memory. There were eyes — and a blemish. It was the pit — the maelstrom — the ultimate abomination. Carter, *it was the unnamable*![493]

Taken together, these four approaches lead to a paradoxical revelation, in which one thinks the thought of the limit of all thought. What is thought is only this absolute inaccessibility, this absolute incommensurability; what is affirmed is only that which is negation.

What results, then, is an enigmatic revelation of the unthinkable — what we've already termed "black illumination." It does not lead to the affirmation of the human within the unhuman, but instead opens onto the quality of *indifference* vis-à-vis the unhuman. The unhuman does not exist for us (the humanism of the unhuman), and neither is it against us (the misanthropy of the unhuman). Nevertheless, it is no doubt for this reason that the instances of black illumination in the horror genre indelibly bear the mark of a generalized misanthropy, that moment when philosophy and horror collapse into each other.

*

Naturhorror. Near the end of the 18th century, the philosopher, novelist, and aphorist Friedrich Schelling sought to formulate a renewed philosophy of nature that would combine the findings of the physical sciences with that of speculative philosophy in the wake of Kant. Kant's critical philosophy had forged a wedge between the world in itself and our perception of the world, but post-Kantian thinkers like Schelling sought ways of bridging Kant's division of self and world. For Schelling, the key intuition was that the self that thinks about the world is also part of the world, and it is a mistake to presume that there is first a separately existing self that then turns towards and reflects on the world as an object. The world that the self thinks about is also "in" the self, and the two share something in common that may not be reducible to either.

What, then, is that "something" that is common to both self and world? For Schelling, "nature" came to signify that commonality — but by nature Schelling does not mean "the outdoors" or forests and oceans, and neither does he mean nature in the sense of a fixed essence (as in "human nature"). Nature for Schelling was that "something" that was not in itself anything, constituted entirely of process, becoming, flux and flow — a "ground" of the world that was also continually ungrounding itself. The stakes of such a philosophy are high, as summarized by philosopher Iain Hamilton Grant in his study *Philosophies of Nature After Schelling*:

> If, in other words, "to philosophize about nature means to create nature," the latter cannot be a nature restricted a priori by the particular physiological means by which it philosophizes. Instead, nature philosophizing must itself be unconditioned, so that the range of instances of natural philosophy must extend beyond the remit of physiologically conditioned particulars such as species, or even phyla.[494]

In his syncretic approach, Schelling incorporated ideas from physics, biology, geology, chemistry, as well as elements from mystical theology and classical myth. Given the questions Schelling is posing, such a philosophy would no longer simply be a philosophy *of* nature, as if the philosopher stood apart from nature. For if the nature that I am thinking about is also in me and coursing through me, then it follows that I am in some way identical with nature, and that nature "thinks" me just as I think nature. As Grant puts it, "what thinks in me is what is outside me." Instead of a philosophy of nature, Schelling proposes a *naturphilosophie*. Thought becomes strangely nonhuman, just as the human being becomes at once that which thinks nature and that which is thought by nature.

But if this is the case, and what thinks in me is also outside me, it is also possible that what is outside me is also outside of my subjective concerns, hopes, and desires, just as what thinks in me is also alien, impersonal, and similarly estranged to the "me" that is thought. My thoughts are not my own, and I am thought by an enigmatic non-entity whose motives may be contrary to my own — or which may have no motives at all. Contra Schelling's romantic conception of the unity of self and world (the nature in me and the nature outside me), there is another kind of "nature," one that courses through self and world, but that does so without aim or end, indifferent to the self's possessive individualism and the species sense of superiority. What thinks in me is what is outside me. Is this not also a description of "nature" as invasive, contagious, engulfing the human being like an overgrown, dilapidated ruin? Would this not transform Schelling's *naturphilosophie* into a *naturhorror*?

Among authors of supernatural horror, no one has examined the role of nature more than Algernon Blackwood. Blackwood's characters frequently discover a nature that is a darker version of Schelling's *naturphilosophie*, and a nature that they are, at the same time, drawn to, often undergoing ambivalent transformations. Lyrical and foreboding, Blackwood's story "The Man Whom the Trees Loved" (1912) tells of a husband and wife enjoying their cabin in the woods. Gradually the husband becomes more and more interested in the trees that surround their house, taking long walks in the forest, becoming silent and preoccupied. He has dreams of the slow and swaying trees, and his dreams begin to blur into his daily life. The couple can't tell, but it seems as if the trees outside their house have moved ever so closer. At night, amid the "strong smell of mould and fallen leaves" the wife feels a presentment of something close but intangible, something linked to the trees outside: "The horrible, dim enchantment of the trees was close about them in the room — gnarled, ancient, lonely trees of winter, whispering round the human life they loved."[495] One night, amid stirring dreams, the wife suddenly awakes. There are wet leaves and dew on her clothing, as if she had been outside. In the dim, moonlit darkness, she glances over at her husband, sound asleep. Then she looks up:

> ...what caught her unawares was the horrid thing that by this fact of a sudden, unexpected waking she had surprised

> these other things in the room, beside the very bed, gathered close about him while he slept ... She screamed before she realised what she did — a long, high shriek of terror that filled the room, yet made so little actual sound. For wet and shimmering presences stood grouped all round that bed. She saw their outline underneath the ceiling, the green, spread bulk of them, their vague extension over walls and furniture. They shifted to and fro, massed yet translucent, mild yet thick, moving and turning within themselves to a hushed noise of multitudinous soft rustling. In their sound was something very sweet and winning that fell into her with a spell of horrible enchantment.[496]

Seamlessly crossing nature outside and nature inside, waking and dreaming, the animate and inanimate, the eerie forest trees in Blackwood's story literally envelop the characters in an intimate, lulling terror, a "horrible enchantment" that pulls the human characters further and further away from the human.

Something similar happens in Izumi Kyōka's story "The Holy Man of Mount Kōya" (1900), which tells the story of a young Buddhist monk making his way to a monastery near the mountain. The monk begins his journey on a road, which then turns to a path, which then vanishes, leaving the monk directionless as he walks into a dense forest. He sees a snake, various insects, and at one point discovers a leech on his arm. Then, inexplicably, a torrent of leeches descends upon him from the trees. Fatigued, delirious, and panic-stricken, "it was then," the monk states, "that the strangest thought occurred to me": "These terrifying mountain leeches had been gathered there since the age of the gods, lying in wait for passersby ... And at the same time, all these enormous trees, large enough to block out even the midday sun, will break into small pieces that will then turn into even more leeches..."[497] Foreboding in its appearance, the forest through which the monk walks literally takes on animalistic properties, the boundary between vegetable, animal, and mineral fading away. Recalling the experience later, the monk solemnly observes:

> The destruction of mankind will not come with the rupture of the earth's fragile crust and with fire pouring down from the heavens. Nor will it come when the waves of the ocean wash over the land. Rather, it will begin with the forests of Hida turning into leeches and end with black creatures swimming in blood and muck. Only then will a new generation of life begin.[498]

This intermingling of forms is at the center of a group of short stories by contemporary horror author and paleontologist Caitlín R. Kiernan. Published in their 2000 collection *Tales of Pain and Wonder*, each of the stories focuses on a particular place where some undefined scientific anomaly is discovered. In the story "In the Water Works (Birmingham, Alabama 1888)," it is the mining site near Red Mountain, at the tip of the Appalachias. There, geology teacher Henry S. Matthews carries out his research under the auspices of the Birmingham Water Works and the Elyton Land Companies, gathering samples, accumulating data, a northerner minding his own business down south. Eventually the miners discover what appears to be a massive fault within the mountain. The foreman asks Matthews to come with them to take a look. As they go deeper and deeper into the mountain, Matthews notices a strange, repulsive, rotten stench, the stench, he thinks of fungoid, mold-ridden rocks. When they finally arrive at the breach, Matthews, still repulsed by the smell, isn't sure what he sees: "...a wide crevice in the wall of the tunnel maybe four feet across and dropping suddenly away into darkness past the reach of the lantern, running west into more blackness but pinching closed near the tunnel's ceiling."[499] The foreman holds Matthews's arm as he slowly leans over into the blackness. He discovers the bottom of the cavern is flooded, the black water infinitely deep. Looking closer, the foreman still holding him, Matthews notices something else:

> At first he doesn't see anything, angle a little less than ninety degrees where black rock meets blacker water, and then he

> does see something and thinks it must be the roots of some plant growing in the pool, or, more likely, running down from the forest above to find this hidden moisture. Gnarled roots as big around as his arm, twisted wood knotted back on itself … But one of them moves, then, abrupt twitch as it rolls away from the others…[500]

Matthews watches in dismay as one of the roots rises out of the water, and, dripping, glides slowly towards him — and on its underside there is a small, fossil-like worm, "coiling and uncoiling, and here are a thousand of them, restless polyps sprouting from this greater appendage, row upon writhing row, and now it's risen high enough that the thing is right in front of him, shimmering in the lantern light, a living question mark."[501]

That question mark is at the center of both the horror genre and philosophy. It demands to be taken both literally and figuratively. And it is a question mark posed to the sciences as well. This is something that American author and purveyor of the paranormal Charles Fort knew well. In a string of books published between 1919 and 1932, Fort, spending hours upon hours in the New York Public Library, amassed material on unexplained phenomena. Scientific papers, philosophy books, news reports, travelogues, even anecdotal accounts — nothing escaped Fort's keen eye, as he gathered data on those phenomena which had been excluded from mainstream scientific systems. Some of his books gathered together data relating to biological anomalies, while others pertained to geological anomalies, and still others to cosmological anomalies. At the center of his project lay a profound interest in the limits of human knowledge:

> All attempted organizations and systems and consistencies, some approximating far higher than others, but all only intermediate to Order and Disorder, fail eventually because of their relations with outside forces. All are attempted completenesses. If to all local phenomena there are always

> outside forces, these attempts, too, are realizable only in the state of completeness, or that to which there are no outside forces.[502]

Such phenomena were that portion of knowledge, which must be excluded in order for systematic knowledge and natural laws to exist at all. Fort is a thinker of the supernatural steeped in the hermetic depths of the archive. His research into the unexplained often points to the unexplainable, and in this sense his books are a compendium of the horizon of human intelligibility. His books read less like coherent theories and more like a dossier facts and figures put in narrative form, an agnostic's archive, the "data of the damned." A deep-seated skepticism undergirds Fort's books: "Nothing has ever been defined. Because there is nothing to define."[503] Or: "Nothing has ever been finally found out. Because there is nothing to find out."[504] Or again: "We are not realists. We are not idealists. We are intermediatists — that nothing is real, but that nothing is unreal: that all phenomena are approximations one way or the other between realness and unrealness."[505] What Fort attempted in works like *The Book of the Damned* was nothing less than a "procession of data that Science has excluded." At the same time, Fort's books are absent of any conclusions, his authorial voice buried in the curation of "damned" facts, as if "the facts themselves" revealed things far more horrific and unmentionable than the fancies of a writer's imagination.

*

An Exegesis on Tentacles. There is never just one tentacle, but many. And yet, the many tentacles always seem to trail off into nothingness, into a distant ocean abyss as black as the ink it secretes. The cephalopod occupies this duality, a multiplicity of seemingly incongruous features — tentacles and multiple "arms" with suckers, a razor-sharp "beak," a complex nervous system, rows of intestinal "teeth," and a formless "head" — whose coherence falls apart once one tries to make sense of the whole creature. Emerging from a lightless ocean depth, the tentacles seem to lead back down to the abyss from which they came, a multiplicity dissipating into a slumberous, slow, and alien depth. When the tentacles are not reaching down, they are reaching up, for prey — fish, crustaceans, a whale, a seaborne ship, a flailing human body. This is the cultural mythos, at least. From medieval Icelandic fables of the Kraken, to Jules Verne's *20,000 Leagues Beneath the Sea*, tentacles envelop human beings in their unhuman embrace, the abyss of the unknown sea reaching up to the surface with a certain inevitability.

At the same time, cephalopods are products of human knowledge-production. We have given them their various names, both scientific and colloquial, and they make appearances in the natural history works of Pliny the Elder and Linnaeus, as well as in the Teuthological studies of modern marine biologists. This has not, however, prevented the periodic (and often dubious) reports of giant squids, which continue to this day. At once products of science and myth, a multiplicity receding into an abyss, an alien creature become a god — these are themes woven into China Miéville's 2010 novel *Kraken*, his own rendition of cephalopod-lore.

Like many of Miéville's novels, the backdrop of *Kraken* is urban London. But counterposed to this is the vast sea. One is bustling with noise, the other enigmatically silent. One is built up or broken down, the other flows, sometimes turbulently and sometimes imperceptibly. In the interzone between city and sea *Kraken* introduces us to a whole bestiary of groups and organizations — the London Natural History Museum, the Darwin Centre, the FSRC (Fundamentalist and Sect-Related Crime Unit), the Krakenist cult, Londonmancers, the Brotherhood of the Blessed Flood, Knuckleheads, Gunfarmers, Chaos Nazis, and other nefarious grifters, gangsters, and cultists, each warring for their own apocalypse. But running through everything is the enigmatic and mute figure of the giant cephalopod, encased in museum glass as visitors gaze at it with equal muteness.

All-touching, all-seeing, an alien intelligence writing with an ink illegible but in the sea, in *Kraken* the cephalopod becomes at once an object of religion and of science — an object of religion because of science. Beneath the all-too-human veneer of urban London patterns emerge, linking city, sea, and the unhuman forms of life that pass between them. As one character notes, "What was squiddity but otherness, incomprehensibility. Why would such a deity understand those bent on its glory? Why should it offer anything? Anything at all?"[506] An old "Londonmancer," deciphering bloody entrails, gives a foreboding reading: "Everything closing down. Something coming up."[507]

But if, for these fringe groups, the cephalopod has become a god, it is not an anthropomorphic or even communicative god. In the library of the Krakenist cult, in a concrete bunker deep underground, we discover a storehouse of "cephalopod folklore" — *Moby Dick*, Jules Verne, the poetry of Hugh Cook and Tennyson, obscure scientific papers, and secret treatises such as the dreaded *Apocrypha Tentacula*. In one of the books we read:

> We cannot see the universe. We are in the darkness of a trench, a deep cut, dark water heavier than earth, presences lit by our own blood, little biolumes, heroic and pathetic. Promethei too afraid or weak to steal fire but able to still glow. Gods are among us and they care nothing and are nothing like us. This is how we are brave: we worship them anyway.[508]

In *Kraken*, the alterity of the cephalopod is matched only by its indifference towards the various groups that attempt to control it. Eventually the enigma of the cephalopod becomes the enigma of the sea itself. At one point in the novel we visit the "Brotherhood of the Blessed Flood," who protect an oracle of the sea. But the sea remains impervious to human demands:

> The sea is neutral. The sea didn't get involved in intrigues, didn't take sides in London's affairs. Wasn't interested. Who the hell could understand the sea's motivations, anyway? And who would be so lunatic as to challenge it? No one could fight that. You don't go to war against a mountain, against lightning, against the sea. It had its own counsel, and petitioners might sometimes visit its embassy, but that was for their benefit, not its. The sea was not concerned: that was the starting point.[509]

The starting point is, then, the indifference of the world. It is an insight found not only in myths and fables but also in treatises of natural history and marine biology. Commenting on the myriad of monsters in the sea, physician Ambroise Paré notes, in his 16th-century *On Monsters and Marvels* (*Des Monstres et Prodiges*), that "awesome things likewise happen on water. For huge flames of fire spreading across the water have been seen issuing from the abysses and whirlpools of the sea — a very monstrous thing — as if the great quantity of water could not stifle the fire; in this God shows himself incomprehensible, as in all his works."[510]

Whether one puts it in the language of fiction or science, the result is the same — the sudden realization of a stark, "tentacular" alienation from the world in which one is enmeshed. For these and other texts the cephalopod stands in as a manifestation of that indifference of the black, inky abyss. And in a modern context it is largely through scientific knowledge-production that this tentacular alienation is made possible. We human beings are, after all, the ones who have dreamed up taxonomies, anatomies, and nomenclatures, making possible the most systematic, rigorous articulation of this alienation. In a sense, the result of scientific classification is not that we as human beings finally find our place in the world, but the reverse — that we increasingly feel ill-at-ease in the world. It is we who are alien.

This is the insight of *Vampyroteuthis Infernalis*, an incomparable and strange work that straddles the line between science and fiction, biology and horror. Published in the 1980s by the philosopher and journalist Vilém Flusser, the *Vampyroteuthis* is written in the language of a biological classification textbook or a marine biology research paper. Appended to it is a report by the Scientific Institute for Paranaturalist Research, a set of anatomical illustrations and accompanying text, both by the artist Louis Bec. The text details the purported discovery of a new species of hypercomplex, "intelligent" cephalopod, dubbed *Vampyroteuthis infernalis* due to its many rows of undulating teeth and the general "voracity of their expression." As a whole, the text is a study in self-reflexivity; the language of biological classification is not simply mocked but respectfully, even enthusiastically employed, to give the reader a sense of the strangeness of life on the planet. The cephalopod is the key figure in the text, at once the most remote from the human being, and yet, as Flusser contends, at the same time uncannily near to us:

> ...the vampyroteuthis is not entirely alien to us. The abyss that separates us is incomparably smaller than that which separates us from extraterrestrial life ... We are pieces of the same game, both constructed of genetic information, and we belong to a branch of the same phylogenetic tree to which its branch belongs. Our common ancestors dominated the beaches of the earth for millions of years, and it was relatively late in the history of life that our paths began to diverge...[511]

As Flusser notes "without any previous knowledge of biology, we feel a sense of belonging to our phylum whenever we step on a mollusk, on the one hand, or when we hear, on the other, a crackling bone under our shoe. We feel a connection with life-forms supported by bones, while other forms of life disgust us." This leads Flusser to the evocative idea of a "biological existentialism": "Though existential philosophy has concerned itself with the idea of disgust, it has never attempted to formulate a category of 'biological existentialism,' to advance something like the following hypothesis: 'Disgust recapitulates phylogenesis.'"[512]

Disgust recapitulates phylogenesis. Flusser is playing on the truism of genetics, "ontogeny recapitulates phylogeny," which argues that the development of the individual organism replays the evolutionary development of its species. Flusser applies this to the affective domain of disgust, so beloved by existentialist thinkers such as Sartre and Camus. The insight of the science of biological classification is, Flusser suggests, to have articulated in great detail the scope and range of human disgust towards that which is not human.

Such disgust is also, of course, a sign of the human being's failure to appreciate that which is not human, other than in terms of its utility for us as human beings. This is especially evident in the many horror tales featuring cephalopods, kraken, giant squids, and other nefarious sea creatures, from the *Orlando Furioso* to tales of nautical horror by the likes of Edgar Allan Poe and William Hope Hodgson. A case in point is the Lovecraft short story "Dagon," published in 1919. The plot of the story is threadbare and found in many of Lovecraft's tales — an unnamed narrator tells of his being lost in a strange and terrifying place, and of the unmentionable things he sees there, which, of course, no one believes once he returns home, driving him to the brink of madness. Disgust pervades the story, from the narrator's first impressions of the strange "island": "When at last I awaked, it was to discover myself half sucked into a slimy expanse of hellish black mire which extended about me in monotonous undulations as far as I could see, and in which my boat lay grounded some distance away … The region was putrid with the carcasses of decaying fish, and of other less describable things which I saw protruding from the nasty mud of the unending plain."[514] Without compass or map, shipwrecked and delirious, the seascape draws the narrator into the depths of cosmic horror: "Perhaps I should not hope to convey in mere words the unutterable hideousness that can dwell in absolute silence and barren immensity."[515]

Though the island appears uninhabited, the remnants of what he does discover make no sense within the ambit of existing human history, archaeology, and science. It is unclear if the "island" is a recent upheaval of rock from a deep-sea volcano. A deep ravine leads to a dark pool and a giant, black, "Cyclopean monolith," covered in strange symbols and depictions of unrecognizable creatures, all unmistakably sculpted by some unnamed and unseen entity.

"Then suddenly I saw it." Something "loathsome" rising to the surface of dark waters, sliding into partial view, a "stupendous monster of nightmares," "gigantic scaly arms" reaching around the monolith, a "hideous" and bowed head, emitting "certain measured sounds." "I think I went mad then." The narrator's frantic escape and subsequent rescue offers no consolation. He is tainted with an anthropocentric disgust that will not go away, and the only thing he is disgusted by more than cephalopod-like creatures from the deep is his own species, unable to comprehend a world both alien and indifferent to the human perspective:

> I cannot think of the deep sea without shuddering at the nameless things that may at this very moment be crawling and floundering on its slimy bed, worshipping their ancient stone idols and carving their own detestable likenesses on submarine obelisks or water-soaked granite. I dream of a day when they may rise above the billows to drag down in their reeking talons the remnants of puny, war-exhausted mankind — of a day when the land shall sink, and the dark ocean floor shall ascend amidst universal pandemonium.[516]

Final words that are at once prayer and indictment.

*

Slow Horror. The horror genre is not typically thought of as a "slow" genre. Indeed, contemporary horror films can often have the feeling of a stimulus-response test, viewers subjected to a series of optical and acoustic triggers, a more clinical version of the scare tactics employed by the William Castle films of the 1960s. While such films do have their place in the horror genre, there is another tradition, where everything happens slowly and inexorably, with a diffuse fatalism that resides at the limits of human comprehension.

This is evident in early horror films, where the minimalist aesthetics of light and shadow produced the moody tone poems of German Expressionist films such as *The Cabinet of Dr. Caligari* (1920) and *Nosferatu* (1922), as well as Carl Th. Dreyer's hallucinatory film *Vampyr* (1932). Less a story and more an extended dream-vision, *Vampyr* is unique in the history of horror film for its ability to make use of camera work, montage, and other early cinema techniques to produce something that manages to tread the fine line of the fantastic with great effect. Much of this is also due to the slow, steady, deliberate cadence of the film, which seems to operate according to its own inner clock, indifferent to the demands of character, plot, or realism.

Even in the wake of the introduction of sound, one finds magical moments of slowness embedded within otherwise traditional narrative cinema. A case in point is *The Black Cat* (1934), a pre-Code film noir directed by Edgar Ulmer, starring Boris Karloff and Béla Lugosi. While it begins innocuously enough — a young American couple on holiday in the remote Hungarian countryside, a chance encounter with Dr. Vitus Werdegast, a gentlemanly Austrian psychiatrist, and a visit to the ultramodern home of troubled architect Hjalmar Poelzig — the story eventually takes us deeper and deeper into recesses of war, trauma, folklore, and the experiments of a shadowy Satanic cult. At one point, the narrative stream breaks off so that Karloff's character can deliver a short but hypnotic, elegiac speech. While he speaks, the film segues to slowly drifting camera shots of empty corridors, accompanied by the *Allegretto* movement from Beethoven's Symphony no.7. In his inimitable, almost tender delivery, Karloff ruminates on the atrocities of war, haunted memories, the struggle with mortality, the loss of a culture, the trauma of living: "Are we not both the living dead? … We shall play a little game, a game of death, if you like…" In terms of the

Still from *Vampyr* (dir. Carl Th. Dreyer, 1932)

plot, the episode is unnecessary. But in terms of the film's mood, it is indispensable.

The slowing of the horror film is especially noticeable in the many J-horror films produced between the 1990s and the early 2000s. In fact, one of J-horror's contributions to both film and the horror genre has been the introduction of an aesthetics of slowness. A case point are the films of director Kiyoshi Kurosawa, whose films *Cure* (1997) and *Pulse* (2001) effectively demonstrate this "slowness" of J-horror cinema. In Kurosawa's films, everything unfolds with a gradual, deliberate, and even eerie patience, as in a dream or a trance state. An auteur, professor, and cinephile, Kurosawa's films point back to classics of Japanese horror film such as *Ugetsu* (1953) and *Kuroneko* (1968), both of which are adaptations of Japanese tales of supernatural horror, as well as to the underappreciated Japanese silent film *A Page of Madness* (1926). Beneath this slowness is an intangible but palpable sense of unease, and in this sense Kurosawa also nods to other directors, from Fritz Lang to Alfred Hitchcock. Kurosawa's films also emerge in an era of global horror film, and there is a sense in which *Cure* and *Pulse* also nod to Herzog's *Nosferatu* (1979), Polanski's *Repulsion* (1965), and the trancelike, hovering tension of Dreyer's *Day of Wrath* (1943).

In Kurosawa's horror films, key plot events rarely happen suddenly or with violence. Instead, his characters gradually become prey to the inevitable unfolding of strange events that will forever lay beyond the scope of their comprehension. This is the case with *Cure*, in which a police detective becomes consumed by his pursuit of a killer who seems to use mesmerism to cast a catatonic, trancelike pall over his victims. In *Pulse*, the motif of the portal to the underworld (*The Sentinel*, *The Amityville Horror*, *The Beyond*) is mapped onto the digital space of webcams, where shadowy, nebulous, quasi-human shapes seem to emerge and recede on the other side of the screen — sometimes seeping through the screen, or drawing others into its black recesses. The realization of what is happening occurs so gradually in these films that by the time the characters begin to figure things out, it is already too late. Am I on the cusp of comprehending what is going on, or have I become a symptom of the very phenomenon I'm investigating? At times this uncertainty spreads outwards like a contagion, metaphysically draping itself over everything. We are all walking around in a trance, we are all fleeting shapes in "the floating world" of the screen. At this point, all the characters can do is passively witness the eerie passing of unreal time before them. The result is hypnotic — everything is in slow-motion; everything is in time-lapse.

Films such as *Cure* and *Pulse* are not the only films to have achieved this "slowing" of the horror genre. It can be seen in Panos Cosmatos's *Beyond the Black Rainbow* (2010), Apichatpong Weerasethakul's *Uncle Boonmee Who Can Recall His Past Lives* (2010), Ana Lily Amirpour's *A Girl Walks Home Alone At Night* (2014), Babak Anvari's *Under the Shadow* (2016), and Lukas

Still from *Pulse* (*Kairo*, dir. Kiyoshi Kurosawa, 2001)

Feigelfeld's *Hagazussa* (2017), as well as the patiently unfolding restraint of Tomas Alfredson's *Let the Right One In* (2008) or in *Only Lovers Left Alive* (2013), directed by the maestro of cinematic dead time, Jim Jarmusch. Films like these exist at the borders of the horror genre, slowing down the industry's imperative for sudden thrills to such a degree that the film becomes less about plot, and more about an atmosphere, extended mood pieces suffused with a different set of affects: bewilderment, dereliction, melancholy, catatonia, a terror of being engulfed in time, the slow horror of living.

If films like these are still horror films, it is perhaps because they reveal something about the nature of time, at once deeply phenomenal yet utterly indifferent to our various attempts to measure, control, and manipulate it for our own ends. Slow horror reveals a world different than the one recast in our own species-specific interests; it gives us a glimpse of world indifferent to the human perspective, a world that exists at the fringes of human comprehension, hidden in time, lost in time, buried in time. The "horror" of films like these is a metaphysical horror, the use of cinematic techniques to slow time beyond the human framework, in the process revealing the relative insignificance of frenetic human activity against the backdrop of deep time, the eeriness of slow decay, an eroding earth, and solar death.

Among critics, cinephiles, and scholars, the discussion over "slow cinema" or "contemplative cinema" has been happening for some time. It is the counterweight to the aesthetics of extreme cinema, with its handheld camerawork, frenetic montage, strobing lights, jagged plot lines, and cacophonous score. It is not uncommon to see the names of Ingmar Bergman, Michelangelo Antonioni, Andrei Tarkovsky, Chantal Ackerman, Béla Tarr, Nuri Bilge Ceylan, and Alexandr Sokurov mentioned in these discussions, along with contemporary films such as *Post Tenebras Lux* (2012) or *Norte, the End of History* (2013). Long takes, minimal camera movement, sparse dialogue, and an almost documentary, observational aesthetics characterizes many of these films. Labyrinthine plots and narrative-driven action give way to a more diffuse, more expansive sense of drifting, floating, or hovering in a state of suspended animation. Slow cinema need not be long cinema; a single scene, a single gesture, a moment extracted out of time often suffices.

In Weerasethakul's film *Cemetery of Splendour* (2015), a town is mysteriously stricken with a sleeping sickness. Doctors are helpless, caregivers are overrun with catatonic patients, and only a local spirit medium is able to "communicate" with the sleepers. In one scene, we see a static shot of rows of beds in a hospital, each bed accompanied by a strange, high-tech monitoring device, variously glowing different colors. The hospital, engulfed by the lush quiet of the jungle, sitting on top of an ancient ritual site, is abandoned except for the sleepers in their beds, the glowing colors of the monitors alternating in a slow cadence of sleep.

*

We Are Not from Here (Ligotti). In a culture that thrives on entrepreneurialism, pharmacology, and self-help, any disposition towards skepticism, cynicism or pessimism is often dismissed as a fancy name for a bad mood. In a culture that prizes the can-do, self-starter attitude, to be "against" is simply to complain — if you're not part of the solution, then you're part of the problem (as one joke goes, "why be part of the problem when you can be the whole problem?"). To live in such a culture is to constantly live in the shadow of an obligatory optimism, a novel type of coercion that is pathologized early on in child education: "Does not like to play with others." Indeed, the idea of an American pessimism would seem to be an oxymoron.

If one were to compile a list of American pessimist philosophers, the list would be short, though Thomas Ligotti's name would likely be on it. To those familiar with his work, Ligotti is known as an author of horror fiction. His 1986 debut *Songs of a Dead Dreamer* immediately set him apart from his contemporaries. Filled with dark, lyrical prose, it displayed an unabashed appreciation for the tradition of the Gothic. It was composed of short texts that were difficult to categorize, and that barely contained narrative or plot. When it was published, *Songs of a Dead Dreamer* stood in direct contrast to horror fiction of the 1980s, which was mostly characterized by slasher-style gore and a more brutalist approach to language. Ligotti's writing, by contrast, tended more towards an effusive, contorted prose that revealed almost nothing — though each of his pieces was steeped in a somber, funeral mood more reminiscent of the tradition of Edgar Allan Poe and H.P. Lovecraft. All the horrors — the real horrors — remained hidden in a stark, unhuman nether region beyond all comprehension, a horror that was, at the same time, instilled directly in the flesh.

In a career spanning over thirty years, Ligotti's work has remained committed to this tradition of supernatural horror, and given the trends, fads, and wild mood swings of the horror genre, such a commitment is an admirable anomaly. Ligotti's *The Conspiracy Against the Human Race* (2010; hereafter *Conspiracy*) is, at first, a puzzling book. For one, it is not a work of horror fiction; for that matter, it's not a work of fiction at all. But to call it a collection of essays or a treatise of philosophy doesn't quite do it justice either. Ligotti does comment at length on the horror genre and on a number of authors, from Ann Radcliffe and Joseph Conrad to Poe and Lovecraft. But *Conspiracy* is not just a writer's memoir of other writers. Ligotti does spend much of the book reflecting on pessimism, reminding us of the freshness of grumpy thinkers like Schopenhauer, while also pointing to more obscure thinkers, such as the Norwegian philosopher and alpinist Peter Wessel Zapffe. But Ligotti's approach is much too eccentric and uncompromising to be considered academic philosophy, and as a book *Conspiracy* is unencumbered by reams of footnotes or jargon-heavy vocabulary. Finally, Ligotti does address a number of topical issues in *Conspiracy* — research in cognitive neuroscience, the anti-natalism debate, global warming and overpopulation, transhumanism, Terror Management Therapy, the popularity of Buddhism, and the self-help boom. But the aim of the book is not simply to be topical, much less to present a "pop" introduction to a misunderstood topic.

So then, what kind of book is *Conspiracy*? It is first and foremost a book about pessimism; but it is also a pessimistic book. While it contains critical insights into pessimist thinking, it also contains stunning indictments of our many pretentions to being human: "As for us humans, we reek of our own sense of being something special"; "What is most uncanny about the self is that no one has yet been able to present the least evidence of it."[517] *Conspiracy* constantly hovers around that boundary between writing *about* pessimism and simply *writing* pessimism, and nowhere is this more evident than in Ligotti's own brand of philosophy, at once uncompromising and yet not without a touch of gallows humor:

> Nature proceeds by blunders; that is its way. It is also ours. So if we have blundered by regarding consciousness as a blunder, why make a fuss over it? Our self-removal from this planet would still be a magnificent move, a feat so luminous it would bedim the sun. What do we have to lose? No evil would attend our departure from this world, and the many evils we have known would go extinct along with us. So why

> put off what would be the most laudable masterstroke of our existence, and the only one?[518]

Different though it is from his fiction, *Conspiracy* is very much a Ligotti book, both in style and in the ideas it contains. *Conspiracy* is, in a way, the logical next step in Ligotti's trajectory as a writer. While the book is "philosophical" in a general sense, in reading *Conspiracy* one gets the feeling that Ligotti has pushed the boundaries of horror fiction to the limit, where the next step would be to abandon the fictional elements altogether, dispensing with narrative, character, and plot, in favor of the *ideas* of horror fiction. It is not difficult to see a continuum stretching from the abstract mood pieces of Edgar Allan Poe, to Lovecraft's "documentary" approach to horror, to the psychological studies of Shirley Jackson and Richard Matheson, to a generation of later 20th century horror authors such as T.E.D. Klein and Kathe Koja. Lovecraft himself noted this in his 1927 essay *Supernatural Horror in Literature*, where he argues for an understanding of the horror genre in terms of thought — and the limits of thought — more than character, setting, or plot. It is an approach that, as Ligotti notes, characterizes nearly all supernatural horror fiction: "In the literature of supernatural horror, a familiar storyline is that of a character who encounters a paradox *in the flesh*, so to speak, and must face down or collapse in horror before this ontological perversion — something which should not be, yet is."[519]

This is horror fiction that is solely concept-driven, and the next step would be to abandon narrative altogether — or, perhaps, to sublimate narrative into a kind of nonfictional horror. In *Conspiracy*, Ligotti's writing moves from horror fiction to a "concept-horror."[520] On one page he will engage in a critical examination of philosophers such as Albert Camus or Miguel de Unamuno, and on the next page his writing will amorphously slide into the prose poetry Ligotti fans will be familiar with: "Then it begins. *This can't be happening*, you think — if you can think at all, if you are anything more than a whirlwind of panic"; "This is the whispering undercurrent that creeps into your thoughts — nothing is safe and nothing is off limits"; "No other life forms know they are alive, and neither do they know they will die. This is our curse alone … Everywhere around us are natural habitats, but within us is the shiver of startling and dreadful things. Simply put: *We are not from here*. If we vanished tomorrow, no organism on this planet would miss us."[521]

It is no surprise that the idea of pessimism lies at the core of *Conspiracy*, and in particular the status of pessimism in an era of radical changes in the environment and global human culture. That idea is encapsulated in what Ligotti calls Zapffe's paradox (named after the philosopher Peter Wessel Zapffe): the height of consciousness is to have revealed the uselessness of consciousness. A variant of this is given by the 19th-century German poet, bank clerk, and suicide Philipp Mainländer, also deeply influenced by Schopenhauer: "the knowledge that life is worthless is the flower of all human wisdom."[522] In Ligotti's exegesis, there is a negativity inherent in everything that exists, from inorganic matter to conscious thought, such that at its most developed state it negates itself (or consumes itself, or fulfills itself). In its most crystalline state, *X* is tantamount to the negation of *X*.

Zapffe is an important figure in Ligotti's book. He not only extends the pessimistic diagnosis of thinkers like Schopenhauer, but he steadfastly refuses any panacea or redemption. In this situation, Zapffe diagnosed the various means that we as human beings have developed for staving off the radically misanthropic tendencies of consciousness (including strategies such as: isolating such thoughts from our everyday lives; anchoring them in belief systems such as religion or science; distracting ourselves with the here and now; and the therapeutic sublimation in artistic expression). Zapffe's conclusions were starkly anti-natalist: not only should we cease from procreating, he suggests, but we should consider the best means by which we as a species can facilitate an extinction that is, in Zapffe's opinion, both inevitable and long overdue.

Zapffe is only one of many personages that makes an appearance in *Conspiracy*. There is, as one might expect, a discussion of

Schopenhauer's thesis that all living beings are blindly driven by an anonymous and indifferent "Will-to-Life." But there is also suicidal Schopenhauerian Philipp Mainländer, who suggested a "Will-to-Die" inherent in all beings, living or not — and who speculated on the possibility of God's suicide to correlate with that of human beings. And then there is the Italian writer and philosopher Carlo Michelstaedter, who offers the idea that human beings are the puppets or playthings of unknown forces that may or may not exist — a conspiracy without conspirators. Such thinkers hold a privileged position for Ligotti. Their brand of pessimism refuses any redemptive move towards something beyond pessimism. Pessimism in this view is not simply a practical form of realism, keeping our feet on the ground and preventing us from getting lost in delusions of grandeur. Pessimism is also not simply another name for secularism, bolstering a renewed faith in human choice and action after the cold shower of the death of God. In short, in Ligotti's hands, pessimism stands in contrast to a "heroic" pessimism that ultimately serves human goals and aspirations.[523]

What remains, then, but the tragic (or, perhaps, the tragicomedic)? In a sense, what characterizes pessimistic philosophies, particularly the kind that Ligotti is drawn to, is that they have internalized a lesson from the literary tradition of supernatural horror — thinkers like Schopenhauer, Mainländer, or Zapffe unknowingly write philosophy as if they were writers of horror fiction; they invoke this shift from a philosophy of horror to a horror of philosophy:

> Consciousness is an existential liability, as every pessimist agrees — a blunder of blind nature, according to Zapffe, that has taken humankind down a black hole of logic. To make it through this life, we must make believe that we are not what we are — contradictory beings whose continuance only worsens our plight as mutants who embody the contorted logic of a paradox. To correct this blunder, we should desist from procreating. What could be more

> judicious or more urgent, existentially speaking, than our self-administered oblivion?[524]

This kind of thinking, in which horror and philosophy mutually imply each other, must also confront the obvious contradictions that are internal to it. *Conspiracy* is fascinating in this sense because Ligotti is constantly aware of building up a thought that must eventually undermine itself (and this is, no doubt, the reason for the carnivalesque, gallows humor that runs through much of the book). At times Ligotti will argue for a relation between the self and the world based on the metaphor of conspiracy — the world as perennially working against us, if only by virtue of the fact that we are mortal beings ephemerally existing in finitude and temporality. But at other moments Ligotti will acknowledge that this too is, in a way, the height of humanist thinking, though a perverted humanism that is still able to conceive of human beings as being the center of the universe (love me, hate me, but let me know that you care...). What remains for Ligotti is a relation between self and world based on neutrality, indifference, anonymity. And perhaps this is the horror of horrors — the blankness of the world, the blindness of being. As a book *Conspiracy* is an expression of the pessimist's dilemma: that the worthlessness of life and its philosophical realization itself tend to become worthwhile. And in this, *Conspiracy* might be characterized as a form of ecstatic pessimism, a pessimism that is resolutely misanthropic and without redemption, but that compelled to bear witness to the failure of thought that constitutes it.

If works of supernatural horror are "philosophical" it is not because they have explained anything — quite the reverse. This is what intimately ties horror to philosophy — not that philosophy, which explains everything, would explain horror, making it both meaningful and useful, but that philosophy — all philosophy — eventually discovers within itself a hard limit to what can be known, what can be thought, and what can be said.

*

Dance of the Void. Ligotti's 1994 book *Noctuary* contains a short piece, "The Puppet Masters." It consists of a brief confession of an unnamed narrator who appears to have secret conversations with the puppets, dolls, and marionettes that lay about his room: "Who else would listen to them and express what they have been through? Who else could understand their fears, however petty they may seem at times?" In an uncanny reversal, the narrator begins to suspect he too is a puppet; and the humanoid puppets are also alarmingly unhuman. They are mute and indifferent, like puppet masters. Doubt piles upon doubt, encroaching on the once self-assured bastion of consciousness:

> Do I ever speak to them of my own life? No; that is, not since a certain incident which occurred some time ago. To this day I don't know what came over me. Absent-mindedly I began confessing some trivial worry, I've completely forgotten what it was. And at that moment all their voices suddenly stopped, every one of them, leaving an insufferable vacuum of silence.[525]

The narrator is lead to a perhaps inevitable conclusion: the puppet without strings, the conspiracy without conspirators.

The figure of the puppet pervades much of Ligotti's fiction and philosophy. While the motif is often interpreted within a human-centered framework (where the puppet and puppeteer are allegories of human power dynamics), for Ligotti the puppet is first and foremost a reminder of a fundamental *depersonalization* that courses through humanity, and perhaps even the nature of existence itself. Human beings, in their most quintessentially "human" moments, reveal a metaphysical awkwardness that suggests how strange and estranged "the human" has always been. For Ligotti, the puppet is an exemplar of a kind of concept-horror, an uncanny manifestation of the lifelike that seems to blatantly contradict what we think we know about the world. "We need to know that puppets are puppets," Ligotti notes. "Nevertheless ... if we look at a puppet in a certain way, we may sometimes feel it is looking back, not as a human being looks at us but as a puppet does."[526] As with the puppet, so with our fraught relationship to an enigmatic, indifferent world in which we find ourselves embedded.

In taking up this theme, Ligotti is also pointing to a long tradition of deeply ambivalent attitudes towards puppets and their avatars (dolls, mannequins, dummys, figurines, and perhaps also automata, robots, androids, and their kin). In the supernatural horror tradition, E.T.A. Hoffmann's story "The Sandman" (1816) is for many the exemplar of this ambivalence, where mechanism and magic combine in the character of Olimpia, who not only plays the harpsichord, but also sings and dances with a coldness that makes her the object of adoration. Hoffmann's story not only gives us the uncannily human qualities of an automaton, but it also shows us the disturbing artifice of human beings and human social behavior, asking us who the real automata are. Likewise, the specters of Industrial automation infuse stories such as Edgar Allan Poe's "The Man That Was Used Up" (1839) with metaphysical reflections on the horrors of an indifferent and mechanistic cosmos, and the absurd futility of human attempts to control and master such forces. Similar themes can be witnessed into the 20th century, in the British horror film *Dead of Night* (1945), the famous *Twilight Zone* episode "The Dummy" (1962), as well as numerous contemporary horror films such as *The Boy* (2017).

Puppets in these and other examples both point to the uncanniness of the puppet as well as the artifice of "real" human beings. However, the puppet draws away from human likeness as much as it approaches the human likeness. It is this strange, dehumanizing aspect of the puppet that is at once the most evocative but also the most disturbing. This is what strikes dramatist and author Heinrich von Kleist, recounted in his short essay "On the Puppet Theater" (*Über das Marionettentheater*, 1810). Kleist is an unwieldly figure, even by German literary standards. He shared early Romanticism's fascination with the limits of human experience, but remained skeptical of its aspirations for the Absolute. His prose writings contain acute criticisms of human behavior and society, but he was as cynical about any claims for "revolution" as he was about the established order of things. His literary output ranks him alongside Goethe, Schiller, and Heine, and yet his "aristocratism" sets him apart from any literary movement or trend. While Kleist's writings do fall into categories — plays, novels, stories, essays — his writing is always diverging from genre restrictions, where fiction is written as nonfiction, and nonfiction as fiction, where philosophical exegesis gives way to the parable or the anecdote, where even personal letters become a literary form in and of themselves.

This is evidenced in Kleist's short essay on puppets. Written as if a diary entry, it recounts (one supposes) Kleist's encounter, one winter evening, with a professional dancer in the city's opera. A conversation ensues between them, the dancer expressing his admiration for the art of puppetry. As Kleist notes, "[h]e assured me that the pantomime of these puppets gave him much pleasure, and suggested in no uncertain terms that any dancer who wished to improve his art might learn all sorts of things from them." A technical discussion elaborates the relationships between the curves and straight lines of the puppet strings, the dancer noting that it is precisely the attachment of the strings to the limbs that gives the puppet is unique sense of grace — the dancer noting that, even if the strings are shaken in a random way, "the whole puppet assumed a kind of rhythmic motion that was very much like a dance."[527]

Listening to the dancer, Kleist seems to intuit the analogies behind the discussion. If a puppet displays such choreographic sensitivity, surely this must be an indication that, in a way, the puppeteer is a kind of dancer themselves? Not so, the dancer replies. The concatenation of line, string, and gravity are a "path of the dancer's soul," and the quality of "dance" we ascribe to the puppet is in actuality "the puppeteer transposing himself into the center of gravity of the marionette; or, in other words, by *dancing* … like the relation of numbers to their logarithms or asymptotes to their hyperbola."[528]

As the discussion wanders more and more into fringe territory, Kleist begins to wonder why the dancer, emblem of high culture that he is, should be so taken by the "low" or popular form of puppetry. To which the dancer matter-of-factly replies, that puppets have two advantages over human beings: first, puppets are "incapable of affectation," and therefore freed of the burdens of consciousness, self-awareness, and ego which, for the dancer, sooner or later seeps into even the most accomplished human performers.

Secondly, the dancer continues, puppets have the advantage of "countergravity." In their contrasting physics of pulling up and letting down, the puppet is oblivious to the laws of gravity, the density of matter, the slothlike inertia of flesh. For the dancer, there is an almost occult transference between the gravity of the puppet and the antigravity of the puppet strings. In that weird space between gravity and antigravity, something impersonal "expresses" itself, something paradoxically expressed via the dehumanized and impersonal qualities of the puppet and its uncanny physics of choreography.

Kleist, struggling to comprehend the dancer's theories, asks, but surely no puppet can ever exceed what the human performer can do? Not so, the dancer replies. When it comes to this impersonal dance, no human being can ever compete with a puppet. "Only a god, on this field of contest, could prove a match for matter; and here is where both ends of the ring-shaped world interlock."[529]

Largely unrecognized in his time, Kleist's writings are today well-established in the European literary canon. To many, however, Kleist is also remembered for this fraught and tragic life. A descendent of Prussian nobility, the young Kleist made several attempts at a military career, all of which ended only in failure and disillusion. As a student his studies included everything from physics to history to Latin to mathematics, but these too he found limiting, and after a few years he left university, eventually taking up a series of middling administrative positions. His wandering soon led him into literary circles (Berlin, Dresden, Paris, Prague, Weimar), where he came into contact with many luminaries of the day. He made attempts to write and produce plays, as well as edit and publish journals. However most of his plays were ignored, and publishing ventures often came to nothing. As his letters reveal, there is the sense that Kleist was, on the one hand, constantly disappointed by life, and, on other hand, that his life was not his own, that he, perhaps like all of us, was subject to larger impersonal forces that could only be dimly intuited. Kleist's despair reached a peak in 1811, while in Berlin, where he seemed to find a kindred spirit in musician Henriette Vogel. Vogel was terminally ill with cancer, and with Kleist, the tragic couple made a suicide pact, which they carried out on the 21st of November.

Historians and scholars have provided every variety of interpretation, both of Kleist's writings and of his life. Suffice it to say that, in many cultures, the double suicide (or "lover's suicide") is a voluntary death of a particular sort. In its cultural representations, the double suicide is often the final act of two lives that are at once intertwined and yet perpetually prey to larger forces — social, existential, or cosmic — which seem to push and pull them within a chaotic physics of the impersonal. The final act is less a rebellion or an act of defiance than a kind of resignation, an almost religious self-abandon of the puppet to the enigmatic forces of gravity and antigravity.

This idea is also found in *Double Suicide*, the 1969 film directed by Masahiro Shinoda. In it, two star-crossed lovers in 18th century Osaka similarly find themselves enmeshed in the moral intricacies of class and social standing. At every turn, their attempts to be together are thwarted by the contingencies of their context. Eventually, the melodrama of futility gives way to a deeper despair, where both parties reach a limit, a point of crisis, beyond which there is only the will to abandon oneself completely. The act of double suicide (*shinjū*) is not only a tragic testimony to societal constraints, but it is also the deeply ambivalent act of giving oneself over to the strange and impersonal forces that condition all of existence, including that of social norms. *Double Suicide* is based on a famous play, *The Love Suicides at Amijima* (1721), written by

Still from *Double Suicide* (*Shinjū Ten no Amijima*, dir. Masahiro Shinoda, 1969)

Chikamatsu Monzaemon. Chikamatsu's play was originally written for *bunraku*, the traditional form of Japanese puppetry theater popular at the time. Known both for its technical virtuosity and its grace of movement, *bunraku* typically involves elaborate puppets operated by one or more puppeteers, clothed in all black so as to disguise their presence and heighten the illusion of the uncanniness of the puppets. In *Double Suicide*, director Shinoda self-consciously references this tradition (especially in the opening credits, where we see *bunraku* puppeteers preparing for a performance). While the film itself follows the lover's melodrama through the heightened artifice of the stage sets (much as in traditional theater), we also see the shadowy figures of the puppeteers, clad in the traditional all-black, moving through the diegetic space of the drama, invisibly pulling and loosening the strings of the human actors.

This conceit — to treat human actors as puppets — gives *Double Suicide* the strange aura that it has, at once impassioned and detached, personal and impersonal. In the film's final scenes, the star-crossed lovers have reached their limit, ready to abandon everything, and for a brief moment, they feel the strings give way, as they flee the cloistered world of the stage sets and run, half-deranged, into the fields. They cross a tall, solitary bridge, two huddled figures. Out of nowhere, they see a black-cloaked figure before them.

*

Monastery Horror. In supernatural horror, the uncertainty that marks "the fantastic" is not only an uncertainty between "it's all in your head" (the uncanny) and "it really happened" (the marvelous), but it is also a lived uncertainty, an existential wavering that is inhabited, a structure of experience into which one is unwillingly thrown that allows, for a brief moment, the collapse of all boundaries. This is likely why so many tales of the supernatural take place in landscapes of solitude such as forests, mountains, deserts, and the sea. But it is also why the fantastic tends to creep forward within human-made structures of solitude, from the proverbial cabin in the woods to the estrangement specific to modern, urban high-rises.

The monastic tradition is a case in point. Monasteries are not simply the backdrop for the drama of spiritual struggle and ascetic practice; as built spaces, they are inseparable from the drama of the spiritual itinerary itself. In early Christianity, the monastery provided a practical means for allowing individuals to pursue their spiritual and ascetic practices.[530] As built spaces, however, the monastery becomes an important factor in that spiritual practice. Partly out of necessity and partly out of a concern for "refusing the world," monasteries are negative spaces, eliminating everything unnecessary from the world of human affairs, life emptied of all its contents so that some other form of life might emerge. The monastery is in this sense life evacuated of all its contents, all hopes, fears, desires, and concerns of living a human life in a human world. Because

Still from *Two Monks* (*Dos Monjes*, dir. Juan Bustillo Oro, 1934)

of this, an abyss always looms within the monastery. Though the monastery is the site of this spiritual training, it is not an endeavor that is without its dangers. The bottom drops out; there is no safety net for the human being that has repudiated both the "human" and "being."

An example of this is given in *Two Monks* (*Dos Monjes*), a 1934 Mexican Gothic melodrama directed by Juan Bustillo Oro. On the surface the plot of *Two Monks* is straightforward. At an unnamed, remote monastery, a monk named Javier begins to display erratic and troubling behavior — despondency, despair, impulsiveness, anger — at one point suddenly attacking another monk, named Juan. Fearing that Javier may be possessed by demons, he is confined to a monastic cell, whereupon he confesses that he and Juan actually know each other, and that the reason for his decision to enter the monastery has to do with a bitter past that they share. Told in flashbacks, we learn of Javier's past, his aspirations to become a composer, his struggle with failing health (he is described as "consumptive"), and the tragic love triangle that involves Ana (a singer), and his childhood friend Juan. Javier's recounting of his past seems to have a curative effect. That is, until Juan recounts his version of events, which disturbingly contradicts nearly everything in Javier's account. By the end of the film, Javier is redeemed through his faith, but not before he descends into a wild delirium that could be either mystical vision or the final effects of his illness.

Two Monks is noteworthy on several accounts. It leverages the dramatic tension of differing points of view within the secluded, solitary space of the monastery. Without external points of reference, all we are left with is the trembling and uncertain narrative accounts of the two monks, each traumatized in different ways by the same experience. Their mutually exclusive accounts push the narrative into a tension-filled zone where the very aspects of the human mind that allow memory are also the same things that undermine it. As Javier recounts his brief and tortured life, the film moves back to the austerity of the monastic cell — as if Javier's memory, however unreliable, is using the barren cell walls as a projection screen. In the monastic cell, reality and fantasy collapse into each other.

Two Monks is noteworthy on a formal level as well. The film uses a double flashback, in effect telling two versions of the same story that negate each other. What's more, when the film cuts back to the despairing solitude of the monastic cell, then returns to the flashback scene, what is gradually produced is a kind of delirium in the film itself, as if, by the film's end, everything — past and present, reality and fantasy, memory and imagination — all of it starts to crumble and implode upon itself. Watching it today, nearly a century after it was made, the entire film seems like an extended dream allegory of the trembling human mind, struggling to comprehend its own limitations before the nebulous and opaque finitude of being human.

In the background of *Two Monks* is the question of the uncertainty of point of view, particularly magnified by the austere solitude of monasticism and the ascetic allure of a life of refusal.

We are never sure, even by the film's deranged and hallucinatory finale, whether or not Javier's account of events is accurate, or if they are fabrications of a solitary consciousness weighed down by worldly remorse and the suffering of life. The hesitation that defines "the fantastic" is woven into the very fabric of genre horror, even if the horrors presented turn out to have quite secular and mundane explanations. Perhaps there is a categorical imperative embedded within this tradition: act as if everything presented to you is *not* what it seems. That forest campsite, a despondent seaside town, a sluggish rural village, an ennui-ridden city street, the cold anonymity of the monastery — these are where the fantastic "takes place," an ephemeral uncertainty rendered topographical. At the site of the fantastic, all the swirling interactions comprising the world suddenly become constricted into a solitude beyond estrangement; in this suspended moment one finds only an indifferent world, an inadequate language, an uncertain self.

The monastic cell is the site of the fantastic, stripped to its bare minimum. Although, as the 6th-century *Rule of Benedict* tells us, there are different kinds of monks — cenobites, who live in cloistered communities with other monks, and anchorites or hermits, who live isolated from others — what they have in common is an ongoing practice of stripping away the self through asceticism and spiritual practice. True to the term, the idea of ascetic practice is borrowed in part from classical Greece, where the term *askesis* was conventionally applied to the discipline and training of athletes and warriors. For early Christian hermits, these ascetic practices — which included prayer, fasting, work, and of course the famous battles with "demons" — are *askesis* in the sense of "spiritual exercise." That is the ideal, at least. What the early monks quickly discovered was that the solitude of the cell and monastery often led to spiritual chaos rather than tranquility. John Cassian, the 4th-century desert monastic, described this state as *accedie* — a complicated term that encompasses listlessness, restlessness, torpor, ennui, and depression.

Sometimes *accedie* could lead a monk astray, causing them to abandon the practice altogether, or, in other cases, to descend into madness, fever, delusion. Sometimes *accedie* could actually lead to spiritual insights, ambiguous though they could be; *accedie* could itself become a practice, an *askesis*. Guibert of Nogent, an 11th-century Benedictine monk, recounts his struggles with *accedie* in his *Monodiae* ("Solitary Songs") in prose that looks ahead to the Gothic novel:

> One night (in winter I believe) I was awakened by an intense feeling of panic. I remained in my bed and felt assured by the light of a lamp close by, which threw off a bright light. Suddenly I heard, not far above me, the clamor of what seemed to me many voices coming out of the dark of night, voices without words. The violence of the clamor struck my temples. I fell unconscious, as if in sleep, and I thought I saw appearing to me a dead man … Terrified by the specter I leapt out of the bed screaming, and as I did so I saw the lamp go out.[531]

A whole tradition of monastery horror could be drawn from passages like this: Gothic classics such as Matthew Lewis's *The Monk* (1795), modern science fiction such as Fritz Leiber's *Gather, Darkness!* (1950) and Walter M. Miller Jr.'s *A Canticle for Leibowitz* (1959), late 20th-century bestsellers such as Umberto Eco's *The Name of the Rose* (1980), and contemporary examples of "the new weird" in fiction, film, and TV.

One work that captures this sense of monastery horror is Michael Cisco's 1999 novel *The Divinity Student*. Told in a series of short prose sections, it recounts in vivid, florid language the strange death and resurrection of an anonymous protagonist known only as "The Divinity Student." Drawn into a network of strange conspiracies, The Divinity Student wanders the desert city of San Veneficio, where he is tasked with compiling the Catalog of Unknown Words, whose true purpose remains enigmatic yet nefarious. From its first passages Cisco's novel refuses any clear distinction between what is "really" happening and what is illusion. Cadavers mingle with old books, and lost words alchemically seep into the narrative with all the solidity of chemical compounds. The result is an unsettling collapse between "it really happened" and "it's all in your head."

Cisco's monastery horror captures the ephemeral and uncertain quality of the fantastic, and sustains it throughout the novel. This is largely due to Cisco's language, which is at once lyrical — at times bordering on prose poetry — and yet at the same time acutely aware of its inability to capture the fantastic. A poetics of uncertainty, a lyricism of failure. Is this not what many authors in the supernatural horror tradition secretly aim for?

Ultimately, these examples of monastery horror point back to the source texts of the hermits and monks in the deserts of 4th and 5th century Egypt. There, the desert becomes much more than a landscape; it is *eremos*, the Greek from which we drive "hermit," but which can also mean "wasteland." For the early "Desert Fathers" and "Desert Mothers," *eremos* indicates not only the desert, but a deserted terrain, a landscape inhospitable to human life, a place without people. The place where one hesitates, like a wandering, peripatetic philosopher having strayed from the path. Once, a hermit living in the deserts of Scetis asked an old hermit there for advice. The old man replied: "Are you still alive? Go and sit in your cell, and think to yourself that you have been in your grave a year already."[532] The hermit returned to his cell, perhaps having learned nothing.

5

AS IF...

As If. In the 1780s, at the peak of an epoch that ceremoniously referred to itself as "Enlightenment," Immanuel Kant was writing about ethics. Of course numerous philosophers, from Socrates to Spinoza, had thought about ethics prior to Kant's time. But during the Enlightenment, which Kant himself would characterize as humanity's coming into "maturity," the stakes were, arguably, different. If the "sleep of reason" did indeed produce monsters, it was time for reason to wake up, and to place itself at the center of the quest for knowledge, the pursuit of truth, and the engaged attitudes of civil society. In conjunction with paradigm shifts in astronomy, physics, mathematics, and medicine, the so-called human sciences would follow suit, with a new philosophy, a new aesthetics, and a new ethics founded exclusively on the authority of human reason, without recourse to religion, myth, or superstition.

But the trick was to develop an ethical philosophy that would go beyond a mere list of "dos" and "don'ts" — a task not only unending but continually subject to amendment and modification. In short, Kant was aware that ethical philosophy needed to move beyond mere *hypothetical* imperatives of the type "if A is the case, then do B." Human beings were not, after all, ethical automata, gears and pulleys cloaked by an anthropomorphic shell. Or were they? Kant's solution was to argue for an ethics that would be unconditional — what was required was not just hypothetical imperatives, but a *categorical* imperative, a "do this" that would apply in each and every case, no matter the details. In his 1785 work *Groundwork for the Metaphysics of Morals* Kant provided several definitions of this categorical imperative. One of them reads: "act only in accordance with that maxim through which you can at the same time will that it become a universal law."[533]

The problem, of course, is that it can be incredibly difficult to behave in this unconditional manner. It requires an almost *religious* devotion to scientific reason and the cold logic of universal moral law. For every example of a categorical imperative (e.g., "One should always tell the truth"; "One should always help others") it is easy, all too easy, to think of exceptions, even compounded ones ("…unless telling the truth does not help others…").

At the core of Kant's approach to ethical philosophy is the problem of the "as if." Kant never says that such moral laws *are* universal … or laws … or even moral. What he says is that one should act with such a level of commitment that one would be prepared to claim universal status for such actions. Act *as if* your actions, and the values behind them, are universally valid. As he notes, "act *as if* the maxim of your action were to become by your will a universal law of nature."[534]

Just pretend it's for real.

Nevertheless, Kant stood by his categorical imperative. The implications not only for the individual citizen but for civil society were obvious. The French Revolution, after all, was just around the corner — as was the Terror. Phantoms lurking around every moral corner in a labyrinth designed by human beings, for human beings, to liberate or to enslave.

*

The Wandering Philosopher. If the Enlightenment was about anything, it was about putting theory into practice, about walking the philosophical walk, about showing that reason was not merely an abstract, intellectual exercise with no impact in the "real" world. And Kant loved to walk. He walked, without exception, every day, through the town of Königsberg, where he lived for most of his life. Whether he *loved* it or not is another question.

Did the 70-year-old philosopher, while he was writing his ethical treatises, encounter annoying or difficult people while on his walks? If so, did he view such unfortunate encounters as opportunities to put his "categorical imperative" to the test?

It was often said that the washerwomen of Königsberg could tell the time of day by when the elderly but able-bodied Kant walked by their houses.

*

Dethroned. It is often said that the philosophy of Kant effected a "Copernican turn" in the history of thought, just as, a generation earlier, the astronomer Nicolaus Copernicus demonstrated that the sun, and not the earth, was at the center of our planetary system. Even though Copernicus displaced the earth — and by extension humanity — from the center of the universe, he also put humanity back in the center by showing how human reason alone — without religion, without scripture, and without the Church — could achieve the *fiat* of scientific explanation.

By the time of the industrial dawn of the 20th century, scientific reason had explained much — perhaps too much. There was talk of relativity, the fourth dimension, the space-time continuum, and the first whispers of quantum uncertainty. The distance separating the scientific picture of reality and the way reality "ought to be" began to grow further and further apart.

An avid science reader and amateur science journalist, H.P. Lovecraft noted these changes taking place. Likely Lovecraft sensed something at once modern and primordial in these epistemic shifts. They seemed to, once again, displace humanity from the center of the universe. Lovecraft's now-celebrated "The Call of Cthulhu" (published in the February 1928 issue of *Weird Tales*), summarized these strange reversals of fortune, noting the hubris of this "placid island of ignorance" on which resides our temporary and fragile systems of knowledge, the humbling effect of "the inability of the human mind to correlate all its contents," the realization of an absolute limit to human knowledge that pointed only to "black seas of infinity" or worse, "terrifying vistas of reality" which reveal with cold precision the insignificance of human life in the vast cosmos.[535]

Should we then suggest another turn in the Copernican revolution, after Copernicus, and after Kant — a "Lovecraftian turn"? Not only are we human beings not at the center of the universe, but we are no longer capable of knowing that we are not at the center. Our highest cognitive faculties, inclusive of scientific rationality, seem only to lead to paradox, opacity, and, strangely, to mystery. The more we know, the less we know — and what we know of this doesn't bode well for humanity, and its self-endowed, species-specific dominion.

Perhaps there is another stage even after this. Not much has changed — no one still really understands quantum physics, and everyday reality shows itself to be stranger than fiction. Except that no one cares, or, indeed, bothers to notice. We have become skilled in selectively ignoring the world, even when it shows itself to be blatantly counterintuitive or indifferent. A new *ignorance* is on the horizon, a "learned ignorance" borne not of a lack of knowledge but of too much knowledge, too much data, too many theories, too little time.

Strangely, Kant already foresaw this, as did mystical philosophers such as Nicholas of Cusa or Meister Eckhart. What Kant termed the "antinomies of reason" were those issues that could be debated forever and never resolved — the existence of God, the origin of the universe, life after death. Don't bother thinking about these things, he advised; leave such questions to the theologians or the astronomers — they are not *philosophical* questions.

The humility of philosophy. With Kant, thought attains a humbleness through its rigor. With Lovecraft, that humility is transformed into futility.

*

The Earth, a Relic. We do Nietzsche a disservice when we credit him for the "death of God." He just happened to be at the scene of the crime, and found the corpse. Actually, it wasn't even murder — it was suicide. Perhaps this is why, around 1885, Nietzsche writes in his notebook: "The opposition is dawning between the world we revere and the world which we live — which we are. It remains for us to abolish either our reverence or ourselves."[536]

*

Phantasms (III). Where ethical philosophy leaves off, supernatural horror begins. Kant: "morality is no phantom…"[537]

*

Delightful Horror, Tranquility in Terror. If we accept the philosophical premises of supernatural horror, it can be difficult to walk away from such works without an acute sense of the senselessness of life — in particular, human life — in its relation to an indifferent cosmos. All the same, human beings and their worldly concerns do populate tales of supernatural horror, and many of them take place within the all-too-familiar confines of meaning-making cultures. In his book *The Fantastic* Tzvetan Todorov notes that the hesitation that defines the "fantastic" is by definition ephemeral. The moment we can rationally explain the fantastic event (it was just a dream; a bit of visual trickery; it was the fourth dimension; I was on drugs — or I am hallucinating when I'm not on drugs?) we then leave the fantastic and enter into the "uncanny." It only seemed supernatural but can actually be explained (and thus, explained away). However, sometimes the fantastic is affirmed as that which exists outside of human comprehension, and here we again leave the fantastic and enter the domain of the "marvelous." It not only seemed, but really is supernatural — but then we have to rethink basic things about what we think we know about the world. Either way, there is a residue of the fantastic that remains at the horizon of intelligibility.

If, as per Lovecraft's description, supernatural horror centers on the "fear of the unknown" and the limit of thought, this limit must also be connected to another limit, the limit of the senses. The failure of thought is indelibly tied to the failure of the senses. The aesthetic correlate of the fantastic is what philosophers like Kant referred to as the sublime. Kant's theory of the sublime is well-known.[538] It involves an experience in which I am overwhelmed by my senses, such that they cannot encompass or apprehend what is given to them. This feeling of being overwhelmed is a result of a contrast of scale or granularity: between my human level of sensing the world, and a nonhuman level "above" or "below" that of the human. For this reason Kant simply defines the sublime as "that which is absolutely great," or conversely, "that which is great beyond all comparison."[539]

At the same time that my senses are overwhelmed, I am still experiencing something, even if what I am experiencing is my senses being overwhelmed. What I "sense" is the failure of the senses. At the limit of the human being's capacity for sensing is the sense of the limit of the senses, and by extension, the thought of the limit of thought. Importantly, Kant qualifies the sublime in terms of negation: "the satisfaction in the sublime in nature is thus only *negative* … a feeling of the deprivation of the freedom of the imagination by itself…"[540]

And yet, this is also the point where the sublime turns from the tragic to the heroic. For Kant, it is precisely in this awareness of its own limits that the human being redeems itself. It is in this awareness, which is not itself sensory — a "supersensible substrate" — that we are able to acknowledge these limits, including the limit of thought. As Kant notes, "even to be able to think the given infinite without contradiction requires a faculty in the human mind that is itself supersensible."[541] The human being's final move is to make of this failure a teaching moment.

I confess I've always found Kant's humanist recuperation of the sublime disappointing. Not that it's wrong — just disappointing. Must the human being always, at whatever cost, attain dominion over the world into which it's thrown, even at the moment that it is overwhelmed and rendered insignificant? Must every failure of human-centrism be obliged to turn into success? The tricky part lies in the quandary Kant describes: the human being at once determined by its limits, and thinking beyond its limits. Perhaps this is why Edmund Burke chose to describe the sublime in deliberately ambiguous, seemingly contradictory ways: a "delightful horror," or alternately, a "tranquility tinged with terror."[542]

*

A Once-Living Shadow. The terms phantasmagoria, phantasm, and phantom all share a common etymological root — the Greek *phantazein* (to make visible) and *phainein* (to show). Strange, then, that the same terms would come to denote precisely that which is not seen, or rather, that which is seen with uncertainty. The tradition of the Gothic novel is replete with phantoms of this type; we as readers are never sure if the characters have actually seen a ghost or have simply misjudged the night wind languorously blowing a curtain.

But every phantom — real or imagined — is doubled, referring to a once-living person as well as being a spectral manifestation in and of itself. Every phantom is literally beside itself, not unlike the many cases of disenchanted doubling in the literature of the fantastic, from Dostoevsky's *The Double* (1846), to Shirley Jackson's *The Bird's Nest* (1954), to D.P. Watt's *The Phantasmagorical Imperative* (2014).

Yakov Petrovich Goliadkin, the middling, reclusive bureaucrat in Dostoevsky's novel, returns home one night after having been chastised by his doctor for his anti-social tendencies. In the snow-lit haze of winter night, Goliadkin begins to feel a palpable sense of unease. Arriving home, he encounters a stranger that is the exact likeness of himself. "All of Mr. Goliadkin's forebodings had come perfectly true. All that he had feared and anticipated had now become reality. His breath broke off, his head spun. The stranger sat before him, also in his overcoat and hat, on his own bed, smiling slightly, narrowing his eyes a little, nodding to him amicably."[543]

To live twice, life redoubled in the minutiae of insignificance. "To be besides oneself" — as one's own shadow, as a doppelgänger, as one who exists twice … perhaps twice more than necessary.

*

Phantasms (IV). The phantasmagorical imperative: everything unreal must appear. The phantom imperative: act as if everything real is unreal.

*

The World Becomes a Phantom. Kant's philosophy is, without a doubt, philosophy in the grand style — rigorous, systematic, an architectonics of part and whole. And, for this reason, a touch naive. For, how many of us are really capable of acting according to the cold logic of reason, irrespective of our individual desires, our fears and tremblings, our displaced egos and species-wide impostor syndromes?

Kant seemed aware of this. Forget about the impossibility of everyone acting according to moral or ethical criteria; simply coming to agreement on what those criteria are — the list of "dos" and "don'ts" — is almost a greater impossibility than the fantasy of everyone behaving accordingly. The stakes are too high, it seems. It only works if *everyone* plays along.

But the truly disturbing thing is not just that other people might not act accordingly, but that the whole nonhuman world may not act accordingly — *that the world itself may not play along*. Objects behaving strangely, familiar places suddenly unfamiliar, the inorganic world suddenly staring back. Kant continues: "It is true that, even though a rational being scrupulously follows this maxim himself, he cannot for that reason count upon every other to be faithful to the same maxim nor can he count upon the kingdom of nature and its purposive order to harmonize with him ... that is, upon its favoring his expectation of happiness..."[544]

*

Spectral Suicide. The 17th century scientist, philosopher, and occultist Athanasius Kircher once designed a novel device using a simple candle-powered magic lantern and glass slide. A product of Kircher's interests in optics, he associated these so-called "phantasmagorias" and their ability to produce lifelike, animate images with a kind of vitalistic life-force. Such devices soon proliferated across the cultural centers of 18th- and 19th-century Europe, including the Parisian Cabaret du Néant, where visitors could enjoy an appropriately scary ghost show along with their absinthe. Soon phantasmagoria and magic lantern shows could be found everywhere, along with stereoscopes and other visual media — many of which could be purchased in the then-popular Parisian arcades, with their rows of equally magical window displays — uncanny mannequins, dismembered hats, shoes, gloves, necklaces, walking canes, eyeglasses, children's toys; all the charms of an era quickly vanishing. It was no wonder that Walter Benjamin, living in Paris in the 1920s, would describe the modern commodities of European cities themselves as so many phantasmagoria.

Predominately used for entertainment purposes, the enchanting qualities of 18th- and 19th-century phantasmagoria were also taken quite seriously by those interested in the occult. In Leipzig, the inventor, occultist, and coffee-shop owner Johann Schröpfer designed his own phantasmagoria, which he shared with his Freemason colleagues. In a chilling sequence of events, Schröpfer would himself become a phantasmagoria. So taken was he by the conjuring powers and lifelike qualities of its spectral images, that, during one demonstration, Schröpfer proclaimed that a dead person could be resurrected through the powers of the phantasmagoria. It is said that, in or around 1774, Schröpfer attempted to prove his theories by killing himself — on stage. (Needless to say, the subsequent revitalization was not successful.)

*

An Argument For or Against the Categorical Imperative. "I haven't read as many books as you have, but if they make you this miserable I don't think I want to."[545]

*

Demon-Haunted (Li He). There is an atmosphere of melancholy that courses through much of Classical Chinese poetry, no doubt influenced in part by the pervasive sense of transiency that marks both Taoist and Buddhist thinking. The famous poem "Encountering Sorrow" (*Li Sao*), thought to have been written in the 3rd century BCE, tells of the hopes, aspirations, disappointments, and despair of a precarious life enmeshed in the human world of human-centered concerns. The twists and turns of fortune, political infighting, insurgency and counterinsurgency, intrigues at court, failed romances and lost loves, factionalism and divisiveness, even the petty resentments that constitute everyday life — all of these are recounted in the poem's 300 lines, as failure eclipses failure, leading the poet to eventually question the value of life itself. Engulfed by despair and inundated with disgust, the poet repudiates the world of human affairs. But where this leads is uncertain. The remaining lines of the poem recount a strange, mythical, fantastical journey that ironically leads back to despair and the limits of human understanding. Is this a dream, or has the poet died?

It is likely that "Encountering Sorrow" was an influence on the poet Li He, who, even by the standards of Classical Chinese poetry, excelled all others in the leaden melancholy and weird imagery of his poems. Born around 790 to a distant branch of nobility, Li

He's life has become the stuff of hagiography. A child prodigy, a promising career lay in front of him, yet his life was marked by disappointment, much of it due to petty jealousies and political scheming surrounding the civil service examination system. Moving from one middling position to another, Li He eventually abandoned civil service completely, retreating to his family's remote, dilapidated estate, located in a forested region of Hunan province. There he wrote many of the poems that mark his distinctive style, in surreal and fantastical imagery that drew as much from ancient myth and the natural surroundings as it did from poets of the Tang period such as Li Bai and Meng Jiao.

Demons, ghosts, nature spirits, cemeteries, forests, the moon, night music, and a whole bestiary of fantastical creatures populate Li He's poetry. In one poem, strange phenomena emerge as a solitary zither plays against the backdrop of a moonlit night:

> Cassia leaves stripped by the wind,
> Cassia seeds fall,
> Blue racoons are weeping blood
> As shivering foxes die.
> […]
> Owls that have lived a hundred years,
> Turned forest demons,
> Laugh wildly as an emerald fire
> Leaps from their nests.[546]

In another, "magic strings" seem to accompany the precise and shadowy procedures of a shamanistic ritual:

> The witch pours out a libation of wine,
> And clouds cover the sky,
> In a jade brazier charcoal burns —
> The incense booms.
> Gods of the sea and mountain demons
> Flock to her seat…[547]

It is lines like these that prompted Li He's contemporaries to describe him as a "demon-haunted" or "demon-cursed" poet, a moniker that seems also to reflect his short and tragic life. We will never know what discourse — Faustian or otherwise — Li He might have had with the beyond. But it seems to have left its mark on him. When Li He died in c.816, he was weathered, white-haired, and not yet 30 years old.

An oft-repeated anecdote paints a picture of Li He in the style of a *poète maudit*: gaunt, sickly, unkempt and fingernails overgrown, brows furrowed and with an enigmatic expression of sorrow and detachment on his face. Each morning he leaves, riding his horse, a tattered brocade bag of paper strips on his back. As he writes poems, he puts them back in his bag, reassembling them once home (or not, as he would just as often abandon the poems altogether in favor of wine). Another anecdote has Li He writing down the poems, and then casually discarding them along the forest floor, as if to suggest an almost ritual act of composting, the poetry destined to disintegrate back into the Earth, like the human corpse itself.

*

Hymn to Horror. "All concepts and with them all principles are nevertheless related to empirical intuitions, i.e. to data for possible experience. Without this they have no objective validity at all, but are rather a mere play, whether it be with representations of the imagination or of the understanding."[548]

Philosophers such as Kant tell us that our senses are like eyeglasses we can never take off. If philosophy is a form of conjuring, then what of physics, which speaks to us cryptically of waves, particles, and strings? Both use reason to reveal to us the most unreasonable of propositions — that the world is not "our" world, but a world bereft of humanity, a world that impassively tolerates the ostentatious stage that we have placed at its center, with us stage center, performing endless soliloquies of impermanence. If philosophy is a form of magic, then physics is a necromancy. Perhaps poetry goes even further — a hymn.

*

Unholy Matter. In the Basilica San Domenico, to the right of the nave, within a reliquary altar, resides the head of Saint Catherine of Siena. Catherine, a 14th-century mystic and theologian, is the author of a number of mystical works, including the *Dialogue of Divine Providence*, and was also active in the religious politics of her time. The head of Catherine — sometimes referred to as the "Holy Head" or "Sacred Head" — is contained in an ornate silver shrine in the form of a miniature Gothic temple. Long said to have miraculous powers, Catherine's head was originally brought to the Basilica by Raymond of Capua, a Dominican monk who was both Catherine's confessor and her hagiographer. Following Catherine's death, there was some dispute about where her remains should reside, be it in Rome, the seat of the Church and the place where Catherine had died, or in Siena, her hometown. According to one oft-repeated account, Raymond, attempting to bring Catherine's body back to Siena, realized that the Church authorities would never allow this. Instead, he detached her head from her body, and, placing it in a sack, carried it out of Rome. But he was stopped by the guards. When they looked in the sack, they saw it was filled with lush, vibrant roses. They returned the sack to Raymond and sent him on his way back to Siena, where, it is said, Catherine's severed head rematerialized from the sack of roses.

The head of Catherine is one of many relics of Christian saints preserved to this day. The list of relics within Christianity alone is long and varied. It includes the hand of Teresa of Avila, the arm of Mary Magdalene, and the famous Shroud of Turin. After the death of Claire of Assisi, it is reported that guards had to be stationed around her body, as followers thronged towards the corpse, attempting to take away bits and pieces of it as holy mementos. When the corpse of Anthony of Padua was discovered to have incorruptible parts — the tongue, jaw, left arm and hand all refused to decay — these were detached from the rest of the corpse and encased in reliquaries. Specially constructed vessels were created for such relics, often with ornate designs which were custom shaped to the body part in question. Tombs long hidden from plain sight were unearthed and put on display, corpses in crypts visible through viewing windows on the floor.

Although the veneration of relics in Christianity began as early as the 3rd century, the practice grew significantly in the later Middle Ages. Though perhaps strange to the modern, secular mind, the theories and practices surrounding relics open onto more general questions concerning our embodied, material existence as human beings — and the limits of our ability to fully comprehend that materiality. The medieval historian Caroline Walker Bynum has done the most to articulate the philosophical, religious, and material aspects of relics such as these. As she notes:

> The transformed statues, chalices, wafers, cloths, relics, and even mounds of earth to which the faithful made pilgrimage in the fourteenth and fifteenth centuries presented a challenge that was theoretical as well as practical for a religion that held that the entire material world was created by and could therefore manifest God … Issues of how matter behaved, both ordinarily and miraculously, when in contact with an infinitely powerful and ultimately unknowable God were key to devotion and theology.[549]

The holy matter that Bynum studies includes "animated statues; bleeding hosts, walls, and images; holy dust or cloth that itself mediated further transformation" in addition to traditional relics (body parts or bones of saints), effluvial relics (material that miraculously secreted or oozed from the bodies of saints or from holy objects), sacramental objects (including the Eucharist), as well as animistic devotional images such as prayer cards and winged altarpieces.

Such instances of holy matter were as much about practice as they were about theory; indeed, the devotional practices surrounding relics often takes precedence over the abstract theological discussions of them. What holy matter reveals is a premodern understanding of materiality that is also, in a way, remarkably contemporary: "In contrast to the modern tendency to draw sharp distinctions between animal, vegetable, and mineral, or between animate and inanimate, the natural philosophers of the Middle Ages understood matter as the locus of generation and corruption."[550] In short, "the basic way of describing matter ... was to see it as organic, fertile, and in some sense alive."[551]

Matter as unstable, unpredictable, fecund, ambivalent — when that matter is the stuff of our own bodies, a novel affect emerges, living matter obeying an occult logic of its own, continuing to live bit by bit, continuing to die bit by bit. Perhaps the various "miracles" that populate supernatural horror are, in a way, variations of holy matter. Except that the world of supernatural horror stories is a secular world, where no one believes, at least not without empirical "proof." And yet, within the horror genre there often occurs strange irruptions of paradoxical matter: from the living dead to the undead, from human-animal metamorphoses to creatures that have no name, from resurrected bodies to autonomous body parts, from ominous and animate objects to accursed secret books, from the atheistic passion plays of "splatterhorror" to the mesmerizing dissipations of "cosmic horror." Matter behaving indifferently to the self-conscious human beings that it composes and decomposes. Unholy matter.

Of Catherine's Sacred Head, enshrined in its uncannily preserved splendor, Raymond of Capua once remarked: "she began to build up in her mind a secret cell which she vowed she would never leave for anything in the world."[552]

*

Qualitas Occulta. We can make a list, a partial list (it will always be partial). There is the *Book of Azathoth*, the *Book of Eibon*, the *Cthäat Aquadingen*, the *Cultes des Ghoules*, *De Masticatione Mortuorum in Tumulis*, *De Vermis Mysteriis*, the *Liber Ivonis*, the

Revelations of Glaaki, the *Unaussprechlichen Kulten*, the Pnakotic Manuscripts, the Sigsand Manuscripts, the G'harne Fragments, the Poakotic Fragments, and then there is, of course, the *Necronomicon*. This is but a short sampling. All real books, each existing within the interconnected stories of "weird fiction" authors spanning generations: William Hope Hodgson, Robert Chambers, H.P. Lovecraft, Greya La Spina, Clark Ashton Smith, Mary Elizabeth Counselman, Frank Belknap Long, Everil Worrell, Robert E. Howard, August Derleth, Brian Lumley, Robert Bloch, Ramsey Campbell, T.E.D. Klein, Thomas Ligotti, Caitlín Kiernan, and possibly uncountable others.

Forbidden books penned by obscure and neglected authors, most of whom have gone mad or mysteriously disappeared. The books themselves are difficult to find; if one is lucky there is a dusty old copy in the Miskatonic University library (though you will most likely find it has mysteriously gone missing). One almost never mentions them casually ("What are you reading?" "Oh, just the *Necromonicon*"). They are mentioned — when they are mentioned — with ominous ceremony. The dreaded *Necronomicon*, the unmentionable *Book of Eibon*, the blasphemous *De Vermis Mysteriis*.

The idea that a person might be driven mad by a book is fantastical, even absurd — especially today, as books themselves seem to be vanishing into an ether of oblique metadata. We are so used to the idea of consuming books for the information they contain that we rarely consider the possibility that the books might in turn consume us. Thomas Frognall Dibdin's *The Bibliomania; or, Book-Madness* (1809) uses a quasi-medical diagnosis to describe individuals literally consumed by books, obsessed not just with their contents, but with their materiality: "There is, first, a passion for Large Paper Copies; secondly, for Uncut Copies; thirdly, for Illustrated Copies; fourthly, for Unique Copies; fifthly, for Copies printed upon Vellum; sixthly, for First Editions; seventhly, for True Editions; and eighthly, for Books printed in the Black-Letter."[553]

Holbrook Jackson's *The Anatomy of Bibliomania* (1930) goes further, tracing that fine line where the love of books (bibliophilia) turns into its dark other of book madness (bibliomania). The madness of possessing books turns with great subtlety into the madness of being possessed by books. Jackson even recounts what is no doubt the pinnacle of bibliomania — the "bibliophages," who are so consumed by their books that they eat them, incorporating them into their anatomies, effacing all distinction between the literal and the figurative, perhaps resulting in an unnamable, material "thing" not unlike that which populates the dimly read pages of forbidden books.

*

Misanthropos. Plutarch tells of how the aging Timon of Athens — or "Timon Misanthropos" — grew weary of the endless hypocrisy and stunning stupidity of human beings, eventually withdrawing from society in disgust. Timon would, however, make occasional appearances. In one instance, we are told that Timon went to the marketplace and stood up at the pulpit, as if to give a speech. The crowd there gathered and fell silent. Had the mysterious recluse who had weathered the Peloponnesian War finally come forward to share his wisdom? Instead, Timon began to casually inform those gathered that in the yard in front of his house there was a marvelous, great fig tree, upon which several people had, in the past, hanged themselves. Since he was about to have the tree cut down, Timon urged all those contemplating suicide to make haste at the opportunity, while it lasts.

When Timon died, he was buried near the sea. Legend has it that, over time, the sea overtook the shore and slowly engulfed his tomb, so that no one could visit it (not that anyone wanted to). Plutarch tells us that the epitaph on the unapproachable tomb read: "Here lies a wretched corpse, of wretched soul bereft. Seek not my name; a plague consume you wicked wretches left."[554]

*

Phantasms (V). …fragile and numinous, tentacles longer than night…

into a dark entry of book madness (bibliomania). The darkness of possessing books turns, with great subtlety, into the madness of being possessed by books. Jackson even recounts what is undoubtedly the pinnacle of bibliomania — the "bibliophagi," who are so consumed by their books that they eat them, incorporating them into their anatomies, effacing all distinction between the literal and the figurative, perhaps resulting in an unnameable, tangential thing not unlike that which populates the dimly read pages of forbidden books.

Misanthropos. Plutarch tells of how the aging Timon of Athens — or "Timon Misanthropos" — grew weary of the endless hypocrisy and ensuing stupidity of human beings, eventually withdrawing from society in disgust. Timon would, however, make occasional appearances. In one instance, we are told that Timon went to the marketplace and stood up in the pulpit, about to give a speech. The crowd there gathered and fell silent. Had the most notorious recluse who had weathered the Peloponnesian War finally come forward to share his wisdom? Instead Timon began to casually inform those gathered that in the yard in front of his house there was a marvelous, gnarling tree, upon which several people had, in the past, hanged themselves. Since he was about to have the tree cut down, Timon urged all those contemplating suicide to make haste at the opportunity, while it lasts.

When Timon died, he was buried near the sea. Legend has it that, over time, the sea overtook the shore and slowly engulfed his tomb, so that no one could view it (not that anyone wanted to). Plutarch tells us that the epitaph on this unapproachable tomb reads: "Here lies a wretched corpse, of wretched soul bereft. Seek not my name; a plague consume you wicked wretches left!"

Nematoform (?). Fragile and gelatinous, tentacles longer than night.

ACKNOWLEDGMENTS

Excerpts from this book have appeared in the following publications: *And They Were Two In One and One In Two* (Schism Press, 2014); *Angelaki* 18.1 (March 2013); *Beyond Biopolitics: Essays on the Governance of Life and Death* (ed. Patricia Clough and Craig Willse [Duke University Press, 2011]); Clive Barker, *Cabal and Other Annotations* (ed. Jason Cook [Fiddleblack Press, 2013]); *Collapse* vol. IV (2008) and vol. VIII (2011); *Configurations* 20.1–2 (2012); *Conveyor Magazine* no. 4 (2012); *Culture Machine* 7 (2005) and 9 (2007); D.P. Watt, *The Phantasmagorical Imperative & Other Stories* (Eageus Press, 2014); *Four by Three Magazine* no. 5 (2016); *Hideous Gnosis – Black Metal Theory* (2010); *Incognetum Hactenus* vol. 3 (2012); *Inflexions* no. 7 (2014); *The Japan Times* (2015–2016); *Laboratory Planet Magazine* (2016); *Leper Creativity: The Cyclonopedia Symposium* (eds. Ed Keller et al. [Punctum Books, 2012]); *Mute Magazine* (2010–2013); *Near East Magazine* (Spring 2015); *Nyx – A Nocturnal* #6 (2012); *Parrhesia* no. 10 (2010) and no. 12 (2011); *Posthumous Life: Theorizing Beyond the Posthuman* (eds. Claire Colebrook and Jami Weinstein [Columbia University Press, 2017]); *Postmedieval* 3.1 (2012); *The Public Domain Review: Selected Essays* (ed. Adam Green [PDR Press, 2016]); *Radical Philosophy* 181 (2013); *Realism, Materialism, Art* (eds. Christopher Cox and Suhail Malik [Sternberg Press, 2014]); *SORT Zine* #4

(2019); *Spaces and Fictions of the Weird and Fantastic* (eds. Julius Greve et al. [Palgrave, 2019]); *Speculative Medievalisms* (eds. Eileen Joy et al. [Punctum Books, 2013]); *Theory After 'Theory'* (eds. Derek Attridge and Jane Elliot [Routledge, 2011]); *Theory, Culture & Society* 26.6 (2009); *Veils – Terence Hannum* (Stevenson Gallery, 2012); *Volume Magazine* #24 (2010); *Zombie Theory: A Reader* (ed. Sara Lauro [University of Minnesota Press, 2017]).

Many of the ideas in this book were presented in lectures at: Amherst College; CUNY Graduate Center; Duke University; Humboldt-Universität; Intermediae-Matadero Madrid; Johns Hopkins University; Kings College London Anatomy Theatre; the London Natural History Museum; The New School; NYU; Society for Literature, Science, and the Arts (SLSA); Southern California Institute of Architecture (SCI-Arc); SUNY-Stony Brook/the AC Institute; Università degli Studi di Napoli; Universität Basel; the University of Aberdeen; the University of California Berkeley; the University of Chicago; the University of Victoria; and the University of Washington.

Thanks to Frank Smecker at Collective Ink.

Special thanks to Tariq Goddard.

Thanks to all those who have, over the years, provided support.

ILLUSTRATIONS

16. Cross-section of Dante's Hell, from Dante Alighieri, *The Divine Comedy 1: Hell*, trans. Dorothy Sayers (New York: Penguin, 1949).
17. Diagram of Hell in the edition of Giorlamo Benivieni, from *Commedia di Dante* (1506).
18. Still from *Zombie* (*Zombi 2*, dir. Lucio Fulci, 1979).
19. Still from *Inferno* (*L'Inferno*, dir. Francesco Bertolini, Aldolfo Padovan, Giuseppe de Liguoro, 1911).
20. Still from *Japanese Hell* (*Jigoku*, dir. Nobuo Nakagawa, 1960).
21. Isabelle Adjani in *Possession* (dir. Andrzej Żuławski, 1981).
22. Conrad Veidt in *The Hands of Orlac* (*Orlacs Hände*, dir. Robert Wiene, 1924).
23. Still from *I Bury the Living* (dir. Albert Brand, 1958).
24. Edith Scob in *Eyes Without a Face* (*Les Yeux sans Visage*, dir. Georges Franju, 1960).
25. Barbara Steele in *The Long Hair of Death* (*I Lunghi Capelli della Morte*, dir. Antonio Margheriti, 1964).
26. Still from *Begotten* (dir. E. Elias Merhige, 1989).
27. Still from *Black Sunday* (*La Maschera del Demonio*, dir. Mario Bava, 1960).
28. Still from "The Hungry Glass," *Thriller!* (dir. Douglas Heyes, 1961).
29. Panel from Junji Ito, *Uzumaki* (1998–1999).
30. Panel from Junji Ito, *Uzumaki* (1998–1999).
31. Still from *Vampyr* (dir. Carl Th. Dreyer, 1932).
32. Still from *Pulse* (*Kairo*, dir. Kiyoshi Kurosawa, 2001).
33. Still from *Double Suicide* (*Shinjū Ten no Amijima*, dir. Masahiro Shinoda, 1969).
34. Still from *Two Monks* (*Dos Monjes*, dir. Juan Bustillo Oro, 1934).

NOTES

1. I use the term "non-philosophical" with caution, in that I wouldn't characterize this study as a work of non-philosophy, at least in the sense used by François Laruelle, in books such as *Principles of Non-Philosophy* (trans. Nicola Rubczak and Anthony Paul Smith [London: Bloomsbury, 2013]). However, I will be taking up a number of the orientations of non-philosophy, primary among them an inquiry into the decisional structure of philosophy (described here in terms of "horror"). For very different, though equally compelling, approaches to the philosophy of horror, see Noël Carroll, *The Philosophy of Horror; or, Paradoxes of the Heart* (New York: Routledge, 1990); Julia Kristeva, *Powers of Horror: An Essay on Abjection*, trans. Leon Roudiez (New York: Columbia University Press, 1982); Thomas Ligotti, *The Conspiracy Against the Human Race* (New York: Hippocampus Press, 2010).
2. For more on the historical relationships between music, magic, and the occult, see Joscelyn Godwin, *Harmonies of Heaven and Earth: Mysticism in Music from Antiquity to the Avant-garde* (Rochester: Inner Traditions, 1987); Gary Tomlinson, *Music in Renaissance Magic* (Chicago: University of Chicago Press, 1994); Penelope Gouk, *Music, Science, and Natural Magic in Seventeenth Century England* (New Haven: Yale University Press, 2009); and Nigel Wilkins, *La Musique du Diable* (Brussels: Mardaga, 1999). Godwin's edited volume *Music, Mysticism, and Magic: A Sourcebook* (London: Routledge, 1986) is still a valuable resource. There

are also several volumes on "black metal theory": *Hideous Gnosis: Black Metal Theory Symposium*, eds. Nicola Masciandaro et al. (n.p.: Hideous Gnosis, 2010); *Melancology: Black Metal Theory and Ecology*, eds. Scott Wilson (Winchester: Zero Books, 2014); and *Mors Mystica: Black Metal Theory*, eds. Edia Connole and Nicola Masciandaro (London: Schism, 2015).

3. Arthur Schopenhauer, "Additional Remarks on the Doctrine of the Suffering of the World," *On the Suffering of the World*, ed. Eugene Thacker, trans. E.F.J. Payne (London: Repeater, 2019), 114–15. In another essay Schopenhauer recapitulates the same idea in more Kantian terms: "Therefore, if anyone ventures to raise the question why there is not nothing at all rather than this world, then the world cannot be justified from itself; no ground, no final cause of its existence can be found in itself." Schopenhauer then adds, with the gallows humor for which he is known: "Life is then given out as a gift, whereas it is evident that anyone would have declined it with thanks, had they looked at it and tested it beforehand" (*On the Suffering of the World*, 75).
4. H.P. Lovecraft, "The Call of Cthulhu," in *The Call of Cthulhu and Other Weird Stories*, ed. S.T. Joshi (New York: Penguin, 1999), 139. In the early story "Facts Concerning the Late Arthur Jermyn and His Family," Lovecraft expresses a similar sentiment: "Life is a hideous thing, and from the background behind what we know of it peer daemoniacal hints of truth which make it sometimes a thousandfold more hideous" (*The Call of Cthulhu and Other Weird Stories*, 14). Lovecraft's voluminous correspondence often expresses this combination of cosmic horror and misanthropy.
5. Athanasius, *The Life of Antony and the Letter to Marcellinus*, trans. Robert C. Gregg (Mahwah: Paulist Press, 1980), Ch. 8, 38.
6. *Mark* 5: 9–10, New International Version. Stephanus New Testament version consulted for koine Greek.
7. Dionysius the Areopagite, *The Divine Names*, trans. Colm Luibheid, in *Pseudo-Dionysius: The Complete Works* (Mahwah: Paulist Press, 1987), 85.
8. Dante Alighieri, *Inferno*, trans. Mark Musa (New York: Penguin, 2003), Canto V: 30–38, 42–47. For this and other references to the *Divine Comedy*, see the edition, *The Divine Comedy: Inferno, Part I: Text*, trans.

with commentary by Charles Singleton (Princeton: Princeton University Press, 1970), and *The Divine Comedy: Inferno, Part II: Commentary*, trans. with commentary by Charles Singleton (Princeton: Princeton University Press, 1970). English editions of the *Inferno* by Kirkpatrick, Musa, Sayers, and Singleton each contain information on the religious, theological, and esoteric aspects of Dante's work. There are also numerous scholarly articles and books on the "mystical" elements of the *Divine Comedy*. A classic study is René Guénon, *The Esoterism of Dante*, trans. Henry D. Fohr and Cecil Bethell (Hillsdale: Sophia Perennis, 1996 [1925]).

9. Nancy Caciola, *Discerning Spirits: Divine and Demonic Possession in the Middle Ages* (Ithaca: Cornell University Press, 2003), 75. For more on the history of demonology and witchcraft, see Sydney Anglo (ed.), *The Damned Art: Essays in the Literature of Witchcraft* (London: Keegan Paul, 1977); Stuart Clark, *Thinking With Demons: The Idea of Witchcraft in Early Modern Europe* (Oxford: Oxford University Press, 1997); Armando Maggi, *Satan's Rhetoric: A Study in Renaissance Demonology* (Chicago: University of Chicago Press, 2001); D.P. Walker, *Unclean Spirits: Possession and Exorcism in France and England in the Late Sixteenth and Early Seventeenth Centuries* (London: Scolar Press, 1981); Michel de Certeau, *The Possession at Loudun*, trans. Michael Smith (Chicago: University of Chicago Press, 2000); and Jeffrey Burton Russell's multivolume study of the demonic in the Western tradition, abridged in *The Prince of Darkness: Radical Evil and the Power of Good in History* (Ithaca: Cornell University Press, 1992). Also see the collections *Witchcraft in Europe, 400–1700: A Documentary History (Second Edition)*, eds. Edward Peters and Alan Charles Kors (Philadelphia: University of Pennsylvania Press, 2001), and *The Witchcraft Sourcebook (Second Edition)*, ed. Brian Levack (New York: Routledge, 2015).
10. Johann Weyer, *On Witchcraft: An Abridged Translation of Johann Weyer's De Praestigiis Daemonium*, ed. Benjamin Kohl and H.C. Erik Midelfort, trans. John Shea, (Segundo: Pegasus Press, 1998), Book V, Ch. 28, 238. See also *Witches, Devils, and Doctors in the Renaissance: Johann Weyer, De Praestigiis Daemonium*, eds. George Mora and Benjamin Kohl, trans. John Shea (Binghamton: Medieval and Renaissance Texts and Studies, 1991).

11. Jean Bodin, *De la Démonomanie des Sorciers* (Paris: Jacques du Puys, 1580), Book II, Ch. 8, 237, translation mine. The original passage reads "…tous les Demons sont malings, menteurs, imposteurs, ennemis du genre humain." However, Bodin continues with the complicated caveat "…et qu'ils n'ont plus de puissance que Dieu leur en permet" ("…and they have no more power than God permits them to have"). See also Jean Bodin, *On the Demon-Mania of Witches*, trans. Randy Scott (Toronto: Centre for Reformation and Renaissance Studies, 1995).
12. Julia Kristeva, *Powers of Horror: An Essay on Abjection*, trans. Leon Roudiez (New York: Columbia University Press, 1982), 1–2. Kristeva's study borrows from philosophy, psychoanalysis, anthropology, and literary studies. Elsewhere in her book Kristeva encapsulates the boundary-transgression of the abject: "The body's inside … shows up in order to compensate for the collapse of the border between inside and outside. It is as if the skin, a fragile container, no longer guaranteed the integrity of one's 'own and clean self' but, scraped or transparent, invisible or taut, gave way before the dejection of its contents" (53). For Kristeva the corpse, biological decay, bodily fluids, and refuse of all types are emblems of the abject in this sense. The idea of the "abject" also looks back to notions of purity and impurity in anthropology, described in Mary Douglas's well-known study *Purity and Danger: An Analysis of Concepts of Pollution and Taboo* (London: Routledge & Keegan Paul, 1966).
13. Schopenhauer, *The World as Will and Representation* I, trans. E.F.J. Payne (New York: Dover, 1969), §71, 409. For this and subsequent references to Schopenhauer's work, I have consulted the standard scholarly edition, *Die Welt als Wille und Vorstellung*, in *Sämtliche Werke*, edited by Arthur Hübscher (Mannheim: Brockhaus, 1988). I have also consulted the more recent English edition *The World as Will and Representation* I, trans. Judith Norman, Alastair Welchman, and Christopher Janaway (Cambridge: Cambridge University Press, 2010).
14. Ibid., 410. Schopenhauer's opaque final words of *The World as Will and Representation* encapsulate this paradoxical affirmation of nothing (*Nichts*) in more cosmic terms: "[W]hat remains after the complete abolition of the Will is, for all who are full of the Will, assuredly nothing. But also conversely, to those in whom the Will has turned and

denied itself, this very real world of ours with all its suns and galaxies, is — nothing" (412).

15. Frances Yates, *The Occult Philosophy in the Elizabethan Age* (London: Routledge, 2001 [1979]), 53–54. Yates's work on the occult remains a reference for study on the topic. See also her books *The Art of Memory* (1966) and *Giordano Bruno and the Hermetic Tradition* (1964). For more recent surveys, see Michael Bailey, *Magic and Superstition in Europe: A Concise History from Antiquity to the Present* (New York: Rowman & Littlefield, 2007); Dan Burton and David Grandy, *Magic, Mystery, and Science* (Bloomington: Indiana University Press, 2003); Nicholas Goodrick-Clarke, *The Western Esoteric Traditions: A Historical Introduction* (Oxford: Oxford University Press, 2008); Antoine Faivre, *Access to Western Esoterism* (Albany: SUNY Press, 1994).
16. Heinrich Cornelius Agrippa, *Three Books of Occult Philosophy*, trans. Eric Purdue (Rochester: Inner Traditions, 2021), Ch. 10, 153. This is a complete translation of the Latin 1533 edition of *De Occulta Philosophia libri III*, the first time all three books appeared together in print. For an alternate edition, see also Henry Cornelius Agrippa, *Three Books of Occult Philosophy*, ed. Donald Tyson, trans. James Freake (Woodbury: Llewellyn, 2005). A spurious *Fourth Book of Occult Philosophy* was published in the years following Agrippa's death. It appeared in at least three different editions, sometimes with the subtitles *On the Divination of the Earth*, or *On the Art of Geomancy*, or *On Ceremonial Magic*. Existing copies suggest that the material was originally excised from the original editions, though for what reasons remains a mystery. However, most scholars suggest that the *Fourth Book* was written by a student or follower of Agrippa. Another hypothesis is that the *Fourth Book* is a retroactively attributed forgery, possibly by a late-19th century author associated with the French Decadent and Symbolist movements. With its interest in alchemy, magic, and the occult, it is no surprise that portions of works by Agrippa and other occult thinkers make cameos in minor works of the period, including the poetry of Jean Richepin and Ephraïm Mikhaël, Élémir Bourges's *Twilight of the Gods* (*Le Crépuscule des Dieux*, 1884), and Donatien Ybbuk's *The Crystalline Substrata; or, the Opacity of Metallic Life* (*Le Substrat de Cristal; ou l'Opacité de la Vie Métallique*, 1898), not

to mention works of the Russian Decadent movement such as Valery Bryusov's *The Fiery Angel* (*Ognenny Angel*, 1908). For those interested in the possible apocrypha of *De Occulta Philosophia*, scans of the Cologne 1533 Latin edition, as well as a 1655 English edition of *The Fourth Book*, are both available at the U.S. Library of Congress website (www.loc.gov).

17. Ibid., 154.

18 Johan Huizinga, *Homo Ludens: A Study of the Play Element in Culture* (Boston: Beacon Books, 1971 [1938]), 10.

19. Ibid. This idea has been incorporated into literary studies of poetry and the poetic act as ritual. See, for instance, Georges Poulet's study *The Metamorphoses of the Circle*, trans. Carly Dawnson and Eliott Coleman (Baltimore: Johns Hopkins University Press, 1966).

20. Ibid.

21. Ibid.

22. Cited in Walter Kaufmann's introduction to Goethe's *Faust*, trans. Walter Kaufmann (New York: Anchor, 1962), 13. For more on the history of the Faust myth, see Elizabeth Butler's comprehensive study *The Fortunes of Faust* (Cambridge: Cambridge University Press, 1952).

23.Christopher Marlowe, *Doctor Faustus and Other Plays*, ed. David Bevington and Eric Rasmussen (Oxford: Oxford University Press, 2008), A 1.1, 12–15. Citations refer to either the 1604 "A" text or the 1616 "B" text.

24. Ibid., A 1.1, 50.

25. Ibid., 51–54.

26. Ibid., B 1.3, 1–15. The iterations of this paradigmatic scene within the horror genre are innumerable. One not insignificant development in recent years has been the abstraction of the magic circle using the language of science, computing, and "dark physics." Popular horror authors such as Stephen King, Peter Straub, and Anne Rice have experimented with stories of this type, in which physics, the occult, and horror intersect in various ways around the idea of a magic circle. The motif is repeated ad nauseum in Garth Marenghi's pulp horror novels, such as *Star Mangler*, *Star Mangler II: Starsplatter*, and *Doomscroller*. In interviews Marenghi discusses his adventures (and misadventures) with magic and the occult. See *A Very Dark Place Indeed: Interviews with the Guru of Gore*, ed. Tariq Goddard (London: Repeater Books, 2026).

27. Goethe, *Faust* I, 382–85.
28. Ibid., 418–21.
29. Ibid., 438.
30. Ibid., 434; 447–48.
31. Dennis Wheatley, *The Devil Rides Out* (Hertfordshire: Wordsworth, 2007), 213–14.
32. Ibid., 221.
33. Ibid., 243.
34. James Blish, *Black Easter, or Faust Aleph-Null* (New York: Avon/Equinox, 1977), 28.
35. Ibid., 131–32.
36. Ibid., 157.
37. Ibid., 163.
38. William Hope Hodgson, *The Casebook of Carnacki — Ghost Finder* (Hertfordshire: Wordsworth, 2006), 45.
39. Ibid., 46.
40. Ibid., 173.
41. Ibid., 180.
42. H.P. Lovecraft, "From Beyond," in *The Dreams in the Witch House and Other Weird Stories*, ed. S.T. Joshi (New York: Penguin, 2005), 24.
43. Ibid. This idea — already latent in the earliest Faust myths — is one that recurs in science fiction that engages with ideas borrowed from fields such as atomic and quantum physics, where it is experiments in particle physics rather than the operations of magic, which open the magic circle. In this sense there is a shift from 19th century science fiction, particularly those works dealing with the end of the world (the comet colliding with the Earth, the heat death of the Sun), influenced by ideas from astrophysics and thermodynamics, to early 20th century weird fiction, influenced by ideas from particle physics, no doubt influenced by popularizations of general relativity and the "fourth dimension." Weird tales such as "From Beyond" or "The Dreams in the Witch House" report anomalies which impossibly emerge from the odd angles in a derelict room, "inorganic masses" described as "prisms, labyrinths, clusters of cubes and planes, and Cyclopean buildings," as well as vague organic forms akin to "bubbles, octopi, centipedes, living Hindoo idols, and intricate Arabesques roused into a kind of ophidian animation" (*The*

Dreams in the Witch House and Other Weird Stories, ed. S.T. Joshi [New York: Penguin, 2004], 305). As with many tales of the weird, the finite and limited human mind is unable to comprehend the dimension that has been opened, and crumbles before "abysses whose material and gravitational properties, and whose relation to his own entity, he could not even begin to explain" (304). All that remains is the dim intuition of "an insight into mathematical depths perhaps beyond the utmost modern delvings of Planck, Heisenberg, Einstein, and de Sitter" (302).

44. Ibid., 25.
45. Ibid., 27.
46. Ibid., 28.
47. Ibid., 26–27.
48. Ibid., 29.
49. Junji Ito, *Uzumaki*, Vol. 1, trans. Yuji Oniki (San Francisco: Viz Media, 2007), 20.
50. Letter from Lovecraft to Farnsworth Wright, 5 July 1927, in H.P. Lovecraft, *Selected Letters II*, 1925–1929, ed. August Derleth and Donald Wandrei (Sauk City: Arkham House, 1968), 150.
51. M.P. Shiel, *The Purple Cloud* (Lincoln: Bison Books, 2000), 41.
52. Ibid., 40.
53. Fred Hoyle, *The Black Cloud* (New York: Signet, 1959), 16.
54. Ibid., 29.
55. Ibid., 105.
56. J.G. Ballard, *The Wind From Nowhere* (Berkeley: Berkeley Medallion, 1966), 101.
57. Ibid., 127.
58. Ibid., 47.
59. Ibid., 42.
60. Fritz Leiber, "The Black Gondolier," in *Night Monsters* (New York: Ace, 1969), 14. Originally published in the anthology *Over the Edge*, ed. August Derleth (Sauk City: Arkham House, 1964).
61. Ibid.
62. Ibid.
63. Ibid., 15. Leiber's story also invites us to rethink technology in terms of accident, disaster, and catastrophe. In our own era, the prevalence of space

debris, oil spills, and nuclear reactor leaks suggest to us that technological breakdown is an integral part of technological innovation, rather than an aberration. Technological disasters such as these prompt reflection on the ways in which the downstream effects of geotechnologies provide the conditions for the emerge of a new class of disaster. The tragic regularity of industrial disasters such as oil spills reveals novel forms of accident disaster that accompany any technology. As philosophers such as Paul Virilio have long noted, every new technology produces new accidents (the derailment, the airplane crash, the computer virus). Weird fiction often takes up this idea and inverts the point of view, highlighting the human-centric bias in the very notion of "accident" or "disaster." This idea — that what is a "disaster" from the human perspective may simply be the elemental aspects of the planet utilizing humanity for its own ends — is eerily evoked in Leiber's story.

64. Carl Schmitt, *Political Theology: Four Chapters on the Concept of Sovereignty*, trans. George Schwab, (Chicago: University of Chicago Press, 2006), 36.
65. Ibid.
66. Ibid., 49.
67. Ibid., 46.
68. Schopenhauer, "On Death and Its Relation to the Indestructibility of Our Inner Nature," *On the Suffering of the World*, 131–32.
69. See *Inferno*, Canto XIV, 22–24: "some souls were stretched out flat upon their backs, / others were crouching there all tightly hunched, / some wandered, never stopping, round and round."
70. For more on blasphemy, religious language, and its relation to heresy in Medieval Christianity, see Jennifer Kolpakoff Deane, *A History of Medieval Heresy and Inquisition* (Lanham: Rowman & Littlefield, 2011), and Malcolm Lambert, *Medieval Heresy: Popular Movement from the Gregorian Reform to the Reformation* (London: Blackwell, 1992). A classic study is Norman Cohn, *The Pursuit of the Millennium* (Oxford: Oxford University Press, 1970).
71. Ibid., Canto XIV, 51. An alternate edition by Mandelbaum translates "Qual io fui vivo, tal son morto" thus: "That which I was in life, I am in death."
72. Upon seeing the bestial figure of Satan, Dante notes "I did not die — I was not living either!" (*Inferno*, Canto XXXIV, 25).

73. Nigel Kneale, *The Quatermass Experiment* (London: Penguin, 1959), 174. In the film Kneale's longer, more deliberate discussion is shortened to the more punchy, noirish hypothesizing of Quatermass alone: "What if there is a form of life in space, not on some planet, but just drifting — not life as we know it — with intelligence, yes — but pure energy, with no organic structure, invisible … it entered the rocket, it found living specimens of our form of life — cell organisms, human … now, if, even by accident, it could enter one of those structures — what a way to invade the Earth!"
74. H.P. Lovecraft, *At the Mountains of Madness*, in *The Dreams in the Witch House and Other Weird Stories*, ed. S.T. Joshi (New York: Penguin, 2004), 271. Literary historians have traced a number of the scientific sources for this and other Lovecraft stories. In the case of *At the Mountains of Madness* the source Lovecraft references the most is the geology article William Dyer et al., "A Hypothesis Concerning Pre-Archaean Fossil Data Found Along the Ross Ice Shelf," *The New England Journal of Geological Science*, 44.2 (1936): 1–17. See also J.P. Drapeau (ed.), *Stranger Science: Influences and Sources of H.P. Lovecraft and the Lovecraft Circle* (Sauk City: Arkham House, 1999).
75. *At the Mountains of Madness*, 330. The creatures that inhabit many of the tales of the weird fiction tradition are the product of both science and the supernatural, a motif that stretches back to Mary Shelley's *Frankenstein*, and which perhaps has its roots in late-medieval commentaries on Aristotelian bestiaries by Arabic philosophers such as Averroës, and in early teratology treatises, such as Ambroise Paré's 16th century work *On Monsters and Marvels* (*Des Monstres et Prodiges*, 157–1585, originally included as part of the treatise *Deux Livres de Chirurgie*), as well as treatises on "occult medicine" such as Gustav Rondelet's *Of the Abyss of Creatures: A Catalog of Natural Monstrosities with regards to Astronomy and Mathematics* (*De Abysso Creaturarum, Catalogus Aberrationum Naturalium quoad Astronomiam et Mathematicam*, c.1580; also known as *Crinis Abyssi*, or "Tendrils of the Abyss").
76. Ibid., 331. Other stories by Clark Ashton Smith, Frank Belknap Long, and Robert E. Howard feature similar combinations of monstrous anatomies. For examples in the supernatural horror tradition, see the tales by Petrus Borel, William Hope Hodgson, Arthur Machen, and Leopoldo

Lugones. This combination of science and the supernatural is also found in H.G. Well's *The Island of Dr. Moreau* (1896), in early 20th century science fiction stories by John W. Campbell, Fritz Leiber, and A.E. van Vogt, and is further explored in late-20th century "slipstream" authors such as Brian Aldiss, William Burroughs, J.G. Ballard, Ursula Le Guin, Joanna Russ, and Octavia Butler.

77. See Graham Priest, *In Contradiction* (Martinus: Nijhoff, 1987). In its simplest form, dialetheism argues that for any proposition X, both X and *not*-X are true. Dialetheism therefore works against the Law of Noncontradiction (defined in Aristotle's *Metaphysics*), but, in order to avoid accepting absolute relativism, it must also accept some form of paraconsistent logic.
78. The idea of body horror produced by science working "too well," is explored in my essay "Biohorror/Biotech," *Paradoxa* 17 (2002): 109–30.
79. These ideas are indebted to Michel Foucault's lectures at the Collège de France, especially the volumes: *Security, Territory, Population: Lectures at the Collège de France, 1977–1978*, trans. Graham Burchell (New York: Palgrave, 2007); and *The Birth of Biopolitics: Lectures at the Collège de France, 1978–1979*, trans. Graham Burchell (New York: Palgrave, 2008). On the philosophical relation between epidemic, medicine, and sovereignty, see my essays "The Shadows of Atheology: Epidemics, Power, and Life in Foucault," *Theory, Culture & Society* 26 (2009): 134–52; and "Biological Sovereignty," *Pli: The Warwick Journal of Philosophy* 17 (2006): 1–21.
80. For a survey, see the collection *Epidemics and Ideas: Essays on the Historical Perception of Pestilence*, ed. Terrence Ranger and Paul Slack (Cambridge: Cambridge University Press, 1992). A great deal of humanities scholarship on epidemics focuses on the impact of metaphors in the modern, germ-theory context, with Susan Sontag's 1979 essay *Illness as Metaphor* as an oft-cited example. Emily Martin's *Flexible Bodies* (Boston: Beacon, 1994), Sander Gilman's *Disease and Representation: Images of Illness from Madness to AIDS* (Ithaca: Cornell University Press, 1988), Laura Otis's *Membranes* (Baltimore: Johns Hopkins University Press, 2000), and Ed Cohen's *A Body Worth Defending* (Duke University Press, 2009) provide views from anthropology, art history, literary studies, and cultural theory.

81. For instance, William Bullein's mid-16th century plague pamphlet, *A Dialogue Against the Fever Pestilence,* uses religious allegory to anthropomorphize plague in terms of greed, selfishness, and the absence of faith.
82. *Exodus* 7:14–12:42, New International Version.
83. *Revelation* 15–16, New International Version.
84. See the accounts collected in *The Black Death*, ed. Rosemary Horrox (Manchester: Manchester University Press, 1994), and in *The Black Death: The Great Mortality, 1348–1350*, ed. John Aberth (Boston: Bedford/St. Martin's, 2005).
85. Here is De Mussis's account, which is thought by most historians to be secondhand: "The dying Tartars, stunned and stupefied by the immensity of the disaster brought about by the disease, and realizing that they had no hope of escape, lost interest in the siege. But they ordered corpses to be placed in catapults and lobbed into the city in the hope that the intolerable stench would kill everyone inside … And soon the rotting corpses tainted the air and poisoned the water supply, and the stench was so overwhelming that hardly one in several thousand was in a position to flee the remains of the Tartar army … No one knew, or could discover, a means of defense" (*The Black Death*, ed. Horrox, 17).
86. John W. Campbell, "Who Goes There?", in *The Best of John W. Campbell* (New York: Ballantine, 1976), 299. Originally published in *Astounding Science Fiction* (August 1938), under the name Don A. Stuart.
87. Ibid.
88. Homer, *The Odyssey*, trans. Robert Fagles (New York: Penguin, 1999), XII.13–15.
89. Ibid., XI.38–42.
90. *1 Corinthians*, 15.38, 42, 44, New International Version.
91. The most compelling account of such debates is Caroline Walker Bynum's study *The Resurrection of the Body in Western Christianity, 200–1336* (New York: Columbia University Press, 1995).
92. Rudolf Otto, *The Idea of the Holy*, trans. John Harvey (London: Oxford University Press, 1958 [1917]), 13. The full title of the book is *The Idea of the Holy: An Inquiry in the Non-Rational Factor in the Idea of the Divine and its Relation to the Rational.*

93. Ibid., 28.
94. This is a theme of much literary criticism on the Gothic novel. See, for instance, the still-relevant anthology *The Gothic Imagination: Essays in Dark Romanticism*, ed. G.R. Thompson (Pullman: Washington State University Press, 1974), as well as David Punter's two-volume study *The Literature of Terror: A History of Gothic Fictions From 1765 to the Present Day* (New York: Addison-Wesley, 1980). For more recent surveys, see: Fred Botting, *Gothic (New Critical Idiom)* (New York: Routledge, 2013); David Punter and Glennis Byron, *The Gothic* (London: Blackwell, 2004). While by many standards outdated and not particularly academic, Montague Summers's 1938 book *The Gothic Quest: A History of the Gothic Novel* remains a point of reference for studies of the literary Gothic. Summers — an English clergyman, author, and amateur occultist — is also known for his studies *The History of Witchcraft and Demonology* (1926) and *The Vampire: His Kith and Kin* (1928).
95. In his lectures on theology, Kant comments on the presumptuousness of absolute knowledge: "God knows all things as they are in themselves a priori and immediately through an intuitive understanding. For he is the being of all beings and every possibility has its ground in him. If we were to flatter ourselves so much as to claim that we know the *modum noumenon* [the mode of things in themselves], then we would have to be in community with God so as to participate immediately in the divine ideas ... To expect this in the present life is the business of mystics and theosophists" (*Lectures on Philosophical Theology*, trans. Allen Wood and Gertrude Clark, [Ithaca: Cornell University Press, 1978], 86).
96. Aristotle, *De Anima*, trans. Hugh Lawson-Tancred (New York: Penguin, 1986), Book II, Section 1, 412a. Many of the issues Aristotle raises concerning the problem of thinking "life itself" are elaborated the commentary tradition on the *De Anima*. Arabic philosophers such as Avicenna and Averroës produced commentaries on the treatise, as did Scholastic theologians from Thomas Aquinas to John Buridan and Nichole Orseme.
97. Aristotle, *De Generatione et Corruptione*, trans. Harold Joachim, in *The Basic Works of Aristotle*, ed. Richard McKeon (New York: Modern Library, 2001), Book I, Section 5, 321a.

98. Ibid., Book I, Section 5, 321b–322a.
99. Today, the different perspectives of biocomplexity, complex adaptive systems, and developmental systems biology, raise these questions. See, for instance, the work of complexity biologist Stuart Kauffman, *The Origins of Order: Self-Organization and Selection in Evolution* (Oxford: Oxford University Press, 1993), and *At Home in the Universe: The Search for the Laws of Self-Organization and Complexity* (Oxford: Oxford University Press, 1996), as well as Richard Sole and Brian Goodwin, *Signs of Life: How Complexity Pervades Biology* (New York: Basic Books, 2000).
100. It's worth noting the longer history of "end of the world" narratives, a tradition that arguably stretches back to apocalyptic theology and deluge myths in different cultures around the world. In the shadow of the 18th century European Enlightenment, a number of 19th century speculative fictions borrowed from apocalyptic and prophetic traditions to produce end of the world scenarios that combined horror, science, and science fiction, including Jean-Baptiste Cousin de Grainville's *The Last Man* (*Le Dernier Homme*, 1805), Mary Shelley's eschatological epic *The Last Man* (1826), Richard Jefferies's *After London* (1885), and Camille Flammarion's *Omega: The Last Days of the World* (*La Fin du Monde*, 1894), in addition to end-of-the-world tales by Edgar Allan Poe, Ivan Turgenev, Horacio Quiroga, Gabriel Tarde, and H.G. Wells.
101. The full title in French is *Recherches sur les Ossements Fossiles de Quadrupèdes, òu l'on Rétablit les Caractères de Plusieurs Espèces d'Animaux que les Révolutions du Globe Paroissent avoir Détruites.*
102. Georges Cuvier, *Recherches sur les Ossemens Fossiles de Quadrupeds* (Paris: Déterville, 1812), "Discours Préliminaire," 2, translation mine.
103. Kant, "The End of All Things" (1794), in *Religion and Rational Theology*, ed. and trans. Allen Wood and George di Giovanni (Cambridge: Cambridge University Press, 2005), 224.
104. Ibid.
105. Ray Brassier, *Nihil Unbound: Enlightenment and Extinction* (London: Palgrave, 2007), 238.
106. Kant, "The End of All Things," 224.

107. John Scottus Eriugena, *Periphyseon (De Divsione Naturae), Liber Tertius*, ed. and trans. I.P. Sheldon-Williams and Ludwig Bieler (Dublin Institute for Advanced Studies, 1981), Book III, 633A, 59.
108. Martin Heidegger, *Being and Time*, trans. Joan Stambaugh (Albany: SUNY Press, 1996), §10, 43–44.
109. Ibid., 46.
110. Emmanuel Levinas, "There is: Existence without Existents," in *The Levinas Reader*, trans. Seán Hand (London: Blackwell, 1990), 30.
111. Ibid., 30; 32.
112. Ibid., 33.
113. Regarding the troubled history of the debate about "mysticism" what is noteworthy is that, during the late-19th and early-20th centuries — at the moment when traditional, institutional Christianity was waning in the face of evolutionary biology, relativity in physics, and industrial Capitalism — one finds a resurgence of interest in alternative spiritualities and mysticism generally, from Spiritualism, Theosophy, and Anthroposophy to the influence of religious ideas imported from Buddhism and classical Indian philosophy: Swami Vivekenanda's *Vedanta Philosophy: An Address Before the Graduate Philosophical Society* (1896), Richard Maurice Burke's *Cosmic Consciousness: A Study in the Evolution of the Human Mind* (1901), William James's *The Varieties of Religious Experience* (1902), Bertrand Russell's *Mysticism and Logic* (1910), Evelyn Underhill's *Mysticism: A Study of the Nature and Development of Man's Spiritual Consciousness* (1911), Oscar Augustín Solari's *Nest of the Phoenix* (1914), Rudolf Otto's *The Idea of the Holy* (1917), D.T. Suzuki's *An Introduction to Zen Buddhism* (1934), and Aldous Huxley's *The Perennial Philosophy* (1945), to name but a few.
114. The poem has never appeared in print, though fragments have appeared in hard-to-find zines such as *Ailing Dancer, HexAgon Saturn, Sad Trad, Nostromo Lament* and *JLP*. The poem itself was initially claimed to be an English translation of an early 19th century text of the "frénétique" school, though literary scholars and historians have since disputed this assertion. See the dossier "The Planets Are Watching," Supplement to issue 4 of the *WinterMute — A Journal of Speculative Poetics*, the relevant

articles collected in the *Arkham Analytica* (vol. IX, "Techniques in Non-Standard Onto-Exhumation").

115. "En una noche oscura, / con ansias, en amores inflamada, / ¡oh dichosa ventura! / salí sin ser notada / estando ya mi casa sosegada." See John of the Cross, *The Dark Night*, in *The Collected Works of St. John of the Cross*, trans. Kieran Kavanaugh and Otilio Rodriguez (Washington D.C.: Institute of Carmelite Studies, 1991), 50.
116. John of the Cross, *The Dark Night*, Book II, Ch. 5, 405.
117. John of the Cross, *The Ascent of Mount Carmel*, in *The Collected Works of St. John of the Cross*, Book I, Ch. 2, 120.
118. John of the Cross, *The Dark Night*, Book II, Ch. 8, 411.
119. Georges Bataille, *Inner Experience*, trans. Leslie-Ann Boldt (Albany: SUNY Press, 1988), 17, italics removed.
120. Bataille, "The Archangelic," in *Collected Poems*, trans. Mark Spitzer (Chester Springs: Dufour, 1998). 65. The key phrase reads "l'excès de ténèbres / est l'éclat de l'étoile." See Bataille, *Oeuvres Complètes* III (Paris: Gallimard, 1974).
121. John of the Cross, *The Ascent of Mount Carmel*, Book I, Ch. 2, 120.
122. Böhme, *The Signature of All Things* (Cambridge: James Clarke, 1969), Ch. III. Commenting on *Genesis*, Böhme refers to "the greatest secret mystery; namely, how the abyss, or the Deity, manifests itself with this eternal generation" (22). In the *Mysterium Magnum* Böhme describes God as both "abyss" and "byss," both the mystery of creation out of nothing, as well as "the eye of the abyss, the eternal chaos." In another treatise, the *Mysterium Pansophicum*, Böhme is more direct: "The Unground is an eternal Nothing."
123. Schopenhauer, "On the Vanity and Suffering of Life," *On the Suffering of the World*, 65.
124. Schopenhauer, *The World as Will and Representation* I, §24, 124.
125. Ibid., §29, 163.
126. Ibid., §24, 124. Remarks like these have influenced later developments in existential psychology and related therapeutic applications. For examples, see Otto Rank, *The Trauma of Birth* (*Das Trauma der Geburt*, 1924); Francis B. Gröss, *Anxiety in the Modern World: An Essay on Pathology* (*Angst in der Modernen Welt, Ein Essay zur Pathologie*,

1929); Viktor Frankl, *Man's Search for Meaning* (*Ein Psychologe erlebt das Konzentrationslager*, 1946); Rollo May, *The Meaning of Anxiety* (1950); Luther Stringfellow and Henry Raglan, *The Shape of Despair: Psychoplasmics and Psychology* (1969); and Ernst Becker, *The Denial of Death* (1973).

127. Schopenhauer, "On the Vanity and Suffering of Life," 75.

128. *Dōgen's Manuals of Zen Meditation*, trans. Carl Bielefeldt (Berkeley: University of California Press, 1990) 147; I have removed translation brackets in the original for readability.

129. Georges Bataille, "La Planète Encombrée," *Oeuvres Complètes* XII (Paris: Gallimard, 1998), 475–77. The article was originally published in *La Cigüe* no. 1 (1958) and is translated as "The Congested Planet," in *The Unfinished System of Nonknowledge*, ed. Stuart Kendall, trans. Michelle Kendall and Stuart Kendall (Minneapolis: University of Minnesota Press, 2001). The phrase "planète encombrée" may also be rendered as the "cluttered planet."

130. Ibid., 222.

131. Ibid.

132. Bataille, *The Accursed Share*, Volume I, trans. Robert Hurley (New York: Zone, 1991), 21. In essays from the 1930s, such as "The Sacred Conspiracy" and "Sacrifices," Bataille takes up the French anthropological approach to the sacred (e.g. Henri Hubert and Marcel Mauss's 1898 essay *Sacrifice: Its Nature and Function*) and elevates it to the cosmic level, which allows him to tease out the quality of the impersonal in theories of the sacred produced from the human-centric point of view. For Bataille, if one regards sacrifice from the enigmatic point of view of the cosmos itself, the ultimate endpoint of the activity of sacrifice is ultimately a necessarily ambiguous form of self-abnegation — but at the species level. It's worth pointing out the intriguing similarities with the work of historian of religion Mircea Eliade, particularly in books such as *The Myth of the Eternal Return: Cosmos and History*, where Eliade notes the dual characteristics of sacrifice — arbitrariness and necessity — as techniques for staving off the threat of nihilism. For Eliade, "suffering is perturbing only insofar as its cause remains undiscovered. As soon as the sorcerer or priest discovers what is causing children or animals to die,

drought to continue, rain to increase, game to disappear, the suffering begins to become tolerable; it has a meaning and a cause … If it was possible to tolerate such sufferings, it is precisely because they seemed neither gratuitous nor arbitrary" (*The Myth of the Eternal Return: Cosmos and History*, trans. Willard Trask [Princeton: Princeton University Press, 1971], 98, 96).

133. Ibid.
134. Ibid., 20. Allan Stoekl examines this theme in his book *Bataille's Peak: Energy, Religion, and Postsustainability* (Minneapolis: University of Minnesota Press, 2008). For recent studies on mysticism, theology, and global climate change, see: Catherine Keller, *Cloud of the Impossible: Negative Theology and Planetary Entanglement* (New York: Columbia University Press, 2014); Mary-Jane Rubenstein, *Strange Wonder: The Closure of Metaphysics and the Opening of Awe* (New York: Columbia University, 2010); John Durham Peters, *The Marvelous Clouds: Towards a Philosophy of Elemental Media* (Chicago: University of Chicago Press, 2016).
135. Ibid., 20–21.
136. Bataille, *Theory of Religion*, trans. Robert Hurley (New York: Zone, 1992), 33, translation modified.
137. Evelyn Underhill, *Mysticism: A Study in the Nature and Development of Man's Spiritual Consciousness* (Cleveland: Meridian, 1963), 4.
138. John of the Cross, *The Ascent of Mount Carmel*, 57.
139. Henry Annesley, *Dark Geomancy; or, Chthonic Mysticism in the Modern Age, With Implications for Cosmic Consciousness* (Arkham: Miskatonic Virtual University Press, 2029 [1927]), 4. It is unclear how deeply ghostwriters such as Annesley shaped the "weird fiction" tradition in the pulps, though Lovecraft does include him as a fictional character in the story "From Beyond," first published in *The Fantasy Fan* (June 1934).
140. Underhill, *Mysticism*, 444.
141. Otto, *The Idea of the Holy*, 70.
142. Keiji Nishitani, *Religion and Nothingness*, trans. Jan Van Bragt (Berkeley: University of California Press, 1983), 89. See also the section "Prayers for Nothing" in this volume.
143. Ibid., 95.

144. Ibid., 96.
145. Ibid., 98.
146. Ibid., 101.
147. Ibid., 102.
148. René Descartes, *Meditations on First Philosophy, With Selections from the Objections and Replies*, ed. and trans. John Cottingham (Cambridge: Cambridge University Press, 1996), 15. The standard scholarly edition is in *Oeuvres de Descartes*, eds. Charles Adam and Paul Tannery (Paris: Vrin, 1976). The publication history of the *Meditations* is not without its complexities. Generally speaking, there are three aspects to the *Meditations*: the original Latin version of the text, the subsequent French translation, and a set of "Objections and Replies" that were the result of Descartes having sent the Latin version of the text to a number of colleagues (which included such luminaries as political philosopher Thomas Hobbes, the astronomer and priest Pierre Gassendi, and the friar and mathematician Marin Mersene).
149. Ibid.
150. Ibid., 17.
151. Ibid., 15.
152. Ibid. See Cottingham's Introduction, as well as Desmond Clarke's *Descartes: A Biography* (Cambridge: Cambridge University Press, 2006). The descriptions of Descartes's nightmares are largely apocryphal, and come mainly from biographies in the wake of his death, though Descartes's own notebooks do contain accounts of his dreams.
153. Thomas De Quincey, "The Last Days of Immanuel Kant," in *The Last Days of Immanuel Kant and Other Writings — De Quincey's Works*, Vol. III (Edinburgh: Adam and Charles Black, 1871), 164. De Quincey — author, opium addict, and friend of the Lake Poets — bases his account on that of Ehregott Andreas Wasianski, pastor and friend of Kant. See also Manfred Kuehn, *Kant: A Biography* (Cambridge: Cambridge University Press, 2002), and Ernst Cassirer, *Kant's Life and Thought*, trans. James Haden (New Haven: Yale University Press, 1981).
154. Ibid., 165.
155. Ibid.
156. E.M. Cioran, *A Short History of Decay*, trans. Richard Howard (New York: Arcade, 2012), 47.

157. Immanuel Kant, "On the Power of the Mind to Master Its Morbid Feelings by Sheer Resolution," in *The Conflict of the Faculties*, in *Religion and Rational Theology*, ed. and trans. Allan W. Wood and George Di Giovanni (Cambridge: Cambridge University Press, 2001), 318. As per the convention of his time, Kant doesn't use the term "depression," but either "melancholia" or "hypochondria."
158. Ibid.
159. Ibid.
160. Kant, *Critique of the Aesthetic Power of Judgment*, trans. Paul Guyer and Eric Matthews (Cambridge: Cambridge University Press, 2000), §29, 157. There are several scholarly editions of this work in German. For this and later references, editions consulted were Immanuel Kant, *Kritik der Urteilskraft*, ed. Gerhard Lehmann (Stuttgart: Reclam, 1963), and Immanuel Kant, *Kritik der Urteilskraft*, ed. Wilhelm Weishedel (Frankfurt: Suhrkamp, 1974). Other English editions of the *Critique of Judgement* consulted include those by J.H. Bernard (1892), James Creed Meredith (1911; 1952), and Werner S. Pluhar (1987).
161. Ibid., 317.
162. Ibid.
163. See Kant, "An attempt at some reflections on optimism…", in *Theoretical Philosophy*, 1755–1770, ed. and trans. David Walford with Ralf Meerbote (Cambridge: Cambridge University Press, 2003).
164. Kant, "The End of All Things," in *Religion and Rational Theology*, 224.
165. De Quincey, "The Last Days of Immanuel Kant," 163.
166. According to Wasianski's account, the words "it is enough" (*es ist genug*) had a humbler origin: they were simply a reply to Wasianski, who was giving the ailing Kant a drink of water. See his *Immanuel Kant in seinen Letzten Lebensjahren* (1804).
167. Friedrich Nietzsche, "On Truth and Lie in an Extra-Moral Sense," in *The Portable Nietzsche*, ed. and trans. Walter Kaufmann (New York: Viking, 1964), 42. For an alternate translation, see "On Truth and Lies in a Nonmoral Sense," in *Philosophy and Truth: Selections from Nietzsche's Notebooks of the Early 1870s*, ed. and trans. Daniel Breazeale (London: Humanities Press, 1979). For this and other references to Nietzsche's works, the standard scholarly edition is Friedrich Nietzsche, *Sämtliche*

Werke, Kritische Studienausgabe, ed. Giorgio Colli and Mazzino Montinari, an English edition of which is being published by Stanford University Press.

168. As a book, *Human, All Too Human* is often passed over in Nietzsche scholarship. While *Beyond Good and Evil* and *The Genealogy of Morals* are frequently taught in the classroom, *Thus Spoke Zarathustra* is popularly read as literature, and late works such as *The Antichrist* and *Ecce Homo* read for their iconoclastic rhetoric. However, a closer look at *Human, All Too Human* not only shows that many of Nietzsche's later concepts were already present there in nascent form, but it also brings much of his later work (especially on the question of nihilism) back within the broader issue of the problem of the human being, set against the backdrop of a vast and indifferent cosmos. Arguably, if there is a Nietzsche for our twenty-first century of planetary disaster, extinction, and the "posthuman," it resides not in his later work, but in the two volumes of *Human, All Too Human*.
169. Friedrich Nietzsche, *Human, All Too Human II and Unpublished Fragments from the Period of Human, All Too Human II* (Spring 1878–Fall 1879), trans. Gary Handwerk (Stanford: Stanford University Press, 2013), 158–59.
170. Ibid., 159.
171. In *Ecce Homo* Nietzsche recounts how, upon the publication of *Human, All Too Human*, he had sent two copies to Wagner, from whom he had definitively separated. By coincidence, Wagner had at the same time sent him a copy of *Parsifal*. Nietzsche describes the coincidence as a moment of dissonance, "as if two swords had crossed."
172. For popular accounts of mycorrhizal fungi and their complex interactions with forest ecologies, see Merlin Sheldrake, *Entangled Life: How Fungi Make Our Worlds, Change Our Minds & Shape Our Futures* (New York: Random House, 2020); Peter Wohlleben, *The Hidden Life of Trees: What They Feel, How They Communicate* (Vancouver: Greystone, 2016); as well as the pioneering research by ecologist Suzanne Simard. While scientific research into the symbiotic properties of fungi (along with moss, lichen, and a variety of epiphytes) has become a highly specialized field in its own right, the general idea can be traced back, not only to 19th century

theories of evolution and "theoretical biology," but to late-19th and early-20th century philosophies inspired by biological theories of vitalism, including Hans Dreisch's *Vitalism as History and Theory* (*Der Vitalismus als Geschichte und als Lehre*, 1905), Johannes Reinke's *Philosophy of Botany* (*Philosophie der Botanik*, 1905), Henri Bergson's *Creative Evolution* (*L'Évolution Créatrice*, 1907), Marlène Dotard's *The Spirit of Microbes, Towards a New Theory of Evoultion* (*L'Ésprit des Microbes, vers une Nouvelle Théorie de l'Évolution*, 1929), and Jakob von Uexküll's *The Life-World of Pathogens* (*Die Lebenswelt der Erreger*, 1933). These and other like-minded books incorporate perspectives from biology, ecology, mathematics, and even ideas borrowed from alternative spiritualities of the period. (It is worth noting that Dreisch and Bergson were deeply interested in "psychical research," both publishing on the topic, as well as serving as prominent members of the Society for Psychical Research.) Contemporary views are given in Christopher Donohue and Charles T. Wolfe (eds.), *Vitalism and Its Legacy in Twentieth Century Life Sciences and Philosophy* (New York: Springer, 2023).

173. Georges Bataille, *Guilty*, trans. Bruce Boone (Venice: Lapis Press, 1988), 12.
174. Dionysius the Areopagite, *The Mystical Theology*, in *Pseudo-Dionysius: The Complete Works*, 135. Elsewhere I have referred to this idea in terms of "ascending negations" and "descending assertions." See also Chapter 2 of *After Life* (Chicago: University of Chicago Press, 2010).
175. Ibid., 136.
176. Ibid., 135.
177. Ibid., 139. For works in the philosophy of religion on apophatic mysticism and negative theology, see Denys Turner, *The Darkness of God: Negativity in Christian Mysticism* (Cambridge: Cambridge University Press, 1995); Dierdre Carabine, *The Unknown God: Negative Theology in the Platonic Tradition* (Leuven: Peeters Press, 1995); Michael Sells, *Mystical Languages of Unsaying* (Chicago: University of Chicago Press, 1994); Sarah Coakley and Michael Strang (eds.), *Rethinking Dionysius the Areopagite* (London: Wiley-Blackwell, 2009). See also Jacques Derrida's essay, "How To Avoid Speaking: Denials," in *Languages of the Unsayable*, eds. Sanford Budick and Wolfgang Iser (Stanford: Stanford University Press, 1987).

178. Vladimir Lossky, *The Mystical Theology of the Eastern Church*, trans. Fellowship of St. Alban and St. Sergius (London: James Clarke & Co., 1957), 28.
179. Meister Eckhart, *Sermon 4*, in *The Complete Mystical Works of Meister Eckhart*, 56. See also the two edited volumes, *Meister Eckhart: The Essential Sermons, Commentaries, Treatises, and Defense*, trans. Edmond Colledge and Bernard McGinn (Mahwah: Paulist Press, 1981), and *Meister Eckhart: Teacher and Preacher*, ed. Bernard McGinn (Mahwah: Paulist Press, 1986). An earlier and widely read selection is *Meister Eckhart: A Modern Translation*, ed. and trans. Raymond Blakney (New York: Harper & Row, 1941). Recently, the long project of producing a standard critical edition of both the Latin and vernacular works has been completed. See *Meister Eckhart: Die Deutschen und Lateinischen Werke. Herausgegeben im Auftrage der Deutschen Forschungsgemeinschaft* (Stuttgart/Berlin: Verlag W. Kohlhammer, 1936–2022).
180. Ibid.
181. Ibid., *Sermon 51*, *The Complete Mystical Works of Meister Eckhart*, 273.
182. For an overview on the role of gender in medieval Christian mysticism, see Bernard McGinn, *The Flowering of Mysticism: Men and Women in the New Mysticism, 1200–1350* (New York: Crossroad, 1998); *Medieval Writings on Female Spirituality*, ed. Elizabeth Spearing (New York: Penguin, 2002); and Caroline Walker Bynum, *Holy Feast and Holy Fast* (Berkeley: University of California Press, 1988). For a consideration of the links between medieval mysticism and postmodern theory, see Amy Hollywood's *Sensible Ecstasy* (Chicago: University of Chicago Press, 2002), where Hollywood discusses, among other things, the relationship between Angela of Foligno and Georges Bataille.
183. Angela had actually outlined thirty stages of her mystical itinerary, though it appears that Brother Arnaldo, unable to make sense of the final stages, attempted to condense them into the seven supplementary stages. Indeed, much of the scholarship on Angela focuses on the unique circumstances of textual production. Reading through the *Memorial*, one often gets the impression of Brother Arnaldo struggling to keep up with Angela's thought.

184. Angela of Foligno, *The Memorial*, in *Complete Works*, trans. Paul Lachance (New York: Paulist, 1993), 128. The critical edition is *Il Libro della Beata Angela da Foligno*, eds. Thier Luger and Abele Calufetti (Rome: Editiones Collegii S. Bonventurae ad Claras Aqas, 1985).
185. Ibid., 176.
186. Ibid., 182.
187. Ibid., 198.
188. Ibid., 202.
189. Ibid., 205.
190. *The Cloud of Unknowing*, ed. James Walsh (New York: Paulist, 1981), 128. A critical edition is *The Cloud of Unknowing (TEAMS Middle English Texts Series)*, ed. Patrick J. Gallacher (Kalamazoo: Medieval Institute Publications, 1997).
191. Ibid., 120.
192. Ibid., 128.
193. Ibid., 130.
194. John of the Cross, *The Dark Night*, Book I, Ch. 8, 375.
195. Ibid., Book I, Ch. 12, 388.
196. Ibid., Book II, Ch. 5, 401, 402.
197. Bataille, *Inner Experience*, trans. Leslie Anne Boldt (Albany: SUNY Press, 1988), 4–5.
198. Bataille, *The Accursed Share*, trans. Robert Hurley (New York: Zone, 1991), 21.
199. Bataille, *L'Archangélique et Autre Poèmes* (Paris: Gallimard, 2008), 32–33, translation mine. The passage reads: "l'excès de ténèbres / est l'éclat de l'étoile / le froid de la tombe est un dé."
200. Bataille, *The Tears of Eros*, trans. Peter Connor (San Francisco: City Lights, 1991), 206–207.
201. Bataille, *Inner Experience*, 17.
202. Ibid., 33.
203. Maurice Blanchot, "The Outside, the Night," in *The Space of Literature*, trans. Ann Smock (Lincoln: University of Nebraska Press, 1982), 163.
204. Novalis, *Hymns to the Night*, trans. Dick Higgins (New York: McPherson & Co., 1988), 11.

205. Blanchot, "The Outside, the Night," 163. See also Blanchot's short unpublished text "The Night Invades" ("La Nuit Envahit…", *Le Dernier Homme: Écrits Posthumes* [Paris: Gallimard, 2023]).
206. While the phrase "invasive species" continues to be contested within the scientific community, it has taken root, due in part to nonspecialist books on the topic, such as Julia Lockwood, *Invasive Species: A Very Short Introduction* (Oxford: Oxford University Press, 2023), and Ken Friers and Anton Tivč, *Strange Life: How Invasive Species Are Redefining Our Ecosystems* (Boston: Darr House Books, 2019). In the 1980s, the International Council for Science organized a series of studies on the impact of invasive species on the environment, culminating in their 1989 report *Biological Invasions: A Global Perspective*, later revised as *Invasive Alien Species: A New Synthesis* (2005). The group has adopted the phrase "Invasive Alien Species" (IAS) to cover a wide range of organisms that adhere to the criteria of nonindigenous species which effect a degradation of the host environment. Similarly, the idea of a possible "Green Plague" has emerged mostly from science journalism, and has been taken up in a number of reports issued by the WHO and affiliate agencies (see, for example, the online publication *Public Health Implications of Invasive Species: A Global Perspective*, published in 2001 and updated thereafter).
207. Blanchot, *Thomas the Obscure*, trans. Robert Lamberton (Barrytown: Station Hill, 1988), 14.
208. Ibid., 169.
209. Rasu-Yong Tugen, *Songs from the Black Moon* (n.p.: gnOme books, 2014), 58. Other small presses that publish anonymous and pseudonymous writing of this kind include Dostoevsky Wannabe, Dreamless Halfsleep, ex.military.io, Éditions Zutique, Schism Press, and ToxiCon Press.
210. Pseudo-Leopardi, *Cantos for the Crestfallen* (n.p.: gnOme books, 2014), Canto XXVIII. The moniker "Pseudo-Leopardi" has actually been applied to a number of Leopardi's recently discovered, unpublished papers on astronomy, astrology, and cryptography (one document even mentions the *poesia della stella nera*, a supposed "secret poetry manual"). It appears that Leopardi had set apart this and other material from the *Zibaldone*, which has since led scholars to dispute their authorship. For

more see Adriano Comasinc et al., "Black Stars, Hidden Texts: On the Philological Status of the Leopardian *Manuale Segreto*," *Il Giornale delle Lettere Italiane dell'Ottocento* (Fall/Winter 2027).

211. Blanchot, "The Outside, the Night," 169.
212. Robert Fludd, *The Technical, Physical and Metaphysical History of the Macrocosm and Microcosm*, in *Robert Fludd (Western Esoteric Masters Series)*, ed. William Huffman (Berkeley: North Atlantic Books, 2001), 74; 62. A synoptic overview is given in Joscelyn Godwin's *The Greater and Lesser Worlds of Robert Fludd: Macrocosm, Microcosm, and Medicine* (Rochester: Inner Traditions, 2019). There are several online versions of the original Latin text with diagrams and illustrations, including a scan of a 1624 edition of the *Utriusque Cosmi*, available at the Wellcome Collection website.
213. The Gospel passages are from *Luke* 23:43–44 and *Matthew* 27:45–46, respectively.
214. See Nicola Masciandaro, "Paradisical Pessimism: On the Crucifixion Darkness and the Cosmic Materiality of Sorrow," *Qui Parle*, Vol. 23 (Fall/Winter 2014), 7. The essay is from Masciandaro's forthcoming book *The Sorrow of Being*.
215. Ibid., 10.
216. Ibid., 11.
217. Nicola Masciandaro, "Secret: No Light Has Ever Seen the Black Universe," in Alexander Galloway, Daniel Colucciello Barber, Nicolas Masciandaro, and Eugene Thacker, *Dark Nights of the Universe* (Miami: [name], 2013), 60–61. This publication collects talks given at an event cosponsored by The Public School New York and Recess Gallery in New York City.
218. François Laruelle, "On the Black Universe in the Human Foundations of Color," trans. Miguel Abreu, in *Dark Nights of the Universe*, 106.
219. Masciandaro, "Secret," in *Dark Nights of the Universe*, 61.
220. For more on the cultural history of the color black, see John Harvey, *The Story of Black* (London: Reaktion, 2013), and Michel Pastoureau, *Black: The History of a Color* (Princeton: Princeton University Press, 2008).
221. See the report by the U.S. Surgeon General Vivek Murthy, "Work and the Loneliness Epidemic," *Harvard Business Review* (September

2017), where Murthy coins the phrase "loneliness epidemic" to describe emergent forms of social alienation in the era of digital connectivity. Around the same time, the British government appointed a "Minister of Loneliness," whose office publishes an annual report on the social, psychological, and economic impact of loneliness (similar initiatives have been established in Brazil, Denmark, Japan, and South Korea). While approaches from psychology, sociology, and philosophy often distinguish between the mood states of "solitude" and "loneliness" (the former seeking freedom from sociality, the latter seeking freedom from isolation), a number of studies have shown that the distinction between them is becoming more complex. Articles appearing in *The Guardian, The New York Times*, and *The Atlantic* have each reported on forms of social withdrawal (dubbed the "new ascetics" or "Doomerists"), echoed in the 2020 study *Lonely People, Lonely Planet: A Survey of Social Anomie in Technology, Work, and Culture*, published by the American Association of Psychologists and Psychiatrists (AAPP).

222. Johann Wolfgang von Goethe, *Theory of Colors*, trans. Charles Lock Eastlake (Cambridge: MIT Press, 1970), 2.

223. *Lonely People, Lonely Planet*, 49. The AAPP study highlights two tends in particular: voluntary social isolation within urban centers (e.g., the phenomenon of *hikikomori* in Japan, or the *sumgyeojin* in South Korea, often confining themselves to a small apartment or a single room), and social withdrawal away from urban centers (e.g., "homesteading" in remote locations such as the Italian alps or lower Cascades). Both tendencies use digital media to document, report, and livestream their daily lives (using lesser-known platforms such as Starliner). In some, more unsettling cases, individuals have undertaken more extreme forms of austerity, including hunger strikes, vows of silence, and "sleep without rest" (sleeping for twenty-four hours or more at a time). In addition, many self-consciously identify with the climate change crisis, sometimes coalescing into loosely knit (online) groups, with names like "Earth Martyrs," "Polygon Grief," or "Daughters of Medea." While efforts are being made to offer healthy solutions for social reintegration, this has been largely undermined by new incentives from Wellness Industry companies like New Path, which offer therapeutically curated

"people purging" retreats (or what some have cynically called "corporate monasticism") which entail long-term, voluntary solitude to treat a number of workplace-associated conditions, from social anxiety disorder to "extinction anxiety" and "S.A.D."

224. Arthur Schopenhauer, *On Vision and Colors*, in *On Vision and Colors by Arthur Schopenhauer and Color Sphere by Philipp Otto Runge*, trans. Georg Stahl (New York: Princeton Architectural Press, 2010), 61.

225. If the visible spectrum has black and white at either pole, then color is some mixture or "fraction" in between. As Schopenhauer notes: "Black and white are not colors in the true sense … because they do not represent fractions, and thus no qualitative division of the retina" (*On Vision and Colors*, 70). Summarizing this polarized nature of the visible spectrum between white and black, Schopenhauer continues: "We have found that, by the qualitatively divided activity of the retina, the appearance of one half is essentially conditioned by the *inactivity* of the other half, at any rate at the same spot. *Inactivity* of the retina is … *total darkness*" (73).

226. See the summary provided in *Invasive Alien Species: A New Synthesis* (Paris: ICS Publications, 2005), as well as *Perspectives on Invasive Species, Astrobiology, and Space Biodiversity* (Dordrecht: Weyland, 2009), a report commissioned by United Nations Environmental Epidemiology Program (UNEEP). The hypothesis concerning a "Green Plague" entails the possibility of a "metastatic invasion," that is, of separate invasive species coalescing into cascading networks of biological overgrowth that have the potential to engulf entire ecosystems (and, in some of the more alarmist speculations, entire habitable areas of the planet itself). These and other ideas have raised "existential threats" (in the jargon of policymakers) as much as biological or epidemiological ones. While outdated from a scientific perspective, a number of historical works on invasive species have been cited by science writers as being relevant for the broader questions posed. See, for instance, *The Ecology of Invasion by Animals and Plants* (1958), by British zoologist Charles Elton; *Decay and Overgrowth in Plant Ecology*, by Canadian botanist Herbert Quain (1949); and *Pathology in Microbial Habitat Development* (1946), by Dutch ecologist Alva Brigham Hansen.

227. An overview is given in Stephanie Rosenthal, *Black Paintings: Robert Rauschenberg, Ad Reinhardt, Mark Rothko, Frank Stella* (Ostfildern: Hatje Cantz, 2007). In the late 1940s Willem De Kooning produced several "black drawings," though these were really expressionist white on a black background. In the 1950s Ellsworth Kelly produced his own, ultraflat black paintings in a series of large canvases, including "Black" (1951), and later in the decade Robert Motherwell produced almost all-black canvases of his giant brush strokes (such as "Iberia no. 18," 1958). Also in the late 50s, Robert Rauschenberg produced a thick, textual canvas of black goop, though the thickness of the paint produced a glossy, reflective surface. Throughout the 1960s several artists produced black paintings with differing degrees of hue and texture, most notably in Ad Reinhardt's abstract black paintings, as well as in Frank Stella's black canvases, which outline subtle geometries in faint white lines. In Japan, several artists working in the Gutai group also produced black paintings with thick, dynamic, performative gestures, as in the paintings by Kazuo Shiraga and Takesada Matsutani.

228. Laruelle, "On the Black Universe," in *Dark Nights of the Universe*, 104.

229. Ibid., 105.

230. Ibid., 105–106. Laruelle continues: "As opposed to the black objectified in the spectrum, Black is already manifested, before any process of manifestation."

231. Aristotle, *Physics*, trans. R.P. Hardie and R.K. Gaye, in *The Complete Works of Aristotle*, ed. Jonathan Barnes (Princeton: Princeton University Press, 1991), Book IV, Section 8, 216a.

232. The secondary literature on nihilism in the work Nietzsche is too voluminous to list here. However, several general studies are worth mentioning within the context of horror and philosophy: Jon Stewart, *A History of Nihilism in the Nineteenth Century* (Cambridge: Cambridge University Press, 2023); Conor Cunningham, *Genealogy of Nihilism: Philosophies of Nothing and the Difference of Theology* (London: Routledge, 2002); Michael Allen Gillespie, *Nihilism Before Nietzsche* (Chicago: University of Chicago Press, 1996); Winfried Schröder, *Moralischer Nihilismus: Radikale Moralkritik von den Sophisten bis Nietzsche*

(Stuttgart: Reclam, 2005). Earlier books on Nietzsche & nihilism by Lev Shestov, Georges Bataille, Karl Löwith, and Pierre Klossowski, are as thought-provoking today as they were when first published. Also still relevant are Heidegger's lectures on Nietzsche and nihilism, delivered between 1940 and 1946: Martin Heidegger, *Nietzsche, Volume IV: Nihilism*, trans. Joan Stambaugh, David Farrell Krell, and Frank A. Capuzzi (New York: Harper & Row, 1982).

233. Martin Heidegger, *Being and Time*, trans. John Macquarrie and Edward Robinson (New York: HarperCollins, 1962), §2, 25–26, italics removed.
234. Heidegger, "What is Metaphysics?", trans. David Farrell Krell, in *Basic Writings* (New York: HarperCollins, 1977), 96.
235. Ibid., 108.
236. *Being and Time*, §62, 356, italics removed.
237. Jean-Paul Sartre, *Being and Nothingness*, trans. Hazel E. Barnes (New York: Washington Square Press, 1984), 36.
238. Ibid.
239. Ibid., 42.
240. Ibid., 49.
241. Alain Badiou, *Being and Event*, trans. Oliver Feltham (New York: Continuum, 2005), 56.
242. Sartre, *Being and Nothingness*, 49.
243. On Eckhart's concept of nothing/nothingness with respect to continental philosophy, see John Caputo, *The Mystical Element in Heidegger's Thought* (New York: Fordham University Press, 1986); Beverly Lanzetta, "Three Categories of Nothingness in Eckhart," *Journal of Religion* 72.2 (1992): 248–68; and Reiner Schürmann, *Meister Eckhart, Mystic and Philosopher* (Bloomington: Indiana University Press, 1978). On Eckhart's relation to Buddhism, see Shizuteru Ueda, "Nothingness in Meister Eckhart and Zen Buddhism," in *The Buddha Eye: An Anthology of the Kyoto School and Its Contemporaries*, ed. Frederick Franck, (Bloomington: World Wisdom, 2004), 157–70.
244. Meister Eckhart, *Sermon 19*, in *The Complete Mystical Works of Meister Eckhart*, 137.
245. Ibid., 140.
246. Ibid., 141.

247. Ibid. On Eckhart's metaphysics of flow, see McGinn, *The Mystical Thought of Meister Eckhart*, 72ff. As McGinn notes, God in Eckhart's writings is at once *bullitio* (overflowing, beneficent, generosity) and *ebullitio* (flowing onward and outward into creatures and the world).
248. Ibid.
249. In this way mysticism can be viewed from the viewpoint of mediation, and the mystical encounter can be regarded as an instance of "media" in a premodern sense, tipping either towards pure continuity ("immediation") or pure inaccessibility ("antimediation"). For more, see my chapter in *Excommunication: Three Inquiries in Media and Mediation*, coauthored with Alexander Galloway and McKenzie Wark (Chicago: University of Chicago Press, 2013), 77ff.
250. Eckhart, *Sermon 97*, in *The Complete Mystical Works of Meister Eckhart*, 469.
251. Eckhart, *Sermon 96*, in *The Complete Mystical Works of Meister Eckhart*, 465.
252. John Caputo notes this apparent duplicity in his comparison of Eckhart and the later Heidegger in his study *The Mystical Element in Heidegger's Thought* (New York: Fordham University Press, 1986).
253. Bernard McGinn, *The Mystical Thought of Meister Eckhart.*
254. Alina Feld, *Melancholy and the Otherness of God: A Study of the Hermeneutics of Depression* (Lanham: Lexington Books, 2011), 136.
255. This is a coinage by François Laruelle to describe the pre-philosophical "decision" of philosophy, the presupposition that anything existent is philosophizable. See the opening sections of his *Principles of Non-philosophy*, trans. Anthony Paul Smith and Nicola Rubczak (New York: Bloomsbury, 2013).
256. James Heisig's book *Philosophers of Nothingness: An Essay on the Kyoto School* (Honolulu: University of Hawaii Press, 2002) is one of the most cogent appraisals of this underread philosophical tradition. See also Robert Carter's *The Kyoto School: An Introduction* (Albany: SUNY Press, 2013). For a sampling of Kyoto School writings, see the anthology *The Buddha Eye: An Anthology of the Kyoto School*, ed. Frederick Franck (World View Press, 2004). For a broader view of the Kyoto School tradition within Japanese philosophy, see *Japanese Philosophy: A Sourcebook*, ed.

James Heisig et al. (Honolulu: University of Hawaii Press, 2011), and Heinrich Dumolin, *Zen Buddhism in the 20th Century*, trans. Joseph O'Leary (New York: Weatherhill, 1992).

257. Masao Abe, *Zen and Western Thought*, ed. William R. LaFleur (Honolulu: University of Hawaii Press, 1989), 133.

258. For recent summaries of the "sixth mass extinction," see Elizabeth Kolbert, *The Sixth Extinction: An Unnatural History* (New York: Henry Holt & Co., 2014); Richard Leakey and Roger Lewin, *The Sixth Mass Extinction: Patterns of Life and the Future of Humankind* (New York: Doubleday, 1995); and Paul Wingall, *Extinction: A Very Short Introduction* (Oxford: Oxford University Press, 2019). It's worth noting the subtle shift in rhetoric in the UN's COP (Conference of the Parties) climate summit meetings, from a language of precautionary or preventive measures ("if we don't do this, then this will happen") to a language of responsive and reactive measures ("when this happens, we should do this"), a shift that seems to indicate a certain tone of inevitability with regard to human extinction. At the same time, a number of big data companies have utilized predictive analytics (including "scenario builders" previously used for conflict escalation with nation-states or terrorist groups) to create simulations for both local and global extinction events. One recent example is the data report generated by analytics company Somnos EDA (often referred to as the "Quiet Earth" report), made available via WikiLeaks. Controversially, the "Quiet Earth" report was commissioned by Polygon Group, a consortium of private sector "climate security" companies with purported ties to the UN Security Council, the SVR RF, and Brazil's ABIN, as well as Blue Origin and GoogleSpace. (It also gained attention for its use of a satellite AI meshwork, developed in response to concerns over "space junk" in the Earth's atmosphere produced by space exploration companies.) Among other things, the "Quiet Earth" report advises investing in climate design technologies to locally modify regions of the planet's still-habitable biosphere, as well as utilizing aspects of computational epidemiology, stem cell research, and regenerative medicine towards a gradual, multigenerational, "phased extinction" of the human species, to the

point where it reaches a homeostasis with the planet's progressively diminishing biodiversity.

259. Nagarjuna, *The Fundamental Wisdom of the Middle Way*, trans. Jay Garfield (Oxford: Oxford University Press, 1995), XXII.11, 61. The secondary scholarship on Nagarjuna's work is vast, and includes notable commentaries by Chandrakirti (c. 7th century), an Indian Buddhist monk and central figure in the Madhyamaka tradition, as well as the commentary by Tsong Khapa (c. 14th–15th century), a key figure in Tibetan Buddhism. For modern commentaries, see Jan Westerhoff, *Nagarjuna's Madhyamaka: A Philosophical Introduction* (Oxford: Oxford University Press, 2009), and Mark Sidertis and Shoryu Katsura, *Nagarjuna's Middle Way: Mulamadhyamajkakarika* (Boston: Wisdom Publications, 2016).
260. Ibid., XIII.7, 36.
261. Quoted in Heisig, *Philosophers of Nothingness*, 44.
262. Ibid., 48.
263. Ibid., 63.
264. One of the issues that Heisig discusses in his book is the conflicted relation between philosophy and politics in modern Japan, particularly surrounding the Kyoto School's ambivalent nationalism. Heisig observes how, for Kyoto School thinkers, religion often comes to serve as a mediator between philosophy and politics, though with varied results. On the one hand, there is a turn towards traditions specific to Japan (from Shinto to Zen Buddhism) as a counterweight to the hegemony of Western philosophy; on the other hand this often has the unfortunate effect of reifying a vague sense of "Asian" or "Eastern." See also James Heisig and John Maraldo (eds.), *Rude Awakenings: Zen, the Kyoto School, and the Question of Nationalism* (Honolulu: University of Hawaii Press, 1995).
265. Keiji Nishitani, *The Self-Overcoming of Nihilism*, trans. Graham Parkes with Setsuko Aihara (Albany: SUNY, 1990), 175.
266. Nishitani, *Religion and Nothingness*, trans. Jan Van Bragt (Berkeley: University of California Press, 1983), 4.
267. Ibid., 48.
268. Ibid., 17–18.

269. Ibid., 112. See also Nishitani's essay "Encounter with Emptiness," in *The Religious Philosophy of Keiji Nishitani: Encounter with Emptiness*, ed. Taitetsu Unno (Berkeley: Asian Humanities Press, 1989).
270. Ibid., 90.
271. Ibid.
272. For historical views, see Georges Minois, *History of Suicide: Voluntary Death in Western Culture*, trans. Lydia G. Cochrane (Baltimore: Johns Hopkins University Press, 1998), and Marizio Barbagli, *Farewell to the World: A History of Suicide*, trans. Lucinda Byatt (London: Polity, 2015). For more on "The Great Dying," see Ashton C. Mott, "Earth Martyrs: Has the Voluntary Extinction Movement Finally Found Its Cause?", *Psychology Today* (November 2024, Supplement). In these and other articles, the term "Great Dying" is used to describe mass suicides motivated in some way by despair over climate change (distinguished from individual, similarly motivated cases of "climate suicide"). While the Voluntary Human Extinction movement has repudiated such actions, their ideas concerning a "phased extinction" of the human species has nevertheless had an influence (as have debates in sociology, psychology, and philosophy around "anti-natalism" and "peak humanity"). In their statements, more radical groups such as Tears of Scipio or Shadow of Sati will incorporate scientific data on the regular periodicity of species extinction on the planet, in addition to offering highly detailed "zero protocols" for coordinating voluntary human extinction events. In addition, such events are often carried out at specifically chosen locales that require a kind of pilgrimage, including archaeo-astronomy sites like Göbekli Tepe (Turkey), Mnajdra (Malta), and Uexactun (Guatemala). Other sites — such as the Aokigahara region on the Japanese island of Honshu — have taken on much of the same aura, due in part to the discoveries of inexplicable, monolithic polyhedrons nested deep within the forest itself (which by most accounts are dismissed as hoaxes).
273. Nishitani, *Religion and Nothingness*, 137.
274. Ibid., 138.
275. Ibid., 97.
276. Ibid., 96–97.

277. Ibid., 123.
278. Heisig, *Philosophers of Nothingness*, 220–21.
279. Ibid., 221.
280. Abe, *Zen and Western Thought*, 126–27. Abe's interest in these ideas is also evident in his work on Dōgen, collected in Masao Abe, *A Study of Dōgen: His Philosophy and Religion*, ed. Steven Heine (Albany: SUNY Press, 1992).
281. Shizuteru Ueda, "'Nothingness' in Meister Eckhart and Zen Buddhism," trans. James Heisig, in *The Buddha Eye: An Anthology of the Kyoto School*, ed. Frederick Franck (New York: Crossroad, 1982), 160, 161. Ueda's work remains underrepresented in English. A student of Nishitani, he studied at the University of Marburg, where he wrote a thesis on Meister Eckhart and Zen Buddhism.
282. Heisig, *Philosophers of Nothingness*, 230.
283. Ibid., 61.
284. The widespread coverage of extremophile research is evidenced by pop science books like Michael Ray Taylor's *Dark Life: Martian Nanobacteria, Rock-Eating Cave Bugs, and Other Extreme Organisms of Inner Earth and Outer Space* (New York: Scribner, 1999), as well as a number of science documentaries, including *Journey into Amazing Caves* (2001). Recent articles include: Nancy Merino et al., "Living at the Extremes: Extremophiles and the Limits of Life in a Planetary Context," *Frontiers in Microbiology* 10 (2019); MacReddy, R.J. et al., "Extremophiles, Astrobiology, and Microbial Deep Time: The Antarctic Case Study," *Nature Astrobiology* 71 (2011); Lynn Rothschild et al., "Life in Extreme Environments," *Nature* 409 (2001). There is a college-level textbook *Physiology and Biochemistry of Extremophiles* (Washington D.C.: ASM Press, 2007), and there exist professional organizations such as the International Society for Extremophiles.
285. European Science Foundation (ESF), *Investigating Life in Extreme Environments — A European Perspective* (Strasbourg: European Science Foundation, 2007), 13. See also the press release from NASA (December 2010; www.nasa.gov), announcing the discovery of an arsenic-based bacterium.
286. Ibid., 15.

287. The most comprehensive book on the topic is Lily Kay, *Who Wrote the Book of Life? A History of the Genetic Code* (Stanford: Stanford University Press, 2000). Also relevant is Evelyn Fox Keller, *Refiguring Life: Metaphors of Twentieth-Century Biology* (New York: Columbia University Press, 1995), and Dorothy Nelkin and Susan Lindee, *The DNA Mystique: The Gene as a Cultural Icon* (New York: W.H. Freeman, 1995).
288. Benjamin Noys, *The Persistence of the Negative* (Edinburgh: Edinburgh University Press, 2010), ix.
289. This hypothesis has led to some concern, especially within fields such as virology, pathogenetics, and epidemiology, over the possibility that extremophiles might evolve to become contagious to human populations. A recent report, *Extremophiles, Epidemiology, and Global Human Health*, organized by the International Consortium for Global Environmental Health (ICGEH), puts the problem plainly: "Those who study epidemic disease are readily familiar with the relative ease with which microbes are able to jump across species barriers, be it 'monkey pox' or 'bird flu.' We are also familiar with both the genetic mechanisms and environmental conditions by which these trans-species contagions are made possible. From a genetic perspective, virulent microbes are extremely simple and effective. A polyhedron protein shell, a single strand of genetic material, and an adaptive host — this, and right environmental conditions, is all that's required. What remains to be seen is whether extremophiles might display this same kind of opportunistic contagion pattern" (14). In a tone that eerily echoes fictional medical thrillers, the authors then ask, "What might be the downstream effects, from a global public health perspective, of a novel contagion from an extremophile 'alien' virus?" (21).
290. For an overview, see Graham Priest, *Beyond the Limits of Thought* (Oxford: Oxford University Press, 2003). One of the most cogent books on the topic is Priest's *In Contradiction: A Study of the Transconsistent* (Oxford: Clarendon, 2006).
291. Laruelle, *Principles of Non-philosophy*, 2, italics removed.
292. Ludwig Wittgenstein, *Tractatus Logico-Philosophicus*, ed. and trans. D.F. Pears and B.F. McGuinness (New York: Routledge & Keegan Paul, 1961), 4.0621, 45.

293. Ibid.
294. This appears to be one of the most perplexing questions within the scientific research on extremophiles, and it is likely the reason that much extremophile research takes place within fields such as astrobiology, as well as in xenobiology and biomathematics. As the authors of the textbook *Extremophile Biology: Life at the Extremes* (Second Edition) (New York: SIP Books, 2015) note: "The very presence of extremophiles on our planet leads us to a crucial question. If these microbes are indeed thriving under conditions previously thought to be inhospitable to biological life, then where did they come from? All the research seems to point to one inescapable conclusion: from outer space. However, this is not some imaginary creation of science fiction, and extremophiles did not arrive on Earth via a Martian invasion or mysterious monolith. Rather, they may have travelled to our planet on one of the many micrometeorites which have routinely entered the Earth's atmosphere since its formation some 4.5 billion years ago. Of course, most of the microbes hitching a ride to the Earth on meteorites don't survive the journey. But some do. And the ones that do, evolve and adapt. The biological probability that this is the case seems supported by research in evolutionary genetics, microbial paleontology, and astrobiology. Such 'visitors' are, quite literally, not of this Earth." (4–5).
295. The phrases "post-Kantian idealism" and "German idealism" are often used interchangeably, though arguably there are reasons for separating them. An excellent overview is provided by Frederick Beiser, *German Idealism: The Struggle Against Subjectivism, 1781–1801* (Cambridge: Harvard University Press, 2008).
296. The most frequently referenced example is in the opening section of Hegel's *Phenomenology of Spirit*, though the *Philosophy of Nature*, part of Hegel's *Encyclopedia of the Philosophical Sciences*, also revisits these themes, from the perspective of Nature as manifest Spirit.
297. Schelling returned again and again to this relationship between Nature and the Absolute, from synoptic overviews such as *First Outline of a System of the Philosophy of Nature*, to the difficult to categorize later work, such as *The Ages of the World*.

298. This phrase plays a key role in Fichte's lectures, some of which are collected in *The Science of Knowing — Fichte's 1804 Lectures on the Wissenshaftslehre.*
299. Here I borrow Steven Shaviro's paraphrase of Whitehead's process philosophy in his book *Without Criteria* (Cambridge: MIT Press, 2012).
300. On life-as-genesis, see Henri Bergson's *Creative Evolution*, as well as much of Gilles Deleuze's work, including his books *Bergsonism*, *Difference and Repetition*, and the two volumes of *Cinema*. On life-as-givenness, see Jean-Luc Marion's *Being Given: Towards a Phenomenology of Givenness*, and Michel Henry's multivolume *Phenomenology of Life*.
301. There is an anecdote often told about Schopenhauer that, while lecturing in Berlin in 1820, he intentionally chose the same time for his lectures as that of Hegel, the more senior and more established of the two. Needless to say, the Hegel lectures continued to draw huge crowds, while Schopenhauer was faced with an empty hall (apparently he gave his lectures anyways).
302. *The World as Will and Representation*, Vol. I, "Appendix: Criticism of the Kantian Philosophy," 429. Schopenhauer borrows the phrase *exemplar vitiis imitabile* from Horace.
303. Ibid., 434, italics removed.
304. Ibid., §7, 25–26.
305. Ibid., §1, 3.
306. Ibid., §24, 124.
307. Ibid., §6, 19.
308. Ibid., §1, 4.
309. Ibid., "Appendix: Criticism of the Kantian Philosophy," 417, italics removed.
310. "On the Vanity and Suffering of Life," *On the Suffering of the World*, 75.
311. *The World as Will and Representation*, Vol. I, §54, 275. I have chosen to translate Schopenhauer's *Wille zum Leben* as Will-to-Life, in order to emphasize the metaphysical stakes of the phrase. The Payne translation renders it "will-to-live," which I have retained in the quotes from this edition. The more recent translation by Judith Norman et al. simply renders the phrase as "will to life." See *The World as Will and Representation*, ed. and trans. Judith Norman, Alastair Welchman,

and Christopher Janaway (Cambridge: Cambridge University Press, 2010).

312. In addition to potential environmental applications (e.g., engineered extremophiles to clean up oil spills or test for ecological toxicity), several "Big Pharma" research initiatives have partnered with global health agencies to use extremophiles for the treatment and prevention of epidemic diseases (e.g., the Global Science Foundation's "Project BioShield," originally initiated by the U.S. Health and Human Services agency in 2004, and subsequently redeployed in the wake of the COVID-19 pandemic). Numerous biotech start-ups (e.g., Exscientia, Lifecore Biomedical, Pharmek-MAB, Somafree Biopharma) have emerged in response to the need for new tools for extremophile-based medical applications, many of them utilizing AI-driven drug discovery platforms. The momentum around AI-based computational biology has also spawned a number of nonmedical applications. A recent example is Lemurian Sky, a small private-sector space company, which has partnered with Polygon Pharmaceuticals (a spin-off startup of Pfizer-Merck) to explore the augmentation of human immunity via stem cell engineering (one application is extended human habitation in extraterrestrial environments). For more, see Raymond Bertram and Tess Ahrim-Hajan, *Maps to the Stars: NASA, Roscosmos, the CNSA, & Space X* (New York: Wiley-Revok, 2020), as well as the streaming docuseries *Off-World: Adventures in Space Capitalism and the Search for Home Beyond the Stars.*

313. *The World as Will and Representation*, Vol. I, §18, 100.

314. Ibid.

315. Ibid., §18, 102–103.

316. Ibid., §54, 275.

317. Schopenhauer's negative approach is a position that is as much about being a curmudgeon as it is about critique — indeed the stylistic innovation in Schopenhauer's writings is to have rendered the two inseparable, culminating in a philosophical pessimism defined as much by writing style as by its conceptual content. This disposition perhaps explains the turn, in Schopenhauer's later writings, towards the "incomplete" form of the aphorism, the fragment, and the parable, as if

Schopenhauer was disputing philosophy's tendency towards totalization at the level of style. Later thinkers influenced by Schopenhauer have taken this tendency in different directions. See, for example, Silas Haslam's *The Tears of Nietzsche* (*Nietzsches Tränen*, 1889), as well as Philipp Mainländer's *The Philosophy of Redemption* (*Die Philosophie der Erlösung*, 1876).

318. *The World as Will and Representation*, Vol. I., §27, 146–47.
319. Ibid., 147.
320. Ibid., 149.
321. Ibid., §23, 113.
322. Ibid., §28, 159–60.
323. Ibid., §58, 322.
324. Ibid., §29, 162.
325. On Schopenhauer's relation to Eastern philosophy, see Peter Abelsen, "Schopenhauer and Buddhism," *Philosophy East and West* 43:2 (1993): 255–78; Urs App, "Schopenhauer's Initial Encounter With Indian Thought," *Schopenhauer-Jahrbuch* Vol. 87 (Würzburg: Köningshuasen & Neumann, 2006), 35–76; Stephen Cross, *Schopenhauer's Encounter With Indian Thought* (Honolulu: University of Hawaii Press, 2003); Moira Nicholls, "The Influences of Eastern Thought on Schopenhauer's Doctrine of the Thing-in-Itself," in *The Cambridge Companion to Schopenhauer*, ed. Christopher Janaway (Cambridge: Cambridge University Press, 1999), 171ff.
326. *The World as Will and Representation*, Vol. I, §71, 410.
327. Ibid., 409.
328. Ibid., 412.
329. Voltaire's satirical attacks against optimism were not limited to *Candide*. For example, his underappreciated science fictional tale *Micromégas* (1752) involves a giant alien visitor to Earth named "Micromégas" (literally, "small-large"), who observes with perplexity the absurd and busied self-importance of earthbound humanity. Voltaire's inversion of the travel narrative was no doubt a jab at the presumptuousness of the Western imperialist expansionism and colonial occupation. More narrowly, the conceit of the "alien ethnographer" allows Voltaire to ridicule and even mock the ideologies of "Enlightened," 18th century

France, views also expressed in his article "Bien (tout est)," part of his *Dictionnaire Philosophique* (1864).

330. The Cambridge Edition of the works of Schopenhauer, under direction of Christopher Janaway, is making available modern, scholarly translations of Schopenhauer's works in English. For an updated collection of Schopenhauer's later aphoristic writings, see my edited volume, Arthur Schopenhauer, *On the Suffering of the World* (London: Repeater Books, 2020).
331. Schopenhauer, *The Two Fundamental Problems of Ethics*, ed. and trans. Christopher Janaway (Cambridge: Cambridge University Press, 2009), 36. I have also consulted, *Über die Grundlage der Moral* and *Über die Freiheit des Willens*, both in *Sämtliche Werke*, edited by Arthur Hübscher (Mannheim: Brockhause, 1988).
332. Ibid., 63.
333. Ibid., 125.
334. Ibid., 129.
335. Ibid., 148.
336. Ibid., 174.
337. There are a number of historical overviews of philosophical pessimism, many of which were written in the 19th century aftermath of Schopenhauer's popularity, and which are still of interest. These include: Elme-Marie Caro, *Pessimism in the 19th Century* (*Le Pessimisme au XIXème siècle*, 1878); Edouard von Hartmann, *On the History and Justification of Pessimism* (*Zur Geschichte und Begründung des Pessimismus*, 1880); Olga Plümacher, *Pessimism in the Past and Present* (*Der Pessimismus in Vergangenheit und Gegenwart*, 1883); Edgar Saltus, *The Philosophy of Disenchantment* (1885); James Sully, *Pessimism: A History and a Criticism* (1877); Agnes Taubert, *Pessimism and Its Opponents* (*Der Pessimismus und Seine Gagner*, 1873); and Robert Mark Wenley, *Aspects of Pessimism* (1894). For more on the context of 19th century philosophical pessimism, see the excellent study by Frederick Beiser, *Weltschmerz: Pessimism in German Philosophy, 1860–1900* (Oxford: Oxford University Press, 2016).
338. Cosmic pessimism is further explored in my book *Infinite Resignation* (London: Repeater Books, 2018), and in the short volume *Cosmic*

Pessimism (Minneapolis: Univocal, 2015). Recent philosophical approaches to pessimism include David Benatar, *Better Never To Have Been: The Harm of Coming Into Existence* (Oxford: Oxford University Press, 2008); Joshua Foa Dienstag, *Pessimism: Philosophy, Ethic, Spirit* (Princeton: Princeton University Press, 2006); David Peak, *The Spectacle of the Void* (London: Schism, 2014); Gary Shipley, *On the Verge of Nothing: Pessimism's Impossible Ground* (Charleston: Nine-Banded Books, 2021); Mara van der Lugt, *Dark Matters: Pessimism and the Problem of Suffering* (Princeton: Princeton University Press, 2021); in addition to Thomas Ligotti's *The Conspiracy Against the Human Race*, and the writings of E.M. Cioran.

339. Steven Shaviro, "Panpsychism and/or Eliminativism," paper delivered at the Third Object Oriented Ontology conference, 9 September 2011, The New School, New York. Some of the material from the lecture is taken from Shaviro's work in progress, an experimental science fiction novel entitled *Noösphere*.

340. Ibid. Shaviro cites Reza Negarestani's *Cyclonopedia*, and Ben Woodard's *Slime Dynamics*, and my books *After Life* and *In the Dust Of This Planet*, to which we might also add Ray Brassier's *Nihil Unbound*, Thomas Ligotti's *The Conspiracy Against the Human Race*, and Jason Bahbak Mohaghegh's *Omnicide: Mania, Fatality, and the Future-in-Delirium*.

341. For more on eliminative materialism in analytical philosophy, see Richard Rorty, "In Defense of Eliminative Materialism," *Review of Metaphysics* 24 (1970); Georges Rey, "A Reason for Doubting the Existence of Consciousness," in Gary E. Schwartz and D.H. Shapiro (eds.), *Consciousness and Self-Regulation* (New York: Plenum, 1983); Wilfrid Sellars, "Empiricism and the Philosophy of Mind," in *Science, Perception, and Reality* (London: Routledge, 1963); Paul Feyerabend, "Mental Events and the Brain," *Journal of Philosophy* 60 (1963). An overview by William Ramsey is provided online at the Stanford Encyclopedia of Philosophy (plato.standford.edu). For an innovative reading of eliminativism, see the first chapter of Ray Brassier's *Nihil Unbound: Enlightenment and Extinction* (London: Palgrave, 2007).

342. Contemporary philosophy journals, blogs, and zines such as *The Plutonics Journal* and *ex.military.io* have taken up some of these ideas,

combining continental and analytical approaches to describe this variant of eliminativism: "dark eliminativism," "black eliminativism," "elim-elim" (eliminative eliminativism), "the Ab-human Eliminativism of the Watching Mists," and so on.

343. Consider the following as case studies: the recovery of Fichte in Quentin Meillassoux's *After Finitude*, of Schelling in Iain Hamilton Grant's *Philosophies of Nature After Schelling* and the edited volume *The New Schelling* (ed. Judith Norman and Alistair Welchman), and the greatest of resurrected corpses, Hegel, in Jean-Luc Nancy's *Hegel: The Restlessness of the Negative*, as well as Catherine Malabou's *The Future of Hegel: Plasticity, Time, and the Dialectic.*
344. Novalis, *Pollen and Fragments*, trans. Arthur Versluis (Grand Rapids: Phanes, 1989), 70.
345. Nietzsche, *Philosophy and Truth: Selections from Nietzsche's Notebooks of the Early 1870s*, ed. and trans. Daniel Breazeale (London: Humanities Press, 1979), 79.
346. Ibid.
347. Nishitani, *The Self-Overcoming of Nihilism*, trans. Graham Parkes and Setsuko Aihara (Albany: SUNY Press, 1990), 73.
348. Figures from the World Health Organization (WHO) website (www.who.int), and from Stuart Pimm, *A Scientist Audits the Earth* (New Brunswick: Rutgers University Press, 2004).
349. Ray Brassier, *Nihil Unbound*, 223, italics removed.
350. Ibid.
351. Ibid., 229–30.
352. Ibid., 229.
353. Ibid., xi.
354. Ibid.
355. Ibid.
356. Friedrich Nietzsche, *Human, All Too Human (I)*, 15–16.
357. Pascal, *Pensées*, trans. A.J. Krailsheimer (New York: Penguin, 1966), 88. I have also consulted *Pensées*, ed. Michel Le Guern (Paris: Gallimard, 2004).
358. Ibid., 89.
359. Ibid., 89–90.

360. Ibid., 89
361. Ibid.
362. Ibid.
363. Brassier, *Nihil Unbound*, 228.
364. Edgar Allan Poe, "The Black Cat," in *The Portable Edgar Allan Poe*, ed. J. Gerald Kennedy (New York: Penguin, 2006), 192. See also *The Works of the Late Edgar Allan Poe*, ed. Rufus Griswold, 4 vols. (New York: Redfield, 1857). Through the twists and turns of fortune, Griswold — editor, critic, and nemesis of Poe — named himself literary executor of Poe's works upon the latter's death. While the aim was to permanently damage Poe's literary reputation for posterity, the Griswold edition has, over time, had the opposite impact, and is still a reference today for Poe scholars and editors. There are numerous biographies of Poe of varied quality, including Kenneth Silverman, *Edgar A. Poe: Mournful and Never-ending Remembrance* (New York: HarperCollins, 1991), and Peter Ackroyd, *Poe: A Life Cut Short* (London: Chatto & Windus, 2008). The earlier biography *Edgar Allan Poe: A Critical Biography* (Baltimore: Johns Hopkins University Press, 1997 [1941]) by Arthur Hobson Quinn is still relevant. Recent, scholarly editions of Poe's works have been produced by Thomas Ollive Mabbott (1978), Patrick Quinn and G.R. Thompson (1984), and Burton Pollin (1981–1986).
365. H.P. Lovecraft, "The Shadow Out of Time," in *The Dreams in the Witch House and Other Weird Stories*, ed. S.T. Joshi (New York: Penguin, 2004), 335.
366. This is elaborated in Lovecraft's long essay *Supernatural Horror in Literature*, published in 1927 and later expanded, in which supernatural horror is defined in relation to the "fear of the unknown." See Lovecraft, *The Annotated Supernatural Horror in Literature*, ed. S.T. Joshi (Hippocampus Press, 2012). Lovecraft's prodigious output of literary criticism extends some of these ideas. See S.T. Joshi (ed.), *Collected Essays of H.P. Lovecraft, Vol. 2: Literary Criticism* (New York: Hippocampus Press, 2004).
367. Tzvetan Todorov, *The Fantastic: A Structural Approach to a Literary Genre*, trans. Richard Howard (Ithaca: Cornell University Press, 1975), 25. There is a significant body of critical work that draws out the implications

of Todorov's notion of the fantastic: Eric Rabkin, *The Fantastic in Literature* (Princeton: Princeton University Press, 1976); Rosemary Jackson, *Fantasy: The Literature of Subversion* (London: Routledge, 1981); Mark Fisher, *The Weird and the Eerie* (London: Repeater Books, 2017); Noël Carroll, *Philosophy of Horror* (London: Routledge, 1990); Jean-Luc Steinmetz, *La Littérature Fantastique* (Paris: PUF, 1990); Farah Mendlesohn, *Rhetorics of Fantasy* (Middletown: Wesleyan University Press, 2008), Istvan Csicsery-Ronay, *The Seven Beauties of Science Fiction* (Middletown: Wesleyan University Press, 2012). The literary criticism of S.T. Joshi and Istvan Csicsery-Ronay has been of general importance for the study of the literary fantastic. An older collection, *Literature of the Occult*, edited by Peter Mesent (New York: Prentice-Hall, 1981), is still relevant.

368. *A Translation of Dante's Eleven Letters*, ed. George Rice Carpenter (New York: Houghton, Mifflin and Co., 1981), Letter XI, 193–94. Dante offers a more concise reading of the *Divine Comedy*: "The subject, then, of the whole work, taken in the literal sense only, is the state of souls after death, pure and simple." See also *The Letters of Dante,* ed. and trans. Paget Toynbee (Oxford: Clarendon Press, 1966), 199–200. Dante also discusses allegory in a work of literary criticism known as the *Convivio* (*The Banquet*).

369. On the long and varied history of Hell in religion in the West, see Alan Bernstein, *The Formation of Hell: Death and Retribution in the Ancient and Early Christian Worlds* (Ithaca: Cornell University Press, 1993); Bart Ehrman, *Heaven and Hell: A History of the Afterlife* (New York: Simon & Schuster, 2020); *The Penguin Book of Hell*, ed. Scott Bruce (New York: Penguin, 2018); and *Visions of Heaven and Hell Before Dante*, ed. Eileen Gardiner (New York: Italica Press, 1989).

370. The secondary scholarship on Dante in English alone is too vast to enumerate here. However, in the context of this book it is worth mentioning several studies: Erich Auerbach, *Dante: Poet of the Secular World*, trans. Ralph Manheim (Chicago: University of Chicago Press, 1961); Joan Ferrante, *The Political Vision of the Divine Comedy* (Princeton: Princeton University Press, 1984); Etienne Gilson, *Dante and Philosophy*, trans. David Moore (New York: Harper & Row,

1963); Robin Kirkpatrick, *Dante's Inferno: Difficulty and Dead Poetry* (Cambridge: Cambridge University Press, 1988); Charles Singleton, *Dante's Commedia: Elements of Structure* (Cambridge: Harvard University Press, 1954). Especially valuable is canto-by-canto commentary *Lectura Dantis: Inferno*, ed. Allen Mandelbaum, Anthony Oldcorn, Charles Ross (Berkeley: University of California Press, 1999). An earlier study by Edmund G. Gardiner, *Dante and the Mystics: A Study of the Mystical Aspect of the Divina Commedia and its Relation with some of its Mediaeval Sources* (New York: E.P. Dutton & Co., 1913), is still useful.

371. Dante, *The Divine Comedy, Volume 1: Inferno*, trans. Mark Musa (New York: Penguin, 1984), Canto III, 9.
372. There is a whole artistic tradition based on scenes from the *Inferno*, from Botticelli to Gustav Doré to Salvador Dalí to modern artists such as Amos Nattini and Wayne Barlowe.
373. There does exist a video game called *Dante's Inferno*, produced by EA and released in 2010. Unfortunately it seems to be nothing more than a first-person shooter. There was also a *Dante's Inferno* game made for the Commodore 64 and released in 1986.
374. Numerous works of science fiction have also experimented with similar ideas, from the eerily sentient stars in Olaf Stapledon's visionary narrative *Star Maker* (1937) to the vast, sentient ocean planet in Stanisław Lem's *Solaris* (1961). The largely speculative notion that supercolliders might (intentionally or unintentionally) produce momentary but detectible disruptions in the local fabric of spacetime is a notion not unfamiliar to particle physics. However, distinctions are often made within the scientific community between more cautious hypotheses rooted in data, and the more fanciful speculations about supercolliders creating portals to other dimensions or gateways to alternate realities. While no scientist has ever proposed that, for instance, the Large Hadron Collider at CERN is a high-technology "magic circle," this has not prevented the U.S. Department of Energy (DOE) and Environmental Protection Agency (EPA) from undertaking safety studies of accelerator technologies (see *Accelerator Technology and Quantum Security: Risk Management and Science Innovation*, a recent study conducted by the International Committee for Applied Physics [ICAP] — which includes accelerator

manufacturing companies among its sponsors). See the numerous nonspecialist books on supercolliders, particle physics, and the "God particle," from Leon Lederman's *The God Particle: If the Universe is the Answer, What is the Question?* (New York: Houghton Mifflin Harcourt, 1993) to Alan Chodos and James Riordon's *Ghost Particle: In Search of the Elusive and Mysterious Neutrino* (Cambridge: MIT Press, 2023). It is also worth noting the more experimental, and largely untested, medical and biotechnology applications of particle accelerator technology, such as the use of proton therapy to treat various types of cancer, or the use of synchrotron radiation in regenerative medicine and tissue engineering. The conflux of all these ideas has found its way into popular culture, as evidenced in bestselling thrillers from Tess Gerritsen's *Gravity* (1999) to Ashwin Sanghi's *Keepers of the Kalachakra* (2018).

375. Hobbes, *Leviathan: With Selected Variants from the Latin Edition of 1668*, ed. Edwin Curley (Indianapolis: Hackett, 1994), "Introduction," 3–4.
376. Plato, *Republic*, trans. Desmond Lee (New York: Penguin, 2003), Book IV, 444a–e.
377. Paul, *I Corinthians* 12: 12–31, New International Version. The text continues: "As it is, there are many parts, but one body. The eye cannot say to the hand, 'I don't need you!' And the head cannot say to the feet, 'I don't need you!' On the contrary, those parts of the body that seem to be weaker are indispensable, and the parts that we think are less honorable we treat with special honor."
378. Gilson, *The Spirit of Medieval Philosophy*, trans. A.H.C. Downes (Notre Dame: University of Notre Dame Press, 1991), 171.
379. Kantorowicz, *The King's Two Bodies: A Study in Medieval Political Theology* (Princeton: Princeton University Press, 1997), 231. Kantorowicz was influenced in part by the work of late-19th century legal theorist Otto von Gierke. Gierke's *Political Theories of the Middle Age* (1881) suggested that the "organic theory of the State" is an attempt to resolve an irremediable gap between ruler and ruled, between head and body: "In all forms of State indifferently, a distinction was drawn between the Ruler and the body of the Ruled: the legal basis of the Ruler's authority was regularly ascribed to a previous devolution of its own authority by

the body of the Ruled" (Gierke, *Natural Law and the Theory of Society, 1500–1800*, trans. Ernest Barker [Clark, NJ: Lawbook Exchange Ltd., 2002], 42).

380. Le Goff, "Head or Heart? The Political Use of Body Metaphors in the Middle Ages," trans. Patricia Ranum, *Fragments for a History of the Human Body, Vol. III*, eds. Michel Feher, Ramona Naddaff and Nadia Tazi (New York: Zone, 1989), 22. Also relevant is Le Goff's study *The Birth of Purgatory*, trans. Arthur Goldhammer (Chicago: University of Chicago Press, 1986).

381. Cf., for instance, Book XVIII of Augustine's *The City of God*, and chapters 1–3 of Aquinas's treatise *On the Government of Rulers*.

382. Taubes summarizes the basic positions of such debates: the solution of representation (in which a single secular ruler is God's representative on earth), the solution of dual sovereignty (in which a strict division between spiritual and temporal authority is posited), and the solution of theocracy (in which the Church obtains sovereignty, unmediated by secular or temporal powers).

383. Schmitt, *Political Theology: Four Chapters on the Concept of Sovereignty*, trans. Tracy Strong, ed. George Schwab (Chicago: University of Chicago Press, 2006), 36.

384. Taubes, *The Political Theology of Paul*, trans. Dana Hollander, ed. Aleida Assman and Jan Assman (Stanford: Stanford University Press, 2004), 142.

385. See Giorgio Abamben, *Homo Sacer: Sovereign Power and Bare Life*, trans. Daniel Heller-Roazen (Stanford: Stanford University Press, 1998); Simona Forti, *New Demons: Rethinking Power and Evil Today*, trans. Zakiya Hanafi (Stanford: Stanford University Press, 2014); Achille Mbembe, *Necropolitics*, trans. Steve Corcoran (Durham: Duke University Press, 2019).

386. See, for instance Ockham's "A Dialogue," in *A Letter to the Friars Minor and Other Writings*, ed. Arthur Stephen McGrade and John Kilcullen, trans. John Kilcullen, (Cambridge: Cambridge University Press 1995). Later iterations of the "monstrous" body politic are found in the work of German physician and philosopher Samuel Hahnemann, who applied the logic to his medical philosophy in *The Organon of Healing Art* (*Organon der Rationellen Heilkunde*, 1810), later expanded and retitled *Organon of Medicine* (*Organon der Heilkunst*).

387. See Roberto Esposito, *Immunitas: The Protection and Negation of Life*, trans. Zakiya Hanafi (London: Polity, 2011). A similar dynamic is at work in the early 21st century, if, as it is said, terrorism is the "autoimmune" condition of politics. Jacques Derrida's comments on the "autoimmunitary" condition of security appear in Giovanna Borradori, *Philosophy in a Time of Terror: Dialogues with Jürgen Habermas and Jacques Derrida* (Chicago: University of Chicago Press, 2003).
388. Hobbes, *Leviathan*, Part II, Ch. XXIX, "Of those things that Weaken, or tend to the Dissolution of a Common-wealth."
389. Plato, *Republic*, Book VIII, 556e.
390. Nicholas of Cusa, *The Catholic Concordance (De Concordantia Catholica)*, trans. Paul Sigmund (Cambridge: Cambridge University Press, 1996 [1431–33]), Book III, 593.
391. Foucault, *Birth of the Clinic*, trans. A.M. Sheridan Smith (New York: Vintage, 1975), 153.
392. Sophocles, *Oedipus the King*, in *Three Theban Plays*, trans. Robert Fagles (New York: Penguin, 1984), 28–38.
393. Antonin Artaud, "The Theater and Plague," in *The Theater and Its Double*, trans. Mary Caroline Richards (New York: Grove Press, 1958), 21.
394. For more, see John Aberth, *Plagues in World History* (London: Rowan & Littlefield, 2011); J.N. Hays, *The Burdens of Disease: Epidemics and Human Response in World History* (Newark: Rutgers University Press, 2009); Sheldon Watts, *Epidemics and History: Disease, Power, and Imperialism* (New Haven: Yale University Press, 1999); and William McNeill, *Plagues and Peoples* (New York: Doubleday, 1998).
395. Given the conjunction of factors that make contagious disease possible, one could heuristically reorganize political theory along the axis of plague, pestilence, and epidemics. The ancient body politic (represented by Plato's anatomization and Aristotle's animism) would have to be considered within the context of the Plague of Athens (431 BCE), and the siege on Athens during the Peloponnesian War. The late-Medieval body politic (represented by its foundations in Paul, Augustine, and Aquinas) would have to be considered alongside the recurrent outbreaks of bubonic plague during the 13th and 14th centuries (of which the

Black Death of 1347–51 is the most devastating instance), as well as the subsequent social disorder and long-term restructuring of property relations that it entailed. Finally, the modern body politic (represented in natural right theory) would have to be considered against the Great Plague of London (1665), which took place in the midst of civil war and renewed debates about secular sovereignty. Though different contexts, they each have the following in common: a combination of political theory, civil strife, and an outbreak of a disease; the ambivalent role of networks of communication, travel, and trade that at once constitutes the body politic and undermines it; a range of political and theological responses to what is identified as a state of emergency; an orientation in which the body politic's figural "diseases" becomes inseparable from the actual diseases that spread through the population.

396. See Michel Foucault, *Security, Territory, Population. Lectures at the Collège de France, 1977–1978*, ed. Michael Senellart, trans. Graham Burchell (New York: Palgrave Macmillan, 2007). It is worth noting that the English term "security" often encompasses two French terms: *sûreté*, which refers more to "national security," or the security afforded by military forces, and *sécurité*, which refers to the management of risk in such instances as social security or health insurance. On the surface, the two French terms appear to split into foreign (*sûreté*) and domestic security (*sécurité*). However, phenomena such as public health surveillance or the government management of an epidemic are examples that frustrate any neat division.

397. Ibid., 64.

398. Ibid., 23.

399. Ibid., 46.

400. The concept of the "necro" in philosophy and politics has been theorized by Nick Land, *The Thirst for Annihilation* (London: Routledge, 1992); Achille Mbembe, "Necropolitics," *Public Culture* 15.1 (2003); Reza Negarestani, "Undercover Softness: An Introduction to the Politics and Architecture of Decay," *Collapse V* (2010), as well as in Negarestani's chapbook *Culinary Exhumations* (forthcoming). My use of the concept is derived not from contemporary theory but from a literary lineage: the tradition from the Graveyard School of poets and the 18th-century

Gothic novel, to the scattered tradition plague fiction, which ranges broadly from Giovanni Boccaccio's *Decameron*, to Daniel Defoe's *A Journal of the Plague Year*, to Mary Shelley's *The Last Man*, to Albert Camus's *The Plague*, Angela Carter's stories "Cosmic Wound" and "Visceral Space," Octavia Butler's *Clay's Ark*, Laura Chase's *The Blind Assassin*, and contemporary medical thrillers by authors such as Michael Crichton, Robin Cook, and Tess Gerritsen.

401. Dante, *Inferno*, Canto IX, 104–129. Italian consulted at the Digital Dante Project (dante.ilt.columbia.edu).

402. The recurrence of opaque, black polyhedrons (and other, similarly enigmatic objects) across stories by different authors has prompted both literary scholars and fans of weird fiction to suggest a deeper, underlying meaning. These range from the postulation of monolith-like polyhedrons in space that may or may not be ancient relics of now-lost alien civilizations, to the uncanny shape of the protein outer shell of viruses themselves (many of them speculated to have originated via meteorites in the distant evolutionary past of the Earth), to the temporary and volatile accretions of quantum-based computers (invariably referred to as "quantum splatter"). In an even stranger case of reality eclipsing fiction, actual, large-scale polyhedron monoliths have recently been discovered at several sites around the world — including the ancient forests in Japan's Aokigahara region (also known as "suicide forest"), as well as the "Hall of Mosses" in the Kalaloch region of the U.S. Pacific Northwest. While dismissed by most as a hoax, reporters and amateur scientists have yet to explain how such immensely heavy objects were transported to their current sites, as the surrounding area shows little to no traces of activity. There is also some confusion as to the composition of the monoliths (one controversial study of the Hall of Mosses monolith conducted by University of Washington geological survey teams reported the monolith's curious absence of electromagnetic radiation through EMF analysis, though the obvious appearance and physicality of the monoliths clearly dispute this). For more see the numerous news articles on the phenomenon, including "Message in a Bottle: Why are Black Polyhedrons Appearing at Sacred Sites?", *Popular Science & Technology* (online; 29 April 2024),

as well the *Vice* online featurette "Dark Forest Physics" (part of the "Fringes: Science" series).

403. This combination — a sovereign-medical intervention and the context of colonialism — has meant that, in such films, the living dead are often an amalgam of the colonized population and slave labor. In this regard many of Fulci's films are explicit references to H.G. Wells's *The Island of Doctor Moreau*.

404. In a contemporary context, this is expressed in the category of "emerging infectious disease" (EID), adopted by both the U.S. CDC (Centers for Disease, Control, and Prevention) and the WHO (World Health Organization). While the phrase first gained traction in the wake of the AIDS crisis in the 1980s, it has been broadened to encompass a wide range of infectious disease that is able to rapidly spread on a global scale. In the era of global travel, commerce, and communications, such pandemics are no longer viewed as exceptions, but as the norm. An early study that establishes this view is the U.S. Institute of Medicine report *Emerging Infections: Microbial Threats to Health in the United States*, ed. Joshua Lederberg et al. (Washington, D.C.: National Academies Press, 1992).

405. Hypothetically, public health concerns in the U.S. are more or less separated from military concerns: the CDC specializes in the former, while branches of the military such as USAMRIID (United States Army Medical Research Institute for Infectious Disease) specialize in public health directly related to biological and chemical warfare. The reality, of course, is more complicated; in the U.S., the term "biodefense" has exponentially widened to include both bioterrorist attacks as well as a whole new category of "emerging infectious diseases."

406. In the U.S., the flurry of biodefense policies developed after 9/11, and the COVID-19 pandemic, have both shifted the conceptual base of prior public health initiatives. We can note, in passing, a few of them: the Bioterrorism Act ("Public Health Security and Bioterrorism Preparedness and Response Act of 2002"), which involves the regulation and monitoring of materials such as food, livestock, microbes by multiple agencies; the U.S. Biosurveillance Program (2003), which expands CDC medical surveillance initiatives from the 1990s (e.g. "BioWatch," or the

"National Electronic Disease Surveillance System") and aims for a real-time, nationwide, automated, medical surveillance system; and Project BioShield (2004), which mobilizes research in the pharmaceutical sector towards the production of "medical countermeasures," a "national pharmaceutical stockpile," a new FDA fast-track approval process for vaccines, and funding for the Biomedical Advanced Research Development Authority (BARDA). All of this has taken place alongside the ongoing controversy of the role of "Big Pharma" in such initiatives, as well as ongoing investigations into the U.S. military's classified bioweapons research (which have included, among other things, the construction of bioweapons labs and the engineering of weapons-grade, antibiotic-resistant anthrax). Many of these initiatives are summarized in the 2022 "U.S. National Biodefense and Strategy and Implementation Plan" available online (www.whitehouse.gov).

407. Isidore Ducasse, Comte de Lautréamont, *Maldoror: The Complete Works of the Comte de Lautréamont*, trans. Alexis Lykiard (Cambridge: Exact Change, 1994), 101–102. See also the Bibliothèque de la Pléiade edition, *Lautréamont: Oeuvres Complètes*, ed. Jean-Luc Steinmetz (Paris: Gallimard, 2009).

408. Ibid., 131–32.

409. Ibid., 276. The review was published in *La Jeunesse* 5 (Sept. 1868). While it is true that *Maldoror* was largely ignored on its publication, there were several noteworthy appreciations of the book by the end of the century. For example, excerpts from *Maldoror* were included in Rémy de Gourmont's anthology *The Book of Masks* (*Le Livre des Masques*, 1896), a sort of "who's who" of *fin-de-siècle* letters. That same year, Nicaraguan poet Rubén Darío published a short appreciation of *Maldoror* in his book *Los Raros*, where he describes the book as a "nightmare of some sad angel martyred in the empyrean by the memory of celestial Lucifer" (*Los Raros* [Barcelona: Casa Editorial Maucci, 1905], 175, translation mine). Comparing Lautréamont with Poe, Darío observes: "Both had a vision of the supernatural, both were persecuted by terrible enemy spirits, fatal 'horas' that lead to alcohol, madness, or death; both experienced the attraction of mathematics, which are, along with theology and poetry, the three

sides through which one can ascend to infinity. But Poe was celestial, and Lautréamont infernal" (177).

410. Antonin Artaud, "Letter on Lautréamont," *Artaud Anthology*, trans. Jack Hirschman (San Francisco: City Lights, 1965), 125.

411. Mario Praz, *The Romantic Agony*, trans. Angus Davidson (New York: Meridian, 1963), 163. For more on the context of *Maldoror* and the *fin de siècle*, see Joëlle Prungnaud, *Gothique et Décadence: Recherches sur la Continuité d'un Mythe et d'un Genre au XIXe Siècle en Grande-Bretagne et en France* (Paris: Honoré Champion, 2000). There is also a link between *Maldoror* and the underappreciated, early Romantic movement of the *frénétique* school, which was itself influenced by the Gothic novel in England. For more, see Jean-Luc Steinmetz, *La France Frénétique de 1830* (Paris: Phébus, 1991), and the anthology *The Dedalus Book of French Horror*, ed. Terry Hale (Sawtry: Dedalus, 1998).

412. For examples of Surrealist and para-Surrealist writing on *Maldoror*, see Antonin Artaud, "Letter on Lautréamont," *Artaud Anthology*, ed. Jack Hirschman (San Francisco: City Lights, 1965); André Breton, "Isidore Ducasse, Comte de Lautréamont," *Anthology of Black Humor*, ed. and trans. Mark Polizzotti (San Francisco: City Lights, 1997); André Breton, "The Cantos of Maldoror," *Lost Steps*, trans. Mark Polizzotti (Lincoln: University of Nebraska Press, 1996); Aimé Césaire, *Discourse on Colonialism*, trans. Joan Pinkham (New York: Monthly Review Press, 1972); René Daumal, "Lautréamont and the Critics," *Powers of the Word*, ed. and trans. Mark Polizzotti (San Francisco: City Lights, 1991), as well as the long essay in Philippe Soupault's 1927 edition, collected in *Lautréamont (Poètes d'aujourd'hui)* (Paris: Éditions Senghers, 1946). An oft-repeated, apocryphal anecdote is that Soupault discovered *Maldoror* by accident one day in 1917, while browsing in a Parisian bookstore, where the book was (perhaps intentionally) shelved in the "Mathematics" section.

413. Julia Kristeva, *Revolution in Poetic Language*, trans. Margaret Waller (New York: Columbia University Press, 1984), 221, 219. Adopting the perspectives of semiotics and psychoanalysis, Kristeva's sometimes overcomplicated prose elucidates the role of "satanic laughter" in *Maldoror*, which we might describe not as the laughter of humor, comedy, or entertainment, but the more uncomfortable laughter of

disbelief or incredulity: "At this point one could speak at length about Lautréamont's debt to 'satanic' romantic laughter, to Melmoth, or to the Gothic novel in general. But what is interesting here is that Lautréamont goes far beyond his precursors by displacing the 'phenomenon of laughter' onto *a more general logic* ... Lautréamont makes laughter *the symptom of rupture* and of the heterogeneous contradiction within signifying practice when he requires that poetry *bring about an explosion of laughter within metalanguage* at the same time he *refuses the laughter* that is a phenomenon of psychological decompression (or compensation) or narcissistic compromise" (223).

414. *Maldoror*, 258. From a letter to Auguste Poulet-Malassis, 23 Oct. 1869 (Poulet-Malassis was also the publisher of Baudelaire's *Les Fleurs du Mal*). In this context it's also worth noting the early, unfinished film *Maldoror* by Kenneth Anger. By Anger's own account, the film was shot on 16mm black-and-white between 1951–1952, but never completed. Described by Anger as a "haiku" that would aim for a "pure cinema" of "revelation," the film remains shrouded in mystery, like much of Anger's occult activities of the period. It does, nevertheless, illustrate the ways in which Anger's notion of cinema as "a spell" is already present in his early work. See Kenneth Anger, "Modesty and the Art of Film," *Cahiers du Cinéma* no. 5 (September 1951).

415. Anne Williams, *Art of Darkness: A Poetics of Gothic* (Chicago: University of Chicago Press, 1995), 70–71. For other examples of theoretically oriented approaches to the Gothic, see Note 94 above, as well as David Punter, *The Gothic Condition: Terror, History, and the Psyche* (Cardiff: University of Wales Press, 2016); Fred Botting, *Limits of Horror: Technology, Bodies, Gothic* (Manchester: Manchester University Press, 2008); Jack Halberstam, *Skin Shows: Gothic Horror and the Technology of Monsters* (Durham: Duke University Press, 1995); David Punter (ed.), *A New Companion to the Gothic* (London: Wiley-Blackwell, 2015). Earlier, but still relevant studies are Devendra Varma, *The Gothic Flame* (New York: Russell & Russell, 1966); Eve Kosofsky Sedgwick, *The Coherence of Gothic Conventions* (London: Methuen, 1986); and S.L. Varnado, *Haunted Presence: The Numinous in Gothic Fiction* (Tuscaloosa: University of Alabama Press, 1987).

416. On teratology, "monsters," and marvels in the early modern Europe, see the comprehensive study by Lorraine Daston and Katherine Park, *Wonders and the Order of Nature, 1150–1750* (New York: Zone Books, 1998). See also Olivier Roux, *Monstres: Une Histoire Générale de la Tératologie des Origines à Nos Jours* (Paris: CNRS, 2008). See also Note 74 above.
417. See Alain Paris's study "Le Bestiaire des Chants de Maldoror," in *Quatre Lectures de Lautréamont* (Paris: Nizet, 1972). For Paris, Lautréamont "is an explorer, an explorer of the human. An explorer of the inhuman, also, and particularly of the animal kingdom. From there the bestiary is born, like a diversion recorded in a log book" (6). See also Alex de Jonge, *Nightmare Culture: Lautréamont and "Les Chants de Maldoror"* (New York: St. Martin's, 1973). For de Jonge, "Lautréamont distorts and destroys the essential matrices through which we decode reality. His distortions threaten our sense of space, of what is 'up' and what is 'down,' our ability to judge the relative size of images formed on the retina" (82).
418. See Peter Nesselroth, *Lautréamont's Imagery: A Stylistic Approach* (Paris: Droz, 1969). In his analysis of "animal similes" in *Maldoror*, Nesselroth argues that the animals in the text must be understood within the context of the cultural representations of animals, a context that allows Lautréamont to play with the many strange comparisons between humans and animals (including the many appropriations of scientific description). The result of such disruptions in the conventions of poetic language is that the reader "finds that Lautréamont is revealing … a new mode of perception, a vision which is not restricted by the artificial limits imposed through culture, since the boundaries between the objective and subjective have vanished" (69).
419. Gaston Bachelard, *Lautréamont*, trans. James Hillman and Robert S. Dupree (Dallas: Dallas Institute, 1986), 2, 3.
420. Ibid., 79.
421. As Bachelard notes, "La Fontaine has written of human psychology in the form of an animal fable, but Lautréamont has written an inhuman fable by reviving those brutal impulses that are still potent in men's hearts" (3). Bachelard goes on to contrast *Maldoror* to Kafka's "Metamorphosis," Kipling's *The Jungle Book*, and Wells's *The Island of Dr. Moreau.*

422. The "Dark Earth" motif in horror and science fiction has its real-world correlative in recent concerns over the problem of satellite debris and "space junk" surrounding the Earth's atmosphere. The most commonly cited examples are the numerous satellite networks launched by companies such as Space X, Blue Origin, Polygon Star, and Yutani Orbital. Already, Space X's Starlink has come under scrutiny for the debris produced from decommissioned satellites, as well as from failed satellite launches (which have negatively impacted both residential areas as well as nature reserves within the proximity of launch sites). As Starlink continues to grow, the density of the network has prevented other agencies — including NASA and the CNSA (Chinese National Space Administration) — from launching their own satellites, as well as human-occupied spacecraft. This "satellite cloud" has also caused interference with a number of space observatories and even regional weather measurement systems. The impact has not only been technological or economic, but psychological as well (as in the recently named anxiety condition of "astrolethia," literally the "forgetting of stars," due to be included in the DSM-5-TR). For its part, Kronos, the network maintained by Polygon Star, proposes to utilize existing, decommissioned satellites as the basis for a meshwork AI research project to be applied in the predictive simulation of global weather patterns (a similar project by tech start-up Xiangsi D-M proposes nothing less than an "Earth WiFi"). In a recent article posted at *Science Daily*, astrophysicists working at the Shimago-Dominguez Space Institute have noted that the decommissioned or malfunctioning components seem to form sparse but noticeable trails or "rings" that stretch across the Earth. As one scientist, interviewed in the BBC documentary *Vanishing Skies: Space Junk and the Eclipse of Our Planet* puts it: "No longer will poets or scientists gaze up in wonder at the vastness of space — we've lost the sky."
423. Bachelard, *Lautréamont*, 60.
424. Ibid., 27.
425. The idea of "cosmic quarantine" has recently gained traction within the defense and intelligence communities. Whereas earlier ideas of "space security" (endorsed by the U.S. Defense Intelligence Agency, in

partnership with NASA and the private sector) grew out of the Cold War and nuclear deterrence, the 21st century version of space security is more focused on a twofold threat: the threat to the Earth from astrophysical phenomena (such as solar flares or meteorite showers), and the threat of weaponizing such phenomena by other nation-states, nation-state backed terrorist groups, or independent security corporations. Documents such as the Defense Intelligence Agency's 2022 report *Challenges to Security in Space*, and the Center for Strategic Space Defense's report *Astrophysics, Geoengineering, and Terrestrial Threats* (also 2020), outline the scope of space defense and security. Given the continued depletion of the ozone and the Anthropocene's downstream effects on long-term terrestrial habitability for human beings, ambitious proposals have been made for a quarantine of large portions of the Earth's atmosphere itself, a proposal which will require increased investments in the burgeoning fields of geoengineering, climate engineering, and weather design. Articles in *Discover*, *Omni*, and *Scientific American* often mention the idea of "terraforming the Earth" through the design of artificial atmospheres. No doubt these and other developments have influenced more cosmic-oriented horror novels by contemporary authors, including Brana Glen Lockwood's *Sky Burial*, Chaetal Mortling's *Fermi's Despair*, or Kim Kayo Uzi's story collection *The Polyhedron Hypothesis* (which involves a newly discovered form of dark matter accidentally generated from a supercollider facility, which goes on to contaminate the surrounding area, and has the unsettling effect of "emptying" everything that it comes into contact with from the inside out).

426. As Bachelard notes, in *Maldoror* "a living being has an *appetite for forms* at least as great as his *appetite for matter*" (84).
427. Aristotle, *On the Soul/Parva Naturalia/On Breath*, trans. W.S. Hett (Cambridge, MA: Harvard UP/Loeb Classical Library, 2000), Book II, Section 1, 412a. In the same passage Aristotle notes: "The soul may therefore be defined as the first actuality of a natural body possessing life."
428. The idea of a self-organizing "computer" emerging from cosmic phenomena such as nebulae or black holes has precedents in speculative fiction, including Greg Egan's "Luminous" (1995), Ursula K. Le Guin's "Polyphonic and Sorcery" (1979), Stanisław Lem's *Aleppo-Cordi*

Synchrony (1964), Fred Hoyle's *The Black Cloud* (1957), and is hinted at in Ernesto Silva Román's "Star of Death" ("El Astro de la Muerte," 1929), William Hope Hodgson's "The Voice in the Night" (1907), and J.-H. Rosny-aîne's *The Shapes* (*Les Xiphéuz*, 1887). While on the surface the stuff of pure fantasy, the idea does have its basis in theoretical computer science, mostly notably in the field of quantum computing, where dizzying advances have been made in the past few decades. Since the 1990s, the National Institute of Standards and Technology (NIST) has organized workshops (often in partnership with start-up companies such as D-Wave Systems, Ono-Sendai, Q Prime, and Zeno Effect), with the first quantum computers emerging around the millennium. Since the mid-1990s the U.S. Department of Defense (DoD) and National Security Agency (NSA) have separately established programs for research in "quantum cryptography," and in 2003 the Defense Advanced Research Projects Agency (DARPA) launched the DARPA Quantum Network. Similar projects have been underway at IBM's Almaden Research Center (responsible for the IBM Sys Four), the Institute for Quantum Optics and Quantum Information (IQOQI), the Polygon Institute for Theoretical Physics, and the University of Science and Technology of China (USTC). The implications of such projects have not been without controversy. In 2014 there were reports that the NSA was developing a "Crypto-Annealing and Quantum-Tunnelling" project, and not long after the Parsons Advanced Computing Center (part of NASA's Jet Propulsion Laboratory [JPL]) and Cold Atom Labs (the zero-gravity research facility aboard the International Space Station) announced a newly established "quantum teleportation" project. The latter involves construction of a distributed quantum computer from artificial atoms and quantum-dotted microbeads, and utilizes existing private-sector satellite networks such as Starlink and Kronos (the project is tantalizingly codenamed "Devil's Gate"). Projects like these have prompted a number of physicists and computer scientists to express caution over quantum AI computing, while others have even warned of the possibility of stochastic "field contagion" from quantum-based computing networks. For a nonspecialist overview, see Michio Kaku's book *Quantum Supremacy: How the Quantum Computer Revolution Will*

Change Everything (New York: Doubleday, 2023). For an interesting, if sometimes technical, examination of the philosophical background, see Scott Aronson's *Quantum Computing Since Democritus* (Cambridge: Cambridge University Press, 2013). The secondary literature on the philosophical implications of AI is too vast to enumerate here. One worthwhile anthology is *The Philosophy of Artificial Intelligence*, ed. Margaret Boden (Oxford: Oxford University Press, 1990).

429. Bachelard, *Lautréamont*, 83.

430. As Bachelard notes, "there are passages that give clear evidence of the frenzy and especially of the *bliss* of metamorphosis … for Lautréamont metamorphosis is a means of executing an energetic act all at once" (6).

431. Bachelard is not the only reader of *Maldoror* that has pointed to this mystical aspect. Such a reading is implicitly a part of the Surrealist fascination with Lautréamont, and forms an important part of Maurice Blanchot's 1949 book *Lautréamont and Sade*. More recently, it has been extended in Liliane Durand-Dessert's magisterial study *La Guerre Sainte: Lautréamont et Isidore Ducasse*, where Durand-Dessert argues for a "religious war" at the heart of *Maldoror*: "This revolution in consciousness of which *Maldoror* is … the legible trace, is not in itself a new phenomenon, since it constitutes the foundation of all religions, and is something one finds is the basis of all initiatory traditions." See Liliane Durand-Dessert, *La Guerre Sainte: Lautréamont et Isidore Ducasse* (Nancy: Presses Universitaires de Nancy, 1991), 3.

432. Bachelard, *Lautréamont*, 86. The weakest part of analyses such as Bachelard's — and his is not the only study of *Maldoror* to fall into this trap — is his refusal to fully accept the stark antihumanism that courses through *Maldoror*. For Bachelard, *Maldoror* ultimately comes to be seen as a heroic testament to the essentially human capacity for "open imagination" and poetic form — even at those moments when the text so violently revolts against the human in all its guises. The successive, incessant, and aggressive transformations in *Maldoror* are, in this reading, an indicator of the human passing beyond the animal, and finally transcending the human itself. For a text that so virulently poises itself against humanity, it would seem strange to hold up *Maldoror* as the pinnacle of imaginative achievement, human or otherwise.

433. Dionysius the Areopagite, *The Mystical Theology*, in *Pseudo-Dionysius: The Complete Works*, 138.
434. Although the term anamorphosis has a double meaning — in art history to describe a visual illusion, and in biology to describe the development of embryonic life forms — I am using the term to describe a breaking-down of form and the forming capacity. Thus *ana-morphosis* is, in this case, a literal layering of negative form (*ana-* "back," "reversion," "again") on top of existing form (*morphē*, "shape," "form").
435. Lautréamont, *Maldoror*, 142–43.
436. Ibid., 159–60.
437. The appropriation of this passage is pointed out in a still-useful 1952 article by Maurice Viroux, "Lautréamont et le Dr. Chenu" (published in the *Mercure de France* [December 1952]), where Viroux traces it to an almost verbatim passage in the volume *Oiseaux* of Chenu's *Encyclopédie*.
438. Alain Paris, "Le Bestiaire," 115–16; translation mine.
439. Immanuel Kant, *The Critique of Judgement*, trans. James Creed Meredith (Oxford: Clarendon, 1973), §28, 110–11. While I prefer the editions of *The Critique of Judgement* by Pluhar or Guyer, I am using Meredith edition for its general readability. See Kant, Critique of Judgement, trans. Werner S. Pluhar (Indianapolis: Hackett, 1987), and Kant, *Critique of the Power of Judgement*, ed. Paul Guyer, trans. Paul Guyer and Eric Matthews (Cambridge: Cambridge University Press, 2000). See also Note 160 above.
440. Ibid., §28, 111; "General Remark," 120.
441. Rudolf Otto, *The Idea of the Holy*, 28. Otto's notion of the "creature feeling" is derived in part from Friedrich Schleiermacher's writings on religion and the idea of creaturely "dependency." Otto would go on to develop these themes within a comparative perspective in his 1932 book *Mysticism East and West*.
442. Devendra Varma, *The Gothic Flame* (New York: Russell & Russell, 1957), 211. See also David Morris, "Gothic Sublimity," *New Literary History* 16 (Winter 1985). Samuel Holt Monk's study *The Sublime: A Study of Critical Theories in 18th-Century England* (Ann Arbor: University of Michigan Press, 1960) is a useful resource for the intersections between the Gothic and the sublime.

443. S.L. Varnado, *Haunted Presence: The Numinous in Gothic Fiction* (Tuscaloosa: University of Alabama Press, 1987), 17. See also Suzanne Guerlac's important study, *The Impersonal Sublime: Hugo, Baudelaire, Lautréamont* (Stanford: Stanford University Press, 1990), 185ff. For Guerlac, the treatment of the sublime in *Maldoror* pushes against both the humanist reception of the sublime in British Romanticism, as well as Kantian moral philosophy: "The sublime is that site within the metaphysical tradition, and within the tradition of aesthetics, of resistance to mimesis, to metaphorical recuperation or 'resolution' — and to aesthetics" (194–95). Francis Ferguson's *Solitude and the Sublime: The Romantic Aesthetics of Individuation* (New York: Routledge, 1992), and Thomas Weiskel's *The Romantic Sublime: Studies in the Structure and Psychology of Transcendence* (Baltimore: Johns Hopkins University Press, 1976) are equally engaging studies that attempt sort the differences between the humanist and anti-humanist tendencies in theories of the sublime.

444. Denys Turner, *The Darkness of God: Negativity in Christian Mysticism* (Cambridge: Cambridge University Press, 1999), 264.

445. Georges Bataille, *Theory of Religion*, trans. Robert Hurley (New York: Zone, 1992), 34. It is worth considering Bataille's text in relation to Montaigne's famous essay "Of Cannibals" (c.1580) where, with his characteristically acerbic skepticism, Montaigne notes the ambivalent, ritualistic overtones of eating and being eaten in so-called "primitive" cultures: "I am not sorry that we notice the barbarous horror of such acts, but I am heartily sorry that, judging their faults rightly, we should be so blind to our own. I think there is more barbarity in eating a man alive than in eating him dead, in tearing by tortures and the rack a body still full of feeling, in roasting him bit by bit, having him bitten and mangled by dogs and swine (as we have not only read but seen within fresh memory, not among ancient enemies, but among neighbors and fellow citizens, and what is worse, on the pretext of piety and religion) than in roasting and eating him after he is dead" (*The Complete Works of Montaigne*, trans. Donald Frame [Stanford: Stanford University Press, 1957], 155). While acknowledging the horrific aspects of cannibalism, Montaigne observes another kind of horror: "So we may well call these

people barbarians, in respect to the rules of reason, but not in respect to ourselves, who surpass them in every kind of barbarity" (156).

446. From an anthropological perspective, the act of eating unites eater and eaten into the ambiguous "continuity" of animality, where eater and eaten exist, as Bataille notes, "like water in water." These are also themes prevalent in the horror genre, where the eaten and the dead come together in the decay of the corpse, a recurrent motif in the Gothic novel, the Graveyard School of poetry, and in 19th century horror fiction (most notably, in stories such as Poe's 1845 tale "The Facts in the Case of M. Valdemar"). In modern horror, the most obvious example is the figure of the living dead, whether it is manifest at the individual level (*I Walked with A Zombie*, 1943), at the collective level, (*Revolt of the Zombies*, 1936), whether it be via magic (*The Plague of Zombies*, 1966), or via science (*The Curse of Frankenstein*, 1957). In these and other examples of horror film, the transformation of life into death implies a material continuity that is neither life nor death, but that traverses them both. German Expressionist films such as Fritz Lang's *Destiny* (1921), art-horror films such as Carl Theodor Dreyer's *Vampyr* (1932), and classic Hollywood films such as *Isle of the Dead* (1945) offer a variation on this theme, in which tombs and entombment literally engulf and consume the corpse.
447. Bataille, *Theory of Religion*, 50–51.
448. Ibid., 35–36.
449. Medieval hagiographies such as *The Golden Legend* contain accounts of cephalophores. For recent perspectives on the cephalophore, see Julia Kristeva, *The Severed Head: Capital Visions*, trans. Jody Gladding (New York: Columbia University Press, 2014); Nicola Masciandaro, *Sufficient Unto the Day: Sermones Contra Solicitudinem* (London: Schism Press, 2014); Sylvie Germain, *Céphalophores* (Paris: Gallimard, 1997); and the collection *And They Were Two In One And One In Two: Beheading and Cinema* (London: Schism Press, 2014).
450. Lafcadio Hearn, "The Reconciliation," in *Shadowings* (Little, Brown & Company, 1919), 10–11.
451. The sobering effect of scientific explanation has long since explained to us the myth of "death-hair." The corpse, no longer taking in fluids, becomes dehydrated. This process of waterloss in the skin (desiccation)

causes the skin to shrivel and shrink, pulling the skin back over the bones. When this happens, the roots of the hair are revealed, giving the illusion of more hair than there is. For an entertaining summary, see Mary Roach's popular book *Stiff: The Curious Lives of Human Cadavers* (New York: Norton, 2003). That said, a film that also deserves mention is a short by John Carpenter titled "The Hair" (part of the 1993 straight-to-video collection *Body Bags*). In it, a balding man gets a hair transplant but later discovers the true secret to the miracle procedure in the innumerable microscopic worms that are growing out of his scalp.

452. Plato, *Parmenides*, in *The Collected Dialogues of Plato*, ed. Edith Hamilton and Huntington Cairns (Princeton University Press, 1961), 130c–d.
453. Pascal, *Pensées*, trans. A.J. Krailsheimer (New York: Penguin, 1966), 165.
454. Jane de la Vaudère, "The Double Star," in *The Double Star and Other Occult Fantasies*, trans. Brian Stableford (n.p.: Snuggly Books, 2018), 50. Originally published in Jane de la Vaudère, *La Mystérieuse* (Paris: Ernest Flammarion, 1901). Along with authors such as Rachilde (Marguerite Vallette-Eymery) and Renée Vivien, Vaudère is an author whose contribution to the literature of the *fin de siècle* has yet to be fully appreciated. A recent study is Sharon Larson, *Resurrecting Jane de la Vaudère: Literary Shapeshifter of the Belle Époque* (Philadelphia: Penn State University Press, 2022).
455. Ibid., 52. The Chimera continues, commenting on the relative insignificance of life on Earth: "Creation is composed of an infinite number of universes, separated from one another by abysms of nothingness, and the world is only a portal by means of which errant souls are precipitated into glory and become stars in their turn" (54–55). A prophetic vision of the planet's demise follows: "the circle of monsters opened, the blue star appeared between two chrysoprase peaks … a thousand strange insects swirled in its radiance like diamond snow" (63).
456. Ibid., 56.
457. Algernon Blackwood, "The Willows," in *Ancient Sorceries and Other Weird Stories*, ed. S.T. Joshi (New York: Penguin, 2002), 56–57.
458. Ibid., 57.
459. Ibid., 54.
460. Lovecraft, *At the Mountains of Madness*, 331.

461. Ibid., 334.

462. Ibid., 334–35.

463. Immanuel Kant, *The Critique of Judgement*, §23, 90. See also Note 439 above.

464. Ibid., 91.

465. Ibid., § 25, 98, italics removed.

466. Lovecraft, *Supernatural Horror in Literature*, 23. S.T. Joshi, the editor of the Lovecraft volumes for Penguin Classics, has written extensively on the "weird" and its difference from the earlier traditions of the Gothic novel and the 19th century tale of terror. See Joshi's studies *The Weird Tale* (Cabin John: Wildside Press, 2003), and *The Evolution of the Weird Tale* (New York: Hippocampus Press, 2004), and his two-volume survey *Unutterable Horror: A History of Supernatural Fiction* (New York: Hippocampus Press, 2014). Two earlier studies also contain insights to Lovecraft as a philosophically minded fiction writer: Barton Levi St. Armand's *The Roots of Horror in the Fiction of H.P. Lovecraft* (Elizabethtown: Dragon Press, 1977), and Maurice Lévy's *Lovecraft: A Study in the Fantastic*, trans. S.T. Joshi (Detroit: Wayne State University Press, 1988).

467. Ibid., 21.

468. Ibid., 23.

469. Lovecraft, "The Shadow Out of Time," in *The Dreams in the Witch House and Other Weird Stories*, ed. S.T. Joshi (New York: Penguin, 2004), 389.

470. Lovecraft, letter to Farnsworth Wright (5 July 1927), *Selected Letters, 1925–1929*, ed. August Derleth and Donald Wandrei (Sauk City: Arkham House, 1968), 150.

471. Lovecraft, letter to James Ferdinand Morton (30 October 1929), *Selected Letters, 1929–1931*, ed. August Derleth and Donald Wandrei (Sauk City: Arkham House, 1974), 39ff.

472. In the history of technology, the standard communications model is usually attributed to the work of mathematician Claude Shannon, who worked as an engineer and cryptographer at Bell Labs during the Second World War. His 1949 paper "A Mathematical Theory of Communication," published in the *Bell System Technical Journal*, contains what is referred to as the "Shannon diagram." The paper was expanded into the book *The Mathematical Theory of Communication* (1949) which is, along with

Norbert Weiner's 1948 book *Cybernetics: Or, Control and Communication in the Animal and the Machine*, an oft-referenced text in the development of modern cybernetics. For more on the history of cybernetics, see Ronald Kline, *The Cybernetics Moment: Or, Why We Call Our Age the Information Age* (Baltimore: Johns Hopkins University Press, 2015); and Steve Joshua Heims, *Constructing a Social Science for Post-War America: The Cybernetics Group, 1946–1953* (Cambridge: MIT Press, 1993).

473. These ideas are expanded in my essay "Dark Media," in *Excommunication: Three Inquiries in Media and Mediation*, coauthored with Alexander Galloway and McKenzie Wark (Chicago: University of Chicago Press, 2013). For more on the relation between media technologies and the supernatural, see Jeffrey Sconce, *Haunted Media: Electronic Presence from Telegraphy to Television* (Durham: Duke University Press, 2000); Siegfried Zielinski, *Deep Time of the Media*, trans. Gloria Custance (Cambridge: MIT Press, 2006); Friedrich Kittler, *Gramophone, Film, Typewriter*, trans. Geoffrey Winthrop-Young and Michael Wutz (Stanford: Stanford University Press, 1999); John Durham Peters, *Speaking Into the Air: A History of the Idea of Communication* (Chicago: University of Chicago Press, 2001); and Akira Mizuta Lippitt, *Atomic Light (Shadow Optics)* (Minneapolis: University of Minnesota Press, 2005).

474. William James, *The Varieties of Religious Experience* (New York: Penguin, 1985), 58. James's book was published in 1902, and based on lectures given at the University of Edinburgh a year prior. See also James's 1897 essay "What Psychical Research Has Accomplished," in his book *The Will to Believe and Other Essays*.

475. Jun'ichirō Tanizaki, *In Praise of Shadows*, trans. Thomas J. Harper and Edward G. Seidensticker (Stony Creek: Leete's Island Books, 1977 [1933]), 13. Interestingly, some of these ideas are already present, though in a different guise, in Tanizaki's 1928 novel *In Black and White*, a murder mystery that features a doppelgänger-like "Shadow Man."

476. Ibid., 35.

477. Fyodor Sologub, "Light and Shadow," in *The Dedalus Book of Russian Decadence*, ed. Kirsten Lodge (Sawtry, Cambs: Dedalus, 2007), 150. Sologub, paragon of the Russian decadent movement, would return to many of these themes in other stories. See, for instance, *The Kiss of the*

Unborn and Other Stories, trans. Murl G. Barker (Knoxville: University of Tennessee Press, 1977).

478. Ibid., 155.
479. Ibid., 156–57.
480. Ibid., 163.
481. Thomas Ligotti, "The Shadow, the Darkness," in *Teatro Grottesco* (London: Vintage, 2008), 259. Motifs of shadow and darkness pervade many of Ligotti's tales, including "The Lost Art of Twilight" (in the 1985 collection *Songs of a Dead Dreamer*), "The Shadow at the Bottom of the World" (in the 1991 collection *Grimscribe: His Life and Works*), and *The Spectral Link* (2014).
482. Ibid., 263.
483. Ibid., 276.
484. Ibid., 276–77.
485. Victor Stoichita, *A Short History of the Shadow*, trans. Anne-Marie Glasheen (London: Reaktion, 1999), 133.
486. Ibid., 150.
487. Kant, "What Does It Mean To Orient Oneself In Thinking?" (1786), in *Religion and Rational Theology*, ed. and trans. Allen W. Wood (Cambridge: Cambridge University Press, 1996), 9.
488. "The Dark," *Lights Out!*, air date 29 December 1937, available online at Archive.org.
489. Edogawa Rampo, "Hell of Mirrors," in *Japanese Tales of Mystery and Imagination*, trans. James Harris (Tokyo: Tuttle, 1956), 115. "Edogawa Rampo" was the penname of Tarō Hirai, who specialized in tales of perverted reasoning and the aesthetic of "ero-guro" (erotic-grotesque). See my article "The Erotic, Grotesque Nonsense of Edogawa Rampo," *Japan Times* (7 January 2017).
490. Ibid., 116.
491. Junji Ito, *Uzumaki* vol. 3, trans. Yuji Oniki (San Francisco: Viz Media, 2008), 150, 218. See also my article, "The Unhuman World of Junji Ito," *Japan Times* (30 January 2016).
492. H.P. Lovecraft, "The Shadow Out of Time," in *The Dreams in the Witch House and Other Weird Stories*, ed. S.T. Joshi (New York: Penguin, 2004), 340, 373, 381, 393.

493. H.P. Lovecraft, "The Unnamable," in *The Dreams in the Witch House and Other Weird Stories*, ed. S.T. Joshi (New York: Penguin, 2004), 89.
494. Iain Hamilton Grant, *Philosophies of Nature After Schelling* (London: Continuum, 2006), 2. For an examination of the links between Schelling's philosophy and modern science fiction and horror, see Ben Woodard's *On an Ungrounded Earth: Towards a New Geophilosophy* (Brooklyn: Punctum, 2013).
495. Algernon Blackwood, "The Man Whom the Trees Loved," in *Ancient Sorceries and Other Weird Stories*, ed. S.T. Joshi (New York: Penguin, 2002), 268, 271.
496. Ibid., 268.
497. Izumi Kyōka, "The Holy Man of Mount Kōya," in *Japanese Gothic Tales*, trans. Charles Shirō Inouye (Honolulu: University of Hawaii Press, 1996), 36–37. Much of the scholarship on Kyōka's tales not only points to the influence of Buddhism and Shinto, but also situates it within the reception of the Gothic novel within early-20th century Japanese literary aesthetics. See, for instance, Inouye's essay "Japanese Gothic," in *A New Companion to the Gothic*, ed. David Punter (London: Wiley-Blackwell, 2015).
498. Ibid., 37.
499. Caitlín R. Kiernan, "In the Water Works (Birmingham, Alabama 1888)," in *Tales of Pain and Wonder* (Atlanta: Meisha Merlin Publishing, 2001), 294. In Kiernan's early collections there is a story cycle that mixes elements of supernatural horror with modern paleontology. See also the stories in *From Weird and Distant Shores* (2002) and *To Charles Fort, With Love* (2005).
500. Ibid., 296.
501. Ibid.
502. Fort, *The Book of the Damned: The Collected Works of Charles Fort* (New York: Tarcher/Penguin, 2008 [1919]), 9. Though more a nonfictional documentarian of the unexplained, Fort's contribution to supernatural horror remains underappreciated. The series of books he published in the early 20th century — *The Book of the Damned* (1919), *New Lands* (1923), *Wild Talents* (1935), and the evocatively titled *Lo!* (1931) — are more dossiers than traditional nonfiction, and represent an

innovation in style and structure that sits somewhere between scientific taxonomy and the tradition of the beast fable. A recent biography is Jim Steinmeyer, *Charles Fort: The Man Who Invented the Supernatural* (New York: Tarcher/Penguin, 2008).

503. Ibid., 13.
504. Ibid., 14.
505. Ibid.
506. China Miéville, *Kraken* (London: Pan Books, 2011), 417. Many of Miéville's novels portray urban environments themselves as characters in the story, either fanning outwards in a network of streets and byways, or stratified vertically in labyrinthine underworlds and cities-within-cities. For examples, see the novels *King Rat* (1998), *Perdido Street Station* (2000), and *The City and the City* (2009).
507. Ibid., 186.
508. Ibid., 106.
509. Ibid., 295.
510. Ambroise Paré, *On Monsters and Marvels*, trans. Janis L. Pallister (Chicago: University of Chicago Press, 1982), 161. Paré's treatise was initially included in his 1573 compendium *Two Books on Surgery* (*Deux Livres de Chirurgie*). A modern edition is *Des Monstres et Prodiges*, ed. Michel Jeanneret (Paris: Gallimard, 2015). A scan of the first edition of *Two Books on Surgery* is available online at the Bibliothèque Nationale de France (www.gallica.bnf.fr). See also Note 74 above.
511. Vilém Flusser and Louis Bec, *Vampyroteuthis Infernalis: A Treatise, with a Report by the Institut Scientifique de Recherche Paranaturaliste*, trans. Valentine A. Pakis (Minneapolis: University of Minnesota Press, 2012), 6.
512. Ibid., 11. Later in the text Flusser gives a more tangible definition: "The more disgusting something is, the further removed it is from humans on the phylogenetic tree."
513. These ideas are echoed in Antonin Artaud's plans for the use of archaeo-astronomy sites as forms of sacrificial theater, mentioned in notebooks and letters of the mid-1930s (the same period as the writings that form his book *The Land of the Tarahumaras*), which recur in his late writings. Artaud's notoriously fractured and oblique writings mention a "Ritual of the black night" and "the eternal death of the sun," a "seraphic

theater of bloodstained stars," that involves "cosmic limbs sacrificed in the House of Flowers," and "burning skies sacred in noonday rot." See Antonin Artaud, *Oeuvres Complètes*, vol. IX (Paris: Gallimard, 1979), and *Cahiers Mexique, 1935–1937* (Paris: Gallimard, 2018), as well as *Watchfiends and Rack Screams: Works from the Final Period*, ed. and trans. Clayton Eshleman with Bernard Bador (Cambridge: Exact Change, 2004), and *A Sinister Assassin: Antonin Artaud's Last Writings*, ed. and trans. Stephen Barber (London: Infinity Land Press, 2022). Artaud was a decisive influence on the development of Butoh in the work of Japanese choreographer Tatsumi Hijikata, particularly in one of his last works, "Earthen Star Statue Ritual." This project has recently been revived by the performance art collective Anni Cyclops/Gori OP, comprised of students in the Hijikata/Ankoku Butoh tradition. The group incorporates elements of Shinto, *suijakutai* anatomy, and Buddhist self-mummification, proposing an ongoing performance of Artaud's plans for cosmic sacrifice in a series of rituals that follow the strange cartographies Artaud laid out in the last notebooks, letters, and sketches (a delirious amalgam based on pre-Columbian astronomy, 12th century treatises on "sand science" [*ilm al-raml*], as well as diagrams of *qi* meridians from traditional Chinese medical texts such as the *De bìng lùn*). For more, see Sondra Fraleigh and Tamah Nakamura, *Hijikata Tatsumi and Ohno Kazuo* (New York: Routledge, 2006), as well as Komoda Jogoro, "Revolting Earth: Disease, Sacrifice, and Cosmos in Tatsumi Hijikata's *Ankoku Butoh*," *Performance Studies Journal* vol. 4.3 (Winter 2011).

514. H.P. Lovecraft, "Dagon," in *The Call of Cthulhu and Other Weird Stories*, ed. S.T. Joshi (New York: Penguin, 1999), 1–2.
515. Ibid., 2.
516. Ibid., 6.
517. Ligotti, *The Conspiracy Against the Human Race*, 52, 101.
518. Ibid., 104.
519. Ibid., 16.
520. For more on the notion of "concept-horror" see the journal *Collapse*, volume IV (2008), published by Urbanomic (www.urbanomic.com).
521. Ligotti, *Conspiracy*, 220, 221.

522. Quoted in Ligotti, *Conspiracy*, 37, from Mainländer's main philosophical work, *Die Philosophie der Erlösung* (*The Philosophy of Redemption*, 1876). A recent critical edition is included in Philipp Mainländer, *Schriften*, ed. Winfried Müller-Seyfarth, vols. I–II (Hildesheim: Georg Olms, 2021). Another variant on the idea is given in Ligotti's own words: "Nonhuman occupants of this planet are unaware of death. But we are susceptible to startling and dreadful thoughts, and we need some fabulous illusions to take our minds off them" (28).
523. This comes through clearly in Ligotti's critical assessment of thinkers such as Unamuno and Camus, as well as his ambivalence towards contemporary scholars such as Joshua Dienstag and William Brashear. The implication is that such approaches to pessimism tend to render it as a form of self-help in disguise, in effect recuperating pessimism's "negativity bias" towards either realistic or even optimistic ends. (We might also add to this list John Gray's deceptively provocative *Straw Dogs*, the tepid utilitarianism of Roger Scruton's *The Uses of Pessimism*, as well as Alain de Botton's patronizingly naïve *Religion for Atheists*, all of which argue in favor of the healthy side effects of pessimist thinking.) It is interesting that a separate, parallel development has emerged in psychology under the names of "defensive pessimism" or "positive pessimism."
524. Ligotti, *Conspiracy*, 51–52.
525. Ligotti, "The Puppet Masters," in *Noctuary* (New York: Carroll & Graf, 1995), 172.
526. Ligotti, *Conspiracy*, 16. Ligotti continues: "Human puppets could not conceive of themselves as being puppets at all, not when they are fixed with a consciousness that excites in them the unshakable sense of being singled out from all other objects in creation. Once you begin to feel you are making a go of it on your own — that you are making moves and thinking thoughts which seem to have originated within you — it is not possible for you to believe you are anything but your own master" (17).
527. Heinrich von Kleist, "On the Puppet Theater," in *An Abyss Deep Enough: The Letters of Heinrich von Kleist, with a Selection of Essays and Anecdotes*, ed. and trans. Philip B. Miller (New York: E.P. Dutton, 1982), 211.
528. Ibid., 212.
529. Ibid., 214.

530. For more on early Christian monasticism, see Derwas Chitty, *The Desert a City: An Introduction to the Study of Egyptian and Palestinian Monasticism Under the Christian Empire* (London: Blackwell, 1977); Marilyn Dunn, *The Emergence of Monasticism: From the Desert Fathers to the Early Middle Ages* (London: Blackwell, 2000); William Harmless, *Desert Christians: An Introduction to the Literature of Early Monasticism* (Oxford: Oxford University Press, 2004).
531. Guibert of Nogent, *A Monk's Confession*, trans. Paul Archamabult (University Park: Penn State University Press, 2006), 51–52.
532. *The Desert Fathers: Sayings of the Early Christian Monks*, ed. and trans. Benedicta Ward (New York: Penguin, 2003), 10. Other collections in English include *The Sayings of the Desert Fathers: The Alphabetical Collection*, trans. Benedicta Ward (Cistercian Publications, 1975), and *Western Asceticism*, ed. and trans. Owen Chadwick (Philadelphia: The Westminster Press, 1958).
533. Kant, *Groundwork of the Metaphysics of Morals*, in *Practical Philosophy*, trans. Mary J. Gregor (Cambridge: Cambridge University Press, 1999), 73.
534. Ibid.
535. Lovecraft, "The Call of Cthulhu," 139.
536. Nietzsche, *Writings from the Late Notebooks*, ed. Rüdiger Bittner, trans. Kate Sturge (Cambridge: Cambridge University Press, 2003), 84.
537. Kant, *Groundwork of the Metaphysics of Morals*, 93.
538. While Kant's *Critique of Judgement* is the most-commonly cited text in this regard, it's also worth noting the much longer discussion of the sublime in Western aesthetics, from Longinus, to Burke, to European Romanticism and beyond. An overview is provided in Robert Doran's *The Theory of the Sublime from Longinus to Kant* (Cambridge: Cambridge University Press, 2015). See also Note 433 above.
539. Immanuel Kant, *The Critique of Judgement*, §25, 131, 132.
540. Ibid., "General Remark," 151–52.
541. Ibid., §26, 138, emphasis removed.
542. Edmund Burke, *A Philosophical Inquiry into the Origin of our Ideas of the Sublime and Beautiful*, ed. David Womersley (New York: Penguin, 1998), Part IV, Section vii, 165.

543. Fyodor Dostoevsky, *The Double and The Gambler*, trans. Richard Pevear and Larissa Volokhonsky (New York: Vintage, 2005), 50.
544. Kant, *Groundwork of the Metaphysics of Morals*, 87–88.
545. Either I read this somewhere, overheard it in a café, or made it up entirely.
546. Li He, "Song of Magic Strings," *The Collected Poems of Li He*, trans. J.D. Frodsham (New York: NYRB, 2016), 221. See also Frodsham's earlier edition *The Poems of Li Ho, 791–817* (Oxford: Clarendon Press, 1970).
547. "Magic Strings," *The Collected Poems of Li He*, 222.
548. Kant, *Critique of Pure Reason*, trans. Norman Kemp Smith (New York: St. Martin's, 1964), I, Part II, Section iii., "The Ground of the Distinction of All Objects in General into Phenomena and Noumena," 259.
549. Caroline Walker Bynum, *Christian Materiality: An Essay on Religion in Late Medieval Europe* (New York: Zone, 2011), 17. Bynum has extended her study of the often strange and enigmatic aspects of religious materiality in her followup book *Dissimilar Similitudes: Devotional Objects in Late Medieval Europe* (New York: Zone, 2022).
550. Ibid., 30.
551. Ibid.
552. Raymond of Capua, *The Life of St. Catherine of Siena*, trans. George Lamb (Ann Arbor: Harvill Press, 1960), 43. See also *Catherine of Siena: The Dialogue*, trans. Suzanne Noffke (Mahwah: Paulist Press, 1980).
553. Thomas Frognall Dibdin, *The Bibliomania; or, Book-Madness; Containing Some Account of the History, Symptoms, and Cure of this Fatal Disease* (London: Longman, Hurst, Rees, and Orme, 1809), 58. Books of this type, which "diagnosed" bibliomania in quasi-medical terms, are also indebted to the long tradition of writing about the love of books, compellingly depicted in Richard de Bury's *Philobiblon* (c.1345).
554. Plutarch, *Plutarch's Lives*, trans. Bernadotte Perrin (Cambridge: Harvard University Press, 1920), *Antony*, LXX 1–4, 297ff. Notable dramatic presentations of Timon include Shakespeare's *Timon of Athens* (c.1606, first published in 1623, though some scholars suggest the play was originally written in collaboration with Thomas Middleton), as well as Thomas Shadwell's *The History of Timon of Athens, the Man-Hater* (1674). Shakespeare was influenced in part by Plutarch's account.

CULTURE, SOCIETY & POLITICS

Contemporary culture has eliminated the concept and public figure of the intellectual. A cretinous anti-intellectualism presides, cheer-led by hacks in the pay of multinational corporations who reassure their bored readers that there is no need to rouse themselves from their stupor. Zer0 Books knows that another kind of discourse — intellectual without being academic, popular without being populist — is not only possible but already flourishing. Zer0 is convinced that in the unthinking, blandly consensual culture in which we live, critical and engaged theoretical reflection is more important than ever before.

CULTURE, SOCIETY & POLITICS

Contemporary culture has eliminated the concept and public figure of the intellectual. A cretinous anti-intellectualism presides, cheer-led by hacks in the pay of multinational corporations who reassure their bored readers that there is no need to rouse themselves from their stupor. Zer0 Books knows that another kind of discourse – intellectual without being academic, popular without being populist – is not only possible: it is already flourishing. Zer0 is convinced that in the unthinking, blandly consensual culture in which we live, critical and engaged theoretical reflection is more important than ever before.

If you have enjoyed this book, why not tell other readers by posting a review on your preferred book site.

You may also wish to subscribe to our Zer0 Books YouTube Channel.